GAMEPLAY GLOSSARY 2

INTRODUCTION 4

SOULCALIBUR IV GAMEPLAY
- Basic Controls & Movement 5
- Defense 7
- Offense 10

SINGLE-PLAYER GAME MODES
- Story 16
- Tower of Lost Souls 17
- Arcade 22
- Honors & Achievements 22

CHARACTER CREATION 24

RETURNING CHARACTERS
- Amy 26
- Astaroth 32
- Cassandra Alexandra 38
- Cervantes de Leon 44
- Hilde (Hildegard von Krone) 50
- Ivy (Isabella Valentine) 56
- Kilik 64
- Lizardman (Aeon Calcos) 70
- Maxi 76
- Heishiro Mitsurugi 82
- Nightmare 88
- Raphael Sorel 94
- Rock (Rock Adams) 100
- Seong Mi-na 106
- Setsuka 112
- Siegfried Schtauffen 118
- Sophitia Alexandra 124
- Taki 130
- Talim 136
- Tira 144
- Voldo 152
- Chai Xianghua 160
- Yoshimitsu 166
- Hong Yun-seong 174
- Zasalamel 180

BOSS CHARACTER
- The Hero King Algol 186

BONUS CHARACTERS
- Angol Fear 192
- Ashlotte Maedel 198
- Kamikirimusi 204
- Scheherazade 214
- Shura 216

GUEST CHARACTERS
- Darth Vader 222
- Yoda 228
- Darth Vader's Secret Apprentice 234

Gameplay Glossary

Term	Definition
8-Way Run	The main movement system in *Soulcalibur IV*, accomplished by holding the D-pad or stick in any direction.
Advantage	Refers to a situation in which your earliest possible action will occur before your opponent's. Usually occurs after guarding or evading the opponent's attack. The opposite of ***disadvantage***.
Aerial Control	A system in place to prevent infinite or extremely long ***juggle*** combos. After getting hit with one hit during a ***juggle***, hold a direction on the D-pad or stick to cause your character to fall in that direction. This can cause subsequent ***juggle*** hits to ***whiff***.
Backward	Refers to directions away from the opponent. Represented as ⇦, ⬃, and ⬁, as this guide assumes your character is on the left side of the screen (often called the 1P side), facing your opponent on the right.
Blockstun	The state in which, after guarding an attuck, your character can do nothing until the blocking animation ends. Lighter attacks cause brief ***blockstun***, while powerful attacks cause lengthy ***blockstun***.
Buffering	Beginning to enter the command for your next action while the current action is still underway. Also refers to using the motion or command for one action as part of the motion or command for another.
Cancel	A generic term that refers to canceling any action with another.
Clash	The situation that occurs when two characters strike one another at approximately the same time. One or both combatants will recoil, no damage done.
Close Range	Refers to pointblank range. Quick ***mid*** attacks and ***throws*** tend to dominate this range.
Combo	A series of attacks that is unavoidable after the first successful hit. ***Combos*** that bounce the opponent into the air are called ***juggles***.
Normal Hit	Striking the opponent while he or she is not actively attacking or moving backward or sideways. The attack delivers normal damage, inflicts normal hitstun, and has normal hit properties.
Counter-Hit	Striking the opponent while he or she is actively attacking or moving backward or to the side. A ***counter-hit*** deals more damage than a ***normal hit***, and can cause an extended ***hitstun*** and inflict special hit properties, such as staggers, bounces, or crumples.
Critical Finish	Unique to *Soulcalibur IV*, these finishing moves can be accomplished by pressing Ⓐ+Ⓑ+Ⓚ+Ⓖ while your opponent reels from a ***Soul Crush***. A ***Critical Finish*** ends the current round.
Crouch	Accomplished by inputting ⬇Ⓖ. ***Crouching*** lowers your character's profile and causes ***high*** attacks and most ***throws*** to ***whiff***.
Damage Scaling	A system that prevents extended ***combos*** or ***juggles*** from being too powerful. As the number of hits in a ***combo*** grows larger, the damage each hit inflicts is reduced.
Dash	Accomplished by tapping the D-pad or stick ⇦, ⇩, ⇨, or ⇧. Also called a ***step***.
Delay	Intentionally delaying inputs during a string or action, causing an attack to execute slightly later than usual. Useful for tricking opponents and scoring ***counter-hits***.
String	A canned sequence of attacks accomplished by inputting certain button combinations. Also referred to as a ***chain***.
Disadvantage	Refers to a situation in which your earliest possible action will occur after your opponent's. Usually occurs after having your attack guarded or evaded. The opposite of ***advantage***.
Footsies	Refers to positional game-play that usually takes place at the edge of each characters' range, in which players try to ***poke,*** counter-***poke,*** and score ***knockdowns***.
"For Free"	A catch-all fighting game term that indicates an action is guaranteed and risk-free, e.g. "after guarding X move, you can land Y combo *for free*."
Forward	Refers to directions toward your opponent. Represented as ⬂, ⇨, and ⬀, as this guide assumes your character is on the left side of the screen (often called the 1P side), facing your opponent on the right.
Fuzzy Guard	A defensive technique that involves holding Ⓖ while switching the D-pad or stick between ⬃, ⇦, and ⬁. This is an ***Option Select*** that can allow defense against incoming threats at different levels simultaneously.
Grapple Break	Refers to pressing Ⓐ or Ⓑ to break the opponent's ***throw*** just as it begins. Ⓐ+Ⓖ throws are broken by tapping Ⓐ, and Ⓑ+Ⓖ throws are broken by tapping Ⓑ.
Guard	Accomplished by holding Ⓖ, guarding blocks incoming attacks, putting your character into ***blockstun*** and negating the attack's damage. ***Unblockables*** and ***throws*** cannot be guarded.
Guard Break	An attack specifically designed to knock away the opponent's ***guard***. Causes no damage if guarded, but can still serve to make the opponent wary of playing defensively.
Guard Cancel	Tapping Ⓖ to interrupt an action before it becomes active. Can be useful to fake out the opponent. Only certain attacks can be guard canceled.
Guard Impact	*Soulcalibur IV*'s system of aggressive defense. ***Repels*** and ***Parries*** are ***Guard Impact*** techniques. A successful ***Guard Impact*** knocks aside the opponent's attack and returns the ***advantage*** to your character.
Guessing Game	A situation in which players are forced to decide between multiple threats or options.
High	An attack that strikes standing or jumping characters, but can be crouched under.
Hit Confirmation	Visually confirming that an attack is successful before initiating follow-up options or strings.
Hit Throw	An attack that can be guarded, but transitions into a ***throw*** upon a successful hit. Also called an ***Attack Throw***.
Hitstun	The state that a character enters upon getting hit by an attack. No actions can be initiated until ***hitstun*** ends. ***Combos*** are possible because of ***hitstun***.
Horizontal Attack	An attack with Ⓐ that can catch opponents using sidesteps or ***8-Way Run*** to evade to the side.
Juggle	A ***combo*** that keeps the enemy airborne.
Jump	A leaping action that goes over ***low*** attacks.
Just	A generic term applied to indicate that an action must be performed with extreme precision, sometimes down to single frames.
Just Frame	An attack that is accomplished only with exact timing. ***Just Frame*** attacks can have a window of as small as one frame (in a game running at 60 frames per second) to be initiated successfully.

Term	Definition
Just Impact	A variation of the ***Repel*** version of a ***Guard Impact***; a ***Just Impact*** occurs when a ***Repel*** is used with exact timing, causes a red flash rather than a green flash, and grants more ***advantage*** to the character using the ***Just Impact***.
Just Ukemi	A version of ***Ukemi*** that requires exact precision, tapping Ⓖ in order to get up exactly as one's character strikes the ground from a ***knockdown***.
Kick	An attack with Ⓚ that uses leg power rather than being weapon-based.
Knockdown	Refers to knocking your opponent to the floor, or getting knocked down. After a ***knockdown*** a character is referred to as being "***floored***." Characters can be struck while ***floored***. Rising from a knockdown is referred to as ***Ukemi***. Guessing games employed against ***floored*** opponents are called ***okizeme***.
Link	An attack that results in a ***combo*** in spite of the attack not being part of a ***string*** or ***chain***. Occurs when the ***hitstun*** caused by an attack is long enough to allow a different attack to connect before ***hitstun*** ends.
Long Range	The range at which all but the very longest-range attacks will ***whiff***.
Low	An attack that must be guarded by crouching, but can be jumped over.
Mashing	Entering inputs very quickly. Sometimes used with certain attacks or combos, and to escape from recoverable staggers and stuns.
Mid	An attack that cannot be crouched, and must be guarded standing.
Mid Range	Just outside of throw range, but not so far that most attacks will whiff.
Mix-up	Same as a guessing game; creating a situation in which your opponent is forced to deal with different options.
Okizeme	A term that refers to the anti-***wakeup*** game, employed against an opponent you have successfully ***floored***.
Option Select	An advanced fighting game concept, critical to successfully employing and defending against ***mix-ups*** and ***guessing games***. An ***Option Select*** is a combination of inputs or actions that defeat or defend against multiple options simultaneously, removing some of the guesswork from playing.
OTG	An acronym for "***off the ground***," refers to continuing a ***combo*** on a ***floored*** opponent.
Parry	A variation of ***Guard Impact*** accomplished by tapping ⇦ or ⬁Ⓖ just as an attack is about to strike your character. If successful, the opponent is thrown to the ground and your character gains the ***advantage***.
Poke	An attack that, due to speed, priority, or range, is relatively safe to use for pressuring or ***zoning*** your opponent.
Priority	The likelihood that one attack will cleanly beat out another.
Repel	A variation of ***Guard Impact*** accomplished by tapping ⇨ or ⬂Ⓖ just as an attack is about to strike your character. If successful, your character will knock aside the opponent's strike with a green flash and gain the ***advantage***. A ***Repel*** executed at the last possible moment becomes a ***Just Impact***, causing a red flash and granting additional ***advantage***.
Reverse Impact	A counter to ***Repels***, ***Reverse Impacts*** are accomplished by tapping ⇨ or ⬂Ⓖ after having *your* strike ***Repelled***. If successful, the opponent's follow-up to his or her ***Repel*** will be knocked aside, and your character retains ***advantage***.
Ring Out	Most stages have edges off of which a character can be knocked, thus removing the character from the field of play. It is possible to win by knocking your opponent off the stage, through ***Ring Out***.
Run	Accomplished by holding ➡ from distance. Your character closes the distance to the other character as quickly as possible. Characters are vulnerable while they run, but some attacks are accessible only during a ***run***.
Soul Crush	Every character has a glowing orb near his or her health gauge. Guarding high-power attacks while this orb glows red results in a ***Soul Crush***. Soul Crushed characters reel, unable to defend or attack, and can lose pieces of armor. Getting ***Soul Crushed*** can lead to a ***Critical Finish*** and the end of the round!
Soul Gauge	The glowing orb near the health gauge. When it's green, this orb is at mid level. Guarding attacks or being ***Guard Impacted*** reduces this gauge, edging its color toward red. Aggressive actions and attacks increase this gauge, edging its color toward blue. A flashing red gauge leaves you susceptible to ***Soul Crushes***, ***Critical Finishes***, and the loss of armor.
Special Low	A ***low*** attack that, unlike other ***lows***, can be guarded standing. ***Special lows*** can still be jumped over as well.
Special Mid	A ***mid*** attack that, unlike other ***mids***, can be guarded crouching.
Stagger	A hit effect, usually accomplished through ***counter-hits***, in which the opponent is stuck in a painful animation for a time, allowing for follow-ups. There are many similar effects, such as ***Stuns*** and ***Crumples***, also usually accomplished through ***counter-hits***.
Step	Another term for ***dash***, this involves tapping ⇦, ⇩, ⇨, or ⇧. Causes a quick ***step*** in the desired direction, possibly evading attacks and gaining better position.
Throw	An attack initiated with Ⓐ+Ⓖ or Ⓑ+Ⓖ. ***Throws*** cannot be guarded. Most throws are targeted at standing opponents and can be avoided by crouching. However, some throws are specifically tailored to hit crouching, jumping, or ***floored*** opponents.
Throw Escape	***Throws*** can be broken by pressing the same attack button that the opponent presses to execute the throw. For example, tap Ⓐ to break an Ⓐ+Ⓖ throw.
Tick	A quick attack used to get the opponent to guard or play passively, in order to set up throw attempts or mix-up options.
Ukemi	Tapping Ⓖ while floored, causing your character to rise, is called ***Ukemi***. Tapping Ⓖ with precision in order to rise quickly after getting ***floored*** by certain attacks is called ***Just Ukemi***.
Unblockable	An attack, animated with a flame effect, that hits opponents who are guarding. ***Unblockables*** must instead be evaded or interrupted with attacks before they strike.
Verification	Also called ***Hit Confirmation***, ***Verification*** refers to confirming that an action is successful before performing desired follow-ups.
Vertical Attack	An attack with Ⓑ that can be avoided by using sidesteps or ***8-Way Run***.
Wakeup	A term referring to an action that causes a character to rise from a ***floored*** position.
Whiff	Any attack that completely misses the opponent, whether intentionally or not.
While Rising	Every character has attacks that are performed first by crouching, then tapping attack buttons as the character rises from crouching to standing again. These are "***While Rising***" attacks. Attacks performed while "***waking up***" from a ***knockdown*** will also be ***While Rising*** attacks.
Zoning	Refers to keeping your opponent in a particular range that is beneficial to your character and game plan, and detrimental to your foe's.

Soulcalibur IV Gameplay

Introduction: A Tale of Souls and Swords

"Chosen by history, a man becomes a warrior. Engraved into history, a warrior becomes a hero."
—14th century troubadour's song

"Transcending history and the world, a tale of souls and swords, eternally retold."
—Late medieval ballad, author unknown

This is the story of two great blades.

Soul Edge, the cursed sword; whispered of in legends the world over, the devourer of souls.

Soul Calibur, the spirit sword; destined to halt the evil of the cursed sword, yet remain unknown to mankind and unsung in history.

For millennia, the two swords fought across countless bloody battlefields, until at the close of the 16th century they were silenced, forced to fuse together into a form unlike anything ever before seen. None knew what desperate struggle continued within that quiet "embrace of souls," but when they were once again freed upon the world, Soul Calibur and Soul Edge were more powerful than ever before.

When Siegfried and Nightmare first stood against each other, each bearing one of the swords, the torrent of power that they unleashed obliterated the Lost Cathedral in which they dueled. When the wave of destruction finally ebbed, they had disappeared, together with the swords they wielded.

No one knew, no one realized that when the minds of Soul Calibur and Soul Edge touched, an ancient taboo had been broken, and the gears of fate had begun to turn. It was this turn of events that the guardians of the spirit sword, a tribe long since lost to history, had feared and sought to prevent, even as they fought the evil of Soul Edge through the ages. When the two opposing blades came together, a consciousness quietly awakened, and none know what final destiny it seeks...

The end game in the ageless conflict between Soul Calibur and Soul Edge is fast approaching, a battle like none history has witnessed before. The great heroes of the age are drawn into the vortex, and together they are driven helplessly toward the terrible denouement.

"Emotions of hope and fear cannot be in themselves good."
—Benedict de Spinoza, from Ethics: Demonstrated by the Method of Geometry

Basic Controls & Movement

1. Movement: Hold for 8-Way Run, tap for steps.
2. Ⓖ: Initiates Guard and defensive actions like Guard Impact.
3. Ⓐ: Performs horizontal attacks.
4. Ⓑ: Performs vertical attacks.
5. Ⓚ: Performs kick attacks.
6. Switch: Switches between characters (when possible).
7. Ⓐ + Ⓖ: Performs a throw.
8. Ⓑ + Ⓖ: Performs a throw.
9. Ⓐ + Ⓑ + Ⓚ: Activates manual skill if available; taunts otherwise (Ⓖ + Ⓚ also taunts).

8-Way Run

Press the D-pad or stick in any direction to initiate an ***8-Way Run***. This is an effective way to dance in and out of your opponent's range, and to potentially sidestep his or her vertical attacks. Getting struck while 8-Way Running in a backward or lateral direction registers as a ***counter-hit***, so beware of moving carelessly! Each character has attacks that can be performed only during an 8-Way Run. You can also access these moves by double-tapping in the appropriate direction. For example, an 8-Way Run horizontal attack executed by tapping Ⓐ while moving laterally into the foreground (toward the screen) is usually notated as ↓Ⓐ. However, it can also be notated (and input) as ⇩⇩Ⓐ.

Step

To initiate a ***step***, tap ⇦, ⇩, ⇧, or ⇨. Your character will initiate a quick dash in the chosen direction. Like 8-Way Run, this is useful for avoiding and baiting moves, or for securing a better position. As with the 8-Way Run, getting hit while dashing backward or to the side results in a ***counter-hit***.

Run

From a great distance, hold → to ***run*** toward the opponent quickly. Specific moves can be performed only while running. Beware of running carelessly, as your character is vulnerable in this state.

Special Skills: Run & Step Speed Up

The Run Speed Up and Step Speed Up skills increase the speed of running and stepping. Make someone like Taki lightning-quick, or turn a lumbering beast like Astaroth into a horrifying speed demon!

Jump

To ***jump***, tap any upward direction while tapping or holding Ⓖ. Jumps leap over low attacks. To attack while jumping, press any upward direction together with Ⓐ, Ⓑ, or Ⓚ. Jumping attacks inflict slightly more damage when initiated jumping forward, and slightly less damage jumping backward. Don't jump carelessly, as it can easily lead to a juggle or a Ring Out loss!

Crouch

Crouching is accomplished by holding ↓ and tapping Ⓖ. This initiates the crouch; to continue crouching, continue holding ↓. Crouching is useful, as it causes high attacks and most throws to miss. Guarding while crouching is also required to block incoming low attacks. Attacks initiated while crouching usually go under incoming high attacks. Many moves are performed by crouching first and then pressing an attack button while returning to a standing state. These attacks are referred to as being executed ***While Rising***. You can also perform While Rising attacks immediately after you use an attack that ends with your character crouching as part of the attack's animation. Some attacks must be performed ***While Crouching***. For these attacks, you initiate a crouch and then input the appropriate commands.

Defense

The Best Offense is a Good Defense
—Frequent Proverbial Misquote

Defense in *Soulcalibur IV* has received many tweaks since the last installment. The introduction of the ***Soul Gauge*** and ***Critical Finish*** attacks adds a new tug-of-war aspect to guarding and passive play. These new wrinkles warrant a refresher course on Soulcalibur defense.

Guard: Ⓖ

Holding Ⓖ puts your character into a guarding state. Simply holding Ⓖ makes your character guard in a standing position, thus blocking high and mid strikes. Holding ⬇Ⓖ guards with your character in a crouched position, which blocks low attacks. A successful guard prevents damage, diminishes your ***Soul Gauge***, and briefly puts your character into a state called ***blockstun***. Your character cannot take action until blockstun ends. Blocking is not effective against throws, ***Guard Breaks*** (animated with a blue lightning effect), and ***Unblockables*** (animated with a flame effect). When in doubt, guarding is often the safest option, but beware that the ***Soul Crush*** system—new to *Soulcalibur IV*—can lead to severe penalties for overly defensive play!

Power Skills: Shave Damage

The Shave Damage set of skills, found in Character Creation mode, emulate the "block damage" found in many other fighting games—your character will dole out small slivers of damage even if attacks are guarded.

Guard Impact

Soulcalibur IV doesn't just offer guarding as the only defensive choice. The ***Guard Impact*** system gives you other options for turning the tables on an aggressive opponent. Guard Impacts can also prove useful while attacking, after having your own strikes guarded. Often, the opponent's first instinct is to take back the initiative with his or her own attacks as soon as possible. While the use of Guard Impact has been important since its introduction to the *Soulcalibur* franchise, it's even more important now with the addition of the ***Soul Gauge*** and ***Critical Finishes***.

REPEL: ⇨ OR ⇘ Ⓖ

Inputting ⇨ or ⇘ Ⓖ causes your character to raise his or her weapon aggressively. If you time and aim this properly, it deflects the opponent's attack with a green flash, granting your character the advantage. High and mid attacks must be Repelled with ⇨Ⓖ, while low attacks must be Repelled with ⇘Ⓖ. A successful Repel decreases your opponent's ***Soul Gauge***. It is possible to cause a ***Soul Crush*** with a Repel! After Repelling the opponent's attack, you can try for a quick follow-up attack or throw—use fast attacks and they may be guaranteed, as the opponent cannot guard while reeling just after getting Repelled. Some slower characters can't land free attacks this way, but they still gain the advantage after a Repel, while skewing Soul Gauges in their favor. Beware that opponents can use a ***Reverse Impact*** to counter attacks that you attempt immediately after a normal Repel (see the following section for details). Finally, a perfectly timed Repel results in a ***Just Impact***, which flashes red instead of green. Note that Guard Breaks can be Repelled normally, but only Just Impacts can Repel Unblockables.

Reverse Impact

Having your attack Repelled is not the end of the world—***Reverse Impacts*** grant the Repelled character some recourse. After getting Repelled, input ⇨ or ⇘ Ⓖ to counter-Repel any attack the opponent tries after his or her initial Repel. Of course, in order to succeed, you must choose the correct hit level. This keeps the momentum exactly where it started: with the initial aggressor. While it's unlikely, note that if you follow up your Reverse Impact with an attack, the opponent can then Reverse Impact in response! To minimize the risk of having your Repels negated with Reverse Impacts, mix-up your choices after a successful Repel. Don't always attack right immediately. Occasionally go for a throw or intentionally delay your attack. Finally, note that only normal Repels, which flash green, can be Reverse Impacted. Repels that flash red, called ***Just Impacts***, cannot be Reverse Impacted.

Just Impact

A normal Repel, which causes a green flash, doesn't necessarily guarantee anything—it simply grants a mild advantage. However, timing a Repel at the last possible moment results in a ***Just Impact***. A Just Impact causes a red flash and leaves the opponent defenseless for a longer period of time, guaranteeing that any character can take advantage—sometimes even with slower moves, like launchers! Any attack landed after a Just Impact registers as a ***counter-hit***, inflicting bonus damage. Finally, Just Impacts are *not* susceptible to ***Reverse Impacts***. Just Impacts are much better than normal Repels, but they are balanced by the extreme precision required to trigger them consistently. While it's not possible to normally Repel Unblockables, it *is* possible to Repel them with ***Just Impacts***. Of course, the exact timing required makes this a risky maneuver!

Impact Skills: Repel

Many of the skills available in Character Creation mode enhance Repels even further. Repels can be tailored to recover a small amount of health, to drain the opponent's health, to happen automatically on occasion when guarding, to always make follow-up attacks into counter-hits, or even to always be Just Impacts!

PARRY: ⇦ OR ⇙ Ⓖ

The ***Parry*** is a lower-risk, lower-reward version of ***Guard Impact***. By tapping ⇦ or ⇙Ⓖ just as an attack strikes your character, you toss the opponent to the ground and gain a great advantage—again, successfully Parrying is hit-level dependent. Fewer positions in fighting games are more advantageous than standing near a grounded opponent. The pressure you can put on a foe from this position is called a ***wakeup game***, or ***Okizeme***. Parries deal no direct damage and have no effect on the Soul Gauge, unlike Repels, but neither are Parries susceptible to Reverse Impacts. Guard Breaks can be Parried, but Unblockables cannot.

The Soul Gauge

The Soul Gauge is the most significant addition to the Soulcalibur IV combat system. This globe-like meter is located next to each character's health bar, at the top of the screen. At the beginning of a round, it is colored green. Guard too many attacks or have your attacks Repelled too often, and it begins to turn red, eventually flashing red. When you attack the opponent frequently, it begins to turn blue before it eventually flashes blue. A flashing blue Soul Gauge is full, while a flashing red Soul Gauge is empty. These two extremes are very important, as only with a flashing red gauge can a character be ***Soul Crushed***!

SOUL CRUSH

Guarding attacks while your character's ***Soul Gauge*** is empty results in a ***Soul Crush***. During a Soul Crush, your character reels, completely vulnerable to attack, and he or she loses a piece of armor. The armor lost corresponds to the incoming attack's hit level. A Soul Crush caused by a high attack removes headwear, for example. The only upside to getting Soul Crushed—provided you survive the ordeal—is that the Soul Gauge resets to green, preventing you from getting Soul Crushed twice in succession. The downside far outweighs this minor benefit. In a Soul Crushed state, you're completely vulnerable to anything the opponent feels like doing: a Ring Out attempt, a launcher into a big juggle, and so on. Most worrisome, he or she can even end the round outright with a ***Critical Finish***! The threat of a Soul Crush, and the likely subsequent Critical Finish, should make you very wary of guarding when your Soul Gauge edges into the red. While it's risky to turn up your offense or to go for Guard Impacts instead of just blocking, it's safer than guarding one too many times and losing a round to an instant kill! Likewise, press the advantage against your adversary when his or her Soul Gauge turns red. However, be aware that your opponent may adjust his or her play style to avoid Soul Crushes and Critical Finishes. Use this against your enemy, avoiding predictable moves that he or she might expect to Guard Impact, counter-hit, or sidestep.

Actions that Increase Soul Gauge, Edging Toward Blue

- Landing attacks
- Having attacks guarded
- Getting Soul Crushed (assuming you survive)
- Naturally increases slowly over time

Actions that Decrease Soul Gauge, Edging Toward Red

- Guarding attacks
- Having attacks Repelled

Armor

Another new aspect of *Soulcalibur IV*, entwined with the ***Soul Gauge***, is the armor system. Armor is no longer strictly cosmetic. Every character has high, mid, and low pieces of armor that can be broken off under certain circumstances! When a character is Soul Crushed, he or she loses armor corresponding to the hit level of the attack that causes the Soul Crush. Thus, a low hit that triggers a Soul Crush destroys low armor, for example. Armor also has a chance to break anytime a character suffers a powerful attack, so armor is frequently destroyed after harsh counter-hits and painful combos. When armor breaks, strikes against the unprotected region deal extra damage. Special Mid and Special Low attacks do not benefit from this damage increase. A small armor indicator appears just below each character's Soul Gauge; it shows which pieces of armor are missing.

Damage with Armor Broken

Broken Armor Location	Damage Percentage
High	111%
Mid	106%
Low	111%

Critical Finish

An extension of the ***Soul Crush*** system, ***Critical Finish*** attacks allow you to end matches instantly after Soul Crushing your foe. Pay attention to the Soul Gauges. If your opponent's Soul Gauge is flashing red, try to make him or her guard an attack. As your enemy reels from the resultant Soul Crush, press Ⓖ+Ⓐ+Ⓑ+Ⓚ. This initiates your character's Critical Finish, an elaborate attack that defeats the enemy outright and ends the current round! Note that it's possible to Soul Crush your foe with a Repel, and then Critical Finish him!

The Soul Still Burns

In Character Creation mode, there are many skills that alter how the Soul Gauge behaves. You can drain the opponent's Soul Gauge more quickly, refill your own more rapidly, begin the round with a blue gauge rather than a green one, or even have stats that improve when your Soul Gauge is in bad shape!

Waking Up: Options While Floored

One of the worst possible positions for your character in any fighting game is to be lying on the ground with your opponent hovering over you. Options while "waking up" are severely limited compared to those available to the character still on his or her feet. However, the situation isn't completely hopeless. You can simply press Ⓖ to rise, but other, more complex and situation-specific options are also available.

ROLLING

By tapping the D-pad or stick ⇦, ⇩, ⇨, or ⇧ you can make your character roll toward or away from the opponent, as well as laterally into the background or foreground. This can be useful if the opponent expects you simply to get up, into the path of his or her attack or throw attempt. Lateral rolls cause your foe's vertical attacks to whiff, while forward and backward rolls can make pouncing attacks miss.

RISING ATTACKS

Floored characters do retain some offensive capability. Pressing Ⓐ, Ⓑ, or Ⓚ while waking up from a knockdown causes your character to perform a "While Rising" attack. Wakeup attacks can be performed after rolls, making them useful for punishing enemy attacks that you evade with a roll. They're also great to use after you intentionally pause before waking up—your opponent may stick out attacks quickly, expecting you to rise into them. In this situation, a delayed rising attack will counter-hit your adversary's whiffed strike.

UKEMI

Any time after you get knocked down, you can rise by pressing Ⓖ. However, pressing Ⓖ just as you hit the ground performs an ***Ukemi***. Ukemi translates as "the art of falling safely." For the purposes of *Soulcalibur IV*, it means that you rise as soon as possible. Tapping ⇦, ⇩, ⇨, or ⇧ along with Ⓖ just as your character hits the ground causes your character to spring up in that direction. Using Ukemi is vital for getting back into the fight quickly and not giving your opponent too much of an advantage for knocking you down. Note that if you Ukemi you cannot use rising attacks.

Just Ukemi

In some situations it's not possible to wake up simply by rising or using Ukemi. This is usually the case while you get bounced off the ground in certain juggle combos. Your character may be on the ground for only a split second before getting launched up into the air again. However, on these occasions you can use what's called ***Just Ukemi*** to attempt to get up in the midst of the combo and avoid the rest of it. The term "Just" when applied in fighting games means that the timing on a given action must be extremely precise. A Just Ukemi involves pressing Ⓖ at the *exact* moment your character hits the ground. For example, the Just Frame version of Amy's ⇨⇨Ⓑ bounces the target off the ground during aerial combos, enabling it to be used up to three times in succession. However, Just Ukemi can be used precisely when the second ⇨⇨Ⓑ slaps a character to the ground, avoiding the remainder of the combo's hits. This is challenging, but there is no reason not to attempt it. Trying for Just Ukemi is better than simply submitting to an extended, damaging juggle! Between Just Ukemi and ***Aerial Control***, you still have some defense even in the middle of a combo.

Aerial Control

While the situation may seem hopeless when you're caught in a juggle combo, it's not. ***Aerial Control*** allows you to escape most juggle combos after the first juggle hit. After you get launched into the air, your foe gets one crack at your character for free. But subsequent hits after the first one are not guaranteed if you pay attention. Simply hold the stick or D-pad in any direction, and your character "twists" in that direction in midair, likely causing more juggle hit attempts to miss. This is a crucial tactic to mitigate the damage you receive when you get launched. If the opponent tries too hard to keep juggling you after you use Aerial Control to tumble out of harm's way, you may be able to hit the ground and rise quickly to retaliate before your foe recovers from his or her attacks!

Offense

In War, the Only Sure Defense is Offense...
—General George S. Patton

Offense is as powerful as ever in *Soulcalibur IV*. With many types of attacks and mix-ups to master, along with the new ***Soul Gauge*** system to deter passive play, attacking is king. Familiarity with the various kinds of strikes aids you in applying them against foes and in defending against them. Notations within this guide that include commands like ←Ⓑ, ↓Ⓐ, Ⓑ+Ⓖ, and so on convey that you simply have to tap the commands. Notations using ←Ⓑ, ↓Ⓐ, and so on indicate that you must press and hold the buttons and directions. Finally, commands notated as ⒷⒶ or ⒶⒷ+Ⓚ indicate that you must press one button very briefly, or "feather" it, before you input the next command as quickly as possible.

Basic Attack Controls

HORIZONTAL ATTACK: Ⓐ

Horizontal attacks are the foundation of an offense. They tend to be faster than vertical attacks, and they have circular properties. Horizontal attacks usually strike opponents using 8-Way Run or sidesteps. Standing Ⓐ is one of the fastest attacks for most characters, and it usually leads to a string of potential attacks that can serve as your offense's foundation. Horizontal attacks whiff more often than other attacks against crouching characters.

VERTICAL ATTACK: Ⓑ

Vertical attacks are usually more powerful than horizontal attacks, inflicting more damage and possessing greater ***Soul Crush*** potential. Also, vertical attacks are less frequently avoidable by crouching. To balance these aspects, vertical attacks can be avoided by using 8-Way Running or sidesteps. Thus, using vertical attacks carelessly can expose you to huge openings and big retribution.

Boost Skills: Strengthen Horizontal/Vertical

Under Boost Skills, you'll find options to enhance all horizontal attacks at the expense of vertical attacks, or vice versa. This can be helpful for characters almost entirely focused on one or the other: Hilde and Raphael for verticals, or Seong Mi-Na and Astaroth for horizontals, to name a few examples. In exchange for the boost to your favored attacks you sacrifice some damage, but it's not the type of damage around which you base your play style.

KICK: Ⓚ

Kicks usually deliver less damage and have shorter range than horizontal and vertical attacks. Kicks make up for this by frequently being faster than their Ⓐ and Ⓑ slash counterparts.

THROWS

Throws, initiated by pressing Ⓐ+Ⓖ or Ⓑ+Ⓖ, are used to damage passive or overly defensive opponents, as they cannot be guarded. However, throws have weaknesses that keep them from dominating. Crouching avoids almost all throws, save for those specifically tailored to snag crouching characters. Finally, throws can be escaped with the correct command. Throws initiated with Ⓐ+Ⓖ are escaped by pressing Ⓐ, while throws initiated with Ⓑ+Ⓖ are escaped by pressing Ⓑ. This holds true for standing and crouching throws, and even a few throws that are intended for use against grounded opponents. Only a few throws cannot be throw escaped, including throws executed from behind.

Special Skills: Auto Grapple Break

Auto Grapple Break, found in Character Creation, allows you to escape throws occasionally—even if you don't try!

Throw Escapes

Just as a throw is initiated, the throw victim has a brief window to input the correct escape command. Pressing either or (depending on which was used in the attacker's throw command) during this window breaks the grapple. When the player inputs the command early in the window, an advantage is given to the would-be throw victim. If he or she inputs the command midway through the window, a match reset will occur, with advantage given to neither character. Finally, late in the window, the throw escapee breaks the throw but is at a disadvantage. Note that certain throws, including air and back throws, cannot be escaped (although Voldo and Astaroth can escape back throws). Finally, both Ⓐ and Ⓑ cannot simply be mashed to escape throws—whichever is pressed first counts as the throw attempt command, and if both are pressed simultaneously a break attempt with Ⓐ is registered.

Attack Types

HIGH

High strikes tend to be faster than other attacks. Characters can avoid them by guarding while standing, or by crouching. This means that high attacks are most likely to connect if your opponent is actively trying to move or attack.

MID

Mid-hitting attacks are usually a little slower than high attacks. But they have an advantage in that they cannot be avoided by crouching. Mids must be guarded while standing, and they strike crouching characters. Note that characters guarding while standing, in anticipation of incoming mid or high attacks, are susceptible to throws.

LOW

Low attacks must be guarded while crouching, and they strike standing characters. Low attacks actually duck under incoming high attacks, striking the opponent and scoring a counter-hit. However, low attacks can be avoided by jumping. Low attacks generally don't have as many string or combo follow-up options as highs and mids. This makes lows most useful for making opponents guess between guarding while standing or crouching, and for striking a foe's high attacks and throw attempts.

SPECIAL MID

Special mids can be guarded standing *or* crouching, unlike normal mids. These attacks are thus most likely to connect while the opponent is trying to maneuver or attack.

SPECIAL LOW

Special lows can be guarded standing *or* crouching. They can also be avoided by jumping, just like normal lows. Because any guard action avoids them, the usefulness of these attacks is limited to going under an opponent's high attacks.

UNBLOCKABLE

Unblockable attacks work as advertised; they cannot be guarded at all. Luckily, Unblockables announce themselves with a flame effect that's hard to miss—a visual queue that says, "Watch out!" Avoid Unblockables by dashing away, sidestepping, striking, or throwing the user before you get hit. Use Unblockables to your advantage by setting them up on floored opponents who are rising ("waking up"), or to keep overly passive rivals on their toes. Unblockables can be Repelled only by ***Just Impacts***, and they cannot be Parried.

Power Skills: Auto Unblockable

In Character Creation mode you'll find the Auto Unblockable skills. These generate a flame effect on your combatant's hands and occasionally turn high-damage attacks into Unblockables automatically. Wait, come back! It's not as strong as it sounds, and it simply adds a new wrinkle to offense.

GUARD BREAK

Some attacks cause the opponent to stagger even if guarded. These attacks, which animate with a blue lightning effect, are called Guard Breaks. While they don't inflict damage, some leave your enemy vulnerable to attack, while others can be useful to gain a little advantage and to keep your opponent wary of playing defensively. For example, Kilik's ⇩⇙⇦Ⓑ Guard Break leaves his enemy vulnerable to a quick ⇨ⒶⒶ string. On the other hand, Seong Mi-na's ⇦⇦Ⓑ doesn't give her a direct opening, but instead leaves her with the advantage needed to stage a follow-up attack. They also deal significant ***Soul Gauge*** damage if guarded, making them helpful when hunting for ***Soul Crush*** and ***Critical Finish*** opportunities.

Power Skills: Guard Breaker

The Guard Breaker skill is found under Power Skills in Character Creation and is activated manually during a match by pressing Ⓐ + Ⓑ + Ⓚ when the Soul Gauge pulses white. It changes all high-damage attacks into Guard Breaks for a brief period. This can be extremely useful, especially for inciting your opponent to panic when his or her Soul Gauge approaches dangerous levels.

THROW

As we discussed previously, throws cannot be guarded and can usually be avoided by crouching. Characters can escape throws with the correct escape command. Mix your throws between Ⓐ+Ⓖ and Ⓑ+Ⓖ to keep the opponent guessing if he or she continually tries to grapple break. Some characters even have throws designed to nab opponents off the ground or out of the air.

HIT THROW

Hit throws, also called attack throws, are moves that resemble strikes. They can be guarded, but when they're successful they lead to a throw animation.

Hit Effects

NORMAL HITS

Normal hits occur when your attack strikes the opponent while he or she is not actively initiating an attack, moving backward, or moving laterally. Successful strikes also register as normal hits if you strike an opponent's attack as it retracts. While many fighting games register a strike against an opposing attack's recovery as a counter-hit, *Soulcalibur IV* does not. You'll most frequently score normal hits simply because the opponent is guarding incorrectly or moving forward.

Normal Hit Damage

Area/State During Normal Hit	Damage Percentage
Front of body, standing	100%
Side of body, standing	105%
Back of body, standing	110%
Front of body, crouching	105%
Side of body, crouching	110%
Back of body, crouching	116%
Jumping up or forward	105%
Jumping backward	116%

Power Skills: Auto Counter

Under Power Skills in Character Creation mode you'll find a set of skills that randomly causes normal hits to register as counter-hits. The benefits to damage output and hitstun are obvious, especially for heavily damaging hits, which benefit more from an increase in damage percentage than lower-damage strikes.

COUNTER-HITS

Counter-hits occur when you strike the opponent while he or she is in the process of performing most actions. An opponent struck while moving forward or merely standing idle cannot be counter-hit; in these instances, the damage that the foe suffers (and the hitstun state that results) simply registers as normal. However, an opponent attempting a throw, starting an attack, or even moving backward or to the side can be counter-hit. This causes the character to take extra damage, and it often leads to special counter-hit-exclusive hitstun states, such as spins and crumples. Because counter-hits lead to significant bonus damage, and they often allow combos when they aren't otherwise possible, hunting for counter-hits (and avoiding enemy counter-hits) is a huge part of *Soulcalibur IV*. Try to sense when your opponent might attack too aggressively, and stick out attacks into your foe's startup. By the same token, don't be too cavalier using your own attacks!

Counter-Hit Damage

Area/State During Counter-Hit	Damage Percentage
Front of body, standing	120%
Side of body, standing	126%
Back of body, standing	132%
Front of body, crouching	126%
Side of body, crouching	132%
Back of body, crouching	139%
Lateral step/8-Way Run	110%
Backward step/8-Way Run	120%
Jumping up or forward	126%
Jumping backward	139%

Impact Skills: Nullify Counter

As the polar opposite to the Auto Counter skill set, Nullify Counter skills randomly downgrade incoming attacks to normal hits when they would otherwise register as counter-hits, bailing you out of additional pain and potential combos.

TYPES OF HITSTUN

When an attack is successful, it sends the opponent into ***hitstun***. There are many types of hitstun. Usually the opponent simply reels for a bit, vulnerable only to quick follow-up string hits, or perhaps nothing at all. Sometimes, with certain attacks (or with attacks that land as counter-hits), hitstun is more significant, leading to a special state usually referred to as a stagger, stun, or crumple. This opens opportunities for extra damage from combos. However, all is not lost for the character trapped in a special stun. Sometimes stuns can be escaped early by spinning the stick or D-pad as quickly as possible while holding Ⓖ. If a player does this quickly enough, he or she may escape the stun before the opposition capitalizes on it. Generally speaking, a player can escape special stun types early when his or her character staggers but does not ultimately fall to the ground. If a stun or crumple ends in a character collapsing to the floor, the stun is not recoverable. Unrecoverable, special stuns are crucial to landing and extending many combos. After a combo begins (or after a Wall Hit), all subsequent combo hits register as counter-hits. Thus, if a move causes a special type of stun on counter-hit, that's the type of stun it will cause within a combo (with few exceptions). Combos can generally continue until you repeat the same type of stun twice. To create truly brutal combos, try finding ways to string many types of moves that cause special (but not the same) staggers. If you have trouble getting moves to connect, try attempting a string with an opponent's back to an arena edge, reducing the distance he or she gets pushed back by the hits. Or try scoring a Wall Hit somewhere in the combo. Combos using staggers, crumples, and stuns are good because they pile on the damage, and because they often give you plenty of time to verify that a combo is working. Finally, note that during crumples and staggers foes are not usually considered standing[md]as they slump to the ground, they're usually considered crouching regardless of their animation. This means that high throws and attacks will whiff, but mid and low attacks, as well as crouching throws, will connect.

Types of Special Hitstun

Effect	Notes
Double Over	Character bends over clutching stomach—recoverable
Crumple	Character collapses to the ground—vulnerable
Fall Back	Character falls backward—recoverable
Hop	Character clutches foot in pain while hopping—vulnerable
Spin	Character spins in place—vulnerable
Tremble	Character shakes in place—vulnerable
Writhing	Character shudders in pain on the ground—vulnerable

Combos

A combo is a succession of hits that are unavoidable after the first hit connects. There are many ways to start combos: from launching moves, after attacks with special stun properties, or even after some throws. After launching an opponent, you're guaranteed one free hit only while the foe is airborne, before he or she can use ***Aerial Control*** to escape. There are a few exceptions to this rule for particular types of launching moves or extremely fast attacks. Combos on the ground usually require the special extended stun properties detailed in the previous section. As a rule, you can extend *Soulcalibur IV* combos provided you use moves that cause a *different* type of stun than the previous moves in the combo. As soon as you repeat a particular stun, the opponent usually slumps to the ground and the combo ends. Finally, note that when we discuss combos, we almost always mean guaranteed ones that the opponent cannot escape. If your opponent isn't mashing out of recoverable stuns or using defensive systems like ***Aerial Control*** and ***Just Ukemi***, it can seem like some "combos" are terrific. However, a savvy player—or even the CPU AI, depending on the difficulty setting—can usually escape them.

Special Skills: Charge Cancel

Attacks have startup, active, and recovery periods. Startup is the period when the attack winds up, before it can actually strike. Hitting a character out of an attack during this period registers as a counter-hit. The active period is the time in which the attack is actually capable of striking. The recovery period is the animation afterward, in which your character returns to a neutral position, able to accept new commands. Normally, you can do nothing until your character finishes recovering—this often leaves you vulnerable and limits combo potential. Imagine if you could perform moves instantly, without having to wait out the recovery period. The Charge Cancel, activated by pressing Ⓐ + Ⓑ + Ⓚ when your Soul Gauge pulses white, allows exactly that! Your character flashes red and instantly returns to a neutral state. This can be useful to create combos that aren't possible otherwise. It's also great for using heavy moves consecutively against a guarding opponent to decimate his or her Soul Gauge. Finally, Charge Cancel comes in handy after your foe guards or dodges one of your attacks that has a lengthy recovery, thus saving you from retaliation!

Gauge Skills: HP Recovery

HP Recovery skills, found in Character Creation, actually return a small amount of life to your character when you're struck with a combo of three hits or more! While it's not a good idea to rely heavily on this crutch, every little bit of life helps...assuming you survive the combo!

JUGGLES

A juggle combo involves launching or bouncing the opponent into the air, then following up with strikes against his or her airborne body. As we mentioned previously, usually you get only one free strike against the airborne opponent before he or she can ***Aerial Control*** away from your combo attempt. For this reason, many juggle combos have only one follow-up hit in the air after a launch or bounce.

Power Skills: Nullify Aerial Control

The Nullify Aerial Control skill, found in Character Creation mode, allows three "free" hits against an airborne opponent before he or she can Aerial Control away. Needless to say, this enhances juggle potential greatly! Combined with Charge Cancel, it's possible to create some absolutely brutal juggles, with greatly enhanced damage and Ring Out potential.

Special Skills: Magnet

The Magnet skill diminishes the ability of *both* characters to juggle, because it reduces the height to which all launching moves loft characters. This can be a terrific skill to equip if your playing style isn't too juggle-dependent, because it limits your opponent's combo potential.

Power Skills: Knockdown

Knockdown is polar opposite to Magnet. The altitude to which characters are juggled, or "bounce" to, is increased. This creates new combo possibilities, especially from attacks that launch just enough to create a knockdown situation, but not enough to juggle otherwise.

WALL HITS

While wall hits are situational and not possible on every stage, they can lead to some of the game's biggest combos and damage potential. A wall hit occurs when you "splat" your foe against a wall with attacks that cause special types of stun. Often, this allows you to score additional hits after attacks that normally just floor the opponent or knock him or her too far away. Additionally, any attack connected after a wall hit has the properties of a counter-hit. Use attacks with special hit properties to keep the foe reeling in different types of stun—combos can continue until you repeat the same type of stun twice.

Ring Outs

A ***Ring Out*** occurs when one character falls off a stage, whether by stepping or jumping off accidentally or getting thrown or knocked off. A Ring Out is an instant loss for the character that falls over the edge. Ring edges can work for and against you. Nothing generates a huge comeback or devastating turnaround loss faster and more unexpectedly than a Ring Out. If you're far behind in a fight and feeling overmatched, it just might play in your favor to lure the battle to a ring's edge and hope for the best. Likewise, if you overmatch your opponent greatly or have a large life lead, there's no reason to tempt fate by skirting the brink. Be aware of the ring's edge at all times and position yourself accordingly.

Special Skills: Nullify Ring Out

Lessen the chances of getting Ringed Out by equipping a Nullify Ring Out skill, found in Character Creation mode. These skills make it much harder to fly off the edge. They cause you to "stick" to the ring by a small amount whenever you're in danger of falling over. Ring Out losses are still very possible, but they happen less often.

Okizeme: The Anti-Wakeup Game

Floored characters are extremely vulnerable, and a large part of effective play is to continue pressuring them, scoring ground hits or additional knockdowns. A rising character may Ukemi to rise quickly, or the foe may wake up guarding, or with rising attacks. Well-timed attacks can beat a rising character's strikes, while Guard Breaks and Unblockables can be useful against foes who simply Ukemi and then guard. Mix between useful low and mid attacks, hopefully sending your opponent to the ground again if he or she guards incorrectly. Once your enemy fears mids like launchers on wakeup, you can simply run up and throw against foes who rise and guard standing, as well. Finally, you can also simply stand nearby, hoping to bait whiffed rising attacks that you can easily punish.

Advantage and Disadvantage

Understanding the notion of advantage and disadvantage is extremely important for improving your fighting game skills. When characters stand idle, they are considered to be "neutral." That is to say, they are doing nothing, ready to accept and execute commands at any time. Once a character initiates a maneuver or attack, he enters startup and recovery periods—the times in which the character's attack or move animates its windup, its active or striking period, and then its recovery. This includes states like hitstun and blockstun. Although the receiving character doesn't actually initiate these states, their animations must play out before the character returns to neutral, ready to accept more commands. With very rare exceptions, characters cannot accept further input during these times. In essence, consider characters "busy" while they perform any action. Advantage and disadvantage, then, refer to what is possible after two characters interact, playing out their respective animations. Depending on each character's actions, one character returns to a neutral state faster than the other. Assuming both characters perform another action as soon as possible, the character who can act first has what is called ***advantage***. The character who will act last has what is called ***disadvantage***.

In practice, this is less complicated than it sounds. Let's say Nightmare pokes at Siegfried with ⇨Ⓚ at close range, hoping to counter-hit Siegfried to the ground if he tries anything:

1 Unfortunately for Nightmare, Siegfried guards. While Nightmare is stuck in the animation for ⇨Ⓚ, Siegfried is stuck in blockstun.

2 Siegfried recovers from blockstun before Nightmare recovers from the animation for ⇨Ⓚ. Siegfried has the ***advantage***; his next actions, executed as quickly as possible, will become active before Nightmare's. Siegfried tries ⇘Ⓑ, knowing that if Nightmare tries an attack the fiend will get counter-hit.

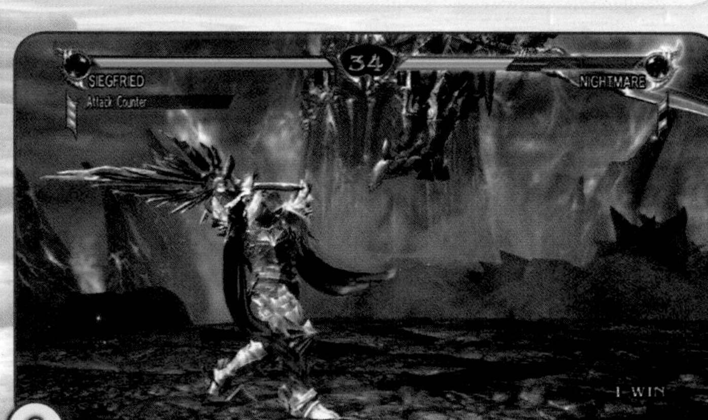

3 Nightmare, being overly aggressive and a little too optimistic, tries to attack after he recovers from his ⇨Ⓚ. However, Nightmare is at a ***disadvantage***, so his attack begins just in time to get counter-hit and launched by Siegfried's ⇘Ⓑ. From here, Siegfriend can add a juggle hit with Ⓑ, smacking Nightmare to the ground. Nightmare paid a heavy price for ignoring his own disadvantage.

This example isn't cut-and-dried, and many variables could come into play. If Nightmare simply guards after his ⇨Ⓚ, he'll block Siegfried's ⇘Ⓑ. However, Siegfried's ⇘Ⓑ changes his stance, and instead of using his Ⓑ follow-up to score a juggle hit, he has many other options to maintain the pressure. Nightmare could also try a Repel or Parry after having his ⇨Ⓚ guarded, and then Siegfried's ⇘Ⓑ gets turned against him. Many outcomes are possible every time two characters interact, and understanding advantage and disadvantage is critical to making good decisions. In general, it pays to be cautious and use defensive options when you're at a disadvantage. Conversely, it's good to be aggressive and use offensive options when you have an advantage. Characters usually have an advantage after they land hits, and they're at a disadvantage after their hits get guarded. There are no universal rules, so practice with your favorite characters and fighting styles, and consult our character chapters for more specific notes and scenarios for each fighter.

Fancy Footwork: The Poking Game

Novice and advanced players alike often underestimate the importance of positioning and patience. Often, the temptation is to rush in and stage your favorite tactics, but a little patience and attentiveness pays off. Based on your opponent's abilities—both the player's and his or her character's—what is your foe's most probable plan? Do you think your adversary knows what you want to do? How is he or she likely to counter? All of these questions are important to consider during a match. Thanks to sidesteps and 8-Way Run, he who hesitates is usually *not* lost. Watch the opponent carefully, and stay on the edge of his or her attack range. Use relatively safe, low-risk moves—referred to as pokes—to gauge a response, to score a knockdown, or to punish your foe's whiffed attacks. Playing the positioning game and going for knockdowns or counter-hits to force your way in, is affectionately called "footsies," or foot games, by the fighting game community. Conversely, keeping enemies out or caging them into a particular distance that's beneficial to your character and detrimental to theirs is called "zoning." Learning patience and playing the position game with your enemy pays huge dividends by making you less predictable, thus making it safer when you finally do rush in and exploit your biggest threats.

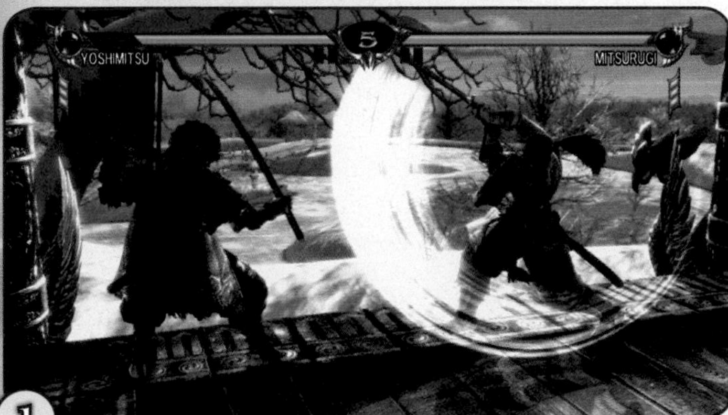

1 Yoshimitsu dances on the edge of Mitsurugi's range, coaxing Mitsurugi into attempting ⇘Ⓑ. However, Yoshimitsu's careful positioning causes Mitsurugi's attack to whiff…

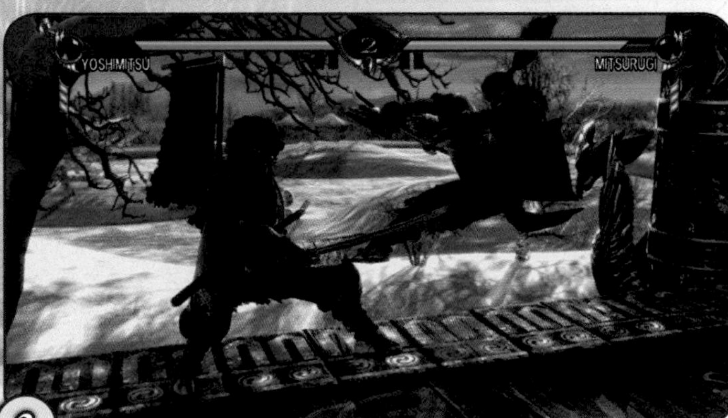

2 …and Yoshimitsu punishes Mitsurugi with ⇦ⓀⒷ, scoring a knockdown and a shot at pressuring Mitsurugi while he's floored.

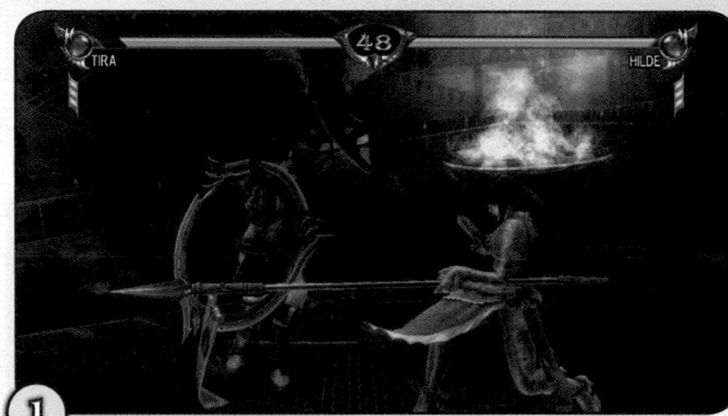

1 Hilde is fantastic at controlling the linear plane, but many of her attacks are susceptible to sidesteps and 8-Way Run. Tira, wielding a weapon with far shorter range, capitalizes on this knowledge by continually using 8-Way Run to avoid Hilde's long, linear pokes.

2 Tira avoids a spear thrust and counterattacks with ⇧Ⓑ (⇩Ⓑ when facing left), launching Hilde during her attack's recovery. Tira can juggle with ⇨⇨Ⓚ, and then establish close range while Hilde rises.

1 Talim is an exclusively short-range character. Against characters with longer weapons, she might not always be able to punish their whiffs, but at least she gets a brief opportunity to rush in. Here, Seong Mi-na uses ⒶⒶ to swipe at Talim, but Talim backpedals to avoid it.

2 Talim uses Seong Mi-na's recovery period to run forward, getting closer to her ideal position—in Seong Mi-na's face.

Single-Player Game Modes

Soulcalibur IV features myriad gameplay modes for the solo gamer. Not only are they expansive and fun, but playing through the various modes also earns gold and unlocks a vast arsenal of equipment, along with numerous bonus characters. You can tweak equipment and appearances in Character Creation mode, and you can even assemble entirely new custom characters! By playing with a given character (or with a custom character patterned after a particular character's style), you'll level up the style of said character. The max level is 9; higher levels allow access to better skills in Character Creation mode. Access to better skills is very important if you want a decent chance at completing some of the harder single-player challenges. Consult the skill tables in our Character Creation chapter for a list of skills and their effects, along with the level required to equip them. Leveling up a given skill doesn't take too long—just keep plugging away with characters using that style in single-player modes.

Story

In Story mode, you select your character and take him or her through five stages, playing out the character's role in the story of *Soulcalibur IV*. The third stage takes place at the Ancient Gate, fighting against a bonus character who will be unlocked if you're victorious. Upon completing the fifth stage, each fighter's ultimate weapon—often a variation of Soul Calibur or Soul Edge—becomes available for purchase in Character Creation mode. Beating Algol as the final boss unlocks him for use in other modes.

Character	Mid-Boss	Boss
Algol	Angol Fear	Siegfried
Amy	Kamikirimusi	Nightmare
Angol Fear	Ashlotte	Algol
The Apprentice	Angol Fear	Algol
Ashlotte	Scheherazade	Algol
Astaroth	Ashlotte	Algol
Cassandra	Kamikirimusi	Algol
Cervantes	Shura	Algol
Darth Vader	Angol Fear	Algol
Hilde	Scheherazade	Nightmare
Ivy	Shura	Nightmare
Kamikirimusi	Shura	Algol
Kilik	Angol Fear	Algol
Lizardman	Ashlotte	Nightmare
Maxi	Ashlotte	Nightmare
Mitsurugi	Kamikirimusi	Algol
Nightmare	Scheherazade	Siegfried
Raphael	Shura	Siegfried
Rock	Ashlotte	Algol
Scheherazade	Angol Fear	Algol
Seong Mi-Na	Shura	Algol
Setsuka	Shura	Algol
Shura	Kamikirimusi	Algol
Siegfried	Scheherazade	Nightmare
Sophitia	Ashlotte	Algol
Taki	Shura	Siegfried
Talim	Ashlotte	Algol
Tira	Kamikirimusi	Siegfried
Voldo	Scheherazade	Nightmare
Xianghua	Kamikirimusi	Algol
Yoda	Scheherazade	Algol
Yoshimitsu	Scheherazade	Algol
Yun-Seong	Kamikirimusi	Nightmare
Zasalamel	Angol Fear	Algol

Tower of Lost Souls

The Tower of Lost Souls offers an extensive challenge that requires the use of modified, buffed custom characters. Whether you're Ascending or Descending, you're continually required to fight a dozen or more fighters in succession, without any sort of breather or health regeneration in between. This makes skills like HP Drain A, equipped in Character Creation mode, absolutely essential. Keep the "Switch" button handy—you don't want to allow characters to die in these modes! Swapping them out when they're at low health helps greatly, as they stay alive and regain vitality, albeit slowly, while they're off-screen. It can be useful to build characters for different roles. For example, set up your first character as an offensive powerhouse, and your second as a defensive stalwart with skills that replenish HP. Use the first character to beat down your foes, swapping to the second character when HP gets low.

Ascend

Ascending the Tower of Lost Souls, you select the floor on which to fight and then your combatants. A few stages allow you to select three fighters, while others allow you to choose only one, but most require you to pick a duo. You must then plow through all the adversaries on a given set of floors, without any rest between battles. Naturally, this makes the lengthy stages in which you can select only one fighter the toughest. Levels 30-32F, 39-41F, 50-52F, and 53-56F force you to fight as many as *fourteen* foes in a row... *solo*. To succeed in these battles, use Character Creation to build a fighter based on the style with which you're most comfortable. Outfit this fighter with equipment that boosts Defense and HP as high as possible—the closer you can get to 200% in each, the better your odds of success. Attack power is less important; damage comes naturally regardless, but survival is the paramount concern, and there are no guarantees. To this end, equip the HP Drain A skill. HP Burst is useful too, but it can leave you extremely vulnerable to Soul Crushes. If you're still having trouble with a given stage, note the genders, styles, and skills of fighters on a given set of stages, and plan accordingly. For example, the Appeal skill can help if most of the fighters are of the opposite gender to your preferred character. Finally, note that every floor in the Tower houses a special piece of equipment that is unlocked if you fulfill certain parameters. These conditions can be as simple as landing a few throws, or as strange as intentionally jumping off a stage!

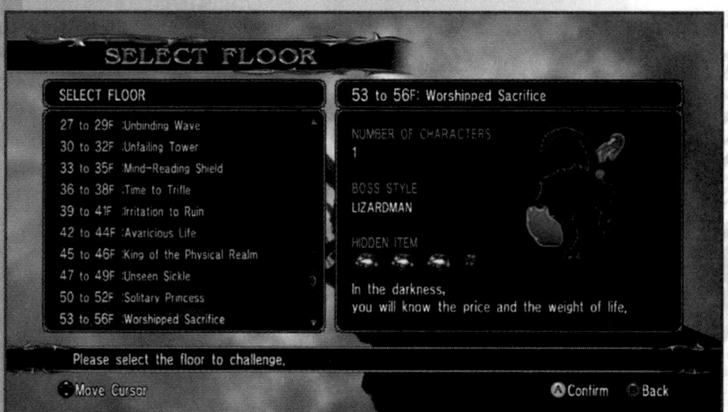

1-2F: LAW OF THE EARTH

Select 2 Fighters

Floor	Foe	Gender	Style	Skills
1F	Helerides	Male	Astaroth	Slow Feet
1F	Rock	Male	Rock	Knock Down, Slow Feet
2F	Revvolk	Male	Zasalamel	Shave Damage C, Slow Feet
2F	Curtana	Female	Rock	Shave Damage C
2F	Astaroth	Male	Astaroth	Shave Damage C, Auto Counter C, Knock Down

1F	Soldier's Hat	Cleared the stage with no damage taken.
2F	Warrior Trousers	Cleared the stage with no Ring Out from either parties.

3-4F: BLADE PIERCING WALL

Select 2 Fighters

Floor	Foe	Gender	Style	Skills
3F	Laldenna	Male	Raphael	Nullify Ring Out C
3F	Farvolte	Male	Siegfried	Nullify Counter C
3F	Vhaju	Male	Cervantes	Nullify Ring Out B, Nullify Counter B, Will Power
4F	Alhabot	Male	Nightmare	Nullify Counter B, Nullify Ring Out B
4F	Hilde	Female	Hilde	Soul Repel, Soul Gauge Boost C, Nullify Ring Out A, Will Power

Floor	Item Reward	Acquisition Method
3F	Pauldron	Switch with an ally more than 2 times.
4F	Warlord's Belt	Performed 3 attack throws.

5-7F: PREDATOR'S FEAST

Select 3 Fighters

Floor	Foe	Gender	Style	Skills
5F	Lizardman	Male	Lizardman	Magnet
5F	Lizardman	Male	Lizardman	Magnet
6F	Lizardman	Male	Lizardman	Venom Fang C, Step Speed Up
6F	Lizardman	Male	Lizardman	Step Speed Up
7F	Lizardman	Male	Lizardman	Step Speed Up, Run Speed Up, Nullify Ring Out A

Floor	Item Reward	Acquisition Method
5F	Clergy Clothes	Defeated an enemy by Ring Out.
6F	Wonder Jacket	Threw an opponent.
7F	Warrior Trousers	Cleared the stage without missing any attacks.

8-10F: AWAKENING DISASTER

Select 2 Fighters

Floor	Foe	Gender	Style	Skills
8F	Dirk	Male	Yun-Seong	Will Power
8F	Elise	Female	Xianghua	Will Power
8F	Marej	Male	Raphael	Will Power, Hyper Mode
9F	Zain	Male	Nightmare	Hysterical Strength, Appeal
9F	Kudi	Female	Seong Mi-Na	Will Power, Appeal
10F	Cervantes	Male	Cervantes	Hysterical Strength, Will Power, Hyper Mode

Floor	Item Reward	Acquisition Method
8F	Armor Ring: Ice Mirror	Switch characters twice.
9F	Scarlett Blossoms	Guarded the opponent's attack 3 times in a row.
10F	Silver Boots	Guarded the opponent's attack 10 times in a row.

11 FLOOR: THREATENING MIRROR

Select 1 Fighter

Floor	Foe	Gender	Style	Skills
11F	Ayala	Female	Seong Mi-Na	Knock Down, Auto Grapple Break C
11F	Certis	Female	Cervantes	Knock Down, Nullify Ring Out C
11F	Rapielle	Female	Tira	Knock Down, Auto Grapple Break C
11F	Angol Fear	Female	Angol Fear	Knock Down, Nullify Ring Out C

Floor	Item Reward	Acquisition Method
11F	Grim Horn	Defeated all enemies with Critical Finish.

12-14F: LIFE ON SAND

Select 2 Fighters

Floor	Foe	Gender	Style	Skills
12F	Claire	Female	Talim	Soul Gauge Damage C
12F	Lydia	Female	Voldo	Soul Gauge Damage B, Soul Gauge Rate Up C
13F	Jiland	Male	Maxi	Soul Gauge Damage B, Soul Gauge Vamp
13F	Enna	Female	Setsuka	Soul Gauge Damage A, Soul Gauge Rate Up B
14F	Henrietta	Female	Ivy	Soul Gauge Damage A, Soul Gauge Recovery C, Nullify Ring Out B
14F	Rusa	Female	Taki	Soul Gauge Damage A, Soul Gauge Rate Up A, Nullify Ring Out A
14F	Tira	Female	Tira	Soul Gauge Boost C, Soul Gauge Damage S, Soul Gauge Recovery B, Nullify Ring Out S

Floor	Item Reward	Acquisition Method
12F	Magus Cloth	Defeated all enemies by Ring Out.
13F	Pegasus Sallet	Destroyed all the walls within the stage.
14F	Stage: Phantom Pavilion - Seesaw	Performed Guard Impact more than 3 times.

15-17F: LIFE TO ENTERTAIN

Select 2 Fighters

Floor	Foe	Gender	Style	Skills
15F	Alastor	Male	Zasalamel	HP Drain S, Nullify Ring Out A
16F	Skeleton	Male	Lizardman	HP Drain A
16F	Skeleton	Male	Cassandra	HP Drain A
16F	Skeleton	Male	Hilde	HP Drain A, Shave Damage C
17F	Curua	Female	Seong Mi-Na	HP Drain A
17F	Ducis	Male	Astaroth	HP Drain A, HP Recovery C
17F	Armaroth	Male	Zasalamel	HP Drain S, Shave Damage C, HP Recovery B

Floor	Item Reward	Acquisition Method
15F	Submissions Belt	Cleared the stage with only Ⓐ & Ⓖ.
16F	Warlord's Pauldrons	Cleared the stage with time remaining at 0.
17F	Arm Bandages	Executed a 5+ combo.

18-20F: NO MAN'S LAND

Select 3 Fighters

Floor	Foe	Gender	Style	Skills
18F	Tomoe	Female	Yoshimitsu	Auto Impact B, Auto Grapple Break B
18F	Ryuki	Male	Mitsurugi	Auto Impact B, Impact Edge, Auto Grapple Break B
19F	Ryouga	Male	Mitsurugi	Auto Impact A, Auto Grapple Break B
19F	Setsuka	Female	Setsuka	Auto Impact A, Impact Heal, Auto Grapple Break A
20F	Sizuku	Female	Taki	Auto Impact S, Impact Edge, Auto Grapple Break A, Impact Heal
20F	Yoshimitsu	Male	Yoshimitsu	Auto Impact S, Impact Heal, Auto Grapple Break S

Floor	Item Reward	Acquisition Method
18F	Kouchu Kabuto	Stood on all corners of the stage.
19F	Longhua Qipao	Switched with an ally more than 5 times.
20F	Life Gem: Sun	Cleared the stage with a Critical Finish.

21-23F: UBER AIRHEAD

Select 2 Fighters

Floor	Foe	Gender	Style	Skills
21F	Seong Mi-Na	Female	Seong Mi-Na	Evil Sword Berserk, Double-Edged Sword, Hyper Mode
21F	Uvall	Male	Rock	Auto Counter B
21F	Veles	Male	Maxi	Auto Unblockable Attack B
22F	Xianghua	Female	Xianghua	Evil Sword Berserk, Double-Edged Sword, Hyper Mode
22F	Yufeng	Male	Zasalamel	Nullify Counter B, Auto Counter C
22F	Xunyu	Male	Astaroth	Nullify Counter A, Auto Counter B
23F	Cassandra	Female	Cassandra	Evil Sword Berserk, Double-Edged Sword, Hyper Mode, Shave Damage S
23F	Helios	Male	Yoshimitsu	Shave Damage C, Impact Edge
23F	Beleth	Male	Mitsurugi	Shave Damage B, Impact Edge

Floor	Item Reward	Acquisition Method
21F	Longhua Qipao	Voluntarily performed a Ring Out.
22F	Honor Boots	Performed more than 4 counter-hits.
23F	Frilled Skirt	Guarded the opponent's attack 3 times in a row.

24-26F: IRON SWORD

Select 1 Fighter

Floor	Foe	Gender	Style	Skills
24F	Gorus	Male	Kilik	Start Dash C, Will Power
24F	Marid	Male	Cervantes	Start Dash B
24F	Jean	Female	Raphael	Nullify Aerial Control, Charge Cancel, Soul Gauge Rate Up C
25F	Astraia	Female	Maxi	Soul Gauge Rate Up A, Soul Gauge Damage A, Charge Cancel
25F	Juno	Female	Siegfried	Soul Gauge Rate Up C, Charge Cancel
25F	Thetis	Female	Mitsurugi	Nullify Aerial Control, Soul Gauge Rate Up C, Charge Cancel
26F	Oruks	Male	Nightmare	Nullify Aerial Control, Charge Cancel, Soul Gauge Rate Up C, Nullify Ring Out A
26F	Castor	Male	Yoshimitsu	Nullify Aerial Control, Soul Gauge Rate Up C, Charge Cancel
26F	Nornen	Female	Xianghua	Nullify Aerial Control, Soul Gauge Rate Up C, Charge Cancel, Double-Edged Sword

Floor	Item Reward	Acquisition Method
24F	Protect Gem: Cardinal Direction	Performed a combo with a total damage over 240.
25F	Zhuque Changpao	Threw 5 times.
26F	Warthog Cuirass	Executed a 10+ combo.

27-29F: UNBINDING WAVE

Select 3 Fighters

Floor	Foe	Gender	Style	Skills
27F	Shura	Female	Shura	Switch Speed Up, Knock Down, Strengthen Vertical
27F	Taki	Female	Taki	Switch Speed Up, Magnet, Strengthen Horizontal
28F	Scheherazade	Female	Scheherazade	Switch Speed Up, Appeal, HP Drain S
28F	Raphael	Male	Raphael	Switch Speed Up, Appeal, Shave Damage S, Nullify Ring Out A
29F	Kamikirimusi	Female	Kamikirimusi	Switch Speed Up, Will Power, Auto Impact A, Impact Edge
29F	Ashlotte	Female	Ashlotte	Switch Speed Up, Hysterical Strength, Auto Impact A, Impact Heal

Floor	Item Reward	Acquisition Method
27F	Iron Gauntlets	Cleared the stage with no damage taken.
28F	Aculeus Suit	Opponent guarded a Guard Break attack at least twice.
29F	Menghu Boots	Switched with an ally more than 5 times.

30-32F: UNFAILING TOWER

Select 1 Fighter

Floor	Foe	Gender	Style	Skills
30F	Ivy	Female	Ivy	HP Recovery C, Auto Grapple Break C
30F	Talim	Female	Talim	HP Recovery B, Auto Grapple Break C, Nullify Ring Out B
30F	Cassandra	Female	Cassandra	Soul Gauge Boost C, HP Recovery C, Auto Impact C, Nullify Ring Out S
31F	Siegfriend	Male	Siegfried	HP Recovery C, Auto Grapple Break C
31F	Yun-Seong	Male	Yun-Seong	HP Recovery B, Auto Grapple Break B
31F	Rock	Male	Rock	HP Recovery B, Auto Grapple Break S
31F	Setsuka	Female	Setsuka	Soul Gauge Boost B, HP Recovery B, Auto Impact B
32F	Sophitia	Female	Sophitia	HP Recovery B, Nullify Ring Out A
32F	Tira	Female	Tira	HP Recovery A, Auto Grapple Break S
32F	Voldo	Male	Voldo	HP Recovery A, Auto Grapple Break S, Nullify Ring Out A
32F	Zasalamel	Male	Zasalamel	Soul Gauge Boost S, Auto Impact S, Nullify Ring Out S

Floor	Item Reward	Acquisition Method
30F	Spirit Gem: Nonuple Heads	Cleared the stage without guarding.
31F	Longming Qipao	Performed 5 or more Just Inputs.
32F	Vane Mask	Performed a low throw.

33-35F: MIND-READING SHIELD

Select 2 Fighters

Floor	Foe	Gender	Style	Skills
33F	Freya	Female	Hilde	Impact Heal, Auto Impact A
33F	Hestia	Female	Taki	Impact Heal, Master Impact
33F	Sallos	Male	Maxi	Impact Heal, Strong Impact
34F	Asrafil	Male	Mitsurugi	Impact Edge, Strong Impact
34F	Mors	Female	Amy	Impact Edge, Master Impact
34F	Seong Mi-Na	Female	Seong Mi-Na	Impact Edge, Auto Impact A
35F	Azalea	Female	Seong Mi-Na	Impact Edge, Master Impact, Auto Impact A
35F	Camilla	Female	Cassandra	Auto Impact A, Impact Edge, Impact Heal
35F	Xianghua	Female	Xianghua	Impact Edge, Impact Heal, Strong Impact, Auto Impact S

Floor	Item Reward	Acquisition Method
33F	Battle Dress	Performed 3 attack throws.
34F	Power Gem: Warrior Princess	Performed Guard Impact more than 3 times.
35F	Warthog Pauldrons	Cleared the stage without switching characters.

36-38F: TIME TO TRIFLE

Select 2 Fighters

Floor	Foe	Gender	Style	Skills
36F	Fenvil	Male	Maxi	Auto Grapple Break S, Soul Gauge Recovery A
36F	Jarvis	Male	Kilik	Nullify Ring Out S, HP Recovery S
36F	Aeolos	Male	Yun-Seong	Soul Gauge Boost S, HP Drain S
37F	Iblis	Male	Yoshimitsu	Auto Grapple Break A, HP Recovery A, Soul Gauge Recovery A
37F	Abigail	Female	Ivy	Nullify Ring Out A, HP Recovery A, Soul Gauge Boost A
37F	Carine	Female	Talim	Auto Grapple Break A, HP Drain A, Soul Gauge Boost A
38F	Eriel	Female	Hilde	Auto Grapple Break S, HP Recovery S, Soul Gauge Recovery S
38F	Hernes	Male	Rock	Nullify Ring Out A, HP Recovery S, Soul Gauge Boost S
38F	Siegfried	Male	Siegfried	Auto Grapple Break S, HP Drain S, Soul Gauge Boost S

Floor	Item Reward	Acquisition Method
36F	Parlor Blouse	Cleared the stage with time remaining at 0.
37F	Siren's Helm	Defeated all enemies with Critical Finish.
38F	Gorgon Fauld	Defeated all enemies by Ring Out.

39-41F: IRRITATION TO RUIN

Select 1 Fighter

Floor	Foe	Gender	Style	Skills
39F	Camio	Male	Voldo	Venom Fang B, Auto Unblockable Attack C
39F	Kalad	Male	Mitsurugi	Venom Fang B, Shave Damage C
39F	Guison	Male	Cervantes	Venom Fang B, Impact Edge
40F	Ainsel	Female	Tira	Venom Fang A, Shave Damage B
40F	Eris	Female	Taki	Venom Fang A, Auto Unblockable Attack B
40F	Callist	Female	Amy	Venom Fang A, Impact Edge
41F	Skeleton	Male	Lizardman	Venom Fang S, Shave Damage A, Impact Edge
41F	Skeleton	Male	Ivy	Venom Fang S, Auto Unblockable Attack A, Impact Edge
41F	Skeleton	Male	Raphael	Venom Fang S, Guard Breaker, Impact Edge

Floor	Item Reward	Acquisition Method
39F	Kingfisher Greaves	Cleared the stage without changing position.
40F	Deer Head	Executed a 5+ combo
41F	Minotaur	Perform 5 or more Just Inputs.

42-44F: AVARICIOUS LIFE

Select 2 Fighters

Floor	Foe	Gender	Style	Skills
42F	Cytherea	Female	Tira	HP Drain B, HP Recovery C
42F	Asphodel	Female	Setsuka	HP Drain B, HP Recovery B, Nullify Ring Out C
42F	Zasalamel	Male	Zasalamel	Life Burst S, Soul Gauge Boost A, Soul Gauge Recovery A, Nullify Ring Out A
43F	Haystir	Male	Yun-Seong	HP Drain A, HP Recovery A, Nullify Ring Out C
43F	Annaretta	Female	Sophitia	HP Burst, Soul Gauge Boost C, Nullify Ring Out B
43F	Talim	Female	Talim	Life Burst S, Soul Gauge Boost A, Soul Gauge Recovery A, Nullify Ring Out A
44F	Eurania	Female	Xianghua	Life Burst S, Soul Gauge Boost S, Soul Gauge Recovery A
44F	Kilik	Male	Kilik	Life Burst S, Soul Gauge Boost S, Soul Gauge Recovery A, Nullify Ring Out A

Floor	Item Reward	Acquisition Method
42F	Demonic Gloves	Cleared the stage without letting opponents invoke a skill.
43F	Repel Gem: Iron Shell	Performed an over-the-back throw.
44F	War Cloak	Cleared the stage with no Ring Out from either party.

45-46F: KING OF THE PHYSICAL REALM

Select 3 Fighters

Floor	Foe	Gender	Style	Skills
45F	Amrita	Female	Taki	Auto Grapple Break S, Nullify Ring Out S, Start Dash B
46F	Malphas	Male	Zasalamel	Auto Grapple Break S, Nullify Ring Out S, Auto Impact B
46F	Raguel	Male	Astaroth	Auto Grapple Break S, Nullify Ring Out S, Hysterical Strength

Floor	Item Reward	Acquisition Method
45F	Tiger Lily Kabuto	Defeated enemies without equipping any skills.
46F	Butterfly Salet	Defeated enemies without equipping any skills.

47-49F: UNSEEN SICKLE

Select 2 Fighters

Floor	Foe	Gender	Style	Skills
47F	Althea	Female	Yun-Seong	Invisible, Soul Gauge Boost C, Nullify Ring Out B
47F	Luph	Male	Rock	Invisible, Soul Gauge Boost C, Nullify Ring Out A
47F	Kilik	Male	Kilik	Invisible S, Soul Gauge Boost C, Nullify Ring Out S, Knock Down
48F	Loki	Male	Cervantes	Invisible, Soul Gauge Boost C, Soul Gauge Recovery A
48F	Elza	Female	Nightmare	Invisible, Soul Gauge Boost C, Soul Gauge Rate Up A
48F	Astaroth	Male	Astaroth	Invisible S, Soul Gauge Boost C, Soul Gauge Rate Up A, Knock Down
49F	Hilde	Female	Hilde	Invisible S, Soul Gauge Boost C, Nullify Ring Out A
49F	Setsuka	Female	Setsuka	Invisible S, Soul Gauge Boost C, Nullify Ring Out A
49F	Zasalamel	Male	Zasalamel	Invisible S, Soul Gauge Boost C, Nullify Ring Out S, Knock Down

Floor	Item Reward	Acquisition Method
47F	Succubus Boots	Threw 5 times.
48F	Life Gem: Jade	Cleared the stage with a character equipped with the skill "Invisible."
49F	Horns of Calamity	Cleared the stage without missing any attacks.

50-52F: SOLITARY PRINCESS

Select 1 Fighter

Floor	Foe	Gender	Style	Skills
50F	Flora	Female	Seong Mi-Na	Double-Edged Sword
50F	Alberic	Male	Maxi	Start Dash B, Step Speed Up, Auto Grapple Break B
50F	Balduin	Male	Siegfried	Will Power, Nullify Ring Out A
51F	Iris	Female	Raphael	HP Recovery A
51F	Jeanne	Female	Sophitia	HP Drain B, Nullify Ring Out B
51F	Apheta	Female	Cassandra	HP Drain A, Nullify Ring Out A
52F	Amy	Female	Amy	Appeal, Venom Fang A, Nullify Ring Out S
52F	Elnathan	Male	Raphael	Appeal, Nullify Counter B
52F	Dean	Male	Raphael	Appeal, Nullify Counter A
52F	Raphael	Male	Raphael	Appeal, Auto Impact A, Impact Heal

Floor	Item Reward	Acquisition Method
50F	Tiger Lily Breastplates	Executed a 10+ combo.
51F	Tiger Lily Fauld	Performed more than 4 counter-hits.
52F	Feathered Wings	Cleared the stage with a Critical Finish.

53-56F: WORSHIPPED SACRIFICE

Select 1 Fighter

Floor	Foe	Gender	Style	Skills
53F	Deanna	Female	Voldo	Shave Damage A, HP Recovery C
53F	Edith	Female	Voldo	Shave Damage B, HP Recovery B
53F	Voldo	Male	Voldo	Shave Damage C, HP Recovery A
54F	Shiun	Male	Yoshimitsu	Auto Impact B, Impact Heal
54F	Mayura	Female	Yoshimitsu	Auto Impact B, Impact Heal
54F	Yoshimitsu	Male	Yoshimitsu	Auto Impact B, Impact Heal
55F	Grima	Male	Astaroth	Nullify Ring Out C, HP Drain B
55F	Herman	Male	Astaroth	Nullify Ring Out B, HP Drain A
55F	Judas	Male	Astaroth	Nullify Ring Out B, HP Drain A
55F	Astaroth	Male	Astaroth	Nullify Ring Out A, HP Drain S
56F	Lizardman	Male	Lizardman	Nullify Ring Out C, Venom Fang C
56F	Lizardman	Male	Lizardman	Nullify Ring Out B, Venom Fang B
56F	Lizardman	Male	Lizardman	Nullify Ring Out A, Venom Fang A
56F	Lizardman	Male	Lizardman	Nullify Ring Out S, Venom Fang S

Floor	Item Reward	Acquisition Method
53F	Blade Ring: Demon Lord	Defeated all enemies by Ring Out.
54F	Leviathan Pauldron	Destroyed all the walls within the stage.
55F	Priestess Kimono	Performed 3 attack throws.
56F	Leviathan Burgonet	Perform a combo with total damage over 240.

57F-59F: ENVOY OF DESTRUCTION

Select 2 Fighters

Floor	Foe	Gender	Style	Skills
57F	Cassandra	Female	Cassandra	Soul Gauge Damage A, Shave Damage B
57F	Sophitia	Female	Sophitia	Shave Damage A, Soul Gauge Boost B, Nullify Ring Out B
57F	Talim	Female	Talim	Soul Gauge Damage B, Soul Gauge Boost A, Nullify Ring Out A
58F	Mitsurugi	Male	Mitsurugi	Soul Gauge Damage A, Shave Damage A, Soul Gauge Recovery A
58F	Setsuka	Female	Setsuka	Auto Unblockable Attack A, Shave Damage A, Soul Gauge Boost A
58F	Cervantes	Male	Cervantes	Soul Gauge Damage A, Guard Breaker, Soul Gauge Boost A
59F	Tira	Female	Tira	Soul Gauge Damage A, Shave Damage A, Soul Gauge Boost A, Nullify Ring Out A
59F	Astaroth	Male	Astaroth	Soul Gauge Damage A, Shave Damage A, Soul Gauge Boost A, Nullify Ring Out A
59F	Nightmare	Male	Nightmare	Soul Gauge Damage S, Shave Damage S, Soul Gauge Boost S, Nullify Ring Out S

Floor	Item Reward	Acquisition Method
57F	Voodoo Armlets	Voluntarily performed a Ring Out.
58F	Tiger Pauldrons	Defeated enemy without equipping any skills.
59F	Voodoo Greaves	Guarded the opponent's attack 10 times in a row.

60F: LAST JUDGEMENT

Select 3 Fighters

Floor	Foe	Gender	Style	Skills
60F	Algol	Male	Algol	Auto Unblockable Attack S, HP Drain S, Soul Gauge Boost S, Nullify Ring Out S

Floor	Item Reward	Acquisition Method
60F	Voodoo Breastplate	Cleared the stage without switching characters.

Descend

Descending into the Tower's basement is just as daunting a proposition as assaulting its upper reaches. You pick two fighters, and then battle through waves of two to four enemies at a time. As with the ascent, there is no health regeneration between battles. Once again, custom-building supercharged characters—preferably with enhanced defense, health, and health regeneration capabilities—is in order. The enemies you face are arranged randomly and are pulled from the same pool of foes you face during the ascent. The biggest challenge here is simply to avoid getting careless. Manage your duo's health, switching them out when necessary to give one or the other a breather, and stay away from ring edges—there is no more frustrating way to end an otherwise fruitful descent than to get thrown off the edge 30 floors down! Every five floors you successfully clear unlocks another special piece of gear for Character Creation mode.

Floor	Reward
B5	Dark Knight's Cloak
B10	Blade Ring: Raging Thunder
B15	Lapin Chapeau
B20	Repel Gem: Fox Demon
B25	Succubus Gauntlets
B30	Demonic Armor
B35	Demonic Pauldrons
B40	Voodoo Crown

Arcade

Arcade Mode duplicates the classic fighting experience of simply plowing through the roster of foes, en route to an end boss and hopefully a high score. Arcade Mode has eight stages. For most characters, the seventh stage takes place in a Star Destroyer, fighting Darth Vader's Apprentice! Defeating Arcade Mode with Darth Vader or Yoda unlocks The Apprentice for use in other game modes. The Apprentice is extremely powerful, and can prove useful in other challenging single-player modes, such as the Tower of Lost Souls. When you play through Arcade Mode with The Apprentice, the seventh stage takes place against Yoda on the Xbox 360 and Darth Vader on the PS3—an Honor is unlocked when you defeat the Apprentice's elders in these encounters.

Honors & Achievements

Various accomplishments unlock Honors, viewable in Museum mode under Battle Records. On the Xbox 360, Honors also unlock Achievements and increase your Gamerscore. On both Xbox 360 and PS3, Honors often unlock new equipment that becomes available in Character Creation mode.

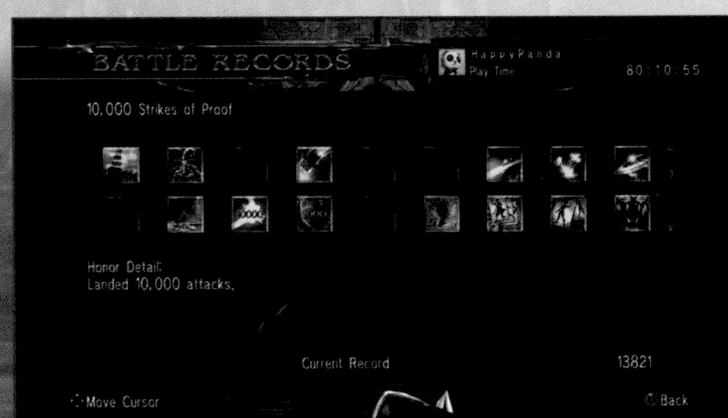

Honor	Requirement	Gamerscore (Xbox 360 only)
10,000 Strikes of Proof	Landed 10,000 attacks.	30
Chosen by History	Created a custom character.	5
Death on the Battlefield	Successfully perform 100 critical finishes.	30
Distance will not Betray	Reached over 10,000 meters in total movement distance in battle.	20
Divine Punishment	K.O. with an Unblockable Attack.	20
Encounter with the Unknown	Fought against Yoda or Vader.	10
Endure 1000	Guarded 1000 times against attacks.	30
Engraved into History	Fight 100 times (Online).	30
Equal Skill and Power	Used all skill points and set up 4 skills.	20
First Step as an Artist	Customized a regular character.	5
Gathering of the Best	Completed CHAIN OF SOULS.	20
Gladiator	Win consecutive ranked matches (Online).	20
Hero King	Level up to 20 (Online).	30
Hero on the Battlefield	Cleared ARCADE MODE with over 450,000 points.	20
Iron Hammer	Landed an attack on a taunting opponent.	10
Legendary Hidden Treasures	Acquired over 30 treasures in TOWER OF LOST SOULS.	20
Like a Flowing Stream	Successfully perform 200 impacts.	20
Looter of the Battlefield	Collect all accessories.	20
Lost in the Moment	Performed 20 Just Impacts.	30
Mad Destroyer	Performed 100 Soul Crushes.	20
May the Force be with You	Cleared STORY MODE with Yoda.	20
Never Ending Advance	Descended 20 floors in TOWER OF LOST SOULS.	20
Numeric God	The last two numbers of total play time and remaining time in a victorious battle was the same.	20
Observer of Souls	Collected all illustrations in Art Gallery.	30
Pursuer of the Secret	Cleared STORY MODE on difficulty: NORMAL.	10
Phoenix	Win with all equipment destroyed.	10
Quick Strike	Performed 5 First Attacks in a row in Arcade.	10
Repel All Blades	Won perfect 30 times.	30
Reversal Wizard	Won 20 matches with low HP.	20
Scorpion's Sting	Won a battle with Critical Finish.	10
Sharpened Teeth	Maximized a style's level.	20
Smasher	Destroy all of the opponent's equipment.	10
Solved the Mystery of the Swords	Cleared STORY MODE on difficulty: HARD.	20
Start of a New Era	Welcome to the new world of Soulcalibur! Started the game after watching the opening movie to the end.	5
Swift Strike	Performed 100 first attacks.	20
Sword Hunter	Collect all weapons for 5 characters.	15
The Controller	Got Soul Calibur (Final Form).	20
Tower's New Guardian	Cleared all upper floors of TOWER OF LOST SOULS.	30
Transcend History and the World	Get all weapons and equipment.	50
Tower of Gold	Acquired over 1,000,000 Gold.	20
Two Cannot Exist Together	Exhaust each other's power.	20
Unknown Swordsman	Win 10 times (Online).	20
Violent Storm	Performed 50 Wall Hits.	20
Wandering Assassin	K.O. opponent with over 20 types of weapons.	10
Wandering Weapon Merchant	Collect 350 pieces of equipment.	20
War Veteran	Cleared ARCADE MODE.	10
Water Moon	Successfully perform 30 grapple breaks.	20
Wild Run to Tragedy	Got Soul Edge (Final Form).	20
World Class Fighter	Fight 20 different fighting styles (Online).	30
World Traveler	Fight on all stages (Online).	30

Character Creation

Soulcalibur IV allows you to either edit an existing fighter or build your own from scratch. After either selecting a *Soulcalibur IV* combatant or choosing a custom character's gender, fighting style, and general traits, you're ushered to the equipment and appearance menu. From here you can modify equipment, weaponry, coloring, aesthetic traits, and skills. Aside from having a big effect on appearance, equipment determines your character's Attack, Defense, and HP stats. Equipment also occasionally adds bonuses to your character's Power, Impact, Boost, Gauge, and Special totals. These figures, along with your fighting style's level, determine which skills you can equip, and how many.

Building a Hero

If you don't plan on playing single-player modes or special online battles—which allow stat bonuses and special effects from armor, weapons, and skills—then build a character however you like, with nothing in mind except fighting style and aesthetics. However, if you plan to play any mode that allows special effects, it's worth the time to build a character with a little more in mind. First things first: pick a fighting style, then ask yourself, is this a heavy-hitting style? A quick, juggle-happy style? A counter-hit reliant style? A style that's great for Soul Crushing? What strengths could I enhance further through skills? It's most important to determine which skills you find essential before you dress a character. Once you know which skills you want to have, you'll know the minimum number of skill points you must get from your armor. It can be hard to strike a balance between desired looks, skill points, and Attack/Defense/HP, so remember that just because you *can* assign four skills doesn't mean you *have to*. Sometimes you can achieve the effect you want with just a few skill slots, thus requiring fewer skill points and making it easier to build toward strong Attack/Defense/HP values. Depending on available gear, you can usually scrounge up roughly 400 skill points total, with a max of around 300 going to any one category. Here are some skill set examples, each pointed toward a specific goal:

Last Gasp: 30 Power, 160 Boost
Will Power
Hyper Mode

Killing Instant Kills: 100 Boost, 140 Gauge
Soul Gauge Recovery A
Soul Gauge Boost A

Every Little Bit Counts: 140 Power, 40 Gauge, 100 Special
Shave Damage A
Venom Fang A

Juggle Fiend: 180 Power, 180 Special
Knock Down
Nullify Aerial Control
Charge Cancel

Impact Happy: 40 Power, 220 Impact, 30 Gauge
Impact Heal
Impact Edge
Strong Impact

Health Springs Eternal: 250 Gauge, 50 Impact
HP Drain A
Impact Heal
HP Recovery A

Soul Destroyer: 190 Gauge, 30 Special
Soul Gauge Vamp
Soul Gauge Damage A

The Unstoppable Force: 270 Power
Auto Unblockable Attack A
Auto Counter A

The Immovable Object: 100 Impact, 175 Special
Nullify Counter A
Magnet
Nullify Ring Out A

Skills

Power Skills

Skill	Description	Power	Impact	Boost	Gauge	Special	Required Level
Shave Damage C	Shave small amount of HP from opponent even if the attack was guarded.	50			20		1
Shave Damage B	Shave HP from opponent even if the attack is guarded.	70			30		3
Shave Damage A	Shave large amount of HP from opponent even if attack was guarded.	100			40		7
Auto Counter C	[Chance] Has a slight chance of turning an attack that lands on the opponent to a counter-hit.	60					2
Auto Counter B	[Chance] Has a chance of turning an attack that lands on the opponent to a counter-hit.	90					4
Auto Counter A	[Chance] Has a high chance of turning an attack that lands on the opponent to a counter-hit.	130					8
Auto Unblockable Attack C	[Chance] Has a slight chance of turning the next high damage attack into Unblockable Attack.	80					2
Auto Unblockable Attack B	[Chance] Has a chance of turning the next high damage attack into Unblockable Attack.	110					5
Auto Unblockable Attack A	[Chance] Has a high chance of turning the next high damage attack into Unblockable Attack	140					9
Knock Down	[Constant] Increase knock down power.	80				30	5
Nullify Aerial Control	[Constant] Opponent is unable to gain aerial control until the character is attacked three times in the air.	100					6
Guard Breaker	[Manual] All high-attack-power moves are Guard Breaks for a set time by pressing Ⓐ+Ⓑ+Ⓚ simultaneously during battle.	90		40			8

Impact Skills

Skill	Description	Power	Impact	Boost	Gauge	Special	Required Level
Nullify Counter C	[Chance] Has a slight chance of turning the opponent's counter-hit into a normal hit.		50				1
Nullify Counter B	[Chance] Has a chance of turning the opponent's counter-hit into a normal hit.		70				3
Nullify Counter A	[Chance] Has a high chance of turning the opponent's counter-hit into a normal hit.		100				6
Auto Impact C	[Chance] Has a slight chance of performing an Impact when an attack is blocked.		60				2
Auto Impact B	[Chance] Has a chance of performing an Impact when an attack is blocked.		90				4
Auto Impact A	[Chance] Has a high chance of performing an Impact when an attack is blocked.		120				8
Impact Heal	[Constant] When an impact is performed, HP is recovered proportional to the strength of the impact.		50		30		3
Impact Edge	[Constant] When an Impact is performed, damage proportional to the strength of the Impact is inflicted on the opponent.		80				4
Strong Impact	[Constant] When an Impact is successful, next attack will turn into a counter-hit.	40	90				5
Master Impact	[Constant] All Impacts will be Just Impacts, but it must be executed within a shorter timeframe.		130				7
Soul Repel	[Manual] Repel any attacks at any time except when in the air.		110				9

Boost Skills

Skill	Description	Power	Impact	Boost	Gauge	Special	Required Level
Hysterical Strength	[Constant] Stats increase inversely to the amount of Soul Gauge remaining.			50			1
Start Dash C	[Constant] At the start of battle, all stats are slightly higher for a set time.			50			1
Start Dash B	[Constant] At the start of battle, all stats are higher for a set time.			60			5
Start Dash A	[Constant] At the start of battle, all stats are much higher for a set time.			80			8
Will Power	[Constant] All stats increase when HP decreases to a set amount.			90			2
Soul Gauge Recovery C	[Constant] Increase the rate at which the Soul Gauge recovers by a small amount.			30	20		2
Soul Gauge Recovery B	[Constant] Increase in the rate at which Soul Gauge recovers.			40	30		4
Soul Gauge Recovery A	[Constant] Large increase in the rate at which Soul Gauge recovers.			50	40		7
Alignment	[Constant] Stats increase or decrease depending on the opponent's alignment (Good/Evil/None).			50			3
Strengthen Horizontal	[Constant] Strengthen horizontal attacks while weakening other attacks.			70			4
Appeal	[Constant] Stats increase when fighting against the opposite gender and decrease when fighting against the same gender.			50			6
Hyper Mode	[Manual] All stats increase for a set time by pressing Ⓐ+Ⓑ+Ⓚ simultaneously during battle.	30		70			6
Strengthen Vertical	[Constant] Strengthen vertical attacks while weakening other attacks.			60			7
Skill Ability Up	[Manual] Enhance the effects of a random skill by pressing Ⓐ+Ⓑ+Ⓚ simultaneously during battle.			80			9

Gauge Skills

Skill	Description	Power	Impact	Boost	Gauge	Special	Required Level
Soul Gauge Boost C	[Constant] Start with the Soul Gauge full.			40	70		1
Soul Gauge Boost B	[Constant] Start with the Soul Gauge full and slightly decrease the amount of damage to the Soul Gauge when blocking opponent's attacks.			50	80		3
Soul Gauge Boost A	[Constant] Start with the Soul Gauge full and decrease the amount of damage to the Soul Gauge when blocking opponent's attacks.			50	100		5
Soul Gauge Damage C	[Constant] Small increase the amount of damage on the opponent's Soul Gauge when an attack is guarded.				40		1
Soul Gauge Damage B	[Constant] Increase the amount of damage on the opponent's Soul Gauge when an attack is guarded.				60		4
Soul Gauge Damage A	[Constant] Large increase the amount of damage on the opponent's Soul Gauge when an attack is guarded.				90		6
HP Drain C	[Constant] When an attack lands on the opponent, HP recovers a small amount (proportional to the damage on the opponent).				60		1
HP Drain B	[Constant] When an attack lands on the opponent, HP recovers a medium amount (proportional to the damage on the opponent).				90		3
HP Drain A	[Constant] When an attack lands on the opponent, HP recovers a large amount (proportional to the damage on the opponent).				120		8
Soul Gauge Rate Up C	[Constant] Small increase in the rate of Soul Gauge recovery when attacking.				30		2
Soul Gauge Rate Up B	[Constant] Increase in the rate of Soul Gauge recovery when attacking.				50		4
Soul Gauge Rate Up A	[Constant] Large increase in the rate of Soul Gauge recovery when attacking.				80		7
HP Recovery C	[Constant] When hit with a combo of 3 or more, HP recovers a small amount (proportional to the total damage of the combo).				50		2
HP Recovery B	[Constant] When hit with a combo of 3 or more, HP recovers a medium amount (proportional to the total damage of the combo).				70		5
HP Recovery A	[Constant] When hit with a combo of 3 or more, HP recovers a large amount (proportional to the total damage of the combo).				100		8
HP Burst	[Manual] Recover HP by pressing Ⓐ+Ⓑ+Ⓚ simultaneously during battle. Soul Gauge will gradually decrease after a set time.				130		6
Soul Gauge Vamp	[Manual] Randomly decrease the opponent's Soul Gauge and absorb part of it by pressing Ⓐ+Ⓑ+Ⓚ simultaneously during battle.				100	30	9

Special Skills

Skill	Description	Power	Impact	Boost	Gauge	Special	Required Level
Switch Speed Up	[Constant] Increase the rate at which Switch Gauge increases during AMB.					80	1
Auto Grapple Break C	[Chance] Has a slight chance of performing a Grapple Break when thrown.		30			30	1
Auto Grapple Break B	[Chance] Has a chance of performing a Grapple Break when thrown.		30			50	3
Auto Grapple Break A	[Chance] Has a high chance of performing a Grapple Break when thrown.		40			70	7
Double-Edged Sword	[Constant] Increase the rate of gain and loss of Soul Gauge.					60	2
Nullify Ring Out C	[Chance] Has a slight chance of preventing a Ring Out.					40	2
Nullify Ring Out B	[Chance] Has a chance of preventing a Ring Out.					70	4
Nullify Ring Out A	[Chance] Has a high chance of preventing a Ring Out.					100	6
Venom Fang C	[Constant] Additional small poison damage to a downed opponent. The poisoned state will stop when the opponent lands an attack or after a set amount of time.	20				50	3
Venom Fang B	[Constant] Additional poison damage to a downed opponent. The poisoned state will stop when the opponent lands an attack or after a set amount of time.	30				70	5
Venom Fang A	[Constant] Additional large poison damage to a downed opponent. The poisoned state will stop when the opponent lands an attack or after a set amount of time.	40				100	8
Magnet	[Constant] Reduce knock down power on both sides.					75	4
Run Speed Up	Increase running speed.					70	6
Invisible	Become invisible for a set amount of time by pressing Ⓐ+Ⓑ+Ⓚ simultaneously during battle.					130	7
Step Speed Up	Increase stepping speed.					70	8
Charge Cancel	[Manual] Cancel a move when used while attacking the opponent by pressing Ⓐ+Ⓑ+Ⓚ simultaneously.					150	9

Amy

Amy

Heard melodies are sweet, but those unheard are sweeter . . .

"Ode on a Grecian Urn," John Keats (1795 - 1821)

Bio

Age:	Unknown
Birthplace:	Rouen, French Empire
Height:	Unknown
Weight:	Unknown
Birth Date:	Unknown
Blood Type:	Unknown
Weapon:	English Sword Rapier
Weapon Name:	Albion
Discipline:	La Rapière des Sorel
Family:	Foster father: Raphael Her real parents are unknown.

Amy

Peace had been restored to the night. With the besieging army crushed, nothing remained to disturb the silence.

Torch lights, far fewer than before, made their way down through the steep ridges. It had seemed a legion of flames encircled the castle, writhing. And now, one by one, the last of them were swallowed into the darkness. Who knew how many lives were lost on this day?

Countless lives had blinked out, like the faint lights of so many fireflies. But one girl, who was gazing out the window coldly, spared not a moment's thought to lament life's transience. Her eyes darted restlessly across the mantle of darkness, as if searching for something.

(Still, no sign of him.)

He had left her, left this castle home behind. She knew he had done it for her sake, because he wanted her to be happy more than anything else in this world. And so he had to leave her side for a little while, in search of something that would protect the bond they shared. She understood. Nonetheless she was restless. The grandest of furnishings and the most lavish of clothes could hardly replace the warmth of his hands.

Amy recalled the days before they arrived in these lands, when they had lived in the west. And she remembered the day he had returned from a long journey. He had collapsed on the floor at once; wherever he had gone, he had incurred deep wounds. A moment's glance had told her they were not ordinary sword wounds. They were infected, and gave off a strange stench. And even after several days they had showed no sign of healing. When she had tried to clean the wounds, the viscous fluid that stuck to her skin was the wrong color: a baleful shade so close to black that it only confirmed her fears.

By the time he had finally taken a turn for the better, the aberrations had spread over his whole body—as well as to the girl who had stayed by his side and nursed him. The shadows that had seeped out of the darkness and immersed them had stained them the same color. That was Soul Edge's power; this phenomenon they called "malfestation." But even without this explanation, Amy already understood that the two of them had stepped beyond the boundaries of humanity.

Remembering the sensation of her own body turning into something foreign from the inside out, Amy gently slumped her shoulders. They may be forced to shun daylight and slake their nightly thirst in secret, but that was fine, so long as he was by her side.

"Be a good girl. I'll be back in a while."

Those were his last words to her, but Amy had to ponder them for a moment. Even the most dutiful fledgling takes flight when the longing for its parents grows too strong.

Again, Amy cast her gaze out the window, across a world stained in darkness.

(The evil blade, Soul Edge. Did he leave so he might find it again?)

Amy left the window and slowly, without the faintest hint of noise, cut across the gloom-filled room. Except for a downcast glance, not a single emotion marred her face.

(How many nights must we wander?)

A single butterfly was being tossed about on the cold night winds, like a lonely star drifting far from heaven; like a soul freed from all its burdens.

Silently, with all her feelings neatly locked away where none could read them, Amy pushed open the door.

Albion

As Raphael fled from the aristocracy where all around had turned on him, Amy appeared and saved his life. Considering he had never had a shred of trust for other human beings, her compassion was a sort of revelation. It would almost be an understatement to say that since that time, he has only lived for her. He gave her this rapier; its name means "the shining one," a perfect expression of his feelings for her.

La Rapière des Sorel

Born among the poor class, Amy grew like a weed. Disliking the soldiers as she did, one rainy day she told a lie in response to a soldier's question. As a result, it managed to save the life of Raphael who was on the run. Raphael dedicated his own life to protecting her in return and taught her the art of self-defense. That proved to be a skill that saved Amy's life.

Raphael was affected by Soul Edge and the Evil Seed and turned evil. Amy, who was nursing him at the time, also received the same evil influence. Now, even though she is no longer human, she still protects the secrets of his teaching.

Command List

Signature Techniques

Name	Command	Attack Level	Damage	Notes
Graceful Cutter	⇙Ⓐ	Low	18	
Triple Botta in Tempo	⇨ⒷⒷⒷ	High, High, Mid	10, 5, 15	Fully combos on counter-hit
Decussate Strike	⇘ⒷⒶ	Mid, Low	20, 26	1st attack stuns on hit
Helm Splitter	⇦ⒷⒷ	High, Mid	14, 16	1st attack stuns on counter-hit, 2nd attack may be delayed
Bella Donna	⇙ⓀⒶ	High, High	12, 12	2nd attack causes recoverable stun on hit, stuns on counter-hit
Advance Splitter Crescendo	→ⒷⒶ	Mid, High	20, 30	2nd attack Guard Breaks and stuns on hit
Soaring Flutter	↘ or ↗Ⓑ	Mid	22	
High Arc	8-Way Run Any Direction Ⓐ+Ⓑ	Mid	26	
Amaryllis Spiral	Amaryllis ⓀⒶ (Just)	Mid, High	10, 9	
Night Toe Kick	Lilith Parry Ⓚ	Mid	20	

Horizontal Attacks

Name	Command	Attack Level	Damage	Notes
Attack au Fer	ⒶⒶ	High, High	8, 10	
Flash Needle	ⒶⒷ	High, Low	8, 10	
Hilt Strike	⇨Ⓐ	High	12	
Air Blade	⇘Ⓐ	Mid	14	
Twirling Talon	⇩Ⓐ	Sp.Low	8	Leaves Amy in crouching state
Graceful Cutter	⇙Ⓐ	Low	18	
Heavy Mandritti	⇦Ⓐ	High	18	Evades vertical attacks
Twirling Talon	While Crouching Ⓐ	Sp.Low	8	
Merciless Stramazone	While Rising Ⓐ	High	20	
Sky Botte	Jumping Ⓐ	High	16 or 18 or 20	Damage varies depending on direction jumped in
Turning Attack au Fer	Backturned Ⓐ	High	10	
Low Turn Attack au Fer	While Crouching Backturned Ⓐ	Sp.Low	12	Leaves Amy in crouching state

Throws

Name	Command	Attack Level	Damage	Notes
Forget Me Not	Ⓐ+Ⓖ	Throw	48	Input Ⓐ to escape
Ephemeral Wing	Ⓑ+Ⓖ	Throw	45	Input Ⓑ to escape
A Lesson in Massacre	Left Side Throw	Throw	52	Same button as throw (Ⓐ or Ⓑ) to escape
Undertaker	Right Side Throw	Throw	50	Same button as throw (Ⓐ or Ⓑ) to escape
Pure Sacrifice	Back Throw	Throw	58	Same button as throw (Ⓐ or Ⓑ) to escape

Vertical Attacks

Name	Command	Attack Level	Damage	Notes
Dui Montante	ⒷⒷ	Mid, Mid	10, 12	
Triple Botta in Tempo	⇨ⒷⒷⒷ	High, High, Mid	10, 5, 15	Fully combos on counter-hit
Double Botta in Tempo ~Amaryllis Spin	⇨ⒷⒷ⇩⇘⇨	High, High	10, 5	Shifts into Amaryllia
Decussate Strike	⇘ⒷⒶ	Mid, Low	20, 26	
Fendante	⇩Ⓑ	Mid	14	Leaves Amy in crouching state
Grave Needle	⇙Ⓑ	Low	16	
Helm Splitter	⇦ⒷⒷ	High, Mid	14, 16	1st attack stuns on counter-hit, 2nd attack may be delayed
Crouching Montante	While Crouching Ⓑ	Mid	12	
Advance Slicer	While Crouching ⇘Ⓑ	Mid	24	Stuns on hit
Shadow Stinger	While Crouching ⇙Ⓑ	Low	24	
Frigid Tap	While Rising Ⓑ	High	16	Causes recoverable stun on hit
Sky Agente	Jumping Ⓑ	Mid	14 or 16 or 18	Damage varies depending on direction jumped in. Stuns on hit (except for ⇘Ⓑ).
Turning Montante	Backturned Ⓑ	Mid	12	
Low Turn Montante	While Crouching Backturned Ⓑ	Mid	16	Leaves Amy in crouching state

Kick Attacks

Name	Command	Attack Level	Damage	Notes
Venom High Kick	Ⓚ	High	8	
Venom Swing Kick	⇨Ⓚ	High	14	Causes recoverable stun on hit
Venom Swing Kick ~Amaryllis Spin	⇨Ⓚ⇩⇘⇨	High	14	Causes recoverable stun on hit, shifts into Amaryllis
Venom Side Kick	⇘Ⓚ	Mid	14	
Sweep Kick	⇩Ⓚ	Low	10	Leaves Amy in crouching state
Bella Donna	⇙ⓀⒶ	High, High	12, 12	2nd attack causes recoverable stun
Dual Stinger Kick	⇦ⓀⓀ	High, Mid	12, 14	
Sweep Kick	While Crouching Ⓚ	Low	10	
High Back Kick	While Rising Ⓚ	Mid	18	
Dark Moon	Jumping Ⓚ	Mid	12 or 14 or 16	Damage varies depending on direction jumped in
Turning Venom High Kick	Backturned Ⓚ	High	10	
Turning Sweep Kick	While Crouching Backturned Ⓚ	Low	14	

Amaryllis

Name	Command	Attack Level	Damage	Notes
Amaryllis Spin	⇩⇘⇨			
Scarlet Night	Amaryllis Ⓐ	Mid, High	15, 20	
Stocatta Slicer	Amaryllis Ⓑ Rapidly	Mid, Mid, Mid, Mid, Mid	5 (first 5 hits), 20	Stuns on final hit
Amaryllis Spiral	Amaryllis ⓀⒶ (Just)	Mid, High	10, 12	
Frigid Moon	Amaryllis ⓀⓀ	Mid, Mid	10, 12	

Biondetta Parry

Name	Command	Attack Level	Damage	Notes
Biondetta Parry	Ⓐ+Ⓑ			Deflects high attacks
Aurora Talon	Biondetta Parry Ⓐ	Mid	30	Stuns on hit
Hidden Thorn	Biondetta Parry Ⓑ	Mid	20	Stuns on hit
Silent Sweep	Biondetta Parry Ⓚ	Low	24	
Lilith Parry	Biondetta Parry Ⓑ+Ⓚ			
Crest Form	Biondetta Parry Ⓐ+Ⓚ			
Amaryllis Spin	Biondetta Parry ⇩⇘⇨			

Lilith Parry

Name	Command	Attack Level	Damage	Notes
Lilith Parry	Ⓑ+Ⓚ			Deflects mid attacks
Arctic Night	Lilith Parry Ⓐ	Mid	16	
Frost Blade	Lilith Parry Ⓑ	High	10	Causes recoverable stun on counter-hit
Night Toe Kick	Lilith Parry Ⓚ	Mid	20	
Biondetta Parry	Lilith Parry Ⓐ+Ⓑ			
Crest Form	Lilith Parry Ⓐ+Ⓚ			
Amaryllis Spin	Lilith Parry ⇩⇘⇨			

Simultaneous Press

Name	Command	Attack Level	Damage	Notes
Biondetta Parry	Ⓐ+Ⓑ			Deflects high attacks
Assalto Montante Crescendo	⇨Ⓐ+ⒷⒶ	Mid, Mid, Low	10, 14, 16	2nd attack stuns on counter-hit
Assalto Montante ~Amaryllis Spin	⇨Ⓐ+Ⓑ⇩⇘⇨	Mid Mid	10, 14	2nd attack stuns on counter-hit, shifts into Amaryllis
Silent Curtsey	⇩Ⓐ+Ⓑ	Low	20	
Bloody Funeral	⇦Ⓐ+Ⓑ	Mid	45	Unblockable
Bloody Funeral ~Amaryllis Spin	⇦Ⓐ+ⒷⒼ			Unblockable. Shifts into Amaryllis.
Dark Abyss	⇧Ⓐ+Ⓑ	Mid	28	Stuns on hit
Frigid Stramazone	While Crouching Ⓐ+ⒷⒶ	Mid, Mid	12, 12	2nd attack may be delayed. Both attacks stun on counter-hit.
Lilith Parry	Ⓑ+Ⓚ			Deflects mid attacks
Falling Prayer	⇨Ⓑ+Ⓚ	Mid	30	Causes recoverable stun on hit
Silent Impale	⇩Ⓑ+Ⓚ	Low	20	Stuns on hit
Stocatta Rampage Crescendo	⇦Ⓑ+ⓀⒷ	Mid x9	5 (first 8 hits), 20	Stuns on hit (8th and 9th attack)
Circular Blitz	Backturned Ⓑ+Ⓚ	Mid	20	Stuns on hit
Circular Blitz ~Amaryllis Spin	Backturned Ⓑ+Ⓚ⇩⇘⇨	Mid	20	Shifts into Amaryllis
Crest Form	Ⓐ+Ⓚ			Evades low attacks
Taunt	Ⓚ+Ⓖ			

8-Way Run

Name	Command	Attack Level	Damage	Notes
Descending Talon	→ or ↘ or ↗Ⓐ	Mid	30	Stuns on hit
Silent Saber	↓ or ↑Ⓐ	High	26	
Heartless Needle	↙ or ↖Ⓐ	Mid	22	
Squalambrato Concierto Crescendo	←ⒶⒷⒶ	Mid, Mid, High	18, 11, 30	3rd attack stuns on hit. 1st attack stuns on counter-hit.
Advance Splitter Crescendo	→ⒷⒶ	Mid, High	20, 30	3rd attack stuns on hit
Advance Splitter ~Step	→Ⓑ⇩ or ⇧	Mid	20	Shifts into sidestep
Soaring Flutter	↘ or ↗Ⓑ	Mid	22	
Broken Thrust	↓ or ↑Ⓑ	Mid	24	
Broken Thrust ~Broken Thrust	↓ or ↑Ⓑ⇩ or ⇧Ⓑ	Mid, Mid	24	Shifts into additional Broken Thrust
Broken Thrust ~Amaryllis Spin	↓ or ↑Ⓑ⇩⇘⇨	Mid	24	Shifts into Amaryllis
Shadow Evade	↓ or ↑ⒷⒼ			
Crimson Slicer	↓ or ↑ⒷⒼⒶ	High	18	
Assault Blade	↓ or ↑ⒷⒼⒷ	Mid	28	Causes recoverable stun
Dread Coffin	← or ↙ or ↖Ⓑ	Mid	25	Stuns on hit
Dread Coffin ~Stocatta Rampage Crescendo	← or ↙ or ↖ Ⓑ Counter-hit During Hit Ⓑ	Mid x10	25, 5 (first 8 hits), 20	Stuns on hit (1st, 8th and 9th)
Night Round Kick	→ or ↘ or ↗Ⓚ	High	22	
Venom Swing Kick	↓ or ↑Ⓚ	Mid	18	
Venom Swing Kick ~Amaryllis Spin	↓ or ↑Ⓚ⇩⇘⇨	Mid	18	Shifts into Amaryllis
Unholy Kick	← or ↙ or ↖Ⓚ	High	30	Leaves Amy facing backwards
High Arc	8-Way Run Any Direction Ⓐ+Ⓑ	Mid	26	
Bleak Touch	→Ⓑ+Ⓚ	Mid	18	Causes recoverable stun on hit
Bleak Touch ~Amaryllis Spin	→Ⓑ+Ⓚ During Hit ⇩⇘⇨	Mid	18	Causes recoverable stun on hit, shifts into Amaryllis
Sliding	While Running Ⓚ	Low	26	

Crest Form

Name	Command	Attack Level	Damage	Notes
Crest Form	Ⓐ+Ⓚ			Evades low attacks
Heel Cutter	Crest Form Ⓐ	Low	12	
Vermillion Fang	Crest Form Ⓑ	Mid, Mid	40	Unblockable
Soaring Dance	Crest Form Ⓚ	Mid, Mid	18, 24	Stuns on hit
Biondetta Parry	Crest Form Ⓐ+Ⓑ			
Lilith Parry	Crest Form Ⓑ+Ⓚ			
Amaryllis Spin	Crest Form ⇩⇘⇨			

Combos

⬂ⒷⒶ, ⬂⬂Ⓑ	**3 hits, 59 Damage**
Counter-hit ⇦Ⓐ, ⇨⇨Ⓐ + Ⓑ	**2 hits, 39 Damage**
⇨⇨Ⓐ, ⬂ⒷⒶ, ⬂⬂Ⓑ	**4 hits, 77 Damage**
⇨⇨Ⓐ + Ⓑ, Ⓑ + Ⓚ, ⬂⬊Ⓑ	**3 hits, 62 Damage**
Ⓐ + ⒷⓀ, ⇨ⒷⒷ	**3 hits, 35 Damage**
Ⓐ + ⒷⒷ, ⬂ⒷⒶ, ⬂⬂Ⓑ	**4 hits, 68 Damage**
⬆ or ⬇ⒷⒼ, Ⓑ, ⇨⇨ⒷⒶ	**3 hits, 60 Damage, first stun is escapable**
⬊Ⓑ, ⇨⇨Ⓑ + Ⓚ, ⇩⬂⇨ⓀⓀ	**4 hits, 52 Damage**
⇦Ⓐ + Ⓑ, ⇨⇨Ⓐ + Ⓑ	**2 hits, 63 Damage**
⇦⇦Ⓚ, ⇧Ⓐ + Ⓑ	**2 hits, 55 Damage**
Backturned Ⓑ + Ⓚ, ⇩Ⓚ	**2 hits, 30 Damage, Ⓑ + Ⓚ must hit enemy's front side.**
Backturned Ⓑ + Ⓚ, ⬃ⓀⒶ, ⇩Ⓑ	**4 hits, 47 Damage, Ⓑ + Ⓚ must hit enemy's back.**
⇦Ⓐ + Ⓑ (wall hit), ⬂⬊Ⓑ, ⇨⇨Ⓐ + Ⓑ, Ⓑ + Ⓚ, ⬂⬊Ⓑ	**7 hits, 85 Damage, must be done near wall**

Close Range

Strike with ⇨ⒷⒷ to start an offense. If it connects as a counter-hit, chain into its Ⓑ follow up (⇨ⒷⒷⒷ). If ⇨ⒷⒷ is guarded, shift into Amy's Amaryllis movement (⇨ⒷⒷ⇩⇘⇨) and go for either its Stocatta Slicer (ⒷⒷ) option, or throw as the movement recovers. Unfortunately, ⇨ⒷⒷ is vulnerable to sidesteps and whiffs against crouched opponents. Be aware of this and use Decussate Strike (⇘ⒷⒶ) to hit crouching foes and ⒶⒶ to stop sidesteps. When the enemy begins to stand again, mix in throws and Silent Impale (⇩Ⓑ+Ⓚ) to keep the foe guessing.

Mid Range

Most of Amy's best techniques are linear, making it difficult to stop the enemy from stepping around them. To compensate, use the Heavy Mandritti (⇦Ⓐ) or Silent Saber (⬇ or ⬆Ⓐ) to deter side movement. The slowest of these options is ⇦Ⓐ, but it leads to bigger damage on a counter-hit; hit your stunned enemy with ⇨⇨Ⓐ+Ⓑ afterward. If an opponent uses quick, horizontal attacks to thwart either of these techniques, or if your foe resorts to backward movement to dodge them, counter with Graceful Cutter (⇙Ⓐ), which is a quick, low slice that ducks under high attacks.

Because Amy's ⇦Ⓐ and ⬇(or ⬆)Ⓐ are high attacks, and because her ⇙Ⓐ is a low strike, your enemy can counter the above strategy by guarding while crouched. Use this opportunity to strike with middle attacks, like the Advance Splitter Crescendo (➡Ⓑ) or Soaring Flutter (↘ or ↗Ⓑ). Another worthwhile middle attack is Falling Prayer (⇨Ⓑ+Ⓚ), as it ducks under high attacks, catches backward movement, and slaps the enemy into a recoverable stun. However, it is very vulnerable to side movement, so use it with caution.

Finally, Amy's Unholy Kick (⬅ or ↙ or ↖Ⓚ) is a long-distance mid attack that launches your enemy on contact. If it hits, juggle with ⇧Ⓐ+Ⓑ afterward for a 2-hit combo. This move is completely safe when gaurded, so attack with Amy's Circular Blitz (backturned Ⓑ+Ⓚ) to counter any attack your foe tries to use to when he or she recovers from guardstun. If the Circular Blitz hits, combo after it with ⇙ⓀⒶ, ⇩Ⓑ. Perform the Turning Sweep Kick (backturned ⇩Ⓚ) to stop enemy attempts to sidestep after the blocked Unholy Kick. If backturned ⇩Ⓚ hits, combo into crouching ⇙Ⓑ. Go for throw attempts when when your opponent is afraid of the Turning Sweep Kick or Circular Blitz.

Long Range

Your goal is to move into mid or close range. Play patiently and hover in and out of your enemy's maximum attack range. If your foe mistakenly attacks when you're out of range, punish the miss with ↘Ⓑ or the High Arc (8-Way Run any direction Ⓐ+Ⓑ) to score a combo and a knockdown. Though it's risky, you can also use ⇩⇘⇨ to quickly approach your enemy. Go for either its Ⓑ option or a throw when you recover. Use ⇩⇘⇨Ⓐ to catch your foe's attempts to sidestep around this maneuver.

Special Tactics

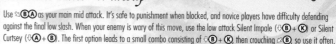

Okizeme: Anti-Wakeup

Use ⇘ⒷⒶ as your main mid attack. It's safe to punishment when blocked, and novice players have difficulty defending against the final low slash. When your enemy is wary of this move, use the low attack Silent Impale (⇩Ⓑ+Ⓚ) or Silent Curtsey (⇩Ⓐ+Ⓑ). The first option leads to a small combo consisting of ⇩Ⓑ+Ⓚ, then crouching ⇙Ⓑ, so use it often.

Another worthwhile option is to use the attacks within Amy's Biondetta Parry (Ⓐ+Ⓑ) stance. Its Hidden Thorn (Ⓑ) option is a mid attack that leads to a stun—follow up with ⇘ⒷⒶ, then ⇘⇘Ⓑ for a 4-hit combo. Its Silent Sweep (Ⓚ) option is a low attack. After the Ⓚ option hits, attack your airborne enemy with ⇨ⒷⒷ⇩⇘⇨ to perform a 3-hit combo. This command also shifts directly into Amy's special movement, leaving her directly next to the fallen enemy.

Despite its above average speed and attack range, Amy's Bloody Funeral (⇦Ⓐ+Ⓑ) Unblockable is linear, making it easy to sidestep in reaction to its wind-up period. However, inputting the command ⇦Ⓐ+ⒷⒼ cancels the attack's starting period and shifts directly into Amy's Amaryllis movement. Use this technique to trick your enemy into sidestepping, then use the Amaryllis's circular Ⓐ option to strike your foe's side movement. When your opponent is afraid to evade the attack, use the Unblockable as you would normally to blow through his or her guard. This tactic is especially powerful near walls, where ⇦Ⓐ+Ⓑ leads to damaging wall combos (refer to Amy's combo section).

Amaryllis

Amy's Amaryllis (⇩⇘⇨) causes her to slide forward at high speed. This movement ducks under high attacks and grants access to three unique attacks: the Scarlet Night (Ⓐ), the Stocatta Slicer (ⒷⒷ), and the Frigid Moon (ⓀⓀ). These options are designed to counter your enemy's attempts to stop the Amaryllis movement. For example, the Stocatta Slicer is the fastest option out of the Amaryllis, stopping your enemy's early attempts to attack. When your enemy hesitates to act, use the Amaryllis to slip into range for a throw. When your enemy sidesteps to avoid both the attack and the throw, use the circular Scarlet Night to hit him or her. Finally, the Frigid Moon is used mainly for combos, such as ↘Ⓑ, ⇨⇨Ⓑ+Ⓚ⇩⇘⇨ⓀⓀ. Its special Just Frame variation, ⇩⇘⇨ⓀⒶ, ends with a safe high attack that can knock enemies into walls. Use this variation accordingly to start wall combinations.

A few of Amy's attacks can shift into this movement. These attacks include her ⇨ⒷⒷ, Assalto Montante Crescendo (⇨Ⓐ+Ⓑ), Bleak Touch (➡Ⓑ+Ⓚ), Night Round Kick (➡Ⓚ), Venom Swing Kick (⬇ or ⬆Ⓚ), and Broken Thrust (⬇ or ⬆Ⓑ). Use these techniques in combination with the Amaryllis to move into close range quickly.

Broken Thrust Options

One of Amy's unique attack options is her Broken Thrust (⬇ or ⬆Ⓑ), which acts as an evasive maneuver that ends with an attack. This attack has three distinct abilities: it can be canceled into the Shadow Evade stance (⬇ or ⬆ⒷⒼ), it can shift into another Broken Thrust (input ⇩ or ⇧Ⓑ during hit), or it can shift directly into the Amaryllis movement. Use these options to stage a confusing guessing game that creates opportunities to score counter-hits and throws.

For example, performing the Broken Thrust and shifting into ⇩⇘⇨ⒷⒷ stops your enemy's immediate attempts to attack your recovery period. When your foe is afraid to attack, shift into back-to-back Broken Thrusts, which you can perform indefinitely in any direction to provoke an enemy attack. When you anticipate another immediate counterattack, shift back into ⇩⇘⇨ⒷⒷ to punish the opponent. When enemies react to the Broken Thrust's starting animation, perform Shadow Evade to dodge any high attacks they perform, and then counter with the Assault Blade (during Shadow Evade Ⓑ). Finally, the Shadow Evade's Ⓐ attack stops attempts to sidestep the Broken Thrust. Use this option to deter that reaction.

Astaroth

...in my bedroom Death dwells,
and wherever I set foot there too is Death!
"Epic of Gilgamesh"

Bio

Age:	Seven years since initial creation
Birthplace:	Unknown (Heretical Order Fygul Cestemus, Grand Shrine of Palgaea)
Height:	6'8"
Weight:	287 lbs.
Birth Date:	September 3
Blood Type:	None
Weapon:	Giant Ax
Weapon Name:	Kulutues
Discipline:	Gyulkus
Family:	None

Astaroth had [illegible] and [illegible] his fate as lore, and the experience left the golem [illegible] of the "gods" inside him—Ker, a servant of the god of destruction. [illegible] In the process, he had been aware of himself to an extent for some time [illegible] impulses. But those scraps of "individuality" were no more than tools that Palgaea [illegible]

When Astaroth learned the truth of his origins—that he had been modeled after a [illegible] fought against that fact for some time afterward, until he had found the human [illegible] the man to the ground, everything inside him turned upside down. Now that [illegible] Cracks began to crisscross Palgaea's puppet, and from behind the fissures Astaroth [illegible]

When the confusion of this metamorphosis had subsided, Astaroth glanced around, but the [illegible] he peered over the tall cliff and down into the rapids below, he realized the man had thrown himself off in [illegible] Astaroth. He thought back on the many atrocities he had committed, all to obtain Soul Edge, [illegible] "master." His chest boiled with rage. He had followed orders without question. He had been used as a [illegible] obeyed, as if it were the only natural thing to do?

His fury swelled in an instant and swept through his new body. From inside, Palgaea's servant Ker let out a shriek of protest, only to be drowned out by Astaroth's rush of emotion. Ker fell silent and yielded control of the golem to these new, ferocious thoughts. Astaroth raised his giant ax, and brought it down with all his might, opening a great fissure in the ground. The earth screamed. What a sight it made; it was as if an earthquake had struck that very spot. He let the rage take him on a wild rampage, and by the time he relented, the landscape was irrevocably changed.

Astaroth committed barbarity after barbarity; slaughtering and pillaging all that he saw. But this he did for his own sake. The fragments of Soul Edge within him had become his flesh and blood; now he constantly hungered for souls, and drank them up greedily. Then, one day, he was greeted by a flurry of black wings. Their master—a mass of evil in the guise of a girl—called herself Tira.

She beckoned to Astaroth in a whisper. "Keep absorbing souls, and who knows how powerful you'll become. Why, who's to say you couldn't even wolf down some old, forgotten god? But you need to feast on more powerful prey. Come. If you seek the power to [illegible] a god, I will show you a better place to go."

Astaroth knew in an instant that the girl before him served Soul Edge. This one seeks to use me just like the last cursed god, he thought. Still, it was true he needed richer pastures from which to reap souls and grow stronger. He watched as the girl turned and pressed onward. Very well, he thought, but I have plans of my own.

Years before, when Nightmare had cloaked Europe in terror, the "Black Giant" Astaroth had wrought havoc in his service. Now, the Black Giant once again set foot in the dark city of Ostrheinsburg. Once again, he entered Nightmare's service, pretending to obey while waiting for the chance to seize his power. This time, however, he had a different purpose, and no soul but his own commanded him.

"Let the fools descend upon Ostrheinsburg; their souls will be mine! I will devour everything, right down to Soul Edge itself."

Kulutues

The name means "merciless destroyer." This giant axe was forged with curses woven into its very blade by the same grand priest of the heathen cult that created Astaroth himself. From the very beginning, it was meant to be wielded by the golem.

Swinging the mighty axe lightly and easily, Astaroth spread mayhem and slaughter far and wide, obeying the commands of Palgaea the Executioner, the god that the cult worshipped. Astaroth grew more powerful and more evil, until eventually the fearsome Black Giant destroyed the cult that had first given him life.

Gyulkus

Astaroth was created by Fygul Cestemus, a heretical cult that called themselves the "guardians of natural order." In the language unique to this cult, gyulkus means "a fight (to protect the temple)," and any battle fought for the sake of the cult was referred to as such.

Kunpaetku, the grand priest of the cult, harbored an ambition to become as powerful as the god they worshipped, the Executioner himself. But the god would not accept such hubris. In retribution, he sent Astaroth, the golem that the cult itself had created, to destroy them and wipe them from the pages of history.

Astaroth has grown mighty, unstoppable. His rage blazes within him and his rampage of destruction consumes everything in its path. His final target is his former master, the Executioner himself: Palgaea.

Command List

Signature Techniques

Name	Command	Attack Level	Damage	Notes
Hades Control	⇦Ⓐ	High	24	Floors on counter-hit
Poseidon Tide Rush (Attack Throw)	⇩⇙⇦Ⓐ	Mid	80	Hit Throw
Hades Ax	ⒷⒷ	Mid, Mid	20, 30	Combos on counter-hit
Bear Fang	⇦Ⓑ	Mid	20	Knocks down on counter-hit
Dark Tamer	⇘ⓀⒶ	Mid, High	18, 36	Combos on counter-hit, 2nd hit knocks down
Titan Ax	Ⓐ+Ⓑ	Mid	25 (48)	Knocks down from long range
Hades Cannon	↓ or ↑Ⓑ	Mid	55 (20)	Launches, does less damage but launches overhead by inputting ↓ or ↑Ⓑ⇦
Bull Rush	→Ⓚ	Mid	26~46	Knocks down
Wicked Judgement	⇨⇘⇩⇙⇦Ⓐ+Ⓖ	Throw	63	Ⓐ breaks throw

Horizontal Attacks

Name	Command	Attack Level	Damage	Notes
Annihilation (Hold)	🅐	High	16	Leaves foe backturned
Annihilation	ⒶⒶ	High, High	16, 24	
Annihilation (Delay)	ⒶⒶ	High, High	16, 24	
Annihilation (Hold)	Ⓐ🅐	High, High	16, 24	Leaves foe backturned
Destruction	ⒶⒷ	High, Mid	16, 20	Combos naturally
Destruction (Delay)	ⒶⒷ	High, Mid	16, 20	2nd hit crumples on counter-hit
Grip Shot to Ax Volcano	⇨ⒶⒷ	High, Mid	10, 20	Combos on counter-hit, 2nd hit launches
Grip Shot to Ax Volcano (Delay)	→ⒶⒷ	High, Mid	10, 20	2nd hit launches
Minotaur Crush	⇘Ⓐ	Mid	18	Causes recoverable stun on counter-hit
Hades Break	⇩Ⓐ	Low	14	
Discus	⇙Ⓐ	Low	25 (35)	Knocks down, leaves Astaroth in crouching state
Double Discus	⇙🅐Ⓐ	Low, Low	35 (45), 35	Both hits knock down, leaves Astaroth in crouching state
Discus Breaker	⇙🅐Ⓑ	Low, Mid	35 (45), 70	1st hit knocks down, 2nd hit is a Guard Break that launches
Hades Control	⇦Ⓐ	High	24	Floors on counter-hit
Hades Control (Hold)	⇦🅐	High	24	Leaves foe backturned
Poseidon Tide Rush (Attack Throw)	⇩⇙⇦Ⓐ	Mid	80	Hit Throw
Poseidon Tide Rush	⇩⇙⇦ⒶⒶⒶⒶⒶⒶ	Mid, Mid, Mid, Mid, Mid Mid	30, 8, 8, 8, 8, 8	Combos naturally
Hades Break	While Crouching Ⓐ	Low	14	Leaves Astaroth in crouching state
Reverse Spiral Ax	While Rising Ⓐ	High	30	Knocks down
Great Annihilation	Jumping Ⓐ	High	30	Knocks down
Reverse Ax Split	Backturned Ⓐ	Low	18	
Lower Hades Split	While Crouching Backturned Ⓐ	Low	22	Leaves Astaroth in crouching state

Vertical Attacks

Name	Command	Attack Level	Damage	Notes
Hades Ax	ⒷⒷ	Mid, Mid	20, 30	Combos on counter-hit
Hades Ax (Hold)	Ⓑ🅑	Mid, Mid	20, 40	Guard Break, 2nd hit launches
Ax Side Cannon	⇨Ⓑ	Mid	20	Crumples on counter-hit
Ax Volcano	⇘Ⓑ	Mid	32	Launches
Ax Volcano (Hold)	⇘🅑	Mid	44	Unblockable, launches
Hades	⇩Ⓑ	Mid	20	Leaves Astaroth in crouching state
Hades (Hold)	⇩🅑	Mid	35	Guard Break, leaves Astaroth in crouching state
Ax Grave	⇙Ⓑ	Low	24	Knocks down, leaves Astaroth in crouching state
Bear Fang	⇦Ⓑ	Mid	20	Knocks down on counter-hit
Bear Fang (Hold)	⇦🅑	Mid	45	Knocks down
Dark Split	While Crouching Ⓑ	Mid	22	Leaves Astaroth in crouching state
Hades Rising	While Rising Ⓑ	Mid	30	
Greater Divide	Jumping Ⓑ	Mid	28	Knocks down
Reverse Dark Split	Backturned Ⓑ	Mid	22	
Lower Dark Split	While Crouching Backturned Ⓑ	Mid	24	Leaves Astaroth in crouching state

Kick Attacks

Name	Command	Attack Level	Damage	Notes
Moloch's Vise	Ⓚ	High	14	
Valarion	🅚	High	34	Hit Throw
Hades Knee	⇨Ⓚ	Mid	18	Knocks down on counter-hit
Dark Tamer	⇘ⓀⒶ	Mid, High	18, 36	Combos on counter-hit, 2nd hit knocks down
Dark Tamer (Delay)	⇘ⓀⒶ	Mid, High	18, 36	Combos on counter-hit, 2nd hit knocks down
Dark Tamer (Hold)	⇘🅚Ⓐ	Mid, High	38, 36	Combos on counter-hit, 2nd hit knocks down
Dark Tamer (Hold)	⇘Ⓚ🅐	Mid, Mid	18, 26	
Dark Tamer (Hold)	⇘🅚🅐	Mid, Mid	38, 26	
Bull Low Kick	⇩Ⓚ	Low	10	
Reverse Tamer	⇙ⓀⒶ	Low, High	26, 30	Combos on counter-hit, 2nd hit knocks down
Command Kicks	⇦ⓀⓀ	Mid, Mid, Mid, Mid	15, 15, 15, 15	
Bull Kick	While Crouching Ⓚ	Low	10	Leaves Astaroth in crouching state
Bull Rush	While Crouching ⇘Ⓚ	Mid	28	Knocks down
Bull Rush (Hold)	While Crouching ⇘🅚	Mid	31	Knocks down
Rising Cyclone	While Rising ⓀⒶ	Mid, Low	18, 30	Combos on counter-hit, 1st hit crumples on counter-hit, 2nd hit knocks down
Great Kick	Jumping Ⓚ	Mid	16	
Reverse Bull Kick	Backturned Ⓚ	High	16	
Lower Sweep	While Crouching Backturned Ⓚ	Low	16	Knocks down, leaves Astaroth in crouching state

Simultaneous Press

Name	Command	Attack Level	Damage	Notes
Titan Ax	Ⓐ+Ⓑ	Mid	25 (48)	Knocks down from long range
Offering	⇘Ⓐ+Ⓑ	Mid	35	Hit Throw on counter-hit
Offering (Hold)	⇘🅐+🅑	Mid	35	Hit Throw
Breath of Hades	⇦Ⓐ+Ⓑ	Mid	20	Knocks down
Breath of Hades (Hold)	⇦🅐+🅑	Mid	50	Unblockable
Guard Crusher	Ⓑ+Ⓚ	High	20	Leaves foe backturned
Body Splash	⇨Ⓑ+Ⓚ	High	28	Deflects vs. high & mid slashes
Body Splash (Hold)	⇨🅑+🅚	High	38	Deflects vs. high & mid slashes
Hades Crush	⇩Ⓑ+Ⓚ	Mid	15	
Hades Crush ~Maelstrom Divide	⇩Ⓑ+ⓀⒶ+Ⓖ	Mid, Throw	15, 30	
Hades Crush ~Hades Destroyer	⇩Ⓑ+ⓀⒷ+Ⓖ	Mid, Throw	15, 30	
Hades Crush ~Bludgeoning Crush	⇩Ⓑ+Ⓚ⇩Ⓐ+Ⓖ	Mid, Throw	15, 35	
Hades Crush ~Drop of Lava	⇩Ⓑ+Ⓚ⇩Ⓑ+Ⓖ	Mid, Throw	15, 45	
Ax Lower Cannon	⇦Ⓑ+Ⓚ	Low, Low, Low	8, 8, 22	Knocks down, leaves Astaroth in crouching state
Ax Lower Cannon (Additional attack)	⇦Ⓑ+ⓀⒷ	Low, Low, Low	8, 8, 21, 22, 39	Hit Throw
Flying Divide	⇙Ⓑ+Ⓚ	Mid	45	Knocks down
Flying Divide (Hold)	⇙🅑+🅚	Mid	55	Guard Break
Demented Moon	⇩⇘⇨Ⓑ+Ⓚ	Mid	110	Unblockable, launches
Side Divide	Backturned Ⓑ+Ⓚ	Mid	27	Leaves Astaroth backturned, crumples on counter-hit
Taunt	Ⓚ+Ⓖ			

8-Way Run

Name	Command	Attack Level	Damage	Notes
Ares Spiral Rage	→ⒶⒷ	Mid, Mid	18, 26	Combos on counter-hit, 1st hit crumples, 2nd hit launches
Ax Blow	↘ or ↗Ⓐ	Mid	26	Causes recoverable stun
Poseidon Crest	↓ or ↑ⒶⒶ	Mid, Mid	16, 16	Combos naturally
Discus	↙ or ↖Ⓐ	Low	25 (35)	Knocks down, leaves Astaroth in crouching state
Hades Divide	←Ⓐ	Mid	20	Leaves foe backturned on normal hit, floors on counter-hit
Hades Divide (Hold)	←🅐	Mid	20	Spins foe
Ax Crash	→Ⓑ	High	35 (45)	Knocks down counter-hit from long range
Ax Volcano	↘ or ↗Ⓑ	Mid	34	Launches
Ax Volcano (Hold)	↘ or ↗🅑	Mid	44	Unblockable, launches
Hades Cannon	↓ or ↑Ⓑ	Mid	55 (20)	Launches, does less damage but launches overhead by inputting ↓ or ↑🅑⇦
Azazel Tackle	↙ or ↖ⒷⓀ	Mid, Mid	36, 30	1st hit aims off-axis
Canyon Creation	←Ⓑ	Mid	40	Knocks down, leaves Astaroth in crouching state
Canyon Creation (Hold)	←🅑	Mid	70	Unblockable, leaves Astaroth in crouching state
Bull Rush	→Ⓚ	Mid	28	Knocks down
Bull Rush (Hold)	→🅚	Mid	50	Launches
Hades Rush	↘ or ↗Ⓚ	Mid	26	Aims off-axis
Hades Rush (Hold)	↘ or ↗🅚	Mid	19	Aims off-axis, launches
Stamp of Hades	↓ or ↑Ⓚ	Mid	30	
Stamp of Hades (Hold)	↓ or ↑🅚	Mid	28	Launches, causes tremor that staggers nearby foes
Lower Command Kick	← or ↙ or ↖Ⓚ	Mid	30	Crumples on counter-hit, leaves Astaroth in crouching state
Titan Swing	↓ or ↑Ⓐ+Ⓑ	High	40 (50)	Knocks down, does extra damage from max range
Titan Swing (Hold)	↓ or ↑🅐+🅑	High	60	Unblockable
Sliding	While Running Ⓚ	Low	22	Knocks down

Throws

Name	Command	Attack Level	Damage	Notes
Maelstrom Divide	Ⓐ+Ⓖ	Throw	55	Ⓐ to break throw
Hades Destroyer	Ⓑ+Ⓖ	Throw	50	Ⓑ to break throw
Beat Down	Left Side Throw	Throw	68	Ⓐ or Ⓑ to break throw
On Silent Wings	Right Side Throw	Throw	62	Ⓐ or Ⓑ to break throw
Death Crush	Back Throw	Throw	70	
Plunging Crush	Against Crouching Foe ⬂Ⓐ+Ⓖ	Throw	50	Ⓐ to break throw
Flood of Lava	Against Crouching Foe ⬂Ⓑ+Ⓖ	Throw	60	Ⓑ to break throw
Bludgeoning Crush	Against Crouching Foe ⇩Ⓐ+Ⓖ	Throw	50	Ⓐ to break throw
Drop of Lava	Against Crouching Foe ⇩Ⓑ+Ⓖ	Throw	60	Ⓑ to break throw
Wicked Judgement	⇨⬂⇩⬃⇦Ⓐ+Ⓖ	Throw	63	Ⓐ to break throw
Flight of the Wicked	⇨⬂⇩⬃⇦Ⓑ+Ⓖ	Throw	33	Ⓑ to break throw
Wrath of the Damned	Against Airborne Foe Ⓐ+Ⓖ	Throw	30	
Titan Bomb	Against Airborne Foe ⇩⇧Ⓑ+Ⓖ	Throw	88 (94)	Does more damage with perfect input
Brutal Grasp	Against Downed Foe's Head ⬃Ⓐ+Ⓖ or ⬃Ⓑ+Ⓖ	Throw	30	Leaves foe standing, Ⓐ or Ⓑ to break throw
Wrath of the Damned	Against Downed Foe ⇩Ⓑ+ⓀⒶ+Ⓖ	Mid, Throw	14, 30	
Burial	Against Downed Foe ⇩Ⓐ+Ⓚ	Throw	35	

Combos

Counter-hit ⇨Ⓑ, ⇩Ⓐ + Ⓖ (Wall Hit), ⬃Ⓐ (or Ⓑ) +Ⓖ

4 hits, 88 damage, leaves foe standing

⇩⇩🅑⇨, ⇩⇧Ⓑ + Ⓖ

2 hits, 90 damage

⇨⬂⇩⬃⇦Ⓑ + Ⓖ, ⇩⇧Ⓑ + Ⓖ (Wall Hit), ⇩Ⓐ + Ⓚ

3 hits, 109 damage, Astaroth's back near wall

⇨⬂⇩⬃⇦Ⓑ + Ⓖ, Ⓐ + Ⓖ (Wall Hit), ⇩Ⓐ + Ⓖ (Wall Hit), ⬃Ⓐ (or Ⓑ) + Ⓖ

5 hits, 88 damage, start with foe's back near wall, leaves foe standing

Counter-hit ⇨Ⓚ, ⇩Ⓐ + Ⓚ

2 hits, 56 damage

Counter-hit ⬂Ⓐ (recoverable stun), While Rising Ⓚ, ⇩Ⓐ + Ⓖ (Wall Hit), ⬃Ⓐ (or Ⓑ) + Ⓖ

5 hits, 86 damage, leaves foe standing

⬂Ⓐ + Ⓖ (Wall Hit), ⬃Ⓐ (or Ⓑ) + Ⓖ

3 hits, 80 damage, start with crouching foe's back near wall, leaves foe standing

↓Ⓚ, ⇨⇨ⒶⒷ, ⇩⇧Ⓑ + Ⓖ

3 hits, 62 damage, first attack is from a few steps away, pounds ground and staggers foe but does no damage

⇦⇦🅐, ⇨⇨ⒶⒷ, ⇩⇧Ⓑ + Ⓖ

4 hits, 82 damage

⇦⇦🅐, ⒶⒷ, ⇩Ⓐ + Ⓖ (Wall Hit), ⬃Ⓐ (or Ⓑ) + Ⓖ

6 hits, 84 damage, leaves foe standing

Ⓑ + Ⓖ (Wall Hit), ⇩Ⓐ + Ⓖ (Wall Hit), ⬃Ⓐ (or Ⓑ) + Ⓖ

5 hits, 124 damage, begin with foe's back near wall, leaves foe standing

⬃🅐Ⓑ, ⇩Ⓑ + ⓀⒶ + Ⓖ

3 hits, 105 damage, delayed Ⓑ must hit

Ⓑ🅑, ⇩⇧Ⓑ + Ⓖ

2 hits, 110 damage, delayed 🅑 must hit

⇩⬂⇨Ⓑ + Ⓚ, ⇩⇧Ⓑ + Ⓖ

2 hits, 180 damage

Close Range

Astarot[redacted]brute of astounding power, but close range is not his ideal fighting distance. Most of his attacks are relatively slow, a[redacted]uicker foes that specialize in short-range guessing games can overwhelm his close-range offense. He's not completely helpless though—Astaroth has a few great close-range options, and his throw game is very strong. When you're pressured up close, use Guard Impacts, the Hades Knee (→Ⓚ), and the Minotaur Crush (↘Ⓐ) as interruption moves to stop the opponent's offensive patterns. Hades Knee comes out very fast and knocks the enemy on his backside, while Minotaur Crush causes a recoverable stun on counter-hit. It's possible to land a Hades Knee during this stun for extra damage. If the enemy relies on high strings to keep you at bay or thwart throw attempts, preemptively use the Reverse Tamer (↙ⓀⒶ), a low-to-high string that results in a great 2-hit combo on counter-hit. Be careful using this string too often; the first hit is low, while the second is high, so if your foe guards the first hit correctly, the follow-up swing whiffs over his head and leaves Astaroth wide open. You can also use →Ⓑ and While Rising Ⓚ as high payoff counter-hit attacks from close range. If either counter-hits, go for a crouching throw while the opponent crumples. While Rising Ⓚ can also lead into the Rising Cyclone chain, ending with a sweeping low (While Rising ⓀⒶ). This combos on counter-hit, and can be useful if you feel the enemy will guard and retaliate.

Astaroth's Hades Ax (ⒷⒷ) string presents great guessing game options if you can get the enemy to hesitate at point-blank range, wary of counter-hits or throws. If enemies are blocking the string, simply begin throwing more often. Once they're worried about guarding the string versus avoiding a throw, use ⒷⒷ to make the second hit into a delayed Guard Break. If they actually get hit by this Guard Break, they'll bounce into the air and you can immediately land Astaroth's Titan Bomb air throw (↓↑Ⓑ + Ⓖ). When you're going for throws, use Flight of the Wicked (→↘↓↙←Ⓑ + Ⓖ) as your first option—Titan Bomb (↓↑Ⓑ + Ⓖ) is a guaranteed follow-up after the toss, making this Astaroth's most damaging grapple. If the foe's back is to a wall, use Ⓐ + Ⓖ instead after Flight of the Wicked, slapping your opponent against the wall and allowing for follow-up throws.

In addition to Great Divide, the Grip Shot to Ax Volcano (→ⒶⒷ) is also a useful close-range string. It combos on counter-hit, an[redacted]elay the second button input, perhaps baiting the enemy into getting counter-hit and launched. The launch [redacted]enough for practical juggles, but it can set up a ground throw or score a Wall Hit. Using →Ⓐ is great as a tick into throw, too—foes expecting →ⒶⒷ will get snagged. Finally, keep an eye out for walls, and try to force your enemy against them. Astaroth has a few attacks and throws that easily score wall hits and can lead to one another, dealing huge chunks of damage very quickly! Consult the Combo section, along with Ashlotte's chapter, for more on throw tactics.

Mid Range

Astaroth grows more comfortable the further he is from his opponent. At mid range, his options open up and he's less susceptible to quick characters. Use Ax Crash (⇨Ⓑ) and Ax Grave (↙Ⓑ) as excellent pokes to interrupt opponents from a few steps away. However, watch out for side movement against both attacks. Destruction (ⒶⒷ) is an excellent string that begins with a high, horizontal swing that snuffs 8-Way Run and sidesteps. Both hits combo even on normal hit, but the second strike also causes a useful stun on counter-hit. Occasionally poke with Ⓐ by itself, then throw the enemy. This trains foes to stick out attacks after they guard Ⓐ, allowing the follow-up Ⓑ poke to counter-hit them when you finally use it.

If foes start to crouch from mid range to avoid Astaroth's high pokes, start using the Flood of Lava (↘Ⓑ + Ⓖ). This leaping throw is designed to go over low attacks and then snag crouching foes from a surprising distance. The Poseidon Tide Rush (↓↙↘Ⓐ) is a horizontal mid with a fairly long wind-up but, if it hits, it results in a very powerful hit throw. Ax Volcano (↘Ⓑ) is a useful launcher that you can delay for a few reasons. If you delay it as long as possible, the launcher becomes an Unblockable that sends the foe soaring skyward, in prime position for a juggle or air throw. If you don't delay it, it still sends opponents upward, long enough to juggle with Bear Fang (←Ⓑ). For a devious alternative, delay the Ax Volcano just long enough so they think you're going for the Unblockable, and then release it early for the normal version. If your foe sticks out a move trying to snuff an Unblockable, he'll get counter-hit for his trouble. Finally, note the Hades Divide (⇦Ⓐ) from mid range. Whether it strikes as a normal or counter-hit this move causes the enemy to spin very quickly, allowing you to combo →→ⒶⒷ, ↓↑Ⓑ + Ⓖ for a monstrous finish!

Long Range

Astaroth's incredible range, power, and horizontal attacks grant him the upper hand in almost any long-range fight. Use Titan Ax (Ⓐ + Ⓑ or ↑Ⓐ + Ⓑ) as your main poke from a distance. Up close, this attack is underwhelming, but from a distance it strikes in a big, horizontal swath at mid level. This move frequently counter-hits for huge damage against foes using 8-Way Run far away, where they feel (unjustifiably) safe. Once you condition the opponent to fear this move, which won't take very long, begin mixing in Discus (↙Ⓐ). This sweeping axe spin knocks enemies down from extremely far away, and even comes with a multi-layered mix-up built in. If enemies attempt to step back from this attack before rushing in after it whiffs, simply follow it up with While Rising Ⓐ. Discus ↙Ⓐ puts Astaroth into a crouch, so all you have to do is press Ⓐ as he rises. Once the enemy is worried about the mix-up between Titan Ax and Discus at long range, begin using ↙ⒶⒶ or Ⓑ for the Double Discus or Discus Breaker. Astaroth winds up his axe sweep a bit longer before unleashing either a second sweep or a crunching overhead Guard Break. Both attacks are deceptively fast after the seemingly slow sweep, and they cause major headaches for your opposition. If enemies adjust to Astaroth's sweep mix-ups, it's time to use Bull Rush (→→Ⓚ). Like many of Astaroth's moves, you can charge this attack by holding Ⓚ. Whether charged or not, Astaroth puts his shoulder down and rushes forward, bulldozing the enemy. The deception here is at the very beginning, when Astaroth slouches over before attacking; he doesn't look too different than he does when he attempts ↙Ⓐ or Ⓐ. Because those moves are low, and →→Ⓚ or Ⓚ is mid, the opponent frequently gets hit while he or she is busy worrying about Astaroth's Discus attacks. Note the ⇘ or ⇗Ⓚ or Ⓚ versions of Bull Rush—Astaroth breaks laterally at the last moment, nailing sidestepping foes if you choose the correct direction! Finally, keep the Hades Cannon (⇩Ⓑ) in mind as an all-purpose ranged deterrent. This reverse hammer swing hits hard and sends the opponent spinning backward in the air like a flipped coin. This arc can even cause a Ring Out on stages with low walls! From mid-arena, input ← just before Hades Cannon strikes. This makes it deliver less damage, but places the opponent directly above Astaroth, ready to be thrown with ↓↑Ⓑ + Ⓖ!

Special Tactics

Okizeme: Anti-Wakeup

Astaroth is a nightmare once he floors his opponent—apologies to Nightmare, an unpleasant dream in his own right. With ground throws that lead to airtight standing throw mix-ups, ground hit throws, bouncing hits into air throws, and heavy hits that strike floored characters, Astaroth can severely punish enemies for making poor decisions as they wake up. The hit throw ↓Ⓐ + Ⓚ features Astaroth spearing foes with the axe head before slamming them back down. Plus, it's quick enough for him to tack on after many knockdowns or juggles. If the enemy is floored with his head facing Astaroth, try for the Brutal Grasp (↙Ⓐ or Ⓑ + Ⓖ) instead. Either command results in the same ground throw, but the enemy must guess which one to try to break. If successful, Astaroth smashes the foe's head into the ground several times before hauling him to his feet…where he can immediately try for a standing throw! Opponents can do little to avoid this mix-up, aside from crouching or attempting to throw break. If they're savvy enough to crouch, mix in quick mid hits, like →Ⓚ, after picking them up, or go for one of Astaroth's crouch throws. From further away, if they're not rising quickly, go for Canyon Creation—⇦Ⓑ, or ⇦Ⓑ to make this move Unblockable. This smashes foes if they rise without rolling to the side. Another interesting striking option is to use the Stamp of Hades (⇩Ⓚ). This unique ground pound attack is a special mid that launches the enemy if it actually hits. But it also staggers foes from even a few steps away—dealing no damage—if the tremor it causes is not guarded crouching. Either way, you get combo follow-up potential. This move usually has too much start-up to use while the opponent is on his feet, but it's ideal to use while he wakes up.

Hades Crush

After inputting ↓Ⓑ + Ⓚ, immediately press any basic standing or crouching throw command: Ⓐ + Ⓖ, Ⓑ + Ⓖ, ↓Ⓐ + Ⓖ, or ↓Ⓑ + Ⓖ. Astaroth performs a quick, effective, close-range stomp and follows with the grab attempt of choice. This has great applications both at close range and against floored opponents. Astaroth can stomp and then grab opponents either crouching or standing, and performing ↓Ⓑ + Ⓚ,Ⓐ + Ⓖ actually bounces floored opponents off the ground and into a unique air throw! Using ↓Ⓑ + Ⓚ and its throw follow-ups greatly aids Astaroth's close-range and Okizeme games. If ↓Ⓑ + Ⓚ strikes as a counter-hit, throw follow-ups are usually guaranteed, leading to huge damage!

Cassandra Alexandra

Cassandra Alexandra

Courage is better than keenest steel,
when bold men bare their brands...
The Lay of Fáfnir, "Poetic Edda"

Bio

Age:	21
Birthplace:	Athens, Ottoman Empire
Height:	5'5"
Weight:	Insists she's lost weight recently
Birth Date:	July 20
Blood Type:	B
Weapon:	Short Sword & Small Shield
Weapon Name:	Digamma Sword & Nemea Shield (Reforged)
Discipline:	Athenian Style
Family:	Father: Achelous Mother: Nike Brother: Lucius

Cassandra Alexandra

Cassandra set out once again for that evil city, hoping to find more clues that would lead her to Soul Edge. But when she arrived, she found it under siege; the neighboring powers had combined their might to destroy it. She feared the battle would reduce the city—and her hopes—to ash; but that passed in a moment since she was soon greeted by the sight of the besieging army fleeing for safety. The allied army had lost. Meanwhile, the citizens continued their indiscriminate rampage, as if possessed. From one of the defeated soldiers, Cassandra learned they had a leader: a swordsman.

As she hurried through the night, a man appeared before her. His eyes were stained red, and their gaze fixed on Cassandra as if focusing all the malice she had felt in the city on her. The weapon she held became hot, alerting her to the fact that this man belonged to the darkness. She had found the city's leader, no question.

"You have a piece of Soul Edge, don't you? I can feel it," he said. Cassandra flinched. How could he know that? From within his overcoat, the man produced a rapier and Cassandra only barely managed to sidestep the thrust that came an instant later. After a fierce flurry of blows—all dealt by her opponent—Cassandra finally succeeded in returning the favor. The man's eyes briefly widened with indignation, and then a sneer crossed his face. He parried her next blow, then leapt back. His coat floated a moment, occluding the moonlight, and then she was alone.

The man's voice rang out. "So, woman, you can ward off evil, though not as strong as the Holy Stone. Interesting. I'll let you live for now."

"You're going to run?! You coward!"

A laugh echoed around her. "I already have what I came for." The meaning of his words sunk in and, panicked, Cassandra searched her tunic, but the fragment of Soul Edge was gone.

The man had toyed with her, and for a moment Cassandra lost her composure, but she pushed those unhelpful feelings down and hurried to the city. As she crept about, doing her best to elude the mad citizens, she made an unexpected discovery: not all of the people had gone mad. A few sane citizens were trying to escape. She came to their defense, and together they put the cursed city behind them.

On the road, the rescued citizens explained that they, too, had been taken by madness, but two travelers, a man and a woman, had released them from the spell with a shining blue crystal they had in their possession. Cassandra recalled that the swordsman had mentioned a "Holy Stone." Certainly with a treasure like that, she could stand against any evil; perhaps she could even use it to destroy Soul Edge.

Cassandra left the citizens in a safe location and set out to learn more about the Holy Stone. First she tried to locate the man and woman who had cured the citizens, but was unsuccessful. It was as though the clues she needed had seen her coming and decided to erase themselves just to vex her. But when she was at her wits' end, she heard a rumor about a man who carried a mass of crystal as tall as himself. The man and his crystal which, lo and behold, shone blue had been spotted on the road to Ostrheinsburg.

Cassandra had a passing knowledge of those baleful castle ruins, but why would the man head there? If the crystal he bore had the power to smite evil, then that could only mean some evil presence lurked in the castle. Could it possibly be Soul Edge?

Cassandra decided to follow the man to Ostrheinsburg. She wanted to rescue her sister from the clutches of destiny; she had joined the battle for Soul Edge with that one wish in mind. But now another emotion was kindled within her, and with every step she took toward Ostrheinsburg, it burned more and more fiercely: rage at the cursed sword, for all the ills it had wrought.

Digamma Sword and Nemea Shield

Cassandra is the younger sister of Sophitia, who received the oracle from Olympus and became a holy warrior. The sword and shield that she used in her battles were later dedicated to a temple.

Though it appeared that she had found happiness, Sophitia was still tormented by thoughts of Soul Edge. Seeing her sister caught up in the wars of the gods, Cassandra was determined to help her. Even as she cursed the gods, she claimed the weapons from the temple.

Cassandra is almost completely untrained in the arts of the sword, and her weapons have sometimes broken under her crude handling.

Natural Movements (Athenian Style)

The ancient Greek goddess of civilization was also a goddess of war. Those who received her divine protection were able to master the Athenian style of combat. But now the Greek gods are forgotten, and no one is left to teach the art. Well, almost no one...

The Olympian god of fire and forge, Hephaestus, despised Soul Edge, for it had been made by the hand of man. He gave several devout believers, warriors all, holy weapons to fight and destroy the cursed sword. These holy warriors learned the ancient sword fighting arts thanks to the divine protection with which their weapons were infused.

Though Cassandra was no devout believer, perhaps the gods felt something for the purity and clarity of her soul.

Command List

Signature Techniques

Name	Command	Attack Level	Damage	Notes
Undertow	⬃Ⓐ	Low	28	
Shield Buster	⇦ⒷⒷⒶ (Just)	Mid, Mid, High	12, 6 35	
Seraphim Heel	⬃Ⓚ	Low	18	Stuns on counter-hit
Angel Snipe	→ or ↘ or ↗Ⓐ	Mid	32	
Rothion Mauler	↘ or ↗Ⓑ	Mid	30	
Hip Bomber	← or ↙ or ↖Ⓑ +Ⓚ	Mid	46	
Luminance Fall	Angel Step ⒶⒷ	Mid, Mid	20, 30	
Angelic Gust	Angel Step 🅑	Mid	20	Stuns on hit
Angel's Embrace	⇨⇨Ⓑ+Ⓖ	Throw	25	Input Ⓑ to escape throw

Horizontal Attacks

Name	Command	Attack Level	Damage	Notes
Slide Flow	ⒶⒶ	High, High	12, 18	
Slide Knee	ⒶⓀ	High, Mid	12, 20	
Slide Knee (Delay)	ⒶⓀ	High, Mid	12, 20	
Shield Slaps	⇨ⒶⒶⒶ	High, High, High	12, 10, 20	Final attack stuns on counter-hit
Shield Slaps (Delay)	⇨ⒶⒶⒶ	High, High, High	12, 10, 20	Final attack stuns on counter-hit
False Slide Kick	⬂ⒶⓀ	Mid, Mid	20, 28	2nd attack can be delayed, causes stun on counter-hit
Under Slide Blade	⇩Ⓐ	Sp Low	12	
Undertow	⬃Ⓐ	Low	28	
Cross Blitz	⇦ⒶⒷ	High, Mid	18, 28	1st attack stuns on counter-hit. Wind-up period for 2nd hit deflects horizontal attacks.
Under Slide Blade	While Crouching Ⓐ	Sp Low	12	
Mirage Satellite	While Rising Ⓐ	Mid	24	Stuns on counter-hit
Mirage Satellite (Hold)	While Rising 🅐	Mid	24	Stuns on hit
Leaping Slide Spin	Jumping Ⓐ	High	26 or 28 or 30	Damage varies depending on direction jumped in
Flipside Slide Blade	Backturned Ⓐ	High	14	
Flipside Under Slide Blade	While Crouching Backturned Ⓐ	Low	16	

Vertical Attacks

Name	Command	Attack Level	Damage	Notes
Dancing Shield	ⒷⒷ	Mid, Mid	10, 20	
Splash Beat	ⒷⓀ	Mid, High	10, 14	
Artemis Dart	⇨Ⓑ	High	30	
Heaven Lift	⬂Ⓑ	Mid	24	Launches on hit
Guardian Strike	⇩ⒷⒷ	Mid, Mid	10, 30	2nd attack stuns on hit
Elfin Thrust (Additional attack)	⇩ⒷⒷ During Hit Ⓚ		10, 30, 10(20)	2nd attack stuns on hit. 3rd attack deals extra damage if timed perfectly (Just Frame).
Guardian Wings	⇩Ⓑ⇧ⒷⒶⒶ	Mid, Mid, High, High	10, 30, 8, 23,	
Under Splash	⬃Ⓑ	Mid	16	
Shield Buster	⇦ⒷⒷⒶ (Just)	Mid, Mid, High	12. 6. 35	
Under Splash	While Crouching Ⓑ	Mid	18	
Shield Swipe	While Crouching ⬂Ⓑ	Mid	18	Deflects vertical attacks (shifts into 30 damage attack)
Pure Stinger	While Crouching ⬃Ⓑ	Low	18	
Heaven's Wing	While Rising Ⓑ	Mid	28	
Leaping Under Splash	Jumping Ⓑ	Mid	24 or 26 or 28	2nd attack stuns on hit
Flipside Sword Splash	Backturned Ⓑ	Mid	12	
Flipside Under Splash	While Crouching Backturned Ⓑ	Mid	18	

Kick Attacks

Name	Command	Attack Level	Damage	Notes
Holy High Kick	Ⓚ	High	12	
Holy Heaven Kick	⇨Ⓚ	Mid	16	
High Knee	⬂Ⓚ	Mid	14	Causes recoverable stun on hit
Spring Under Kick	⇩Ⓚ	Low	14	
Seraphim Heel	⬃Ⓚ	Low	18	Stuns on counter-hit
Seraphim Turning Kick	⇦Ⓚ	High	20	Causes recoverable stun
Spring Under Kick	While Crouching Ⓚ	Low	14	
Holy Ax Kick	While Rising Ⓚ	Mid	18	
Falling Angel	Jumping ⓀⒷ	Mid, Mid	28, 55	2nd attack is unblockable, stuns on hit
Flipside High Kick	Backturned Ⓚ	High	14	
Flipside Spring Under Kick	While Crouching Backturned Ⓚ	Low	12	

Simultaneous Press

Name	Command	Attack Level	Damage	Notes
Tempest	Ⓐ+Ⓑ	Mid, Mid	10, 20	
Cascade Blade	⇧Ⓐ+ⒷⓀ	Mid, Low	24, 15	
Temporal Ascension	Ⓑ+ⓀⒷ	Mid, Mid	20, 20	
Temporal Ascension (Hold)	Ⓑ+Ⓚ🅑	Mid, Mid	20, 30	
Shield Upper	⇩Ⓑ+Ⓚ	Mid	12	Stuns on counter-hit
Destined Greatness	⇦Ⓑ+Ⓚ	Mid	14(20)	Wind-up period deflects vertical attacks, shifts into attack that stuns on hit
Gaia Quake	⇧Ⓑ+Ⓚ	Mid	30	
Gaia Quake (Hold)	⇧🅑+🅚	Mid	50	Unblockable
Heavenly Strike	Backturned Ⓑ+Ⓚ	Mid	28	Causes uncontrollable air state on aerial hit
Holy Purification	⇦Ⓐ+Ⓚ	High	16	Wind-up period deflects horizontal attacks, shifts into unblockable attack
Seraphim Sault	⇧Ⓐ+ⓀⓀ	Mid, Mid	18, 20	
Seraphim Sault (Delay)	⇧Ⓐ+ⓀⓀ	Mid, Mid	18, 20	
Taunt	Ⓚ+Ⓖ			

8-Way Run

Name	Command	Attack Level	Damage	Notes
Angel Snipe	→ or ↘ or ↗Ⓐ	Mid	32	
Shield Slap	↓ⒶⒶ	High, High	12, 8	1st attack stuns on hit
Shield Slap (Inverse)	↑ⒶⒶ	High, High	12, 8	1st attack stuns on hit
Elfin Twister	← or ↙ or ↖Ⓐ	Mid	28	
Shield Nova	→Ⓑ	Mid	20	Stuns on hit
Rothion Mauler	↘ or ↗Ⓑ	Mid	30	Launches on hit
Holy Smash	↓ or ↑Ⓑ	Mid	20	
Holy Smash (Hold)	↓ or ↑🅑	Mid	30	Guard Breaks
Zephyros Wheel	← or ↙ or ↖Ⓑ	Mid	26	Launches on hit
Heaven's Guardian	←🅑Ⓐ	Low, Mid	35, 42	Unblockable. Input Ⓖ to cancel.
Hip Charge	→Ⓚ	Mid	28	Causes recoverable stun on counter-hit
Hip Charge ~Facing Away	→🅚	Mid	28	Causes recoverable stun on counter-hit. Leaves Cassandra backturned.
Seraphim Kicks	↘ or ↗ⓀⓀ	Low, High	16, 32	
Seraphim Tornado	↘ or ↗ⓀⒶ+Ⓚ	Low, Mid	16, 30	
Seraphim Sault	↓ or ↑ⓀⓀ	Mid, Mid	20, 28	
Seraphim Sault (Delay)	↓ or ↑ⓀⓀ	Mid, Mid	20, 28	
Leaping Heaven	← or ↙ or ↖Ⓚ	High	40	
Stardust Strike	→Ⓐ+Ⓑ	Mid	35	
Elfin Dance (Additional attack)	→Ⓐ+Ⓑ During Hit ⇦		35, 10(20)	Input second attack perfectly for additional damage
Angel's Judgement	→ or ↘ or ↗ Ⓑ+ⓀⒶⒷ	Mid, High, Mid	34, 10, 24	1st and 2nd attack stun on counter-hit
Angel's Hook	→ or ↘ or ↗ Ⓑ+ⓀⒶⓀ	Mid, High, Low	34, 10, 10	1st and 2nd attack stun on counter-hit
Divine Fall	↓ or ↑Ⓑ+Ⓚ	Mid	30	Stuns on hit
Hip Bomber	← or ↙ or ↖ Ⓑ+Ⓚ	Mid	46	
Sliding	While Running Ⓚ	Low	26	

Throws

Name	Command	Attack Level	Damage	Notes
Meteor Shower	Ⓐ+Ⓖ	Throw	50	Input Ⓐ to escape
Seraphim Blade Twist	Ⓑ+Ⓖ	Throw	55	Input Ⓑ to escape
Guardian Revenge	Left Side Throw	Throw	58	Same button as throw (Ⓐ or Ⓑ) to escape
Seraphim Hammer	Right Side Throw	Throw	62	Same button as throw (Ⓐ or Ⓑ) to escape
Exile Order	Back Throw	Throw	60	Same button as throw (Ⓐ or Ⓑ) to escape
Guardian's Knee	Against Crouching Foe ⇩Ⓐ+Ⓖ	Throw	35	Input Ⓐ to escape
Seraphim Cyclone	Against Crouching Foe ⇩Ⓑ+Ⓖ	Throw	60	Input Ⓑ to escape
Angel's Embrace	⇨⇨Ⓑ+Ⓖ	Throw	25	Input Ⓑ to escape

Angel Step

Name	Command	Attack Level	Damage	Notes
Angel Step	⇩⇘⇨			Deflects high attacks
Luminance Fall	Angel Step ⒶⒷ	Mid, Mid	20, 30	
Angel's Exile	Angel Step Ⓑ	Mid	32	
Angelic Gust	Angel Step 🅑	Mid	20	Stuns on hit
Tornado Feint	Angel Step Ⓚ	Mid	36	
Angel Step ~Sidestep	Angel Step ⇩ or ⇧			
Luminance Fall	Angel Step ⇩ or ⇧ ⒶⒷ	Mid, Mid	20, 30	
Guardian Wings	Angel Step ⇩ or ⇧ ⒷⒶⒶ	Mid, High, High	38, 8, 23	
Falling Angel	Angel Step ⇩ or ⇧ ⓀⒷ	Mid, Mid	38, 55	2nd attack is unblockable

Angelic Twirl

Name	Command	Attack Level	Damage	Notes
Angelic Twirl	⇩⇙⇦			Deflects high attacks
Luminance Fall	Angelic Twirl ⒶⒷ	Mid, Mid	20, 30	
Angel's Exile	Angelic Twirl Ⓑ	Mid	32	
Angelic Gust	Angelic Twirl 🅑	Mid	20	Stuns on hit
Tornado Feint	Angelic Twirl Ⓚ	Mid	36	

Combos

⇘Ⓑ, ⇦ⒷⒷⒶ (Just)
4 hits, 60 Damage
⇙Ⓐ, While Rising Ⓑ
2 hits, 49 Damage
Counter-hit ⇩Ⓑ + Ⓚ, ⇦ⒷⒷⒶ (Just)
4 hits, 38 Damage
Counter-hit ⇦ⒶⒷ, ⇦ⒷⒷⒶ (Just)
5 hits, 61 Damage
⇘Ⓚ, ⇘ⒶⓀ, ⇦ⒷⒷⒶ (Just)
6 hits, 67 Damage, 1st stun is recoverable
⇩⇘⇨Ⓑ, ⇩Ⓑ⇧ⒷⒶⒶ
5 hits, 64 Damage
While Rising Ⓐ, ⇨ⒶⒶⒶ, ⇦ⒷⒷⒶ
7 hits, 62 Damage
⇨⇨Ⓑ + Ⓖ, ⇦ⒷⒷⒶ (Just)
4 hits, 64 Damage
↘ or ↗Ⓑ, ⇦⇦Ⓑ + Ⓚ
2 hits, 66 Damage
↘ or ↗Ⓑ, ⇨⇨Ⓐ + Ⓑ⇦ (Just)
2 hits, 74 Damage
Counter-hit Ⓑ + ⓀⒷ, back-turned Ⓑ + Ⓚ
3 hits, 67 Damage

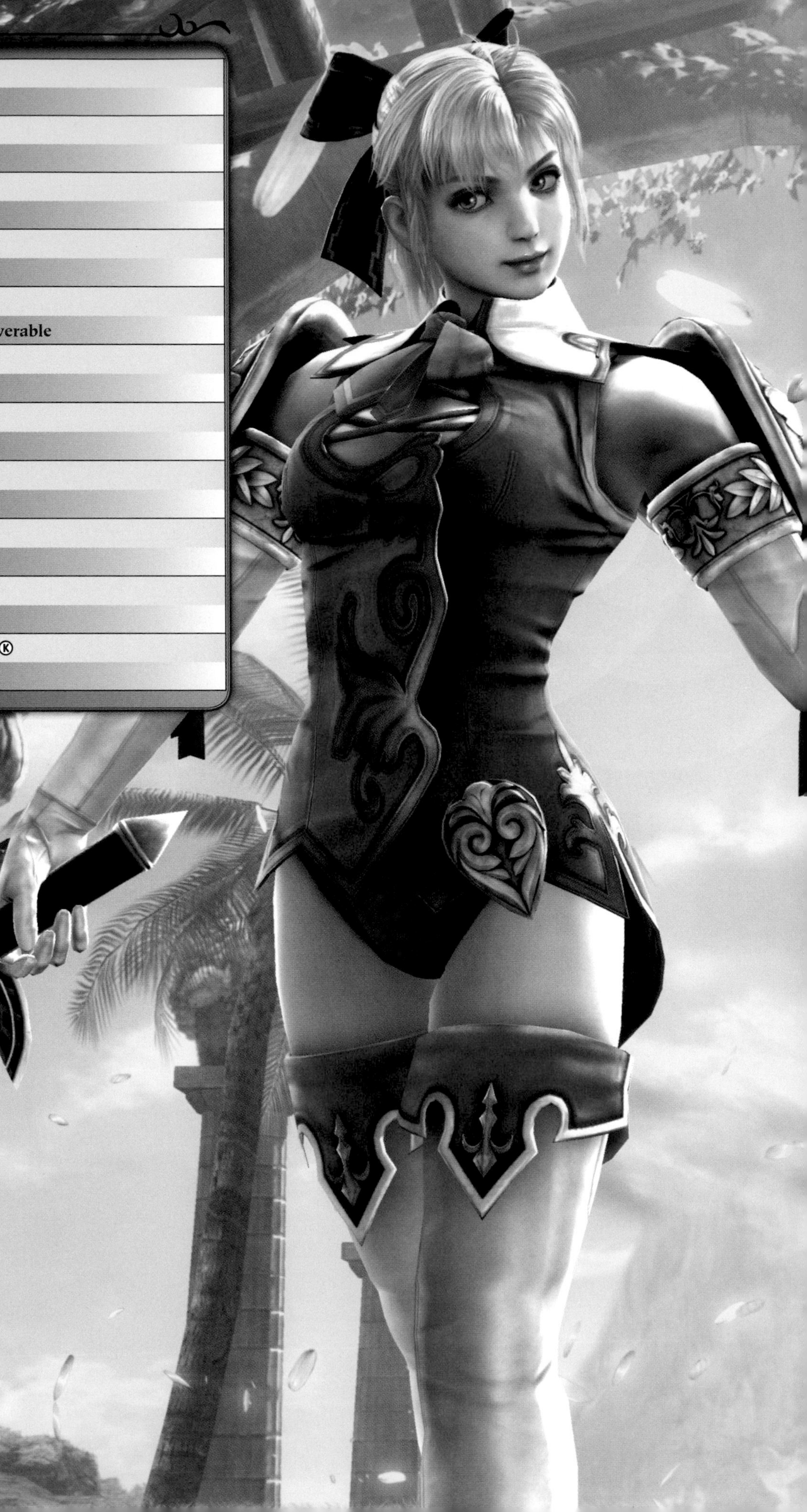

Close Range

Cassandra has a variation of Sophitia's move set, but with several major tweaks. Her attacks are almost entirely geared toward close range, having none of the powerful mid-range attacks Sophitia has. This makes it very difficult to establish close range with her, but once you do, she's extremely effective.

Pay close attention to your enemies' habits. If they tend to stand often, use the low-hitting Undertow (⬃Ⓐ) to catch them off guard. If it hits, combo your fallen enemy with While Rising Ⓑ. Against enemies reacting to your low attack with vertical strikes, sidestep or start your offense with Cassandra's ⒶⒶ string to preemptively stop their attacks. This string also counters sidesteps. On a successful hit, stage a follow-up attack consisting of the Elfin Thrust (⇩ⒷⒷ during hit Ⓚ), ⬃Ⓐ, or False Slide Kick (⬂ⒶⓀ). The flexible ⇩ⒷⒷⓀ(Just) fully combos on counter-hit and against crouching characters, so use it above all other options. When attacking with it, perform ⇩Ⓑ by itself and verify whether it hits. If it connects as a counter-hit or against a crouching character, chain into its Ⓑ extension then tap Ⓚ as the second hit connects to perform a 3-hit combo. When blocked, delay the input for the Ⓑ extension to stop your enemy's attempts to attack your recovery. When your foe is afraid of the follow-up, perform ⇩Ⓑ by itself, then go for the Angel's Embrace (⇨⇨Ⓑ+Ⓖ) or the Heaven Lift (crouching ⬂Ⓑ). Be cautious when using ⇩ⒷⒷ, as the second hit is extremely unsafe when blocked. Avoid performing the second hit if you aren't in a position to take risks.

You can initiate the second hit of ⬂ⒶⓀ very late. Use this to lure out enemy counterattacks. If it connects as a counter-hit, attack your stunned foe with ⇦ⒷⒷⒶ. When your adversary is afraid of the second hit, perform ⬂Ⓐ by itself and then go for Cassandra's ⇨⇨Ⓑ+Ⓖ throw.

When on the defensive—if your enemy guards one of your attacks—use Angelic Twirl (⇩⬃⇦) to deflect incoming mid attacks. If you successfully counter an attack, perform its Angel's Exile (during Angelic Twirl 🅑) to punish your foe's deflected move. Follow up with ⇦ⒷⒷⒶ for a combo. If your opponent keeps you locked down with high attacks, strike with the Shield Upper (⇩Ⓑ+Ⓚ) to duck under your foe's move. Combo your stunned enemy with ⇦ⒷⒷⒶ if it connects as a counter-hit.

Mid Range

Plow your way into close range. Use Artemis Dart (⇨Ⓑ) as a general poking attack to keep your enemy from making any sudden aggressive movements. If your opponent relies on 8-Way Run to approach you, attack with ⬃Ⓐ, ⇨⇨Ⓐ, or the Cross Blitz (⇦ⒶⒷ) to counter-hit his or her movement. The riskiest of these is ⇦ⒶⒷ, but it leads to this powerful combo on counter-hit: ⇦ⒶⒷ, ⇦ⒷⒷⒶ(Just Frame). Back out of your opponent's attack range if you believe he is going to attack. If his attack misses, punish it with the Stardust Strike (→Ⓐ+Ⓑ during hit ⇦) or Angelic Gust(⇩⬂⇨Ⓑ). When the enemy is wary of your mid-range offense, use the Angel Step (⇩⬂⇨) to slip into close range. Come out of the dash with Cassandra's Angel's Exile (🅑) attack, or simply throw your enemy as you recover. If 🅑 hits, crush your foe with the combo ⇩Ⓑ⇧ⒷⒶⒶ to score a knock down.

Long Range

Cassandra has few worthwhile attack options at this distance. Your best choice is to carefully move your way into a more viable position. The Angel Step, though risky, has high deflect properties and the ability to shift into sidesteps to avoid vertical attacks. It's your safest means to approach your enemy if he or she isn't expecting it. An even riskier option is to use the Seraphim Sault (⇧Ⓐ+ⓀⓀ) to kick your way into close range. Perform the first kick by itself (⇧Ⓐ+Ⓚ) to leap over high attacks. If it happens to hit on a counter-hit, input Ⓚ to combo into the second attack. When blocked, delay the second attack to bait and counter your opponent's attempts to attack the first kick's recovery period. When your foe is afraid of the kick extension, go for ⇧Ⓐ+Ⓚ by itself, then simply throw when you recover to catch your opponent's defensive stance.

Special Tactics

Okizeme: Anti-Wakeup

Train your foes to block high with ⇩ⒷⒷⓀ (Just). Go for ⬃Ⓐ when they're afraid of the mid strike. Both options are fairly safe and lead to a ton of damage on a successful hit. If your opponent is scared of your low attack, go for the Rothion Mauler (↘Ⓑ), a powerful launcher that leads to a free ⇦⇦Ⓑ+Ⓚ on a successful hit. This combo deals massive damage and is perfect for scoring Ring Outs when you're three or fewer character lengths from an arena's edge. Though it's easy to read, this attack leaves Cassandra at a slight advantage when blocked, enabling her to stage a follow-up attack.

As an alternate low option, use Seraphim Kicks (↘ or ↗Ⓚ). If it connects as a counter-hit, chain into its Ⓚ extension (↘ⓀⓀ) for a 3-hit combo. String into its mid follow-up if blocked (↘ⓀⒶ+Ⓚ). Although it's difficult to implement, using ↘Ⓚ by itself and then immediately performing a throw afterward may hit your enemy if he or she is expecting the Ⓐ+Ⓚ follow-up attack.

If you ever go for a throw, use Angel's Embrace (⇨⇨Ⓑ+Ⓖ). This throw leaves your enemy vulnerable to a combo, which is ⇨⇨Ⓑ+Ⓖ, ⇦ⒷⒷⒶ. Use it in combination with Cassandra's Ⓐ+Ⓖ throw to avoid Grapple Breaks. This is the perfect option to go for after your enemy blocks ⇩Ⓑ, assuming he or she is afraid of its follow-up attack.

Deflection

Cassandra's Angel Step (⇩⬂⇨) and Angelic Twirl (⇩⬃⇦) are both special movements with deflection properties. Angel Step ⇩⬂⇨ has high deflect properties, while Angelic Twirl ⇩⬃⇦ deflects mid attacks. Both techniques are necessary tools for approaching your enemy or escaping harm. If either movement deflects an attack, shift into its 🅑 option to stun your enemy. Take advantage of the stun and link into ⬂ⒶⓀ, ⇦ⒷⒷⒶ to score a combo.

Many of Cassandra's attacks have deflection properties as well. For example, her crouching Shield Swipe (⬂Ⓑ) deflects middle attacks while also ducking under high moves, a useful tool for staging counterattacks when you don't have an advantage to work with. It's especially powerful when you perform it after ⇩Ⓑ is guarded. Use it to stop your enemy's attempts to counterattack with a ⒷⒷ string or a powerful launcher.

Cervantes de Leon

Cervantes de Leon

Bio

Age:	48 (Aging has stopped)
Birthplace:	Valencia, Spanish Empire
Height:	5'10"
Weight:	176 lbs.
Birth Date:	January 1
Blood Type:	None
Weapon:	Longsword & Pistol Sword
Weapon Name:	Acheron & Nirvana
Discipline:	Memories of Soul Edge
Family:	Father: Killed in battle Mother: Deceased He slaughtered his whole crew when he claimed Soul Edge, although he remembers none of it.

But the other has a heart of iron, and his spirit within him is pitiless as bronze: whomsoever of men he has once seized he holds fast: and he is hateful even to the deathless gods.

"Theogony," Hesiod (c. 700 BC)

Once there was a dread pirate who [illegible] defeated once, [illegible] were [illegible] weapon, [illegible] evil blade and attain the ultimate power, [illegible] Needless to say, his own body, which had [illegible] predicament; his flesh could decay at any moment. He had [illegible]

Cervantes had mastered Soul Edge's technique of [illegible] numbers than ever to hold it together. The souls he absorbed [illegible] unnatural shapes. In the form of ghastly apparitions, the souls [illegible] found himself once again a mighty pirate in command of an undead armada.

However, it was not enough. To face a being powerful enough to seal [illegible] strength. Then he remembered. When the evil blade was [illegible] thus far, but now... Could there be any sacrifice more worthy than [illegible] moment he pinpointed Ivy's location. While she had seemingly [illegible] already exceeded the boundaries of humanity. As he made a blood offering of his [illegible] the seed, and now the time had come to harvest, the way one might pluck the ripest of fruit. [illegible] he had dared imagine. It felt right. How could one soul be so succulent? More and more [illegible] knew what to do with. Once he eliminated his one rival, that wretched spirit sword, [illegible]

But just when it seemed time for him to make his move, calamity struck a second time. [illegible] response, the Soul Edge he carried tried violently to tear itself from his grip. He knew why. [illegible] freed itself from the spirit sword and regained its full power! His own Soul Edge [illegible] other half. After a brief deliberation, Cervantes decided to let his sword go. For if he did, Soul Edge would [illegible] no idea who to thank for this happy turn of events.

As he watched the sword streak across the sky, Cervantes fell into reflection. Once the cursed sword was [illegible] own—and what an easy task it would be! He felt the sheer power within his body and form. [illegible] was tempered anew. As proof, Cervantes took out the longsword he had kept close at hand during his [illegible] sooner had he clutched the sword's hilt than evil coursed through the blade, turning it black [illegible] it had become a cursed weapon. Such evil, such raw, overwhelming power. Now that he had [illegible] stop him. Cervantes held his old blade high aloft—and where did it point? The cursed capital, [illegible]

"Wait and see, Soul Edge. I'll be the one to claim you, and all the world with you!"

Cervantes de Leon

Acheron

The longsword Cervantes wielded before claiming Soul Edge. While it could never match the cursed sword's power, it ranked among the finest of mortal weapons. Acheron was there when Cervantes's connection with Soul Edge brought him back to life, and now the blade has been cursed by the same evil that fills its master.

Cervantes still seeks to dominate Soul Edge completely, but in the meantime he has no qualms about making do with this old friend.

Nirvana

A rare and singular sword with a pistol installed in its hilt. Like Acheron, it has been cursed: the bullets it fires are packed with evil.

Soul Edge's Memory

The great pirate Cervantes who spread fear as he crossed the Atlantic Ocean. After he was defeated, his body became infused with thousands of fragments of the evil sword and he literally became one with the evil.

His power was now that of the Cervantes himself along with the power of all the souls that Soul Edge has consumed over the years. One blow from the fencing master Cervantes is both sharper and more powerful than any other swordsman.

Command List

Signature Techniques

Name	Command	Attack Level	Damage	Notes
Wave Break	⬃Ⓐ	Low	26	Knocks down, leaves Cervantes in crouching state
Cannonball Lifter	⬂Ⓑ	Mid	18 (24)	Launches and does extra damage at close range
Bloody Hilt Kick	⇦ⒷⓀ	Mid, High	16, 22	Combos on counter-hit, 2nd hit leaves both characters backturned
Scissor Wave	⬂Ⓐ+Ⓑ	Mid, Mid	15, 12	
Flying Dutchman	While Crouching Ⓐ+ⒷⒷ (Mash)	Mid, Mid, Mid, Mid, Mid, Mid, Mid	6, 6, 6, 6, 6, 6, 20	Guard Break
Law of Pirates	While Rising ⒷⒷ	Mid, Mid	15, 35	1st hit launches, 2nd hit launches on counter-hit, leaves Cervantes in crouching state
Lagging Wave	➡Ⓐ	High	30	Knocks down
Bile Lunges	➡Ⓑ	Mid	25, (48)	Hit throw if close
Geo Da Ray	Dread Charge Ⓑ	Mid	30	Launches, hold Ⓑ to redirect off walls

Horizontal Attacks

Name	Command	Attack Level	Damage	Notes
Soul Swing	ⒶⒶ	High, High	10, 11	Combos naturally
Pirate's Cross	ⒶⒷ	High, Mid	10, 25	
Anchor Gusty Kick	ⒶⓀ	High	28	
Gentle Wave	⇨Ⓐ	High	14	Leaves foe sideturned
Scissor Lifter	⬂ⒶⒷ	Low, Mid	14, 16	Just Frame Ⓑ for extra damage and launch
Laser Wave	⇩Ⓐ	Sp.Low	10	
Wave Break	⬃Ⓐ	Low	26	Knocks down
Crush Keel	⇦Ⓐ	High	17	Backturns foe on normal hit, crumples foe on counter-hit
Crush Keel (Hold)	⇦🅐	High	17	Crumples foe
Laser Wave	While Crouching Ⓐ	Sp.Low	10	
Cursed Blow	While Rising Ⓐ	Mid	18	Spins foe
Soul Wipe Riptide	Jumping Ⓐ	High	24	
Aft Soul Wipe	Backturned Ⓐ	High	12	
Sub Laser Wave	While Crouching Backturned Ⓐ	Low	14	

Vertical Attacks

Name	Command	Attack Level	Damage	Notes
Wild Storm	ⒷⒷⒷ	Mid, Mid, Mid	13, 13, 24	Combos on counter-hit, knocks down
Storm Flare	ⒷⒷ⇦Ⓑ+Ⓚ	Mid, Mid, Mid	13, 13, 45	First 2 hits combo naturally, 3rd hit is a Guard Break
Surprise Wave	ⒷⒶ	High	16	Causes foe to spin and crumple on counter-hit, teleports Cervantes if struck during retraction by high slashes
Head Snap Kick	ⒷⓀ	Mid	28	Knocks down
Storm Generate	Ⓑ⇩	Sp.Mid	5	Hit throw against airborne foes
Storm Generate (Attack Throw)	Against Airborne Foe Ⓑ⇩		20	Hit Throw against airborne foes
Sail Nautilus (Hold)	⇨🅑	Mid	25	Crumples foe
Sail Nautilus	⇨ⒷⒷ	Mid, Mid	20. 25	Combos on counter-hit
Sail Nautilus (Hold)	⇨Ⓑ🅑	Mid, Mid	20, 15, 15, 20	Last 3 hits combo naturally
Cannonball Lifter	⬂Ⓑ	Mid	18 (24)	Launches and does extra damage at close range, press Ⓑ for follow-up attack during counter-hit
Cannonball Lifter (Follow-up Attack 1)	Counter-hit ⬂Ⓑ Ⓑ (Just)	Mid, Mid	28, 35	
Cannonball Lifter (Follow-up Attack 2)	Counter-hit ⬂Ⓑ ⇦Ⓑ (Just)	Mid, Mid	28, 20	
Spike Anchor	⇩Ⓑ	Mid	20	Leaves Cervantes in crouching state
Bloody Hoist	⬃Ⓑ	Mid	24	Knocks down, leaves Cervantes in crouching state
Bloody Hilt Kick	⇦ⒷⓀ	Mid, High	16, 22	Combos on counter-hit, 2nd hit leaves both characters backturned
Slay Storm	While Crouching Ⓑ	Mid	16	Leaves Cervantes in crouching state
Law of Pirates	While Rising ⒷⒷ	Mid, Mid	15, 35	1st hit launches, 2nd hit launches on counter-hit, leaves Cervantes in crouching state
Deck Lifter	Jumping Ⓑ	Mid	20	Launches
Aft Blade Storm	Backturned Ⓑ	Mid	15	
Sub Slay Storm	While Crouching Backturned Ⓑ	Mid	18	Leaves Cervantes in crouching state

Kick Attacks

Name	Command	Attack Level	Damage	Notes
Anchor Kick	Ⓚ	High	14	
Anchor Knee Kick	⇨Ⓚ	Mid	16	
Anchor Middle Kick	⬂Ⓚ	Mid	15	
Anchor Bow Kick	⇩Ⓚ	Low	11	Leaves Cervantes in a crouching state
Anchor Marooned Kick	⬃Ⓚ	Low	18	Leaves Cervantes in a crouching state
Anchor Steep Kick	⇦ⓀⓀ	High, Mid	16, 16	Combos on counter-hit
Vile Slide	⇦⇩⬃Ⓚ	Low	25	Crumples on counter-hit
Vile Tornado	⇦⇩⬃ⓀⒷⒷ	Low, High, High	10, 20, 20	First 2 hits combo, 3rd hit is Unblockable
Anchor Bow Kick	While Crouching Ⓚ	Low	11	Leaves Cervantes in a crouching state
Anchor Revive Kick	While Rising Ⓚ	Mid	21	
Cannon Launch Kick	Jumping Ⓚ	Mid	18	
Aft Anchor Kick	Backturned Ⓚ	High	16	
Sub Anchor Bow Kick	While Crouching Backturned Ⓚ	Low	12	Knocks down, leaves Cervantes in crouching state

Simultaneous Press

Name	Command	Attack Level	Damage	Notes
Full Sail Hoist	Ⓐ+Ⓑ	Mid	18	Causes recoverable stun
Gale Slash	⇨Ⓐ+ⒷⒷ	Mid, Mid	14, 20 (30)	Extra hit and damage with Just Frame input on 2nd hit
Scissor Wave	⬂Ⓐ+Ⓑ	Mid, Mid	12, 15	
Fregata Slicer	⇩Ⓐ+Ⓑ	Mid	20	Crumples foe on counter-hit, leaves Cervantes in a crouching state
Eternal Curse	⬃Ⓐ+Ⓑ	Mid	30	Unblockable, launches
Dark Geo Da Ray	⇦Ⓐ+Ⓑ	Mid, Mid, Mid	10, 20, 22	Guard Break, launches
Iceberg Circular	⇧Ⓐ+Ⓑ	Mid	28	Launches
Flying Dutchman	While Crouching Ⓐ+Ⓑ	Mid, Mid, Mid, Mid, Mid, Mid, Mid	6, 6, 6, 6, 6, 6, 20	
Flying Dutchman	While Crouching Ⓐ+ⒷⒷ (Mash)	Mid, Mid, Mid, Mid, Mid, Mid, Mid	6, 6, 6, 6, 6, 6, 20	Guard Break
Pirate's Tactics	Ⓑ+Ⓚ			Deflects vertical slashes and teleports Cervantes behind foe
High Tide Anchoring	⇩Ⓑ+Ⓚ	Mid	33	
High Tide Anchoring (Hold)	⇩🅑+🅚	Sp.Mid	38	Knocks down
Shadow Flare	⇦Ⓑ+Ⓚ	Mid	45	Guard Break
Shadow Flare (Hold)	⇦🅑+🅚	Mid	45	Guard Break, falls behind foe
Killer X Crawler	⇧Ⓑ+Ⓚ	Mid	36	Knocks down
Pressure Astern	⇧🅑+🅚	Mid	28	Knocks down
Aft Dread Pressure	Backturned Ⓑ+Ⓚ	Mid	20	
Pirate's Scheme	Ⓐ+Ⓚ			Deflects horizontal high and mid slashes and teleports Cervantes behind foe
Genocidal Culverin	⇨Ⓐ+Ⓚ	High	60	Unblockable
Anchor Bow Heel	⇦Ⓐ+Ⓚ	Mid	25	Launches on counter-hit, deflects vs. horizontal high and mid slashes
Bloody Culverin	⇧Ⓐ+Ⓚ	High	15	Unblockable
Dark Flame	Backturned Ⓐ+Ⓚ			Teleports behind foe, facing them
Dark Flame (Hold)	Backturned 🅐+🅚			Teleports behind foe, backturned
Taunt	Ⓚ+Ⓖ			

Throws

Name	Command	Attack Level	Damage	Notes
Sadistic Cross	Ⓐ+Ⓖ	Throw	50	Ⓐ to break throw
Turbulence Lift	Ⓑ+Ⓖ	Throw	10	Launches
Figurehead Break	Left Side Throw	Throw	55	Ⓐ to break throw
Jolly Roger Hoist	Right Side Throw	Throw	58	Ⓑ to break throw
Flush Flood	Back Throw	Throw	60	
Curse of the Ancient Mariner	While Crouching ⬂⇩⬂Ⓑ+Ⓖ	Throw	69	Ⓑ to break throw

8-Way Run

Name	Command	Attack Level	Damage	Notes
Lagging Wave	→Ⓐ	High	30	Knocks down
Dishonest Wave	↘ or ↗Ⓐ	High	35	Knocks down, deflect vs. horizontal high slashes
Bridgette Slice	↓Ⓐ	Mid, High	15, 20	Knocks down
Tornado Slice	↑Ⓐ	High, Mid	15, 20	Knocks down
Gibbering Torpedo	↙ or ↖ⒶⒶ	Low, Low	15, 27	Combos on counter-hit, 2nd hit launches
Gibbering Pressure	↙ or ↖ⒶⒷ	Low, Mid	15, 25	
Merciless Wave	←Ⓐ	High	38	Knocks down
Cannonball Split	←ⒶⒷ	Mid	43	Hit throw
Merciless Needle	←ⒶⒷⒷ	Mid, Mid	X, 16	Follow-up if hit throw is blocked
Bile Lunges	→Ⓑ	Mid	25, (48)	Becomes hit throw if close enough
Cannonball Lifter	↘ or ↗Ⓑ	Mid	18 (24)	Launches and does extra damage from close range
Storm Nest	↓ or ↑Ⓑ	Low	15	Crumples on counter-hit
Storm Nest (Attack Throw)	Against Downed Foe ↓ or ↑Ⓑ		25	Hit throw against downed foes, launches
Riot Storm	↙ or ↖Ⓑ	Mid	34	Launches on counter-hit
Bow Breaker	←Ⓑ	Mid	35	
Head Scratch Kick	→ or ↘ or ↗Ⓚ	Mid	16	Crumples on counter-hit
Anchor Side Kick	↓ or ↑Ⓚ	Mid	22	Deflects vs. horizontal highs and mids
Anchor Swirl Kick	↙ or ↖Ⓚ	Low	22	
Galleon Sinker	←Ⓚ	Mid	28	Causes back slide on counter-hit
Windmill	→Ⓐ+Ⓑ	Mid, High	15, 15	Launches
Cross Bone Divider	←Ⓐ+Ⓑ	Mid	35	Launches
Cross Bone Divider (Hold)	←🅐+🅑	Mid	50	Unblockable, launches
Sliding	While Running Ⓚ	Low	26	Knocks down

Dread Charge

Name	Command	Attack Level	Damage	Notes
Dread Charge	⇩⬃⇦			Initiates Dread Charge
Dread Slash	Dread Charge Ⓐ	High	55	Unblockable
Geo Da Ray	Dread Charge Ⓑ	Mid	30	Launches, hold 🅑 to redirect off walls
Geo Da Ray	Dread Charge Ⓑ (Perfect ⇩⬃⇦Ⓑ input)	Mid	17, 10, 6	Launches
Geo Da Ray	Dread Charge Ⓑ (Perfect ⇩⬃⇦Ⓑ input) ⇩⇧Ⓑ	Mid, Mid	17, 10, 6, 18	
Geo Da Ray	Dread Charge ⇩ or ⇧Ⓑ		30	Aims off-axis
Rolling Slapper	Dread Charge Ⓚ	Mid	20, 20	
Tornado Swell	Dread Charge Ⓑ+Ⓚ		22, 22, 22	
Anchor Whirlpool	Dread Charge Ⓐ+Ⓚ	Low	20	Knocks down
Dark Flame	Dread Charge ⇨			Teleports forward

Combos

↘Ⓑ, ⇧Ⓐ + Ⓚ, ↘Ⓐ + Ⓑ	4 hits, 52 damage
Counter-hit ↘Ⓑ, ⇩⇙⇦, Ⓑ + Ⓚ	4 hits, 79 damage
⇦⇦ⒶⒷ, Ⓑ⇩	2 hits, 63 damage
Ⓑ + Ⓖ, Ⓑ + Ⓚ (late)	4 hits, 55 damage
While Rising Ⓐ, ⇦ⓀⓀ	3 hits, 45 damage
↘ⒶⒷ (Just), ⇧Ⓐ + Ⓚ, ⒶⒶ	6 hits, 51 damage
⇦⇦Ⓐ + Ⓑ, ⇩⇙⇦,Ⓑ + Ⓚ	4 hits, 86 damage
⇨⇨Ⓑ (Wall Hit), ⒷⒷⒷ	6 hits, 86 damage
Counter-hit ⇦Ⓐ, ⇩Ⓐ + Ⓑ, While Rising Ⓐ, Ⓐ	4 hits, 60 damage
Counter-hit ⒷⒶ, ⇩Ⓐ + Ⓑ, While Rising Ⓐ, ⇦ⓀⓀ (Wall hit), ↘Ⓑ, ⇩⇙⇦, Ⓑ + Ⓚ	10 hits, 90 damage

Close Range

Cervantes has a terrific offense from any range. Up close, build his attack patterns around the Soul Swing (ⒶⒶ) and Wild Storm (ⒷⒷⒷ). Soul Swing is a fast, high-striking string that combos even on normal hit and will stop side movement. However, enemies can crouch to avoid it—counter this by using the Wild Storm. This string is made up of three mid hits that combo on counter-hit or against crouching enemies. Input ⒷⒷ and wait to see if they're hitting before you input the third Ⓑ press, because the third hit is unsafe to retaliation if guarded. If the enemy is guarding correctly, either cut the string short or end the string with the Storm Flare (← Ⓑ + Ⓚ), a falling Guard Break that keeps the enemy off balance. Use this sparingly, as it can be sidestepped easily. The Cannonball Lifter (↘ Ⓑ) is also useful up close, whether against crouching opponents or after guarding the opponent's attacks and gaining the advantage. It's unsafe to quick attacks if guarded, but it leads to big juggles on either normal or counter-hit. (Consult the Combos section of this character profile.)

Fregata Slicer (↓ Ⓐ + Ⓑ) is another great option at close range. It's a fast mid attack that puts Cervantes into a crouching animation, making subsequent While Rising attacks easy to perform. Cervantes is safe if the attack is guarded. If it lands as either a normal or counter-hit, Cervantes is in the driver's seat. Fregata Slicer on normal hit smacks opponents onto their backsides, and puts Cervantes in command of a sizeable advantage…enough so that While Rising Ⓐ counter-hits anything the opponent tries that isn't guarding. If While Rising Ⓐ counter-hits, tack on ← ⓀⓀ for extra damage. If Fregata Slicer strikes as a counter-hit right off the bat, the enemy is put into a stagger state that allows While Rising Ⓐ to combo, leading to yet another stagger state, from which ← ⓀⓀ will combo as well. This is already plenty of damage from using Fregata Slicer as a safe poke, but the combo can get bigger and bigger if ← ⓀⓀ knocks the enemy into a wall. Finally, while Cervantes is safe from retaliation after a guarded Fregata Slicer, he's still at a disadvantage. So, don't perform While Rising follow-ups, or you'll just get counter-hit when the opponent tries to reclaim momentum after guarding your attack.

When you're at a mild but not punishable disadvantage, such as after a guarded ⒶⒶ Soul Swing, keep Pirate's Scheme (Ⓐ + Ⓚ) and Pirate's Tactics (Ⓑ + Ⓚ) in mind up close. Both of these moves have special deflection properties. Pirate's Scheme causes Cervantes to hold his blades aloft, waiting for incoming high and mid horizontal attacks. Pirate's Tactics is designed to counter high and mid vertical attacks. If the appropriate attack strikes against Pirate's Scheme or Tactics, Cervantes immediately warps behind the opponent, ready to strike his or her flank. However, note that neither of these special actions deflect kicks.

Mid Range

With his long range and great speed, Cervantes is formidable from mid range too. The Scissor Lifter (↘ ⒶⒷ) is a great tool to score combos even on normal hit. While it's unsafe if blocked, the first hit is low and the second is mid, making this a difficult sequence to guard properly. Normally, on contact this chain simply flips foes over Cervantes's head for a 2-hit combo. But if you press Ⓑ with perfect timing Cervantes flashes white and performs an extra hit while flipping the opponent upward, after which you can juggle with ↑ Ⓐ + Ⓚ, ⒶⒶ. The Scissor Lifter is avoidable through side movement, so occasionally mix in Gibbering Torpedo (⇙ or ⇘ ⒶⒶ). This attack is unsafe to counterattack if guarded, just like Scissor Lifter, but it has two low hits that can catch side movement, and it pops up foes for a juggle with ↘ Ⓐ + Ⓑ even on normal hit. If you fear the opponent will guard correctly, use Gibbering Pressure (⇙ or ⇘ ⒶⒷ) occasionally instead. The first hit is the same but, instead of performing a second sweep, Cervantes turns around and strikes with a mid that floors opponents if they're watching out for a second low attack.

For another mix-up between an attack that strikes side movement at mid range versus one that punishes opponents trying to crouch under circular attacks, use Merciless Wave (← ← Ⓐ) and Merciless Needle (← ← ⒶⒷⒷ). Merciless Wave is a high-hitting slash that floors opponents using sidesteps or 8-Way Run. Merciless Needle first fakes Merciless Wave before it goes for a mid-striking hit throw. If Merciless Needle is guarded, Cervantes instead performs two safe blocked strikes, wearing down the enemy's Soul Gauge without leaving him open.

Long Range

Being far away isn't Cervantes's preference, but he's no slouch from a distance either, and he has many options for getting inside easily. Keep the Genocidal Culverin (→ Ⓐ + Ⓚ) in mind—it's an Unblockable gunshot that you should use to catch opponents that aren't paying attention. It's avoidable through side movement, so don't get too careless with its use. The Shadow Flare ← Ⓑ + Ⓚ is another attack that's great for closing distance quickly. Cervantes warps above the enemy before falling with a Guard Break. Like the Genocidal Culverin, this move can be sidestepped. Finally, keep ← ↓↙ Ⓚ in mind as a useful poke from a distance. It's a sliding kick that's safe if guarded as long as you use it from the edge of its range. Plus, it will stagger the enemy if it strikes as a counter-hit. Dread Charge (↓↙←) moves are also useful from long range—Geo Da Ray (↓↙←, Ⓑ) insures Cervantes can get to his opponents quickly from anywhere. However, be careful of using it on stages without walls, where Cervantes can easily hurl himself off the stage inadvertently!

Special Tactics

Okizeme: Anti-Wakeup

Many of Cervantes's attacks and combos crumple the enemy at his feet, and he has many options to maintain the pressure afterward. Dread Stance attacks are effective against opponents waking up, especially because they'll see Cervantes entering the stance and feel pressured to guard or retaliate correctly. High Tide Anchoring (↓Ⓑ + Ⓚ) can either simply strike floored opponents or it can be charged while they rise. If they don't guard low once they're on their feet, this attack's tremor will stagger them, allowing you to combo with ⒷⒷⒷ. The Storm Nest (⇩ or ⇧ Ⓑ) is also useful against grounded foes. If it strikes enemies before they begin to rise, Cervantes stabs them and flips them up into a hit throw, where you can juggle with combinations like ↑ Ⓐ + Ⓚ, ↘ Ⓐ + Ⓑ. Finally, keep Pressure Astern (↗ Ⓑ + Ⓚ) in mind to use occasionally against foes waking up far away.

Dread Charge

Cervantes's signature stance, initiate the Dread Charge by inputting the motion ↓↙←. From here, Cervantes has a number of options. Inputting Ⓑ initiates the Geo Da Ray, which is also available in an amped-up Guard Break form by inputting ← Ⓐ + Ⓑ (or in a lightning-fast Just Frame version by performing ↓↙← Ⓑ perfectly). This torpedo charge across the screen floors the opposition and can be followed with a combo if you're quick. The Ⓐ + Ⓚ Anchor Whirlpool attack initiates a sweep kick that knocks down even on normal hit, while Ⓐ initiates the Unblockable high Dread Slash. Simply holding → causes Cervantes to teleport toward his foe. Mixing up these options, especially after flooring opponents, keeps them on their toes and Cervantes in control of the match.

Hildegard von Krone

Hildegard von Krone

Age:	18
Birthplace:	Wolfkrone Kingdom
Height:	5'3"
Weight:	110 lbs.
Birth Date:	August 13
Blood Type:	AB
Weapon:	Sword & Lance
Weapon Name:	Glänzende Nova & Frischer Himmel
Discipline:	Groß Erbschaft
Family:	Father, the king (victim of malfestation, now imprisoned by necessity)

Bio

Death, be not proud, though some have called thee
Mighty and dreadful, for thou art not so...
"Holy Sonnet X," John Donne (1572 - 1631)

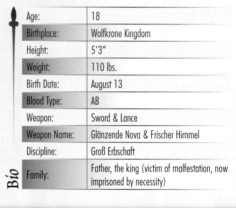

Hildegard von Krone

Hildegard von Krone lowered her head before the cold iron bars of the cell.

"Father, we leave today. Our kingdom shall be victorious. This I swear to you, upon the honor of our family's name."

There was no answer, just an animal growl devoid of all human reason. In the closed stone chamber, not a single torch flickered. Only the faithful moon, shining silver and weak through a small window set high in the wall, offered any light at all.

It was an audience beyond the public gaze. Though "audience," Hilde realized, was far too grand a word for the encounter that took place in this chamber at the very top of the castle tower, the chamber in which the king of Wolfkrone was sent to live out his days. Hilde's father—the great king, the great warrior—was no more. Lost in a fog of madness, he could not even recognize his own daughter when she stood before him.

Hilde had lost him on that horrible day when the light of destruction had swept across the kingdom. Though she was still but a child, the reins of the kingdom were thrust into her hands. Gathering allies and power about her, she managed to cling to the throne and at the same time save the kingdom from the grotesque hordes that were being led by the Azure Knight. Her youth was sacrificed to war, and she was tempered in the fires of battle.

How many times had Hilde almost given up the struggle? Though she knew nothing could be changed, she could not help but dream of how things would be if her father—her strict, fair and kind-hearted father—were still king. But she pushed those thoughts from her mind. The survival of the kingdom depended on her now. Weakness was not an option.

Yet in those moments when Hilde was alone with her father, she longed to renounce everything and give in to her weaknesses. To once again be the meek, frightened little girl who knew that she could rely on the absolute protection of her father.

But, it was not to be. Hilde raised her head and slowly stood up.

Her world was different now. Hilde was no longer the little girl whose father taught her fencing in jest. The sword she wielded was a bolt of lightning that cut down all those tainted by evil, and the lance in her hand was a symbol of her kingdom which, when raised aloft in battle, summoned great warriors to her side. She had become strong. Strong enough to rule her father's nation, but one aspect of Hilde had not changed. The nobility of the wolf, inherited from her father, still flowed in her veins, as it had in the veins of every king and queen that had ruled Wolfkrone.

With a murmured prayer and a final glance at her father, Hilde turned on her heels to leave the room that only she could enter. An inhuman shriek followed her as she passed through the door, but her face betrayed no reaction.

Hilde had to purify herself before leading her army to battle.

She bathed alone. She felt no shame in exposing the wounds that covered her body; it was the sorrowful, pitying gazes of her servants that she could not bear. As Hilde poured the ice-cold water over her skin, her mind was as chilled and cleansed as her body.

It was the moment just before dawn and the garden was as still as a grave. The moon that attended Hilde's quiet ritual would soon slip below the horizon. The night belonged to "them." When the sun set, they emerged from the ruins of Ostrheinsburg Castle, a deadly threat to the land. The people of the kingdom barricaded themselves into their homes and brave soldiers patrolled the villages, watching over them.

Whenever Hilde thought of her devastated realm, sorrow gripped her heart. Once upon a time, it was a rich, bountiful land, but now the hopes of her subjects rested on her shoulders. She must restore its former glory for the men, who in times of peace tilled the soil, but now had taken up the sword to fight with her.

The time was at hand; the tides were changing. Hilde thought of recent events; patrols reporting bizarre sights, such as thousands of objects in the sky, shining with an evil light, hurtling toward the ruined castle like wasps swarming a nest. And then there was the encounter with that man.

Her purification complete, Hilde left the garden and entered her chambers. Immediately, her servants began to prepare her for battle in silence.

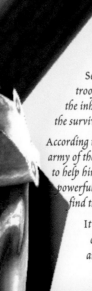

Several days earlier, Hilde and her soldiers had come to the assistance of a troop of mercenaries traveling through Wolfkrone. They had been attacked by the inhabitants of the ruined castle and many of their number were slain. Among the survivors was a woman who had information that was of great interest to Hilde.

According to her, a man called Siegfried had entered the cursed city alone to face the army of the Azure Knight. The woman told Hilde in a quiet voice that she had tried to help him but he had refused her. She just was not strong enough, but Hilde was powerful. Perhaps she could help him instead? Hilde immediately sent out patrols to find the man. She could not let one who fought for the same cause die in vain.

It was not long before Hilde found Siegfried and contrived to meet him on the outskirts of Ostrheinsburg. However, the knight clad in the cold, crystal armor would have nothing to do with her.

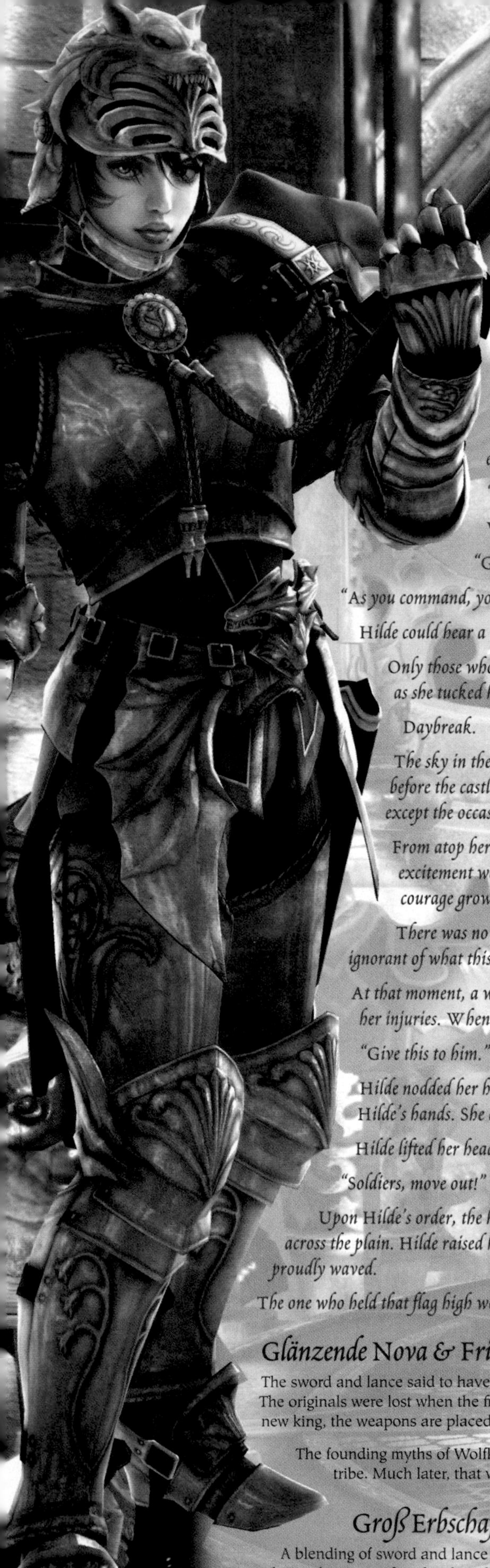

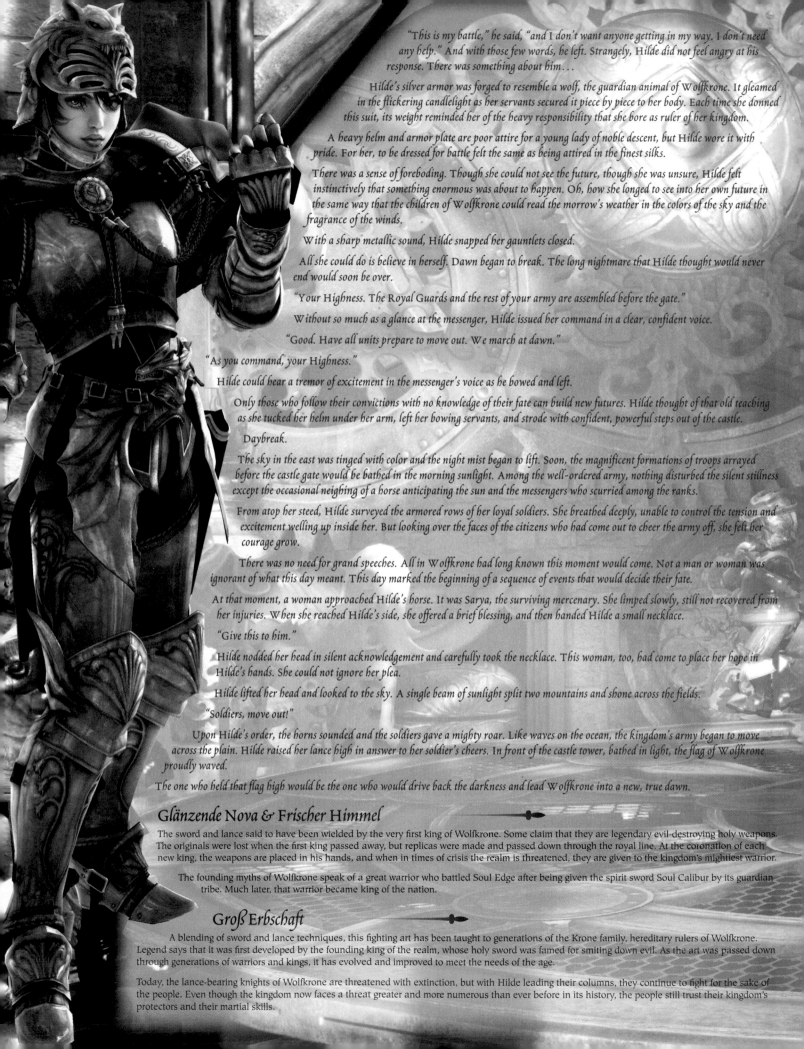

"This is my battle," he said, "and I don't want anyone getting in my way. I don't need any help." And with those few words, he left. Strangely, Hilde did not feel angry at his response. There was something about him...

Hilde's silver armor was forged to resemble a wolf, the guardian animal of Wolfkrone. It gleamed in the flickering candlelight as her servants secured it piece by piece to her body. Each time she donned this suit, its weight reminded her of the heavy responsibility that she bore as ruler of her kingdom.

A heavy helm and armor plate are poor attire for a young lady of noble descent, but Hilde wore it with pride. For her, to be dressed for battle felt the same as being attired in the finest silks.

There was a sense of foreboding. Though she could not see the future, though she was unsure, Hilde felt instinctively that something enormous was about to happen. Oh, how she longed to see into her own future in the same way that the children of Wolfkrone could read the morrow's weather in the colors of the sky and the fragrance of the winds.

With a sharp metallic sound, Hilde snapped her gauntlets closed.

All she could do is believe in herself. Dawn began to break. The long nightmare that Hilde thought would never end would soon be over.

"Your Highness. The Royal Guards and the rest of your army are assembled before the gate."

Without so much as a glance at the messenger, Hilde issued her command in a clear, confident voice.

"Good. Have all units prepare to move out. We march at dawn."

"As you command, your Highness."

Hilde could hear a tremor of excitement in the messenger's voice as he bowed and left.

Only those who follow their convictions with no knowledge of their fate can build new futures. Hilde thought of that old teaching as she tucked her helm under her arm, left her bowing servants, and strode with confident, powerful steps out of the castle.

Daybreak.

The sky in the east was tinged with color and the night mist began to lift. Soon, the magnificent formations of troops arrayed before the castle gate would be bathed in the morning sunlight. Among the well-ordered army, nothing disturbed the silent stillness except the occasional neighing of a horse anticipating the sun and the messengers who scurried among the ranks.

From atop her steed, Hilde surveyed the armored rows of her loyal soldiers. She breathed deeply, unable to control the tension and excitement welling up inside her. But looking over the faces of the citizens who had come out to cheer the army off, she felt her courage grow.

There was no need for grand speeches. All in Wolfkrone had long known this moment would come. Not a man or woman was ignorant of what this day meant. This day marked the beginning of a sequence of events that would decide their fate.

At that moment, a woman approached Hilde's horse. It was Sarya, the surviving mercenary. She limped slowly, still not recovered from her injuries. When she reached Hilde's side, she offered a brief blessing, and then handed Hilde a small necklace.

"Give this to him."

Hilde nodded her head in silent acknowledgement and carefully took the necklace. This woman, too, had come to place her hope in Hilde's hands. She could not ignore her plea.

Hilde lifted her head and looked to the sky. A single beam of sunlight split two mountains and shone across the fields.

"Soldiers, move out!"

Upon Hilde's order, the horns sounded and the soldiers gave a mighty roar. Like waves on the ocean, the kingdom's army began to move across the plain. Hilde raised her lance high in answer to her soldier's cheers. In front of the castle tower, bathed in light, the flag of Wolfkrone proudly waved.

The one who held that flag high would be the one who would drive back the darkness and lead Wolfkrone into a new, true dawn.

Glänzende Nova & Frischer Himmel

The sword and lance said to have been wielded by the very first king of Wolfkrone. Some claim that they are legendary evil-destroying holy weapons. The originals were lost when the first king passed away, but replicas were made and passed down through the royal line. At the coronation of each new king, the weapons are placed in his hands, and when in times of crisis the realm is threatened, they are given to the kingdom's mightiest warrior.

The founding myths of Wolfkrone speak of a great warrior who battled Soul Edge after being given the spirit sword Soul Calibur by its guardian tribe. Much later, that warrior became king of the nation.

Groß Erbschaft

A blending of sword and lance techniques, this fighting art has been taught to generations of the Krone family, hereditary rulers of Wolfkrone. Legend says that it was first developed by the founding king of the realm, whose holy sword was famed for smiting down evil. As the art was passed down through generations of warriors and kings, it has evolved and improved to meet the needs of the age.

Today, the lance-bearing knights of Wolfkrone are threatened with extinction, but with Hilde leading their columns, they continue to fight for the sake of the people. Even though the kingdom now faces a threat greater and more numerous than ever before in its history, the people still trust their kingdom's protectors and their martial skills.

Command List

Signature Techniques

Name	Command	Attack Level	Damage	Notes
Raging Volcano	⇦ⒶⓀ	High, Mid	22, 15	
Lightning Horn	→ⒷⒷⒷ	High, Mid, High	12, 10, 18	
White Torch	⇘ⒷⒶ	Mid, High	20, 24	
Double Kick	⇗ⓀⓀ	Low, Mid	12, 15	2nd attack stuns on counter hit
Fire Strike	⇩Ⓐ+Ⓚ	Low	24	
Noble Heart	↘ or ↗Ⓚ	Mid	24	Causes recoverable stun on hit
Fire Heel	↓ or ↑ⓀⒶ	Mid, High	15, 18	
Thunder Wolf	→ or ↘ or ↗ Ⓐ+Ⓑ	Mid	32	Stuns on hit
Mystic Star	Ⓐ 2 seconds, then release During Hit Ⓐ	Mid, Mid	15. 14	1st hit Guard Breaks, 2nd hit is unblockable
Moonlit Dance	Ⓑ 2 seconds, then release During Hit Ⓑ	Mid, Mid	10, 15	1st attack stuns on hit

Kick Attacks

Name	Command	Attack Level	Damage	Notes
Iron Kick	Ⓚ	High	14	
Drill Knee	→Ⓚ	Mid	18	
Metal Kick	⇘Ⓚ	Mid	15	
Shadow Kick	⇩Ⓚ	Low	12	
Double Kick	⇗ⓀⓀ	Low, Mid	12, 15	2nd attack stuns on counter hit
Knight Heel	⇦Ⓚ	High	20	
Shadow Kick	While Crouching Ⓚ	Low	12	
Shining Kick	While Rising Ⓚ	Mid	20	
Sickle Kick	⇙Ⓚ	Mid	28	
Tornado Kick	⇧ or ⇖Ⓚ	High	22 or 26	Damage varies depending on direction jumped in
Back Kick	Backturned Ⓚ	High	16	
Back Low Kick	While Crouching Backturned Ⓚ	Low	12	

Horizontal Attacks

Name	Command	Attack Level	Damage	Notes
Fire Slash	ⒶⒶ	High, High	8, 12	
Fire Strike	→Ⓐ	High	20	
Hilt Strike	⇘Ⓐ	Mid	24	
Fire Shadow	⇩Ⓐ	Sp.Low	8	
Blazing Shadow	⇙Ⓐ	Low	20	
Raging Volcano	⇦ⒶⓀ	High, Mid	22, 15	
Thundering Volcano	While Crouching Ⓐ	Sp.Low	8	
Rising Fire	While Rising Ⓐ	High	25	
Leaping Slash	Jumping Ⓐ	High	22 or 26 or 30	Damage varies depending on direction jumped in
Back Slash	Backturned Ⓐ	High	10	
Back Low Slash	While Crouching Backturned Ⓐ	Low	12	

Simultaneous Press

Name	Command	Attack Level	Damage	Notes
Royal Windmill	Ⓐ+Ⓑ	Mid, Mid	5, 10	
Double Falcon	→Ⓐ+Ⓑ	Mid, Mid	12, 22	2nd attack stuns on hit
Eagle Talon	⇩Ⓐ+ⒷⓀ	Low, Mid	20, 12	1st attack stuns on hit
Eagle Talon (Cancel)	⇩Ⓐ+ⒷⓀⒼ	Low	20	Cancels 2nd attack
Eagle Talon ~Back Facing	⇩Ⓐ+ⒷⓀ⇦Ⓖ	Low	20	Cancels 2nd attack. Leaves Hilde backturned.
Pulverize	⇦Ⓐ+Ⓑ	Mid	28	Stuns on hit
Golden Heart	While Rising Ⓐ+Ⓑ	Mid	18	Causes recoverable stun
Iron Tower	Against midair opponent Ⓑ+Ⓚ	High	12, 12	Only hits airborne enemies. Shifts to throw on hit.
Double Avalanche	⇨Ⓑ+Ⓚ	Mid	35	Stuns on hit. Evades low attacks.
White Stone	⇩Ⓑ+Ⓚ	Low	20	
Noble Kick	⇦Ⓑ+Ⓚ	Mid	18	
Back Assault	Backturned Ⓑ+Ⓚ	Mid	18	Stuns on hit
Burning Blade	Ⓐ+Ⓚ	Mid	26	
Fire Flash	→Ⓐ+Ⓚ	High, High	6, 10	
Fire Strike	⇩Ⓐ+Ⓚ	Low	24	
Taunt	Ⓚ+Ⓖ			

Vertical Attacks

Name	Command	Attack Level	Damage	Notes
Roaring Horn	ⒷⒷ	Mid, Mid	12, 18	
Lightning Horn	→ⒷⒷⒷ	High, Mid, High	12, 10, 18	
White Torch	⇘ⒷⒶ	Mid, High	20, 24	
White Impale	⇘ⒷⒷ	Mid, Mid	20, 14	
Glorious Hammer	⇩Ⓑ	Mid	16	
Peregrine Falcon	⇙Ⓑ	Low	14	
Hilt Crush	⇦Ⓑ	High	15	
Crown Split	While Crouching Ⓑ	Mid	16	
Wind Horn	While Rising Ⓑ	High	23	
Leaping Strike	Jumping Ⓑ	Mid	18 or 22 or 26	Damage varies depending on direction jumped in
Back Horn	Backturned Ⓑ	Mid	20	
Back Low Horn	While Crouching Backturned Ⓑ	Mid	18	

8-Way Run

Name	Command	Attack Level	Damage	Notes
Runnine Blaze	→ or ↘ or ↗(A)	High	25	
Dancing Torch	↓ or ↑(A)(A)	High, High	18, 15	
Warrior Dance	↓ or ↑(A)(B)	High, Mid	18, 20	
Brute Strike	←(A)	Mid	28	
Lion's Fang	→(B)	Mid	25	
Roaring Fang	↘ or ↗(B)	Low	16	
Circling Hilt	↓ or ↑(B)	Mid	26	
Black Crystal	↙ or ↖(B)	Mid	24	
Elk Rush	←(B)	Mid	22	
Knee Assault	→(K)	Mid	18	
Noble Heart	↘ or ↗(K)	Mid	24	Causes recoverable stun on hit
Fire Heel	↓ or ↑(K)(A)	Mid, High	15, 18	
Spiral Sweep	↙ or ↖(K)	Low	20	
Iron Heel	←(K)	High	16	
Thunder Wolf	→ or ↘ or ↗ (A)+(B)	Mid	32	Stuns on hit
Sliding Kick	While Running (K)	Low	26	

Throws

Name	Command	Attack Level	Damage	Notes
Devine Bolt	(A)+(G)	Throw	55	Input (A) to escape
March of Triumph	(B)+(G)	Throw	50	Input (B) to escape
Victorious Ruler	Left Side Throw	Throw	58	Same button as throw ((A) or (B)) to escape
Royal Seal	Right Side Throw	Throw	60	Same button as throw ((A) or (B)) to escape
Road to Glory	Back Throw	Throw	65	Same button as throw ((A) or (B)) to escape
Heart of Justice	⇨⇦(B)+(G)	Throw	35(92)	Input (B) to escape. Throw initiates an additional attack when it tosses enemy into a wall. Use throw when Hilde's back is against a wall to do this.

Charge Techniques

Name	Command	Attack Level	Damage	Notes
Mystic Star (Stage 1)	Hold (A) 1 second, then release	Mid	20	Causes recoverable stun on counter hit
Mystic Star (Stage 2)	Hold (A) 2 seconds, then release, During Hit (A)	Mid, Mid	15. 14	1st hit Guard Breaks, 2nd hit is unblockable. Deflects high horizontal attacks.
Mystic Star (Stage 3)	Hold (A) 3 seconds, then release	Mid	20	Deflects high horizontal attacks
Moonlit Dance (Stage 1)	Hold (B) 1 second, then release	Mid	20	Causes recoverable stun on hit
Moonlit Dance (Stage 2)	Hold (B) 2 seconds, then release, During Hit (B)	Mid, Mid	10, 15	1st attack causes stun on hit
Moonlit Dance (Stage 3)	Hold (B) 3 seconds, then release	Mid	20	
Dragon Breath (Stage 1)	While Crouching hold (A) 1 second, then release	Mid	20	Causes recoverable stun on counter hit
Dragon Breath (Stage 2)	While Crouching hold (A) 2 seconds, then release	Mid	24	Causes stun on counter hit. Deflects high horizontal attacks.
Dragon Breath (Stage 3)	While Crouching hold (A) 3 seconds, then release, (K)(A)	High, Mid, Low	18, 15, 21	2nd and 3rd attacks stun on counter hit
Dragon Breath (Stage 3)	While Crouching hold (A) 3 seconds, then release, (K)(B)	High, Mid, Mid	18, 15, 18	2nd attack stuns on counter hit
Seiren's Call (Stage 1)	While Crouching hold (B) 1 second, then release, (B)	Mid, Mid	15, 16	
Seiren's Call (Stage 2)	While Crouching hold (B) 2 seconds, then release	Mid	18	
Seiren's Call (Stage 3)	While Crouching hold (B) 3 seconds, then release, (B) During Hit (A)	Mid, Mid Mid	18, 21, 15	1st attack stuns on hit. Final attack is unblockable.

Combos

Counter-hit ⇘(A), ⇨(A) + (K)

3 hits, 44 damage

⇨(B) + (K), ⇦(A) + (B)

2 hits, 54 damage

⇨⇨(A) + (B), ⇦(A) + (B)

2 hits, 54 damage

Stage 3 Mystic Star, ⇦(B) + (K)

2 hits, 39 damage

Stage 3 Moonlit Dance, (B) + (K), ⇦(A) + (B)

3 hits, 68 damage

Stage 3 Moonlit Dance, (B) + (K), Stage 2 Moonlit Dance, Stage 2 Mystic Star

6 hits, 74 Damage, use (B) + (K) command to charge for second Moonlit Dance

Counter-hit Stage 2 Dragon Breath, ⇗(K)(K), ⇩(B) + (K)

4 hits, 60 damage

Counter-hit Stage 2 Dragon Breath, ⇘(B)(A)

3 hits, 63 damage

Stage 2 Moonlit Dance, Stage 3 Mystic Star, ⇦(A) + (B)

4 hits, 45 damage, must begin charging for both attacks at same time

⇦⇦(K), Stage 2 Moonlit Dance, Stage 3 Mystic Star, ⇦(A) + (B)

5 hits, 69 damage, must begin charging for both attacks before ←←(K)

Counter-hit Stage 3 Dragon Breath (K)(B), (B) + (K), ⇦(A) + (B)

5 hits, 78 Damage

Counter-hit Stage 3 Dragon Breath (K)(B), (B) + (K), Stage 2 Moonlit Dance, Stage 2 Mystic Star

8 hits, 79 Damage, re-press buttons after releasing them to quickly start charging again

Close Range

This isn't Hilde's most effective distance, but she does have a few interesting options at her disposal. Your objective is to pressure your enemies into attacking when they're at a disadvantage, enabling you to land a counter-hit. Do this by using the few attacks in Hilde's arsenal that leave her at an advantage. For example, Hilde's Royal Windmill (Ⓐ+Ⓑ) is a mid attack that gives her the advantage even if blocked. This enables her to safely commence a secondary attack. Additionally, the input for this technique, Ⓐ+Ⓑ, enables you to start charging for her Mystic Star (hold Ⓐ for 1~3 seconds, then release) or Moonlit Dance (hold Ⓑ for 1~3 seconds, then release). After the Royal Windmill makes contact with your foe, attack with the Blazing Shadow (⇗Ⓐ), Noble Kick (⇦Ⓑ+Ⓚ), ⇩Ⓐ+Ⓚ, a throw, or the Mystic Star. Use ⇗Ⓐ to duck under high attacks, counter-hitting foes and enabling ⇨Ⓐ+Ⓚ to link afterward for a 3-hit combo. Using ⇦Ⓑ+Ⓚ stops any of your enemy's attempts to counterattack, but it yields less damage than the other options. Use the Mystic Star to stop your enemy's attempts to sidestep ⇗Ⓐ or ⇦Ⓑ+Ⓚ. It causes a recoverable stun on counter-hit, allowing you to link directly into the Moonlit Dance for a giant combo.

As an alternate attack opening, strike with ⒶⒶ, which is used to preemptively stop slower attacks while also countering sidesteps. If it hits your enemy, go for the same options you would after Ⓐ+Ⓑ. This attack leaves Hilde at a disadvantage when it's blocked though, so take a defensive stance. Use ⇗Ⓐ to counter high attacks and Guard Impacts to deal with your enemy's ⇩Ⓐ.

Mid Range

Your focus is to charge for a Stage 3 Mystic Star, which is Hilde's strongest means of countering sidesteps at this distance. This enables you to use her vertical attacks more frequently, which miss against circular movement. The best time to charge is before the round starts, or after striking your enemy with one of her attacks. Because you can't attack with horizontals when you're charging for this move, hold Ⓐ while you use her Ⓑ and Ⓚ techniques. Hilde's better attack options are the Lightning Horn ⇨ⒷⒷ, Roaring Fang (➘ or ➚Ⓑ), Iron Heel (←Ⓚ), and Roaring Horn (ⒷⒷ). Use ⇨ⒷⒷ whenever you anticipate a forward movement from your enemy. If it connects as a counter-hit, string into its Ⓑ extension (⇨ⒷⒷⒷ) for a 3-hit combo. If it doesn't hit, you may opt to start holding Ⓑ afterward to charge for the Moonlit Dance. Back up when you recover and watch your enemy's actions. If your foe tries to mount an immediate counterattack when you recover, backing up will cause his or her attack to whiff, enabling you to punish with the Moonlit Dance. Use ➘Ⓑ to hit opponents who tend to stand often, and mid-hit ⒷⒷ as a direct counter to those looking for ➘Ⓑ. Employ ←Ⓚ to punish missed high attacks, which leads to a free Stage 2 Moonlit Dance if you happen to be holding a charge for it.

Whenever you anticipate a sidestep or an 8-Way Run attempt, punish it with a Stage 3 Mystic Star. Hit your fallen enemy after the attack with ⇨Ⓐ+Ⓑ for additional damage. Because this attack requires a charge, you may not always have access to it. In those cases, use Hilde's Raging Volcano (⇦ⒶⓀ), a 2-hit combination that links together off a counter-hit.

Long Range

Despite her incredible attack range, Hilde's long-range offense is linear, making it very difficult for her to deal with 8-Way Run. Your objective is to move into mid range, where Hilde's horizontal attacks are effective. Your only means of doing this is through careful movement. The only time worth attacking is when your enemy makes an aggressive movement toward you; otherwise it's too unsafe to commit to a vertical attack. Strike with ⇨Ⓑ or →Ⓐ+Ⓑ when this moment arises to counter enemy movement. If ⇨Ⓐ+Ⓑ hits, link into ⇨Ⓐ+Ⓑ for a 2-hit combo.

Special Tactics

Okizeme: Anti-Wakeup

Hilde's anti-wakeup options are limited to the Eagle Talon (⇩Ⓐ+ⒷⓀ), Fire Strike (⇩Ⓐ+Ⓚ), Ⓐ+Ⓑ, and White Torch (⇘ⒷⒶ). Her most damaging low attack is ⇩Ⓐ+ⒷⓀ, which is safe when guarded. It has the unique ability to cancel the second attack (⇩Ⓐ+ⒷⓀⒼ), which may surprise a defending enemy and open him up to throw attempts, though this is generally not recommended. Hilde's basic launching attack is ⇘ⒷⒶ, which inflicts noteworthy damage on hit. It's initially safe when blocked, but it's possible for your opponent to duck under the second high strike. Compensate for this by occasionally using the White Impale (⇘ⒷⒷ) mid variation to dissuade these attempts.

The Way of the Spear

Hilde uses an attack type completely new to the Soul Calibur series. Pressing and holding either Ⓐ or Ⓑ for 1~3 seconds, then releasing the button, initiates a special attack. The longer you hold the button, the more effective the attack is, often changing its hit properties, attack range, and damage output. Note that holding a button prevents you from using other attacks associated with it, thus limiting your offensive capabilities. Spend some time in training mode to learn to fight with the other available buttons while you hold a charge. Initiating the command to charge these techniques also performs an attack, leaving you vulnerable if you attempt it at an inopportune time. Bypass this issue by inputting the command during other attacks, or by pressing and holding Ⓐ or Ⓑ while guarding. You can't attack while you're guarding, so pressing the button won't initiate an attack. Be sure to press your chosen attack button *after* you press the Ⓖ button, or else you'll initiate a throw. Similarly, in many cases, it's important to abandon an attack in the midst of charging it in order to free up the button for important strikes. Simply releasing the button initiates the attack, possibly leaving you vulnerable if your enemy is looking for it. Hold the Ⓖ button before you release Ⓐ or Ⓑ to safely drop your charge.

In most cases, we recommend that you fight while holding only one attack type, compensating for the limitation by being aware of your weaknesses. For example, holding a charge with the Ⓐ button eliminates your horizontal attacks, making it difficult to punish 8-Way Run movement and sidesteps. On the other hand, holding the Ⓑ button puts your vertical attacks on hold, hurting your overall attack range and ability to deal with crouching opponents. Remember that both limitations last only until you obtain a charge for the attacks you want, in which case you gain access to an especially powerful vertical or horizontal attack.

Although it's exceedingly difficult, you can play with only kick attacks in order to charge for both the Mystic Star (Ⓐ button) and the Moonlit Dance (Ⓑ button). If you can withstand the limitations, hitting your enemy with a Stage 3 Mystic Star or a Stage 2 Moonlit Dance leads to giant combos with both charged. For example, successfully landing a Stage 3 Mystic Star against a sidestepping or crouching enemy leads to a free Stage 2 Moonlit Dance, which picks up the enemy off of the ground and launches him or her into the air. Though it's challenging, you can immediately start charging for a Stage 2 Mystic Star immediately after releasing the button for the first, allowing you to juggle with another Mystic Star after the Moonlit Dance. The end result is this combo: Stage 3 Mystic Star, Stage 2 Moonlit Dance, Stage 2 Mystic Star. The same idea applies when you hit your enemy with a Stage 2 Moonlit Dance. Release Ⓑ to initiate the attack, then immediately press it again, not only to initiate the Stage 2 Moonlit Dance's extension, but also to start charging for another Moonlit Dance. This allows you to perform the combinations like Stage 2 Moonlit Dance, Stage 3 Mystic Star, Stage 2 Moonlit Dance, and then a Stage 2 Mystic Star.

Finally, two ultra-powerful versions of the Mystic Star and Moonlit Dance gain Unblockable properties. Perform these attacks by holding the corresponding button for roughly 25 seconds. Although they aren't easy to do, these attacks are absurdly powerful, obliterating 75% of the enemy's life bar in a single hit. Don't forget about them if you happen to be charging for a long time.

Ivy

Ivy

No coward soul is mine
"No Coward Soul Is Mine," Emily Bronte (1818 - 1848)

Bio

Age:	32
Birthplace:	London, British Empire
Height:	5'10"
Weight:	128 lbs.
Birth Date:	December 10
Blood Type:	Unknown
Weapon:	Snake Sword
Weapon Name:	Valentine (Ivy Blade)
Discipline:	Unrelated Link
Family:	Adoptive parents: Deceased Father: Cervantes Mother: Deceased

For how long could she cling to life?

This terrible uncertainty shadowed Ivy's every step. But she knew the answer to that question lay in the hands of fate, and no human mortal, no matter how wise, could answer it for her. All she could do was keep moving forward, one step at a time, and not waste a moment of whatever time she had left.

With only the few clues she had gleaned from the book that the man with the scythe had burned, Ivy set out, not just to find Soul Edge, but also to discover a way to destroy it. She had heard rumors that the answers she sought were in a great empire to the East. There could be found a temple that had been corrupted by evil and fallen into chaos, a temple that had safeguarded a certain weapon. She followed the trail of rumors until she met a man who claimed he had had been banished from the temple and now lived there tending the graves. He told her of the spirit sword.

However, this presented a new problem. The blood of the cursed sword that coursed through Ivy's veins would prevent her from ever wielding the spirit sword. Even if she could find it, she would not be able to use it to destroy the cursed sword.

Ivy brought her journey to an end and returned to her family mansion. A brilliant scientist, she once again delved into her alchemic research. Her failures far outnumbered her successes, but at length she finally began to close in on the answer. Had she been allowed to complete her experiments, Ivy may well have achieved her goal, but it was not to be. An uninvited guest interrupted her work. It was the man whose soul was closest to her own—Cervantes, her own cursed, inhuman father. He had come to rob his own flesh-and-blood, to take his daughter's soul so that he might become more powerful.

Ivy's priceless collection of documents and tomes were torn apart, their pages scattered. The heavy laboratory table was scarred and broken, and glasses and phials lay in fragments on the floor. The walls, floor, and ceiling all bore the signs of terrible violence; nothing survived of her alchemic laboratory. And Ivy herself hovered on the brink of death.

The man had almost consumed her entire soul, but Ivy had one last chance, a desperate trump card that might save her life. As she hovered on the edge of death, she struggled to play it. She had been researching the secret of life itself, trying to find the means to fabricate a being that could wield the spirit sword. Ivy used the artificial soul that had been meant to animate it to save her own life. But, the research had been incomplete. Death would come to her, sooner or later.

Ivy took up the living snake sword that was her other half. She had lost much of the soul that connected her to the weapon, but it still responded to her. Yes, she could fight with it. And the new soul she had created, even though mixed with Ivy's original cursed soul, remained pure. Perhaps she could wield the spirit sword after all?

Ivy had one objective. She would fulfill her oath and destroy Soul Edge. Resolutely, she set out on her last journey.

Valentine

Ivy, a skilled alchemist, created this living snake sword specifically to destroy Soul Edge. Able to transform into sword or whip at will, the living weapon even acts of its own volition to protect its mistress. But the power of the cursed sword was used in its creation.

When Ivy learned that the blood of the cursed sword flowed through her veins, she was thrown into a despair that lasted years. She began to detest her own weapon, which shared her same evil fate. Eventually, however, she emerged from her self-imposed prison. She renamed her sword Valentine, and made it a symbol of her will to deny the imperatives of fate.

Unrelated Link

Ivy created a living weapon to destroy the cursed sword, and then set out to study the sword fighting arts so that she could unleash its full potential. But no school of warfare existed that could teach her how to wield such a unique weapon. After an exhaustive search of ancient and modern texts from around the world, she at last found the answer in a document from ancient China that described fencing arts hitherto unknown in the West. She combined them with battle-whip techniques to develop her unique fighting art.

She had invented a fighting art in which both she and her weapon could magically transform themselves. They were a perfect match. How ironic that the blood of Soul Edge that coursed through their veins was what united them so.

Command List

Signature Techniques

Name	Command	Attack Level	Damage	Notes
Reveal Thyself	Coiled Ⓑ+Ⓚ			Shifts to Sword
Know Thyself	Coiled Ⓐ+Ⓚ			Shifts to Whip
Dashing Wind	Coiled ⇨ⒶⓀ	High, High	12, 12	Combos on counter-hit, causes recoverable stun
Venom Lash	Coiled ⇩⬃⇦Ⓑ	Mid, Mid	14, 16	Combos naturally, launches if it strikes a stunned foe
Force Pledge (Additional attack)	Coiled ↘ or ↗ Ⓑ (Mash)	Mid, Mid	35	Knocks down
Piercing Madness	Sword ⇨🅑	Mid, Mid	15, 15	Guard Break, causes brief stagger
Royal Huntress	Sword ⇩Ⓐ+Ⓚ	Low	19	Knocks down
Dark Wings	Sword → or ↘ or ↗Ⓐ	Mid	30	Crumples on counter-hit
Rushing Raven	Whip ⇨Ⓑ	High	20	Knocks down
Raging Gnome	Whip →Ⓐ+Ⓑ	Mid, Mid, Mid	25, 15, 35	Combos naturally, 3rd hit is Guard Break
Summon Suffering	Whip ⬃⇩⬂⇨⬃⬁⬂ Ⓑ+Ⓖ	Throw	80	Ⓑ to break throw

Horizontal Attacks - Coiled

Name	Command	Attack Level	Damage	Notes
Doomed Mark	Coiled ⒶⒶ	High, High	8, 12	Combos naturally
Biting Raven	Coiled ⒶⒶ+Ⓚ	High, High	8, 10	Combos on counter-hit, changes to Whip
Dashing Wind	Coiled ⇨ⒶⓀ	High, High	12, 12	Combos on counter-hit, 2nd hit causes recoverable stun
Damned Mark	Coiled ⬂Ⓐ	Mid	18	Causes recoverable stun on normal hit, forward crumple on counter-hit
Cursed Mark	Coiled ⇩Ⓐ	Sp.Low	9	Leaves Ivy in crouching state
Hidden Gnome	Coiled ⬃Ⓐ	Low	10	Does extra damage and launches on counter-hit
Dark Gathering	Coiled ⇦Ⓐ	High	30	Guard Break, knocks down
Pecking Raven	Coiled While Crouching Ⓐ	Sp.Low	9	Leaves Ivy in crouching state
Demented Loop	Coiled While Rising ⒶⒶ	Mid, Mid, High	16, 10, 25	Last 2 hits combo naturally
Rising Raven	Coiled Jumping Ⓐ	Mid	26	
Reverse Raven	Coiled Backturned Ⓐ	High	10	
Deep Curse	Coiled While Crouching Backturned Ⓐ	Low	14	Leaves Ivy in crouching state

Vertical Attacks - Coiled

Name	Command	Attack Level	Damage	Notes
Immortal Gale	Coiled ⒷⒷ	Mid, Mid	13, 17	Combos on counter-hit
Ivy Thrust	Coiled ⇨Ⓑ	Mid	24	
Cursed Heavens	Coiled ⬂Ⓑ	Mid	25	Launches
Curse Brand	Coiled ⇩Ⓑ	Mid	16	Leaves Ivy in crouching state
Splashing Apas	Coiled ⬃ⒷⒷ+Ⓚ	Mid, Mid	10, 21	Combos naturally, changes to Sword
Dark Moon	Coiled ⇦Ⓑ	High, Mid	12, 12	Combos on counter-hit
Piercing Bolt	Coiled ⇩⬂⇨ⒷⒷ	Mid, Mid	12, 29	Combos naturally
Venom Lash	Coiled ⇩⬃⇦Ⓑ	Mid, Mid	14, 16	Combos naturally, launches if it strikes a stunned foe
Venom Lash ~Serpent's Embrace	Coiled ⇩⬃⇦🅑	Mid, Mid	14, 16	Combos naturally, changes to Serpent's Embrace, launches if it strikes a stunned foe
Immortal Flow	Coiled While Crouching Ⓑ	Mid	16	
Shameless	Coiled While Rising Ⓑ	Mid	28	Knocks down
Ivy Brambler	Coiled Jumping Ⓑ	Mid	36	Knocks down
Reverse Immortal	Coiled Backturned Ⓑ	Mid	12	
Deep Immortal	Coiled While Crouching Backturned Ⓑ	Mid	18	Leaves Ivy in a crouching state

Kick Attacks - Coiled

Name	Command	Attack Level	Damage	Notes
Night Swallow	Coiled Ⓚ	High	13	
Raven Catcher	Coiled ⇨Ⓚ	High	26	
Flying Night Swallow	Coiled ⬂Ⓚ	Mid	18	
Charmer Silhouette	Coiled ⇩Ⓚ	Low	9	
Raven Knee	Coiled ⬃Ⓚ	Mid	21	Causes backward crumple
Evil Sparrow	Coiled ⇦Ⓚ	Mid	24	Knocks down on counter-hit
Charmer Silhouette	Coiled While Crouching Ⓚ	Low	9	
Rising Cross	Coiled While Rising Ⓚ	Mid	16	
Rising Mind Shatter	Coiled Jumping Ⓚ	Mid	22	Knocks down
Reverse Night Swallow	Coiled Backturned Ⓚ	High	18	
Deep Silhouette	Coiled While Crouching Backturned Ⓚ	Low	12	Knocks down, leaves Ivy in crouching state

Simultaneous Press - Coiled

Name	Command	Attack Level	Damage	Notes
God Whisper	Coiled Ⓐ+ⒷⒶ	Mid, Low, Sp.Mid	15, 10, 15	Launches, combos on normal hit
Embrace of Lust	Coiled ⇨Ⓐ+Ⓑ	Mid	40 (34)	Hit throw, does more damage from long range, leaves foe backturned from close range
Heel Explosion	Coiled ⇦Ⓐ+Ⓑ	Mid	80	Unblockable, knocks down
Asylum	Coiled While Rising Ⓐ+Ⓑ	Mid, Mid, Mid, Mid	9x4	Combos naturally
Viper Tail	Coiled Backturned Ⓐ+Ⓑ	Mid	30	Launches
Reveal Thyself	Coiled Ⓑ+Ⓚ			Changes to Sword
Know Thyself	Coiled Ⓐ+Ⓚ			Changes to Whip

8-Way Run - Coiled

Name	Command	Attack Level	Damage	Notes
Raven's Egg	Coiled →Ⓐ	High	29	Knocks down
Tezhas Raven	Coiled ↘ or ↗Ⓐ	Mid	25	Crumples on counter-hit
Coating Tezhas	Coiled ↓ or ↑Ⓐ	High	18	Leaves foe backturned
Wolf Lash	Coiled ← or ↙ or ↖Ⓐ	High	26	Spins foe
Freeze Gaze	Coiled →ⒷⒶ	Mid, Mid	18, 20	Combos on counter-hit
Force Pledge	Coiled ↘ or ↗Ⓑ	Mid	20	Knocks down
Force Pledge (Additional attack)	Coiled ↘ or ↗Ⓑ (Mash)	Mid, Mid	35	Knocks down
Landing Embrace	Coiled ↓ or ↑Ⓑ	Mid	35	Guard Break, knocks down
Blazing Sword	Coiled ← or ↙ or ↖ⒷⒷ	Mid, Mid	15, 15	Combos naturally, launches
Mind Shatter	Coiled → or ↘ or ↗Ⓚ	High	30	Knocks down
Hammering Raven	Coiled ↓ or ↑Ⓚ	Mid	24	Knocks down
Vanishing Cloak	Coiled ← or ↙ or ↖Ⓚ	Mid	20	

Horizontal Attacks - Sword

Name	Command	Attack Level	Damage	Notes
Ominous Mark	Sword ⒶⒶ	High, High	8, 14	Combos naturally
Cross Madness	Sword ⇨Ⓐ	Mid	24	
Raven Gash	Sword ⇘Ⓐ	Mid	22	Causes recoverable stun
Cursed Mark	Sword ⇩Ⓐ	Sp.Low	12	
Crimson Scar	Sword ⇙Ⓐ	High	15	Knocks down on normal hit, causes stagger on counter-hit
Menace Slice	Sword ⇦Ⓐ	High	18	Knocks down
Pecking Raven	Sword While Crouching Ⓐ	Sp.Low	12	
Menace	Sword While Rising Ⓐ	Mid	24	
Rising Raven	Sword Jumping Ⓐ	Mid	26	
Reverse Raven	Sword Backturned Ⓐ	High	10	
Deep Curse	Sword While Crouching Backturned Ⓐ	Low	14	Leaves Ivy in crouching state

Vertical Attacks - Sword

Name	Command	Attack Level	Damage	Notes
Carving Strike	Sword ⒷⒷ	Mid, Mid	12, 20	Combos naturally
Ivy Sting	Sword ⇨Ⓑ	Mid	15	
Piercing Madness	Sword ⇨Ⓑ	Mid, Mid	15, 15	Guard Break, causes brief stagger
Ivy Lick	Sword ⇨Ⓑ⇧	High	15	Hit throw against airborne opponent
Silhouette	Sword ⇨Ⓑ⇧Ⓚ	High, Low	15, 20	Combos naturally
Dominance	Sword ⇘Ⓑ	Mid	22	Launches on counter-hit
Twisted Dominance	Sword ⇩Ⓑ	Mid	18	
Poison Leaf	Sword ⇙Ⓑ	Low	26	Knocks down
Ivy Bite	Sword ⇦Ⓑ	High	17	
Immortal Flow	Sword While Crouching Ⓑ	Mid	16	
Ivy Masquerade	Sword While Crouching ⇘Ⓑ	Low	22	
Pride	Sword While Rising Ⓑ	Mid	28	Launches overhead at extremely close range, causes backward stagger from further away
Rising Ivy	Sword Jumping Ⓑ	Sp.Mid	18	
Reverse Immortal	Sword Backturned Ⓑ	Mid	12	
Deep Immortal	Sword While Crouching Backturned Ⓑ	Mid	18	Leaves Ivy in crouching state

Kick Attacks - Sword

Name	Command	Attack Level	Damage	Notes
Night Swallow	Sword Ⓚ	High	16	
Raven Catcher	Sword ⇨Ⓚ	High	26	
Rage Kick	Sword ⇘Ⓚ	Mid	17	
Charmer Silhouette	Sword ⇩Ⓚ	Low	12	
Dark Cage	Sword ⇙ⓀⒷⓀ	Mid, High, Low	16, 10, 20	2nd hit is hit throw against airborne foes
Evil Sparrow	Sword ⇦Ⓚ	Mid	24	
Ivy Sweep	Sword ⇩⇙⇦Ⓚ	Low	10	Crumples on counter-hit, hit throw against grounded foes
Charmer Silhouette	Sword While Crouching Ⓚ	Low	12	
Rising Cross	Sword While Rising Ⓚ	Mid	16	
Rising Mind Shatter	Sword Jumping Ⓚ	Mid	22	Knocks down
Reverse Night Swallow	Sword Backturned Ⓚ	High	18	
Deep Silhouette	Sword While Crouching Backturned Ⓚ	Low	12	Knocks down, leaves Ivy in crouching state

Simultaneous Press - Sword

Name	Command	Attack Level	Damage	Notes
Crucifixion	Sword Ⓐ+Ⓑ	Mid	57	Knocks down
Crucifixion (Hold)	Sword 🅐+🅑	Mid	78	Unblockable, knocks down
Embrace of Guilt	Sword ⇨Ⓐ+Ⓑ	Mid	27 (42)	Becomes a hit throw and does extra damage at close range
Razor's Bite	Sword ⇩Ⓐ+Ⓑ	Low	30	Knocks down
Asylum	Sword While Rising Ⓐ+Ⓑ	Mid, Mid, Mid, Mid	9x4	Combos naturally
Viper Tail	Sword Backturned Ⓐ+Ⓑ	Mid	30	Launches
Serpent's Embrace	Sword Ⓑ+Ⓚ			Shifts to Serpent's Embrace
Fear's Void	Sword ⬃ or ⇩ or ⬂Ⓑ+Ⓚ	Sp.Mid	35	Knocks down
Gnome Huntress	Sword ⬂🅑+🅚	High	40	Unblockable
Ivy Lick	Sword ⇧Ⓑ+Ⓚ	High	5	Hit throw against airborne foes
Silhouette	Sword ⇧Ⓑ+ⓀⓀ	High, Low	5, 20	Combos naturally, 1st hit is hit throw against airborne foes
Know Thyself	Sword Ⓐ+Ⓚ			Shifts to Coiled
Royal Huntress	Sword ⇩Ⓐ+Ⓚ	Low	19	Knocks down

8-Way Run - Sword

Name	Command	Attack Level	Damage	Notes
Dark Wings	Sword → or ↘ or ↗Ⓐ	Mid	26	Crumples on counter-hit
Cursed Soul	Sword ↓ or ↑Ⓐ	Mid	28	Backturns foe
Doomed Mark	Sword ← or ↙ or ↖Ⓐ	High	26	Spins foe
Lost Pledge	Sword →Ⓑ	High	36	Knocks down
Dominance	Sword ↘ or ↗Ⓑ	Mid	22	Launches on counter-hit
Serpent's Breath	Sword ↓ or ↑Ⓑ	Mid	22	Launches
Poison Leaf	Sword ↙ or ↖Ⓑ	Low	26	Knocks down
Moaning Mark	Sword ←Ⓑ	Mid	22	Causes crumple
Wondergale	Sword → or ↘ or ↗Ⓚ	Mid	18	Knocks down on counter-hit
Royal Huntress	Sword ↓ or ↑Ⓚ	Low	14	Knocks down
Diving Raven	Sword ← or ↙ or ↖Ⓚ	Mid	35	Knocks down, leaves Ivy in downed state

Kick Attacks - Whip

Name	Command	Attack Level	Damage	Notes
Night Swallow	Whip Ⓚ	High	13	
Raven Catcher	Whip ⇨Ⓚ	High	26	
Flying Night Swallow	Whip ⬂Ⓚ	Mid	18	
Charmer Silhouette	Whip ⇩Ⓚ	Low	9	
Raven Knee	Whip ⬃Ⓚ	Mid	21	Causes crumple
Evil Sparrow	Whip ⇦Ⓚ	Mid	24	Knocks down on counter-hit
Charmer Silhouette	Whip While Crouching Ⓚ	Low	9	
Rising Cross	Whip While Rising Ⓚ	Mid	16	
Rising Mind Shatter	Whip Jumping Ⓚ	Mid	22	Knocks down
Reverse Night Swallow	Whip Backturned Ⓚ	High	18	
Deep Silhouette	Whip While Crouching Backturned Ⓚ	Low	12	Knocks down

Vertical Attacks - Whip

Name	Command	Attack Level	Damage	Notes
Poison Apas	Whip ⒷⒷ	Mid, Mid	11, 17	Combos on counter-hit
Rushing Raven	Whip ⇨Ⓑ	High	20	Knocks down
Dashing Wings	Whip ⇨ⒷⒶ+Ⓑ	High x5, Mid x4	42	Guard Break, knocks down
Drowning Madness	Whip ⬂Ⓑ	Mid	24	Causes crumple on counter-hit
Drowning Madness ~Serpent's Embrace	Whip ⬂🅑	Mid	24	Causes crumple on counter-hit, shifts to Serpent's Embrace
Aqua Worshipper	Whip ⇩Ⓑ	Mid	14	
Poison Ivy	Whip ⬃Ⓑ	Low, Sp.Mid, Sp.Mid	12, 10, 10	Combos naturally
Red Moon	Whip ⇦Ⓑ	High, High	10, 10	Combos naturally, backturns foe
Aqua Worshipper	Whip While Crouching Ⓑ	Mid	14	
Ivy Masquerade	Whip While Crouching ⬂Ⓑ	Low	22	Crumples on counter-hit
Masquerade ~Suppressed Exile	Whip While Crouching ⬂🅑	Low, Mid	22	Crumples on counter-hit
Masquerade ~Exile	Whip While Crouching ⬂🅑Ⓐ+Ⓑ	Low, Mid	22, 15	1st hit crumples on counter-hit, 2nd hit launches
Cagemaster	Whip While Rising ⒷⒷ	Mid, High, High	15, 5, 15, 10	Combos naturally, launches
Ivy Brambler	Whip Jumping Ⓑ	Mid	36	Knocks down
Reverse Immortal	Whip Backturned Ⓑ	Mid	12	
Deep Immortal	Whip While Crouching Backturned Ⓑ	Mid	18	Leaves Ivy in crouching state

Horizontal Attacks - Whip

Name	Command	Attack Level	Damage	Notes
Danger Range	Whip ⒶⒶ	High, High	8, 10	Combos naturally
Intertwined Paths Alpha2	Whip ⇨ⒶⒶ	High, Mid, High	12, 12, 28	Last 2 hits combo on normal hit, all 3 hits combo on counter-hit
Dancing Tezhas	Whip ⬂Ⓐ	Mid	22	Crumples on counter-hit
Ancient Worshipper	Whip ⇩Ⓐ	Sp.Low	8	
Ancient Wheel	Whip ⬃ⒶⒶ	Low, Low	14, 10	Combos on counter-hit, leaves Ivy in crouching state
Deceitful Raven	Whip ⇦Ⓐ	High	18	Sideturns foe
Serpent's Venom	Whip ⇩⬃⇦Ⓐ	High	80	Unblockable, knocks down
Ancient Worshipper	Whip While Crouching Ⓐ	Sp.Low	8	
Hunting Raven	Whip While Rising Ⓐ	Mid	24	Sideturns foe on counter-hit
Rising Raven	Whip Jumping Ⓐ	Mid	26	
Reverse Raven	Whip Backturned Ⓐ	High	10	
Deep Curse	Whip While Crouching Backturned Ⓐ	Low	14	Leaves Ivy in crouching state

Simultaneous Press - Whip

Name	Command	Attack Level	Damage	Notes
Flaming Descent	Whip Ⓐ+Ⓑ	Mid, Mid	10, 30	Combos naturally, knocks down
Dancing Gnome	Whip ⇨Ⓐ+Ⓑ	Mid, Mid	10, 10	Combos naturally, knocks down
Dancing Gnome (Hold)	Whip ⇨🅐+🅑	Mid, Mid, Mid, Mid, Mid	5x5	Unblockable, knocks down
Suppressed Exile	Whip ⬂Ⓐ+Ⓑ	Mid	48	Unblockable, launches
Exile	Whip ⬂Ⓐ+Ⓑ Ⓐ+Ⓑ	Mid	15	Launches
Spiral Punishment	Whip ⇦Ⓐ+ⒷⒷ	Mid x7	5x7	Combos naturally, knocks down
Asylum	Whip While Rising Ⓐ+Ⓑ	Mid, Mid, Mid, Mid	9x4	Combos naturally
Viper Tail	Whip Backturned Ⓐ+Ⓑ	Mid	30	Launches
Reveal Thyself	Whip Ⓑ+Ⓚ			Shifts to Coiled
Ivy Lash	Whip ⇨Ⓑ+Ⓚ	Mid	20	Shifts to Coiled
Biting Ivy Inner	Whip ⇨Ⓑ+Ⓚ ⇩ or ⇧	Mid, Mid	20, 20	Drags whip sideways to strike sidesteps, shifts to Coiled
Stinging Souls	Whip ⬃ or ⇩ or ⬂ Ⓑ+Ⓚ	Mid	20	Does extra damage and launches on counter-hit
Taunt	Ⓚ+Ⓖ			

8-Way Run - Whip

Name	Command	Attack Level	Damage	Notes
Flaming Wings	Whip → or ↘ or ↗Ⓐ	High	28	Knocks down
Insanity Light	Whip ↓ or ↑Ⓐ	Mid	28 (43)	Spins foe from long range, is a hit throw at close range
Insanity Feast	Whip ↓ or ↑Ⓐ⇦	Mid	48	Does extra damage as hit throw and leaves Ivy backturned
Lamenting Tail	Whip ↙ or ↖Ⓐ	Low	42~47	Hit throw
Venom Strike	Whip ←Ⓐ	High	30	Guard Break, knocks down
Venom Strike ~Serpent's Embrace	Whip ←🅐	High	30	Guard Break, knocks down, shifts to Serpent's Embrace
Aqua Clipper	Whip →Ⓑ	Mid	22	Crumples
Drowning Madness	Whip ↘ or ↗Ⓑ	Mid	19	Crumples
Drowning Madness ~Serpent's Embrace	Whip ↘ or ↗🅑	Mid	19	Crumples, shifts to Serpent's Embrace
Darkside	Whip ↓ or ↑Ⓑ	Mid	25	Launches
Intertwined Paths	Whip ← or ↙ or ↖ⒷⒷ	Mid, Mid	20, 15	Combos naturally, knocks down
Intertwined Paths (Delay)	Whip ← or ↙ or ↖ⒷⒷ(Delay)	Mid, Mid	20, 15	Combos naturally, knocks down
Mind Shatter	Whip → or ↘ or ↗Ⓚ	High	30	Knocks down
Hammering Raven	Whip ↓ or ↑Ⓚ	Mid	24	Knocks down
Vanishing Cloak	Whip ← or ↙ or ↖Ⓚ	Mid	20	
Raging Gnome	Whip →Ⓐ+Ⓑ	Mid, Mid, Mid	25, 15, 35	Combos naturally, 3rd hit is Guard Break
Exile ~Suppressed Exile	Whip ←Ⓐ+Ⓑ	Mid, Mid	25, 48	2nd hit is Unblockable, launches
Exile	Whip ←Ⓐ+Ⓑ Ⓐ+Ⓑ	Mid, Mid	15, 25	Combos naturally, 2nd hit launches

8-Way Run

Name	Command	Attack Level	Damage	Notes
Sliding	While Running Ⓚ	Low	26	Knocks down

Throws

Name	Command	Attack Level	Damage	Notes
Primal Dominance	Ⓐ+Ⓖ	Throw	45	Ⓐ to break throw
Dominion Throw	Ⓑ+Ⓖ	Throw	50	Ⓑ to break throw
Heartless Guide	Left Side Throw	Throw	55	Ⓐ or Ⓑ to break throw
Sunset Cradle	Right Side Throw	Throw	60	Ⓐ or Ⓑ to break throw
Sweet Dominance	Back Throw	Throw	68	
Calamity Symphony	Sword ⬂⇩⬃⇦⬂⬀⬃ Ⓐ+Ⓖ	Throw	80	Ⓐ to break throw
Summon Suffering	Whip ⬃⇩⬂⇨⬃⬁⬂ Ⓑ+Ⓖ	Throw	80	Ⓑ to break throw

Ivy

Special

Name	Command	Attack Level	Damage	Notes
Serpent's Embrace	Sword Ⓑ+Ⓚ			Shifts to Serpent's Embrace
Wind Embrace	Serpent's Embrace Ⓐ During Hit ⇩⬂⇨Ⓐ	High, Mid	5, 20, 28	Combos naturally, shifts to Whip
Mistress' Justice	Serpent's Embrace ⒷⒷⒷ	Mid, Mid, Mid	8, 8, 20	Combos naturally, knocks down
Howling Spirits	Serpent's Embrace Ⓑ⇨Ⓑ⇦Ⓑ⇨Ⓑ ⇦Ⓑ(Just)	Mid, Mid, Mid, Mid, Mid	8, 8, 8, 8, 20	Inputs after first attack are Just Frames
Charging Serpent	Serpent's Embrace Ⓚ or ⇨⇨Ⓚ	Mid	25	Launches on counter-hit
Released Souls	Serpent's Embrace Ⓐ+Ⓑ	Mid	80	Unblockable, knocks down
Stinging Souls	Serpent's Embrace Ⓑ+Ⓚ	Mid	25	Launches and does extra damage on counter-hit
Stinging Souls	Serpent's Embrace ⇨Ⓑ+Ⓚ	Mid	25	Launches and does extra damage on counter-hit
Stinging Souls	Serpent's Embrace ⇦Ⓑ+Ⓚ	Mid	25	Launches and does extra damage on counter-hit
Lamenting Tail	Serpent's Embrace Ⓐ+Ⓚ	Low	46	Hit throw

Close Range

With her variable weapon, Ivy is comfortable at any range. In close, stick to Sword and Coiled—use Ⓑ+Ⓚ to shorten Valentine from Whip, to Coiled, to Sword if necessary. Ivy has many linear mid attacks that lead to flashy juggles and good damage. She also has the two most damaging throws in the game. An extremely attentive enemy may try to avoid these options by guarding high or sidestepping when in doubt, simultaneously looking to break throws with Ⓐ when Ivy uses Sword and Ⓑ when she uses Whip. To thwart such opponents, you'll have to strike low.

In Sword form, Royal Huntress (⬇ or ⬆Ⓚ) is an excellent sweep that floors the enemy even on normal hit, and it snuffs sidestep attempts and high chains. For an alternative with bigger payoff, Hidden Gnome (Coiled ⇙Ⓐ) counter-hits attacks or sidestep attempts and launches the opponent high into the air, in prime position for a juggle. The follow-up launch on this attack occurs only in the event that the move counter-hits, and the range is extremely short. So, keep that in mind. God Whisper (Coiled Ⓐ+ⒷⒶ) is another Coiled move that deserves mention for snagging sidesteps and striking low. This three-part attack strikes mid-low-special mid very quickly, making it difficult to block. It cannot be avoided through side movement, and it can lead to juggles if the opponent does not use Aerial Recovery. God Whisper is relatively safe if blocked, depending on how close Ivy is to the opponent. There are instances where the foe can hit Ivy with a quick attack after guarding, but by no means does this diminish the attack's usefulness. If you happen to get caught in a close-range battle while using Whip, Danger Range (Whip ⇙ⒶⒶ) is a useful ducking double sweep. While the sweep is recovering, either perform Cagemaster (Whip While Rising ⒷⒷ) for a potential juggle starter, or tap Ⓑ+Ⓚ to shift from Whip to Coiled, which is much more conducive to point-blank combat. Continue pressuring adversaries by performing Demented Loop (Coiled While Rising ⒶⒶ) as Ivy rises from Danger Range. Demented Loop hits mid-mid-high and knocks down if successful, allowing you to swap back to Whip and a long-distance game if you like (Ⓐ+Ⓚ). Once you've conditioned your foes to fear your tactics after they eat Whip ⇙ⒶⒶ up close, you can simply forego the above and go for a Summon Suffering throw.

With the enemy worried about low threats, and wary of using side movement for fear of getting counter-hit, it's time to employ Ivy's mid options. Raven Gash (Sword ⇘Ⓐ) is a gut punch using the hilt of Ivy's blade that puts the enemy into a recoverable stun on contact. If your foe doesn't shake out quickly, you can link ⇘Ⓑ to launch him or her into a juggle. Note that Sword ⇘Ⓑ doesn't launch on its own; it requires a counter-hit to launch, or it must strike a staggered opponent. However, Serpent's Breath (Sword ⬇ or ⬆Ⓑ) does launch even on normal hit. Cursed Heavens (Coiled ⇘Ⓑ) can also start juggles easily with a normal hit. Many of Ivy's better juggles require that you quickly shift forms mid-juggle. This can take some practice, but just remember that sword changes can happen anytime. Finally, Ivy has two more harsh close-range threats: Calamity Symphony (Sword ⇘⇩⇙⇦⇘⇙⇗Ⓐ+Ⓖ) and Summon Suffering (Whip ⇗⇩⇘⇨⇙⇗⇘⇘Ⓑ+Ⓖ). These two throws have daunting motions, but as with her form changes, practice makes perfect. Actually, you don't have to complete the motions that quickly, and you can just roll the entire motion instead of tapping the final portions, if that works better for you. Additionally, you can input the command for these throws while your most recent attack recovers. For example, using Sword ⇘Ⓐ up close usually leaves Ivy with the advantage. She can time a Calamity Symphony to strike opponents just as they mash out of their stun, snagging them as they return to standing guard. Both of these throws inflict 80 damage, making them the most powerful grabs in the game. When enemies guard high, worried about mid pokes and launchers, they're completely susceptible to these attacks.

Combos

Counter-hit Sword ⇨Ⓑ (recoverable stun), ⇨Ⓑ
4 hits, 59 damage
Sword While Rising Ⓑ, ⇩Ⓐ + Ⓑ
2 hits, 55 damage
Counter-hit Sword ⇩⇙⇦Ⓚ, ⇩⇙⇦Ⓚ
5 hits, 45 damage
Counter-hit Sword ➡Ⓐ, ⇩⇙⇦Ⓚ
5 hits, 67 damage
Sword ⇘Ⓐ (recoverable stun), ⇘Ⓑ, Ⓐ + Ⓚ (switch to Coiled), ⇦Ⓑ, Ⓑ + Ⓚ (switch to Sword), ⇩⇙⇦Ⓚ
8 hits, 64 damage
Coiled ⇘Ⓑ, Ⓑ + Ⓚ (switch to Sword), ⇩⇙⇦Ⓚ
5 hits, 66 damage
Sword ⇘Ⓐ (recoverable stun), Ⓐ + Ⓚ (switch to Coiled), ⇩⇙⇦Ⓑ, ⇦Ⓑ + Ⓚ, ⇦Ⓑ, Ⓑ + Ⓚ (switch to Sword), ⇩⇙⇦Ⓚ
11 hits, 69 damage
Whip ⇨⇨Ⓑ, ⇘Ⓐ, Ⓑ + Ⓚ (switch to Coiled), ⇩⇘⇨ⒷⒷ
4 hits, 64 damage
Counter-hit Coiled ⇙Ⓐ, (slight step forward) ⇦Ⓑ, Ⓑ + Ⓚ (switch to Sword), ⇩⇙⇦Ⓚ
8 hits, 85 damage
Counter-hit Coiled ⇨ⒶⓀ (recoverable stun), ⇦Ⓑ, Ⓑ + Ⓚ (switch to Sword), ⇩⇙⇦Ⓚ
9 hits, 99 damage, leave a brief gap between final two attacks
Whip ⬇ or ⬆Ⓑ, Ⓑ + Ⓚ (switch to Coiled), ⇦Ⓑ, Ⓑ + Ⓚ (Switch to Sword), ⇩⇙⇦Ⓚ
7 hits, 79 damage
Counter-hit Whip While crouching ⇘Ⓑ, Ⓐ + Ⓑ, ⇨ⒷⒶ + Ⓑ
4 hits, 52~84 damage
Sword ⇦⇦Ⓑ, ⇨Ⓑ (recoverable stun), ⇦⇦Ⓐ, Ⓐ + Ⓚ (switch to Coiled), ⇨ⒶⓀ (recoverable stun), ⇩⇙⇦Ⓑ, ⇦Ⓑ + Ⓚ, ⇦Ⓑ, Ⓑ + Ⓚ (switch to Sword), ⇩⇙⇦Ⓚ
16 hits, 102 damage

Mid Range

Strike low and snuff side movement from mid range with Danger Range (Whip ⇙ⒶⒶ) or Lamenting Tail (⬋ (or ⬉Ⓐ). The first is the same double sweep mentioned in the Close Range tactics section. The second is a low-striking hit throw with surprising reach. Supplement these low, circular threats with Crucifixion (Sword Ⓐ+Ⓑ) and Tezhas Raven (Coiled ⬊ or ⬈Ⓐ). The first is a lunging mid attack with slight delay but a big payoff. It snuffs side movement and crouches, knocks down even on normal hit, has huge Ring Out potential, and delivers buckets of damage for a single attack. It can also be charged, becoming Unblockable! The second is a little less risky, simply an effective mid-striking circular poke with good range. Dark Gathering (Coiled ⇔Ⓐ) is a high-hitting circular Guard Break. While it can be avoided by crouching, it still snuffs sidesteps, and you can use it to pressure foes trying to guard your other mid-range pokes. Once the enemy stops using side movement, mix in Landing Embrace Guard Break (Coiled ⬇ or ⬆Ⓑ) and Ivy's Blazing Sword double-hitting launcher (Coiled ⬅ⒷⒷ). Both of these attacks are linear mids, so make sure the enemy isn't continually sidestepping before you employ them.

Mid range and further out is also the place to employ Whip—cycle through to it with Ⓐ+Ⓚ or swap to it quickly with Biting Raven (Coiled ⒶⒶ+Ⓚ). Many useful, far-reaching attacks are found here. Examples include Darkside (⬇ or ⬆Ⓑ), a linear whip smash that leads to a juggle, and Insanity Light (⬇ or ⬆Ⓐ), a far-reaching circular attack that automatically becomes a hit throw if close enough. Of extra interest, Venom Strike (⬅Ⓐ) is a high, circular Guard Break that allows Ivy to enter her Serpent's Embrace stance simply by holding Ⓐ! Drowning Madness (Whip ⇖Ⓑ) works similarly. This linear mid attack looks like a launcher but causes the enemy to crumple forward even on normal hit. If you hold Ⓑ, Ivy goes into Serpent's Embrace. From here, ⒷⒷⒷ combos on the slumping character. Or you can try Ⓑ⇨Ⓑ⇨Ⓑ⇨Ⓑ⇨Ⓑ if you have stellar timing—every input after the first one is a Just Frame! If your foe guards while you transition into Serpent's Embrace, try Ⓐ+Ⓚ for a low hit throw that mirrors Ivy's Whip (⬋ or ⬉Ⓑ), or Ⓐ+Ⓑ for a far-reaching, circular Unblockable.

Long Range

Whip form comes into its own when Ivy is far away from the opposition. Ivy Sting (⇨Ⓑ) is a high-striking linear poke that is easily sidestepped, but it floors the enemy from almost a full arena away! Ivy Masquerade (While Crouching Whip ⇘Ⓑ) is an interesting long-range low poke. Hold Ⓑ and Ivy lets her whip fall where she swings it, charging an explosive Unblockable along its path. If you'd like to interrupt this Unblockable and spring the whip back, creating a launcher, press Ⓐ+Ⓑ while the Unblockable charges. Inputting ⇘Ⓐ+Ⓑ accesses this same sequence without the low poke to start. Raging Gnome (Whip ➡Ⓐ+Ⓑ) is a long-range 3-part Guard Break that acts like a geyser. The linear mid ⬇ or ⬆Ⓑ can launch from a huge distance, while ⬇ or ⬆Ⓐ remains a great anti-sidestep option. Ivy can play keep-away with just about anyone, using her superior speed to outpace other long-range characters. However, as mentioned above, she's just as comfortable moving into close range. Transitioning between the two is as easy as scoring a knockdown and cycling through her sword forms.

Special Tactics

Okizeme: Anti-Wakeup

More than almost any other character, Ivy can confuse and confound grounded enemies. Her God Whisper (Coiled Ⓐ+ⒷⒶ) strikes mid, low, then special mid very quickly. It's an extremely good move to use just as an enemy starts to rise nearby. Depending on how quickly the enemy rises, and how long you wait to perform the move, it's nearly impossible for your adversary to know whether to block the mid or the low first (if the mid whiffs before your foe is actually on his feet). If either of the first two attacks hits, the opponent gets popped up—while he or she can Aerial Recover away, you can try for juggle hits here, or rush forward as your enemy lands. This puts the enemy right back where he was: at Ivy's feet, where you can make your hapless victim guess which way to block or Repel against God Whisper again! If the enemy is floored a few steps away, you can pressure or hit with Dancing Gnome (Whip ⇨Ⓐ+Ⓑ), a 2-hit rolling mid attack that can be charged, becoming Unblockable. Finally, keep in mind Ivy Sweep (Sword ⇩⇙⇦Ⓚ) against enemies floored near you. You can often tack on this hit throw to the end of juggle combos that leave the foe underfoot, and it inflicts excellent damage.

Taming the Whip

If Ivy has a weakness, it's that she is one of the most complicated characters in Soul Calibur IV, and it's impossible to simply select her and do well immediately. She has answers for any situation, but they require intimate familiarity with the different forms of her living, changing sword, Valentine. Ivy begins each round with the sword in a curled-up, Coiled form. Through various attacks or inputting certain commands, the sword can also enter an extended Whip form, or a solid, short Sword form. Ivy also has a special stance, the Serpent's Embrace, in which she stretches the whip behind her back. Pressing Ⓐ+Ⓚ together cycles her whip through its forms, from Sword to Coiled to Whip. Likewise, pressing Ⓑ+Ⓚ contracts in the opposite direction, from Whip to Coiled to Sword, and then finally to Serpent's Embrace. These commands can be input on their own or even during Ivy's attacks, changing Valentine on the fly. This is necessary for some combos and pressure patterns. Swapping in mid-attack can also be desirable if the complexion of a match changes quickly. A long-range standoff might quickly become a short-range brawl, for example. As you might expect, Whip is most effective from a distance, while Sword is best at point-blank range. The curled Coiled offers a mix of both worlds, while the utility of Serpent's Embrace is situational. Each form of Valentine has its own move set and intricacies. When in doubt, Coiled is the most versatile, but all of Valentine's forms have merit.

Command	Form Valentine Shifts To
Ⓑ+Ⓚ	Whip > Coiled > Sword > Serpent's Embrace
Ⓐ+Ⓚ	Sword > Coiled > Whip
Coiled ⇙ⒷⒷ+Ⓚ	Sword
Coiled ⒶⒶ+Ⓚ	Whip
Coiled ⇩⇙⇦Ⓑ	Serpent's Embrace
Whip ⬅Ⓐ	Serpent's Embrace
Whip ⇘Ⓑ	Serpent's Embrace

Ivy

Kilik

Kilik

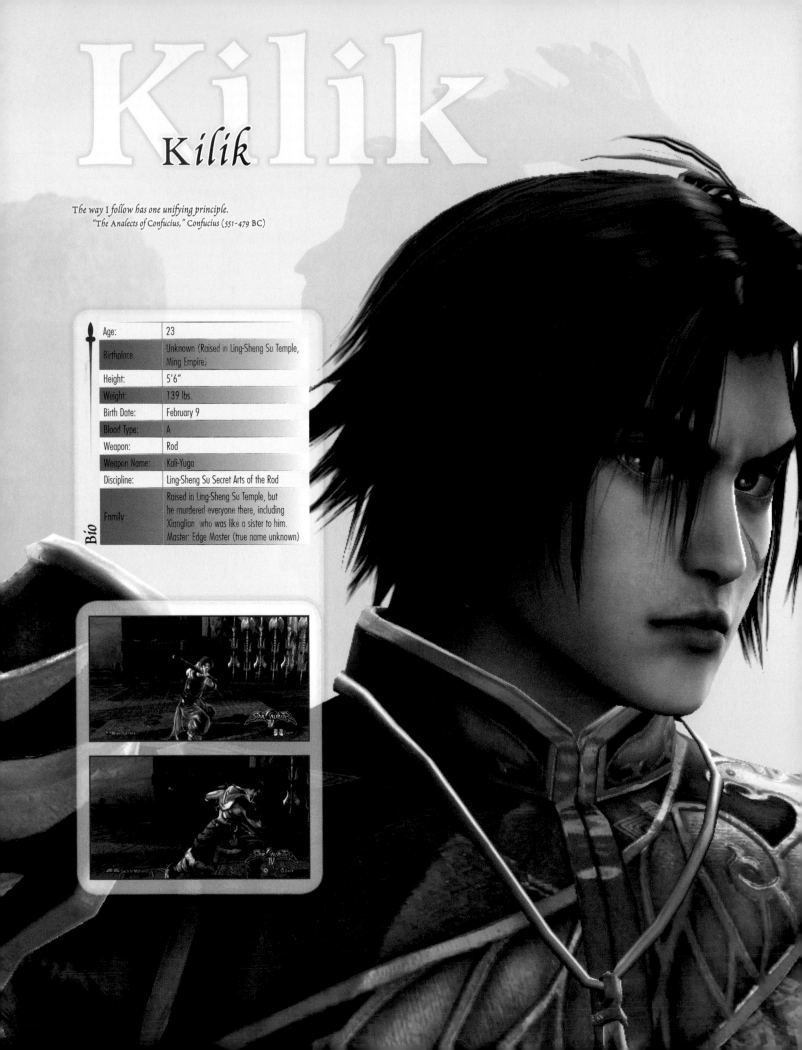

The way I follow has one unifying principle.
"The Analects of Confucius," Confucius (551-479 BC)

Bio

Age:	23
Birthplace:	Unknown (Raised in Ling-Sheng Su Temple, Ming Empire)
Height:	5'6"
Weight:	139 lbs.
Birth Date:	February 9
Blood Type:	A
Weapon:	Rod
Weapon Name:	Kali-Yuga
Discipline:	Ling-Sheng Su Secret Arts of the Rod
Family:	Raised in Ling-Sheng Su Temple, but he murdered everyone there, including Xianglian, who was like a sister to him. Master: Edge Master (true name unknown)

"Kilik?" Xianghua called, but he did not hear.

His body having once been profaned by the Evil Seed sown by Soul Edge, Kilik devoted himself to war against the cursed blade. With the help of Xianghua and the spirit sword she held, he had emerged victorious once; but in the several years since, Soul Edge had regained its power and yet again threatened the world. Still, Kilik had not idled those years away either; having trained hard and mastered the art of purging evil, he had taken an oath to purify Soul Edge once and for all. Only then could he atone for the lives he took while evil had hold of his soul.

If there was one answer Kilik arrived at, after witnessing the battle between the spirit sword and cursed sword firsthand—and after probing the evil essences within his own body as he tempered his mind—it was this: Soul Calibur was a being extremely similar to Soul Edge. While their alignments differed, that was all; their essential natures were the same. Though known as a "spirit sword"—a force for good—it would take only one malicious wielder with a will stronger than the sword's to bend the blade toward evil. Yet, the converse must also hold true. The key lay in balancing the two blades' torrential power, finding the one point where their opposed mights would cancel each other out, stemming the flood to create waters calm as a mirror.

Since entering Europe, Kilik had been aware of several pursuers on their tail. Who they were, he could not say, but he had no desire to involve others in this battle, least of all those in ignorant pursuit of one blade or the other. He had done his best to keep himself and his companion hidden...

"Kilik!" Xianghua called again. This time her sharper tone gave Kilik a start.

"Oh. Sorry, I was lost in thought."

"Well, just as long as you're on your toes when it counts. For my sake," she added with a smile. Kilik had been traveling with Xianghua since reuniting with her during his quest to find the cursed sword. She herself had once clutched the other blade, Soul Calibur, but remained unaware of the spirit sword's dangers.

Kilik was slow, but not stupid; he knew Xianghua had feelings for him. For his part, he felt a warm sentiment toward her that undeniably lent calm to his heart. But his affection for her was much closer to the attachment one feels toward a blood relative. Something about Xianghua—though he could not explain exactly what—reminded Kilik of Xianglian, the woman he had once loved as an older sister. And perhaps seeing Xianglian in Xianghua was what prevented him from perceiving her as a woman in her own right; for train as he may, temper his mind as he might, he could never erase the pain in his heart. Each of Xianghua's smiles only brought back memories of his past, of when he murdered Xianglian with his own hands.

Kilik

From this Kilik took resolve. As the Conciliator, he faced a brutal road ahead. Could he find and maintain just the right equilibrium to keep the scales from tipping toward one great force or the other? He believed he could, if he made full use of the evil infesting his body. His mentor, Edge Master, had lived an eternity that way. Why not Kilik as well?

He cast a glance to Xianghua, who stood at his side. She flashed a speculative smile in return.

(I cannot involve Xianghua in the fate I have chosen for myself.)

And then there was Maxi. Kilik thought of his old traveling companion. He had not seen Maxi since their parting in India. A strong man like him would not readily give in to Soul Edge's charms; he must have had his reasons. What was he doing now? Beneath these dark skies, it was almost as if Kilik could make out his friend's figure in pursuit of that faintest light: vengeance.

One night, the two caught sight of a meteor shower falling westward. Within the stunning lights, they could sense Soul Edge's evil energy, and knew they must make haste on their quest. Ostrheinsburg, the final battleground, drew ever closer. Yet Kilik was determined to move on alone when the time came; he would cast away the happiness of humanity and become a part of nature. Never again would the spirit sword and the cursed sword cast their shadows on the human realm. He knew this was the only way to protect those dear to him.

Kali-Yuga

One of the tools of war known as the Three Treasures. It was in the keeping of Ling-Sheng Su Temple, once home to a renowned line of warriors, until the temple was reduced to ruins and it came to rest in the hands of Kilik, the last of their people. The rod has the ability to store power, be it good or evil; thus both it and its wielder were filled with Soul Edge's evil when the temple was destroyed. Sensing the Kali-Yuga might turn into a second Soul Edge, Kilik began learning how to control the evil, and thus his and the weapon's destinies became intertwined.

After much training—and with the help of another of the Three Treasures, the Dvapara-Yuga—Kilik learned how to purify evil, but the malice within the Kali-Yuga runs deep, and has yet to be fully expunged.

Ling-Sheng Su Temple Staff Jutsu

Edge Master, the famous sword monk. This old man was headed to Ling-Sheng Su Temple as a military advisor. The "Three Treasures" had been stored there from some time ago.

The Krita-Yuga (sword), The Kali-Yuga (staff), and the Dvapara-Yuga (mirror). All those who train at the Ling-Sheng Su Temple one day hope to inherit one of these. They are, in all ways, the very highest form of sword technique and staff technique that exists in the world.

The Three Treasures each find their own inheritors who come to the holy place to study the secret arts under the sword monk. The inheritor of the Staff Arts was Kilik. As the only survivor of Ling-Sheng Su Temple, he faces his own destiny.

Command List

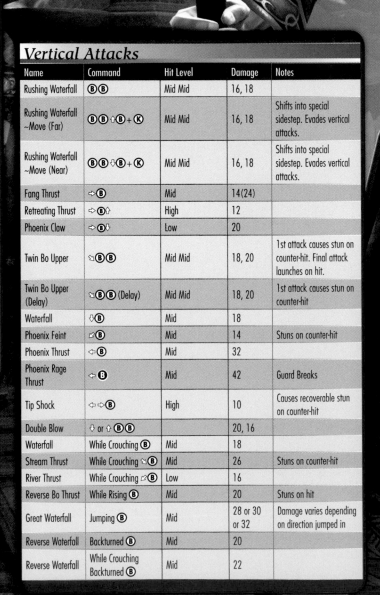

Signature Techniques

Name	Command	Hit Level	Damage	Notes
Bo Rush Combo	ⒶⒶⒷ	High High Mid	12, 8, 22	Fully combos on counter-hit
Raging Phoenix Combo	⇨ⒶⒶⒶ	High High High	14, 10, 20	
Twin Bo Upper	⬂ⒷⒷ	Mid Mid	18, 20	1st attack stuns on counter-hit
Dragon Glide Bo	→ⒶⒶ	High Low	20, 40	
Raven Slaughter	↓ or ↑Ⓑ	Mid	25	
Absolute Truth ~Monument	⇩Ⓑ+Ⓚ	Mid	26	Stuns on counter-hit. Shifts to Monument.
Monument	⇩⬂⇨			Deflects horizontal attacks
Circular Strike	Monument stance Ⓐ	Mid	20	Stuns on hit
Retreating Hilt	Monument stance Ⓑ	Low	24	

Horizontal Attacks

Name	Command	Hit Level	Damage	Notes
Bo Rush Combo	ⒶⒶⒷ	High High Mid	12, 8, 22	Fully combos on counter-hit. Final attack launches on hit.
Bo Rush ~Move (Far)	ⒶⒶ⇧Ⓑ+Ⓚ	High High	12, 8	Shifts into special sidestep. Evades vertical attacks.
Bo Rush ~Move (Near)	ⒶⒶ⇩Ⓑ+Ⓚ	High High	12, 8	Shifts into special sidestep. Evades vertical attacks.
Twin Phoenix	ⒶⒷⒷ	High High Mid	14, 10, 28	1st attack causes stun on counter-hit
Raging Phoenix Combo	⇨ⒶⒶⒶ	High High High	10, 10, 20	
Mid Sweep	⬂Ⓐ	Mid	18	
Inner Peace	⇩Ⓐ	Low	18	
Lower Bo Slice	⬃Ⓐ	Low	16	
Escaping Bo	⇦Ⓐ	High	28	
Lower Bo Slice	While Crouching Ⓐ	Low	18	
Ling Sheng Slash	While Rising Ⓐ	Mid	24	
Scattering Bo	Jumping Ⓐ	Mid	20 or 22 or 24	Damage varies depending on direction jumped in
Reverse Bo Tap	Backturned Ⓐ	High	14	
Reverse Lower Bo Slice	While Crouching Backturned Ⓐ	Low	22	

Vertical Attacks

Name	Command	Hit Level	Damage	Notes
Rushing Waterfall	ⒷⒷ	Mid Mid	16, 18	
Rushing Waterfall ~Move (Far)	ⒷⒷ⇧Ⓑ+Ⓚ	Mid Mid	16, 18	Shifts into special sidestep. Evades vertical attacks.
Rushing Waterfall ~Move (Near)	ⒷⒷ⇩Ⓑ+Ⓚ	Mid Mid	16, 18	Shifts into special sidestep. Evades vertical attacks.
Fang Thrust	⇨Ⓑ	Mid	14(24)	
Retreating Thrust	⇨Ⓑ⇧	High	12	
Phoenix Claw	⇨Ⓑ⇩	Low	20	
Twin Bo Upper	⬂ⒷⒷ	Mid Mid	18, 20	1st attack causes stun on counter-hit. Final attack launches on hit.
Twin Bo Upper (Delay)	⬂ⒷⒷ (Delay)	Mid Mid	18, 20	1st attack causes stun on counter-hit
Waterfall	⇩Ⓑ	Mid	18	
Phoenix Feint	⬃Ⓑ	Mid	14	Stuns on counter-hit
Phoenix Thrust	⇦Ⓑ	Mid	32	
Phoenix Rage Thrust	←Ⓑ	Mid	42	Guard Breaks
Tip Shock	⇦⇨Ⓑ	High	10	Causes recoverable stun on counter-hit
Double Blow	⇩ or ⇧ ⒷⒷ		20, 16	
Waterfall	While Crouching Ⓑ	Mid	18	
Stream Thrust	While Crouching ⬂Ⓑ	Mid	26	Stuns on counter-hit
River Thrust	While Crouching ⬃Ⓑ	Low	16	
Reverse Bo Thrust	While Rising Ⓑ	Mid	20	Stuns on hit
Great Waterfall	Jumping Ⓑ	Mid	28 or 30 or 32	Damage varies depending on direction jumped in
Reverse Waterfall	Backturned Ⓑ	Mid	20	
Reverse Waterfall	While Crouching Backturned Ⓑ	Mid	22	

Kick Attacks

Name	Command	Hit Level	Damage	Notes
Sheng Front Kick	Ⓚ	High	12	
Sheng Illusion Kick	ⓀⒷ	High Low	15, 15	
Sheng Lung Kick	⇨Ⓚ	Mid	30	
Sheng Lung Kick Combo	⇘ⓀⒷ	Mid High	15, 20	
Sheng Su Low Kick	⇩Ⓚ	Low	12	
Sheng Side Kick	⇗Ⓚ	Mid	14	
Hawk Claw	⇦ⓀⒷ	High Low	26, 28	2nd attack stuns on counter-hit
Hawk Claw (Delay)	⇦ⓀⒷ (Delay)	High Low	26, 28	2nd attack stuns on counter-hit
Sheng Su Low Kick	While Crouching Ⓚ	Low	12	
Sunrise Kick	While Rising Ⓚ	Mid High	15, 15	
Phoenix Splits	Jumping Ⓚ	High	14 or 16 or 18	Damage varies depending on direction jumped in
Reverse Sheng Su Kick	Backturned Ⓚ	High	14	
Reverse Sheng Su Low Kick	While Crouching Backturned Ⓚ	Low	12	

Simultaneous Press

Name	Command	Hit Level	Damage	Notes
Bo Smack Down	Ⓐ+Ⓑ	High High High High High High	10, 10, 8, 8, 8, 8	Final attack stuns on hit
Biting Phoenix	⇨Ⓐ+Ⓑ	Mid Mid Mid Mid Mid	15, 15, 10, 10, 15	
Trick Bo	⇘Ⓐ+Ⓑ	Low	32	Shifts into throw at close distances. Input Ⓐ to escape throw.
Lower Bo Smackdown	⇩Ⓐ+Ⓑ	Low Low Low Low	8, 8, 18, 18	
Dirty Bo	⇗Ⓐ+Ⓑ	Low	47	Shifts into throw at close distances. Input Ⓑ to escape throw.
Phoenix Flare ~Raven Slaughter Thrust	⇦Ⓐ+ⒷⒷⒷ	Mid Mid Mid Mid Mid Mid	15, 15, 15, 15, 24, 20	May input ⒷⒷ during 2nd hit instead of 4th
Pounding Stones	While Crouching Ⓐ+Ⓑ	Mid Mid Mid	20, 21	1st attack stuns on hit
Heaven Monument	While laying down Ⓐ+Ⓑ	Mid	75	Unblockable
Heaven Monument (Cancel)	While laying down Ⓐ+ⒷⒼ			
Heaven Monument Fall	While laying down Ⓐ+ⒷⓀ	Low	30	
Asura Dance	Ⓑ+Ⓚ⇨Ⓑ ⇦⇩⇨Ⓑ	Mid Mid Mid	23, 10, 36	Deflects horizontal attacks
Yin Rising	⇨Ⓑ+Ⓚ	Mid Mid	14, 18	2nd attack stuns on hit
Playful Phoenix	⇘Ⓑ+Ⓚ	Low	24	
Playful Phoenix ~Fall	⇘Ⓑ+Ⓚ			Leaves Kilik lying on floor
Absolute Truth	⇩Ⓑ+Ⓚ	Mid	26	Stuns on counter-hit
Absolute Truth ~Monument	⇩Ⓑ+Ⓚ	Mid	26	Stuns on counter-hit. Shifts into Monumnet.
Playful Phoenix	⇗Ⓑ+Ⓚ	Low	24	
Playful Phoenix ~Lay	⇗Ⓑ+Ⓚ			Leaves Kilik lying on floor
Phoenix Lunge	⇦Ⓑ+Ⓚ	Low	35	
Asura Clairvoyance	Backturned Ⓑ+Ⓚ ⇦Ⓑ⇦⇩⇨Ⓑ	Mid Mid Mid	25, 10, 36	
Phoenix Cross	Ⓐ+Ⓚ	Mid Mid	20, 25	
Mountain Breaker	⇨Ⓐ+Ⓚ	Low High	22. 33	
Wave Divide	⇩Ⓐ+Ⓚ	Low	33	
Phoenix Tail	⇦Ⓐ+Ⓚ	Low Low	20, 20	
Rising Flare	While laying down Ⓐ+Ⓚ	Low	36	
Taunt	Ⓚ+Ⓖ			

8-Way Run

Name	Command	Hit Level	Damage	Notes
Dragon Glide Bo	→ⒶⒶ	High Low	20, 40	
Roundhouse Bo	↘ or ↗Ⓐ	High	24	
Wind Divide Flare	↓ or ↑ⒶⒶⒶ	Mid Low Low	16(20), 16, 36	1st attack deals additional damage from max range
Mountain Carve	↓ or ↑ⒶⒷ	Mid Mid	16(20), 28	1st attack deals additional damage from max range
Ling Sheng Slice	↙ or ↖Ⓐ	Low	22	
Cross Tide	←ⒶⒶ	Mid Low	18, 20	
Cross Tide (Delay)	←ⒶⒶ (Delay)	Mid Low	20, 28	
Yin and Yang	←ⒶⒷ	Mid	70	Unblockable. Causes stun against enemies lying down.
Heavy Bo	→ or ↘ or ↗Ⓑ	Mid	18(43)	Shifts into special attack on counter-hit
Raven Slaughter	↓ or ↑Ⓑ	Mid	25	Launches on hit
Lower Bo Feint	↙ or ↖Ⓑ	Low	20	Stuns on hit
Stream Thrust	←Ⓑ	Low	25	
Rising Phoenix	→ or ↘ or ↗ⓀⓀⒷ	Mid Mid Mid Mid	15, 10, 15, 30	
Sheng Su Thrust	↓ or ↑ⓀⒷ	Low Mid	18, 28	
Sheng Heh Kick	← or ↙ or ↖Ⓚ	Mid	30	Stuns on hit
Sliding	While Running Ⓚ	Low	26	

Monument

Name	Command	Hit Level	Damage	Notes
Monument	⇩⇘⇨			Deflects horizontal attacks
Circular Strike	Monument stance Ⓐ	Mid	20	Stuns on hit
Retreating Hilt	Monument stance Ⓑ	Low	24	
Scythe	Monument stance Ⓚ	High High	10, 14	
Heaven Monument	Monument stance Ⓐ+Ⓑ		45	Unblockabkle
Heaven Monument (Cancel)	Monument stance Ⓐ+ⒷⒼ			
Heaven Monument Fall	Monument stance Ⓐ+ⒷⓀ	Low	30	
Festival of the Damned	Monument stance Ⓐ+Ⓖ ⇦⇨Ⓐ⇦⇩⇨Ⓑ		30	Input Ⓐ to escape throw after first attack
Festival of the Dead	Monument stance Ⓑ+Ⓖ⇦⇨Ⓑ		50	Input Ⓑ to escape throw after first attack
Monument ~Move (Far)	Monument stance ⇧Ⓑ+Ⓚ			Shifts into special sidestep. Evades vertical attacks.
Monumen ~Move (Near)	Monument stance ⇩Ⓑ+Ⓚ			Shifts into special sidestep. Evades vertical attacks.

Throws

Name	Command	Hit Level	Damage	Notes
Light Breeze	Ⓐ+Ⓖ	Throw	55	Input Ⓐ to escape
Heaven Dance	Ⓑ+Ⓖ	Throw	50	Input Ⓑ to escape
Cutting Sadness	Left Side Throw	Throw	60	Same button as throw (Ⓐ or Ⓑ) to escape
Summer Gale	Right Side Throw	Throw	65	Same button as throw (Ⓐ or Ⓑ) to escape
Phoenix Pounce	Back Throw	Throw	65	Same button as throw (Ⓐ or Ⓑ) to escape
Festival of the Damned	⇩⇘⇨Ⓐ+Ⓖ ⇦⇨Ⓐ⇦⇩⇨Ⓑ	Throw	30	Input Ⓐ to escape throw after first attack
Festival of the Dead	⇩⇘⇨Ⓑ+Ⓖ ⇦⇨Ⓑ	Throw	50	Input Ⓑ to escape throw after first attack

Back Parry

Name	Command	Hit Level	Damage	Notes
Back Parry	⇩⇙⇦			Deflects vertical attacks
Parry Sweeper	Back Parry Ⓐ	Low	25	
Parry Bolt	Back Parry Ⓑ	Mid	40	Guard Breaks
Parry Kick	Back Parry Ⓚ	Mid	26	

Combos

Counter-hit ⒶⒶⒷ, ⇨ⒶⒶ

5 hits, 59 Damage

Counter-hit ⇘ⒷⒷ, ⇨ⒶⒶ

5 hits, 50 Damage

While Rising Ⓑ, ⇨⇨Ⓑ

2 hits, 54 Damage

↓ or ↑Ⓑ, ⇘ⓀⒷ, ⇩Ⓑ

4 hits, 62 Damage

⇩⇘⇨Ⓐ, ⇦⇨Ⓑ, ⇨ⒶⒶⒶ

2 hits, 42 Damage

↙ or ↖Ⓑ, ⇨⇨Ⓑ

3 hits, 27-30 Damage

Tap ⇩ⒷⒷ (Counter-hit), ⇩Ⓑ

3 hits, 52 Damage

Counter-hit ⇙Ⓑ, ⇩⇩Ⓑ, ⇘ⓀⒷ, ⇩Ⓑ

5 hits, 61 Damage

⇩⇘⇨Ⓐ + Ⓖ⇦⇨Ⓐ⇦⇙⇩⇘⇨Ⓑ, run forward, ⇘ⓀⒷ, ⇩Ⓑ

6 hits, 70 Damage

Close Range

Kilik has a small handful of abilities that are effective at close range, but his lack of a safe launcher makes it difficult for him to deal heavy damage from this position. Your goal is to reposition yourself away from your enemy via a knockdown. Achieving this relies on your ability to use Kilik's defensive options. His Monument stance (⇩⇘⇨), for instance, can be used when you're at a disadvantage to deflect horizontal attacks. After a successful deflection, attack with the stance's Circular Strike (Ⓐ) to stun your foe, leaving him or her open to an additional ⇦⇨Ⓑ, then ⇨ⒶⒶⒶ for a 5-hit combo. If your enemy doesn't initiate an attack, mix between the Monument's mid Ⓐ or low Ⓑ attacks. The Back Parry ability (⇩⇙⇦) has a similar use, but instead deflects vertical attacks. Upon a successful deflection, shift into its Ⓚ option to hit your vulnerable opponent.

If you anticipate a high attack but aren't willing to risk using the Monument stance, which is vulnerable to throws, crouch under the strike and use the Reverse Bo Thrust (While Rising Ⓑ). It causes a stun on a successful hit, enabling you to link ⇨⇨Ⓑ afterward for big damage. Your enemy may try to sidestep this attack if he or she sees it coming, in which case use the Raging Phoenix Combo (⇨ⒶⒶⒶ) to counter-hit your foe's movement.

Mid Range

Kilik's biggest advantage is his unparalleled ability to control side movement. His flexible ⒶⒶ string is his best means to do this. If it connects on a counter-hit, chain into its launcher extension (ⒶⒶⒷ) and juggle your enemy with ⇨ⒶⒶ. If ⒶⒶ connects normally, use the hit advantage to stage a follow-up attack: Perform Tip Shock (⇦⇨Ⓑ) to preemptively stop enemy mid attacks—on counter-hit, combo ⇩⇩Ⓑ, ⇘ⓀⒷ, ⇩Ⓑ. Alternatively, to stage a 2-way mix-up, vary between the low ⇩Ⓐ and the mid While Rising Ⓑ—link into ⇨⇨Ⓑ if it hits. When ⒶⒶ is blocked, use Kilik's Monument (⇩⇘⇨) and Back Parry (⇩⇙⇦) to deflect attacks while mounting a counter offensive.

The threat of the aforementioned string will eventually convince your enemies to take countermeasures. Their best options include crouching under it or backing out of its range. If you anticipate a crouch, hit your enemy with Biting Phoenix (⇨Ⓐ+Ⓑ) or While Rising Ⓑ to deal massive damage. A more flexible option is to use the Wind Divide Flare (⬇ or ⬆ⒶⒶⒶ) or Mountain Carve (⬇ or ⬆ⒶⒷ). Both strings start with the same mid hit and lead into either a mid or low attack. If your enemy positions himself outside your Ⓐ attack's range, use the low Stream Thrust (⬅Ⓑ) to catch him standing.

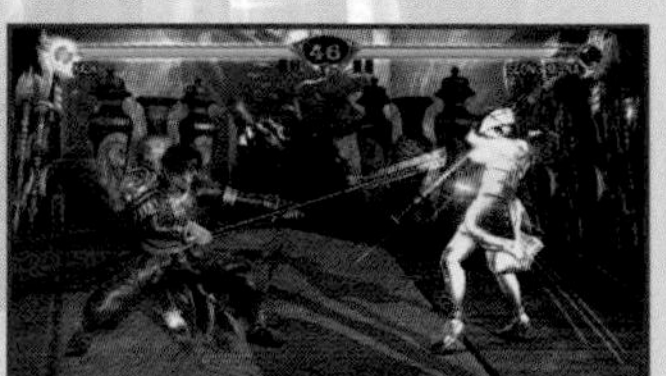

Long Range

Your objective is to deter 8-Way Run and sidesteps, which are dangerously effective against many of Kilik's long-range attacks. Use Dragon Glide Bo (➡ⒶⒶ) to counter these actions for massive damage. It leaves Kilik safe to attack if it's blocked, though it's possible for your enemy to crouch under the first hit and counterattack before the second swing. If you ever anticipate this countermeasure, use the mid Phoenix Thrust (⇦Ⓑ) to stop it. You can charge this attack (⇦ Ⓑ), improving its damage output and turning it into a Guard Break. Mix between this attack and the low-hitting ⬅Ⓑ.

Special Tactics

Okizeme: Anti-Wakeup

Use the Trick Bo (⇘Ⓐ+Ⓑ) or Dirty Bo (⇙Ⓐ+Ⓑ) if your enemy guards high on wakeup. Both attacks are special low hits with throw extensions. It's possible for the enemy to escape the throw segments, so vary between both versions, which have different escape commands. When your enemy is afraid of either of those techniques, attack with the mid-hitting Phoenix Flare (⇦Ⓐ+Ⓑ). Chain into its Raven Slaughter Thrust (⇦Ⓐ+ⒷⒷⒷ) extension if the first two hits connect. The opening attack is safe to punishment, so don't perform the Raven Slaughter Thrust if it's blocked.

Implement Kilik's Festival of the Damned (⇩⇘⇨Ⓐ+Ⓖ⇦⇨Ⓐ⇦⇙⇩⇘⇨Ⓑ) and Festival of the Dead (⇩⇘⇨Ⓑ+Ⓖ⇦⇨Ⓑ) throws against opponents with strong guarding habits. The Festival of the Damned leads to aerial combos, such as run up ⇘ⓀⒷ, ⇩Ⓑ, which inflicts extremely high damage.

Wall Game

Kilik has several attacks that cause a wall stun. The best of these attacks include his ⇨Ⓐ+Ⓑ and ⇨Ⓚ. You can land these attacks after knocking your enemy into a stun with counter-hit ⇙Ⓑ, potentially leading to wall combos. For example, land a counter-hit ⇙Ⓑ near a wall, then hit your enemy with ⇨Ⓐ+Ⓑ before he recovers. When he hits the wall, strike your stunned enemy with ⇘ⒷⒷ, ⇘ⒷⒷ, ⇨⇨Ⓑ. This basic combo deals massive damage to your adversary.

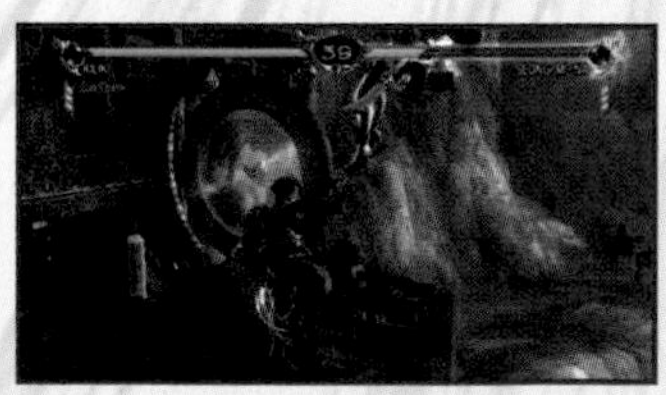

Kilik

Aeon Calcos - Lizardman

Aeon Calcos -

It is usually the case that our powers of imagination work better in the darkness than in the light.

"The End of All Things," Immanuel Kant (1724 - 1804)

Bio

Age:	36 (the last 7 years of which were spent in this form)
Birthplace:	Sparta, Ottoman Empire
Height:	5'11"
Weight:	190 lbs.
Birth Date:	June 23
Blood Type:	None
Weapon:	Single-Handed Ax & Small Shield
Weapon Name:	Grudge Ax & Aya Shield
Discipline:	Rapid Ares Style
Family:	He must have one, waiting in his homeland, but...

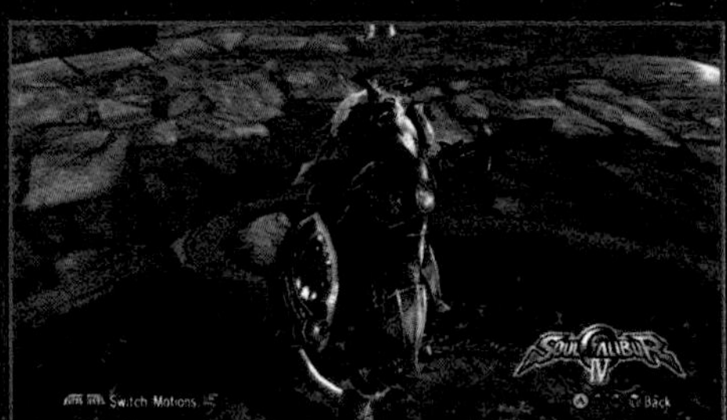

Lizardman

[illegible]

[illegible]

[illegible]

[illegible]

[illegible] Calcos, to the [illegible].

Before he knew it, [illegible] the cult's [illegible] and [illegible] as much as himself [illegible] who was [illegible] were looking for a [illegible]

In the past he had [illegible] gave himself over to [illegible] heathens, he bared his fangs [illegible] cover of darkness, his monstrous pack [illegible] Death itself returned.

It always happened in the dead of night, when his sleep grew [illegible] be: the sensations and memories of being human, [illegible] chaotic reality so like a nightmare. What sort of [illegible] endless blankness. And when he tried to sum up his thoughts, [illegible] were lost to him. Just like a moth-eaten tome, missing words [illegible] meaning. Beset by a fierce agitation, he tried [illegible] with his own name.

It was too late. The water jar holding his memories had [illegible] nearly all of them had leaked away. Only a [illegible] a desperate panic. He'd lost something, something so [illegible] that he could not find the word. A [illegible] unconsciously. "Wait," he thought. "It's on the tip of my tongue. . ."

Then—yes!—he remembered. "My soul! What has become of my soul?" [illegible] of his memories led him to the single drop remaining at the bottom of the jar [illegible] vestiges of the obsession he had once held: Soul Edge. The name [illegible] the top of his mind. "Yes!" he thought. "That is where my soul lies!" [illegible] repeating the words, to hold them fast lest they flicker and disappear: "My soul. Soul Edge. [illegible] My soul. Soul Edge. . ."

(My. . .my soul. Must find it. Once the sun has risen. . .)

And with that last thought, he exhaled, shut his eyes, and [illegible]

However, the next time he opened his eyes, all his human thoughts and memories [illegible] for one earnest hope left by his human heart, powerful enough to [illegible]

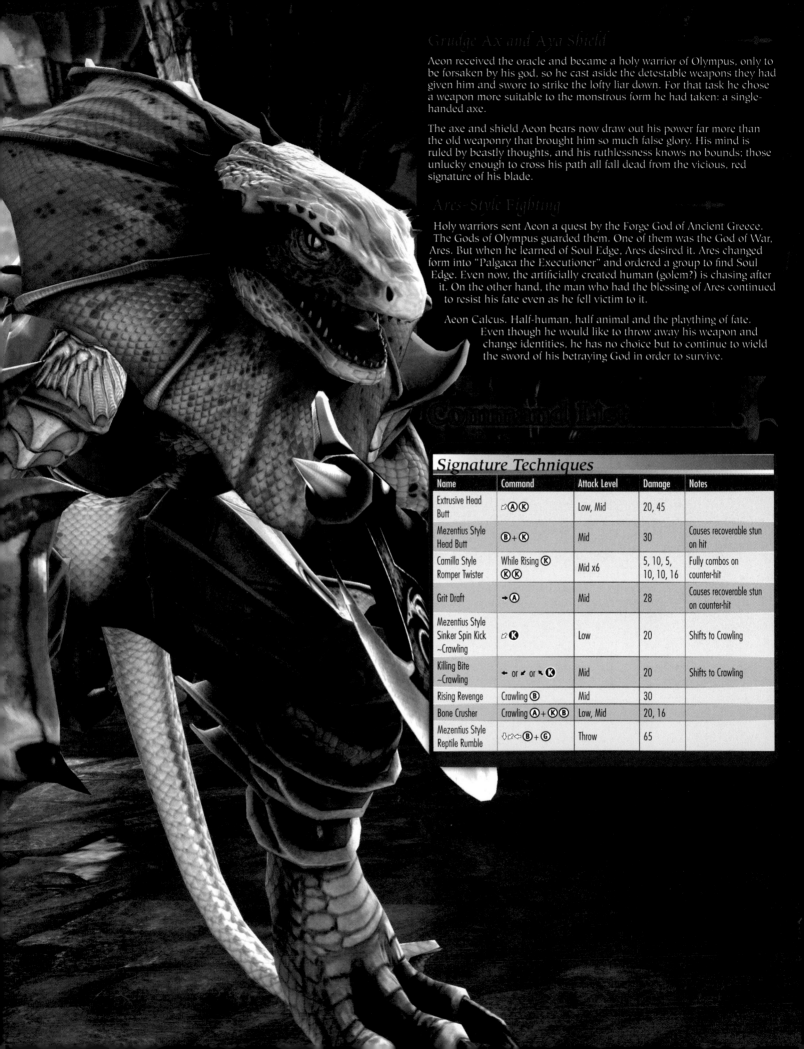

Grudge Ax and Aya Shield

Aeon received the oracle and became a holy warrior of Olympus, only to be forsaken by his god, so he cast aside the detestable weapons they had given him and swore to strike the lofty liar down. For that task he chose a weapon more suitable to the monstrous form he had taken: a single-handed axe.

The axe and shield Aeon bears now draw out his power far more than the old weaponry that brought him so much false glory. His mind is ruled by beastly thoughts, and his ruthlessness knows no bounds; those unlucky enough to cross his path all fall dead from the vicious, red signature of his blade.

Ares-Style Fighting

Holy warriors sent Aeon a quest by the Forge God of Ancient Greece. The Gods of Olympus guarded them. One of them was the God of War, Ares. But when he learned of Soul Edge, Ares desired it. Ares changed form into "Palgaea the Executioner" and ordered a group to find Soul Edge. Even now, the artificially created human (golem?) is chasing after it. On the other hand, the man who had the blessing of Ares continued to resist his fate even as he fell victim to it.

Aeon Calcus. Half-human, half animal and the plaything of fate. Even though he would like to throw away his weapon and change identities, he has no choice but to continue to wield the sword of his betraying God in order to survive.

Command List

Signature Techniques

Name	Command	Attack Level	Damage	Notes
Extrusive Head Butt	⇙Ⓐ Ⓚ	Low, Mid	20, 45	
Mezentius Style Head Butt	Ⓑ+Ⓚ	Mid	30	Causes recoverable stun on hit
Camilla Style Romper Twister	While Rising Ⓚ Ⓚ Ⓚ	Mid x6	5, 10, 5, 10, 10, 16	Fully combos on counter-hit
Grit Draft	→Ⓐ	Mid	28	Causes recoverable stun on counter-hit
Mezentius Style Sinker Spin Kick ~Crawling	⇙Ⓚ	Low	20	Shifts to Crawling
Killing Bite ~Crawling	← or ↙ or ↖ Ⓚ	Mid	20	Shifts to Crawling
Rising Revenge	Crawling Ⓑ	Mid	30	
Bone Crusher	Crawling Ⓐ+Ⓚ Ⓑ	Low, Mid	20, 16	
Mezentius Style Reptile Rumble	⇩⇙⇦Ⓑ+Ⓖ	Throw	65	

Horizontal Attacks

Name	Command	Attack Level	Damage	Notes
Refrain Axe	ⒶⒶ	High, High	10, 10	
Aigis Hook	→Ⓐ	High	16	
Lumber Axe	↘Ⓐ	Mid	30	
Lower Celtis	↓Ⓐ	Sp.Low	10	
Extrusive Head Butt	↗ⒶⓀ	Low, Mid	20, 45	
Turnus Style Blade Edge	←Ⓐ	High	32	
Lower Celtis	While Crouching Ⓐ	Sp.Low	10	
Sandstorm Axe	While Rising Ⓐ	High	26	
Spinning Edge Hopper	Jumping Ⓐ	High	26 or 28 or 30	Damage varies depending on direction jumped in
Rear Side Edge	Backturned Ⓐ	High	12	
Rear Base Current	While Crouching Backturned Ⓐ	Low	14	

Vertical Attacks

Name	Command	Attack Level	Damage	Notes
Scale Strike	ⒷⒷ	Mid, Mid	14, 16	
Spot Strike	→Ⓑ	Mid	26	
Rising Grit	↘Ⓑ	Mid	30	
Mezentius Style Shield Blast	↓ⒷⓀ	Sp.Low, Mid	10, 30	
Base Scale Axe	↗Ⓑ	Mid	16	
Shield Clipper	←Ⓑ	High	20	Stuns on counter-hit
Base Axe	While Crouching Ⓑ	Mid	18	
Tail Weapon Gazer	While Rising Ⓑ	Mid	16	
Base Axe Hopper	Jumping Ⓑ	Mid	25 or 26 or 28	Damage varies depending on direction jumped in
Rear Scale Axe	Backturned Ⓑ	Mid	16	
Rear Base Axe	While Crouching Backturned Ⓑ	Mid	18	

Kick Attacks

Name	Command	Attack Level	Damage	Notes
Gloom High Kick	Ⓚ	High	14	
Gloom Front Kick	→Ⓚ	Mid	30	Stuns on counter-hit
Gloom Front Kick (Hold)	→Ⓚ	High	30	
Lizard Stamp Kick	↘Ⓚ	Mid	18	
Romper Base Kick	↓Ⓚ	Low	12	
Mezentius Style Sinker Spin Kick	↗Ⓚ	Low	20	
Mezentius Style Sinker Spin Kick ~Crawling	↗Ⓚ	Low	20	Shifts to Crawling
Mezentius Style Lightning Head Masher	←Ⓚ	High	20	
Lizard Low Kick	While Crouching Ⓚ	Low	12	
Camilla Style Romper Twister	While Rising Ⓚ ⓀⓀ	Mid x6	5, 10, 5, 10, 10, 16	Fully combos on counter-hit
Side Arch Kick	Jumping Ⓚ	Mid	14 or 16 or 18	Damage varies depending on direction jumped in
Rear Gloom High Kick	Backturned Ⓚ	High	16	
Rear Lizard Low Kick	While Crouching Backturned Ⓚ	Low	12	

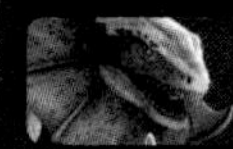

Simultaneous Press

Name	Command	Attack Level	Damage	Notes
Axe Hopper	Ⓐ+Ⓑ	Mid	28	
Mezentius Style Head Butt	Ⓑ+Ⓚ	Mid	30	Causes recoverable stun on hit
Mezentius Style Sand Roll	↗Ⓑ+Ⓚ	Low	48, 16	Unblockable
Mezentius Style Sand Roll ~Crawling	↗Ⓑ+ⓀⒼ			Shifts to Crawling
Sand Revenger	←Ⓑ+Ⓚ	Mid	30	
Quick Sand Revenger	←Ⓑ+ⓀⒼ	Mid	30	Leaves Lizardman lying face down
Sand Revenger ~Crawling	←Ⓑ+Ⓚ	Mid	30	Shifts into Crawling
Mezentius Style Desert Threat	↑Ⓑ+Ⓚ	Mid	30	
Mezentius Style Desert Threat (Hold)	↑Ⓑ+Ⓚ	Mid	50	Unblockable
Spiral Tail	Backturned Ⓑ+Ⓚ	Low	20	Stuns on counter-hit
Mezentius Style Twister High Kick	Ⓐ+Ⓚ	High	30	Stuns on hit
Taunt	Ⓚ+Ⓖ			

8-Way Run

Name	Command	Attack Level	Damage	Notes
Grit Draft	→Ⓐ	Mid	28	Causes recoverable stun on counter-hit
Spiral Draft	↘ or ↗Ⓐ	High	30	
Spiral Draft ~Crawling	↘ or ↗Ⓐ	High	30	Shifts to Crawling
Reverse Double Shield Swing	↓ⒶⒶ	High, High	20, 10	1st attack knocks down on counter-hit
Double Shield Swing	↑ⒶⒶ	High, High	20, 10	1st attack knocks down on counter-hit
Mezentius Style Sweeper	↙ or ↖ⒶⓀ	Low, Low	16, 28	
Camilla Style Rising Lizard	←ⒶⒷ	Mid, Mid	20, 30	1st attack stuns on counter-hit
Camilla Style Rising Lizard (Hold)	←ⒶⒷ	Mid, Mid	20, 30	1st attack Guard Breaks, stuns on hit
Turnus Style Dune Smash	→Ⓑ	Mid	30	
Mezentius Style Camel Blow	↘ or ↗Ⓑ	Mid	20	
Sandland Predator (Additional attack)	↘ or ↗Ⓑ During Hit Ⓑ		23, 7	
Sandland Predator (Additional attack) ~Crawling	↘ or ↗Ⓑ During Hit Ⓑ		23, 7	Shifts to Crawling
Mezentius Style Shield Jolt	↓ or ↑Ⓑ	High	20	
Mezentius Style Shield Cannon	↙ or ↖Ⓑ	Mid	21	
Rumbling Axe	←Ⓑ	Mid	30	
Mezentius Style Grit Blast	→ or ↘ or ↗Ⓚ	Mid	36	
Mezentius Style Scale Twister	↓ or ↑Ⓚ	Mid	20	Causes stun on hit
Killing Bite	← or ↙ or ↖Ⓚ	Mid	20(30)	Shifts to special throw on ground hit
Killing Bite ~Crawling	← or ↙ or ↖Ⓚ	Mid	20(30)	Shifts to special throw on ground hit. Shifts to Crawling.
Turnus Style Screw Shot	→Ⓐ+Ⓑ	Mid	42	
Mezentius Style Double Rising Beat	↘ or ↗Ⓐ+Ⓑ	Mid, Mid	15, 38	
Mezentius Style Shield Rush	→Ⓑ+ⓀⒶⒷ	Mid, High, Mid	22, 8, 15	Fully combos on counter-hit
Mezentius Style Shield Rush (Delay)	→Ⓑ+ⓀⒶⒷ	Mid, High, Mid	22, 8, 15	Fully combos on counter-hit
Sliding	While Running Ⓚ	Low	26	

Throws

Name	Command	Attack Level	Damage	Notes
Mezentius Style Sand Tomb	Ⓐ+Ⓖ	Throw	50	Input Ⓐ to escape
Mezentius Style Sand Bomb	Ⓑ+Ⓖ	Throw	55	Input Ⓑ to escape
Mezentius Style Santana Storm	Left Side Throw	Throw	55	Same button as throw (Ⓐ or Ⓑ) to escape
Mezentius Style Sadistic Rush Lift	Right Side Throw	Throw	60	Same button as throw (Ⓐ or Ⓑ) to escape
Mezentius Style Scale Brusher	Back Throw	Throw	60	Same button as throw (Ⓐ or Ⓑ) to escape
Mezentius Style Reptile Rumble	⇩⬃⇦Ⓑ+Ⓖ	Throw	65	Input Ⓑ to escape

Crawling

Name	Command	Attack Level	Damage	Notes
Crawling	⇩⬂⇨			Evades high attacks and some mid attacks
Sidewinder	Crawling stance Ⓐ	Low	15	
Rising Revenge	Crawling stance Ⓑ	Mid	30	
Scale Ram	Crawling stance Ⓚ	Mid	20	
Scale Shield	Crawling stance Ⓐ+Ⓑ			Guard Impact. Deflects Mid and low attack types.
Rolling Revenge	Crawling stance Ⓑ+Ⓚ	Mid	20	
Bone Crusher	Crawling stance Ⓐ+ⓀⒷ	Low, Mid	20, 16	

Combos

⬂Ⓑ, ⬂⬂Ⓐ + Ⓑ

3 hits, 66 Damage

↘ or ↗ⒷⒷ (Just), ⇦⇦Ⓚ

2 hits, 60 Damage

↘ or ↗ⒷⒷ (Just), Ⓑ,Ⓑ + Ⓚ

3 hits, 72 Damage

Counter-hit ⇦Ⓑ, ⇦⇦Ⓚ

2 hits, 49 Damage

Ⓐ + Ⓚ, ⇦⇦Ⓚ

2 hits, 53 Damage

Counter-hit ⇨Ⓚ, ⇦⇦ⒶⒷ, Ⓐ + Ⓑ

4 hits, 87 Damage

↓ or ↑Ⓑ, ⇨⇨Ⓐ + Ⓑ

2 hits, 49 Damage

Counter-hit ⇨⇨Ⓑ + ⓀⒶⒷ, Ⓖ (cancel back-turned state), Ⓐ + Ⓑ, ⇨⇨Ⓚ

6 hits, 104 Damage, possible to Just Ukemi after Ⓐ + Ⓑ

⇩⬂⇨, Ⓑ + Ⓚ, Ⓐ

2 hits, 30 Damage

⇩⬂⇨, Ⓐ + ⓀⒷ, ⇨⇨Ⓚ

3 hits, 59 Damage

Close Range

Lizardman thrives at close range, where his easy-to-use mix-up options come into play. The goal is to lock your enemy into attack patterns and stage varying mix-ups that ultimately lead to a knockdown. Start your offense with the sidestep-crushing ⒶⒶ. On a successful hit, follow up with the Mezentius Style Reptile Rumble (↓↙← Ⓑ+Ⓖ), Extrusive Head Butt (↙ⒶⓀ), or the Mezentius Style Shield Blast (↓ⒷⓀ). Use the versatile ↓ⒷⓀ more than the other options, as it fishes for crouching states and counter-hits. Attack with a standalone ↓Ⓑ, and if it connects as a counter-hit or against a crouching enemy, chain into its Ⓚ extension for a 2-hit combo. When blocked, use the Ⓚ extension to stop your enemy's immediate attempts to attack your recovery. When your opponent is afraid of the follow-up, perform ↓Ⓑ then go for a Camilla Style Romper Twister (While Rising ⓀⓀ) or Lizardman's ↓↙← Ⓑ+Ⓖ throw. If While Rising ⓀⓀ hits on a counter-hit, chain into its Ⓚ extension for a 6-hit combo. Also use While Rising Ⓐ after ↓Ⓑ to stop attempts to sidestep your secondary attacks.

If your enemy tries to duck under your ⒶⒶ string, attack with ⒷⒷ or ↓Ⓑ. If your enemy manages to guard one of your attacks, shift into Crawling (↓↘→) to duck under high attacks—punish your foe with Ⓐ+ⓀⒷ, →→Ⓚ. Or you can sidestep into ↘Ⓑ then ↘↘Ⓐ+Ⓑ to counter most vertical attacks.

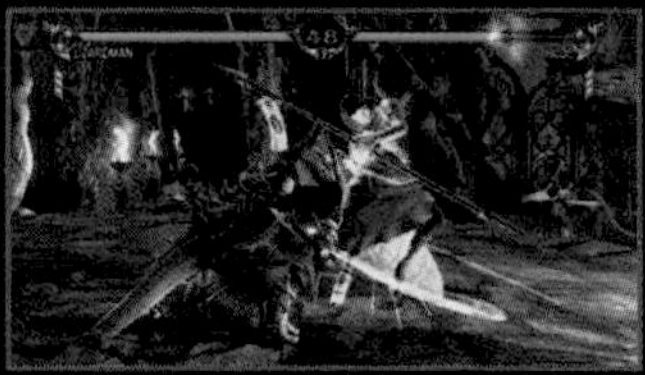

Mid Range

Establish close range or knock down your enemy at all costs. There are three ways to accomplish this: You can catch your enemy's 8-Way Runs via the Grit Draft (⇨Ⓐ) or Spiral Draft (⇘or⇗Ⓐ). Another option is to punish a whiffed move with Turnus Style Screw Shot (⇨Ⓐ+Ⓑ) or Rising Grit (↘Ⓑ). Finally, you can force your way in with the Mezentius Style Shield Rush (⇨Ⓑ+ⓀⒶ). Dissuading your foe's use of 8-Way Run is your first priority. The mid hit ⇨Ⓐ causes a recoverable stun on counter-hit, allowing for possible follow-up combos and a knockdown. The most flexible option is ⇘Ⓐ, which knocks down and shifts into Lizardman's Crawling stance, enabling him to immediately stage an anti-wakeup attack. If it's blocked, use the Crawling stance's Ⓐ+Ⓑ to Guard Impact mid attacks. Or punish your foe's missed high attacks with the Bone Crusher (Ⓐ+ⓀⒷ), as the Crawling stance ducks under high attacks.

When your enemy is scared to use 8-Way Run, you can use the risky ⇨Ⓑ+ⓀⒶ to move into attack range. If it happens to strike your enemy as a counter-hit, chain into its Ⓑ follow-up (⇨Ⓑ+ⓀⒶⒷ) to launch your enemy for a combo. When blocked, perform the Ⓑ extension extremely late to lure out enemy attacks, or throw your enemy when he or she is afraid of the string's final hit.

Perform ↙ⒶⓀ to slip under opponents using horizontal attacks to keep you out, or shift into ↓↘→ and crawl your way into close range. Use the stance's Ⓐ+Ⓚ or Ⓑ+Ⓚ option to stage a basic mix-up.

Long Range

Because of Lizardman's paucity of long-range moves, this is a problematic distance. Your objective is to establish close range via a knockdown, which is difficult to do. Rely on ⇨Ⓐ to stun 8-Way Run movement for a combo, or force your way in with ⇨Ⓑ+ⓀⒶ. If your enemy ever misses an attack with heavy recovery, attack with ←←Ⓑ then ↘↘Ⓐ+Ⓑ to punish it for big damage.

Special Tactics

Okizeme: Anti-Wakeup

ur objective is simple: mix up your actions between ↘Ⓑ, ↙ⒶⓀ, and ↓↙← Ⓑ + Ⓖ. The most flexible of these options is ↘Ⓑ. Use it often to condition your enemy into blocking high, then attack with ↙ⒶⓀ. If your enemy consistently guards ↙ⒶⓀ, use ⇙ⒶⓀ instead to throw off your foe's blocking patterns. You can also replace ↙ⒶⓀ with ↙Ⓚ occasionally, which shifts into Lizardman's Crawling stance. On a successful hit, pursue your grounded enemy with the stance's Ⓐ + ⓀⒷ or Ⓚ options.

If your enemy is especially afraid of your low attacks, go for the mid-hitting Mezentius Style Head Butt (Ⓑ + Ⓚ) or the Sandland Predator (⇘ⒷⒷ Just Impact). When it hits, Ⓑ + Ⓚ causes a recoverable stun, allowing you to possibly land a follow-up combo. It also leaves Lizardman at a slight advantage when blocked, enabling you to salvage your attack. If this happens, follow-up with →Ⓑ to stop your foe's counterattacks, or go for ↘Ⓑ or ↙ⒶⓀ when your opponent is playing passively. The powerful ↘ⒷⒷ has a hit-throw extension that shifts into Lizardman's special stance. It leads to some of his strongest combos, like ⇘ⒷⒷ (Just), Ⓑ, Ⓑ + Ⓚ.

Crawling

Lizardman's Crawling (↓↘→) stance positions him extremely low to the ground, enabling him to crawl under most horizontal attacks. This is useful for getting close to enemies reliant on horizontal attacks. Several options are at his disposal from this stance. For example, Rising Revenge (Ⓑ) is a middle attack that leaps over low attacks. The Scale Ram (Ⓚ) option is the most flexible mid hit in the stance; it leaps over some crouching attacks and leaves Lizardman at an advantage when it's blocked. Attack with Ⓐ after it's blocked to stop your enemy's attempts to attack. Rolling Revenge (Ⓑ + Ⓚ) is the strongest mid option out of the stance; it allows for small follow-up combos, but leaves him at disadvantage when it's guarded. Sidewinder (Ⓐ) and Bone Crusher (Ⓐ + ⓀⒷ) are both low attacks, Ⓐ being the fastest move in the stance, while Ⓐ + ⓀⒷ leads to its most damaging combo: Ⓐ + ⓀⒷ, then →→Ⓚ. Finally, Ⓐ + Ⓑ initiates a Guard Impact out of the stance, which is Lizardman's only defense when his Ⓐ, Ⓐ + ⓀⒷ, or Ⓑ + Ⓚ options are guarded. Use these options together to counter your enemy's actions.

In addition to its myriad abilities, several of Lizardman's attacks shift directly into this stance. The strongest of these attacks is his Sand Revenger (←Ⓑ + Ⓚ) and Killing Bite (⇦ or ⇗ or ⇘Ⓚ). These techniques leave Lizardman at a massive advantage even when guarded, making them perfect for starting a Crawling offense.

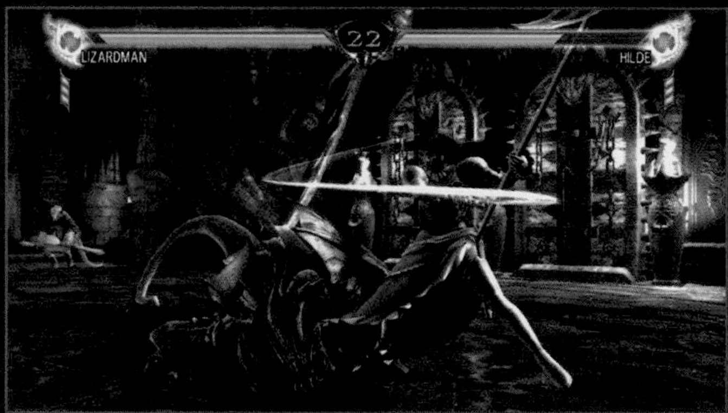

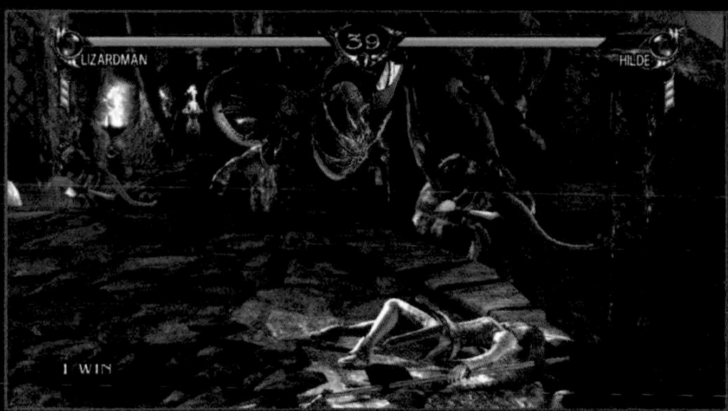

Maxi

Strides a stranger, the heart within him, A wilder thing than wind or billows

"Die Nacht am Strande" Heinrich Heine (1797-1856)

Bio	
Age:	28
Birthplace:	Shuri, Ryukyu Kingdom
Height:	5'8"
Weight:	126 lbs.
Birth Date:	May 1
Blood Type:	O
Weapon:	Nunchuk
Weapon Name:	Soryuju
Discipline:	Shissen Karihadi
Family:	Parents: Deceased His crew, who were like family, were slain by Astaroth.

[illegible] appeared, a strange feeling of [illegible]

[illegible]

[illegible]

[illegible]

Maxi struggled to keep the smile on his face as he [illegible] Kilik and Xianghua [illegible] sensed the [illegible] emanating from Maxi's body. [illegible] mirror Dvapara-Yuga could purify evil energy.

"No, it's buried inside me. There's no way to get it out." (And my body can no longer live without it.)

Maxi took a step back. The wind was growing stronger. The clouds were [illegible] the canopy of the [illegible]

"I'm sorry, but I cannot go with you."

And so saying, Maxi turned his back on his friends and their memories, and left them to their [illegible].

Instead of returning to town, Maxi went to the woods and took shelter from the squall. [illegible] in the darkness [illegible] visitor.

"What do you want?"

As Maxi spoke, he swung his weapon at the girl menacingly, but his visitor dodged and sidestepped the blow.

"What kind of greeting is that?"

So said the mysterious young girl in a startled voice. A sinister aura surrounded her, the foreboding that [illegible]. There was no question, the same evil that tainted the grotesque beast had also poisoned her.

"Don't look down upon me. You and I are more alike than you know. It was easy to find you. I just had to follow [illegible]."

In response to her taunts, Maxi glared at her in cold silence. But she pretended not to notice. She let out a [illegible]

"I know about him, you know. That mud puppet you're chasing."

Little light penetrated the canopy of the evergreen forest as it trembled in the beating rain, but her dark form [illegible]. The disciple of the cursed sword whispered seductively that the enemy against whom he had sworn revenge was growing stronger; that his current strength was no match for that monster; that there was only one way—Soul Edge. Only with the power of the cursed sword [illegible].

Through the rain, Maxi could faintly hear the crashing of the waves. The two continued to stand within striking distance. If they were to engage, only one would survive.

(Incredible, just incredible!)

The messenger of the cursed sword, Tira, was calm on the surface, but inside, her heart danced. This man was far more than she dared to hope. She must have him. It was a gamble to bring up Soul Edge. Once he had completed his quest to avenge his friends, he would [illegible] Soul Edge, the weapon that was her lord and master. Despite the evil shard inside his body, he still had not lost his mind. He was a dangerous element in the equation, but she wanted him, in spite of—no, because of the danger. His powerful soul only made him a more [illegible] offering.

Maxi continued to stare her down in silent malice, but his face betrayed what he really wanted. Tira had him now, and she licked her lips in anticipation. Finally, she told him of that cursed land.

"Ostrheinsburg! That's where you'll find both Soul Edge and your revenge! Come! Come to me, avenger! I'll be waiting!"

Maxi listened as her triumphant laughter faded slowly into the distance, accompanied by the hoarse cawing of crows. The rain had stopped, but the menacing dark clouds lingered in the sky, blocking the rays of the sun.

His mind was made up.

(Kilik, Xianghua... forgive me.)

He would do what he must to gain the power he needed, even if it meant severing ties with his friends, even if it was a trap, even if this journey would lead him outside the boundaries of humanity.

(It's so dark.)

Maxi noticed now that the path leading deeper into the forest was covered by folded curtains of blackness. It was darker than anything he had ever seen, but he would brave the darkness. Each step he took was heavy and slow, and his legs seemed to creak with pain. But he did not stop. Slowly, the sound of the waves receded into the distance behind him.

Maxi

Soryuju

Maxi crafted these nunchaku, reminders of his oath of vengeance, with his own two hands. Their name means "the dragons, reborn, will gather," an expression of his determination to fulfill that oath.

The burden has grown heavy of late, forcing him to make hard choices: to avenge friends of the past, he has had to part ways with friends of the present. In his hands, Soryuju continues to howl.

Shissen Karihadi

He uses the nunchaku fighting style that he learned in the Ryukyan Islands where he was raised.

Its unique characteristic is that it has very flowing style moves. As its name implies, there are seven stances from which an attack can suddenly come forth like a flash. Furthermore, Maxi has moves from other disciplines mixed in with his own.

That's proof of the fact that he continues to refine his own techniques as he gains experience from his life.

Command List

Signature Techniques

Name	Command	Attack Level	Damage	Notes
Serpent's Pleasure	Ⓐ+Ⓑ	Mid, Mid	18, 29	
Striking Snake	↘ or ↗Ⓐ	High	20	
Dragon Cannon	→ or ↘ or ↗Ⓑ +Ⓚ	Mid	38	Launches on hit
Nunchaku Slap ~Fury Kicks	⇦ⒶⓀⓀ	High, Low, High	18, 14, 28	
Venom Fangs ~Wing Sobat	ⒷⒷⒷⓀ	Mid, Mid, Mid, High	14, 12, 16, 25	
Snake Kiss ~Star Gale	⇦ⒷⓀ	Mid, High	14, 45	2nd attack guard Breaks. Input Ⓖ to cancel pose after Star Gale.
Twin Snakes ~Wavering Light	ⒶⒶⒷ+Ⓚ	High, High	10, 8	Final stance deflects mid attacks
Shin Breaker	Wavering Light Ⓐ	Low	28	Stuns on counter-hit
Wavering Dream ~Right Outer	Wavering Light Ⓑ ⒷⒶ	Mid, Mid, Mid, Mid, High	3, 3, 3, 3, 16	

Horizontal Attacks

Name	Command	Attack Level	Damage	Notes
Twin Snakes ~Right Cross	ⒶⒶ	High, High	10, 8	Shifts to Right Outer.
Stone Wall ~Left Outer	ⒶⓀ	High, Mid	12, 16	2nd attack stuns on hit. Shifts to Left Outer.
Lunging Snake ~Right Outer	⇨Ⓐ	High	14	Shifts to Right Outer
Lotus ~Behind Lower	⬂Ⓐ	Mid	18	Causes recoverable stun on counter-hit. Shifts to behind Lower.
Tongue	⇩Ⓐ	Sp.Mid	10	
Snake Scythe	⬃Ⓐ	Low	18	
Nunchaku Slap ~Behind Lower	⇦Ⓐ	High	18	Shifts to behind Lower
Nunchaku Slap to Steel Dragon ~Left Outer	⇦ⒶⒷ	High, High	18, 32	Shifts to Left Outer
Dandy Surprise ~Behind Lower	⇩⬂⇨Ⓐ	Low, Low, Low, Low, Low	8, 8, 8, 8, 8	Shifts to Behind Lower
Tongue	While Crouching Ⓐ	Sp.Low	10	
Rope Dancer ~Right Outer	While Crouching ⬂Ⓐ ⒶⒶ	Low, Low, Low	6, 6, 6	Shifts to Right Outer
Scythe Fang ~Left Outer	While Crouching ⬃ⒶⒷ	Low, Mid	18, 26	Shifts to Left Outer
Purity Cross ~Right Cross	While Rising Ⓐ	High	35	Shifts to Right Outer
Leaping Snake	Jumping Ⓐ	High	18 or 22 or 26	Damage varies depending on direction jumped in
Reverse Snake	Backturned Ⓐ	High	12	
Reverse Tongue	While Crouching Backturned Ⓐ	Low	13	

Vertical Attacks

Name	Command	Attack Level	Damage	Notes
Venom Fangs ~Left Outer	ⒷⒷ	Mid, Mid	14, 12	Shifts to Left Outer
Dragon Backfist	⇨ⒷⒷⒷ	Mid, Mid, High	10, 10, 28	Fully combos on counter-hit
Rising Fang ~Right Outer	⬂Ⓑ	Mid	22	Shifts to Right Outer
Falling Fang	⇩Ⓑ	Mid	14	
Inner Biting Upper	⬃Ⓑ	Mid	18	
Snake Kiss ~Left Outer	⇦Ⓑ	Mid	14	Shifts to Left Outer
Mantis Lunge ~Left Inner	⇩⬂⇨Ⓑ	Mid, Mid, Mid	8, 8, 8	Final attack stuns on hit. Shifts to Left Inner.
Crouching Inner Upper	While Crouching Ⓑ	Mid	14	
Rolling Biting Upper ~Left Inner	While Rising Ⓑ	Mid	20	Shifts to Left Inner
Falling Sky	Jumping Ⓑ	Mid	28 or 32 or 36	Damage varies depending on direction jumped in
Reverse Snake Bite	Backturned Ⓑ	Mid	16	
Reverse Biting Upper	While Crouching Backturned Ⓑ	Mid	17	

Kick Attacks

Name	Command	Attack Level	Damage	Notes
Fang Scratch	Ⓚ	High	14	
Left Roundhouse	⇨Ⓚ	High	22	
Snap Kick	⬂Ⓚ	Mid	14	
Illusion Kick ~Right Outer	⇩ⓀⒷ	Low, Mid	14, 20	Shifts to Right Outer
Illusion Low Kicks	⇩ⓀⓀ	Low, Low	14, 16	
Quick Slice	⬃Ⓚ	Low	10	
Right Roundhouse	⇦Ⓚ	High	26	
Hurricane	⇩⬂⇨Ⓚ	Mid, Mid, Mid, Mid	14, 10, 10, 10	Final attack stuns. Input Ⓖ during any hit to cancel following attack.
Hurricane (Cancel)	⇩⬂⇨ⓀⒼ	Mid	10	May be canceled during any hit
Quick Slice	While Crouching Ⓚ	Low	10	
Dragon Scream	While Rising ⓀⓀ	Mid, High	16, 22	
Reverse Roundhouse	Jumping Ⓚ	Mid	18 or 22 or 26	Damage varies depending on direction jumped in. ⬂Ⓚ loses launch properties.
Reverse Fang Scratch	Backturned Ⓚ	High	16	
Reverse Illusion Kick	While Crouching Backturned Ⓚ	Low	12	

8-Way Run

Name	Command	Attack Level	Damage	Notes
Snake's Tale	→Ⓐ	Mid, High	10, 18	
Striking Snake	↘ or ↗Ⓐ	High	20	
Northern Lights ~Left Inner	↓Ⓐ	Mid	16	Stuns on counter-hit. Shifts to Left Inner.
Northern Lights (Reverse)	↑Ⓐ	Mid	16	Stuns on counter-hit
Wave Slice	↙ or ↖Ⓐ	Low	30	
Propeller Nunchaku ~Right Outer	←ⒶⒷ	High, Mid, Sp.Mid, Sp.Mid	15, 5, 5, 5	Shifts to Right Outer
Steel Dragon ~Left Outer	→Ⓑ	High	32	Shifts to Left Outer
Branding Nunchaku ~Left Inner	→Ⓑ⇦	Mid, Mid, Mid, Mid, Mid	10, 30, 14, 14, 14	Shifts to Left Inner
Branding Nunchaku (Cancel)	→Ⓑ⇦ Ⓖ	Mid	10, 30	
Return of Fear ~Behind Lower	↘ or ↗Ⓑ	Mid	28	Shifts to Behind Lower
Cobra's Temple ~Right Cross	↘ or ↗ⒷⒶ	High	22	Shifts to Right Cross
Mark of the Beast	↓ or ↑Ⓑ	Mid, Mid, Mid, Mid	8, 8, 10, 10	Final attack stuns on hit
Reverse Snake Cross ~Right Cross	↙ or ↖Ⓑ	Mid	25	Shifts to Right Cross
Serpent's Breath ~Right Outer	←Ⓑ	Mid	34	Stuns on hit. Shifts to Right Outer.
Dragon Roar	→Ⓚ	High	28	
Back Kick	↘ or ↗Ⓚ	Mid	18	
Guillotine Kick	↓ or ↑ⓀⓀ	Low, Mid	15, 21	
Stone Kick	← or ↙ or ↖Ⓚ	High	27	
Dragon Cannon	→ or ↘ or ↗Ⓑ +Ⓚ	Mid	38	
Sliding	While Running Ⓚ	Low	26	

Simultaneous Press

Name	Command	Attack Level	Damage	Notes
Serpent's Pleasure	Ⓐ+Ⓑ	Mid, Mid	18, 29	
Serpent's Pleasure (Cancel) ~Right Cross	Ⓐ+ⒷⒼ	Mid	18	Shifts to Right Cross
Backfist Blow ~Behind Lower	⇨Ⓐ+Ⓑ	High	30	
Rage of Pleasure	⇦Ⓐ+Ⓑ	Mid, Mid	14, 14	
Rage of Pleasure (Hold)	⇦🅐+🅑	Mid, Mid	18, 14	1st attack Guard Breaks, makes 2nd attack a guaranteed hit
Dragon's Brand ~Left Inner	While Rising Ⓐ+Ⓑ	Mid	28	Causes recoverable stun on counter-hit
Dragon's Brand (Hold) ~Left Inner	While Rising 🅐 +🅑	Mid	36	Causes recoverable stun on counter-hit. Shifts to Left Inner.
Fury ~Right Outer	Ⓑ+ⓀⒷⒷ ⒷⒶ	Mid x 9	44(58)	Input final 3 commands with Just Frame timing for additional damage. Shifts to Right Outer.
Tiger Slaughter	⇩Ⓑ+ⓀⒷ	Low, Low	12, 18	1st attacks stuns against enemies lying on ground (⇩Ⓑ+Ⓚ cannot be done by itself for this to work)
Twisted Loop	⇦Ⓑ+Ⓚ	Mid	37, 12	Unblockable. Input Ⓖ to cancel.
Reverse Blow	Backturned Ⓑ+Ⓚ	Mid	38	Guard Breaks, stuns on hit
Left Inner	Ⓐ+Ⓚ or ⇧Ⓐ +Ⓚ			
Guillotine Dance	⇙Ⓐ+Ⓚ	Low, High	18, 24	
Right Outer ~Behind Lower	⇩Ⓐ+Ⓚ			
Taunt	Ⓚ+Ⓖ			

Throws

Name	Command	Attack Level	Damage	Notes
Falling Heaven Dragon	Ⓐ+Ⓖ	Throw	50	Input Ⓐ to escape
Lynching	Ⓑ+Ⓖ	Throw	50	Input Ⓑ to escape
Dragon Destroyer	Left Side Throw	Throw	60	Same button as throw (Ⓐ or Ⓑ) to escape
Leaving the Dragon Nest ~Behind Lower	Right Side Throw	Throw	55	Same button as throw (Ⓐ or Ⓑ) to escape
Parting the Waves	Back Throw	Throw	65	Same button as throw (Ⓐ or Ⓑ) to escape

Maxi

Right Outer

Name	Command	Attack Level	Damage	Notes
Dragon Bite ~Behind Lower	Right Outer Ⓐ	High	16	Shifts to Behind Lower
Dragon Bite	Right Outer ⒶⓀ	High, Mid	16, 20	
Dragon Bite (Hold)	Right Outer Ⓐ 🅚	High, Mid	16, 30	2nd attack Guard Breaks
Black Serpent ~Right Cross	Right Outer Ⓑ	Mid	24	Causes Recoverable stun on hit. Shifts to Right Cross.
Dragon Twister ~Left Outer	Right Outer ⓀⒶ	Mid, High, Mid	20, 20, 16	Final attack stuns on hit. Shifts to Left Outer.
Falling Dragon	Right Outer Ⓚ⇩Ⓐ	Mid, Low	20, 24	
Dragon Shadow ~Right Outer	Right Outer ⓀⒷ	Mid, Mid	20, 30	Final attack stuns on hit. Shifts to Right Outer.
Dragon Pounce	Right Outer ⓀⓀ	Mid, Mid	20, 18	
Dragon Pounce (Hold)	Right Outer Ⓚ 🅚	Mid, Mid	20, 30	
Right Outer ~Wavering Light	Right Outer Ⓑ + Ⓚ			Deflect mid attacks

Left Outer

Name	Command	Attack Level	Damage	Notes
Bloody Cross	Left Outer ⒶⓀ	Low, Mid	18, 25	
Wing Slice ~Right Cross	Left Outer Ⓑ	Mid	16	
Wing Sobat	Left Outer ⒷⓀ	Mid, High	16, 25	
Star Gale	Left Outer Ⓚ	High	45	Guard Breaks
Left Outer ~Wavering Light	Left Outer Ⓑ + Ⓚ			Deflects mid attacks

Left Inner

Name	Command	Attack Level	Damage	Notes
Serpent's Desire ~Behind Lower	Left Inner ⒶⒶ	Mid, Mid	14, 14	Shifts to Behind Lower
Serpent's Desire	Left Inner ⒶⒶⒷ	Mid, Mid, Mid	14, 14, 31	Final attack stuns on hit
Serpent's Desire (Delay)	Left Inner ⒶⒶⒷ (Delay)	Mid, Mid, Mid	14, 14, 30	
Serpent's Desire (Hold)	Left Inner ⒶⒶ 🅑	Mid, Mid, Mid	40	Final attack Guard Breaks
Canyon Carve ~Behind Lower	Left Inner Ⓑ	Mid	28	Shifts to Behind Lower
Canyon Carve (Cancel) ~Left Inner	Left Inner ⒷⒼ			Shifts to Left Inner
Canyon Carve (Hold)	Left Inner 🅑	Mid	38	Guard Breaks
Canyon Carve (Hold Cancel) ~Right Outer	Left Inner 🅑Ⓖ			Shifts to Right Outer
Wheel Kick	Left Inner Ⓚ	Mid	15	Stuns on counter-hit
Left Inner ~Wavering Light	Left Inner Ⓑ + Ⓚ			Deflects mid attacks

Right Cross

Name	Command	Attack Level	Damage	Notes
Tiger Pounce	Right Cross Ⓐ	Mid, Mid	15, 26	Both attacks stun on hit
Raging Ocean ~Right Cross	Right Cross ⒶⒶ	High	25	Shifts to Right Cross
Striking Fear ~Behind Lower	Right Cross ⒶⒷ	Mid	30	Shifts to Behind Lower
Double Hammer ~Left Outer	Right Cross Ⓑ		34	Guard Breaks, stuns on hit. Shifts to Left Outer.
Dragon Star	Right Cross ⓀⓀ Ⓚ(Just)	Low, Mid, High	14, 16,30	Final attack Guard Breaks
Right Cross ~Wavering Light	Right Cross Ⓑ + Ⓚ			Deflects mid attacks

Behind Lower

Name	Command	Attack Level	Damage	Notes
Water Cutter ~Left Inner	Behind Lower Ⓐ	Mid	18	Stuns on counter-hit. Shifts to Left Inner.
Nunchaku Lick ~Right Outer	Behind Lower Ⓑ	Low	16	Shifts to Right Outer
Fury Kicks	Behind Lower ⓀⓀ	Low, High	14, 28	
Behind Lower ~Wavering Light	Behind Lower Ⓑ + Ⓚ			Deflects mid attacks

Wavering Light

Name	Command	Attack Level	Damage	Notes
Shin Breaker	Wavering Light Ⓐ	Low	28	Stuns on counter-hit
Wavering Dream ~Right Outer	Wavering Light Ⓑ ⒷⒶ	Mid, Mid, Mid, Mid, High	3, 3, 3, 3, 16	
Black Lotus	Wavering Light Ⓚ	High	28	

Combos

⇘Ⓑ, Ⓐ
2 hits, 38 Damage
Counter-hit ⇘Ⓑ, Ⓑ
2 hits, 45 Damage
⇦ⒶⒷ, Ⓑ
3 hits, 61 Damage
Counter-hit ⇩⇩ⒶⓀ, ⇦ⒷⒷⓀ
5 hits, 54 Damage
Counter-hit ⇩⇩ⒶⓀ, Ⓑ + ⓀⒷⒷⒷⒶ, back-turned Ⓑ + Ⓚ
12 hits, 59 Damage
Counter-hit ⇧⇧Ⓐ, ⇨Ⓐ, ⒶⓀ
4 hits, 54 Damage
During Right Outer Ⓚ🅚, ⇨⇨Ⓑ + Ⓚ
3 hits, 73 Damage, second hit can be escaped with Just Ukemi
During Wavering Light ⒷⒷⒶ, back-turned Ⓑ + Ⓚ
7 hits, 65 Damage
Counter-hit ⇘Ⓐ, Ⓐ, ⒶⒶⒷ
5 hits, 65 Damage, first stun is recoverable
Counter-hit While Rising Ⓐ + Ⓑ, ⒶⒶⒷ
4 hits, 69 Damage, first stun is recoverable
⇦Ⓑ + Ⓚ, back-turned Ⓑ + Ⓚ
3 hits, 83 Damage, wait for enemy to hit ground before performing Ⓑ + Ⓚ

Close Range

Complex and always changing, Maxi's fighting style thrives at pointblank range. His main attack method is through his stances, which shift in and out of each other as he uses various strings. His strongest stance is the Right Cross, which is used mainly off of his Ⓐ Ⓐ string. This is the ideal chain to start an offensive because of its fast starting speed and ability to counter sidesteps. Regardless of whether your attack hits, stage a secondary offensive based on your enemy's anticipated defense measures. If you believe your foe will try to attack your recovery with a quick high string, perform the Dragon Star (during Right Cross Ⓚ Ⓚ Ⓚ) to duck under it; input Ⓖ after the final kick to cancel the taunt animation. Verify whether the first kick hits before you perform the remainder of the string. If you believe the enemy will try to stop your offense with a crouching attack, initiate the Double Hammer (during Right Cross Ⓑ) to leap over it. This attack is also a Guard Break that shifts into Maxi's Left Outer stance. So, if it's blocked, use the advantage to stage an attack; use Ⓑ Ⓚ to stop counterattacks or Ⓐ Ⓚ to hit standing opponents. Attack with the Tiger Pounce (during Right Cross Ⓐ) when your enemy is afraid of the low Dragon Star string.

Because Maxi's Ⓐ Ⓐ string hits high, it's vulnerable to crouching attacks. Compensate for this problem with the mid-hitting Rising Fang (↘ Ⓑ), which shifts into the Right Outer stance. Its importance stems from the ability to verify whether it has hit and select actions depending on the outcome. If it hits as a counter-hit, perform Right Outer's Black Serpent (Ⓑ) to slap your enemy to the ground. On a normal hit, perform the Dragon Bite (during Right Outer Ⓐ) to land a 2-hit combo. Then commence a second attack with either its mid-hitting Ⓚ extension or Behind Lower's Ⓚ Ⓚ string. When blocked, input Ⓐ Ⓚ to counter-hit attempts to quickly attack the Rising Fang's recovery. When your foe is afraid to attack, throw after you recover, or perform the Dragon Pounce (during Right Outer Ⓚ Ⓚ) to leap over crouching attacks aimed at punishing your throw or Ⓐ Ⓚ attack. Juggle after the Dragon Pounce with → → Ⓑ+Ⓚ for heavy damage.

Finally, attack with Maxi's ↓ Ⓚ Ⓚ and ↓ Ⓚ Ⓑ strings as an alternate method of making your enemy vulnerable to mid attacks. If the second hit of ↓ Ⓚ Ⓑ hits, follow up with → → Ⓑ+Ⓚ for a 2-hit combo.

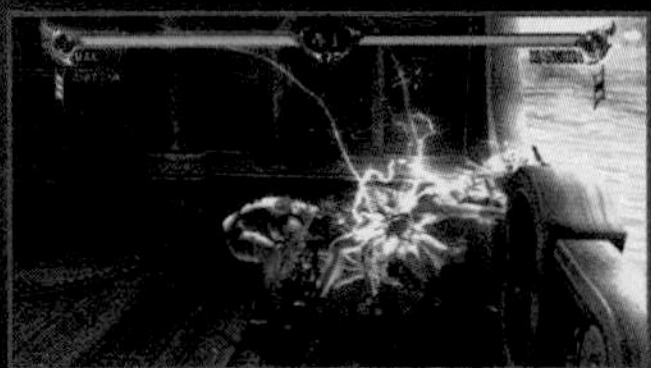

Mid Range

Your objective is to establish close range by knocking down your enemy, or by moving in when there's a gap in your foe's offense. Maxi has a lot of trouble at this distance, where his main attack options are completely ineffective. This is due to the terrible recovery time and attack range on many of his attacks. Because of this, you'll have to make due with just a small number of attacks. Dance in and out of your enemy's maximum attack range and closely watch his actions. If your foe mistakenly attacks when you're out of range, punish his recovery with ⇘ (or ⇙) Ⓐ or ⇘ (or ⇙) Ⓑ. To deal with an opponent's 8-Way Run usage, attack with either → → Ⓐ or ← ← Ⓐ Ⓑ. Using ← ← Ⓐ Ⓑ shifts into Right Outer, enabling you to utilize its close-range attack options regardless of whether it hits. Using ⇩ (or ⇧) Ⓐ also counters sidesteps and allows for follow-up combos (counter-hit ⇩ Ⓐ, Ⓚ, ← Ⓑ Ⓑ Ⓚ), but its slow wind-up time makes it difficult to land. If your enemy reacts to these attack methods with quick, horizontal strikes, like the universal Ⓐ Ⓐ string, either crouch and punish with While Rising Ⓚ Ⓚ or use ↘ Ⓐ+Ⓚ to slip under the opponent's string and knock him down. Finally, ⇗ (or ⇘) Ⓐ is a low attack with a ton of range. Use it from as far away as possible to control your enemy's movements and to catch standing guard attempts.

Long Range

Maxi's only means of punishing missed attacks is → → Ⓚ, a high jump-kick that knocks down on hit. Its high hit property makes it impossible to use against missed low attacks, so use it only against whiffed mids and highs. If you aren't willing to wait things out, attack with the mid Reverse Snake Cross (⇗ or ⇘) Ⓑ) or the Cobra's Temple (⇖ or ⇙ Ⓖ Ⓐ), both of which shift into the Right Cross stance. Cobra's Temple ducks under high attacks and stops sidesteps, so use it over the other option. If it's blocked, use the opportunity to stage an attack with the Right Cross options. Shift into the Ⓑ option if your enemy tries to do a low Ⓐ out of block-stun. Use its Ⓑ+Ⓚ deflect to stop verticals—hit Ⓚ after the deflect to punish the foe's move. Or use the Ⓚ Ⓚ Ⓚ string if the opponent uses his standing Ⓐ Ⓐ string. The Cobra's Temple is a high attack, so if you anticipate that your enemy will try to crouch under it, use the Reverse Snake Cross instead.

Special Tactics

Okizeme: Anti-Wakeup

The Rising Fang (↘ Ⓑ) is your most flexible mid attack. Use it on wakeup in the same way you would at close range. An alternate mid option is the Stone Kick (⇨ or ⇗ or ⇘ Ⓚ). Though it's less flexible than ↘ Ⓑ, it's safe when blocked and launches your enemy on a successful hit, enabling you to follow up with → → Ⓑ+Ⓚ for heavy damage. Go for this option when you're certain of a hit. When your enemy is afraid of this move, strike with the Guillotine Dance (↘ Ⓐ+Ⓚ), a quick low attack that hits for a ton of damage.

Pure Soul Loops

Maxi shifts into stances after many of his attacks, giving him access to new techniques. He doesn't idle in one stance indefinitely. Instead, he shifts between one to three stances before returning to a neutral position. However, it's possible to repeatedly and indefinitely cycle through stances by holding a direction after entering a stance. This process is called a "Pure Soul Loop." The order in which he progresses through stances depends on the direction held. This constant shifting initially makes it difficult to determine which attacks are available at any given time. However, you *can* learn the order in which the stances progress, enabling you to get the attacks you want when you need them. The following chart illustrates the order in which each command progresses through stances.

Pure Soul Loop Chart

Loop	Command	Stance Order
Pure Soul Loop	1	During stance ⇨: (Right Outer, Behind Lower, Right Cross) Repeat.
Pure Soul Loop	2	During stance ⇦: (Behind Lower, Left Outer, Right Cross) Repeat.
Pure Soul Loop	3	During stance ⇧: (Left Inner, Behind Lower, Right Outer) Repeat.
Pure Soul Loop	4	During stance ⇩: (Right Outer, Behind Lower, Left Inner) Repeat.

Heishiro Mitsurugi

Heishiro Mitsurugi

One should not look for anything else in the Way of the Samurai.
"Hagakure" Chapter I: 140, Tsunetomo Yamamoto (1659 - 1719)

Bio

Age:	29
Birthplace:	Bizen, Japan
Height:	5'7"
Weight:	143 lbs.
Birth Date:	June 8
Blood Type:	AB
Weapon:	Katana
Weapon Name:	Shishi-Oh
Discipline:	Tenpu-Kosai-Ryu Kai
Family:	Immediate family: All taken by sickness

Mitsurugi could feel the fire burning deep within his heart. The enemy he had long sought was close at last. Now everywhere he went, he heard the tales of tragedy and horror. The closer he drew to that place, the more the scars of violence lay upon the land. Unconsciously, his pace began to quicken.

Once, Mitsurugi had traveled the world so that he might learn how to defeat the rifle. But when at last he no longer feared that dreadful weapon, he continued his journey, seeking ever-stronger enemies to challenge. Yet no matter how powerful he became, no matter how polished his skills, he hungered for more. He thirsted for those moments when a mere flick of the wrist, a glint of light on a blade, separated life from death. At no other time did life's flame burn so brightly. But few opponents could give him what he sought, and the hollow, empty days stretched out before him.

In battle after battle, Mitsurugi learned that no matter how powerful the weapon a man bears, it is meaningless if he does not have the strength to match it. As time passed, and the old stories about Soul Edge and the Azure Knight began to fade from people's memories, even Mitsurugi lost interest in the legendary sword that was rumored to be the most powerful weapon of all.

More than ever before, Mitsurugi hungered for that ultimate moment in combat when life hung in the balance. But it was harder and harder to find, and though he desperately cut down foe after foe, they never lit a fire in his cold heart. Mitsurugi was a man turned an ogre, lusting only for the power of battle. It was then that he heard whispered voices, speaking among the shadows.

"Number Four. This must be the man who carries a fragment of Soul Edge," said the voice of a young woman.

"Indeed it is, Number Five," said another voice. It was an older man, standing deeper in the shadows. "You, there. You're going to tell us everything you know about your power and its connection to Soul Edge."

Mitsurugi answered by swinging his sword in a shining arc. In the heavy air, the two sides fought a deadly dance. The katana flashed once, twice, thrice, and two assassins lay dead at his feet.

"Bah. They were too weak."

Mitsurugi produced a bundle from within his tunic. He had almost forgotten about it, it was a metal shard, a fragment of Soul Edge.

"Useless junk."

So muttering, Mitsurugi was about to throw the bundle away, but then a strange sensation swept over him and the metal shard shone with an unholy brilliance. Unthinkingly, Mitsurugi let go of the fragment, and before his eyes, the unbelievable happened. The metal shard shone brighter still, leapt into the air, and flew toward the sky in the west.

Suddenly, Mitsurugi saw a vision of the Azure Knight with Soul Edge held in his gauntleted fist.

So Mitsurugi went west, following the rumors and tales. If the knight had indeed returned, perhaps he could at last slake his thirst, if only for a while. The shadow of the Azure Knight stretched deep and dark across his path, and the rumors he heard were more terrible than he could have imagined. The lands ahead of him were gripped in terror, and hordes of grotesque monsters and mad warriors were gathering there. But Mitsurugi was not afraid. On the contrary, the more he heard, the more his heart beat in excitement and anticipation.

At last he arrived at the cursed city that rose like a dagger from the flat plains, shrouded in a foreboding aura. Light gleamed from the metal of his blade and Mitsurugi trembled with joy. Oh, he knew whence this excitement came. No human adversary had been worthy of his skills. But this time, it was different!

Heishiro Mitsurugi

Shishi-Oh

Mitsurugi had a voracious appetite for learning sword fighting arts that would enable him to defeat the rifle, such as "iai," the simultaneous drawing and striking of the sword. He also sought a sword that was a match for his skills. After fighting many duels and battles with many different blades, he finally chose Shishi-Oh as his weapon.

Shishi-Oh has never since left Mitsurugi's side. The day he finally proved that he could defeat a rifle with only a sword, it was Shishi-Oh that he held in his hand.

A Japanese katana called "Shishi-Oh" is known to exist today, but it is not believed to be the same Shishi-Oh that Mitsurugi himself wielded.

Tenpu-Kosai-Ryu Kai

Though born a simple farmer, the young Mitsurugi soon exchanged his plowshare for a sword. His natural reflexes and physical gifts helped him survive while he honed his sword fighting skills on the countless battlefields that served as his training ground. He did not fight with the refined polish and smooth movements of the dojo sensei; his technique was crude, but deadly practical.

To cultivate a sophisticated facade and sell himself as a mercenary, he gave his rough fencing skills a name: Tenpu-Kosai-Ryu. But as time passed, Mitsurugi came to fear the power of the rifle and devoted himself to overcoming that threat. He crossed swords with every dueling master he could find, greedily absorbing their knowledge. Ultimately, he developed his techniques enough to add the suffix "Kai" ("improved") to the name of his school.

In the many years since, he has learned to move and fight like no other warrior, and Mitsurugi can now boast he fears no weapon—not even the rifle.

Command List

Signature Techniques

Name	Command	Attack Level	Damage	Notes
Stalk Reaper	⇩ⓀⒷ	Low, Mid	10(14), 18(22)	Perform input as slow as possible for additional damage (removes knockdown properties)
Sudden Gale	→Ⓐ	Mid	32	Causes recoverable stun on counter-hit
Divine Tale	↘ or ↗Ⓑ	Mid	38	
Drawn Breath ~Mist	⇦🅐	High	20	Shifts to Mist
Hell Divide ~Mist	←Ⓑ	Mid	24	Shifts to Mist
Water Parting Thrust	Mist stance ⓀⒷ	Low, High	14, 20	
Reaver ~Relic	⇨🅐	High	14	Shifts to Relic
Fire Brand	Relic stance Ⓑ	Mid	24	

Horizontal Attacks

Name	Command	Attack Level	Damage	Notes
Twin Splinters	ⒶⒶ	High, High	10, 10	
Reaver	⇨Ⓐ	High	14	
Reaver ~Relic	⇨🅐	High	14	Shifts to Relic
Splitting Gold	⇘Ⓐ	High	12	Stuns on counter-hit
Knee Slice	⇩Ⓐ	Sp.Low	10	
Shin Slicer	⇙Ⓐ	Low	30	
Shin Slicer (Hold)	⇙🅐	Low	35	
Shin Slicer Feint	⇙ⒶⒷ	Mid	30	Guard Break, recoverable stun on hit
Drawn Breath	⇦Ⓐ	High	20	
Drawn Breath ~Mist	⇦🅐	High	20	Shifts to Mist
Knee Slice	While Crouching Ⓐ	Sp.Low	10	
Trunk Slicer	While Rising Ⓐ	Mid	26	
Field Reave	Jumping Ⓐ	High	26 or 31 or 36	Damage varies depending on direction jumped in
Reverse Slice	Backturned Ⓐ	High	12	
Hidden Slice	While Crouching Backturned Ⓐ	Low	12	

Vertical Attacks

Name	Command	Attack Level	Damage	Notes
Forced Prayer Divide	ⒷⒷ	Mid, Mid	12, 16	
Mask	Ⓑ⇨	High	20	Stuns on counter-hit
Feint L	ⒷⒶ	Mid	28	Stuns on counter-hit
Gleaming Hilt	⇨Ⓑ	Mid	18	Stuns on counter-hit
Lion's Clutch	⇨ⒷⒶ+Ⓖ	Mid, Throw	18, 30	Stuns on counter-hit
Korefuji	⇨ⒷⒷ+Ⓖ	Mid, Throw	18, 35	Stuns on counter-hit
Heaven Cannon	⇘Ⓑ	Mid	20	
Rust	⇩Ⓑ	Mid	14	
Crest Cannon	⇙Ⓑ	Mid	18	
Wind Hole Vortex	⇦Ⓑ	Mid	24	Stuns on counter-hit
Wind Hole Vortex ~Mist	⇦🅑			Shifts to Mist
Step Stone Divide	⇩⇘⇨Ⓑ	Mid	25	
Step Stone Divide (Hold)	⇩⇘⇨🅑	Mid	40	
Upper Arch	While Crouching Ⓑ	Mid	15	
Time Hole	While Crouching ⇘Ⓑ	High	30	
Wing Blade ~Cold Stitch	While Crouching ⇙ⒷⒷ	Mid, Mid	24, 10	2nd attack stuns on aerial hit
Wing Blade ~Cold Stitch (Hold)	While Crouching ⇙Ⓑ🅑	Mid, Mid	24, 28	2nd attack Guard Breaks, stuns on aerial hit
Wind Divide	While Rising Ⓑ	Mid	22	
Shearing Knot	Jumping Ⓑ	Mid	22 or 27 or 32	Damage varies depending on direction jumped in
Reverse Divide	Backturned Ⓑ	Mid	16	
Hidden Divide	While Crouching Backturned Ⓑ	Mid	16	

Kick Attacks

Name	Command	Attack Level	Damage	Notes
Snap Kick	Ⓚ	High	14	
Obedience	ⓀⒷ	Mid, Mid	18, 30	2nd attack stuns on hit
Wheel Kick	⇨Ⓚ	High	18	
Front Kick	⇘Ⓚ	Mid	14	
Stalk Reaper	⇩ⓀⒷ	Low, Mid	10(14), 18(22)	Perform input as slow as possible for additional damage (removes knockdown properties)
Hem Stitch	⇙Ⓚ	Low	10	
Bullet Cutter	⇦ⓀⒷ	Mid, Mid	18, 28	
Hem Stitch	While Crouching Ⓚ	Low	10	
Front Kick	While Rising Ⓚ	Mid	16	
Jump Kick	Jumping Ⓚ	Mid	15 or 20 or 25	Damage varies depending on direction jumped in
Reverse Kick	Backturned Ⓚ	High	16	
Hidden Kick	While Crouching Backturned Ⓚ	Low	12	

Simultaneous Press

Name	Command	Attack Level	Damage	Notes
Steel Slicer	(A)+(B)	Mid, Mid	16, 20	
Triple Steel	(A)+(B) During Hit (B) (Just)	Mid, Mid, Mid	16, 20, 24	
Purifying Thrust	(A)+(B)⇨	Mid	55	
Dividing Thrust	(A)+(B)→	Mid	50	
Cold Stitch	⇩(A)+(B)	Mid	20	
Shin Vanish	While Crouching ⇙(A)+(B)	Low	28	
Wheel Slash	⇖ or ⇧ or ⇗(A)+(B)	Mid	44	Stuns on hit
Disembowel	(B)+(K)	High	28	Deflects vertical attacks, Stuns on hit
Mist	⇨(B)+(K)			Shifts to Mist
Relic	⇦(B)+(K)			Shifts to Relic
Samurai Tackle	Backturned (B)+(K)	Mid	28	Stuns on hit
Steel Roll	(A)+(K)	Mid	40	Deflect mid and high vertical attacks
Taunt	(K)+(G)			

8-Way Run

Name	Command	Attack Level	Damage	Notes
Sudden Gale	→(A)	Mid	32	Causes recoverable stun on counter-hit
Drawn Air	↘ or ↗(A)	Mid	26	
Drawn Air ~Relic	↘ or ↗(A)	Mid	26	Shifts to Relic
Rib Ripper	↓ or ↑(A)	Mid	20	Stuns only when used against stunned enemy
True Vacuum	↙ or ↖(A)	Low	32	
Ear Slicer	←(A)(A)	High, High	11, 29	2nd attack stuns on hit
Lantern Divide	→(B)(B)	Mid, Mid, Mid	24, 5, 20	
Divine Tale	↘ or ↗(B)	Mid	38	
Hell Flash	↓ or ↑(B)	Mid	28	Stuns on hit
Blunt Flames	↙ or ↖(B)(A)(B)	Mid, High, Mid	16, 14, 30	2nd attack stuns on counter-hit. 3rd attack stuns on hit.
Hell Flash ~Mist	↙ or ↖(B)(A)	Mid, High	16, 14	Shifts to Mist. 2nd attack stuns on counter-hit.
Hell Divide ~Mist	←(B)	Mid	24	Shifts to Mist. Stuns against enemies lying on ground
Rising Knee	→ or ↘ or ↗(K)	Mid	16	
Wheel Kick	↓ or ↑(K)	High	20	
Stalk Spin ~Relic	↙ or ↖(K)	Low	16	Shifts to Relic
Bullet Cutter	←(K)(B)	Mid, Mid	18, 28	
Phoenix Tail	8-Way Run Any Direction (A)+(B)	Mid	42	Stuns on hit
Phoenix Tail (Cancel)	8-Way Run Any Direction (A)+(B)(G)			
Driving Stitch	↓ or ↑(B)+(K)	Mid	26	Stuns on hit
Prime Moon Shadow	↓ or ↑(A)+(K)	High	30	Stuns on hit
Sliding	While Running (K)	Low	26	

Throws

Name	Command	Attack Level	Damage	Notes
Sea of Madness	(A)+(G)	Throw	40	Input (A) to escape
Zen Blade	(B)+(G)	Throw	50	Input (B) to escape
Gates of Hell	Left Side Throw	Throw	65	Same button as throw ((A) or (B)) to escape
8th Bill of Punishment	Right Side Throw	Throw	50	Same button as throw ((A) or (B)) to escape
Divine Gift	Back Throw	Throw	60	Same button as throw ((A) or (B)) to escape

Full Moon Death

Name	Command	Attack Level	Damage	Notes
Full Moon Death	⇨⇘⇩⇙⇦(B)			
Full Moon Death ~Full Moon Death	Full Moon Death stance ⇨⇘⇩⇙⇦			
Full Moon Disembowel	Full Moon Death stance (B)	Mid	65	Unblockable

Relic

Name	Command	Attack Level	Damage	Notes
Relic	⇦ or ←(B)+(K)			
Relic Step (Advance)	Relic stance ⇨⇨			
Relic Step (Retreat)	Relic stance ⇦⇦			
Relic ~Jump	Relic stance ⇖ or ⇧ or ⇗			
Relic ~Duck	Relic stance ⇩			
Parting Arc	Relic stance (A)	Sp.Mid, High	4, 16	
Parting Arc ~Mist	Relic stance (A)	Sp.Mid, High	4, 16	Shifts to Mist
Fire Brand	Relic stance (B)	Mid	24	
Relic Low Kick	Relic stance (K)	Low	24	
Relic Low Kick ~Relic	Relic stance (K)	Low	24	
Fire Cannon ~Relic	Relic stance (A)+(B)	High	26	Guard Break, stuns on hit
Cannon Divide ~Relic	Relic stance (A)+(B) (release early or late)	Mid	60(72)	Unblockable. Hold input for entire duration for full damage.
Blazing Steel	Relic stance (A)+(B) (release before full charge)	Low, Low	70	Unblockable
Mist	Relic stance (B)+(K)			Shifts to Mist
False Purification	Relic stance (A)+(B)+(K)		60	Deflects vertical attacks

Heishiro Mitsurugi

Mist

Name	Command	Attack Level	Damage	Notes
Mist	⇨ or ➡Ⓑ+Ⓚ			
Mist Step (Advance)	Mist stance ⇨⇨			
Mist Step (Retreat)	Mist stance ⇦⇦			
Mist ~Jump	Mist stance ⇖ or ⇧ or ⇗			
Mist ~Duck	Mist stance ⇩			
Full Moon Divide	Mist stance Ⓐ	High	24	
Wind Stitch	Mist stance ⒷⒷⒷ	High, High, High	8,8,10	
Wind Stitch ~Relic	Mist stance ⒷⒷ🅑	High, High, High	8,8,10	Shifts to Relic
Wind Torture	Mist stance Ⓑ⇦Ⓑ	High, Mid	8, 56	
Mist Pursuit	Mist stance ⒷⓀ	High, Low	8, 14	
Heavenly Dance	Mist stance ⇨ⒷⒷ	Mid, Mid	20, 30	
Heavenly Dance (Delay)	Mist stance ⇨ⒷⒷ	Mid, Mid	20, 20	
Heavenly Dance ~Relic	Mist stance ⇨🅑	Mid	20	Shifts to Relic
Purifying Thrust	Mist stance ⇦Ⓑ	Mid	48	
Dividing Thrust	Mist stance ⇦Ⓑ⇨	Mid	38	
Water Parting Thrust	Mist stance ⓀⒷ	Low, High	14, 20	
Divide	Mist stance Ⓐ+Ⓑ	Mid	30	Stuns on hit
Relic	Mist stance Ⓑ+Ⓚ			Shifts to Relic
Lion's Clutch	Mist stance Ⓐ+Ⓖ	Throw	35	
Korefuji	Mist stance Ⓑ+Ⓖ	Throw	40	

Combos

⇘Ⓑ, ⇦⇦ⒶⒶ

3 hits, 47 Damage

⇩ⓀⒷ, ⇨⇨Ⓚ

3 hits, 39 Damage, final attack can be avoided with Just Ukemi

Counter-hit ⇨⇨Ⓐ, Ⓐ + ⒷⒷ (Just)

4 hits, 80 Damage, first stun is escapable

Counter-hit ⇨⇨Ⓐ, ⇩⇩Ⓐ, ⇘Ⓐ, ⇦⇦Ⓑ, ⇨Ⓑ

5 hits, 82 Damage, first stun is escapable

Counter-hit ⇘Ⓐ, ⇦⇦Ⓑ, ⇨Ⓑ

3 hits, 42 Damage

During Mist, counter-hit ⒷⒷ🅑, 🅐, ⇨Ⓑ

6 hits, 65 Damage

During Mist, Ⓐ + Ⓑ, ⇘Ⓐ, ⇦⇦Ⓑ, ⇨ⒷⒷ

5 hits, 70 Damage

Counter-hit crouching ⇙Ⓑ🅑, ⇦⇦Ⓑ, ⇨Ⓑ

4 hits, 81 Damage

Counter-hit ⇨⇨Ⓐ, ⇩⇩Ⓐ, ⇙⇙Ⓑ🅐, Ⓑ⇦Ⓑ ➡ (wall hit), ⇘Ⓐ, ⇦⇦Ⓑ, ⇨ⒷⒷ

11 hits, 107 Damage, first stun is escapable

Close Range

The versatile Mitsurugi can play from any position, but his strongest is close range. Your objective is to condition your enemy into crouching with Mitsurugi's (A)(A) string or low attacks. This opens the window to landing Mitsurugi's Heaven Cannon (⇘(B)) or Splitting Gold (⇘(A)). Start your attack with (A)(A) to keep foes from sidestepping. If the attack hits, stage a secondary mix-up consisting of the Stalk Reaper (⇩(K)(B)), ⇗(A), ⇘(B), or a throw. If you're certain your enemy is looking to sidestep the ⇘(B) option, counter-hit his or her movement with ⇘(A). Go for ⇦⇦(B), ⇨(B) afterward to land heavy damage and a knockdown. If (A)(A) is blocked, crouch to avoid high attacks, or use Disembowel ((B)+(K)) to deflect mid strikes. Perform crouching Wing Blade ~Cold Stitch (while crouching ⇗(B)(B)) if you see a high attack whiff over you. This counter-hits your foe and allows the following combo: ⇗(B)(B), ⇨⇨(A)+(B).

As an alternate attack method, perform the Drawn Breath (⇦ (A)) or Hell Flash (↙ or ↖(B)(A)) to shift into the Mist stance. Throw after you enter the stance, or perform the Mist's (B)(B)(B) string to counter-hit quick standing attacks. This string shifts into the Relic stance, so if it hits, link into the Relic's (A) attack for a 5-hit combo. If your opponent tries to crouch (A) to stop the throw or the string, tap ⇧ to jump over it, then land and go for a mix-up. Vary between the Mist's mid Divide ((A) + (B)) or low Water Parting Thrust ((K)(B)) when you face opponents that are good at escaping throws. If (A) + (B) hits, combo ⇘(A), ⇦⇦(B), ⇨(B)(B). Use the Mist's Full Moon Divide ((A)) option to counter your foe's attempts to sidestep any of the above options.

Mid Range

Your goal is to establish close range. Do this by knocking down your enemy or by scaring your foe into guarding high so that you can move in with the Drawn Breath or Hell Flash. Stay out of your enemies' attack distance and carefully watch their actions. If they stick out any attacks, punish them with the Hell Flash (⬇ or ⬆(B)) or the Bullet Cutter (⇦(K)(B)). Stop slower strikes preemptively with the Mask ((B)⇨), which leads to giant combos on counter-hit, such as (B)⇨, ⇘(A), ⇦⇦(B), ⇨(B). Against careful players reliant on 8-Way Run or sidesteps to move around, use Sudden Gale (⇨⇨(A)) to counter-hit their movements. Follow up with the (A) + (B)(B) Just Frame extension. Never let foes think that they're safe. Pressure them with ⬇(B) to get them to stand, then go for ⇗(A) to knock them down or make them guard your ⇦ (A) to start a Mist stance offense.

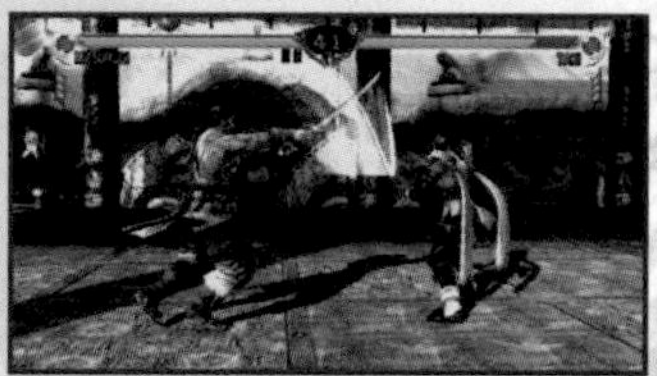

Long Range

Mitsurugi's options are extremely limited from long range. Move into mid or close range through careful movement and baiting enemy attacks. Move in and out of your opponent's attack range to coerce him into attacking. If he whiffs a move, crush it with the Phoenix Tale (During 8-Way Run (A) + (B)). The Phoenix Tale can also be faked by inputting (G) just before the slash hits. This is horrifyingly useful for quickly moving into close range while luring your opponent into guarding high. Attack with ⇩(K)(B) or a throw afterward for stunning results. If your foe uses a lot of circular movement, go for ⇗(A) to hit him. You can also use this to slip under long-range horizontals.

Special Tactics

Okizeme: Anti-Wakeup

Your basic attack options include ⇩(K)(B), ⇘(B), and ⬇ or ⬆(B)+(K). The slowest attack of this group is ⬇(B)+(K), but it leads to massive combos on a successful hit. Link after it with ⇘(B), ⇦⇦(A)(A) to perform a 4-hit combo.

Another versatile option is ⇗(A). This tricky low attack shifts into a mid-hitting Guard Break (input ⇗(A)(B)), which is difficult to block if enemies expect the low variation—link into ⇨⇨(B)(B) if this attack hits. You can also charge ⇗(A) by holding down the command, slowing its attack speed to make it look like you're going for the mid variation.

Attack with the mid Cold Stitch (⇩(A) + (B)) when you're unsure of a successful hit. Though it doesn't inflict much damage, it's completely safe when guarded, and it leaves Mitsurugi with a massive advantage when it hits, allowing to you follow up with a throw without the risk of counterattack. Your opponent's only means of avoiding the throw is to break it or crouch under it. Counter crouch attempts by attacking with ⇘(B), and mix between both throw options to lower the risk of escapes.

Relic

The Relic stance acts as defensive posture to counter your enemy's actions. Though the options out of it are not mix-up heavy, they can stop any countermeasure your foes have up their sleeves. For example, input ⇩ to duck under your foe's fast high attacks. When his or her attack whiffs overhead, press (A) to punish the opponent's move with the Relic's fastest attack. Use the Parting Arc ((A)) to also stop sidestep attempts. To counter low or middle attacks, input (A)+(B)+(K) to initiate the False Purification deflect. Also use Relic's Fire Brand ((B)) attack to sidestep passed verticals.

When your enemy is afraid of the above counter options, you can then take advantage of Relic's low (K), mid (B), and its (A)+(B) Guard Break. In particular, (A)+(B) shifts back into the Relic stance, enabling you to score a free (A) when your enemy is open.

Nightmare

Lo! the fell monster with the deadly sting!
Who passes mountains, breaks through fenced walls
And firm embattled spears, and with his filth
Taints all the world!

"La Divina Commedia: Inferno" Canto 17, Dante Alighieri (1265–1321)

Bio

Age:	Existed since ancient times as Soul Edge
Birthplace:	Unknown
Height:	5'6"
Weight:	212 lbs.
Birth Date:	Unknown
Blood Type:	None
Weapon:	Soul Edge (Zweihander type)
Weapon Name:	Soul Edge
Discipline:	The Memories that Stain his Armor
Family:	All life is but prey to satiate his hunger.

Soul Edge, the Cursed Sword

They said it was the greatest of all weapons. They said it was the weapon of heroes. Soul Edge, a weapon steeped in history and shrouded in legend. But the truth is that it is a cursed sword, which controls those who would wield it and consumes the souls of those it cuts down.

It began, in ancient times, as nothing but a commonplace battle sword. But the more battlefields it saw, the more blood that it tasted, the more Soul Edge began to control the men who wielded it, pushing them to feed it more of the souls that its insatiable thirst demanded. It learned to transform itself to best suit the fighter who held it, so that together they could slay even more victims. Human war conceived and gave birth to this monstrous existence.

The evil sword continues to grow. Countless souls, countless hates, countless sorrows swirl within its hard metal embrace.

The Memories that Stain His Armor

Nightmare, the Azure Knight, and his reign of terror appeared quite suddenly in Europe. In reality, the knight was Siegfried, his soul possessed by the cursed sword Soul Edge. Driven mad by the knowledge that he had slain his father, Siegfried was all too ready to believe the lies Soul Edge whispered in his ear that if only he harvested enough souls, his slain father would be resurrected.

In the fight with the spirit sword Soul Calibur, he was finally released from the spell. Soul Edge was smashed into shards and the demon that wielded it disappeared. But the evil memories lingered, surviving within the azure armor. None of the evil, none of the atrocities was forgotten. The memories of Siegfried, of the people who had suffered under his tyranny, and of the cursed sword itself, all lived on. The sword in the armor willed an immortal sorcerer named Zasalamel to come to it. Zasalamel, who sought to use the power of both good and evil, enabled the cursed sword's spirit to obtain a new temporary vessel.

And so the cursed sword was freed. Soul Edge is whole once more, and soon the world will again be hurled into a maelstrom of blood and chaos.

Command List

Signature Techniques

Name	Command	Attack Level	Damage	Notes
Right Slasher	→ or ↘ or ↗Ⓐ	High	34	
Rook Splitter	↓ or ↑Ⓑ	Mid	38	
Shadow Slicer ~Grim Stride	⇙Ⓐ⇨	Low	32	Shifts to Grim Stride
Ether Splitter ~Grim Stride	↘ or ↗Ⓑ⇨	Mid	21	Shifts to Grim Stride
Grim Launcher ~Night Side Stance	Grim Stride Ⓑ	Mid	30	Launches on counter-hit
Soul Wave	Grim Stride Ⓐ+Ⓑ	Mid	30	Leaves Nightmare in powered up state
Death Smash ~Night Side Stance	⇖Ⓑ	Mid	16(26)	Shifts to Night Side Stance. Guard Breaks when powered up. Launches and deals additional damage at close distances.
Night Side Stance	Standing or While Crouching Ⓑ+Ⓚ			
Cannonball Feint ~Night Side Stance	Night Side Stance Ⓐ	Mid	20	Shifts to Night Side Stance
Skull Chopper	Night Side Stance ⒷⒶ	High	32(42)	Input as fast as possible for additional damage

Horizontal Attacks

Name	Command	Attack Level	Damage	Notes
Slash Cross	ⒶⒶⒷ	High, High, Mid	14, 16, 30	3rd hit stuns
Slash Cross (Delay)	ⒶⒶⒷ	High, High, Mid	14, 16, 30	3rd hit stuns
Slash Cross ~Night Side Stance	Ⓐ	High	14	Shifts to Night Side Stance
Triple Grounder	Ⓐ⇩ⒶⒶ	High, Low, Low	14, 18, 28	
Bloody Hilt	ⒶⒷ	High	22	
Bloody Hilt ~Night Side Stance	ⒶⒷ	High	22	Shifts to Night Side Stance
Quick Neck Buster	ⒶⒼⒶ	High	28(32)	Guard Breaks. Perform input as fast as possible for additional damage.
Quick Temple Buster	⇨Ⓐ	High	28	
Mail Crusher	⇖ⒶⒶ	Mid, Mid	20, 280	1st attack stuns on counter-hit
Death Grounder	⇖Ⓐ⇩Ⓐ	Mid, Low	20, 26	1st attack stuns on counter-hit
Death Grounder ~Grim Stride	⇖Ⓐ⇩Ⓐ⇨	Mid, Low	20, 26	1st attack stuns on counter-hit. Shifts into Grim Stride.
Jade Slicer	⇩Ⓐ	Low	18	
Shadow Slicer	⇙Ⓐ	Low	32	
Shadow Slicer (Hold)	⇙Ⓐ	Low	52	Guard Breaks
Jade Crusher	⇙ⒶⓀ	High	60	
Shadow Slicer ~Grim Stride	⇙Ⓐ⇨	Low	32	Shifts into Grim Stride
Back Blade	⇦Ⓐ	High	36	Guard Breaks, stuns on hit
Leg Slash	While Crouching Ⓐ	Low	12	
Death Rage	While Rising ⒶⒶ	Mid, Mid	20, 30	
Death Rage ~Grim Stride	While Rising Ⓐ Ⓐ→	Mid	20	Shifts to Grim Stride
Fatal Spin Slash	Jumping Ⓐ	High	28 or 30 or 32	Damage varies depending on direction jumped in
Turning Head Slash	Backturned Ⓐ	High	18	
Turning Leg Slash	While Crouching Backturned Ⓐ	Low	14	

Vertical Attacks

Name	Command	Attack Level	Damage	Notes
Knight Breaker	ⒷⒷⒷ	Mid, Mid, Mid	15, 10, 25	3rd attack stuns on hit. String fully combos on counter-hit.
Backspin Temple Buster	ⒷⒶ	High	28	Stuns on hit
Backspin Temple Buster ~Grim Stride	ⒷⒶ⇨	High	28	Stuns on hit. Shifts to Grim Stride.
Quick Revenge	⇨Ⓑ	Mid	20	
Quick Revenge (Additional attack)	⇨Ⓑ During Hit Ⓑ (Just)	Mid, Mid	20, 21	Guard Breaks when Nightmare is powered up
Death Smash	⇘Ⓑ	Mid	16(26)	Launches and deals additional damage at close distances. Guard Breaks when Nightmare is powered up.
Death Smash ~Night Side Stance	⇘🅑	Mid	16(26)	Shifts to Night Side Stance. Launches and deals additional damage at close distances. Guard Breaks when Nightmare is powered up.
Shadow Buster	⇩Ⓑ	Mid	20	
Reaver	⇙Ⓑ	Mid	24	Causes recoverable stun on counter-hit
Reaver ~Night Side Stance	⇙🅑	Mid	24	Stuns on counter-hit. Shifts to Night Side Stance.
Midnight Launcher	⇦Ⓑ	Mid	36	Guard Breaks
Split Buster	While Crouching Ⓑ	Mid	23	
Death Horn Charge	While Crouching ⇘Ⓑ	Mid	40	
Upper Claw	While Rising Ⓑ	Mid	16	Stuns on counter-hit. Always stuns when Nightmare is powered up.
Upper Claw ~Night Side Stance	While Rising 🅑	Mid	16	Stuns on counter-hit. Shifts into Night Side Stance.
Fatal Buster	Jumping Ⓑ	Mid	26 or 28 or 30	Damage varies depending on direction jumped in
Turning Sword Buster	Backturned Ⓑ	Mid	20	
Turning Shadow Buster	While Crouching Backturned Ⓑ	Mid	22	

Grim Stride

Name	Command	Attack Level	Damage	Notes
Grim Stride	⇩⇘⇨			
Grim Fang	Grim Stride Ⓐ	High	16	Stuns on counter-hit. Deflects mid attacks.
Grim Launcher	Grim Stride Ⓑ	Mid	30	Launches on counter-hit
Grim Launcher ~Night Side Stance	Grim Stride 🅑	Mid	30	Launches on counter-hit. Shifts to Night Side Stance.
Grim Launcher ~Grim Stride	Grim Stride Ⓑ⇨	Mid	30	Shifts to Grim Stride
Grim Roundhouse	Grim Stride ⓀⓀ	Mid, High	10, 13	
Soul Wave	Grim Stride Ⓐ+Ⓑ	Mid	30	Leaves Nightmare in powered up state

Kick Attacks

Name	Command	Attack Level	Damage	Notes
Dark High Kick	Ⓚ	High	14	
Jade Strike	⇨Ⓚ	High	20	
Dark Middle Kick	⇘Ⓚ	Mid	16	
Dark Middle Kick (Hold)	⇘🅚	Mid	30	
Stomping	⇩Ⓚ	Low	14	
Stomping (Hold)	⇩🅚	Low	22	Unblockable
Grind Low Kick	⇙Ⓚ	Low	12	
Double Death Claw	⇦ⓀⓀ	Mid, High	16, 20	Second attack may be delayed, fully combos on counter-hit
Double Death Thrust	⇦🅚Ⓑ	Mid, Mid	18, 21	
Double Death Thrust (Additional attack)	⇦🅚Ⓑ During Hit Ⓑ (Just)	Mid, Mid, Mid	20, 21, 21	
Grind Low Kick	While Crouching Ⓚ	Low	12	
Phantom Knee	While Rising Ⓚ	Mid	24	
Fatal Brave Kick	Jumping Ⓚ	Mid	14 or 18 or 20	Damage varies depending on direction jumped in
Turning Dark High Kick	Backturned Ⓚ	High	18	
Turning Dark Low Kick	While Crouching Backturned Ⓚ	Low	12	

Simultaneous Press

Name	Command	Attack Level	Damage	Notes
Soul Wave	Ⓐ+Ⓑ	Mid	30	Nullifies 1 hit (Nightmare still receives damage, but continues attack), deflects all following attacks after first nullification. Leaves Nightmare in powered up state.
Dark Soul Impact	⇘Ⓐ+Ⓑ	Low	34	
Soul Smasher	⇩Ⓐ+Ⓑ	Mid	10(32)	Performs special hit throw against fallen enemies (leaves Nightmare powered up after it hits)
Soul Blaze	⇦Ⓐ+Ⓑ	Mid	48	Unblockable. Input Ⓖ to cancel.
Soul Wave	Backturned Ⓐ+Ⓑ	Mid	30	Leaves Nightmare in powered up state
Night Side Stance	While Standing or While Crouching Ⓑ+Ⓚ			
Bloody Jade Impact	⇩Ⓑ+Ⓚ	Mid	30	Guard Breaks
Dark Bite	Backturned Ⓑ+Ⓚ	High	43	Special hit throw. Can grab airborne enemies.
Dark Bite	Ⓐ+Ⓚ	High	40	
Taunt	Ⓚ+Ⓖ			

8-Way Run

Name	Command	Attack Level	Damage	Notes
Right Slasher	→ or ↘ or ↗Ⓐ	High	34	
Shadow Cross Divide	↓ or ↑ⒶⒷ	High Mid	18, 26	2nd attack stuns on hit
Alternate Cross	← or ↙ or ↖Ⓐ	High	36	
Hell Slayer	→Ⓑ	Mid	36	Guard Breaks when Nightmare is powered up
Ether Splitter	↘ or ↗Ⓑ	Mid	21	
Ether Splitter ~Grim Stride	↘ or ↗Ⓑ⇨	Mid	21	Shifts to Grim Stride
Rook Splitter	↓ or ↑Ⓑ	Mid	38	
Darkness Impact	↙ or ↖Ⓑ	Low	24	
Shadow Breaker	←ⒷⒷ	Mid, Mid	30, 33	2nd attack stuns on ground hit
Shadow Breaker ~Night Side Stance	←ⒷⒷ	Mid, Mid	30, 30	2nd attack stuns on ground hit. Shifts to Night Side Stance.
Shoulder Rush	→ or ↘ or ↗Ⓚ	Mid	20	
Shoulder Rush ~Grim Stride	→ or ↘ or ↗Ⓚ⇨	Mid	20	Shifts into Grim Stride
Jade Smasher	↓ or ↑Ⓚ	Mid	28	
Jade Smasher ~Grim Stride	↓ or ↑Ⓚ⇨	Mid	28	Shifts into Grim Stride
Darkside Kick	↙ or ↖Ⓚ	Mid	24	
Drop Kick	←Ⓚ	High	46	Guard Breaks
Flying Edge	→Ⓐ+Ⓑ	Mid	48	
Cannonball Splitter	→Ⓑ+Ⓚ	Mid, Mid, Mid	10, 10, 25	Leaves Nightmare in crouching state
Sliding	While Running Ⓚ	Low	26	

Night Side Stance

Name	Command	Attack Level	Damage	Notes
Night Side Stance	While standing or While Crouching Ⓑ+Ⓚ			
Cannonball Feint	Night Side Stance Ⓐ	Mid	20	
Cannonball Feint ~Night Side Stance	Night Side Stance Ⓐ	Mid	20	Shifts into Night Side Stance
Phantom Impact	Night Side Stance Ⓑ	Low	28	
Skull Chopper	Night Side Stance ⒷⒶ	High	32(42)	Perform input as fast as possible for additional damage (Just)
Night Front Kick	Night Side Stance Ⓚ	High	16	Stuns on counter-hit
Phantom Splitter	Night Side Stance Ⓐ+Ⓑ	Mid	26	Guard Breaks when Nightmare is powered up
Grim Stride	Night Side Stance ⇩⬂⇨			

Throws

Name	Command	Attack Level	Damage	Notes
Shoulder Claw Throw	Ⓐ+Ⓖ	Throw	55	Input Ⓐ to escape
Soul Devour	Ⓑ+Ⓖ	Throw	50	Input Ⓑ to escape
Doom's Invitation	Left Side Throw	Throw	55	Same button as throw (Ⓐ or Ⓑ) to escape
Unholy Terror	Right Side Throw	Throw	65	Same button as throw (Ⓐ or Ⓑ) to escape
Witch Hunt	Back Throw	Throw	65	Same button as throw (Ⓐ or Ⓑ) to escape
Flap Jack	While Crouching Ⓐ+Ⓖ	Low	30	Input Ⓐ to escape
Over Toss	While Crouching Ⓑ+Ⓖ	Low	20	Input Ⓑ to escape
Soul Smasher	Against Downed Foe ⇩Ⓐ+Ⓑ	Throw	32	Leaves Nightmare in powered up state.

Combos

⬃Ⓑ, Ⓚ
2 hits, 40 Damage
Counter-hit ⬃Ⓑ, Ⓐ + Ⓑ, ⇩Ⓐ + Ⓑ
3 hits, 68 Damage
While Rising Ⓑ, ⒷⒶ (Just)
2 hits, 51 Damage
Counter-hit While Rising Ⓑ, Ⓐ + Ⓑ, ⇩Ⓐ + Ⓑ
3 hits, 58 Damage
⬂Ⓑ, ⒷⒶ⬂ⒷⒷⒶ (Just)
2 hits, 61 Damage
⇨⇨Ⓐ, ⇩⬂⇨ⓀⓀ
3 hits, 54 Damage
⬃Ⓐ →, ⓀⓀ
3 hits, 53 Damage
⇨⇨Ⓑ, Ⓐ + Ⓚ
2 hits, 68 Damage
⇨⇨Ⓑ, While Rising Ⓑ, ⒷⒶ (Just)
3 hits, 77 Damage, input ↓ⒼⒷ to quickly perform While Rising attack
↘ or ↗Ⓑ →, Ⓑ + Ⓚ
3 hits, 56 Damage
⇩⬂⇨, Ⓑ →, ⓀⓀ
3 hits, 49 Damage
Counter-hit ⇩⬂⇨, Ⓐ, ⇦ⓀⓀ
3 hits, 49 Damage
ⒷⒶ →, Ⓐ, ⒶⒷ, Ⓚ, ⇩Ⓐ + Ⓑ
5 hits, 77 Damage, must be performed against wall

Close Range

Nightmare's close-range options are quite powerful, but their horrendous starting speeds make it difficult to use them in any situation where he hasn't knocked down his enemy. Thus, he has a difficult time against speedy characters at close range, like Taki, who relies on fast, high attacks to pin down her enemy. That said, your objective is to either knock down your enemy or escape to a further distance away. Effectively using Nightmare's defensive options is the key here. The most prominent of these is his Upper Claw (While Rising B). If it strikes as a counter-hit, launch your enemy with A+B, then ↓A+B. This combo inflicts massive damage to the enemy while knocking down him or her next to you, the perfect position for staging an anti-wakeup attack. A second, more risky way of stopping an offense is the Soul Wave (A+B) explosion, which deflects high attacks while blasting your foe away from you. This also leaves Nightmare in a powered-up state (see Soul Wave Power-Ups), the perfect opportunity to pursue your fallen enemy.

An advanced way to punish throw attempts and some close-range attacks is to use Backspin Temple Buster (BA⇨). This attack moves Nightmare backward while performing a high slash, evading and stunning your opponent. When it hits, hold ⇨ to shift into the Grim Stride, and then link KK for a 3-hit combo. Against cornered opponents it's possible to link into the Grim Stride's A attack, which leaves the enemy vulnerable to A, K, ↓A+B.

If all else fails, rely on Guard Impacts and sidesteps to avoid enemy attack. If you ever see a gap in your foe's offense, back-step out of attack range or use the Shoulder Rush (⇨K⇨) to shift into an aggressive posture. Nightmare's AB is also useful for switching into an aggressive stance at this distance. If it hits your enemy, link into the Night Side Stance's Night Front Kick (K) attack to knock down your foe. When blocked, take advantage of the stance's Phantom Impact (B) and Cannonball Feint (A) options to stage a basic 2-way guessing game.

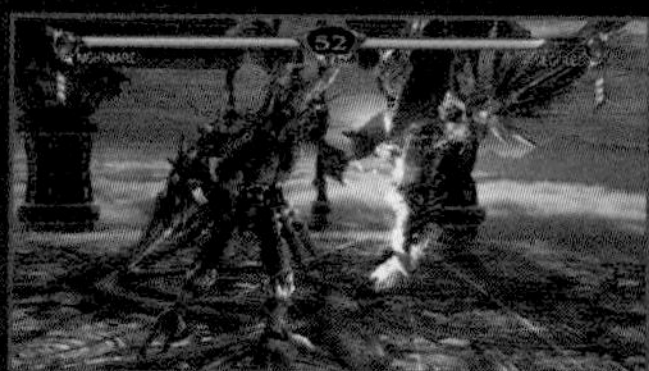

Mid Range

Your strategy is to stop your enemy's attempts to circle around your attacks, scaring him or her into fighting on a linear path. This opens the opportunity to use the more threatening options in Nightmare's arsenal, which are vulnerable to sidesteps. A powerful means of stopping side movement is the Shadow Cross Divide (⇩or⇧AB). Both of this string's hits combo together on counter-hit for a ton of damage. It is vulnerable to fast attacks when blocked, making it risky to use. A safer way to accomplish your objective is to use Nightmare's A slash, a horizontal attack that shifts into his Night Side Stance. It not only deters sidesteps, but it also starts a varied offense that potentially leads to big damage. For example, attack your enemy with Nightmare's A swing, then use the Night Side Stance's mid-hitting A or low-hitting B options to stage a basic 2-way guessing game. The A option counters sidesteps and also shifts back into the Night Side Stance. If the slash hits your enemy, link into the Night Front Kick (during Night Side Stance K) to score a 2-hit combo. When it's blocked, use the K attack to stop your foe's attempts to attack your recovery. Strike with the Night Side Stance's A or B options when enemies are afraid to attack. Note that the Night Side Stance can also shift into the Grim Stride. Use it to quickly approach and surprise your enemy with its many options.

Because the aforementioned circular attacks hit high, and because your foe can't sidestep, his or her counter to the situation is to crouch. Use this to your advantage and attack with the mid strings ↘AA and ↘A↓A. Both options start with the same hit and then end with a mid or low attack. The ↘A↓A string shifts into the Grim Stride, enabling you to combo its KK string on a successful hit. If your enemy is near a wall, go for the Quick Revenge (→B during hit B mid attack, which inflicts massive damage while also setting up a wall stun. Mix between these actions and Nightmare's potent low attacks, like his Darkness Impact (⇙or⇘B) or Shadow Slicer (↙A), to crack through your foe's defense plan.

Long Range

Though they're risky, Nightmare has many high-damage options at this distance. Your goal is to rapidly move in and out of your enemy's maximum attack distance to coerce a sporadic attack. If your foe misses a move, punish him with ⇖ (or ⇗) B⇨, B+K. In cases where you time ⇖B⇨ poorly and your enemy blocks it, use the Grim Slide to move into close range. Come out of the movement with its A option to deflect high or middle attacks, the mid-hitting B option, or let the slide recover and perform the Flap Jack (↓A+G).

If your enemy's side movements give you trouble, use the Right Slasher (⇖ or ⇨ or ⇗A) to stop them. On a successful hit, input ↓↘→KK afterward to score a 3-hit combo. The threat of this attack opens the window to other options, such as Dark Soul Impact (↘A + B), or to simply use ⇖B⇨ to move into close range with the Grim Stride.

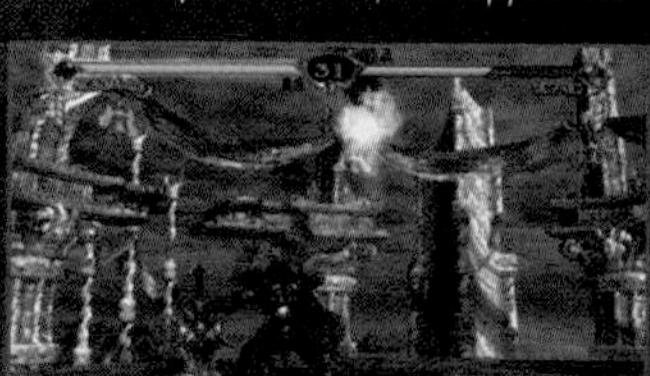

Special Tactics

Okizeme: Anti-Wakeup

Nightmare's basic anti-wakeup options revolve around the Shadow Slicer (↙A) and Midnight Launcher (←B). The low hit ↙A shifts into the Grim Stride (↙A⇨), allowing damaging combos on a successful hit, such as ↙A⇨, KK. You can also charge this attack (↙A) to change it into a Guard Break, a useful option that allows follow-up Grim Slide attacks when ↙A is blocked. The mid Guard Break attack ←B launches your foe into the air. Both moves have a blue lightning effect during their wind-up period, making it difficult for your enemy to distinguish between them. Use both of these options when your enemy is knocked away from you, like after you land a counter-hit Double Death Claw (←KK).

The mid attack Reaver (↙B) is another strong option that shifts directly into the Night Side Stance. If it successfully hits, immediately perform the Night Front Kick (during Night Side Stance K) to score a 2-hit combo. When guarded, vary between the Night Side Stance's low attack (B) and mid attack (A) options. The A option shifts back into the Night Side Stance, enabling you to combo its K attack if it hits. Furthermore, if AB manages to connect as a counter-hit, link directly into the Night Side Stance's A+B launcher, and then stab your falling foe with ↓A+B for a 3-hit combo. This combo leaves your enemy directly next to you, enabling you to go for ↙B again, or the low attack of your choice, preferably the Flap Jack.

Use Nightmare's Flap Jack (↓A + G or ↓B + G) as the low-hitting counterpart to ↙B. Both versions of the throw carry different properties. The ↓A + G version is even useful for scoring a Ring Out near an arena's edge.

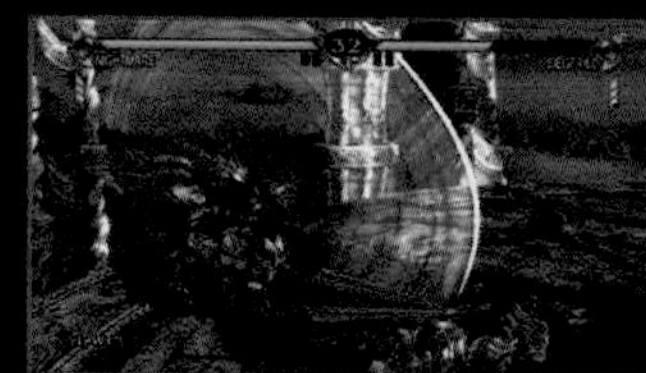

Grim Stride Options

Inputting the command ↓↘→ initiates the Grim Slide, a forward dash with three distinct attacks: the high Grim Fang (A), the Grim Launcher (B), and the combo-oriented Grim Roundhouse (KK). The Grim Fang is the most important of these options, as it hits sidesteps, stuns on counter-hit, and deflects mid and high attacks. Use it to counter your enemy's attempts to stop the Grim Stride. On a successful counter-hit, link into ←KK for a 3-hit combo. It's considered a high hit, so your foe's counter for it is to simply crouch or guard. If your opponent tries to crouch, use the Grim Launcher mid attack. Hold ⇨ if it hits, and perform the Grim Roundhouse to combo your fallen enemy.

The Grim Stride leaves Nightmare in a crouching state near the end of its recovery. This is particularly useful for initiating the low Flap Jack throw (↓A+G or ↓B+G). Use this technique to go for the low attack when your adversary is wary of the mid-hitting Grim Launcher.

Soul Wave and Soul Smasher Power-Ups

Nightmare's A+B and ↓A+B (on successful ground hit only) power up many of his attacks, improving their damage and giving most of them the ability to Guard Break. The attacks it enhances include his ↘B, →BB(Just), ⇨B, While Rising B, and Night Side Stance A+B. Keep this in mind after a successful power-up.

Nightmare

Raphael Sorel

Raphael Sorel

The dictates of the heart are the voice of fate.

"Wallenstein," Friedrich Schiller (1759 - 1805)

Bio

Age:	32
Birthplace:	Rouen, French Empire
Height:	5'10"
Weight:	159 lbs.
Birth Date:	November 27
Blood Type:	A
Weapon:	English Sword Rapier
Weapon Name:	Flambert
Discipline:	La Rapière des Sorel
Family:	Foster daughter: Amy

He looked heavenward. The full moon— [illegible] darkness of the forest, he had at [illegible] as a Holy Stone with the power to [illegible] Soul Calibur had [illegible] Soul Edge's [illegible]

To Raphael, Amy was everything. He had even since [illegible] creating a world Amy could call home. But a greater power [illegible] transformed began to come to their senses. [illegible] there existed something stronger than the evil sword. Soul Edge [illegible] another way! And thus, after routing the forces surrounding the town, [illegible] learned was called the "Holy Stone."

As he searched for this stone, or something similar to it, Raphael [illegible] ends meet to possibly concern themselves with the sort of power he [illegible] those who traveled from land to land, hoping for news from the outside. He [illegible] towns and forced to live in the forest, feared and alienated for their [illegible] susceptible to Soul Edge's effects over the past few years, surely they [illegible]

Here the shards of the cursed sword Raphael had been collecting [illegible] necessary, he slowly closed in on those he sought, until at long last [illegible] out some time ago, who called themselves the "guardians of the spirit sword." [illegible] lived meager lives even as they prayed for the day they could return to the outside world. [illegible] and all; and as for the spirit sword, why, that had been lost to them long ago. They did, however, [illegible] Raphael all about Soul Calibur, the one weapon that could stand against the evil sword Soul Edge. [illegible]

A mad grin crossed his face then, and his sword flashed crimson. The guardians had no further [illegible] power in their place. And thus these people, who had lived in secret for so long, were [illegible] night sky and an eerily sanguine moon.

It was stunning. As Raphael savored this taste of bliss, countless lights [illegible] then he remembered what lay in that direction: Ostrheinsburg, where he had once confronted Soul Edge. [illegible] between the stars in the sky, and he knew exactly what it was. Soul Edge was reviving. If Soul Calibur [illegible] inevitably appear there.

Draped in moonlight, Raphael began to cackle. He would give Amy her perfect world, and none of the [illegible] able to stop him. Any star with the insolence to try to [illegible]

Flambert

Raphael lost everything from his old life, even his own family name, and left the home of his birth with nothing; nothing, that is, except his rapier.

Even as a child he was in constant danger of assassination by those close to him. Though he shunned the senseless feuds and plots of noble society, he still continued to study the fencing arts that were such an essential part of every young nobleman's education.

Raphael has sworn himself to Amy, and his sharp-pointed blade is now his faithful ally in his quest to make their dreams become reality.

La Rapière des Sorel

The now-vanished Sorel family developed this fencing style for rapiers during the turmoil and tumult of mediaeval France.

The scheming Sorel family had always favored the long, thin rapier, handing down its own fencing style from father to son. In the chaotic noble society of the time, it was occasionally necessary to dispatch a political opponent or defend oneself from attack, and for this purpose it was useful to have a sword that could precisely pierce the chinks of armor that many people wore as part of their daily wardrobe.

Raphael was brought up in this world of betrayal and violence, and like all future heads of the Sorel family, he was trained in la Rapière des Sorel.

But it was a time of change, when heavy firearms were starting to appear and thick

Command List

Signature Techniques

Name	Command	Attack Level	Damage	Notes
Quick Botta	⇨ⒷⒷⒷ	High, High, Mid	10, 8 20	Fully combos on counter-hit
Affondo Fendante	⇩⇘⇨Ⓑ	Mid	40	Stuns on hit
Pirouette Sweep	⇙Ⓚ	Low	24	
Crimson Moon	↘ or ↗ⓀⒷ	Mid, Mid	16, 23(30)	Input 2nd attack with perfect timing for additional damage (Just Frame)
Broken Thrust ~Preparation	⇘Ⓑ	Mid	20	Shifts to Preparation
Wicked Thrust ~Preparation	⇦Ⓑ	High	18	Causes recoverable stun on hit. Shifts to Preparation.
Rapid Assault	Preparation ⒷⒷⒷ Ⓑ (Just)	High, High, Mid, Mid	10, 18, 20, 30	Final attack stuns on hit
Repost Thrust	Preparation Ⓐ + Ⓑ	Mid	35	Stuns on hit

8-Way Run

Name	Command	Attack Level	Damage	Notes
Lunging Press	→ or ↘ or ↗Ⓐ	High	28	
Merciless Stramazone	↓ or ↑ⒶⒶ	High, High	14, 16	
Deadly Strikes Crescendo	↓ or ↑ⒶⒷⒷ	High, Low, Mid	14, 14, 30	Final attack stuns on hit
Squalambrato Concierto	← or ↙ or ↖ⒶⒷ	Mid, Mid	30, 16	Both attacks stun on counter-hit
Squalambrato Concierto ~Preparation	← or ↙ or ↖ⒶⒷ	Mid, Mid	30, 16	Both attacks stun on counter-hit. Shifts to Preparation.
Dread Coffin	→Ⓑ	Mid	20	Stuns on hit
Dread Coffin ~Preparation	→Ⓑ	Mid	20	Stuns on hit. Shifts to Preparation.
Death Guise	↘ or ↗Ⓑ	Low	22	
Quick Mandritti	↓ or ↑Ⓑ	Mid	20	Stuns on counter-hit
Quick Mandritti ~Vurkolak Envelopment	↓ or ↑Ⓑ	Mid	20	Stuns on counter-hit. Shifts to Vurkolak Envelopment.
Dark Abyss	↙ or ↖Ⓑ	Mid	34	Stuns on hit
Preparation Parry ~Cranial Scraper	←Ⓑ	Mid	60	Deflects low attacks. Shifts to special attack if it hits at close range.
Venom Side Kick	→Ⓚ	High	18	
Crimson Moon	↘ or ↗ⓀⒷ	Mid, Mid	16, 22(30)	Input 2nd attack with perfect timing for additional damage (Just Frame)
Venom Roundhouse	↓ or ↑Ⓚ	High	20	Stuns on hit
Dark Moon	← or ↙ or ↖Ⓚ	Mid	18	
Wyvern's Tail	↓ or ↘ or → or ↗ or ↑Ⓐ + Ⓑ	Mid	32	
Wyvern's Tail (Cancel)	↑ or ↗ or → or ↘ or ↓Ⓐ + ⒷⒼ			
Bloody Funeral	← or ↙ or ↖ Ⓐ + Ⓑ	Mid	65	
Bloody Funeral ~Preparation	← or ↙ or ↖ Ⓐ + ⒷⒼ			Shifts to Preparation
Sliding	While Running Ⓚ	Low	26	

Horizontal Attacks

Name	Command	Attack Level	Damage	Notes
Attack au Fer	ⒶⒶ	High, High	10, 10	
Flash Needle	ⒶⒷ	High, Low	10, 16	
Hilt Strike	→Ⓐ	High	16	Stuns on counter-hit
Spinal Crusher	↘Ⓐ	Mid	24	
Cleaving Talon	↓Ⓐ	Sp.Low	10	
Heel Snipe	↙Ⓐ	Low	18	
Heavy Mandritti	←Ⓐ	High	22	
Low Tondo Roversi	While Crouching Ⓐ	Sp.Low	10	
Violent Blood	While Rising Ⓐ	Mid	20	
Sky Botte	Jumping Ⓐ	High	17 or 21 or 25	Damage varies depending on direction jumped in
Turning Attack au Fer	Backturned Ⓐ	High	12	
Low Turn Attack au Fer	While Crouching Backturned Ⓐ	Low	14	

Vertical Attacks

Name	Command	Attack Level	Damage	Notes
Roaring Stocatta	ⒷⒷ	Mid, Mid	12, 18	
Quick Botta	→ⒷⒷⒷ	High, High, Mid	10, 8 20	Fully combos on counter-hit
Quick Botta ~Preparation	→ⒷⒷ	High, High	10, 8	Shifts to Preparation
Broken Thrust	↘Ⓑ	Mid	20	
Broken Thrust ~Preparation	↘Ⓑ	Mid	20	Shifts to Preparation
Fendante	↓Ⓑ	Mid	20	
Grave Needle	↙ⒷⒷ	Low, Low	10, 10	
Wicked Thrust	←Ⓑ		18	Causes recoverable stun on hit
Wicked Thrust ~Preparation	←Ⓑ	High	18	Causes recoverable stun on hit. Shifts to Preparation.
Affondo Fendante	↓↘→Ⓑ	Mid	40	Stuns on hit
Crouching Montante	While Crouching Ⓑ	Mid	18	
Affondo Fendante	While Crouching ↘ⒷⒷ	Low, Mid	20, 30	2nd attack stuns on hit
Advance Slicer	While Rising Ⓑ	Mid	22	Stuns on counter-hit
Sky Agente	Jumping Ⓑ	Mid	21 or 25 or 29	Damage varies depending on direction jumped in. Stuns on hit (except ↖Ⓑ).
Turning Montante	Backturned Ⓑ	Mid	14	
Low Turn Montante	While Crouching Backturned Ⓑ	Mid	20	

Kick Attacks

Name	Command	Attack Level	Damage	Notes
Venom High Kick	Ⓚ	High	19	
Venom Toe Kick	→Ⓚ	Mid	20	
Venom Kick	↘Ⓚ	Mid	20	
Sweep Kick	↓Ⓚ	Low	14	
Pirouette Sweep	↙Ⓚ	Low	24	
Venom Heel	←Ⓚ	High	20	
Sweep Kick	While Crouching Ⓚ	Low	12	
High Toe Kick	While Rising Ⓚ	High	18	
Dark Moon	Jumping Ⓚ	Mid	17 or 21 or 25	Damage varies depending on direction jumped in
Turning Venom High Kick	Backturned Ⓚ	High	21	
Turning Sweep Kick	While Crouching Backturned Ⓚ	Low	16	

Simultaneous Press

Name	Command	Attack Level	Damage	Notes
Assalto Montante Crescendo	Ⓐ+ⒷⒶ	Mid, Mid, Low	10, 20, 20	2nd attack stuns on counter-hit
Spinning Affondo Thrust	↓Ⓐ+Ⓑ	Low	35	
Quick Parade	←Ⓐ+Ⓑ			Deflects horizontal attacks. Shifts into attack after successful deflect. Input Ⓑ to finish attack.
Blood Roar	↑Ⓐ+Ⓑ	High, Mid	15, 22	Deflects horizontal attacks
Vurkolak Envelopment	Ⓑ+Ⓚ			Evades vertical attacks
Cantarella Needle (Advance)	→Ⓑ+Ⓚ	Mid	20	Stuns on counter-hit
Cantarella Needle (Right)	↓Ⓑ+Ⓚ	Mid	20	Stuns on counter-hit
Cantarella Needle (Left)	↑Ⓑ+Ⓚ	Mid	20	Stuns on counter-hit
Cantarella Needle (Retreat)	←Ⓑ+Ⓚ	Mid	20	Stuns on counter-hit
Cantarella Needle (Retreat)	Backturned Ⓑ+Ⓚ	Mid	20	Stuns on counter-hit
Strigoii Envelopment	Ⓐ+Ⓚ			Teleports to current position
Strigoii Envelopment	Ⓐ+Ⓚ→			Teleports directly in front of enemy
Strigoii Envelopment	Ⓐ+Ⓚ←			Teleports behind enemy
Taunt	Ⓚ+Ⓖ			

Throws

Name	Command	Attack Level	Damage	Notes
Death Puppet	Ⓐ+Ⓖ	Throw	55	Input Ⓐ to escape
Unending Stings	Ⓑ+Ⓖ	Throw	50	Input Ⓑ to escape
A Lesson in Massacre	Left Side Throw	Throw	62	Same button as throw (Ⓐ or Ⓑ) to escape
Undertaker	Right Side Throw	Throw	60	Same button as throw (Ⓐ or Ⓑ) to escape
Pure Sacrifice	Back Throw	Throw	65	Same button as throw (Ⓐ or Ⓑ) to escape

Vurkolak Envelopment

Name	Command	Attack Level	Damage	Notes
Vurkolak Envelopment	Ⓑ+Ⓚ			Evades vertical attacks
Howling Wolf	Vurkolak Envelopment Ⓐ	Mid, High	10, 11	
Midnight Stocatta Crescendo	Vurkolak Envelopment ⒷⒷ	High, Mid	10, 30	2nd attacks stuns on hit
Pirouette Kick	Vurkolak Envelopment Ⓚ	Mid	30	
Mermet de Vec	Vurkolak Envelopment Ⓐ+Ⓖ or Ⓑ+Ⓖ	Throw	50	Same button as throw (Ⓐ or Ⓑ) to escape

Preparation

Name	Command	Attack Level	Damage	Notes
Preparation	↘Ⓑ or →Ⓑ or ⇨ⒷⒷ			
Ebony Stock	Preparation Ⓐ	Mid	28	Stuns on counter-hit
Rapid Assault	Preparation ⒷⒷⒷ Ⓑ (Just)	High, High, Mid, Mid	10, 8, 20, 30	Final attack stuns on hit
Dark Stinger Crescendo	Preparation ⓀⓀ	Low, Low	15, 15	Both attacks stun on hit. 2nd attack stuns on ground hit.
Repost Thrust	Preparation Ⓐ+Ⓑ	Mid	35	Stuns on hit. Evades high attacks.
Strigoii Envelopment	Preparation Ⓑ+Ⓚ			Evades vertical attacks

Shadow Evade Alpha

Name	Command	Attack Level	Damage	Notes
Shadow Evade Alpha	Preparation ⇩			Evades high attacks
Bloody Slicer	Shadow Evade Alpha Ⓐ	High	18	
Assault Blade	Shadow Evade Alpha Ⓑ	Mid	22	Stuns on counter-hit
Assault Blade ~Preparation	Shadow Evade Alpha Ⓑ	Mid	22	Stuns on counter-hit. Shifts to Preparation.
Hemlock Kick	Shadow Evade Alpha Ⓚ	High	14	Causes recoverable stun on hit
Shadow Evade Beta	Shadow Evade Alpha ⇩			Evades high attacks
Bloody Assault	Shadow Evade Beta Ⓐ	Mid	26	
Bloody Terror	Shadow Evade Beta Ⓑ	Mid	30	Stuns on hit
Bella Donna Kick	Shadow Evade Beta Ⓚ	High	16	Stuns on hit
Shadow Evade Alpha	Shadow Evade Beta ⇩			Evades high attacks

Combos

↘Ⓑ, ⒷⒷ
3 hits, 38 Damage
Counter-hit ↓ or ↑Ⓑ, ⒷⒷ (Just)
3 hits, 55 Damage
⇨⇨Ⓐ + Ⓑ, Ⓑ + Ⓚ
2 hits, 46 Damage
Counter-hit While Rising Ⓑ, ⇩Ⓐ + Ⓑ
2 hits, 52 Damage
→Ⓑ, ⓀⓀ, ⇩Ⓐ + Ⓑ
4 hits, 51 Damage
Counter-hit, ⇩ or ⇧Ⓑ + Ⓚ, ↘Ⓑ, ⒷⒷⒷⒷ (Just)
6 hits, 65 Damage
⇦Ⓑ, Ⓐ, ↘Ⓑ, ⒷⒷⒷⒷ (Just)
7 hits, 60 Damage, first stun is recoverable
Counter-hit ↓ or ↑Ⓚ, ↘Ⓑ, Ⓐ, ↘Ⓑ, ⒷⒷⒷⒷ (Just)
8 hits, 78 Damage
During Shadow Evade II Ⓑ, ↘Ⓑ, Ⓐ, ↘Ⓑ, ⒷⒷⒷⒷ (Just)
8 hits, 84 Damage

Close Range

Raphael's attack strategy revolves around his Preparation stance, which enables him to initiate back-to-back attacks at high speed. However, the stance's options and the attacks that shift into it have a single glaring flaw: almost all are linear. Your first priority is to dissuade your enemy from sidestepping the opening attacks that lead into Preparation. The speedy AA string is your safest means to do this, though its high attack level makes it vulnerable to crouching attacks. When you're wary of the enemy ducking under strikes, use the mid-hitting Squalambrato Concierto (⇨AB), which has a much longer wind-up period but inflicts more damage against sidesteps than AA. This chain also shifts into Raphael's Preparation stance.

When the enemy is reluctant to sidestep, start your offense with the Quick Botta (→BB) or Broken Thrust (↘B). Use the speedy →BB to stop your enemy's attacks preemptively, though it misses against crouching opponents. Attack with the middle-hitting ↘B to counter a foe's crouch. If it connects, do Preparation's BB string to perform a 3-hit combo. Use Preparation's other options when ↘B is blocked (refer to the Preparation tactic section). When your enemy is afraid of middle attacks, use Raphael's Grave Needle (↙BB) low attack to crush his or her high guard.

Mid Range

Raphael's fast running speed supplements your strategy at this distance, which is to deter circular movement while evading your enemy's attacks. Stop your enemy's sidesteps with ⇦AB, Heavy Mandritti (←A), and Merciless Stramazone (⇩or⇧AA). This scares your enemies into fighting on a linear plane, making it easier to avoid their attacks with backward movement. Punish their missed attacks with ↘B, BB to deal heavy damage and to move into close range. Use Quick Mandritti (⇩or ⇧B) instead whenever you dodge an attack with side movement. If the attack hits your enemy, perform BB(Just Frame) for a 3-hit combo. Your enemy may use high horizontal attacks to keep you from sidestepping, in which case use Wicked Thrust (←B) as a direct counter. It ducks under high attacks, stuns the enemy, and shifts into the Preparation stance, allowing you to score a giant combo on a successful hit (←B, A, ↘B, BBBB).

Long Range

Raphael has very few options at this distance. Your goal is to move into mid or close range via a knockdown, or by simply running into range when your enemy is afraid to attack. Attack missed moves with the Dread Coffin (⇨B), or catch your opponent off guard with ↓A+B. Because both options are linear, use Lunging Press (⇨A) to counter-hit opponents that try to sidestep either move. Unfortunately, the ⇨A attack is very vulnerable when guarded, so use it only when you're sure of a successful hit.

Special Tactics

Okizeme: Anti-Wakeup

Your main two attack options are ↙BB and ↘B. The most flexible of the two options is ↘B thanks to its high damage output and ability to shift into Preparation. If it connects, link into Preparation's BB string. Use it to condition your enemy into guarding high, then attack with ↙BB.

Preparation

Use Preparation's stance options either to press an advantage on hit, score combos, or to evade counterattacks when on the defensive. Which option you choose depends on whether or not the attack shifting into the stance hits. For example, successfully hitting with Broken Thrust (↘B) allows you to link into Preparation's BB string, scoring a 3-hit combo. Then BB shifts back into Preparation, leaving you with enough advantage to stage a follow-up attack. This is the best time to go for Preparation's middle Ebony Stock (A) option, the low Dark Stinger Crescendo (KK) option, or to let Preparation recover and go for a throw. Also use the BB option to maintain a continual offense when your enemy isn't willing to crouch. Attack with the Rapid Assault (BBBB(Just Frame)) to stymie your foe's attacks after they block your BB string, or to heavily damage someone trying to crouch.

You need defensive options when your opening attack is guarded. Use Preparation's Repost Thrust (A+B) attack to duck under and counter quick, high attacks, such as AA strings. Preparation's Shadow Evade Alpha (during Preparation ↓) also dodges high attacks, which can then be punished with its B option for bigger damage—shift into Preparation and link BB when it hits. Against vertical attacks, cancel Preparation into the evasive Strigoii Envelopment (B+K). If you successfully dodge the attack, punish it with the BB(Just Frame) option. If your enemy doesn't attempt an attack, go for either A+G or its A attack.

Learning to use Preparation's Ebony Shock (A) is your biggest concern. Its purpose is to preemptively stop enemy attacks, resulting in an extended stun caused by the counter-hit. Unfortunately, this move leaves Raphael vulnerable to attack when guarded, and at a disadvantage on normal hit. Therefore, it's important to condition your enemy with Preparation's other options before committing to the attack. Also, take defensive measures on a normal hit to counter your enemy's offense without sacrificing momentum. Techniques with deflect properties, like the Blood Roar (↑A+B), Quick Parade (←A+B), and Preparation Parry (⇨B), are helpful for countering quick high or low attacks when you're at a disadvantage. Also use Raphael's Vurkolak Envelopment stance to avoid vertical strikes.

One of Preparation's major weaknesses is its lack of circular attacks, making its many options vulnerable to sidesteps. To counter this problem, enter Preparation, then immediately shift into B+KA. This should counter most attempts to sidestep past your attacks.

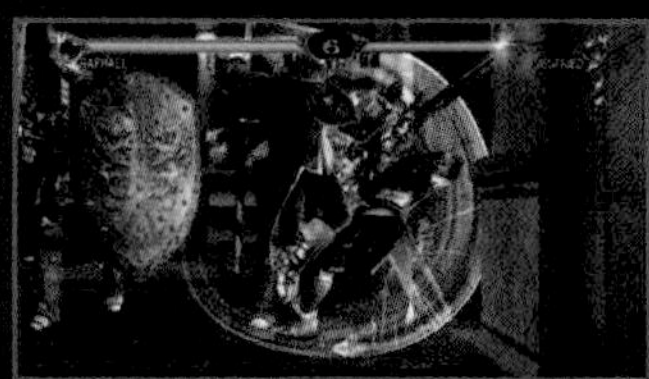

Cantarella Needle

Using the Canterella Needle is an advanced way to punish side movement. You can perform this unique ability in four directions (← or ↓ or → or ↑B+K), enabling you to counter enemy sidesteps at close distances. A successful counter-hit results in an especially long stun, allowing you to perform this combo: ↘B, BBBB(Just). This is easily the most damaging way to stop sidesteps. The drawback is the immense risk involved with using the attack, as it leaves you vulnerable if you perform it in the wrong direction.

Rock

...he who is patient, free from hatred and fear, he is called learned.
"Dhammapada"

Bio	
Age:	42
Birthplace:	London, British Empire (Raised in the New World)
Height:	5'9"
Weight:	187 lbs.
Birth Date:	December 14
Blood Type:	Unknown
Weapon:	Giant Mace
Weapon Name:	Onslaught
Discipline:	Self-Taught
Family:	Parents: Whereabouts unknown The Native American boy he was raising, Bangoo, just recently came of age.

Was he truly a father Bangoo could be proud of? Rock needed proof, and so he continued his hunt for Soul Edge. However, an unexpected road block had cut that search short: as he crossed the Alps and headed south, he had been ambushed by a man even more gargantuan than himself, and lost.

By throwing himself off the cliff into the river below, he had narrowly escaped his unknown foe. The enemy's identity and intentions concerned Rock, but first he needed to heal his battered body. Fortunately, he had stayed in these mountains before and knew the lay of the land well. As he pushed his way deeper into the mountains, he arrived at a secluded hot spring known only to the wild animals. A sojourn here for some rest ought to speed his healing.

Sometimes wounded animals would visit the spring, but otherwise he had no visitors, just peace. Here fierce carnivores never attacked the weaker animals. All the wildlife respected each other's territory, so there were no conflicts.

Rock spent the days soaking in the healing waters and hunting for herbs to prepare salves. He lived only to tend to his wounds, which gave him plenty of time to organize his thoughts. Needless to say, most of the time they wandered toward his assailant. Such a terrible foe. In the New World, Rock had been called the "White Giant." So who was this "Black Giant"? He had fought without honor and sought only to kill. Where had such brutality come from?

There was another thing: the assailant's fighting style was far too similar to Rock's own. It went further than just their similar size and weapons; for no discernible reason, his attacker had come at him with the same exact techniques and moves that Rock himself had devised. Rock had felt as though he was facing his own dark side. True, one could try to duplicate another's maneuvers, but match the finer quirks and nuances? Never. And certainly not if those maneuvers took years of work to develop. No matter how similar the silhouette of each leaf on a tree may appear at first glance, a closer examination always reveals subtle differences. Such is the way of nature. But that monster had copied Rock's every move perfectly.

It was unnatural.

Then there was the attacker's merciless nature. He was dangerous, too dangerous to be allowed to run loose. If people have roles to play, responsibilities to bear, then perhaps this Black Giant was Rock's burden. When he faced the beast again, he would not lose. Not even the most ferocious opponent could scare him. Even the most solid-looking boulders crumble when struck in the right place. If he uses my techniques, Rock thought, then I already know his weaknesses. With new resolve, he waited for his wounds to heal and strength to return to his limbs before putting the hot spring behind him.

Rock assumed that chasing after the Black Giant would mean abandoning his search for Soul Edge. But it was not long before he discovered an unexpected connection between those two seemingly separate purposes. Because the monster, named Astaroth, had entered the service of an Azure Knight headquartered in Ostrheinsburg Castle. Now Astaroth was assisting his lord, day and night, in a great massacre they called a "soul hunt." And his master, this Azure Knight, was none other than Soul Edge's wielder.

While surprised at the way these pieces had fallen into place, Rock also began to feel that some much greater force—perhaps it could be called fate—was the architect of it all. For Rock, his journey was becoming less and less about simply testing himself or finding "proof," but instead something much bigger.

Onslaught

The heathen cult Fygul Cestemus had dragged Rock back into Soul Edge's tangled fate, and when he rescued Bangoo from their nefarious clutches, his favorite weapon was broken. After deciding to live with Bangoo in Scandinavia, Rock recast the broken axe and created an enormous mace. From the leftover fragments he crafted a second mace, which he gave to Bangoo, but in time, the boy no longer needed it; under Rock and harsh Mother Nature's care, he had grown into a strong man.

After the two parted, Rock set out again to find Soul Edge and fulfill his oath, the giant mace he created in hand.

Own Style

Since Rock was washed up on an unknown land, he was forced to rely upon his God-given physical strength to survive. One blow from the man they call the "White Giant," coupled with the force of a weapon, can deliver an incredible amount of destructive power.

For Rock, his fighting style is both a way to defend himself and an extremely natural way of fighting born of need. As a way of showing respect to foes that fought with honor against him, he adorns himself with their skin and skulls.

Signature Techniques

Name	Command	Attack Level	Damage	Notes
Wild Tusk	⇦Ⓑ	High	16	Knocks down on counter-hit
Wild Knuckle	⇦ⓀⒶ	Mid, High	16, 18	Combos on counter-hit, 2nd hit causes backflop
Storm Gust	Ⓐ+Ⓑ	Mid	25 (48)	Causes more damage and knocks down from long range
Horizontal Sweep Kick	⇩Ⓐ+Ⓚ	Low	20	Causes backflop, leaves Rock in crouching state
Shoulder Tackle	While Crouching ⇘Ⓚ	Mid	22	Knocks down
Spike Hammer	➡Ⓑ	Mid	24	Causes backward stagger on counter-hit
Falling Moon	⇨⇘⇩⇙⇦Ⓑ+Ⓖ	Throw	30 (50)	Hold Ⓑ after starting throw increase damage and create a Guard Break, Ⓑ to break throw
Double Slams	Against Downed Foe's Legs ⇘Ⓑ+Ⓖ	Throw	40	Ⓑ to break throw

Horizontal Attacks

Name	Command	Attack Level	Damage	Notes
Gale Ax	ⒶⒶ	High, High	16, 24	Combos on counter-hit
Grip Hammer	⇨ⒶⒶ	High, High	10, 18	Combos on counter-hit, 2nd hit causes backflop
Grip Clutch	⇨Ⓐ⇩Ⓐ+Ⓖ or ⇩Ⓑ+Ⓖ	High, Throw	10, (20)	Throw aims at crouching characters
Hammer Blast	⇘Ⓐ	Mid	26	Causes recoverable stun on counter-hit
Horizon Hammer	⇩Ⓐ	Low	14	
Cyclone Hammer	⇙Ⓐ	Low	25	Knocks down
Rock Knuckle	⇦Ⓐ	High	26	Causes backflop
Spiral Surge	⇩⇙⇦ⒶⒶⒶ	Mid, Mid, Mid	15, 5, 20	
Horizon Hammer	While Crouching Ⓐ	Low	14	Leaves Rock in crouching state
Reverse Spiral Hammer	While Rising Ⓐ	Mid	20	Causes recoverable stun on counter-hit
Jumping Tomahawk	Jumping Ⓐ	High	30	Knocks down
Reverse Breeze Hammer	Backturned Ⓐ	High	18	
Reverse Horizon Hammer	While Crouching Backturned Ⓐ	Low	22	Leaves Rock in crouching state

Kick Attacks

Name	Command	Attack Level	Damage	Notes
Rock Front Kick	Ⓚ	High	14	
Rock Knee	⇨Ⓚ	Mid	18	Causes back slide on counter-hit
Rock Middle Kick	⇘Ⓚ	Mid	18	
Rock Middle Kick (Hold)	⇘🅚	Mid	38	
Rock Bear Kick	⇩Ⓚ	Low	10	
Horizontal Clip Kick	⇙Ⓚ	Low	10	
Horizontal Clutch	⇙Ⓚ⇘Ⓐ+Ⓖ or ⇘Ⓑ+Ⓖ	Low, Throw	10, (10 or 36)	Throw aims at downed foe's legs
Ground Clutch	⇙Ⓚ⇙Ⓐ+Ⓖ or ⇙Ⓑ+Ⓖ	Low, Throw	10, (15 or 40)	Throw aims at downed foe's head
Wild Knuckle	⇦ⓀⒶ	Mid, High	16, 18	Combos on counter-hit, 2nd hit causes backflop
Wild Clutch	⇦Ⓚ⇩Ⓐ+Ⓖ or ⇩Ⓑ+Ⓖ	Mid, Throw	16, (20)	Throw aims at crouching foe
Rock Bear Kick	While Crouching Ⓚ	Low	10	Leaves Rock in crouching state
Shoulder Tackle	While Crouching ⇘Ⓚ	Mid	22	Knocks down
Round Rock Kick	While Rising Ⓚ	Mid	16	Causes backward crumple on counter-hit
Guts Buster	Jumping Ⓚ	Mid	16	
Rolling Rock Kick	Backturned Ⓚ	High	16	
Reverse Bear Kick	While Crouching Backturned Ⓚ	Low	16	Knocks down

Simultaneous Press

Name	Command	Attack Level	Damage	Notes
Storm Gust	Ⓐ+Ⓑ	Mid	25 (48)	Causes more damage and knocks down from long range
Brave Fang	⇨Ⓐ+Ⓑ	Mid, Mid	15, 20	Combos on counter-hit, 2nd hit knocks down
Brave Fang (Hold)	⇨🅐+🅑	Mid, Mid	15, 20	2nd hit is a Guard Break that knocks down
Tidal Wave	⇦Ⓐ+Ⓑ	Mid	20	Causes crumple
Rock Fall	Ⓑ+Ⓚ	Mid	28	Knocks down
Rock Fall (Hold)	🅑+🅚	Mid	38	Guard Break, knocks down
Avalanche Press	⇨Ⓑ+Ⓚ	Mid	30	Causes backward crumple
Rocking Hilt	⇩Ⓑ+Ⓚ	Mid	28	Guard Break, causes recoverable stun
Ultimate Volcano	⇩⇘⇨Ⓑ+Ⓚ	Mid	110	Unblockable, launches
Reverse Rock Fall	Backturned Ⓑ+Ⓚ	Mid	28	Knocks down
Reverse Rock Fall (Hold)	Backturned 🅑+🅚	Mid	38	Guard Break, knocks down
Horizontal Sweep Kick	⇩Ⓐ+Ⓚ	Low	20	Knocks down, leaves Rock in crouching state
Taunt	Ⓚ+Ⓖ			

8-Way Run

Name	Command	Attack Level	Damage	Notes
Swing Cannon	→ or ↘ or ↗ⒶⒷ	Mid, Mid	18, 18	Combos naturally, both hits crumple on counter-hit
Hunter's Spin	↓ or ↑Ⓐ	Mid	20	
Cyclone Hammer	↙ or ↖Ⓐ	Low	25	Knocks down, leaves Rock in crouching state
Rock Tomahawk	←Ⓐ	Mid	20 (30)	Knocks down on counter-hit or from max range
Rock Tomahawk (Hold)	←Ⓐ	Mid	20	Spins foe
Spike Hammer	→Ⓑ	Mid	24	Causes backward crumple on counter-hit
Raging Volcano	↘ or ↗Ⓑ	Mid	20	Causes forward crumple
Giganto Spike	↓ or ↑Ⓑ	Mid	44	Knocks down
Megaton Spike	↙ or ↖Ⓑ	Mid	22	Causes backward crumple on counter-hit
Megaton Spike (Hold)	↙ or ↖Ⓑ	Mid	28	Guard Break, knocks down
Warcry Hammer	←ⒷⒷ	Mid, Mid	16, 13	Combos on counter-hit, 2nd hit launches
Long Horn	→ or ↘ or ↗Ⓚ	Mid	30	Launches
Kneel Kick	↓ or ↑Ⓚ	Mid	26	Knocks down
Rock Stomp Kick	↙ or ↖Ⓚ	Mid	30	Knocks down
Eagle Kick	←Ⓚ	Mid	22	Causes forward crumple on counter-hit
Hurricane Hammer	↓Ⓐ+Ⓑ	High	40 (50)	Knocks down, does extra damage from max range
Hurricane Hammer (Hold)	↓Ⓐ+Ⓑ	High	80	Unblockable, knocks down
Reverse Hurricane Hammer	↑Ⓐ+Ⓑ	High	40 (50)	Knocks down, does extra damage from max range
Reverse Hurricane Hammer (Hold)	↑Ⓐ+Ⓑ	High	80	Unblockable, knocks down
Sliding	While Running Ⓚ	Low	22	Knocks down

Throws

Name	Command	Attack Level	Damage	Notes
Rock Slam	Ⓐ+Ⓖ	Throw	40	Ⓐ to break throw
Canyon Dive	Ⓑ+Ⓖ	Throw	55	Ⓑ to break throw
Horn Fling	Left Side Throw	Throw	60	Ⓐ or Ⓑ to break throw
Face Crush Throw	Right Side Throw	Throw	60	Ⓐ or Ⓑ to break throw
Atomic Drop Maximum	Back Throw	Throw	50	
Falling Moon	⇨⇘⇩⇙⇦Ⓑ+Ⓖ	Throw	30 (50)	Hold Ⓑ after starting throw increase damage and create a Guard Break, Ⓑ to break throw
Maximum Bone Crusher	Against Crouching Foe ⇩Ⓐ+Ⓖ	Throw	20	Ⓐ to break throw
Slam Vortex	Against Crouching Foe ⇩Ⓑ+Ⓖ	Throw	20	Launches, Ⓑ to break throw
Rock Eruption	Against Downed Foe's Legs ⇘Ⓐ+Ⓖ	Throw	10	Launches, Ⓐ to break throw
Double Slams	Against Downed Foe's Legs ⇘Ⓑ+Ⓖ	Throw	36	Ⓑ to break throw
Tri-Horn Stampede	Against Downed Foe's Head ⇗Ⓐ+Ⓖ	Throw	40	Ⓐ to break throw
Gigantic Eruption	Against Downed Foe's Head ⇗Ⓑ+Ⓖ	Throw	15	Launches

Vertical Attacks

Name	Command	Attack Level	Damage	Notes
Rock Assault Crusher	ⒷⒷ	Mid, Mid	20, 20	Combos on counter-hit
Hammer Thrust	⇨Ⓑ	Mid	20	Causes forward crumple on counter-hit at close range
Raging Volcano	⇘Ⓑ	Mid	20	Causes forward crumple
Mountain Crusher	⇩Ⓑ	Mid	20	
Boulder Crush	⇗ⒷⒷ	Mid, High	16, 18	Combos on counter-hit, 2nd hit causes backward crumple
Wild Tusk	⇦Ⓑ	High	16	Knocks down on counter-hit
Peak Split	While Crouching Ⓑ	Mid	22	Leaves Rock in crouching state
Sunrise Hammer	While Rising Ⓑ	Mid	34	Launches
Wood Chopper	Jumping Ⓑ	Mid	28	Knocks down
Reverse Rock Split	Backturned Ⓑ	Mid	22	
Reverse Peak Split	While Crouching Backturned Ⓑ	Mid	24	Leaves Rock in crouching state

Combos

⇘Ⓑ, ⇙Ⓐ + Ⓖ	**2 hits, 60 damage**
⇘Ⓑ, ⇙Ⓑ + Ⓖ, (just as foe lands) ⇘Ⓐ + Ⓖ, ⇨Ⓑ + Ⓚ	**4 hits, 53 damage**
Counter-hit ←Ⓚ, ⇙Ⓐ + Ⓖ	**2 hits, 66 damage**
Counter-hit ←Ⓚ, ⇙Ⓑ + Ⓖ, (just as foe lands) ⇘Ⓑ + Ⓖ	**3 hits, 77 damage**
Counter-hit ⇨Ⓚ, ⇘Ⓑ + Ⓖ	**2 hits, 57 damage**
Counter-hit ⇨Ⓚ, ⇘Ⓐ + Ⓖ, step forward, ⇙Ⓐ + Ⓖ	**3 hits, 71 damage**
Counter-hit While Rising Ⓐ, ⇩Ⓐ + Ⓖ	**2 hits, 44 damage**
Counter-hit While Rising Ⓐ, ⇩Ⓑ + Ⓚ, ⇦ⓀⒶ, ⇘Ⓐ + Ⓖ, step forward, ⇙Ⓑ + Ⓖ, ⇨Ⓑ + Ⓚ	**7 hits, 84 damage, first 2 hits cause recoverable stuns**
Counter-hit ⇦ⓀⒶ, ⇘Ⓐ + Ⓖ, step forward, ⇙Ⓐ + Ⓖ	**4 hits, 87 damage**
⇦Ⓐ, ⇘Ⓐ + Ⓖ, step forward, ⇙Ⓑ + Ⓖ, ⇨Ⓑ + Ⓚ	**4 hits, 74 damage**
⇨Ⓑ + Ⓚ, ⇘Ⓐ + Ⓖ, step forward, ⇙Ⓐ + Ⓖ	**3 hits, 80 damage**
Counter-hit ⇨⇨ⒶⒷ, (step forward) ⇘Ⓑ + Ⓖ	**3 hits, 64 damage**
←Ⓐ, ⒶⒶ	**3 hits, 52 damage**
↓ or ↑Ⓑ, ⇙Ⓑ + Ⓖ, (just as foe lands) ⇘Ⓑ + Ⓖ	**3 hits, 95 damage**
Counter-hit ⇘Ⓐ, ⇘Ⓑ, ⇙Ⓑ + Ⓖ, (just as foe lands) ⇘Ⓐ + Ⓖ, ⇨Ⓑ + Ⓚ	**5 hits, 75 damage, ↘Ⓐ causes recoverable stun**
⇩Ⓑ + Ⓚ, ⇨⇨ⒶⒷ, (step forward) ⇘Ⓐ + Ⓖ, ⇨Ⓑ + Ⓚ	**5 hits, 71 damage, ↓Ⓑ + Ⓚ causes recoverable stun**
⇩Ⓐ + Ⓚ, ⇙Ⓑ + Ⓖ, (just as foe lands) ⇘Ⓑ + Ⓖ	**3 hits, 71 damage**

Close Range

If you like throws, Rock is your man. He doesn't have many conventional combos, or even strings that lead to 2-hit combos. Up close, his attacks usually aren't even safe from counterattack if guarded. More than any other character, Rock depends on throws, heavy single hits, knockdowns, Guard Breaks, and counter-hits that lead to ground throws. When striking up close, rely on Rock's Brave Fang (⇨Ⓐ+Ⓑ). This attack features two linear mid strikes. If you hold Ⓐ+Ⓑ, Rock charges up the second attack, turning it into a Guard Break. If Brave Fang strikes as a counter-hit, both hits will combo. Learn to hold down Ⓐ+Ⓑ; if you confirm that the first hit lands as a counter-hit, simply release the buttons early for a 2-hit combo. If the enemy is guarding, charge up the attack for the Guard Break. If your foe blocks the Guard Break, Rock gains a great opportunity to throw. To get a quick Guard Break on its own at close range, use the Rock Hilt (⇩Ⓑ+Ⓚ). If this hits, or if the enemy tries to guard crouching, he or she is put into a recoverable stun. Regardless of what happens, hit or blocked, Rock is in a good position to try for a throw immediately, as long as the foe doesn't sidestep. If the enemy pressures Rock up close, aware that most of his attacks are slow, try to interrupt them with the Rock Knee (⇨Ⓚ). If this strikes as a counter-hit, the enemy slumps to the ground and you can immediately go for ⇘Ⓐ or Ⓑ+Ⓖ to ground throw him or her for big damage. Vary which ground throw you use so the enemy doesn't get used to breaking one or the other. Because Rock lacks a large arsenal of great combos or strings, setting up staggers into ground throws is a big part of his offense.

To stop 8-Way Run or steps, the Grip Hammer (⇨ⒶⒶ) causes a 2-hit combo against side movement (or on counter-hit) and leads to a guaranteed ground throw attempt with ⇘Ⓐ or Ⓑ+Ⓖ. Both hits are high, but if you suspect the opponent will crouch, input the command ⇨Ⓐ⇘Ⓐ or Ⓑ+Ⓖ. Rock winds up for the first swing, but instead of performing the follow-up hit, he goes for a crouch throw!

Mid Range

Like many slower characters that wield large weapons, Rock is more comfortable the further away he gets from his adversary. Rock's premier tool from mid range is the Swing Cannon (→ or ↘ or ↗ⒶⒷ). This mid-to-mid chain combos on normal hit, but causes a slow crumple on counter-hit. During this crumple, you can either go for a crouching throw, or let your foe collapse a little further and go for a ground throw. There is plenty of time to verify what's happening when you strike with Swing Cannon, making it a great poking string. Although the first hit is semi-circular, it's avoidable through sidestepping. The Rock Tomahawk (←Ⓐ) is effective for killing sidesteps at mid range—it's a mid, so it can't be crouched under. As a counter-hit against, say, an opponent using side movement, it knocks down on contact. If you hold Ⓐ to charge the move, it spins the enemy. From a fully-charged spin ←Ⓐ, it's possible to link ⒶⒶ afterward for a very strong, simple combo.

Rock naturally loses a bit of leverage away from his opponents, as he can't normal throw them, but he has many ways to set up ground throws. After you use Rock Tomahawk to condition the enemy not to rely on side movement, it's safe to poke with Rock Assault Crusher (ⒷⒷ). This mid, linear string isn't safe up close, but it has surprising reach. It teaches the opponent to stand up, giving the Rock Knuckle (⇦Ⓐ) a chance to connect. This high, winding haymaker strikes the enemy hard, knocking him or her to the turf and guaranteeing Rock a shot at either his ⇘Ⓐ+Ⓖ or ⇘Ⓑ+Ⓖ ground throw. The Rock Knuckle can even nail sidesteps and 8-Way Run, but is a little slow to use for this purpose exclusively. For a mid-hitting alternative to the Rock Knuckle, try the Rock Stomp (←Ⓚ). Rock hops forward and plants his foot in the opponent's gut, crumpling the victim to the floor on counter-hit. Just like Rock Knuckle, this crumple guarantees Rock a ground throw. Here, you must use either ⇗Ⓐ+Ⓖ or ⇗Ⓑ+Ⓖ. ⇘Ⓐ or Ⓑ+Ⓖ is for snagging floored enemies by the legs, while ⇗Ⓐ or Ⓑ+Ⓖ picks up foes by their head. The ⇗Ⓑ+Ⓖ and ⇘Ⓐ+Ⓖ ground throws have a twist. Rock begins by picking up the enemy and hurling him or her into the air. Rock lacks great juggle tools but can still deal big damage here. Step forward as the enemy falls and perform another ground throw just as your foe hits the ground—he or she cannot escape! Rock's ⇩Ⓑ+Ⓖ crouch throw also tosses the foe skyward, but not in the correct position to land another toss.

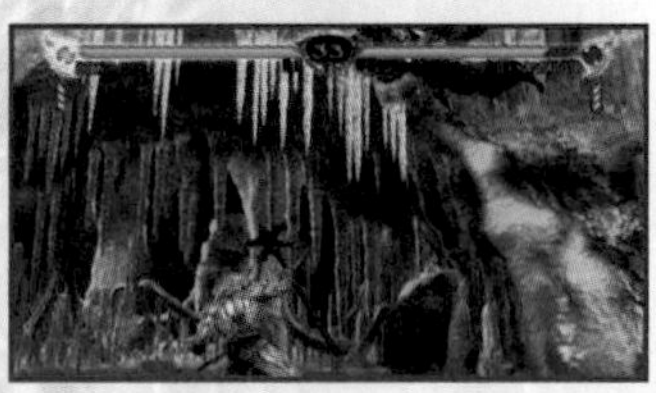

Long Range

Rock's options from far away are similar to Astaroth's. His Storm Gust (Ⓐ+Ⓑ or ⇧Ⓐ+Ⓑ) emulates the Titan Ax. This mid-striking swing is most effective at its max range, and it's great for punishing side movement, crouching, and for scoring Ring Outs. Inputting ⇧ changes the direction from which Rock swings, and therefore changes the direction in which he sends the enemy sailing. If you're certain the enemy will use side movement despite the threat of Wild Hammer, Hurricane Hammer (↓ or ↑Ⓐ+Ⓑ) is also great. It's not as versatile because it can be crouched under, but you can also charge it by holding Ⓐ+Ⓑ, turning it into an Unblockable. As a low-striking variant to these, the Cyclone Hammer (⇗Ⓐ) is a hammer sweep with big range. Cyclone Hammer puts Rock into a crouch animation, from which you can quickly produce three terrific moves. One of them is the Shoulder Tackle (While Crouching ⇘Ⓚ), a mid that charges forward and floors the enemy. The Reverse Spiral Hammer (While Rising Ⓐ) leads to a free crouching throw if it counter-hits. The third is the Sunrise Hammer (While Rising Ⓑ), a long-range linear launcher that leads to a free ground throw. Select a follow-up option to the Cyclone Hammer accordingly if you believe the enemy will rush in to retaliate. When the combination of Wild Hammer and Cyclone Hammer makes the foe wary of sidestepping, begin using the Giganto Spike (↓ or ↑Ⓑ), an overhead, linear smash. Finally, to easily transition from long range to a close-range, throw-oriented game, use either the Long Horn (↘ or ↗Ⓚ), which emulates Astaroth's Bull Rush, or Avalanche Press (⇨Ⓑ+Ⓚ). This is a running elbow drop that strikes from very far away, cannot be crouched, and leads directly to a guaranteed ground throw—use ⇘Ⓐ or Ⓑ+Ⓖ.

Special Tactics

Okizeme: Anti-Wakeup

Rock puts the enemy between a hard place and…uh, *him*, when both combatants are on the ground. If they don't rise immediately, the choice is easy—target legs with ⇘Ⓐ or Ⓑ+Ⓖ and faces with ⇗Ⓐ or Ⓑ+Ⓖ. Remember that the ⇗Ⓑ+Ⓖ and ⇘Ⓐ+Ⓖ variants are the same, hurling the enemy upward and giving you a juggle opportunity. You can also target grounded foes with the Rock Fall (Ⓑ+Ⓚ), a pouncing flop that you can charge by holding the buttons, turning it into a Guard Break. If your foe rises quickly, simply throw him, or mix-up between ←Ⓐ and Horizon Hammer (⇩Ⓐ), one of the best low-hitting pokes in the game.

Caught Between Rock and a Hard Place

As we discussed, few of Rock's attacks are completely safe from retaliation if guarded, and he doesn't have many conventional combos. What he *does* have is a huge arsenal of Guard Breaks and a throw for any situation. Using these attack types means that you don't have to worry about being safe if the opponent guards—neither Guard Breaks nor throws are guardable. Of course, savvy enemies will use sidesteps or Guard Impacts to avoid Guard Breaks, and will crouch under or break throws. Rock's ←Ⓐ, ⇦Ⓐ, and ⇨ⒶⒶ are excellent for solving the sidestep problem. Avoiding Guard Impacts is mostly a matter of varying your timing. They are inevitable to some degree if the enemy is focused on abusing them, but you can make your foe pay frequently by simply not attacking when you otherwise would. When your opponent's Guard Impact attempt whiffs, throw him. To counter crouching enemies, mix in mid attacks liberally, or bust out a crouching throw (⇩Ⓐ or Ⓑ+Ⓖ) to remind the enemy that they exist. Finally, vary between Ⓐ+Ⓖ and Ⓑ+Ⓖ throws, minimizing the risk that your throws will get stuffed.

Rock

Seong Mi-Na

"The sun beyond the mountains glows;
The Yellow River seawards flows.
You can enjoy a grander sight
By climbing to a greater height."
"On the Stork Tower," Wang Zhihuan (688-742)

Bio

Age:	23
Birthplace:	Jirisan, Korea
Height:	5'4"
Weight:	106 lbs.
Birth Date:	November 3
Blood Type:	A
Weapon:	Zanbatou (Halberd)
Weapon Name:	Scarlet Thunder
Discipline:	Seong Style Longsword & Rod Arrangement
Family:	Father: Seong Han Myong Mother & Brother: Deceased

i-Na

Soul Edge drove its wielders mad and harvested the souls of all who drew near. The sword was a destroyer of nations!

So said the hermit sword master of the mountain temple and Seong Mi-na was shaken to the core. For many years she had pursued Soul Edge, always believing that its power was just, that it was the savior of her nation. All that time, only to be told that the sword was pure evil?

It was unthinkable, but Mi-na knew the old man spoke the truth. He had a persuasiveness that hinted at a wisdom accumulated over untold years.

Mi-na took her leave of the old master and left the temple. She thought about Hong Yun-seong again. He had been a student at her father's Seong Dojang. But more than a fellow student, he had been like a younger brother to her. He must still be searching for Soul Edge, ignorant of the truth she had just learned! She had to find him and warn him, but how? There was only one way: she, too, would follow the trail of Soul Edge, and eventually her path would surely cross that of Yun-seong. There was not a moment to lose. She had to reach him before he found the sword!

Istanbul, a cultural melting pot bridging the worlds of Asia and Europe. Here, in the city where East meets West, Mi-na picked up Yun-seong's trail. She learned of a youth, accompanied by a young girl, who had pestered a sailor from Egypt in a bar for rumors and information about Soul Edge. The youth carried a sword that reflected the deepest feelings of its wielder. When she heard this, Mi-na knew immediately that the sword was White Storm, which she had given to Yun-seong.

For weeks Mi-na searched the ships returning from Egypt until at last she found him. But without even allowing Yun-seong a moment to enjoy their reunion, she immediately launched into a lecture.

"Soul Edge is an evil power that brings only disaster. There's no way that thing will save our country!"

It had been some time since Yun-seong had been subjected to Mi-na's scolding, which perhaps increased his reaction, for while he listened to her without dissent, his face clearly showed otherwise. By the next morning, he had disappeared.

"He scurries away like a rabbit," sighed Mi-na. Talim, the young girl with whom Yun-seong had traveled, spoke to her.

"He's headstrong, but a good person. In the end, I'm sure he'll make the right decision."

Talim, too, had sensed the danger of Soul Edge and had tried to warn Yun-seong. But he refused to be swayed, and remained determined to complete his quest and see the sword for himself, with his own eyes. However, upon seeing the scars in Egypt left by Soul Edge's passing, Yun-seong had appeared deep in thought.

Mi-na couldn't help but admire Yun-seong's strength of conviction. Back in the days of the Dojang, he was a boastful student, overly proud of his raw, untried skills, but it seemed that his journey had matured him. Yun-seong had left to continue his quest. She had to follow him, so that she could be at his side and help him make the right choice when the time came.

Mi-na and Talim shared what they knew. Talim told her of a vision she had had of a sword that was Soul Edge's complete opposite. Mi-na was fascinated by the story. If such a weapon did exist, then perhaps it could be the Sword of Salvation? Talim noted that such enormous power, whether wielded for good or evil, was extremely dangerous. But still, if such a weapon existed, and if it was capable of defeating Soul Edge, could Mi-na really afford to ignore it altogether?

Mi-na left Talim, and continued her pursuit of Yun-seong. Asking at every inn and town about Soul Edge and the weapon that could defeat it, she traveled on; her journey taking her further and further west. She found no trace of the weapon of which Talim had spoken, but she continued to draw closer and closer to the cursed sword. The information she gathered was leading her toward the Azure Knight, who had once again appeared in Ostrheinsburg in the Holy Roman Empire. The sword that he wielded had to be Soul Edge. The terrible stories surrounding the knight himself, the destructive power of his sword, the inhuman horde that served him—all were ominous signs worthy of the cursed sword. And she also heard of swordsmen and warriors who seemed mysteriously drawn to Ostrheinsburg, like moths to a flame.

Mi-na still had not found the power that would enable her to defeat the cursed sword, but it was too late for that now. Yun-seong had to be ahead of her. Perhaps he was already in Ostrheinsburg. She had to hurry!

Mi-na began to run. She had to find Yun-seong before it was too late!

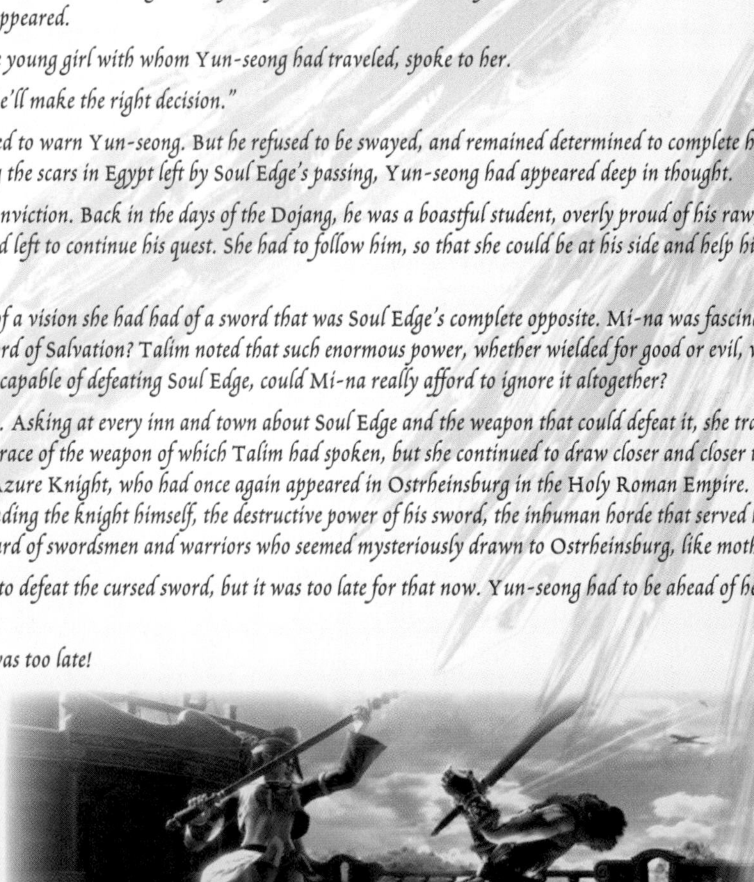

Scarlet Thunder

In Korea, this zanbatou belonged to Seong Han Myong, who was often styled a "demon among warriors." It is a family treasure that has been passed down through the house of Seong for generations.

Mi-na began her study of the martial arts under her father at a very young age. It is said she came by the weapon during this time; one might even say it watched over her as she grew into a fine woman. Later, she chose this same zanbatou to accompany her on her many travels.

Seong-Style Longsword Technique & Ling Shen Su Style Staff

The esteemed Seishiki Dojang in Korea. Mi-na is the only daughter of its head sensei, Seong Han Myeong. Since she was young, she has been trained in the use of the Great Sword and literally grew up with the Seong-Style family Great Sword technique. On a quest to find the Soul Edge, the sword she believed would save her country, she meets with other great world champions. Feeling somewhat weak in comparison to them, she set out on a journey where she gained great experience and learned many new techniques. She refused to reveal her secrets to a man who tried to force her to do so, and he took a sacred sword from the temple and left with it. Her fate is intertwined deeply with the Soul Edge, and her mastery of the staff technique learned from the lost Ling-Sheng Su Temple helped her in her journey.

Command List

Signature Techniques

Name	Command	Attack Level	Damage	Notes
Whirling Fangs	ⒶⒶⒷ	High, High, Mid	12,10,20	Fully combos on counter-hit
Strangling Slash	⬁Ⓐ	Mid	20(22)	Causes stun on counter-hit from max range
Thrusting Fang	⇨ⒷⒷ	Mid, Mid	15(20),30	1st attack causes recoverable stun on normal hit from max range, 2nd hit always stuns
Check Mate	⇦ⓀⒷ	Mid, Mid	14,16	2nd attack stuns on hit. Deflects high attacks
Double Hilt	⇨Ⓑ+Ⓚ	High, High	10,16	Stuns on counter-hit
Lightning Fang	While Crouching ⬀Ⓑ	Low	15	
Liquid Rising	While Crouching ⬀ⓀⓀ	Low, Mid	14,18	2nd attack stuns on hit
Lightning Thrust	➡Ⓑ	High	15(25)	Stuns and inflicts additional damage from max range

Horizontal Attacks

Name	Command	Attack Level	Damage	Notes
Whirling Fangs	ⒶⒶⒷ	High, High, Mid	12,10,20	Fully combos on counter-hit
Hilt Kick	⇨ⒶⓀ	Mid, High	10, 18	2nd attack stuns on counter-hit
Strangling Slash	⬁Ⓐ	Mid	20(22)	Stuns on counter-hit from max range
Root Fang	⇩Ⓐ	Low	10(20)	Deals additional damage from max range
Fang Sweep	⬀Ⓐ	Low	18(26)	
Shadow Step Slice	⇦Ⓐ	Low	14	
Knee Slicer	While Crouching Ⓐ	Sp.Low	12	
Twin Fang Strike	While Rising ⒶⒶ	Mid, Mid	14, 16	
Giant Fang	Jumping Ⓐ	Mid	24 or 26 or 28	Damage varies depending on direction jumped in
Reverse Dance Blade	Backturned Ⓐ	High	14	
Reverse Biting Strike	While Crouching Backturned Ⓐ	Low	22	

Vertical Attacks

Name	Command	Attack Level	Damage	Notes
Meteor Shower	ⒷⒷⒷ	Mid, Mid, Mid	15, 15(18), 28	2nd attack causes recoverable stun at max range. 3rd attack stuns on hit.
Retreating Divide	Ⓑ⇦Ⓑ	Mid, High	15, 14	Shifts into back jump on hit
Hidden Fang	⇨ⒷⒶ	Mid, Low	15(20), 20	1at attack causes recoverable stun at max range
Thrusting Fang	⇨ⒷⒷ	Mid, Mid	15(20), 30	1st attack stuns at max range. 2nd attack stuns on hit.
Lifting Heavens	⇘Ⓑ	Mid	19	Launches at max range
Thrust Kick	⇘ⒷⓀ	Mid	20	
Air Parting	⇩Ⓑ	Mid	16	
Dancing Fang Sweep	⇙ⒷⒶ	Mid, Low	14, 24	
Back Step Fang	⇙ⒷⒷ	Mid, High	14, 10	
Dancing Blade Kick	⇙ⒷⓀ	Mid, Mid	14, 30	
Retreating Fang	⇦Ⓑ	High	13	Shifts into back dash on counter-hit
Air Parting	While Crouching Ⓑ	Mid	16	
Lightning Fang	While Crouching ⇙Ⓑ	Low	15	
Lifting Wing	While Rising Ⓑ	Mid	20(25)	Launches at max range
Giant Air Parting	Jumping Ⓑ	Mid	28 or 32 or 36	Damage varies depending on direction jumped in
Reverse Air Parting	Backturned Ⓑ	Mid	17	
Reverse Air Parting	While Crouching Backturned Ⓑ	Mid	16	

Kick Attacks

Name	Command	Attack Level	Damage	Notes
Snap Kick	Ⓚ	High	12	
Celestial Kick	⇨Ⓚ	Mid, High	10, 20	Deflects mid attacks
Belly Crush Spin Kick	⇘ⓀⓀ	Mid, High	12, 15	2nd hit stuns on counter hit
Earth Kick	⇩Ⓚ	Low	12	
Rock Breaker	⇙Ⓚ	Low	16	
Check Mate	⇦ⓀⒷ	Mid, Mid	14, 16	2nd attack stuns on hit, deflects high attacks
Check Mate (Delay)	⇦ⓀⒷ	Mid, Mid	14, 16	2nd attack stuns on hit, deflects high attacks
Earth Kick	While Crouching Ⓚ	Low	12	
Liquid Rising	While Crouching ⇙ⓀⓀ	Low, Mid	14, 18	2nd attack stuns on hit. 1st attack doesn't knockdown from max range.
Shattering Kick	While Rising Ⓚ	Mid	24	
Giant Rising Kick	Jumping Ⓚ	Mid	12 or 14 or 16	Damage varies depending on direction jumped in
Reverse Snap Kick	Backturned Ⓚ	High	14	
Reverse Earth Kick	While Crouching Backturned Ⓚ	Low	12	

Simultaneous Press

Name	Command	Attack Level	Damage	Notes
Double Fang	Ⓐ+Ⓑ	High, High	10, 30	
Fang Barrage	⇨Ⓐ+Ⓑ	Mid, Mid, Mid	10, 10, 30	
Opening Treasure	⇘Ⓐ+Ⓑ	Low	10, 5, 12	Shifts into hit throw at close distances. Input Ⓐ to escape second attack.
Sweeping Blade	⇩Ⓐ+Ⓑ	Low	30(36)	
Sweeping Blade (Cancel)	⇩Ⓐ+ⒷⒼ			
Holding Treasure	⇙Ⓐ+Ⓑ	Low	10, 7, 7, 21	Shifts into hit throw at close distances. Input Ⓑ to escape final attack.
Dancing Crane	⇦Ⓐ+ⒷⒶⒷ	Mid, Mid, High, Mid	10, 10, 15, 25	Final hit Guard Breaks
Dancing Crane (Cancel)	⇦Ⓐ+ⒷⒶⒷⒼ	Mid, Mid, High	10, 10, 15	
Heavy Crane	⇦Ⓐ+Ⓑ ⇦Ⓐ+Ⓑ	Mid × 7	10, 10, 11, 14, 14, 14	
Seong's Crushing Long Blade	⇗Ⓐ+Ⓑ	Mid	140	Unblockable
Seong's Quick Long Blade(Cancel)	⇗Ⓐ+ⒷⒼ			
Seong's Quick Long Blade	⇗Ⓐ+ⒷⒷ	Mid	50	Guard Break
Radiant Wing	⇧Ⓐ+Ⓑ	Mid	25	
Heaven's Wheel	Ⓑ+Ⓚ	Mid, Mid	19, 28	1st attack stuns on hit
Double Hilt	⇨Ⓑ+Ⓚ	High, High	10, 16	2nd attack stuns on counter hit
Glory Fan	⇩Ⓑ+Ⓚ	Mid, Mid, Mid	15, 26	1at attack stuns on hit
Glory Fan (Cancel)	⇩Ⓑ+ⓀⒼ	Mid	15	Stuns on hit
Retreating Sands	⇦Ⓑ+Ⓚ	Mid, Mid, Mid	10, 10, 10	Final hit stuns. Deflects mid vertical attacks.
Leaping Horse Vault	⇖ or ⇧ or ⇗ Ⓑ+Ⓚ(⇦ or ⇨) Ⓑ(⇦ or ⇨) Ⓑ	Mid, Mid, Mid	18, 16, 23	
Leaping Horse Vault	Backturned Ⓑ+Ⓚ	Mid	20	Stuns on hit
Circular Blade Kick	Ⓐ+Ⓚ	Mid	30	
Dark Curtain	⇩Ⓐ+Ⓚ	Low, High	16, 25	
Power Fang Sweep	⇦Ⓐ+Ⓚ	Low, Low	10, 20	
Taunt	Ⓚ+Ⓖ			

8-Way Run

Name	Command	Attack Level	Damage	Notes
Circular Heaven Slash	→Ⓐ	Mid	18(28)	Inflicts additional damage from max range
Heavy Willow Divide	↘ or ↗ⒶⒶ	Mid, Mid	15, 26	
Strangling Flower	↓ or ↑Ⓐ	High, High	10, 12	
Sparrow Sweep	↙ or ↖Ⓐ	Low	14	
Wing Cross	←ⒶⒶ	Mid, Low	14, 16	
Wing Cross (Delay)	←ⒶⒶ	Mid, Low	14, 16	
Lightning Thrust	→Ⓑ	High	15(25)	Inflicts additional damage and stuns on hit from max range
Lifting Heavens	↘ or ↗Ⓑ	Mid	19	Launches on hit from max range
Shadow Fang	↓ or ↑Ⓑ	Low	10(18)	
Top Hammer Fang	↙ or ↖Ⓑ	Mid	15(25)	Stuns on hit. Deals additional damage and longer stun from max range.
Roaring Heaven	←Ⓑ	Mid	20(36)	Guard Break.
Circular Heaven Spin Kick	→ⓀⓀⓀ	Mid, Mid, High	14, 12, 20	1st hit causes recoverable stun on counter hit, 3rd hit causes stun on counter hit
Circular Heaven Spin Kick (Delay)	→ⓀⓀⓀ	Mid, Mid, High	14, 12, 20	1st hit causes recoverable stun on counter hit, 3rd hit causes stun on counter hit
Spring Splash Esoterica	↘ or ↗ⓀⒷ	Mid, Mid	12, 20	
Dark Sweep	↓ or ↑Ⓚ	Low	18	
Thunder Kick	← or ↙ or ↖Ⓚ	Mid	26	Stuns on hit
Spinning Divide	→Ⓐ+Ⓑ	Mid	34	
Power Spinning Divide	←Ⓐ+Ⓑ	Mid	44	
Sliding	While Running Ⓚ	Low	26	

Throws

Name	Command	Attack Level	Damage	Notes
Dropping Embrace	Ⓐ+Ⓖ	Throw	55	Input Ⓐ to escape
Crushing Soul	Ⓑ+Ⓖ	Throw	50	Input Ⓑ to escape
Riding Mustang	Left Side Throw	Throw	65	Same button as throw (Ⓐ or Ⓑ) to escape
Mi-na Frankensteiner	Right Side Throw	Throw	60	Same button as throw (Ⓐ or Ⓑ) to escape
Stalk Cutter	Back Throw	Throw	68	Same button as throw (Ⓐ or Ⓑ) to escape

Combos

⇘Ⓑ, ⇧Ⓐ + Ⓑ
2 hits, 51 damage, ↘Ⓑ must hit from max distance
⇘Ⓑ, ⇨⇨Ⓑ, While Crouching ⇗Ⓑ
3 hits, 63 Damage, →→Ⓑ must hit from max range
Counter-hit ⇦ⓀⒷ, ⇘ⓀⓀ, ⇘⇘ⓀⒷ
6 hits, 66 Damage
⇨Ⓚ, ⇨ⒶⓀ
4 hits, 49 Damage
⇦Ⓑ + Ⓚ, ⇘Ⓑ
4 hits, 43 Damage
⇦Ⓐ + Ⓚ, ⇘Ⓑ
3 hits, 44 Damage
Counter-hit ⇨Ⓚ, ⇧Ⓐ + Ⓑ
3 hits, 46 Damage
Counter-hit ⇨⇨ⓀⓀⓀ, ⇨Ⓑ + Ⓚ, ⇘Ⓑ
6 hits, 56 Damage
↙ or ↖Ⓑ, ⇨⇨ⓀⓀⓀ, ⇨Ⓑ + Ⓚ, ⇘⇘ⓀⒷ
8 hits, 71 Damage, replace ↘↘ⓀⒷ with ⇘Ⓑ against small characters

Close Range

Seong Mi-na isn't cut out for close-quarters fighting. Keep your close-range attacks to a minimum and look for an opportunity to reposition further away from your enemy. When you're on the defensive, use the Check Mate (⇦ⓀⒷ) string's high deflect properties to counter speedy horizontal attacks. A successful deflection leads to the powerful counter-hit combo ⇦ⓀⒷ, ⇘ⓀⓀ, ⇨Ⓚ. When you block one of your enemy's attacks, use a back step or the Back Step Fang (⇙ⒷⒷ) to escape to your ideal fighting distance: mid and long range. If it makes contact with your enemy, ⇙ⒷⒷ causes Seong Mi-na to initiate a backward jump. Use this intentionally to make escapes when necessary.

Mid Range

Seong Mi-na's Whirling Fangs (ⒶⒶ) string is her easiest means to start an offense at this distance. Its purpose is to dissuade sidesteps and to stop mid attacks preemptively. If it connects on a counter-hit, chain into its Ⓑ extension (ⒶⒶⒷ). Whenever the ⒶⒶ string is blocked, use ⇦ⓀⒷ as a defensive measure to stop high counterattacks. Or chain into the ⒶⒶⒷ extension if your opponent isn't looking for the third hit. Your adversary's options to counter this string include crouching under it or using a Guard Impact. Attack with the Lifting Heavens (⬂Ⓑ) to launch crouching characters for a combo—juggle your enemy with ⇧Ⓐ+Ⓑ. Dash up and throw your enemy if you anticipate a Guard Impact. A more flexible way to deter crouching is to use Seong's Thrusting Fang (⇨ⒷⒷ) or Hidden Fang (⇨ⒷⒶ) combos. Both strings start with the same mid attack and end with either a mid or low strike. Vary between both options to keep your foe guessing.

Long Range

This is one of Seong Mi-na's strongest positions. Her long reach makes it difficult for enemies to evade attacks through back steps, so they often resort to using circular movement to get around your attacks. Focus on deterring their side movements with the Sparrow Sweep (↙ or ↖Ⓐ) or →Ⓐ. Replace these attacks with the damage-heavy Heavy Willow Divide (↘ or ↗ⒶⒶ) string when you're certain of a sidestep or run. This attack is unsafe when guarded, so use it when you're sure of a hit.

When your foes are wary of circular attacks, look for their attempts to back away from your striking range. This is a common reaction to high-priority attacks, as it causes the attack to miss, enabling the defender to hit the missed move, or to move into a closer position as you recover. Use the high-hitting Lightning Thrust (→Ⓑ) to counter this reaction, which knocks down on counter-hit and allows an unavoidable crouching ⬀Ⓑ follow-up.

Special Tactics

Okizeme: Anti-Wakeup

Though it's not very damaging, the Wing Cross (←ⒶⒶ) is useful as an anti-wakeup mid attack. Its natural mid-to-low hit progression is difficult for novice players to defend. This move leaves Seong in a crouching state. If it hits, initiate a follow-up attack consisting of the Shattering Kick (While Rising Ⓚ), a throw, or Liquid Rising (While Crouching ⬀ⓀⓀ).

Your low attacks of choice are Power Fang Sweep (⇦Ⓐ+Ⓚ) and Dark Curtain (⇩Ⓐ+Ⓚ). When blocked, ⇦Ⓐ+Ⓚ is safe to retaliation, but its overall starting period is much longer. It also leads to a short combo consisting of ⇩Ⓐ+Ⓚ, then ⬂Ⓑ. The quicker ⇩Ⓐ+Ⓚ inflicts more immediate damage, but the second hit whiffs against crouching opponents, leaving it vulnerable when guarded. Both options are fairly easy to read, so you may opt to use ⇦Ⓐ instead, which moves Seong backward while performing a quick low attack. Use this in combination with a quick back step followed by ⬂Ⓑ. Both options stage a basic offense while moving Seong out to a more reliable position.

Varied Range Property

Many of Seong Mi-na's moves have stronger hit properties when done from as far away as possible. For example, her ⬂Ⓑ doesn't knock down the enemy if performed at pointblank range. However, it launches the enemy into the air and inflicts more damage if only the very tip of her weapon hits. This causes Seong to be weaker at close distances, further fortifying the notion that you should always position Seong away from her enemy.

Setsuka

Setsuka

[illegible]

Setsuka's heart stirred. She was closing in on him. [illegible] facing Mitsurugi. He was a demon, they said. She was no match for him [illegible] surrounding him defied reason. Not only had he never lost a duel, [illegible] services as a mercenary, and deliberately joined outnumbered forces to fight [illegible]

What purpose could there be in diving headlong into death's grasp like that? [illegible] But Setsuka could not care less about Mitsurugi's motivations. If he was [illegible] would happily rise to the challenge.

But one thing still made Setsuka uneasy: she would have to surpass her [illegible] matter how many great warriors the world held, the foe [illegible] had taught her. But could she surpass him? She would never be able [illegible]

Her master's words echoed in Setsuka's mind, "It is not for vengeance [illegible] and that thought weighed heavy on her heart. But she had chosen to [illegible] cost her humanity. And once she set her mind to something, she was [illegible] breath with the mantle of grief still about her. [illegible]

Which is precisely why I must become stronger, Setsuka thought.

And so she did. By putting faith in herself, Setsuka put faith in her master [illegible] translated into peerless skill with a blade. Each [illegible] once sought.

Then, at last, Setsuka learned of Mitsurugi's [illegible] Knight her foe pursued, had made the [illegible] his stronghold. [illegible] Excitement quickened her heart, and Setsuka [illegible]

It is a flower because it is hidden.
If it were not hidden, it would not be a flower.
"Fushi kaden," Zeami Motokiyo (c. 1363 - c. 1443)

Bio

Age:	24
Birthplace:	Unknown (Raised in Japan)
Height:	5'6"
Weight:	115 lbs.
Birth Date:	Unknown
Blood Type:	A
Weapon:	Iai sword hidden in an umbrella
Weapon Name:	Ugetsu Kageuchi
Discipline:	Shinden Tsushima-ryu Battoujyutsu
Family:	No family Master who raised her: Deceased

Ugetsu Kageuchi

Though a Battoujyutsu master, the man's duel with Heishiro Mitsurugi cost him his life. As he died, he gave a sword to his beloved ward and pupil. Wrapped in the kimono her teacher left her, Setsuka swore vengeance; to keep that secret safe, she took the sword to a certain smith and had him conceal it within an umbrella, clothing it in a mantle of elegance, just like herself.

Since the blade is a "kageuchi," or rejected blade, somewhere there must be a superior "shinuchi." The name of the smith who made the blade is unknown.

Shinden Tsushima-ryu Battoujyutsu

As her name indicates, she is a practitioner of the divine art of Battoujyutsu (the art of cutting with the blade). But since Battoujyutsu was just being developed at that time, it is probably nothing more than a story made up to achieve and justify her rank.

The art had its origin in assassination, and is dedicated to shortening the length of time between drawing the blade and making the cut, and to kill with a single strike. But instead of being something which was a sword technique or as a martial art with katas, its use of old songs and ways of speaking is probably reflective of the art of concealing.

Setsuka's master was from a family that accepted dirty work, but had strong misgivings about the corruption of the Daimyo and his followers who handed down death sentences and, in righteous indignation, threw away his family name and left home.

But that was not what he said to his student, Setsuka. For Setsuka, who had studied the Battoujyutsu in earnest as a sword technique, it was her link to her master and proof of life itself.

Her teacher recognized her skill while he was alive.

Now she has sharpened her sword in preparation for vengeance and it is sharper than it has ever been before...

Command List

Signature Techniques

Name	Command	Attack Level	Damage	Notes
Tousled Hair Slash	⇨ⒶⒶ	High, Mid	16, 22	Combos naturally
Sakura Air Combo	⇗ⒶⒶⒶ	Low, Mid, High	14, 16, 16	2nd and 3rd inputs must be Just Frames for full damage
Winter Funeral	ⒷⒶ	Mid	40	Knocks down
Reverse Blade	⇗ⒷⒷ (Just)	Mid, Mid	10, 20	Requires a Just Frame input, crumples
Shade Buster	While Crouching ⇘ⒶⒷ	Mid	30	Knocks down
Shade Thrust	While Crouching ⇘ⒷⒷ (Just)	Mid, Mid	14, 16	Combos naturally, 2nd hit knocks down, 2nd hit must be input as a Just Frame
Willow Splitter	→ or ↘ or ↗Ⓐ	High	28	
Rising Crescent	↘ or ↗Ⓑ	Mid	22	Launches on normal hit, crumples on counter-hit
Crimson Death	⇩⇗⇦Ⓑ+Ⓖ	Throw	34	Ⓑ to escape throw

Horizontal Attacks

Name	Command	Attack Level	Damage	Notes
Petal Slash	ⒶⒶ	High, High	10, 10	Combos naturally
Rising Red Moon	ⒶⒼⒷ	Mid	22	Launches
Mourning Thrust	ⒶⒷ	Mid	26	Knocks down
Tousled Hair Slash	⇨ⒶⒶ	High, Mid	16, 22	Combos naturally
Willow Slash	⇘Ⓐ	Mid	20	
Grasscutter	⇩Ⓐ	Sp.Low	10	
Sakura Air Combo	⇗ⒶⒶⒶ	Low, Mid, High	14, 16, 16	2nd and 3rd inputs must be Just Frames for full damage
Winter Stitch	⇦Ⓐ	High	18	Sideturns foe on normal hit, causes spin crumple on counter-hit
Stalk Clipper	While Crouching Ⓐ	Sp.Low	10	Leaves Setsuka in crouching state
Shade Buster	While Crouching ⇘ⒶⒷ	Mid	30	Knocks down
Crescent Slash	While Rising Ⓐ	High	28	Backturns foe
Blossom Slicer	Jumping Ⓐ	High	26	Sideturns foe
Winter Breeze	Backturned Ⓐ	High	12	
Blind Grasscutter	While Crouching Backturned Ⓐ	Sp.Low	10	Leaves Setsuka in crouching state

Vertical Attacks

Name	Command	Attack Level	Damage	Notes
Wingbeat Slicer	ⒷⒷ	Mid, Mid	14, 16	Combos naturally
Winter Funeral	ⒷⒶ	Mid	40	Knocks down
Moonlight Thrust	⇨Ⓑ	Mid	20	
Air Blade	⇘Ⓑ	Mid	22	Launches
Waterfowl Slice	⇩Ⓑ	Mid	16	Leaves Setsuka in crouching state
Reverse Blade	⇗ⒷⒷ (Just)	Mid, Mid	10, 20	Combos naturally, 2nd hit crumples, 2nd hit must be input as a Just Frame
Heartening Strike	⇦Ⓑ	High	20	
Petal Slicer	While Crouching Ⓑ	Mid	16	
Shade Thrust	While Crouching ⇘ⒷⒷ (Just)	Mid, Mid	14, 16	Combos naturally, 2nd hit knocks down, 2nd hit must be input as a Just Frame
Crescent Blade	While Rising Ⓑ	Mid	20	Causes backward crumple on normal hit, flopping crumple on counter-hit
Willow Divide	Jumping Ⓑ	Mid	22	
Silver Slicer	Backturned Ⓑ	Mid	15	
Windbeat Strike	While Crouching Backturned Ⓑ	Mid	18	Leaves Setsuka in crouching state

Kick Attacks

Name	Command	Attack Level	Damage	Notes
Rising Sun Kick	Ⓚ	High	12	
Knee Seduction	⇨Ⓚ	Mid	12	Crumples on counter-hit
Oiran Heel Kick	⇘Ⓚ	Mid	16	
Crouching Side Kick	⇩Ⓚ	Low	10	Leaves Setsuka in crouching state
Back Rising Sun Kick	⇗Ⓚ	High	20	Causes backward crumple
Setsuka Stomp	⇦Ⓚ	High	24	Causes recoverable flop
Shin Kick	While Crouching Ⓚ	Low	10	Leaves Setsuka in crouching state
Rising Front Kick	While Rising Ⓚ	Mid	18	
Oiran Rising Heel	Jumping Ⓚ	Mid	22	Knocks down
Rising Moon Kick	Backturned Ⓚ	High	16	
Blind Shin Kick	While Crouching Backturned Ⓚ	Low	12	Knocks down, leaves Setsuka in crouching state

Simultaneous Press

Name	Command	Attack Level	Damage	Notes
Mirror Blade	Ⓐ+Ⓑ		20~86	Deflects and counters mids
Half Moon Shadow	⇩Ⓐ+Ⓑ	Low	28	Causes foot crumple
Rising Moon	While Crouching ⬂Ⓐ+Ⓑ	Mid	20	Causes backward crumple
Sakura Fury Combo	Ⓑ+Ⓚ⇨⬃Ⓑ ⬃⬃Ⓐ+Ⓑ	Mid, Mid, Mid	24, 18, 33	Sequence occurs only on successful hit, requires extremely fast input
Silver Moon Combo	Ⓑ+Ⓚ⇨⬃Ⓑ ⇦⇦Ⓑ+Ⓚ	Mid, Mid, Mid	24, 18, 40	Sequence occurs only on successful hit, requires extremely fast input
Crescent Lash	⇩Ⓑ+Ⓚ	Mid	18	Knocks down
Rainy Moon	Backturned Ⓑ+Ⓚ Ⓑ (Just)	Mid, Mid	20, 20	Combos naturally, knocks down, 2nd hit must be input as Just Frame
Ring of Heaven	Ⓐ+Ⓚ			Movement
Breaking Wave	Ⓐ+ⓀⒶ	High	20	Spins foe
Island Divide	Ⓐ+ⓀⒷ	Mid	20	Knocks down
Ring of Heaven	Backturned Ⓐ+Ⓚ			Movement
Taunt	Ⓚ+Ⓖ			

Throws

Name	Command	Attack Level	Damage	Notes
Crescent Sweep	Ⓐ+Ⓖ	Throw	25	Ⓐ to escape throw
Moon Wind	Ⓑ+Ⓖ	Throw	55	Ⓑ to escape throw
Shadow Descent	Left Side Throw	Throw	59	Ⓐ or Ⓑ to escape throw
Vermilion Moon	Right Side Throw	Throw	65	Ⓐ or Ⓑ to escape throw
Snow Gate	Back Throw	Throw	60	
Crimson Death	⇩⬃⇦Ⓑ+Ⓖ	Throw	34	Ⓑ to escape throw

Special

Name	Command	Attack Level	Damage	Notes
Twilight Haze	⇩⬂⇨			Ducking movement
Dawn Haze	⇩⬃⇦			Ducking movement, leaves Setsuka in crouching state

8-Way Run

Name	Command	Attack Level	Damage	Notes
Willow Splitter	→ or ↘ or ↗Ⓐ	High	28	
Shadow Cutter	↓ or ↑Ⓐ	High	18	Spins and crumples foe, leaves Setsuka backturned
Horizon Sweeper	↙ or ↖Ⓐ	Low	28	Trips on normal hit, back flops on counter-hit, leaves Setsuka in a crouching state
Mist Cutter	←ⒶⒶ	High, High	14, 18	Combos naturally, knocks down
Sakura Twister	→ⒷⒶ	Mid, High	15, 20	Combos naturally, knocks down
Rising Crescent	↘ or ↗Ⓑ	Mid	22	Launches on normal hit, crumples on counter-hit
Double Silver Stab	↓ or ↑ⒷⒷ	Mid, High	18, 26	Combos naturally, knocks down
Crescent Strike	↙ or ↖Ⓑ	Mid	26	Launches
Moon Shadow Strike	←ⒷⒶ	Mid, Mid	18, 20	Combos naturally, knocks down
Shade Roundhouse	→ or ↘ or ↗Ⓚ	High	26	Spins foe
Heel Hook Kick	↓ or ↑Ⓚ	Mid	22	Knocks down
Backspin Snow Sweeper	↙ or ↖Ⓚ	Low	20	Leaves Setsuka in crouching state
Shadow Hunter	←ⓀⒷ	High, Mid	18, 24	Combos naturally
Full Moon Divide	→ or ↘ or ↗ Ⓐ+Ⓑ	Mid	30	Guard Break, knocks down
Shade Dancer	↓ or ↑Ⓐ+ⒷⒶ	Mid, High	10, 20	Combos naturally, both hits knock down
Blazing Moon	←Ⓐ+Ⓑ	Mid	30, 30	Unblockable, knocks down
Blind Heaven	→Ⓑ+Ⓚ	Mid	30	Knocks down, leaves Setsuka backturned
Silver Shadow	←Ⓑ+Ⓚ	High	36	Crumples foe
Sliding Scraper	While Running Ⓚ	Low	26	Knocks down

Combos

⇩Ⓐ + Ⓑ, While Rising Ⓑ

2 hits, 35 damage

↘ or ↗Ⓑ, ⇨ⒶⒶ

3 hits, 48 damage

↘ or ↗Ⓑ, ⒷⒶ

2 hits, 54 damage

Counter-hit ↘ or ↗Ⓑ, ⇨Ⓚ, ⇩Ⓐ + Ⓑ

3 hits, 54 damage

↙ or ↖Ⓑ, ⒷⒶ

2 hits, 59 damage

ⒶⒼⒷ, ⒷⒶ

2 hits, 65 damage

While Crouching ⬂Ⓐ + Ⓑ, ⇨⇨ⒷⒶ

3 hits, 47 damage

Counter-hit ↓ or ↑Ⓐ, Ⓑ + ⓀⒷ (Just)

3 hits, 60 damage

Counter-hit ↙ or ↖Ⓐ, ⬃ⒷⒷ (Just)

3 hits, 49 damage, pause briefly after 1st hit to let Setsuka rise from crouching

⬃ⒷⒷ (Just), ⇨Ⓚ, ⇩Ⓐ + Ⓑ

4 hits, 48 damage

Counter-hit ⇦Ⓐ, ⬂⬂Ⓑ, ⇨⇨ⒷⒶ

4 hits, 67 damage

Counter-hit ⇦Ⓐ, ⬂⬂Ⓑ, ⇨Ⓚ, ⬃ⒷⒷ (Just)

5 hits, 67 damage

Counter-hit ⇦Ⓐ, Ⓑ + Ⓚ⇨⬃Ⓑ⇦⇦Ⓑ + Ⓚ

3 hits, 82 damage

Counter-hit ⇦Ⓐ, ⇦⇦ⒷⒶ (Wall Hit), ⬂⬂Ⓑ, ⇨⇨ⒷⒶ (Wall Hit), ⇩Ⓐ + Ⓑ

9 hits, 81 damage

Close Range

Setsuka is focused on close-range fighting. Stylish parasol in hand, she comes equipped with a plethora of Just Frame attacks, safe offensive options, short but technical and damaging combos, and an exclusive counter that builds up strength the more frequently it is employed. This is the Mirror Blade (Ⓐ+Ⓑ). When executed, Setsuka twirls her blade rapidly, deflecting and retaliating against all mid-level attacks. Once this counter is utilized six to eight times within the same match, it becomes extremely powerful, performing Setsuka's brutal Silver Moon Combo automatically. There is much to be said for a 90-damage counter! However, there is also much risk associated in building Mirror Blade up to that level. It may be prudent to abuse the Mirror Blade only against foes who consistently and predictably go for mid attacks, like launchers, usually when you are at a mild disadvantage, such as after your own attack is guarded. Against seasoned foes that more frequently mix in highs, lows, and throws, overusing this counter gets you into trouble!

Setsuka has very powerful linear pokes. To use them effectively, you must first insure the opponent cannot sidestep without retribution. Punish side movement attempts at close range with the Winter Stitch (← Ⓐ). Setsuka steps back slightly and slashes with a high attack that causes the enemy to spin and flop backward on counter-hit. She can capitalize on this with strong combos, making enemies think twice about carelessly using 8-Way Run or attacks in the future. Once the enemy is afraid of using sidesteps and 8-Way Run in close quarters, begin using throws and strong linear mid attacks, like Rising Crescent (⇘Ⓑ), which launches on counter-hit and crumples on normal hit. Either way, Setsuka gets a combo out of it.

Setsuka has many more great linear, close-range sequences. Reverse Blade (↙ⒷⒷJust) is a mid-hitting string that is completely safe if you perform the Just Frame follow-up. Plus, it leads to combos through a crumple on both normal and counter-hit. The Sakura Air Combo (↙ⒶⒶ Just Ⓐ Just) hits low, then mid, then high. After the first input, the following two inputs must *both* be performed as Just Frames, with extreme precision. If you do this successfully, Setsuka will slash three times, traveling from low to high, flashing white and sparking lightning on the last hit. This move can be difficult to employ effectively, but it's a crucial portion of her close-range game. Mixing up between this and the mid-striking Silver Moon Combo (which is safe if blocked) essentially gives her a 47-damage low and an 86-damage mid! Beware that both the first and second hits of the Sakura Air Combo are unsafe to retaliation if blocked, though the low-to-mid sequence is difficult for the enemy to block. The move is safer if you get a Just Frame input on the second attack. The third attack, which *requires* a Just Frame input, cannot be performed if the enemy is guarding. If you have problems with this attack, you probably just need to slow down your inputs—try to hit Ⓐ exactly as Setsuka strikes her opponent on the follow-up swings.

Mid Range

Setsuka wants to be close to her opponents. Wait patiently for adversaries to attack carelessly, and punish their whiffed moves with Blind Heaven (⇨Ⓑ+Ⓚ). This mid-striking lunge knocks them down and leaves Setsuka back-turned upon completion. If the enemy blocks Blind Heaven, simply guard if you think he'll try a mid or low. Or try for Rainy Moon (back-turned Ⓑ+ⓀⒷ Just) if you anticipate a high string or throw attempt. Rainy Moon goes under these attacks and knocks the opponent to the turf, assuming you get the Just Frame input for the follow-up. For a slightly less risky whiff punisher, try the Shade Buster (While crouching ↘ ⓐⒷ). Setsuka uses her parasol to strike with a mid that knocks down the enemy. Shade Buster is a While Crouching move, which would make it inaccessible for most characters while dancing in and out of the opponent's range, trying to bait attacks. However, two of Setsuka's commands send her quickly into a brief crouching state: the ↓↘→ Twilight Haze and the ↓↙← Dawn Haze. From Dawn Haze, she can easily access While Rising and While Crouching attacks simply by performing their commands just after Dawn Haze. Thus, a command of ↓↙←↘ ⓐⒷ results in a quick Shade Buster anytime it's needed.

If the enemy relies on side movement to avoid these options, retaliate with the Winter Funeral (ⓑⒶ). Setsuka lunges forward and slams the enemy to the ground even on normal hit. Winter Funeral is a mid and cannot be crouched under. It also delivers very impressive damage for a single normal attack. It's not safe from quick retaliation if guarded, but this is still an excellent move, especially from the edge of its deceptively long range.

Finally, keep the Full Moon Divide (⇨ or ⇘ or ⇙ Ⓐ+Ⓑ) ready. This long-reaching, quick Guard Break does wonders for getting inside on defensive opponents or those waiting to block Winter Funeral or Blind Heaven and counterattack.

Long Range

Setsuka has limited options at long range. As with mid range, she should focus on using Blind Heaven to counter-poke and establish close range, where her offense thrives. She can also use her Ring of Heaven leap (Ⓐ+Ⓚ) into its high-hitting Breaking Wave Ⓐ attack from afar. If enemies use 8-Way Run or sidesteps, this attack will hit them and send them into a spin. This puts Setsuka into her favorite position: pointblank range, sitting on a grip of advantage.

Special Tactics

Okizeme: Anti-Wakeup

Use Hall Moon Shadow (↓Ⓐ+Ⓑ) to strike grounded foes or to punish those that rise and immediately guard high. The Ⓑ Island Divide option out of the Ring of Heaven (Ⓐ+Ⓚ) strikes mid and pops up grounded foes. The bounce isn't enough to capitalize with a juggle, but it essentially resets the wakeup situation while scoring you some damage. Against foes rising from a few steps away, try mixing up between Winter Funeral (ⓑⒶ) and Full Moon Divide (⇨ or ⇘ or ⇙ Ⓐ+Ⓑ). The first blasts them back down if they don't guard high, and the second punishes them for exactly that.

Fingers of Lightning

Setsuka's Silver Moon (Ⓑ+Ⓚ→↙Ⓑ←←Ⓑ+Ⓚ) and Silver Fury (Ⓑ+Ⓚ→↙Ⓑ↙↙Ⓐ+Ⓑ) combos work in a unique way. Both of them deal huge damage (Moon slightly more than Fury), can be executed only if the first hit strikes successfully, and must be performed *very* quickly with no gaps. The commands are relative to Setsuka and her opponent—this guide and the in-game movelist assumes Setsuka is on the left, facing right. The twist here is that the camera angle changes midway through these sequences, so the commands as listed are a little deceiving. That is to say, the relative directions for the →↙Ⓑ portion are not the same as the directions for the ←←Ⓑ+Ⓚ or ↙↙Ⓐ+Ⓑ portions. In other words, assuming you aren't looking at the screen at all, or you don't know Setsuka switches to the other side partway through, the commands *feel like* Ⓑ+Ⓚ→↙Ⓑ→→Ⓑ+Ⓚ and Ⓑ+Ⓚ→↙Ⓑ↘↘Ⓐ+Ⓑ. Don't worry; this isn't as confusing when you actually try to perform these moves! You have such a short window on these commands that you won't have time to worry about the side to which Setsuka swaps. Just remember and perform a command confidently through muscle memory. Practice makes perfect—eventually, mastery of these moves gives Setsuka one of the most powerful close-range pokes in the game!

Siegfried

Thou therefore rise: vanish thy weariness
By the mind's effort, in each struggle form'd
To vanquish.

"La Divina Commedia: Inferno" Canto 24, Dante Alighieri (1265 - 1321)

Bio

Age:	23
Birthplace:	Ober-Getzenberg, Holy Roman Empire
Height:	5'6"
Weight:	110 lbs.
Birth Date:	February 6
Blood Type:	A
Weapon:	Soul Calibur (Zweihander type)
Weapon Name:	Soul Calibur
Discipline:	Self-Taught
Family:	Mother: Margaret Father: Frederick (murdered by Siegfried)

Someone was calling him, but he could not clearly hear it. He strained to see, but could see nothing. Then the voice came again, and this time he could hear every word.

"So, you would throw away our friendship?"

"Yes. No one will ever again be a part of my life. Every man or woman who has known me has ultimately fallen to death's touch. So, go. Leave me. Forget you ever knew me."

The voice that had replied was his own. He began to lose his consciousness, his focus wavered, and then another voice came to him from behind.

"I have seen what you have done. Now you devote your life to atoning for your sins and redeeming your soul. Are you not as much a victim of that sword as the others?"

"No, no! No matter what beguiling words you whisper, my sins cannot be forgiven. I-I slew my father with my own bloodied hands. No cursed sword forced me to do that!"

As Siegfried spoke his answer, the man who questioned him faded from his vision, to be replaced once more by the memories of that night. The wind blew the clouds from the face of the moon, and suddenly the head that he held triumphantly aloft was brilliantly revealed. He saw the face, and there was no denying the truth. It was his father. His heart was in agony as if it had been pierced by a white-hot blade.

Siegfried jerked upright, as if yanked by a puppeteer's string. The full moon bathed his face in light. It had been a dream. He was alone.

He pressed his hand against the armor that covered his heart. A terrible scar marked him there. The maelstrom of power unleashed when Soul Calibur and Soul Edge clashed in the Lost Cathedral had torn his body apart. His long quest to destroy the cursed sword had been so nearly completed; redemption had been within his grasp, yet, in that moment, he had died, the scream of frustration at his failure silenced on his lips. Perhaps the spirit sword responded to that outpouring of emotion, for the sword whose destiny it was to destroy the cursed sword resonated with Siegfried's soul. It chose Siegfried for its master, and in doing so saved his life.

Siegfried thought again of the dream he had just seen. He thought of the people who had once stood by him, and the people he had left. And the one who still followed him, despite knowing that Siegfried was none other than Nightmare.

Bathed in the moonlight, Siegfried looked up into the night sky. He knew now what he must do. He would brush aside the outstretched hands that tried to help him. Once, not so long ago, he had stood at the center of the terror that Nightmare wrought. The enemy he now faced was that cursed devourer of souls, Soul Edge. Awaiting him was the maelstrom of destruction unleashed at the cathedral.

Soul Calibur shone with a cold light in his hand. Siegfried made up his mind to become like the sword. No one would touch his heart, no man or woman would sway him from his path, until the cursed sword was destroyed for all time. Images of his brothers-in-arms, comrades, even friends that might have been—and, of course, his father—flashed one by one through his mind. He was alone, and he had no choice but to be alone, for he would never again hurt those he loved.

Siegfried turned his gaze away from the heavens. Before him a black shadow lay heavy over the cursed city of Ostrheinsburg. His journey of repentance was coming to an end.

Soul Calibur, the Spirit Sword

A sword forged in the ancient past, in the time of heroes. Its great mission is to defeat Soul Edge. It is the alter ego of the cursed sword and, like its dark adversary, has the power to transform itself in response to the spirit of the warrior who wields it. For generations, a guardian tribe protected its purity, but in time the tribal line died out and with it the sword's last protectors.

When Siegfried, who had once been possessed by the cursed sword, took up the spirit blade, it responded to his soul and became a great destroyer of evil. Even as Soul Edge grew powerful beyond all reckoning, so did Soul Calibur respond and grow stronger in turn. They say it is has become far more than a mere sword; it is the crystallized embodiment of near limitless power.

Self-Taught

A brigand in his youth who later became a mercenary-for-hire, Siegfried learned the art of sword fighting on the battlefield. His weapon has cut down enemies, crushed opposition, and at times served as a shield to protect his very life.

He spent his youth in careless pillaging and plundering, until one day he unknowingly murdered his own father. The shock caused him to create false memories and his life became a ceaseless, bloody quest to find Soul Edge. The sword twisted his mind, he became the Azure Knight, Nightmare, and he began a rampage of destruction and tyranny that would last for years.

Finally, he escaped the grip of the cursed sword and began the long, arduous task of atoning for his wicked deeds. He still fights for his soul today.

Command List

Signature Techniques

Name	Command	Attack Level	Damage	Notes
Double Grounder Beta	⇗ⒶⒶ	Low, Low	16, 27	
Rook Splitter	➔Ⓑ	Mid	32(42)	Damage varies depending on the distance it hits at
Maelstrom	While Rising ⒶⒶ	Mid, Low	20, 30	
Sky Splitter ~Chief Hold	⇘🅑	Mid	18(28)	Launches and deals more damage at close distances. Shifts to Chief Hold.
Rising Hilt ~Chief Hold	While Rising 🅑	Mid	22	Stuns on counter-hit. Shifts to Chief Hold.
Terror Stomper (Hold)	Chief Hold 🅑	Mid	20(30)	Guard Breaks. Deals additional damage and launches at a close distance.
Terror Slap	Chief Hold Ⓐ+Ⓑ	High	40	
Over Toss	While Crouching Ⓑ+Ⓖ	Low	20	

Horizontal Attacks

Name	Command	Attack Level	Damage	Notes
Slash Impact	ⒶⒶⒷ	High, High, Low	18, 14, 24	
Slash Impact ~Base Hold	ⒶⒶ🅑	High, High, Low	18, 14, 24	Shifts to Base Hold
Slash Impact ~Side Hold	🅐	High	18	Shifts to Side Hold
Quick Backspin Slash	ⒶⒼⒶ	High	30	
Quick Backspin Slash ~Reverse Side Hold	ⒶⒼ🅐	High	30	Shifts to Reverse Side Hold
Quick Spin Slash	⇨Ⓐ	High	20(24)	Deals additional damage at a close distance
Quick Spin Slash ~Side Hold	⇨🅐	High	20(24)	Deals additional damage at a close distance. Shifts to Side Hold.
Armlet Crusher	⇘Ⓐ	Mid	32	
Leg Slash	⇩Ⓐ	Low	14	
Double Grounder Beta	⇗ⒶⒶ	Low, Low	16, 27	
Piercing Hilt	⇦Ⓐ	High	18	Causes recoverable stun on counter-hit
Piercing Hilt ~Reverse Side Hold	⇦🅐	High	18	Causes recoverable stun on counter-hit. Shifts to Reverse Side Hold.
Leg Slash	While Crouching Ⓐ	Low	14	
Maelstrom	While Rising ⒶⒶ	Mid, Low	20, 30	
Maelstrom (Cancel)	While Rising ⒶⒶ⇩	Mid	20	Leaves Siegfried in crouching state
Maelstrom ~Side Hold	While Rising 🅐	Mid	20	Shifts to Side Hold
Fatal Spin Slash	Jumping Ⓐ	High	28 or 30 or 32	Damage varies depending on direction jumped in
Turning Head Slash	Backturned Ⓐ	High	20	
Turning Leg Slash	While Crouching Backturned Ⓐ	Low	16	

Vertical Attacks

Name	Command	Attack Level	Damage	Notes
Armor Breaker	ⒷⒷⒷ	Mid, Mid, Sp.Mid	16, 14, 24	
Armor Breaker ~Base Hold	🅑	Mid	16	Shifts to Base Hold
Armor Breaker ~Chief Hold	ⒷⒷ🅑	Mid, Mid, Sp.Mid	16, 14, 24	Shifts to Chief Hold
Buster Grounder	Ⓑ⇩Ⓐ	Mid, Low	16, 30	
Buster Grounder (Hold)	Ⓑ⇩🅐	Mid, Low	16, 40	Guard Breaks
Buster Grounder ~Chief Hold	Ⓑ⇩Ⓐ⇦	Mid	16	Shifts to Chief Hold
Gauntlet Buster	Ⓑ⇨	Mid	20	
Rampart Buster	Ⓑ⇦	Mid	42(48)	Perform as fast as possible for additional damage (Just Frame)
Piercing Strike	⇨Ⓑ	Mid	35(40)	Inflicts additional damage from a distance
Sky Splitter	⇘Ⓑ	Mid	18(28)	Deals additional damage and launches at close range
Sky Splitter ~Chief Hold	⇘🅑	Mid	18(28)	Deals additional damage and launches at close range. Shifts to Chief Hold.
Shadow Buster	⇩Ⓑ	Mid	18	
Shadow Buster ~Base Hold	⇩🅑	Mid	18	Shifts into Base Hold
Thrust Throw	⇗Ⓑ	Mid	28, 35	Shifts into special hit throw at close distances
Triple Headbutt	⇦ⒷⒷⒷ	Mid, Mid, Mid	12, 16, 20	
Earth Divide	⇩⇘⇨Ⓑ	Mid	50(75)	Unblockabkle. Input Ⓖ to cancel. Deals increased damage at close distances.
Split Buster	While Crouching Ⓑ	Mid	18	
Split Buster ~Base Hold	While Crouching 🅑	Mid	18	Shifts to Base Hold
Rising Hilt	While Rising Ⓑ	Mid	22	Stuns on counter-hit
Rising Hilt ~Chief Hold	While Rising 🅑	Mid	22	Stuns on counter-hit. Shifts to Chief Hold.
Fatal Buster	Jumping Ⓑ	Mid	24 or 28 or 32	Damage varies depending on direction jumped in
Turning Sword Thrust	Backturned ⒷⒷ	Mid, Low	18, 24	
Turning Shadow Buster	While Crouching Backturned Ⓑ	Mid	20	

Kick Attacks

Name	Command	Attack Level	Damage	Notes
Dark High Kick	Ⓚ	High	12	
Dark Toe Kick	⇨Ⓚ	High	18	Causes recoverable stun on counter-hit
Axle Head Upper	⇘ⓀⓀⒷ	Mid, Low, Mid	16, 14, 20	Final attack stuns on hit
Stomping	⇩Ⓚ During Hit ⓀⓀⓀⓀ	Low, Low, Low, Low, Low	10, 6, 4, 4, 4	Final attack stuns on counter-hit
Dark Low Kick	⇗Ⓚ	Low	14	
Darkside Kick	⇦Ⓚ	Mid	22	Knocks down on counter-hit
Dark Low Kick	While Crouching Ⓚ	Low	14	
Rising Night Kicks	While Rising Ⓚ	Mid, Mid	10, 12	
Fatal Brave Kick	Jumping Ⓚ	Mid	14 or 18 or 22	Damage varies depending on direction jumped in
Turning Dark High Kick	Backturned Ⓚ	High	14	
Turning Dark Low Kick	While Crouching Backturned Ⓚ	Low	12	

8-Way Run

Name	Command	Attack Level	Damage	Notes
Assault Slap	→ or ↘ or ↗Ⓐ	High	30	
Alternate Cross	↓ or ↑Ⓐ	Mid	36	
Backspin Slash	← or ↙ or ↖Ⓐ	High	20	Stuns on hit
Backspin Slash ~Reverse Side Hold	← or ↙ or ↖🅐	High	20	Shifts to Reverse Side Hold
Rook Splitter	→Ⓑ	Mid	32(42)	Damage varies depending on the distance it hits at
Sky Splitter	↘ or ↗Ⓑ	Mid	20(30)	Inflicts additional damage and launches at close distances
Sky Splitter ~Chief Hold	↘ or ↗🅑	Mid	20(30)	Inflicts additional damage and launches at close distances. Shifts to Reverse Side Hold.
Phalanx Buster	↓Ⓑ	Mid	27	
Phalanx Buster ~Side Hold	↓🅑	Mid	27	Shifts to Side Hold
Phalanx Buster	↑Ⓑ	Mid	27	
Phalanx Buster ~Reverse Side Hold	↑🅑	Mid	27	Shifts to Reverse Side Hold
Illusion Edge	↙ or ↖Ⓑ	Mid	20	Stuns on counter-hit
Illusion Edge ~Chief Hold	↙ or ↖🅑	Mid	20	Stuns on counter-hit. Shifts to Chief Hold.
Fatal Dive	←Ⓑ	Mid	38	Input Ⓖ to cancel and shift to Chief Hold
Fatal Dive ~Base Hold	←🅑	Mid	38	Shifts to Base Hold
Fatal Drive	←ⒷⒷ	Mid, Mid	38, 30	
Fatal Drive ~Chief Hold	←Ⓑ🅑	Mid, Mid	38, 30	Shifts to Chief Hold
Shoulder Charge Strike	→ or ↘ or ↗ⓀⒶ	Mid, High	16, 25	
Spinning Cross Combo	↓ or ↑ⓀⒶⒶⒷ	High, High, High, Mid	20, 15, 14, 36	Final attack stuns on hit
Spinning Cross Combo ~Chief Hold	↓ or ↑Ⓚ🅐	High, High	20, 15	Shifts to Chief Hold
Spin Slash Double Grounder	↓ or ↑ⓀⒶ ⇩ⒶⒶ	High, High, Low, Low	20, 15, 20, 35	
Spinning Phantom Combo	↓ or ↑ⓀⒶ ⇩ⒶⒶ	High, Low, Low	18, 20, 35	
Spin Kick Combo	↓ or ↑ⓀⓀ	High, Mid	20, 22	
Spin Kick Combo (Delay)	↓ or ↑ⓀⓀ	High, Mid	20, 22	
Fatal Brave Kick	↙ or ↖Ⓚ	High	23	
Drop Kick	←Ⓚ	High	43	
Flying Edge	→Ⓐ+Ⓑ	Mid	44	
Sliding	While Running Ⓚ	Low	26	

Simultaneous Press

Name	Command	Attack Level	Damage	Notes
Blaze Wind ~Side Hold	Ⓐ+Ⓑ	Mid, Mid, Mid	15, 15, 20	Shifts to Side Hold
Blaze Storm	Ⓐ+ⒷⒶ	Mid, Mid, Low	15, 15, 20	
Dark Soul Impact	⇩Ⓐ+Ⓑ	Low	34	
Dark Soul Impact ~Base Hold	⇩🅐+🅑	Low	34	Shifts to Base Hold
Base Hold	Ⓑ+Ⓚ			Deflects low attacks
Reverse Side Hold	⇨Ⓑ+Ⓚ			
Chief Hold	⇩ or ⇧Ⓑ+Ⓚ			Movement acts as a sidestep (evades vertical attacks)
Side Hold	⇦Ⓑ+Ⓚ			
Chief Hold	Backturned Ⓑ+Ⓚ			
Spinning Cross Combo	Ⓐ+ⓀⒶⒶⒷ	High, High, High, Mid	18, 15, 14, 36	Final attack stuns on hit
Spinning Cross Combo ~Chief Hold	Ⓐ+Ⓚ🅐	High, High	18, 15	Shifts to Chief Hold
Spin Slash Double Grounder	Ⓐ+ⓀⒶ⇩ⒶⒶ	High, High, Low, Low	18, 15, 20, 35	
Spinning Phantom Combo	Ⓐ+ⓀⒶ⇩ⒶⒶ	High, Low, Low	18, 20, 35	
Taunt	Ⓚ+Ⓖ			

Throws

Name	Command	Attack Level	Damage	Notes
Hilt Impact	Ⓐ+Ⓖ	Throw	50	Input Ⓐ to escape
Nightmare Killer	Ⓑ+Ⓖ	Throw	55	Input Ⓑ to escape
Calamity Fall	Left Side Throw	Throw	60	Same button as throw (Ⓐ or Ⓑ) to escape
Unholy Terror	Right Side Throw	Throw	60	Same button as throw (Ⓐ or Ⓑ) to escape
Witch Hunt	Back Throw	Throw	68	Same button as throw (Ⓐ or Ⓑ) to escape
Flap Jack	While Crouching Ⓐ+Ⓖ	Low	30	Input Ⓐ to escape
Over Toss	While Crouching Ⓑ+Ⓖ	Low	20	Input Ⓑ to escape

Base Hold

Name	Command	Attack Level	Damage	Notes
Base Hold	Ⓑ+Ⓚ			Deflect low attacks
Reborn Slasher	Base Hold Ⓐ	High	34	
Reborn Kaiser	Base Hold Ⓑ	Mid	28	
Reborn Basher	Base Hold Ⓚ	Mid	32	
Reborn Basher (Hold)	Base Hold 🅚	Mid, Mid, Mid	25, 15, 16	
Landing Slasher	Base Hold Ⓐ+Ⓑ	Low	42	
Landing Slasher ~Reverse Side Hold	Base Hold Ⓐ+ⒷⒼ			Shifts to Reverse Side Hold

Reverse Side Hold

Name	Command	Attack Level	Damage	Notes
Reverse Side Hold	⇨ or ➡Ⓑ+Ⓚ			
Geist Slasher	Reverse Side Hold Ⓐ	High	38	
Geist Slasher ~Base Hold	Reverse Side Hold 🅐	High	38	Shifts to Base Hold
Geist Strike	Reverse Side Hold Ⓑ	Mid	18(28)	Stuns on hit. Deals additional damage when it hits at a close distance.
Geist Spinning Low Kick	Reverse Side Hold Ⓚ	Low	20	Stuns on hit
Geist Spinning Low Kick ~Reverse Side Hold	Reverse Side Hold 🅚	Low	20	Stuns on hit. Shifts to Reverse Side Hold.
Fiend Shatter	Reverse Side Hold Ⓐ+Ⓑ	Mid	48	
Reverse Side Hold	Reverse Side Hold ⇨Ⓑ+Ⓚ			

Chief Hold

Name	Command	Attack Level	Damage	Notes
Chief Hold	⇩ or ⇧ or ⬇ or ⬆ Ⓑ+Ⓚ			Movement acts as a sidestep (evades vertical attacks)
Terror Circular	Chief Hold Ⓐ	High, Mid	27, 21	
Terror Circular ~Side Hold	Chief Hold 🅐	High	27	Shifts to Side Hold
Terror Stomper	Chief Hold Ⓑ	Mid	20(30)	Stuns and deals additional damage when it hits at close distances
Terror Stomper (Hold)	Chief Hold 🅑	Mid	35(40)	Guard Breaks. Deals additional damage and launches at a close distance
Knee Kick Rush	Chief Hold ⓀⓀ	Mid, High	15, 14	2nd attack knocks down on counter-hit
Knee Kick Stomper	Chief Hold ⓀⒷ	Mid, Mid	10, 22	2nd attack stuns on counter-hit
Knee Kick Stomper ~Base Hold	Chief Hold Ⓚ🅑	Mid, Mid	10, 22	2nd attack stuns on counter-hit. Shifts to Base Hold.
Terror Slap	Chief Hold Ⓐ+Ⓑ	High	40	
Chief Hold	Chief Hold ⇩ or ⇧ Ⓑ+Ⓚ			Movement acts as a sidestep (evades vertical attacks)

Side Hold

Name	Command	Attack Level	Damage	Notes
Side Hold	⇦ or ⬅Ⓑ+Ⓚ			
Double Grounder Beta	Side Hold ⒶⒶ	Low, Low	21, 36	
Double Grounder Beta ~Reverse Side Hold	Side Hold 🅐	Low	21	Shifts to Reverse Side Hold
Reaver	Side Hold Ⓑ	Mid	30(35)	Deflects high attacks. Stuns and inflicts less damage if it hits from max range.
Reaver ~Base Hold	Side Hold 🅑	Mid	30(35)	Deflects high attacks. Stuns and inflicts less damage if it hits from max range.
High Kick Beta	Side Hold Ⓚ	High	14	Stuns on counter-hit
Fiend Shatter	Side Hold Ⓐ+Ⓑ	Low	36	Stuns on hit

Combos

⇘🅑, during Chief Hold Ⓑ
2 hits, 49 Damage
Counter-hit, ⇘🅑, during Chief Hold Ⓐ + Ⓑ
2 Hits, 65 Damage
Counter-hit ⇨Ⓚ, ⇘🅑, Ⓐ + Ⓑ
3 Hits, 72 Damage, first stun is escapable
During Reverse Side Hold 🅚, during Reverse Side Hold Ⓐ + Ⓑ
2 Hits, 53 Damage
During Reverse Side Hold Ⓑ, ⇨⇨Ⓑ
2 hits, 49 Damage
During Side Hold 🅑, Ⓚ
2 hits, 63 Damage, first attack must hit from a distance
During Side Hold counter-hit Ⓚ, ⇨⇨ⓀⒶ
3 hits, 50 Damage
During Base Hold Ⓑ, ⇨⇨Ⓐ + Ⓑ
3 hits, 72 Damage
Counter-hit ⬋🅑, Ⓚ🅑, Ⓚ
3 hits, 66 Damage
While Rising 🅑, Ⓑ
2 hits, 36 Damage
Counter-hit While Rising 🅑, Ⓚ🅑, Ⓚ
4 hits, 68 Damage
⇦⇦Ⓐ, ⇨⇨Ⓑ
2 hits, 54 Damage
⇦⇦Ⓐ, ⇗⇗🅑, Ⓚ🅑, Ⓚ
5 hits, 75 Damage

Close Range

Though close range is not Siegfried's best position, his easy-to-use attack options enable him to inflict big damage for little effort. Use the Flap Jack (While Crouching Ⓐ+Ⓖ or Ⓑ+Ⓖ) or Double Grounder Beta (⬀ⒶⒶ) to catch standing adversaries off guard. Exploit the Armlet Crusher (⬂Ⓐ) or the Thrust Throw (⬀Ⓑ) against crouching opponents. The Armlet Crusher and Thrust Throw are both vulnerable to standing Ⓐ strings when guarded, so use the Illusion Edge~Chief Hold (↖ or ↙Ⓑ) instead if you're looking for a safer option. If it strikes as a counter-hit, follow up with the Knee Kick Stomper~Base Hold (during Chief Hold ⓀⒷ), then the Reborn Basher (during Base Hold Ⓚ) for a 4-hit combo.

An advanced way of attacking from this position is with the Piercing Hilt (⇦Ⓐ), which is used to preemptively stop enemy attacks. It shifts into the Reverse Side Hold stance and also causes a recoverable stun on counter-hit, enabling follow-up stance attacks to occasionally combo. If it successfully connects as a normal or counter-hit, attack with the Geist Spinning Low Kick (during Reverse Side Hold Ⓚ) or the mid Geist Strike (during Reverse Side Hold Ⓑ). Both options lead to combinations on a successful hit, and both link if the Piercing Hilt happens to connect on a counter-hit. Its only major weakness is the heavy disadvantage it creates when guarded. If this happens, take defensive measures by using the Geist Spinning Low Kick to duck under high counterattacks. Shift into the Chief Hold stance (⇩ or ⇩Ⓑ+Ⓚ) to avoid vertical attacks, or shift into the Side Hold stance (⇦Ⓑ+Ⓚ) to evade your enemy's ⇩Ⓐ attacks. Whenever an attack is dodged, use each stance's native attacks to punish your recovering foe.

Mid Range

As Siegfried's strongest position, always fall back into mid range when you're unsure of the opposition's strategy. Siegfried's safest option is to use 8-Way Run to hover outside the enemy's attack range and lure out missed strikes. You can then punish missed attacks with the Sky Splitter for heavy damage. If you want to preemptively stop your enemy from attacking with a standing horizontal attack, use the Illusion Edge~Chief Hold (↖ or ↙Ⓑ). If it strikes as a counter-hit, follow up with the Knee Kick Stomper~Base Hold (during Chief Hold ⓀⒷ), then the Reborn Basher (during Base Hold Ⓚ) for a 4-hit combo.

When enemies are afraid to initiate an offense, harass them with strings to pressure them into making a move. A single standing Ⓑ is useful for this, as it shifts directly into the Base Hold stance. When Ⓑ is guarded, follow up with either the Reborn Basher (during Base Hold Ⓚ) extension or the Landing Slasher (during Base Hold Ⓐ+Ⓑ) to begin a basic mid or low offense. The Landing Slasher is fairly slow, though, so occasionally use the Ⓑ⇩Ⓐ string as an alternate low variation. You can also input Ⓑ⇩Ⓐ⇦ To fake the low extension and shift into the Chief Hold stance. Attack with the stance's mid Terror Stomper (during Chief Hold Ⓑ) to slice your crouching opponent.

Defensive players often rely on 8-Way Run to evade some of the preceding options. Use Siegfried's Assault Slap (⇨⇨Ⓐ) or the Quick Spin Slash (⇨Ⓐ) to counter their attempts to circle around you. A far more damaging and flexible option is the Maelstrom (While Rising ⒶⒶ), which fully combos on counter-hit against sidesteps. You can verify whether the attack has connected on a counter-hit and follow up with varying options depending on the outcome. If the attack hits normally, input ⇩ before Siegfried performs the second strike to cancel it (While Rising ⒶⒶ⇩). This leaves Siegfried in a crouching state, enabling you to go for his mid-hitting Rising Hilt (While Rising Ⓑ) to trick players expecting the Maelstrom's second low attack. If the Rising Hilt hits, attack with the Terror Stomper (during Chief Hold Ⓑ) for a 2-hit combo. You can add further confusion to this tactic by using the crouching state to go for Siegfried's Flap Jack, which hits players expecting the Rising Hilt.

Long Range

Focus on using the Dark Soul Impact (⇩Ⓐ+Ⓑ) and Piercing Strike (⇨Ⓑ) to attack from this distance. Dark Soul Impact hits low, while the Piercing Strike is a mid attack. Advanced players may rely heavily on 8-Way Run to evade these attacks, so compensate by using full circular strikes, like the Assault Slap (⇨⇨Ⓐ), to hit them. You may opt to use Siegfried's ⒶⒶ string instead, which is less prone to heavy punishment if it misses.

Special Tactics

Okizeme: Anti-Wakeup

The ultimate goal is to scare your opponents into guarding low, which you can do by pressuring them with Siegfried's Flap Jack (While Crouching Ⓐ+Ⓖ), Over Toss (While Crouching Ⓑ+Ⓖ), or ⬀Ⓚ. When you believe your opponent is going to crouch, attack with the mid-hitting Sky Splitter (⬂Ⓑ), which leads to short aerial combos.

Because Siegfried's low-hitting options aren't as threatening as his mid attacks, your foe may opt to guard high more often than normal. Mix throws into your attack options to further confuse your enemy's defense. When you believe the enemy is looking to counter the throw, quickly stick out the Dark Toe Kick (⇨Ⓚ) to stop the attempt. This kick causes an escapable stun on counter-hit, opening the opportunity to strike your enemy with a Sky Splitter combo if he or she doesn't escape.

Sky Splitter Usage

The Sky Splitter is Siegfried's most important attack, largely because of its high damage output and flexibility. This versatility stems from its ability to shift directly into Siegfried's Chief Hold stance, which is performed by inputting the command ⬂Ⓑ. You should always initiate this shift, as the Chief Hold stance maneuvers can either defend against enemy counterattack or inflict extra damage on a successful hit. For example, if the slice hits your foe on a counter-hit, follow up with the Chief Hold's Terror Slap (during Chief Hold Ⓐ+Ⓑ) to knock your enemy out of the air. If the Sky Splitter is guarded, perform the Knee Kick Rush (during Chief Hold ⓀⓀ) to defend against enemy counterattack. Also use the Terror Circular attack (during Chief Hold Ⓐ) to catch your opponent's attempts to sidestep around the Terror Stomper or Knee Kick Rush follow-ups.

Keep in mind that, regardless of the defensive actions you take, the Sky Splitter is always vulnerable to quick horizontal strikes when blocked. Use it in a reactionary manner against missed attacks to reduce risk of counterattack.

Reverse Side Hold Tactics

If at any point your adversary is afraid to stop your forward movements, force your way into close range by using the Reverse Side Hold stance. This is especially useful after using standing Ⓐ or Ⓑ as a long-range poke, which enters one of Siegfried's alternate stances. After the stance change, you can quickly shift into the Reverse Side Hold. After the forward movement, initiate either the Geist Spinning Low Kick (during Reverse Side Hold Ⓚ) or the mid-hitting Geist Strike (during Reverse Side Hold Ⓑ). The Geist Spinning Low Kick shifts back into the Reverse Side Hold stance, so if it hits, use the stun it causes to follow up with an unavoidable Fiend Shatter (during Reverse Side Hold Ⓐ+Ⓑ). The Geist Strike stuns when it hits, allowing you to link into ⇨⇨Ⓑ afterward for heavy damage. If you believe your opponent will try to sidestep either of the above options, use the Geist Slasher (during Reverse Side Hold Ⓐ) to catch his or her circular movement.

Soul Crush Tactics

Many of Siegfried's basic strikes inflict massive Soul Gauge damage. Attacks like ⇨Ⓑ, ⇨⇨Ⓑ, ⬃Ⓐ, and ⇨⇨Ⓐ are especially powerful, though many aren't safe when guarded. Instead of focusing on forcing your enemy to guard these attacks, which happens naturally during the heat of battle, set up the charged version of Siegfried's Terror Stomper (during Chief Hold Ⓑ). This slash leaves Siegfried at an advantage, enabling you to follow up with additional strikes. A useful way of setting it up is to land ⬂Ⓑ on a normal hit; then hit your airborne foe with the Chief Hold's Ⓚ. When you recover from the kick, start charging for the Terror Stomper as your enemy is falling. As long as your foe doesn't Aerial Recover away from you, he should have no choice but to guard the attack as he stands up. Stay close to your enemy after backward recovery attempts by shifting into the Reverse Side Hold stance.

Sophitia Alexandra

Sophitia Alexandra

The mind is its own place, and in itself
Can make a Heaven of Hell, a Hell of Heaven.
"Paradise Lost" John Milton (1608 - 1674)

Age:	25
Birthplace:	Athens, Ottoman Empire
Height:	5′6″
Weight:	Refuses to say
Birth Date:	March 12
Blood Type:	B
Weapon:	Short Sword & Small Shield
Weapon Name:	Omega Sword & Elk Shield
Discipline:	Athenian Style
Family:	Husband: Rothion Daughter: Pyrrha Son: Patroklos

Omega Sword and Elk Shield

These holy weapons were forged by Sophitia's husband Rothion using iron given to her by Hephaestus, the Greek god of fire and forge. They were crafted with the greatest of care, the grips and balance made to be a perfect fit for Sophitia's size and strength.

Far away in the lands of Athens, Rothion prays for the safety of his wife and daughter, while Sophitia takes up her sword, prepared to commit any sin to save her daughter.

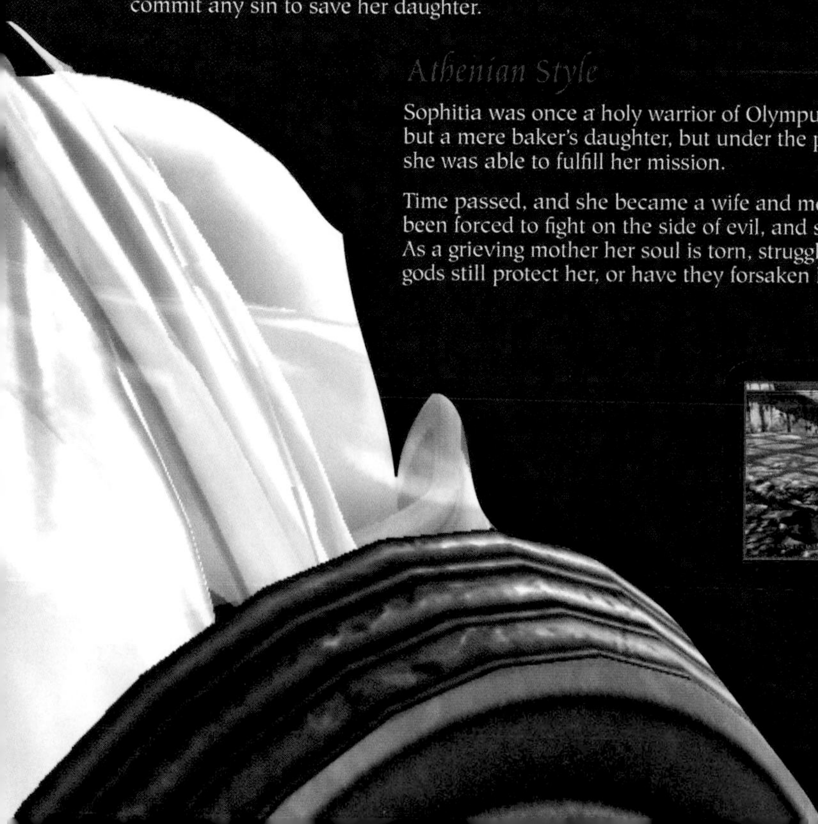

Athenian Style

Sophitia was once a holy warrior of Olympus. Though deeply devout, she was no fighter. Indeed, she was but a mere baker's daughter, but under the protection of the goddess Athena and the divinity within her, she was able to fulfill her mission.

Time passed, and she became a wife and mother of two. But, precisely because she is a mother, she has been forced to fight on the side of evil, and she is more skilled now in the arts of combat than she ever was. As a grieving mother her soul is torn, struggling under the weight of her cruel fate. Do those ancient Greek gods still protect her, or have they forsaken her forever?

Command List

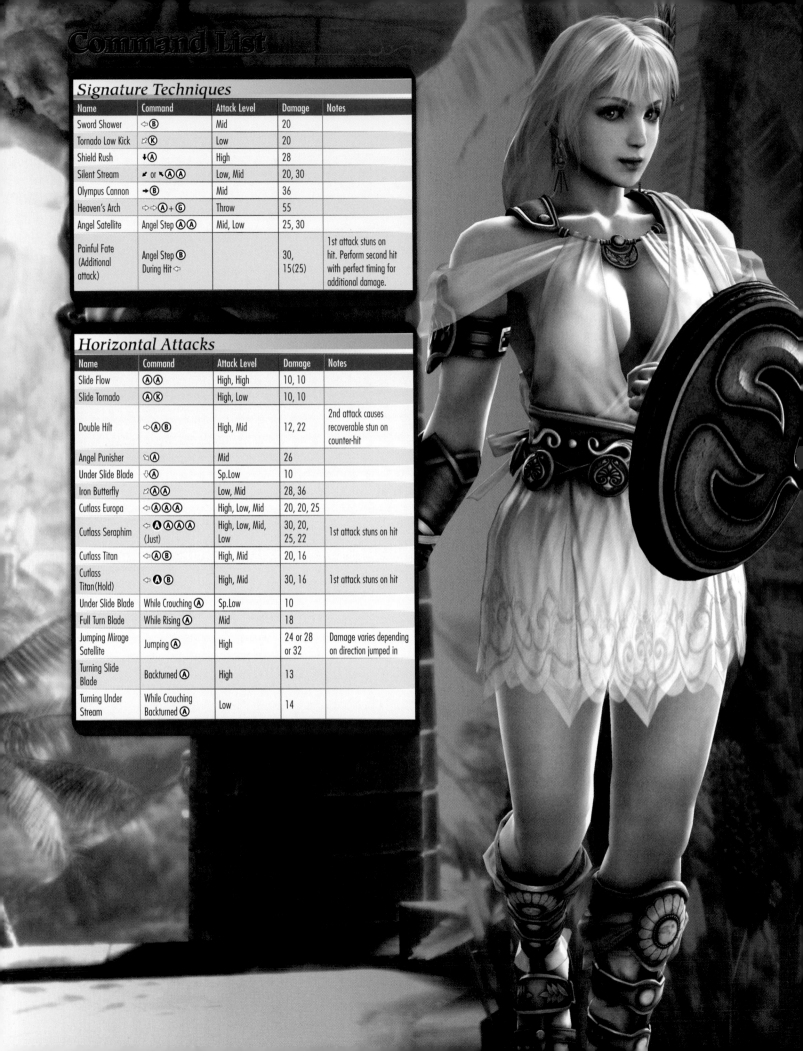

Signature Techniques

Name	Command	Attack Level	Damage	Notes
Sword Shower	⇦Ⓑ	Mid	20	
Tornado Low Kick	⇗Ⓚ	Low	20	
Shield Rush	⬇Ⓐ	High	28	
Silent Stream	⬋ or ⬉ⒶⒶ	Low, Mid	20, 30	
Olympus Cannon	➡Ⓑ	Mid	36	
Heaven's Arch	⇨⇨Ⓐ+Ⓖ	Throw	55	
Angel Satellite	Angel Step ⒶⒶ	Mid, Low	25, 30	
Painful Fate (Additional attack)	Angel Step Ⓑ During Hit ⇦		30, 15(25)	1st attack stuns on hit. Perform second hit with perfect timing for additional damage.

Horizontal Attacks

Name	Command	Attack Level	Damage	Notes
Slide Flow	ⒶⒶ	High, High	10, 10	
Slide Tornado	ⒶⓀ	High, Low	10, 10	
Double Hilt	⇨ⒶⒷ	High, Mid	12, 22	2nd attack causes recoverable stun on counter-hit
Angel Punisher	⇙Ⓐ	Mid	26	
Under Slide Blade	⇩Ⓐ	Sp.Low	10	
Iron Butterfly	⇗ⒶⒶ	Low, Mid	28, 36	
Cutlass Europa	⇦ⒶⒶⒶ	High, Low, Mid	20, 20, 25	
Cutlass Seraphim	⇦ 🅐ⒶⒶⒶ (Just)	High, Low, Mid, Low	30, 20, 25, 22	1st attack stuns on hit
Cutlass Titan	⇦ⒶⒷ	High, Mid	20, 16	
Cutlass Titan(Hold)	⇦ 🅐Ⓑ	High, Mid	30, 16	1st attack stuns on hit
Under Slide Blade	While Crouching Ⓐ	Sp.Low	10	
Full Turn Blade	While Rising Ⓐ	Mid	18	
Jumping Mirage Satellite	Jumping Ⓐ	High	24 or 28 or 32	Damage varies depending on direction jumped in
Turning Slide Blade	Backturned Ⓐ	High	13	
Turning Under Stream	While Crouching Backturned Ⓐ	Low	14	

Vertical Attacks

Name	Command	Attack Level	Damage	Notes
Ascend Splash	ⒷⒷ	Mid, Mid	14, 22	
Angel's Flow	ⒷⓀ	Mid, High	14, 18	
Impaling Strike	Ⓑ⇩ⒷⒷⒷ ⇩⇘⇨Ⓑ	Low, Low, Low, Low, Mid	10, 8, 8, 8, 30	Perform all inputs with Just Frame timing to allow 5th attack to combo against grounded enemies. Final attack stuns on hit.
Quick Strike	⇨Ⓑ	Mid	28	
Paladin Purifier	⇘Ⓑ	Mid	28	
Guardian Strike	⇩ⒷⒷ	Sp.Low, Mid	10, 30	2nd attack stuns on hit
Painful Fate (Additional attack)	⇩ⒷⒷ During Hit ⇦	Sp.Low, Mid	10, 30, 15(25)	2nd attack stuns on hit. Perform third hit with perfect timing for additional damage.
Guardian's Judgment	⇩Ⓑ⇧ⒷⒶⓀ	Sp.Low, Mid, High, High	10, 30, 12, 20	
Under Splash	⇙Ⓑ	Mid	16	
Sword Shower	⇦Ⓑ	Mid	20	
Under Splash	While Crouching Ⓑ	Mid	17	
Guardian Strike	While Crouching ⇙ⒷⒷ	Sp.Low, Mid	10, 30	2nd attack stuns on hit
Painful Fate (Additional attack)	While Crouching ⇙ⒷⒷ During Hit ⇦	Sp.Low, Mid	10, 30, 15(25)	2nd attack stuns on hit. Perform third hit with perfect timing for additional damage.
Exile	While Rising Ⓑ	Mid	17	
Jumping Under Splash	Jumping Ⓑ	Mid	24 or 28 or 32	Damage varies depending on direction jumped in
Turning Sword Splash	Backturned Ⓑ	Mid	18	
Turning Under Splash	While Crouching Backturned Ⓑ	Mid	16	

Simultaneous Press

Name	Command	Attack Level	Damage	Notes
El Fortune	Ⓐ+Ⓑ	18, 9, 26		Deflects vertical strikes. After deflect, input ⒶⓀ for additional hits.
Twin Step Grace	⇘Ⓐ+Ⓑ	Mid, Mid	15, 38	1st attacks stuns on hit
Mirage Satellite	While Rising Ⓐ+Ⓑ	Mid	20	
Mirage Satellite(Hold)	While Rising Ⓐ+Ⓑ	Mid	20	Unblockable. Stuns on hit.
Temperance Strike	Ⓑ+ⓀⒷ	Mid, Mid	16, 30	2nd attack stuns on hit
Painful Fate (Additional attack)	Ⓑ+ⓀⒷ During Hit ⇦		16, 30, 15(25)	2nd attack stuns on hit. Perform third hit with perfect timing for additional damage.
Angel Press	⇦Ⓑ+Ⓚ	Mid	26	
Angel Fall	⇧Ⓑ+Ⓚ	Mid	30	
Angel Fall(Hold)	⇧Ⓑ+Ⓚ	Mid	50	Unblockable
Guardian Upper	While Rising Ⓑ+Ⓚ	Mid	26	
Hip Charge	Backturned Ⓑ+Ⓚ	Mid	30	Causes recoverable stun on hit
Tornado High Kick	Ⓐ+Ⓚ	High	20	
Tornado Feint	Ⓐ+ⓀⓀ	Mid	40	
Angel Stroke	⇧Ⓐ+ⓀⒶⒷ	Mid, Low, Mid	10, 10, 20, 24	
Angel Fall	⇧Ⓐ+ⓀⒷ	Mid, Mid	10, 10, 40	Final attack stuns on hit
Angel's Sault	⇧Ⓐ+ⓀⓀ	Mid, Mid	10, 10, 16	
Taunt	Ⓚ+Ⓖ			

Kick Attacks

Name	Command	Attack Level	Damage	Notes
Kick Duo	ⓀⓀ	High, Mid	8, 12	
Flapping Heel Kick	⇨Ⓚ	Mid	15	
Angel Side Kick	⇘Ⓚ	Mid	18	
Spring Under Kick	⇩Ⓚ	Low	8	
Tornado Low Kick	⇙Ⓚ	Low	20	
Tornado Low Kick(Hold)	⇙Ⓚ	Low	30	
Temple Kick	⇦Ⓚ	High	10	Evades highs and deflects low attacks. Stuns on counter-hit.
Spring Under Kick	While Crouching Ⓚ	Low	8	
Rising Temple	While Rising Ⓚ	Mid	20	
Holy Crest Kick	Jumping Ⓚ	Mid	20 or 24 or 28	Damage varies depending on direction jumped in
Turning Holy High Kick	Backturned Ⓚ	High	16	
Turning Angel Sweep	While Crouching Backturned Ⓚ	Low	12	

8-Way Run

Name	Command	Attack Level	Damage	Notes
Silent Cross	→ or ↘ or ↗Ⓐ	Mid	26	
Shield Rush	↓Ⓐ	High	28	
Inverse Shield Rush	↑Ⓐ	High	28	
Silent Stream	↙ or ↖ⒶⒶ	Low, Mid	20, 30	
Silent Stream (Hold)	↙ or ↖Ⓐ🅐	Low, Mid	20, 50	Unblockable
Reverse Mirage	←Ⓐ	Mid	18	
Reverse Mirage (Counter)	←Ⓐ		21, 16	
Heaven's Gate	←ⒶⒷ	Mid	56	Unblockable. Launches on hit. Input Ⓖ to cancel.
Olympus Cannon	→Ⓑ	Mid	36	
Ascension	↘ or ↗Ⓑ	Mid	21	
Elk Strike	↓ or ↑Ⓑ	High	20	
Elk Strike (Hold)	↓ or ↑🅑	High	30	Guard Breaks
Guardian Upper	← or ↙ or ↖Ⓑ	Mid	22	
Plasma Blade	→ or ↘ or ↗Ⓚ	Mid	16	
Angel Side Kick	↓ or ↑Ⓚ	Mid	20	
Holy Punishment	← or ↙ or ↖Ⓚ	Mid	20	Stuns on counter-hit
Lodestar Strike	→Ⓐ+Ⓑ	High	42	
Twin Step Grace	While Running (except →) Ⓐ+Ⓑ	Mid, Mid	14, 34	1st attack stuns on hit
Jet Stream Rush	→ or ↘ or ↗ Ⓑ+ⓀⒶⒷ	Mid, High, Mid	22, 8, 15	Fully combos on counter-hit
Jet Stream Rush (Delay)	→ or ↘ or ↗ Ⓑ+ⓀⒶⒷ	Mid, High, Mid	22, 8, 15	Fully combos on counter-hit
Olympus Shower	← or ↙ or ↖ or ↓ or ↑Ⓑ+Ⓚ	Mid	38	
Sliding	While Running Ⓚ	Low	26	

Throws

Name	Command	Attack Level	Damage	Notes
Widow Maker	Ⓐ+Ⓖ	Throw	40	Input Ⓐ to escape
Widow Maker	Ⓐ+Ⓖ↓	Throw	35	Input Ⓐ to escape
Holy Cracker	Ⓑ+Ⓖ	Throw	40	Input Ⓑ to escape
Heaven To Hell	Holy Cracker ⇩Ⓐor ⇩Ⓑ	Throw	25	Same button as throw (Ⓐ or Ⓑ) to escape
Round Knocker	Left Side Throw	Throw	40	Same button as throw (Ⓐ or Ⓑ) to escape
Broken Promise	Right Side Throw	Throw	70	Same button as throw (Ⓐ or Ⓑ) to escape
Bottoms Up	Back Throw	Throw	35	Same button as throw (Ⓐ or Ⓑ) to escape
Heaven's Arch	⇨⇨Ⓐ+Ⓖ	Throw	55	Input Ⓐ to escape

Angel Step

Name	Command	Attack Level	Damage	Notes
Angel Step	⇩⬂⇨			Evades high attacks
Angel Satellite	Angel Step ⒶⒶ	Mid, Low	25, 30	
Angel's Strike	Angel Step Ⓑ	Mid	30	Stuns on hit from close range
Painful Fate (Additional attack)	Angel Step Ⓑ During Hit ⇦		30, 15(25)	Perform second hit with perfect timing for additional damage
Holy Arrow Kick	Angel Step Ⓚ	Mid	30	
Angel Step ~Sidestep	Angel Step ⇩ or ⇧			Evades vertical attacks
Angel Satellite	Angel Step ⇩ or ⇧ⒶⒶ	Mid, Low	25, 30	
Jet Stream Rush	Angel Step ⇩ or ⇧ⒷⒶⒷ	Mid, High, Mid	26, 8, 15	Fully combos on counter-hit
Jet Stream Rush (Delay)	Angel Step ⇩ or ⇧ⒷⒶⒷ	Mid, High, Mid	26, 8, 15	Fully combos on counter-hit
Holy Crest Kick	Angel Step ⇩ or ⇧Ⓚ	Mid	20	Stuns on hit

Twin Angel Step

Name	Command	Attack Level	Damage	Notes
Twin Angel Step	⇩⬂⇨⇩⬂⇨			Evades high attacks
Twin Angel Step	Angel Step ⇩ or ⇧⇩⬂⇨			
Seraphim Blade	Twin Angel Step ⒶⒶ	Mid, High	20, 20	1st attack stuns on hit. 2nd attack stuns on counter-hit.
Seraphim Strike	Twin Angel Step Ⓑ	Mid	50	Stuns on hit
Painful Fate (Additional attack)	Twin Angel Step Ⓑ During Hit ⇦		50, 15	1st attack stuns on hit
Angel Arc (Additional attack)	Twin Angel Step Ⓑ During Hit ⇦ (Just)		50, 30	1st attack stuns on hit
Tornado Feint	Twin Angel Step Ⓚ	Mid	30	
Twin Angel Step ~Sidestep	Twin Angel Step ⇩ or ⇧			

Combos

⬂Ⓑ, ⬂Ⓐ + Ⓑ
3 hits, 65 Damage

⇨⇨Ⓑ, ⬂Ⓐ + Ⓑ
3 hits, 72 Damage

Counter-hit ⇦Ⓚ, ⇦⇦Ⓚ, ⇨⇨Ⓑ
3 hits, 51 Damage

Counter-hit ⇦ⒶⒷ, ⇦Ⓑ
3 hits, 54 Damage

While Rising 🅐 + 🅑, ⇨⇨Ⓑ
2 hits, 48 Damage

Counter-hit ⇨⇨Ⓑ + ⓀⒶⒷ, Ⓖ (to turn around from back-turned state), ⬂Ⓐ + Ⓑ
6 hits, 94 Damage

Back-turned Ⓑ + Ⓚ, ⇩Ⓑ ⇧ⒷⒶⓀ
5 hits, 75 Damage

Twin Angel Step ⒶⒶ, ⇩⬂⇨Ⓑ
3 hits, 64 Damage

Close Range

The versatile Sophitia can fight at any distance, but her strongest options are available when she's next to her enemy. Start an offense with ⒶⒶ, which counters your enemy's sidesteps and slower attacks. If it hits, stage a second attack consisting of the Iron Butterfly (↙ⒶⒶ) or Guardian Strike (↓ⒷⒷ). Sophitia's most flexible mid attack is ↓ⒷⒷ, which is used to fish for crouching states and counter hits. Attack with a standalone ↓Ⓑ. If it connects as a counter-hit or against a crouching character, chain into its Ⓑ extension for a 2-hit combo. Tap ← as the second hit connects to perform a third hit. When blocked, use the delay-able Ⓑ extension to stop your enemy's immediate attempts to attack your recovery. When your foe is afraid of the follow-up, perform ↓Ⓑ by itself, then go for a throw or crouching ↙ⒷⒷ. Keep in mind that ↓ⒷⒷ is extremely unsafe to counterattack if blocked, so never perform the second hit if you want to avoid heavy damage. Furthermore, Sophitia's Temperance Strike (Ⓑ+Ⓚ) has the exact same extension as ↓ⒷⒷ (Ⓑ+ⓀⒷ). Use this string to leap over anticipated low attacks.

Your enemy may try to crouch under your ⒶⒶ string and punish it with a rising attack. To prevent this from happening, use Sophitia's Double Hilt (→ⒶⒷ) string, which starts with a high attack and ends with a mid. This string tricks players into ducking under the first high hit and using a rising attack. The opponent's attack is then stopped by the mid-hitting segment of Sophitia's string, which counter-hits and stuns the player.

If your offense is ever blocked, fall back on Sophitia's defensive options. Use the Temple Kick (←Ⓚ) to deflect low attacks, which leads to the following combo on counter-hit: ←Ⓚ, ←←Ⓚ, →→Ⓑ. Though it's risky, El Fortune (Ⓐ+Ⓑ) deflects vertical attacks for massive damage; input ⒶⓀ after the uppercut to finish the string.

Mid Range

Your goal is to knock down your enemy to initiate a wake-up attack. There are several ways to accomplish this: You can cautiously move around and punish your enemy's missed moves with Olympus Cannon (⇨Ⓑ); juggle with ↘Ⓐ+Ⓑ after it hits. Or you can use Lodestar Strike (→→Ⓐ+Ⓑ). Another option is to slip under a high attack with the Angel Step (↓↘→). Finally, you can actively attack. You should use all options together in some shape or form to confuse your enemy. When you take an aggressive stance, stop your enemy's 8-Way Run movements with Cutlass Titan (←ⒶⒷ) and Cutlass Europa (←ⒶⒶⒶ). Cutlass Titan ←ⒶⒷ fully combos on counter-hit, enabling you to score an additional ←Ⓑ afterward for a 3-hit combo. Cutlass Europa ←ⒶⒶⒶ is a low variation to use when your enemy expects the mid-hitting version. Also, use the low Silent Stream (⇗ or ⇘ⒶⒶ) to stop 8-Way Run, which shifts into a final mid attack. When you believe your enemy is afraid of the mid hit, input ⇗ⒶⒶ to shift into an unblockable variation of the string.

When enemies are reluctant to use circular movement, use the Quick Strike (→Ⓑ) to harass them. This is meant to irritate them into attacking. Periodically move out of their attack range to give them room to hang themselves. If they initiate an attack, punish it with →→Ⓑ. Furthermore, if you're willing to take a risk, charge in with Jet Stream (→→Ⓑ+ⓀⒶ). If it happens to strike your enemy on a counter-hit, chain into its Ⓑ follow-up (→→Ⓑ+ⓀⒶⒷ) to launch for a combo. When blocked, perform the Ⓑ extension extremely late to lure an attack, or throw when the opponent is afraid of the string's final hit.

Long Range

Because Sophitia has very few worthwhile options at this distance, focus on establishing mid or close range. Use Reverse Mirage (⇦Ⓐ) to deter your enemy's sidesteps, then use the Angel Step or →→Ⓑ+ⓀⒶ to move in. When the Angel Step recovers, throw your enemy or perform one of its techniques to counter an enemy attack.

Special Tactics

Okizeme: Anti-Wakeup

Sophitia's best anti-wakeup options include ↙ⒶⒶ, ↓ⒷⒷ, and Ⓐ+Ⓖ. Condition your enemies with the flexible ↓ⒷⒷ string, then attack with ↙ⒶⒶ when they're standing. Also use ↑Ⓐ+Ⓚ as an alternate mid attack. If the kick hits, chain into its Ⓚ extension (↑Ⓐ+ⓀⓀ). When blocked, input ⒶⒷ to go for a low-hitting extension, or Ⓑ for its mid option. Finally, Ⓐ+Ⓖ is an interesting throw that leaves Sophitia at an advantage with her enemy directly next to her. This position enables you to attack again with either another throw or ↓ⒷⒷ. If you anticipate a sidestep in this situation, perform ←ⒶⒷ to counter-hit.

Angel Step

The evasive Angel Step (↓↘→) ducks under high attacks while moving Sophitia forward. This is highly useful for quickly slipping into close range when your enemy isn't expecting it. What's more, it's possible to sidestep during this move by inputting ↓ or ↑, which enables you to dodge attacks aimed at hitting the Angel Step. If you manage to dodge an attack, punish it with the Angel Step's Ⓑ option. If not, let the movement recover and throw your enemy.

Taki

...only the person who can remain essentially silent can essentially act.
"A Literary Review," Soren Aabye Kierkegaard (1813 – 1855)

Bio

Age:	29
Birthplace:	Fu-Ma No Sato, Japan
Height:	5'7"
Weight:	117 lbs.
Birth Date:	Unknown
Blood Type:	A
Weapon:	Ninja Sword x 2
Weapon Name:	Rekki-Maru & Mekki-Maru
Discipline:	Musoh-Battoh-Ryu
Family:	Immediate family: All taken by sickness Master: Toki (Taki has opposed him since she left the clan.)

Taki

Whether used for good or evil, too much power can only lead to disaster.

Taki pursued Soul Edge, the sword that had driven her master mad and turned him into a monster. Purifying the fragments of the cursed sword in every place that she found them, she eventually came to the Lost Cathedral. When Taki saw the two swords locked in the Embrace of Souls, she learned at last of the spirit sword, a weapon that was able to resist the evil of the cursed sword.

Taki was there when the two opposing swords were unleashed, and Siegfried and Nightmare fought, but the battle did not end as she had hoped. Instead of destroying each other, Soul Calibur and Soul Edge grew more powerful than ever before, and together sparked a cataclysm.

Taki had to draw on all her strength and skills to escape being destroyed by the maelstrom, and the experience taught her just how dangerous the spirit sword was. The Lost Cathedral had been obliterated, but Soul Calibur and Soul Edge survived. Even now, the dreadful power of the two swords linked them, and brought them closer. They would both have to be consigned to oblivion, one at a time, lest they should come together again.

Perhaps it was the torrent of power that had engulfed it, but the evil impregnated in the enchanted Mekki-Maru blade had become stronger. Taki's favored weapon, Rekki-Maru, also sensed the power of Soul Edge growing ever stronger. Her weapons were drawn to Soul Edge; pointing like a divining rod toward the lands of Ostrheinsburg. She learned that Siegfried was heading to the same location. There was no more time! She set out on her own journey, but then a man stood before her, blocking her path.

This man knew that Nightmare was none other than Siegfried himself, but he still believed in Siegfried, the man. He wanted his friend to fight the battle, and he could not allow Taki to stand in his way. He fought well and with courage, but in the end, what could he do before the flashing speed of Mekki-Maru?

"If you had been there then, he might have kept his humanity. But, that's all in the past now."

Taki left him alive, and turned back toward the dark, evil stench that cloaked Ostrheinsburg like a funeral shroud.

She witnessed everything at the Lost Cathedral. Siegfried was seemingly torn asunder by the overwhelming torrent of power. His soul should have been extinguished from the world, but the spirit sword intervened and kept him alive. Siegfried survived by a twisted act of providence, but would he be able to cling to his human reason and somehow control the immense power that resided within him?

She could not leave that answer to chance. She made her decision; this was not the time for mercy. She would do what must be done.

Rekki-Maru

A sword forged by Taki herself while a member of the Fu-Ma clan, its demon-ward blade can detect strong auras and unquiet atmospheres and transmit those feelings to its mistress Taki. The sword was shattered once when it was crossed with Soul Edge, but Taki later repaired it. It is Taki's preferred weapon, and it never leaves her side.

Mekki-Maru

This is the enchanted sword that bewitched the master of the Fu-Ma ninjas and drove Taki to become a fugitive from the same clan. When she fused a fragment of the evil Soul Edge into Mekki-Maru, it surged with a power that even she could not control.

During her long flight from the Fu-Ma clan pursuers, Taki slowly honed her mental and spiritual strength until she could exert enough control over Mekki-Maru to use it in battle. She has covered its scabbard with charms and tokens, but its power is so great that even she only dares use it in crucial situations.

Musoh-Battoh-Ryu

It is believed that this fighting style was developed in ancient Japan by the demon-exterminating ninjas of the legendary Fu-Ma clan, but no one has been able to prove that the Fu-Ma clan even existed. Surviving contemporary records contain only vague references to the group. Though the name Musoh-Battoh-Ryu is widely known from stories and legends, few believe that the martial art ever existed. But if it did indeed exist, we can assume it was the culmination of all sword techniques, physical disciplines, and magic-ward arts developed by the shadowy Fu-Ma clan.

Command List

Signature Techniques

Name	Command	Attack Level	Damage	Notes
Shadow Ripper	ⒶⒶⒷ	High, High, Mid	8, 8, 18	
Ninja Cannon: Double	⇦Ⓐ+ⒷⒷ	Low, Low	10, 11	
Assassin's Revenge	→Ⓑ During Hit Ⓐ	Mid, Mid	25, 10	Both attacks stun on hit
Assassin's Secret ~Possession	⬂ⒷⓀ⇩⬃⇦	Mid, Mid	14, 15	2nd attack stuns on counter-hit. Shifts to Possession.
Lightning Scroll ~Possession	⬃ⒷⒶ⇩⬃⇦	Mid, High	14, 10	2nd attack stuns on counter-hit. Shifts to Possession.
Possession Strike	Possession Ⓚ	High	16	Causes recoverable stun on hit
Hover Falcon	Hover Ⓐ	Low, Low	20, 15	1st attack stuns on hit
Crossing the Cliff	⇨⇨Ⓑ+Ⓖ	Throw	58	

Horizontal Attacks

Name	Command	Attack Level	Damage	Notes
Shadow Ripper	ⒶⒶⒷ	High, High, Mid	8, 8, 18	
Shadow Ripper (Delay)	ⒶⒶⒷ	High, High, High	8, 8, 13	
Shadow Rush	ⒶⒷⓀ	High, Mid, High	8, 12, 15	
Shadow Rush ~Possession	ⒶⒷ⇩⬃⇦	High, Mid	8, 12	Shifts to Possession
Shadow Cannon	ⒶⒷ⇦Ⓐ+Ⓑ	High, Mid, Low	8, 12, 15	
Lightning Blaze	ⒶⒷ⇦Ⓐ+ⒷⒶ	High, Mid, High	8, 12, 10	
Shadow Shrine	Ⓐ⇨	Mid, Mid	32(34)	2nd attack stuns on counter-hit. Input ⇨ just as Ⓐ hits for Just Frame version. Input Ⓑ+Ⓚ, ⇩ or ⇧Ⓑ+Ⓚ after hit to shift to Wind Roll.
Wind Scroll	⇨Ⓐ	Mid	20	Causes recoverable stun on counter-hit
Wind Scroll ~Possession	⇨Ⓐ⇩⬃⇦	Mid	20	Shifts to Possession in backturned position
Earth Scroll	⬂ⒶⓀ	Low, Low	12, 12	2nd attack can be delayed
Shadow Split	⇩Ⓐ	Sp.Low	8	
Reaping Hook	⬃Ⓐ	Low	25	
Curse ~Possession	⇦Ⓐ	Low	18	Shifts Possession
Shadow Split	While Crouching Ⓐ	Sp.Low	8	
Shadow Claw	While Rising ⒶⒶⒶ	Mid, High, Mid	14, 8, 23	Final attack stuns on hit
Shadow Claw ~Possession	While Rising ⒶⒶ⇩⬃⇦	Mid, High	14, 8	Shifts to Possession
Falling Scroll	Jumping Ⓐ	Mid	18 or 20 or 22	Damage varies depending on direction jumped in
Reverse Shadow	Backturned Ⓐ	High	10	
Reverse Shadow Split	While Crouching Backturned Ⓐ	Low	12	

Vertical Attacks

Name	Command	Attack Level	Damage	Notes
Shadow Scroll	ⒷⒶⒶ	Mid, High, Low	10, 8, 34	
Shadow Banishment	ⒷⒶⓀ	Mid, High, High	10, 8, 26	Fully combos on counter-hit
Shadow Banishment (Hold)	ⒷⒶ🅚	Mid, High, High	10, 8, 36	
Heavy Shadow	ⒷⒶ⇨Ⓚ	Mid, High, Mid	10, 8, 26	Fully combos on counter-hit
Shadow Scroll ~Possession	ⒷⒶ⇩⬃⇦	Mid, High	10, 8	Shift to Possession
Lightning Strike	ⒷⒷⒷ	Mid, Mid, Mid	10, 15, 26	
Lightning Strike (Delay)	ⒷⒷⒷ	Mid, Mid, Mid	10, 15. 26	
Lightning Strike ~Possession	ⒷⒷⒷ⇩⬃⇦	Mid, Mid	10, 15	Shift to Possession. Must input ⇩⬃⇦ before final attack hits.
Oppression	ⒷⓀ	Mid, High	10, 25	
Oppression (Hold)	Ⓑ🅚	Mid, High	10, 35	
Blood Scroll	ⒷⓀⒶ	Mid, High, High	10, 25, 8	
Silence	⇨Ⓑ	Mid	21	
Assassin's Secret	⬂ⒷⓀ	Mid, Mid	14, 15	2nd attacks stuns on counter-hit
Assassin's Secret ~Possession	⬂ⒷⓀ⇩⬃⇦	Mid, Mid	14, 15	2nd attacks stuns on counter-hit. Shifts to Possession.
Vacuum	⇩Ⓑ	Mid	16	
Dark Slicer	⇩ⒷⒶ	Mid High	16, 8	
Dark Slicer ~Possession	⇩ⒷⒶ⇩⬃⇦	Mid High	16, 8	Shifts to Possession
Lightning Scroll	⬃ⒷⒶ	Mid High	14, 10	2nd attack stuns on counter-hit
Lightning Scroll ~Possession	⬃ⒷⒶ⇩⬃⇦	Mid High	14, 10	2nd attack stuns on counter-hit. Shifts to Possession.
Demon Fangs	⇦Ⓑ	Mid	30	Stuns on hit
Seal of the Fire Dragon	⇦⬃⇩⬂⇨Ⓑ	Mid	50	Unblockable. Input Ⓖ to cancel.
Free Shadow	While Crouching Ⓑ	Mid	12	
Darkness Banishment	While Rising ⒷⒷ	Mid Low	13, 15	2nd attack stuns on counter-hit
Windfall	Jumping Ⓑ	Mid	14 or 16 or 18	Damage varies depending on direction jumped in
Shadow Mekki-Maru	Backturned ⒷⒶ	Mid, High	17, 8	
Shadow Mekki-Maru ~Possession	Backturned ⒷⒶ⇩⬃⇦	Mid, High	17, 8	Shifts to Possession
Darkness Shatter	While Crouching Backturned Ⓑ	Mid	18	
Darkness Shatter ~Possession	While Crouching Backturned Ⓑ⇩⬃⇦	Mid	18	Shifts to Possession

Kick Attacks

Name	Command	Attack Level	Damage	Notes
Haste	ⓀⓀⓀ	High, High, High	9, 9, 9	
Water Haste	ⓀⓀ⇩Ⓚ	High, High, Low	9, 9, 10	
Advancing Cloud Scroll	Ⓚ⇩	Mid, Mid	17, 13	2nd attack stuns on counter-hit
Divine Punishment	⇨Ⓚ	Mid	18	
Divine Punishment ~Mekki-Maru	⇨ⓀⒶ	Mid, High	18, 8	
Divine Punishment ~Possession	⇨ⓀⒶ⇩↙⇦	Mid, High	18, 8	Shifts to Possession
Rapid Destruction	↘ⓀⓀⓀ	Mid, Mid, Mid	12, 10, 20	
Rapid Destruction ~Wind Roll 1	↘ⓀⓀⒷ+Ⓚ	Mid, Mid	12, 10	Shifts Wind Roll
Rapid Destruction ~Wind Roll 2	↘ⓀⓀ⇩ or ⇧Ⓑ+Ⓚ	Mid, Mid	12, 10	Shifts Wind Roll
Punishing Strike	⇩ⓀⓀ	Low, Mid	10, 15	
Sealing Punishment	↙Ⓚ	Low	9	
Water Kick	⇦ⓀⓀ	High, Low	17, 12	
Sealing Punishment	While Crouching Ⓚ	Low	9	
Divine Cannon	While Rising Ⓚ	Mid	12	Stuns on counter-hit
Haste Alternate	Jumping ⓀⓀⓀ	High, Low, High	12, 10, 18	
Haste Alternate ~Possession	Jumping ⓀⓀ⇩↙⇦	High, Low	12, 10	Shifts to Possession
Punishing Wind	Backturned Ⓚ	High	11	
Reverse Seal Punishment	While Crouching Backturned Ⓚ	Low	12	

Throws

Name	Command	Attack Level	Damage	Notes
Strangulation Blade	Ⓐ+Ⓖ	Throw	47	Input Ⓐ to escape
Departure in Fire	Ⓑ+Ⓖ	Throw	52	Input Ⓑ to escape
Cellar Drop	Left Side Throw	Throw	58	Same button as throw (Ⓐ or Ⓑ) to escape
Jute Burial	Right Side Throw	Throw	63	Same button as throw (Ⓐ or Ⓑ) to escape
Dropping the Bottle	Back Throw	Throw	60	Same button as throw (Ⓐ or Ⓑ) to escape
Crossing the Cliff	⇨⇨Ⓑ+Ⓖ	Throw	58	Input Ⓑ to escape

Simultaneous Press

Name	Command	Attack Level	Damage	Notes
Ninja Cannon	Ⓐ+Ⓑ	Low	11	
Ninja Cannon ~Mekki-Maru	Ⓐ+ⒷⒶ	High	11, 8	
Ninja Cannon ~Mekki-Maru ~Possession	Ⓐ+ⒷⒶ⇩↙⇦	High	11, 8	Shifts to Possession
Ninja Cannon: Fury	⇨Ⓐ+Ⓑ	Low	15	Unblockable
Fog Blanket	⇩Ⓐ+Ⓑ	Mid	24	Stuns on hit
Ninja Cannon: Double	⇦Ⓐ+ⒷⒷ	Low, Low	10, 11	
Shadow Hunt	⇦Ⓐ+ⒷⒶ	High	10, 8	
Shadow Hunt ~Possession	⇦Ⓐ+ⒷⒶ⇩↙⇦	High	10, 8	Shifts to Possession
Poison Dart	While Crouching ↙Ⓐ+Ⓑ	Sp.Mid	10	Stuns enemies lying on ground
Heavy Burden	Backturned Ⓐ+Ⓑ	Mid	14	
Fog Blanket	Backturned ⇩Ⓐ+Ⓑ	Mid	39	Stuns on hit
Wind Roll 1	Ⓑ+Ⓚ			
Wind Roll 2	⇩ or ⇧Ⓑ+Ⓚ			
Reverse Mill	Ⓑ+ⓀⒷ+Ⓚ			
Reverse Mill	Backturned Ⓑ+Ⓚ			
Stalker	Ⓐ+Ⓚ			
Stalker	⇦Ⓐ+Ⓚ			
Stalker	⇩ or ⇧Ⓐ+Ⓚ			
Divine Cannon Combo	While Crouching ⇩Ⓐ+ⓀⓀ	Low, Mid	10, 14	2nd attack stuns on counter-hit
Stalker	Backturned Ⓐ+Ⓚ			
Stalker	Backturned ⇩ or ⇧ Ⓐ+Ⓚ			
Taunt	Ⓚ+Ⓖ			

Stalker

Name	Command	Attack Level	Damage	Notes
Stalker	Ⓐ+Ⓚ			
Stalker	⇦Ⓐ+Ⓚ			
Stalker	⇩ or ⇧Ⓐ+Ⓚ			
Stalker	Backturned Ⓐ+Ⓚ			
Stalker	Backturned ⇩ or ⇧ Ⓐ+Ⓚ			
Stalker Blade	Ⓐ+ⓀⒶ	Mid	35	Stuns on hit
Stalker Thunder	Ⓐ+ⓀⒷ	Mid	55	
Stalker Tree Spirit	Ⓐ+ⓀⓀ	Mid, Mid	10, 10	
Stalker Drop	Against Airborne Foe Ⓐ+ⓀⒷ+Ⓖ	Throw	44	
Reverse Stalker Drop	Against Airborne Foe Backturned Ⓐ+Ⓚ Ⓑ+Ⓖ	Throw	48	
Stalker ~Reverse Mill	Ⓐ+ⓀⒷ+Ⓚ			Shifts to Reverse Mill

8-Way Run

Name	Command	Attack Level	Damage	Notes
Scroll of Darkness	→Ⓐ	Mid	30	Stuns on hit
Burning Misery	↘ or ↗ⒶⒷⒷⒷ	High, Mid, Mid, Mid	12, 8, 10, 12	All attacks within string can be performed with Just Frame timing, causing the final hit to stun
Burning Misery (Hold)	↘ or ↗🅐ⒷⒷⒷ	High, Mid, Mid, Mid	12, 8, 10, 12	
Burning Misery (Hold) ~Possession	↘ or ↗Ⓐ⇩⇙⇦	High	12	Shifts to Possession
Piercing Wind	↑ or ↓Ⓐ	High	16	Stuns on counter-hit
Bamboo Cutter	← or ↙ or ↖Ⓐ	High	18	
Assassin's Revenge	→Ⓑ During Hit Ⓐ	Mid, Mid	25, 10	Both attacks stun on hit
Assassin's Strike	↘ or ↗Ⓑ	Mid	40	Stuns on hit
Illusion Scroll	↓ or ↑Ⓑ	Mid, Mid	10, 24	
Seal	← or ↙ or ↖Ⓑ	Mid	25	
Hurricane Punishment	→Ⓚ	Sp.Mid, Sp.Mid	15, 15	
Whirling Misery	↘ or ↗Ⓚ	Mid, High	10, 16	2nd attack stuns on hit
Storm Cloud Scroll	↓ or ↑ⓀⒶ	High, High, Mid	14, 14, 26	2nd hit stuns on counter-hit
Storm Cloud Scroll ~Wind Roll 1	↓ or ↑ⓀⒷ+Ⓚ	High, High	14, 14	2nd hit stuns on counter-hit. Shifts to Wind Roll.
Storm Cloud Scroll ~Wind Roll 2	↓ or ↑Ⓚ⇩ or ⇧Ⓑ+Ⓚ	High, High	14, 14	2nd hit stuns on counter-hit. Shifts to Wind Roll.
Heavy Burden	↙ or ↖Ⓚ	Mid	16	Stuns on hit
Mat	←Ⓚ During Hit Ⓚ	Mid, Mid	18, 18	1st attack stuns on hit
Mat ~Possession	←Ⓚ⇩⇙⇦	Mid	18	1st attack stuns on hit. Shifts to Possession.
Vacuum Drop Kick	While Running ⓀⒷ	Low, Low, Mid	30, 16	Shifts to Stalker state

Wind Roll 1

Name	Command	Attack Level	Damage	Notes
Wind Roll 1	Ⓑ+Ⓚ			
Fan Dance	Wind Roll Ⓐ	Mid, Mid	15. 20	
Wind Death Sault	Wind Roll ⒷⒷⒷ	Mid, High, Mid	34, 8, 50	Fully combos on counter-hit. Final attack stuns against enemies lying on the ground.
Wind Sealing Rush	Wind Roll ⒷⓀ During Hit Ⓑ	Mid, High, High	34, 12, 22	
Wind Stealth Launch	Wind Roll Ⓚ	High	30	
Bow Breaker	Wind Roll Ⓐ+Ⓖ	Throw	40	
Return of the Sun	Wind Roll Ⓑ+Ⓖ	Throw	38	
Wind Roll 1 ~Possession	Wind Roll ⇩⇙⇦			Shifts to Possession
Wind Roll 1 ~Wind Roll 2	Wind Roll ⇩ or ⇧ Ⓑ+Ⓚ			Shifts to Wind Roll
Reverse Mill	Wind Roll Ⓑ+Ⓚ			Shifts to Wind Roll
Wind Roll 2	⇩ or ⇧Ⓑ+Ⓚ			
Wind Roll 2 ~Possession	Wind Roll 2 ⇩⇙⇦			Shifts to Possession
Wind Roll 2 ~Wind Roll 1	Wind Roll 2 Ⓑ+Ⓚ			Shifts to Wind Roll
Wind Roll 2 ~Wind Roll 2	Wind Roll 2 ⇩ or ⇧Ⓑ+Ⓚ			Shifts to Wind Roll
Reverse Mill	Wind Roll 2 ⇦Ⓑ+Ⓚ			Shifts to Wind Roll

Reverse Mill

Name	Command	Attack Level	Damage	Notes
Reverse Mill	Ⓑ+ⓀⒷ+Ⓚ			
Reverse Mill	Backturned Ⓑ+Ⓚ			
Weaving Blades	Reverse Mill Ⓐ	Low, High	10, 16	
Assassin's Feather	Reverse Mill Ⓑ	Mid	30	
Reverse Lightning	Reverse Mill Ⓚ	Mid	40	
Reverse Mill ~Wind Roll 1	Reverse Mill Ⓑ+Ⓚ			Shifts to Wind Roll
Reverse Mill ~Wind Roll 2	Reverse Mill ⇩ or ⇧Ⓑ+Ⓚ			Shifts to Wind Roll

Possession

Name	Command	Attack Level	Damage	Notes
Possession	⇩⇙⇦			
Possession Quake	Possession Ⓐ	High, High	5, 5	
Dream Scroll	Possession Ⓑ	Mid	32	
Possession Strike	Possession Ⓚ	High	16	Causes recoverable stun on hit
Dragon Wheel	Possession ⇘ or ⇧ or ⇗Ⓚ	Mid	15	
Exorcism	Possession Ⓐ+Ⓑ	Mid	50	
Wind Stalker ~Possession	Possession Ⓑ+Ⓚ	Throw	45	Unblockable
Wind Stalker ~Possession	Backturned Possession Ⓑ+Ⓚ	Throw	45	Unblockable
Possession Rush	Possession ⇨⇨			Evades high attacks
Possession Step	Possession ⇩ or ⇧			Evades vertical attacks
Silent Mist	Possession ⇩⇙⇦			

Hover

Name	Command	Attack Level	Damage	Notes
Hover	Possession ⇩⇘⇨			
Hover Falcon	Hover Ⓐ	Low, Low	15, 20	1st attack stuns on hit
Hover Lightning	Hover Ⓑ	Mid	25	Stuns on hit. Leaves Taki in crouching state.

Combos

↓ or ↑Ⓑ, ⒶⒶ

4 hits, 41 Damage

↓ or ↑Ⓑ, Ⓐ⇨ (Just)Ⓑ + ⓀⒷ

6 hits, 48 Damage

⇦Ⓐ + ⒷⒷ,Ⓐ + Ⓚ,Ⓑ + Ⓖ

3 hits, 69 Damage

Counter-hit while rising Ⓚ, ⇙ⒷⒶ⇩⇙⇦Ⓑ

4 hits, 52 Damage

Counter-hit ↓ or ↑Ⓐ, backturned Ⓐ + Ⓑ, Ⓐ ⇨Ⓑ + ⓀⒷ

5 hits, 55 Damage

Counter hit ↘ or ↗Ⓐ⇩⇙⇦, Ⓐ

3 hits, 24 Damage

⇩⇙⇦, ⇩⇘⇨Ⓑ, While Crouching ⇩Ⓐ + ⓀⓀ, ⇙ⒷⒶ⇩⇙⇦, Ⓑ

6 hits, 64 Damage

Backturned Ⓑ + ⓀⓀ, Ⓐ + ⓀⒷ + Ⓖ

2 hits, 84 Damage

Close Range

The general aim is to confuse your enemy's defense using Taki's mid-hitting strings. This ultimately allows you to set up her powerful low attacks, like the Ninja Cannon (Ⓐ+Ⓑ) or the final hit of her Shadow Scroll (ⒷⒶⒶ) string. For example, her ⒶⒷ string shifts into either the Ninja Cannon or her Possession stance (ⒶⒷ⇩⬃⇦). Both options have slow starting periods, so use the ⒶⒷⓀ variation to stop your opponents' immediate attempts to counterattack. When they play defensively, focus on chaining into Possession's Ⓑ attack, which is a mid hit. When your enemy is afraid of mid attacks, perform the Ninja Cannon variation of the string (ⒶⒷ⇨Ⓐ+Ⓑ) to nail your standing foe, setting him or her up for an aerial combo—catch the launched enemy with the Reverse Stalker Drop (Ⓐ+ⓀⒷ+Ⓖ).

Also, use Taki's ⒷⒶ string as a secondary option. If it connects as a counter-hit, string into its Shadow Banishment extension (ⒷⒶⓀ) for a 3-hit combo. When guarded, vary between the ⒷⒶⒶ variation, which hits low, or the mid-hitting ⒷⒶ⇨Ⓚ. It's also possible to shift into Possession after the second hit, so use its Ⓑ extension often to keep your offense moving.

Both of the aforementioned strings include high attacks under which your foes can crouch. To prevent enemies from using this to their advantage, use Taki's Lightning Strike (ⒷⒷⒷ) string. You can delay this combination's final hit, which is useful for luring your enemy into attacking after the second hit. When your opponent is afraid to attack at all, perform ⒷⒷ, then immediately throw or perform the Earth Scroll (⬂ⒶⓀ) when you recover to damage your standing enemy.

Mid Range

Your goal is to knock down your enemy or to slip into close range when he or she is afraid to attack. Taki's quick walking speed is invaluable in this capacity, as it facilitates moving in and out of your enemy's maximum attack distance. Keep your distance and focus on tagging your foe with Taki's Assassin's Revenge (⇨⇨Ⓑ during hit Ⓐ) whenever he or she misses an attack. Also, attack with the Illusion Scroll (⬇or⬆Ⓑ) if you sidestep any attacks. It leads to a basic but damaging combo consisting of ⬆Ⓑ, ⒶⒶ. Finally, The Reaping Hook (⬀Ⓐ) is a necessary tool for stopping your adversary's circular movements. It also ducks under high attacks and hits low, so use it often.

Long Range

Taki has very few effective options at this distance. It's best to play conservatively and wait for a moment to hit your enemy with ⇨⇨ⒷⒶ, which enables you to move in to a closer position. If you're feeling edgy, use Taki's Wind Roll (Ⓑ+Ⓚ) to quickly approach your enemy. Come out of the roll with the Fan Dance (during Wind Roll Ⓐ) attack, or simply recover and throw. This tactic is vulnerable to circular movement and early low attacks, so don't use it if the enemy is aware of its weaknesses.

Special Tactics

Okizeme: Anti-Wakeup

Use ⬂Ⓐ as your main low attack. If this attack hits, chain into its Ⓚ extension to score a 2-hit combo. When your enemy guards the attack, delay the Ⓚ input or use the crouching state from ⬂Ⓐ to perform While Rising Ⓚ. Mix between this option and the mid-hitting Assassin's Secret (ⒷⓀ⇩⬃⇦), which shifts into Taki's Possession stance.

Possession Notes

One of Taki's more powerful options is the highly flexible Possession stance (⇩⬃⇦). Its purpose is to counter any of your enemies' actions, an act that ultimately breaks down their defenses. The Possession Quake (Ⓐ) option, for example, counters sidesteps and your enemy's fastest defensive actions. Make Taki's strongest mid attack, the Dream Scroll (Ⓑ), one of your staple options. The Possession Strike (Ⓚ) attack causes a recoverable stun, possibly leading to combos. Lastly, use the Exorcism (Ⓐ+Ⓑ) Unblockable as a last resort to blast through a passive enemy's defenses.

Inputting ⇩⬂⇨ causes Taki to teleport into the air, another option out of the stance. Two attacks are available while Taki is airborne: the Hover Lightning (Ⓑ) mid attack or the low-hitting Hover Falcon (Ⓐ). The initial teleport animation also avoids some attacks, which can then be punished with the Ⓑ option. Use the stun from the attack to combo While Crouching ⇩Ⓐ+ⓀⓀ, ⬀ⒷⒶ⇩⬃⇦Ⓑ. Additionally, you can fake the teleport by inputting ⇩⬃⇦ during Possession. Use this option to scare your foe into taking a defensive stance, then crush your unsuspecting foe with one of Taki's other Possession skills.

Wind Scroll Uses

Taki's Wind Scroll (⇨Ⓐ) causes a recoverable stun on counter-hit. This is useful in close-range counter-hit situations as a means to possibly score combos, assuming your opponent doesn't escape the stun—go for ⬀ⒷⒶ⇩⬃⇦Ⓑ on a successful hit. Interestingly enough, inputting ⇨Ⓐ⇩⬃⇦ shifts the attack into the Possession stance while Taki is facing *away from her enemy*. Though this property may seem useless, this is the perfect opportunity to go for Possession's rarely used Wind Stalker (Ⓑ+Ⓚ), the Unblockable back-flip attack.

Talim

Talim

If I were a swift cloud to fly with thee...
"Ode to the West Wind," Percy Bysshe Shelley (1792 - 1822)

Bio

Age:	15
Birthplace:	Village of the Wind Deity, Southeast Asia
Height:	4'9"
Weight:	93 lbs.
Birth Date:	June 15
Blood Type:	Unknown
Weapon:	Elbow Blade x 2
Weapon Name:	Loka Luha & Syi Salika
Discipline:	Dance of Death
Family:	Father: Sanput Mother: Lidi Grandmother & Village Elder: Kalana Bird: Alun

Talim

It was the same dream that visited her.

Amidst a blue light that brought to mind shimmering waters, a single blade shone brilliantly. The evil on the wind smothered and died when touched by the waves emanating from it. The sword dazzled her, and when she held up her hand to shade her eyes...

She woke. She had only glimpsed the sword for one hallucinatory moment upon saving the boy being ravaged by Soul Edge, but it came back to Talim time and again in her sleep.

"Hey, you awake?" The voice belonged to Hong Yun-seong, a young man she had passed her days with while helping the boy. He, too, had been on a journey in search of Soul Edge, and asked to travel with Talim. At first she had been put off by his forcefulness, but she saw no downside to working together with someone who shared her goals. Besides, Talim had sized up Yun-seong at a glance. He had seemed so eager to attain Soul Edge's power, and despite her best efforts to preach the cursed sword's dangers to him, she could not be sure he had taken a single word seriously. How could she rest easy if she left him to his own devices? So she had agreed to continue the journey together.

Soon Talim and Yun-seong entered Istanbul, gateway to Europe. While gathering information from the merchants and sailors whose business took them from land to land, they heard stories of an ancient shrine that had been destroyed in Egypt, which lay beyond the sea. According to the rumors, this temple made of solid stone had been felled by blows from a sword. Absurd, it seemed... unless the sword in question was Soul Edge. Talim suggested to Yun-seong that they head to Egypt, and so it was that the two boarded a vessel.

Lingering within the ruined shrine was the same evil energy that she had felt countless times in the past; this was indeed Soul Edge's work. Talim, upon seeing Yun-seong's fascinated reaction to the carnage, gave him an even sterner lecture than ever about the sword's dangers, but as usual her companion showed no sign of caring. Despite her repeated warnings, she had been sidestepped again.

Upon returning to Europe, they found Yun-seong's kinswoman, Seong Mi-na, waiting. All the rowdiness Talim had grown accustomed to had faded at once before this new visitor. So, Talim thought, he does listen to someone. Watching Mi-na push him around like a child amused her so much, she could no longer contain her laughter. A pleasant wind blew between the two; Talim could tell they were like siblings.

But the next day, Yun-seong vanished. He must have sensed Mi-na would try to take him back to their homeland, and fled in the night. While Talim was a bit soured by his decision to leave her without so much as a goodbye, the dumbfounded look on Mi-na's face worried her more. Clearly Mi-na never imagined Yun-seong would run from her, which only went to show how serious he was about finding Soul Edge and seeing for himself whether it was good or evil. Some people never learn. Still...

"He's headstrong," Talim said, "but he's a good person. In the end, I'm sure he'll make the right decision." She knew his single-mindedness was also his greatest virtue.

And so the two parted ways: Mi-na left in search of Yun-seong, while Talim went on alone. She knew following Yun-seong would lead her to Soul Edge, but she needed to look into something first. The sword that shone blue—her vision—what did it mean? She had little luck finding the answer. Even the most knowledgeable sailors and oldest keepers of lore had never heard of any such sword. But Talim believed in the power within her as a Babaylan priestess. The scene she kept seeing in her heart must have some meaning, some vital truth it was trying to impart.

One night, a restlessness woke her, and she beheld a wondrous sight. Countless lights shot into the west, like a meteor shower; it was beautiful, but Talim sensed an outpouring of evil in the skies. Something evil had summoned forth its kindred from the darkness. Talim remembered the fragment of Soul Edge she carried. No sooner had she taken it out then it emitted a powerful wave and hurtled away, disappearing into the void of the sky. The winds blew too strong; an ill omen. She sensed Soul Edge had grown in power; time was running short. She must go and find it, now.

From that day, the vision visited her daily. The shining blue sword whose power at first seemed so pure grew more formidable before her, until finally it seemed capable of wiping away all existence around it. Was it responding to the evil blade? Talim grew anxious; if this was a vision of the near future then it was more than just a revelation. It was a warning; for power too great would only warp nature. The most important thing in this world was balance. Even if a great power were to enforce harmony, if that power itself were to fall out of balance, it would bring untold calamity.

Uneasy, Talim glanced up at the skies. As the winds circled the world, she could hear them screaming.

Loka Luha and Syi Salika

There exists a pair of ceremonial weapons called elbow blades. A wind-worshipping people who dwell in the heart of an island in Southeast Asia use these weapons during their ritual sword dances. For ages, the blades have been passed down through a line of Babaylan priestesses.

As the last rightful descendant of their house, Talim has inherited Loka Luha and Syi Salika; when she fights with them, the winds of the world obey and edge their blades.

Wind Offering Dedication Dance

Southeast Asia, encroached upon by Western powers. Even in this time of upheaval, the people who worshipped the wind would not give up their faith. Those who traveled the world using the power of the wind, they protected the legend and they had a sword dance, which was a dedication to the Wind. But sometimes the violent winds blow. That sword dance contained the power of the wind itself.

To the average person, it may seem no more than a dance, but the priestess Talim actually controls the winds and is protected by them.

Command List

Signature Techniques

Name	Command	Attack Level	Damage	Notes
Air Blade Thrust	⇦ⒷⒷ	Mid, Mid	16, 16	Both attacks stun on counter-hit
Blade Cyclone	↘ or ↗Ⓐ	Mid, Mid	14, 21	1st attack causes recoverable stun on hit
Paayon Thrust	→Ⓑ	High	28	
Rapid Espada ~Wind Charmer	ⒶⒶ⇨ⒷⒶ ⇩ or ⇧	High, High, Mid, High	8, 9, 14, 16	Final attack causes recoverable stun on counter-hit. Shifts to Wind Charmer.
Spinning Low Hiwa ~Wind Charmer	⬃Ⓐ⇩ or ⇧	Low	18	Stuns on counter-hit. Shifts to Wind Charmer.
Gust Slicer ~Wind Charmer	⬁ⒷⒶ⇩ or ⇧	Mid, High	14, 16	1st attack causes recoverable stun on counter-hit. Shifts to Wind Charmer.
Turning Kali Strikes ~Wind Charmer	Wind Charmer ⒶⒶ ⇩ or ⇧	High, High	10, 8	Shifts to Wind Charner
Twirling Wind	Wind Charmer Ⓚ	Mid	16	
Flowing Gale Hook ~Wind Sault	→Ⓐ⇨	High, High	10, 16	Shifts to Wind Sault
Double Inwardi	Wind Sault Ⓐ	Low	20	Stuns on counter-hit
Double Bartikal	Wind Sault Ⓑ+Ⓚ	Mid	30	Stuns on hit

Talim

Vertical Attacks

Name	Command	Attack Level	Damage	Notes
Kampilan Slicer	ⒷⒷ	Mid, Mid	12, 13	
Turning Witik Blow ~Face Away	⇨Ⓑ	Mid	21	Leaves Talim backturned
Gust Slicer ~Face Away	⇙ⒷⒶ	Mid, High	14, 16	1st attack stuns on counter-hit. Leaves Talim back-turned.
Gust Slicer ~Wind Charmer	⇙ⒷⒶ⇩ or ⇧	Mid, High	14, 16	Shifts to Wind Charmer. 1at attack stuns on counter-hit.
Gust Slicer (Hold) ~Face Away	⇙Ⓑ🅐	Mid, High	14, 26	1at attack stuns on counter-hit. 2nd attack causes stun on hit. Leaves Talim back-turned.
Gust Slicer ~Wind Charmer	⇙Ⓑ🅐⇩ or ⇧	Mid, High	14, 26	1at attack stuns on counter-hit. 2nd attack causes stun on hit. Shifts to Wind Charmer.
Satik	⇩Ⓑ	Mid	14	
White Wind	⇘Ⓑ	Mid	18	
Air Blade Thrust	⇦ⒷⒷ	Mid, Mid	16, 16	Both attacks stun on counter-hit
Air Blade Thrust (Hold)	⇦Ⓑ🅑	Mid, Mid	16, 25	1st attack stuns on counter-hit, 2nd attack Guard Breaks and stuns on hit
Blue Sky	⇩⇙⇨Ⓑ	Mid	15	Launches on hit
Blue Sky (Hold)	⇩⇙⇨🅑	Mid	22	Launches on hit
Satik	While Crouching Ⓑ	Mid	16	
Rising Baraw	While Crouching ⇙ⒷⒷ	Mid, Mid, Mid	8, 8, 5	Final hit stuns on counter-hit
Rising Baraw (Delay)	While Crouching ⇙ⒷⒷ	Mid, Mid, Mid	8, 8, 5	Final hit stuns on counter-hit
Rising Baraw ~Wind Sault	While Crouching ⇙ⒷⒷ⇨	Mid, Mid, Mid	8, 8, 5	Shifts to Wind Sault. Final hit stuns on counter-hit.
Rising Baraw ~Wind Leap	While Crouching ⇙ⒷⒷ⇦	Mid, Mid, Mid	8, 8, 5	Shifts to Wind Leap. Final hit stuns on counter-hit.
Rising Elbow Blade	While Rising Ⓑ	Mid	18	
Swift Leap	Jumping Ⓑ	High	28	
Baraw Punch Turn	Backturned Ⓑ	Mid	24	Stuns on hit
Baraw Punch Turn ~Wind Charmer	Backturned Ⓑ⇩ or ⇧	Mid	24	Stuns on hit
Turning Satik	While Crouching Backturned Ⓑ	Mid	16	

Horizontal Attacks

Name	Command	Attack Level	Damage	Notes
Swift Espada	ⒶⒶⒷ	High, High, Sp.Mid, High	8, 9, 6, 12	Fully combos on counter-hit
Rapid Espada	ⒶⒶ⇨ⒷⒶ	High, High, Mid, High	8, 9, 14, 16	Final attack causes recoverable stun on counter-hit
Rapid Espada (Delay)	ⒶⒶ⇨ⒷⒶ	High, High, Mid, High	8, 9, 14, 16	Final attack causes recoverable stun on counter-hit
Rapid Espada ~Wind Sault	ⒶⒶ⇨ⒷⒶ⇨	High, High, Mid, High	8, 9, 14, 16	Final attack causes recoverable stun on counter-hit. Shifts to Wind Sault.
Rapid Espada ~Wind Leap	ⒶⒶ⇨ⒷⒶ⇦	High, High, Mid, High	8, 9, 14, 16	Final attack causes recoverable stun on counter-hit. Shifts to Wind Leap.
Rapid Espada ~Wind Charmer	ⒶⒶ⇨ⒷⒶ ⇩ or ⇧	High, High, Mid, High	8, 9, 14, 16	Final attack causes recoverable stun on counter-hit. Shifts to Wind Charmer.
Mirror Fan Strikes	⇨ⒶⒶ	High, High	16, 20	
Mirror Fan Kick	⇨ⒶⓀ	High, Mid	16, 12	
Razor Gale ~Face Away	⇙Ⓐ	High, High	12, 12	Leaves Talim in backturned position
Tuhod Slicer	⇩Ⓐ	Sp.Low	8	
Spinning Low Hiwa	⇘Ⓐ	Low	18	Stuns on counter-hit
Spinning Low Hiwa ~Wind Charmer	⇘Ⓐ⇩ or ⇧	Low	18	Stuns on counter-hit. Shifts to Wind Charmer.
Witik Sweep	⇦ⒶⒶ	High, Low	18, 22	
Witik Stomp	⇦ⒶⓀ	High, Mid	18, 20	
Witik Stomp ~Face Away	⇦Ⓐ🅚	High, Mid	18, 22	Leaves Talim in backturned position
Tuhod Slicer	While Crouching Ⓐ	Sp.Low	8	
Left Witik	While Rising Ⓐ	Mid	20	
Jumping Witik	Jumping Ⓐ	High	16 or 18 or 20	Damage varies depending on direction jumped in
Jumping Witik ~Wind Sault	Jumping Ⓐ⇨	High	16 or 18 or 20	Damage varies depending on direction jumped in. Shifts to Wind Sault.
Jumping Witik ~Wind Leap	Jumping Ⓐ⇦	High	16 or 18 or 20	Damage varies depending on direction jumped in. Shifts to Wind Leap.
Jumping Witik ~Wind Charmer	Jumping Ⓐ⇩ or ⇧	High	16 or 18 or 20	Damage varies depending on direction jumped in. Shifts to Wind Charmer.
Olisi Turn	Backturned Ⓐ	High	30	
Olisi Turn (Hold)	Backturned 🅐	High	40	
Turning Tuhod Slicer	While Crouching Backturned Ⓐ	Sp.Low	10	

Kick Attacks

Name	Command	Attack Level	Damage	Notes
High Sipa	Ⓚ	High	12	
Side Sipa	⇨Ⓚ	Mid	18	Causes recoverable stun on counter-hit.
Inner Sipa	⬂Ⓚ	Mid	14	
Low Sipa Sweep	⇩Ⓚ	Low	12	
Sipa Trip	⬃Ⓚ	Low	16	
Roundhouse Sipa	⇦Ⓚ	High	12	
Low Sipa Sweep	While Crouching Ⓚ	Low	11	
Front Sipa	While Rising Ⓚ	Mid	16	
Sipa Jump	Jumping Ⓚ	Mid	12 or 16 or 20	Damage varies depending on direction jumped in.
Diving Wind Kick	Backturned Ⓚ	High	18	
Turning Sipa Sweep	While Crouching Backturned Ⓚ	Low	12	

Simultaneous Press

Name	Command	Attack Level	Damage	Notes
Ice Wind Combo	Ⓐ+Ⓑ⇩⬂⇨Ⓐ ⇩⬂⇨Ⓑ	Mid x9	5, 5, 5, 3, 3, 3, 8, 8, 10	Final attack stuns on hit, causes special launch against enemies lying on ground
Shearing Blades	⇨Ⓐ+Ⓑ	Mid	30	Stuns on hit.
Rapid Force	⇩Ⓐ+Ⓑ	Mid	24	Launches on counter-hit.
Rapid Force ~Wind Sault	⇩Ⓐ+Ⓑ⇨	Mid	24	Launches on counter-hit. Shifts to Wind Sault.
Rapid Force ~Wind Leap	⇩Ⓐ+Ⓑ⇦	Mid	24	Launches on counter-hit. Shifts to Wind Leap.
Twin Baraw Lift	⬃Ⓐ+Ⓑ	Mid	18	Stuns on hit. Launches on counter-hit.
Twin Espadas ~Face Away	⇦Ⓐ+Ⓑ	Mid, Mid	14, 16	Leaves Talim in backturned position.
Desert Gust	While Rising Ⓐ+Ⓑ	High, Mid	10, 20	Deflects vertical attacks.
Ice Wind Combo	Backturned Ⓐ+Ⓑ ⇩⬂⇨Ⓐ⇩⬂⇨Ⓑ	Mid x9	5, 5, 5, 3, 3, 3, 8, 8, 10	Final attack stuns on hit, causes special launch against enemies lying on ground
Raging Wind	Ⓑ+Ⓚ	Mid	50	Unblockable. Input Ⓖ to cancel attack (leaves Talim in crouching state).
Wind Sault	⇨Ⓑ+Ⓚ			
Wind Charmer ~Wind Sault	⇩ or ⇧Ⓑ+Ⓚ			Shifts to Wind Sault.
Wind Leap ~Wind Sault	⇦Ⓑ+Ⓚ			Shifts to Wind Sault.
Wind Leap	Backturned Ⓑ+Ⓚ			Evades low attacks.
Wind Leap (Hold)	Backturned 🅑+🅚			Evades low attacks.
Razor Storm	Backturned Ⓑ+Ⓚ Ⓐ+Ⓑ	Mid, Mid, Mid, Mid	8, 8, 8, 8	Final hit Guard Breaks, stuns on hit.
Razor Storm (Hold)	Backturned 🅑+🅚 Ⓐ+Ⓑ	Mid, Mid, Mid, Mid	8, 8, 8, 8	Unblockable. Stuns on hit.
Wind Dance	Ⓐ+Ⓚ	High, High	12, 12	2nd attack stuns on counter-hit.
Taunt	Ⓚ+Ⓖ			

8-Way Run

Name	Command	Attack Level	Damage	Notes
Flowing Gale Hook	→Ⓐ	High, High	10, 16	
Flowing Gale Hook ~Wind Sault	→Ⓐ⇨	High, High	10, 16	Shifts to Wind Sault.
Flowing Gale Hook ~Wind Leap	→Ⓐ⇦	High, High	10, 16	Shifts to Wind Leap.
Blade Cyclone	↘ or ↗Ⓐ	Mid, Mid	14, 21	1st attack causes recoverable stun.
Crosswind	↓ or ↑Ⓐ	High, High	12, 16	
Spinning Low Hiwa	↙ or ↖Ⓐ	Low	16	Stuns on counter-hit.
Spinning Low Hiwa ~Wind Charmer	↙ or ↖Ⓐ⇩ or ⇧	Low	16	Stuns on counter-hit. Shifts to Wind Charmer.
Double Abaniko	←ⒶⒶ	High, Mid	20, 20	2nd attack stuns on hit.
Double Abaniko (Hold)	←Ⓐ🅐	High, Mid	20, 30	2nd attack stuns on hit.
Paayon Thrust	→Ⓑ	High	28	
Gust Hook	↘ or ↗Ⓑ⇨Ⓑ	Mid, Mid	20, 20(30)	Perform input with perfect timing for additional damage (Just).
Rising Gale	↓ or ↑Ⓑ	Mid, Mid	15, 18	
Rising Gale ~Wind Sault	↓ or ↑Ⓑ⇨	Mid, Mid	15, 18	Shifts into Wind Sault.
Rising Gale ~Wind Leap	↓ or ↑Ⓑ⇦	Mid, Mid	15, 18	Shifts into Wind Leap.
Isa Hampas ~Face Away	↙ or ↖Ⓑ	Mid	20	Leaves Talim in backturned state.
Isa Hampas ~Wind Sault	↙ or ↖Ⓑ⇨	Mid	20	Shifts to Wind Sault.
Isa Hampas ~Wind Leap	↙ or ↖Ⓑ⇦	Mid	20	Shifts to Wind Leap.
Isa Hampas ~Wind Charmer	↙ or ↖Ⓑ⇩ or ⇧	Mid	20	Shifts to Wind Charmer.
Vertical Abaniko	←Ⓑ	Mid	28	Stuns on hit.
Vertical Abaniko ~Wind Sault	←Ⓑ⇨	Mid	28	Stuns on hit. Shifts to Wind Sault.
Vertical Abaniko ~Wind Leap	←Ⓑ⇦	Mid	28	Stuns on hit. Shifts to Wind Leap.
Vertical Abaniko ~Wind Charmer	←Ⓑ⇩ or ⇧	Mid	28	Stuns on hit. Shifts to Wind Charmer.
Parabolic Sipa	→Ⓚ	Mid	15	
Parabolic Sipa ~Face Away	→🅚	Mid	15	Leaves Talim backturned.
Sipa Slash	↘ or ↗ⓀⒶ	High, Low, Low	16, 8, 8	
Sipa Windmill	↑ or ↓Ⓚ	High	18	
Sweeping Breeze	↙ or ↖ⓀⒶ	Low, High	15, 18	
Sipa Rising	←Ⓚ	Mid, High	14, 18	
Ice Wind	→Ⓐ+Ⓑ	Mid	32	Guard Breaks.
Ice Wind ~Face Away	→Ⓐ+ⒷⒼ			
Twin Espadas ~Face Away	←Ⓐ+Ⓑ	Mid, Mid	12, 16	Leaves Talim in backturned position.
Sipa Slide	While Running Ⓚ	Low	26	

Throws

Name	Command	Attack Level	Damage	Notes
Tagga Na Kamay	Ⓐ+Ⓖ	Throw	48	Input Ⓐ to escape.
Monsoon	Ⓑ+Ⓖ	Throw	52	Input Ⓑ to escape.
Tower Kick	Left Side Throw	Throw	60	Same button as throw (Ⓐ or Ⓑ) to escape.
Piggyback Tulison	Right Side Throw	Throw	58	Same button as throw (Ⓐ or Ⓑ) to escape.
Diving Wind Kick Throw	Back Throw	Throw	58	Same button as throw (Ⓐ or Ⓑ) to escape.
Monsoon Season	⇩⇘⇨Ⓑ+Ⓖ ⇩⇙⇦Ⓐ or Ⓑ	Throw	40, 20	Input Ⓑ to escape first throw, same button as throw (Ⓐ or Ⓑ) to escape second attack.

Wind Charmer

Name	Command	Attack Level	Damage	Notes
Wind Charmer ~Wind Sault	⇩ or ⇧ or ⬇ or ⬆ Ⓑ+Ⓚ			
Turning Kali Strikes ~Face Away	Wind Charmer ⒶⒶⒷ	High, High, Mid	10, 8, 16	
Turning Kali Strikes ~Wind Charmer	Wind Charmer ⒶⒶ ⇩ or ⇧	High, High	10, 8	Shifts to Wind Charmer.
Baraw Strikes	Wind Charmer ⒷⒷ	Mid, Mid	12, 16(26)	Input with Just Frame timing for 2nd attack to deal additional damage and gain Guard Break and launch properties.
Rising Baraw Slice	Wind Charmer ⒷⒷ (Delay)	Mid, Mid	12, 26	2nd attack Guard Breaks, stuns on hit.
Twirling Wind	Wind Charmer Ⓚ	Mid	16	Evades high attacks.
Tuhod Strike	Wind Charmer Ⓐ+Ⓚ	Low	24	
Tagga	Wind Charmer Ⓐ+Ⓖ or Ⓑ+Ⓖ	Throw	35	Leaves Talim in backturned state.

Wind Sault

Name	Command	Attack Level	Damage	Notes
Wind Sault	⇨ or ➡Ⓑ+Ⓚ			
Double Inwardi	Wind Sault Ⓐ	Low	20	Stuns on counter-hit.
Double Inwardi ~Wind Charmer	Wind Sault Ⓐ⇩ or ⇧	Low	20	Stuns on counter-hit. Shifts to Wind Charmer.
Swift Leap	Wind Sault Ⓑ	High	22	
Swift Leap (Additional attack)	Wind Sault Ⓑ During Hit Ⓚ (Just)	High, Mid	22, 22	
Layout ~Wind Sault (Only During Hit)	Wind Sault Ⓚ	High	20	Shifts back into Wind Sault on a successful hit.
Rolling Storm	Wind Sault Ⓐ+Ⓑ	Mid, Mid, Mid	10, 10, 10	
Double Bartikal	Wind Sault Ⓑ+Ⓚ	Mid	30	Stuns on hit.
Double Bartikal ~Wind Sault	Wind Sault Ⓑ+Ⓚ During Hit ⇨	Mid	30	Stuns on hit.
Reversing Wind	Wind Sault Ⓐ+Ⓚ	Mid	22	

Wind Leap

Name	Command	Attack Level	Damage	Notes
Wind Leap ~Wind Sault	⇦ or ⬅Ⓑ+Ⓚ			
Swooping Blade	Wind Leap Ⓐ	Low	20	Stuns on hit, leaves Talim in crouching state.
Paayon Thrust	Wind Leap Ⓑ	High	30	
Leaping Double Sipa	Wind Leap Ⓚ	Mid, Mid	18, 15	1st attack stuns on hit.
Whirlwind Hambalos	Wind Leap Ⓐ+Ⓑ	Mid	85	Unblockable.
Whirlwind Hambalos ~Wind Sault	Wind Leap Ⓐ+ⒷⒼ			Shifts into Wind Sault.

Combos

⬊Ⓑ⇨Ⓑ (Just), ⇩Ⓚ
4 hits, 49 Damage
⇗Ⓐ⬇ or ⬆, ⒶⒶ
3 hits, 36 Damage
⇨⇨Ⓑ, ⇩Ⓐ + Ⓑ
2 hits, 44 Damage
Wind Leap Ⓚ, ⇨➡Ⓑ, ⇩Ⓐ + Ⓑ
4 hits, 49 Damage
During Wind Charmer Ⓐ + Ⓚ, ⇩Ⓐ + Ⓑ
2 hits, 42 Damage
⬇ or ⬆Ⓑ ➡, during Wind Sault Ⓚ, Ⓐ + Ⓑ
5 hits, 56 Damage
⬇ or ⬆Ⓑ ➡, during Wind Sault ⒷⓀ (Just)
4 hits, 64 Damage, final hit can be avoided with Just Ukemi
⇩⇘⇨Ⓑ, ⇨⇨Ⓑ, ⇩Ⓐ + Ⓑ
3 hits, 66 Damage
Counter-hit crouching ⇘ⒷⒷ ➡, Ⓚ, Ⓐ + Ⓑ
6 hits, 50 Damage
During Wind Leap Ⓐ, ⇘ⒷⒷ ➡, Ⓐ + Ⓚ, ⇩Ⓚ
6 hits, 51 Damage
While Rising Ⓐ + Ⓑ, ⇘⇘Ⓐ
4 hits, 54 Damage
During Wind Charmer ⒷⒷ (Just), ⒶⒶⒷ
6 hits, 60 Damage
Back-turned Ⓑ, ⇘Ⓑ 🅐⇩, ⒷⒷ (Just), ⒶⒶⒷ
8 hits, 71 Damage, release ⇘Ⓑ🅐 just before full charge

Close Range

Talim's biggest asset is her ability to break down her enemy's defenses through a rapid series of attacks. This talent stems from her myriad special movements that enable her to evade attacks while also staging an offense. Her many combinations that shift into these movements further supplement this ability. Talim's most valued attacks are those that inflict quick and easy damage, and then shift into one of her special movements. For example, her Rapid Espada (ⒶⒶ⇨ⒷⒶ) combination is useful for starting an offense while also catching close-range sidestep attempts. The final hit of the string shifts directly into her Wind Sault, Wind Leap, and Wind Charmer skills, giving her many options to work with on guard or hit. Attack with the first two hits of the string (ⒶⒶ), performing the remainder of the hits only in specific situations. If the string's first hit connects as a counter-hit, input Ⓑ to initiate the Swift Espada (ⒶⒶⒷ). When ⒶⒶ is blocked, throw your enemy when you recover, or delay the Rapid Espada's ⇨ⒷⒶ extension to lure your enemy into attacking. On either a normal or counter-hit, always shift into the Wind Charmer (ⒶⒶ⇨ⒷⒶ⇩ or ⇧) and go for one of its many options. If the final hit is blocked, shift into the Wind Leap (ⒶⒶ⇨ⒷⒶ⇨) to avoid enemy counterattacks.

Many of the Rapid Espada's attacks are high hits. If your foe tries to crouch under the string's second attack, use the deceptive Witik Stomp (⇦ⒶⓀ) to counter. Its first high attack looks similar to the Rapid Espada's opening strike, which effectively lures your enemy into crouching and taking a hit from its mid-hitting second kick. This kick also leaps over most crouching attacks, making it the perfect crouch deterrent. If it hits, follow up with ⇖⇖Ⓐ to score a 3-hit combo. Use the low Witik Sweep (⇦ⒶⒶ) when your opponent is afraid of the Witik Stomp, or return to pressuring your foe with the Rapid Espada. Conditioning enemies to stand also leaves them vulnerable to other low moves, such as the Sweeping Breeze (↙ or ↖ⓀⒶ) or Spinning Low Hiwa (⇙Ⓐ).

Talim's back-turned attacks, and the techniques that leave her in a back-turned position, are also important to her close-range game. Skills that leave her back-turned include the Gust Slicer (⇖ⒷⒶ), the Turning Witik Blow (⇨Ⓑ), and the Razor Gale (⇖Ⓐ). The Gust Slicer and Turning Witik Blow are both mid attacks used for hitting crouching opponents, while the Razor Gale acts as an alternate sidestep deterrent to the Rapid Espada. If any of these attacks successfully hit, stage a low or mid offense consisting of either the Turning Sipa Sweep (back-turned While Crouching ⇩Ⓚ) or the Baraw Punch Turn (back-turned Ⓑ). The Baraw Punch Turn leads to massive combos on hit, so condition your foe into standing with the Turning Sipa Sweep to land it. If any of these attacks are guarded, attack with the Turning Sipa Sweep to slip under your enemy's high counterattacks, or the Razor Storm (back-turned Ⓑ+ⓀⒶ+Ⓑ) to leap over ⇩Ⓐ attacks. The Razor Storm Guard Breaks when it's blocked, so use the advantage to score a free ⇩Ⓐ, or go for one of Talim's throw options, which can't be crouched under because of the heavy advantage.

The flexible Gust Slicer is the most important of the above attacks. Use it when you anticipate an attempt to block one of your low attacks, or to crouch under the first hit of your Rapid Espada. If it hits, input ⇩ or Ⓑ to shift into the Wind Charmer to stage a follow-up attack. Perform the combo ↘ⒷⒶ⇩(release Ⓐ just before it's fully charged) ⒶⒶⒷ if the Gust Slicer connects as a counter-hit. In cases where it's guarded, use your back-turned options to fend off enemy counterattack, or perform a late shift into the Wind Charmer to avoid vertical slashes. When foes are afraid of your countermeasures, shift into the Wind Charmer to keep your offense rolling. The Gust Slicer's only weakness is its second strike, a high move that's vulnerable to crouching. Occasionally attack with the similar-looking Gust Hook (↘ or ⇘Ⓑ⇨Ⓑ(Just)) to train enemies into standing during the second hit.

Mid Range

Your objective is to knock down your enemy with the Blade Cyclone (↘ or ↗Ⓐ) or to run into close range when your enemy is afraid of your offense. Stay out of your foe's attack range using 8-Way Run, and use the Crosswind (⬇ or ⬆Ⓐ) to strike his or her attempts to move around. If you anticipate an enemy vertical attack, step around it with 8-Way Run and punish it with ↘Ⓐ. The Blade Cyclone also evades high horizontal attacks while also stopping sidesteps, so you can use it in anticipation against most of your enemy's attacks. Its only weaknesses are its heavy recovery period and its poor attack range. If you ever anticipate a high attack from outside the Blade Cyclone's attack distance, duck under it and attack with the Rising Baraw (While Crouching ⇘ⒷⒷ). This string fully combos on counter-hit, allowing you to perform the following combo: While Crouching counter-hit ⇘ⒷⒷ⇨, Ⓚ, Ⓐ+Ⓑ. It's also possible to delay this attack's second input, performing it only when you confirm the first is connecting on a counter-hit. This is useful to trick your enemy into thinking you're stopping your attack short, and then performing its second hit when you lure out a counterattack.

The Crosswind attack is vulnerable to crouching opponents. If you ever anticipate this countermeasure, attack with the powerful Gust Hook (↘ or ⇘Ⓑ⇨Ⓑ(Just)). The Just Frame version of this attack enables you to follow up with an additional ⇩Ⓚ after it hits, leading to high damage. When your foe is wary of this attack, go for Talim's Spinning Low Hiwa (↙ or ↖Ⓐ⇩) to catch your opponent standing.

Long Range

Talim is weak at long distances, so muscle your way into close or mid range by any means necessary. For instance, her Paayon Thrust (➡Ⓑ) is risky because of its high hit property, but its massive traveling distance and quick speed makes it ideal for punishing your opponent's missed moves. If it ever hits, attack your fallen enemy with ⇩Ⓐ+Ⓑ⇨ for a 2-hit combo. In cases where the Paayon Thrust can't hit a crouching move, use Shearing Blades (⇨Ⓐ+Ⓑ) instead.

As an alternate means of getting close, use Talim's Wind Sault to leap toward your enemy. During the flip, initiate either Ⓐ or Ⓑ+Ⓚ to initiate a low or high attack. If the Ⓐ option hits, input ⇩ to shift into her Wind Charmer stance and link ⒶⒶ for a 3-hit combo. If Ⓑ+Ⓚ hits, perform ⇨ then Ⓐ+Ⓑ to do a 4-hit combo. Strike with the Wind Sault's Ⓚ option if your enemy ever tries to stick out an early attack to stop it. If Ⓚ hits, immediately input Ⓑ+Ⓚ to combo.

Special Tactics

Okizeme: Anti-Wakeup

Aside from the Gust Slicer (⇘ⒷⒶ), use the Rapid Force (⇩Ⓐ+Ⓑ) as a secondary mid attack against crouching opponents. If it hits, shift into Talim's Wind Sault (⇩Ⓐ+Ⓑ→) and go for one of its many options. When it's blocked, change into her Wind Leap (⇩Ⓐ+Ⓑ←) to evade enemy counterattack. If ⇩Ⓐ+Ⓑ connects as a counter-hit, shift into the Wind Sault and immediately perform Ⓐ+Ⓑ for a 4-hit combo.

Attack with the Spinning Low Hiwa (⇙Ⓐ) when your enemy is looking for mid attacks. Always shift into the Wind Charmer stance (⇙Ⓐ↓ or ↑) regardless of whether it hits. If it does hit, link directly into the Wind Charmer's ⒶⒶ string for a 3-hit combo. If it connects on a counter-hit, shift into the Wind Charmer and link ⒶⒶⒷ. When it doesn't connect, vary between the Tagga (during Wind Charmer, Ⓐ+Ⓖ or Ⓑ+Ⓖ) and her ⒷⒷ or Ⓚ attacks.

Against opponents who guard often, use the Ice Wind (→Ⓐ+Ⓑ). This technique is a mid-hitting Guard Break with a wind-up period that looks similar to ⇙Ⓐ, enabling you to use it in conjunction with ⇙Ⓐ to stage a basic mid or low anti-wakeup attack. When it's blocked, use the Guard Break advantage to follow up with a throw or ⇩Ⓐ+Ⓑ for a basic 2-way mix-up. It's also possible to cancel ⇨→Ⓐ+Ⓑ before it hits by pressing Ⓖ, leaving Talim in a back-turned state. Use this ability to scare your enemy into guarding high, then attack with a throw or one of Talim's many back-turned mid or low attacks.

Wind Charmer Notes

The Wind Charmer (⇩ or ⇧Ⓑ+Ⓚ) movement acts as a sidestep with a unique set of attacks. Aside from evading vertical attacks, its main purpose is to facilitate a continued offense off of specific techniques. Use the ⒶⒶ option to stop immediate attempts to counter the movement. It also shifts back into the Wind Charmer (ⒶⒶ⇧ or ⇩) to allow continued momentum. Use the string's ⒶⒶⒷ variation to stop immediate attempts to attack the Wind Charmer animation after ⒶⒶ. The second hit of the Wind Charmer's Baraw Strikes (ⒷⒷ) can be delayed, turning it into a Guard Break attack. Inputting the second Ⓑ just as the first attack hits performs the Just Frame version of the attack, giving the second attack its Guard Break properties while enabling both hits to combo on a normal hit. This is the Wind Charmer's most powerful mid attack, as it leads to follow-up juggle combos; hit your airborne opponent with ⒶⒶⒷ afterward. The quick Twirling Wind (Ⓚ) mid attack evades high strikes and causes wall hits, making it useful when attacking at a disadvantage. The Tuhod Strike (Ⓐ+Ⓚ) option is a slow low attack, which you should use only as a last resort to hit defensive players—it leads to an additional ⇩Ⓐ+Ⓑ follow-up on a successful hit. Finally, the Tagga (Ⓐ+Ⓖ or Ⓑ+Ⓖ) are both throw options that leave Talim in a back-turned state. Use the advantage you're left with to strike with Talim's back-turned attacks.

Wind Sault Notes

The forward flipping Wind Sault (⇨Ⓑ+Ⓚ) is useful for leaping over horizontal and low ground attacks. If you successfully jump over an attack, perform the Rolling Thunder (during Wind Sault Ⓐ+Ⓑ) to damage your foe. If your opponent doesn't perform an attack, salvage your offense and input either Ⓐ to go for a low attack, or Ⓑ+Ⓚ to initiate a mid hit. If the Ⓐ option hits, tap ⇩ or ⇧ to shift into Wind Charmer stance and link ⒶⒶ for a 3-hit combo. Inputting → after Ⓑ+Ⓚ shifts back into the Wind Sault, enabling you to combo directly into a Rolling Storm on hit (during Wind Sault Ⓐ+Ⓑ). Use the Layout (during Wind Sault Ⓚ) to counter your enemy's earliest attempts to stop the Wind Sault movement. It's usually safe when blocked, and also shifts back into the Wind Sault when it hits, enabling you to link into Ⓑ+Ⓚ for a basic 2-hit combo. The Wind Sault's Swift Leap (Ⓑ during hit Ⓚ) option is used strictly for combinations. For example, Talim's Rising Gale (↑ or ↓Ⓑ→) shifts directly into the Wind Sault, allowing her to hit an airborne enemy with the ⒷⓀ follow-up.

The Wind Sault's attack options are quite strong against opponents rising from a knockdown. This is specifically useful after combos that end with ⇩Ⓐ+Ⓑ⇨ hitting a floored enemy. For example, strike your foe with ⇨⇨Ⓑ, then hit his or her grounded body with ⇩Ⓐ+Ⓑ⇨. If your enemy Ukemis forward, backward, or neutral, you'll be in the perfect position to mix-up between the Wind Sault's Ⓑ+Ⓚ and Ⓐ options. However, if your opponent Ukemis to the right or left, your Ⓑ+Ⓚ attack will miss. If you anticipate a right or left Ukemi, replace Ⓑ+Ⓚ with the mid-hitting Ⓐ+Ⓑ, which is easier to react to and block, but still catches your enemy off guard if he or she is scared of the low Ⓐ option.

Wind Leap Notes

Wind Leap (⇦Ⓑ+Ⓚ) is a backward jump that evades attacks. This is useful for evading and countering attacks when you're at a disadvantage. For example, it's handy after foes block the final hit of Talim's ⒶⒶ⇨ⒷⒶ string. After you initiate the leap, verify whether you've successfully dodged an attack, then choose one of its many follow-ups. If your foe attacked, perform the Wind Leap's Paayon Thrust (Ⓑ) or Leaping Double Sipa (Ⓚ) attacks to punish the missed move. Use the Ⓐ option to slip under and counter high attacks. In cases where your opponent doesn't attack, perform either the low-hitting Ⓐ option or Ⓚ for a mid attack. If the Swooping Blade (Ⓐ) option connects, combo your enemy with While Crouching ⇘ⒷⒷ→Ⓐ+Ⓚ, then ⇩Ⓚ. If the Ⓚ option hits, juggle your enemy with ⇨⇨Ⓑ then ⇩Ⓐ+Ⓑ. Note that the Wind Leap shifts directly into the Wind Sault if no attack is performed. Use the Wind Sault's attack options in addition to the Wind Leap's when the enemy doesn't miss an attack.

Tira

Tira

Did you glimpse that black shadow flit across the sky to the west? Turn your back upon it and face the east. Do you see those outstretched wings, black as coal, the dark birds alighting heavily on the ground? They are the watchers, infected servants of the evil sword, and today, too, they beat their ill-omened wings and bring information from around the globe to Ostrheinsburg. There, squatting at the summit of the ruined tower! Do you see the solitary woman, her ear cocked toward the cries and caws of her flock? Now, she stands and turns. Yes, it is Tira.

"He is coming! He is coming!"

"The fool. That sword cannot save him this time!"

Tira

"Prophet!" said I, "thing of evil!—prophet still, if bird or devil!—
Whether Tempter sent, or whether tempest tossed thee here ashore…

"The Raven," Edgar Allan Poe (1809 - 1849)

Bio

Age:	17
Birthplace:	Unknown
Height:	5'3"
Weight:	95 lbs.
Birth Date:	Unknown
Blood Type:	AB
Weapon:	Ring Blade
Weapon Name:	Eiserne Drossel
Discipline:	Dance of Death
Family:	No family, but now accompanied by a flock of watchers.

Eiserne Drossel

The ring blade of Tira, loyal servant of Nightmare and mistress of the flock of watchers. She has carried this mysterious sword since the time when she was still human, before she became infected by the evil of Soul Edge. It is a weapon unique to the Bird of Passage, an organization of assassins, and indeed it was they who gave it to her. With it, Tira harvested many lives. She killed the targets assigned to her by the organization. She killed her new friends and family who had taken her in when she had nowhere to go.

Now, it is souls that Eiserne Drossel harvests. Offered up in sacrifice to Nightmare—to Soul Edge—these souls are taken from both indiscriminately chosen victims and from those who would dare challenge her master.

Dance of Death

Bird of Passage was a shadowy organization of assassins that stalked medieval Europe, and whose deadly assassin arts made death a vivid spectacle. Their techniques were developed both to guarantee the death of their targets and also reveal exactly who had committed the deed. They controlled the world of man from the shadows, but each killing sent a message as clear and unequivocal as a royal decree.

Among the unique special arts taught by the Bird of Passage group were those that governed the use of the ring blade. The curved blade would flash in a sweet harmony of movement that bewitched those unfortunate enough to witness it. Mesmerized by the dance, the helpless victim would be cut down and the Bird of Passage would retract its claws into the darkness to await the next summons.

Command List

Signature Techniques

Name	Command	Attack Level	Damage	Notes
Low Swoop	Jolly Side ⇙(A)	Low	22	
Piercing Talon Strike	Jolly Side ←(K)(B)	Mid, Mid	16, 24	
Flageolette Fin	Jolly Side → or ↘ or ↗(A)(A)	Mid, Mid	16, 21	
Bremen Fortissimo	Jolly Side ←(K)	High	15	Causes recoverable Stun. May switch to Gloomy Side.
Gestopft Madness (Hold)	Jolly Side (A)+(K)	High, High, High	15, 15, 15	Deflects high or mid verticals and horizontals. May switch to Gloomy Side. Causes stun on aerial hit.
Shriek Noise	Gloomy Side →(A)(A) Rapidly	High, Mid, High, High, High	13, 8, 8, 8, 8	Inflicts additional damage and hits the faster (A) is tapped
Oratorio Halcyon	Gloomy Side ⇦(B) (B)(B) (Just)	Mid, Mid, Mid	14, 15, 14	2nd attack stuns as hit. 3rd attack Guard Breaks.
Chattering Pinion	Gloomy Side ←(A)	Mid	26	
Hiisi Baroque	Gloomy Side →(B)	Mid, Mid, Mid	8, 4, 10	Final hit stuns as counter-hit
Hell's Barkarole	Gloomy Side →(K)	Mid	24(53)	Shifts to special hit throw on counter-hit or against aerial enemies.

Horizontal Attacks

Name	Command	Attack Level	Damage	Notes
Harmonic Wing	Jolly Side (A)(A)	High, High	8, 8	
Snare Robin	Jolly Side ⇨(A)(B)	High, Low	14, 18(37)	2nd attack shifts into launcher on counter-hit
Fin Beat	Jolly Side ⇘(A)	Mid	18	
Ptarmigan Polka	Jolly Side ⇩(A)(B)	Low, Mid	9, 14	2nd attack may be delayed, stuns on hit
Ptarmigan Polka ~Gestopft Madness	Jolly Side ⇩(A)(B)(A)+(K)	Low, Mid, High	9, 14, 15	2nd attack may be delayed, stuns on hit. May shift to Gloomy Side.
Ptarmigan Polka ~Gestopft Madness (Hold)	Jolly Side ⇩(A)(B)(A)+(K)	Low, Mid, High, High, High	9, 14, 15, 15, 15	2nd attack may be delayed, stuns on hit. May shift to Gloomy Side.
Low Swoop	Jolly Side ⇙(A)	Low	22	
Menuett Dance	Jolly Side ⇦(A) During Hit (A) (Just)	High, High, High	14, 8, 8	Stuns on hit. Causes uncontrollable aerial stun against midair enemies.
Low Pitch Flap	Jolly Side While Crouching (A)	Sp.Low	10	
Snare Clap	Jolly Side While Rising (A)	Mid	18	
Flitting Feather	Jolly Side Jumping (A)	Mid	10 or 14 or 18	Damage varies depending on direction jumped
Retrograde Wing	Jolly Side Backturned (A)	High	10	
Low Retro Flap	Jolly Side While Crouching Backturned (A)	Sp.Low	14	
Harmonic Wing	Gloomy Side (A)(A)	High, High	10, 12	
Shriek Noise	Gloomy Side ⇨(A)(A) Rapidly	High, Mid, High, High, High	13, 8, 8, 8, 8	Inflicts additional damage and hits the faster (A) is tapped
Fin Beat	Gloomy Side ⇘(A)	Mid	26	
Low Pitch Flap	Gloomy Side ⇩(A)	Sp.Low	10	
Low Swoop	Gloomy Side ⇙(A)	Low	22	
Menuett Dance	Gloomy Side ⇦(A) During Hit (A) (Just)	High, High, High	14, 8, 8	Stuns on hit. Causes uncontrollable aerial stun against midair enemies.
Wailing Minerva	Gloomy Side ⇨⇨⇨(A)	High	22 or 24 or 26	The amount of times ⇨ is inputted before (A) determines damage. 2 times is 20, 3 times is 22, 4 times is 24, 5 times is 26.
Chattering Pinion	Gloomy Side ⇦⇦⇦(A)	Mid	26 or 28 or 30 or 36	The amount of times ⇦ is inputted before (A) determines damage. 2 times is 26, 3 times is 28, 4 times is 30, 5 times is 36.
Low Pitch Flap	Gloomy Side While Crouching (A)	Sp.Low	10	
Snare Clap	Gloomy Side While Rising (A)	Mid	22	
Flitting Feather	Gloomy Side Jumping (A)	Mid	10 or 14 or 18	Damage varies depending on direction jumped in
Retrograde Wing	Gloomy Side Backturned (A)	High	10	
Low Retro Flap	Gloomy Side While Crouching Backturned (A)	Sp.Low	14	

Vertical Attacks

Name	Command	Attack Level	Damage	Notes
Two-Step Beak	Jolly Side ⒷⒷ	Mid, Mid	13, 13	
Dark Elegy	Jolly Side →Ⓑ	Mid	18	
Hi-Wind Albatross	Jolly Side →Ⓑ↑	High	12	
Beakbreak Toss	Jolly Side ↘Ⓑ	Mid	18	
Lowdown Neb	Jolly Side ↓Ⓑ	Mid	14	
Low Pitch Pointe	Jolly Side ↙Ⓑ	Sp.Mid	16	
Back Step Pizzicato	Jolly Side ←Ⓑ	Mid	15	
Lowdown Neb	Jolly Side While Crouching Ⓑ	Mid	14	
Uplift Neb	Jolly Side While Rising Ⓑ	Mid	20(64)	Stuns on hit. Shifts into special attack on counter-hit.
Uplift Neb	Jolly Side Jumping Ⓑ	Mid	16(59) or 18(61) or 20(64)	Stuns on hit (except for ↘Ⓑ). Shifts into special attack on counter-hit. Damage varies depending on direction jumped.
Retrograde Beak	Jolly Side Backturned Ⓑ	Mid	15	
Low Retro Neb	Jolly Side While Crouching Backturned Ⓑ	Mid	18	
Two-Step Terror	Gloomy Side ⒷⒷ	Mid, Mid	15, 17	
Elegy Claw	Gloomy Side →ⒷⓀ	Mid, Low	25, 24	
Quick Elegy Claw	Gloomy Side →ⒷⓀ	Low	24	
Hi-Wind Albatross	Gloomy Side →Ⓑ↑	High	16	
Beakbreak Toss	Gloomy Side ↘Ⓑ	Mid	20	Stuns on hit
Lowdown Neb	Gloomy Side ↓Ⓑ	Mid	16	
Low Pitch Pointe	Gloomy Side ↙Ⓑ	Sp.Mid	20	
Oratorio Halcyon	Gloomy Side ←Ⓑ ⒷⒷ (Just)	Mid, Mid, Mid	14, 15, 14	2nd attack stuns as hit. 3rd attack Guard Breaks.
Hiisi Baroque	Gloomy Side →→→Ⓑ	Mid, Mid, Mid, Mid	, 4, 4, 12	The amount of times → is inputted before Ⓑ determines hits and damage. 2 times is 3-hits, 3 times is 4-hits, 4 times is 5-hits, 5 times is 6-hits. Final hit stuns as counter-hit with →→Ⓑ only.
Chattering Thrust	Gloomy Side ←←←Ⓑ	Mid	20 or 25 or 30 or 35	The amount of times ← is inputted before Ⓑ determines damage. 2 times is 20, 3 times is 25, 4 times is 30, 5 times is 35.Stuns on hit. Deflects high attacks.
Lowdown Neb	Gloomy Side While Crouching Ⓑ	Mid	14	
Uplift Neb	Gloomy Side While Rising Ⓑ	Mid	24(68)	Stuns on hit. Shifts into special attack on counter-hit.
Uplift Neb	Gloomy Side Jumping Ⓑ	Mid	16(59) or 18(61) or 20(68)	Stuns on hit (except for ↘Ⓑ). Shifts into special attack on counter-hit. Damage varies depending on direction jumped.
Retrograde Beak	Gloomy Side Backturned Ⓑ	Mid	15	
Low Retro Neb	Gloomy Side While Crouching Backturned Ⓑ	Mid	18	

Kick Attacks

Name	Command	Attack Level	Damage	Notes
High Note Kick	Jolly Side Ⓚ	High	12	
Fear Pecker	Jolly Side →Ⓚ	Mid	16	Stuns on hit
Cadence Side Kick	Jolly Side ↘Ⓚ		24	
Low Pitch Claw	Jolly Side ↓Ⓚ	Low	10	
Claw Kick	Jolly Side ↙Ⓚ	Low	13	
Claw Kick ~Gestopft Madness	Jolly Side ↙ⓀⒶ+Ⓚ	Low, High	13, 15	May shift to Gloomy Side
Claw Kick ~Gestopft Madness (Hold)	Jolly Side ↙ⓀⒶ+Ⓚ	Low, High, High, High	13, 15, 15, 15	May shift to Gloomy Side
Piercing Talon Strike	Jolly Side ←ⓀⒷ	Mid, Mid	16, 24	
Low Pitch Claw	Jolly Side While Crouching Ⓚ	Low	10	
Swing Kick	Jolly Side While Rising Ⓚ	Mid	16	
Flickering Heelkick	Jolly Side Jumping Ⓚ	Mid	15(42)	Shifts to special attack on counter-hit. Leaves Tira in Updraft state.
Retrograde Kick	Jolly Side Backturned Ⓚ	High	15	
Low Retro Claw	Jolly Side While Crouching Backturned Ⓚ	Low	12	
High Note Kick	Gloomy Side Ⓚ	High	12	
Fear Pecker	Gloomy Side →Ⓚ	Mid	22	Stuns on hit
Snare Claw	Gloomy Side ↘Ⓚ	Mid	14	
Divisi Claw Wing	Gloomy Side ↘ⓀⒶ	Mid, High	18, 14	2nd attack stuns on counter-hit
Low Pitch Claw	Gloomy Side ↓Ⓚ	Low	10	
Claw Kick	Gloomy Side ↙Ⓚ	Low	13	
Claw Kick ~Gestopft Madness	Gloomy Side ↙ⓀⒶ+Ⓚ	Low High	13, 15	May shift to Jolly Side
Claw Kick ~Gestopft Madness (Hold)	Gloomy Side ↙ⓀⒶ+Ⓚ	Low High, High, High	13, 15, 15, 15	May Shift to Jolly Side
Piercing Talon Strike	Gloomy Side ←ⓀⒷ	Mid, Mid	16, 24	
Hell's Barkarole	Gloomy Side →→→Ⓚ	Mid	24(53) or 27(57) or 30(61) or 33(54)	The amount of times → is inputted before Ⓚ determines damage. 2 times is 24, 3 times is 27, 4 times is 30, 5 times is 33.Shifts into special attack on counter and aerial hit.
Bremen Fortissimo	Gloomy Side ←←←Ⓚ	High	18 or 19 or 20 or 22	The amount of times ← is inputted before Ⓚ determines damage. 2 times is 18, 3 times is 19, 4 times is 20, 5 times is 22. May shift to Jolly Side.
Low Pitch Claw	Gloomy Side While Crouching Ⓚ	Low	10	
Swing Kick	Gloomy Side While Rising Ⓚ	Mid	22	Causes recoverable stun on counter-hit
Flickering Heelkick	Gloomy Side Jumping Ⓚ	Mid	15(42)	Shifts to special attack on counter-hit. Leaves Tira in Updraft state.
Retrograde Kick	Gloomy Side Backturned Ⓚ	High	15	
Low Retro Claw	Gloomy Side While Crouching Backturned Ⓚ	Low	12	

Simultaneous Press

Name	Command	Attack Level	Damage	Notes
Cross Wing Legato	Jolly Side Ⓐ+Ⓑ	Mid, Mid	11, 14	
Blazing Cadenza	Jolly Side ⇨Ⓐ+Ⓑ	Mid	65	Unblockable. Input Ⓖ to cancel.
Tenuto Sweep	Jolly Side ⇩Ⓐ+Ⓑ	Low	24	Deflects vertical attacks
Shredding Vibrato	Jolly Side ⇦Ⓐ+Ⓑ	Mid, Mid, Mid, Mid, Mid	4, 4, 4, 4, 4	Stuns on hit
Shredding Vibrato (Hold)	Jolly Side ⇦🅐+🅑	Mid, Mid, Mid, Mid, Mid	4, 4, 4, 4, 4	Guard Breaks, stuns on hit
Einsatz Calcatrix	Jolly Side Ⓑ+Ⓚ		48	Nullifies all mid and high attacks. Shifts to Gloomy Side upon absorbing hit. Deflects and counters attacks while changing state. Input Ⓐ+Ⓚ during Gloomy shift to initiate Gestopft Madness.
Somersault Scratch	Jolly Side ⇦Ⓑ+Ⓚ	Mid, Mid	10, 12	
Chattering Cantabile ~Updraft	Jolly Side While Rising Ⓑ+Ⓚ	Mid, Mid, Mid, Mid	10, 8, 7, 5	Leaves Tira in Updraft state
Retro Noise	Jolly Side Backturned Ⓑ+ⓀⒷ	Mid, Mid	18, 26	
Retro Noise ~Gestopft Madness	Jolly Side Backturned Ⓑ+ⓀⒷⒶ+Ⓚ	Mid, Mid, High	18, 26, 15	May shift to Gloomy Side
Retro Noise ~Gestopft Madness (Hold)	Jolly Side Backturned Ⓑ+ⓀⒷ 🅐+🅚	Mid, Mid, High, High, High	18, 26, 15, 15, 15	May shift to Gloomy Side
Gestopft Madness	Jolly Side Ⓐ+Ⓚ	High	15	Deflects high or mid verticals and horizontals. May switch to Gloomy Side. Causes stun on aerial hit.
Gestopft Madness (Hold)	Jolly Side 🅐+🅚	High, High, High	15, 15, 15	Deflects high or mid verticals and horizontals. May switch to Gloomy Side. Causes stun on aerial hit.
Gestopft Madness	Jolly Side Backturned Ⓐ+Ⓚ	High	15	Deflects high or mid verticals and horizontals. May switch to Gloomy Side. Causes stun on aerial hit.
Gestopft Madness (Hold)	Jolly Side Backturned 🅐+🅚	High, High, High	15, 15, 15	Deflects high or mid verticals and horizontals. May switch to Gloomy Side. Causes stun on aerial hit.
Cross Wing Legato	Gloomy Side Ⓐ+Ⓑ	Mid, Mid	11, 14	
Blazing Cadenza	Gloomy Side ⇨Ⓐ+Ⓑ	Mid	65	
Deadly Arietta	Gloomy Side ⇩Ⓐ+Ⓑ	Mid	24	Launches on counter-hit
Deadly Arietta ~Gestopft Madness	Gloomy Side ⇩Ⓐ+ⒷⒶ+Ⓚ	Mid, High	24, 15	May shift to Jolly Side
Deadly Arietta ~Gestopft Madness (Hold)	Gloomy Side ⇩Ⓐ+Ⓑ🅐+🅚	Mid, High, High, High	24, 25, 25, 25	May shift to Jolly Side
Shredding Vibrato	Gloomy Side ⇦Ⓐ+Ⓑ	Mid, Mid, Mid, Mid, Mid	4, 4, 4, 4, 4	Stuns on hit
Shredding Vibrato (Hold)	Gloomy Side ⇦🅐+🅑	Mid, Mid, Mid, Mid, Mid	4, 4, 4, 4, 4	Guard Breaks, stuns on hit
Grim Reaper	Gloomy Side Ⓑ+Ⓚ		50	Deflects all low and mid attacks, then shifts into special throw. Shifts to Jolly Side during attack, and then randomly back to Gloomy Side as it finishes.
Somersault Scratch	Gloomy Side ⇦Ⓑ+Ⓚ	Mid, Mid	10, 12	
Chattering Cantabile ~Updraft	Gloomy Side While Rising Ⓑ+Ⓚ	Mid, Mid, Mid, Mid	10, 8, 7, 5	Leaves Tira in Updraft state
Retro Noise	Gloomy Side Backturned Ⓑ+ⓀⒷ	Mid, Mid	18, 26	
Retro Noise ~Gestopft Madness	Gloomy Side Backturned Ⓑ+Ⓚ ⒷⒶ+Ⓚ	Mid, Mid, High	18, 26, 15	May shift to Gloomy Side
Retro Noise ~Gestopft Madness (Hold)	Gloomy Side Backturned Ⓑ+Ⓚ Ⓑ🅐+🅚	Mid, Mid, High, High, High	18, 26, 15, 15, 15	May shift to Gloomy Side
Gestopft Madness	Gloomy Side Ⓐ+Ⓚ	High	15	Deflects high or mid verticals and horizontals. May switch to Gloomy Side. Causes stun on aerial hit.
Gestopft Madness (Hold)	Gloomy Side 🅐+🅚	High, High, High	15, 15, 15	Deflects high or mid verticals and horizontals. May switch to Gloomy Side. Causes stun on aerial hit.
Gestopft Madness	Gloomy Side Backturned Ⓐ+Ⓚ	High	15	Deflects high or mid verticals and horizontals. May switch to Gloomy Side. Causes stun on aerial hit.
Gestopft Madness (Hold)	Gloomy Side Backturned 🅐+🅚	High, High, High	15, 15, 15	Deflects high or mid verticals and horizontals. May switch to Gloomy Side. Causes stun on aerial hit.
Taunt	Ⓚ+Ⓖ			

8-Way Run

Name	Command	Attack Level	Damage	Notes
Flageolette Fin	Jolly Side → or ↘ or ↗ⒶⒶ	Mid, Mid	16, 21	
Groove Step	Jolly Side ↓ or ↑Ⓐ	Mid	28	
Undertone Rectrix	Jolly Side ↙ or ↖Ⓐ	Low	18	
Canary Waltz C-Dur	Jolly Side ←ⒶⒶ	High, Mid	14, 28	2nd attack Guard Breaks
Canary Waltz C Minor	Jolly Side ←Ⓐ⇩Ⓐ	High, Low	14, 18	
Canary Waltz E Major	Jolly Side ←ⒶⒷ	High, Mid	14, 16	
Wild Beat Neb	Jolly Side → or ↘ or ↗Ⓑ	Mid	20(22)	↘ or ↗ inflict additional damage
Wild Beat Neb ~Gestopft Madness	Jolly Side → or ↘ or ↗ⒷⒶ+Ⓚ	Mid, High	22, 15	May shift to Gloomy Side
Wild Beat Neb ~Gestopft Madness (Hold)	Jolly Side → or ↘ or ↗ⒷⒶ+Ⓚ	Mid, High, High, High	22, 15, 15, 15	May shift to Gloomy Side
Double Rhythm	Jolly Side ↓ or ↑Ⓑ	Mid, Mid	11, 15	2nd attack stuns on counter-hit
Strayed Robin	Jolly Side ← or ↙ or ↖Ⓑ	Low	18	Shifts into launcher extension on counter-hit
Parrot Scratch	Jolly Side →Ⓚ	Mid, High	10, 14	2nd attack stuns on counter-hit
Rhythmic Hook	Jolly Side ↘ or ↗Ⓚ	Mid	20	
Cadence Back Kick	Jolly Side ↓Ⓚ	High	15	
Ring Con Sordino	Jolly Side ↑Ⓚ	Low	16	
Parakeet Scratch ~Blind Stance	Jolly Side ↙ or ↖Ⓚ	Mid, Mid	10, 14	2nd attack stuns on counter-hit
Bremen Fortissimo	Jolly Side ←Ⓚ	High	15	Causes recoverable stun on hit. May shift to Gloomy Side.
Bremen Fortissimo (Hold)	Jolly Side ←Ⓚ	High	15	Causes recoverable stun on hit. May shift to Gloomy Side.
Chattering Tear	Jolly Side While Running Ⓚ	Low	26	
Wailing Minerva	Gloomy Side → or ↘ or ↗Ⓐ	High	20	
Noise Break	Gloomy Side ↓ or ↑Ⓐ	High	32	Causes uncontrollable aerial stun against midair enemies
Undertone Rectrix	Gloomy Side ↙ or ↖Ⓐ	Low	18	
Chattering Pinion	Gloomy Side ←Ⓐ	Mid	26	
Hiisi Baroque	Gloomy Side →Ⓑ	Mid, Mid, Mid	8, 4, 10	Final hit stuns on counter-hit
Chattering Mandible	Gloomy Side ↘ or ↗Ⓑ	Mid	36	
Staccato Ravage	Gloomy Side ↓Ⓑ	Mid	34	Guard Breaks. Stuns against enemies lying on the ground.
Peregrine Rhythm	Gloomy Side ↑Ⓑ	Mid	20	
Strayed Robin	Gloomy Side ↙ or ↖Ⓑ	Low	18(38)	Shifts to special launcher on counter-hit
Chattering Thrust	Gloomy Side ←Ⓑ	Mid	20	Stuns on hit
Hell's Barkarole	Gloomy Side →Ⓚ	Mid	24(53)	Shifts into special attack on counter or serial hit
Rhythmic Hook	Gloomy Side ↘ or ↗Ⓚ	Mid	20	
Cadence Back Kick	Gloomy Side ↓Ⓚ	High	21	
Ring Con Sordino	Gloomy Side ↑Ⓚ	Low	16	
Parakeet Scratch ~Blind Stance	Gloomy Side ↙ or ↖Ⓚ	Mid, Mid	10, 20	2nd attack stuns on counter-hit
Bremen Fortissimo	Gloomy Side ←Ⓚ	High	18	May shift to Jolly Side
Glissando Claw	Gloomy Side While Running Ⓚ	Low	26	

Throws

Name	Command	Attack Level	Damage	Notes
Death Spindle	Ⓐ+Ⓖ	Throw	45	Input Ⓐ to escape
Poison Apple	Ⓑ+Ⓖ	Throw	50	Input Ⓑ to escape
Sweet Lullaby	Left Side Throw	Throw	55	Same button as throw (Ⓐ or Ⓑ) to escape
Bloody Tale	Right Side Throw	Throw	60	Same button as throw (Ⓐ or Ⓑ) to escape
Glass Slippers	Back Throw	Throw	63	Same button as throw (Ⓐ or Ⓑ) to escape

Updraft

Name	Command	Attack Level	Damage	Notes
Updraft	⇖ or ⇧ or ⇗Ⓑ+Ⓚ			
Diving Wing Flap	Updraft Ⓐ	Mid	22	
Diving Talon Thrust	Updraft Ⓑ	Mid	36	Guard Breaks, stuns on hit
Claw Dive	Updraft Ⓚ	Mid	21	

Combos

Jolly Side, ⇨⇨Ⓑ, Ⓐ + Ⓑ
3 hits, 37 Damage
Jolly Side, Counter-hit ⇘Ⓑ, Ⓐ + Ⓑ
3 hits, 39 Damage
Jolly Side, ⇨⇨Ⓑ, ⇦⇦Ⓚ (switches to Gloomy Side), ⇨⇨Ⓑ
5 hits, 49 Damage
Jolly Side, ⇙Ⓐ, ⇩⇩Ⓑ
3 hits, 41 Damage
Jolly Side, ↑Ⓚ (↓Ⓚ when facing left), ⇩⇩Ⓑ
3 hits, 36 Damage
Gloomy Side, ⇙Ⓐ, ⇨⇨⇨⇨⇨Ⓑ
7 hits, 57 Damage
Gloomy Side, ↑Ⓚ (↓Ⓚ when facing left), ⇨⇨⇨⇨⇨Ⓑ
7 hits, 51 Damage
Gloomy Side, ⇘Ⓑ, ⇦⇦⇦⇦⇦Ⓚ, ⇨⇨⇨⇨⇨Ⓑ
8 hits, 57 Damage
Gloomy Side, Counter-hit While Rising Ⓚ, ⇧⇧Ⓑ, ⇨⇨Ⓚ
3 hits, 70 Damage, first stun is recoverable
Gloomy Side, Counter-hit ↑Ⓑ (↓Ⓑ when facing left), ⇩⇩Ⓐ, ⇦ⒶⒶ (Just), ⇦⇦⇦⇦⇦Ⓚ, ⇨⇨⇨⇨⇨Ⓑ
12 hits, 80 Damage
Gloomy Side, Counter-hit ⇦ⒷⒷⒷ, ⇗Ⓚ, during Updraft Ⓚ, ⇨⇨⇨⇨⇨Ⓑ
14 hits, 73 Damage
Gloomy Side, ⇦⇦Ⓑ, ⇙⇙Ⓚ, Ⓑ + ⓀⒷ
5 hits, 60 Damage
Gloomy Side, ⇦Ⓐ + Ⓑ, ⇙↙Ⓚ, back-turned Ⓑ + ⓀⒷ (wall hit), Ⓐ + Ⓚ, ⇨→Ⓑ
15 hits, 72 Damage, must be performed near wall
Gloomy Side, ⇦Ⓐ + Ⓑ, ⇦ⒶⒶ (Just), ⇨ⒶⒶⒶⒶ (wall hit), ⇦ⒷⒷⒷ (Just), ⇗Ⓚ, during updraft Ⓚ, ⇨→Ⓑ
27 hits, 87 Damage, must be performed near wall

Close Range

Tira's two modes of attack, Jolly Side and Gloomy Side, greatly affect her strategy at this distance; refer to the section devoted to Jolly and Gloomy Side tactics. She's generally more effective at close range in Gloomy Side, where many of her high-damage combo starters reside. Unfortunately, the life loss from Gloomy Side's attacks makes it very risky to fight from this position. It's generally better to focus on scoring a knockdown from mid range and saving your close-range options for an anti-wakeup attack. Play defensively and look for an opportunity to knock down your enemy. If you're getting assaulted with high attacks, crouch under them and perform the Uplift Neb (While Rising Ⓑ) to counter-hit for massive damage. Sidestep against vertical attacks and punish their recovery with Beakbreak Toss: ↘Ⓑ, follow-up with Ⓐ+Ⓑ in Jolly Mode or →→Ⓑ in Gloomy. If you ever anticipate an enemy sidestep, attack with ⒶⒶ to hit your foe. On a successful hit, follow-up with an attack consisting of ↘Ⓑ, Ptarmigan Polka (↓ⒶⒷ) (Jolly only), or the Ring Con Sordino (⇧Ⓚ, ⇩Ⓚ when facing left).

If ⒶⒶ is guarded, fall back on defensive measures, such as Guard Impacts or sidesteps. If you happen to be in Gloomy Side from this position, use Tira's Ⓑ + Ⓚ against incoming attacks. It counters all mid and low attacks for massive damage, quickly turning the tables of a bad situation.

Mid Range

When you're in Tira's Jolly Side stance, use her Double Rhythm (⇧ or ⇩Ⓑ) to harass your enemy while you move around with 8-Way Run. When you anticipate a counterattack, dodge or back away from your foe's move, then use Flageolette Fin (→→ⒶⒶ) to punish it. If you anticipate a sidestep or a slow attack, counter it with ↓Ⓐ. Perform the Ⓑ extension (↓ⒶⒷ) if it connects on a counter-hit. You can perform the command ↓ⒶⒷⒶ+Ⓚ for a chance to shift into Tira's Gloomy Mode, though you're left at a disadvantage. Use the Snare Robin (→Ⓐ) as an alternate method of countering sidesteps. If it connects as a counter-hit, verify the hit and chain directly into its extension (→ⒶⒷ) for a 2-hit combo. If →Ⓐ connects as a normal hit, follow up with a guessing game consisting of a throw or a delayed version of the Ⓑ extension. If the low strike connects as a counter-hit, the enemy will be launched, allowing you to connect with Tira's Ⓑ + Ⓚ back-turn attack. The final hit of this string also leaves Tira in a crouching state, which allows her to go for a While Rising Ⓑ, Ring Con Sordino (↑↑Ⓚ), or a throw mix-up when Ⓑ connects on a normal hit. If ↑↑Ⓚ hits, immediately perform ↓↓Ⓑ to score a 3-hit combo. As a third means of countering sidesteps, use Menuett Dance (←Ⓐ during hit Ⓐ). This leaves your foe vulnerable to the combo ←ⒶⒶ, ⒶⒶ.

Tira's Gloomy Side attacks are better used at close range, though she does have a few options to work with at this distance. Use Wailing Minerva (⇨Ⓐ) as a tool for preemptively stopping aggressive movements, and Hell's Barkarole (⇨Ⓚ) to punish your opponent's missed moves. You can replace the Hell's Barkarole with Peregrine Rhythm (⇧Ⓑ, or ⇩Ⓑ when facing left), which leads to juggle combos, like ←←←←←Ⓚ, →→→→→Ⓑ. The combo possibilities get even bigger if the attack connects on a counter-hit: ↓↓Ⓐ, ←ⒶⒶ(Just), ←←←←←Ⓚ, then →→→→→Ⓑ. The Peregrine Rhythm, however, is difficult to use because of its direction-swapping command, so spend time getting used to it in training mode.

Like in Jolly Side, deter sidesteps and 8-Way Run with ←ⒶⒶ (Just). Use the Divisi Claw Wing (↘ⓀⒶ), which leads to less damage but can't be crouched under because of its starting mid hit. Attack with the mid-hitting Elegy Claw (→Ⓑ) when your opponent isn't sidestepping. Go for its low kick extension →ⒷⓀ if your foe tends to stand after blocking →Ⓑ. You can fake →Ⓑ and immediately shift into its low extension by inputting →ⒷⓀ, which may catch your enemy off guard. When fending off your enemy's horizontal attacks, crouch under them and perform the Swing Kick (While Rising Ⓚ). This technique knocks the enemy into a recoverable stun on counter-hit (in Gloomy Side only), enabling you to link into ⇧Ⓑ (⇩Ⓑ when facing left), then →→Ⓚ for massive damage.

Long Range

Your goal is to knock down your enemy or to slip into mid range when there's a gap in your enemy's offense. The preferred way to do this with Tira's Jolly Side stance is to land her Wild Beat Neb (⇨Ⓑ) launcher, which enables her to juggle with Gestopft Madness (Ⓐ+Ⓚ) and possibly change to Gloomy Side. This enables you to immediately stage an anti-wakeup attack with Gloomy Side's powerful options. Play cautiously and rely heavily on 8-Way Run to avoid enemy attack. If your foe misses a move, punish it with ⇨ⒶⒶ or ⇨Ⓑ. The ⇨ⒶⒶ option is much faster and less vulnerable to side movement, but it leads to less damage and no possibility of a Gloomy Side change. Against highly mobile players, occasionally attack with Low Swoop (↙Ⓐ) to catch them while they're standing. When it hits, strike your fallen enemy with ↓↓Ⓑ for a damaging combo. When your enemy is afraid of the low attack, use ⇨Ⓑ to hit him while he's crouching—follow up with Ⓐ+Ⓑ or Ⓐ+Ⓚ for an aerial combo.

Special Tactics

Okizeme: Anti-Wakeup

In both Jolly and Gloomy side, use the mid ↘Ⓑ and the low ⇧Ⓚ (⇩Ⓚ when facing left). If ↘Ⓑ connects, hit your stunned enemy with Ⓐ + Ⓑ (→→Ⓑ in Gloomy Side). The fast, low attack ⇧Ⓚ leads to additional damage in both Jolly and Gloomy Side. In Jolly Side, follow up with ↓↓Ⓑ to hit your grounded enemy. In Gloomy Side, do →→Ⓑ. Occasionally replace ↘Ⓑ with ←ⓀⒷ when you're directly next to your enemy. It leads to an additional →→Ⓑ ground hit in Gloomy Side, or ↓↓Ⓑ in Jolly. Replace ⇧Ⓚ with ↙Ⓐ when attacking from slightly farther away.

One of Tira's more devastating Gloomy Side attacks is her mid-hitting Staccato Ravage (⇩Ⓑ, or ⇧Ⓑ when facing left). It's an extremely fast Guard Break. It leaves Tira at a massive advantage when blocked, enabling her to stage a follow-up attack consisting of a throw, ↘Ⓑ, ←ⒷⒷⒷ(Just), or ⇧Ⓚ(⇩Ⓚ when facing left). Use the ←ⒷⒷⒷ option to counter-hit your enemy's attempts to attack when he or she recovers. If it hits on a counter-hit, blast your airborne foe with ↗Ⓚ, Ⓚ, →→Ⓑ.

Jolly and Gloomy Sides

Tira has two attack modes at her disposal, Jolly Side and Gloomy Side, which she swaps between at random when she gets hit or when she performs certain attacks. These modes have different sets of techniques, even having a few duplicates with slightly different properties. At a base level, Gloomy Mode is generally the stronger pick of the two, having a better variety of attacks that lead to heavy damage. However, many of these attacks absorb Tira's life when she uses them. This also happens in Jolly Side after certain attacks that have a chance to change to Gloomy Side. For example, Bremen Fortissimo (⇦Ⓚ), Gestopft Madness (Ⓐ + Ⓚ), Ⓐ+Ⓚ, and ⇨Ⓑ (Gloomy Side only) absorb Tira's life. They also carry a chance to switch Tira to the opposite stance, which happens at random. Tira's Einsatz Calcatrix (Jolly Side Ⓑ + Ⓚ) and Grim Reaper (Gloomy Side(Ⓑ + Ⓚ), which have deflect and counter properties against most attack types, also change her stance upon a successful counter, though she randomly changes back to the stance in which she uses the attack.

It's important to learn to use both stances because of the erratic nature in which Tira changes modes. Your attack set often changes. It's helpful to recognize when you're most likely to change modes, as well as how to use those instances to your advantage. For example, Tira's ⇦Ⓚ in Jolly Side normally causes her to enter a recovery state. However, if the attack changes her to Gloomy Side, the recovery period is nullified, enabling you to exploit the recoverable stun and start a combo with Gloomy Side's options. A less risky way of using this to your advantage is to land Jolly Side's ⇨Ⓑ to launch your enemy, and then performing ⇦Ⓚ (←←Ⓚ for a faster input). Using ⇦Ⓚ causes a special knockdown state against airborne opponents, which is just long enough to allow Tira to recover from her head butt if her stance change fails. Interestingly enough, if the head butt manages to change your state to Gloomy Side, immediately perform →→Ⓑ to combo your fallen enemy.

In addition to combinations that enable you to safely change stances, several of Tira's strings chain directly into her Ⓐ+Ⓚ or Ⓐ+Ⓚ, a second head butt attack that wastes life for the possibility of a stance change. This ability deflects high attacks and then shifts into the ⇦Ⓚ head butt. Use this specifically to deflect incoming attacks when certain strings are blocked, or to safely change stances after the attack knocks down your enemy. Some of the strings that chain into this move are the Retro Noise (back-turned Ⓑ+ⓀⒷⒶ+Ⓚ), the Claw Kick (↙ⓀⒶ+Ⓚ), the Wild Beat Neb (⇨ⒷⒶ+Ⓚ, Jolly Side only), and Ptarmigan Polka (↓ⒶⒷⒶ+Ⓚ, Jolly Side only).

Voldo

I saw Eternity the other night,
Like a great ring of pure and endless light,
All calm, as it was bright...

"The World," Henry Vaughan (1622 - 1695)

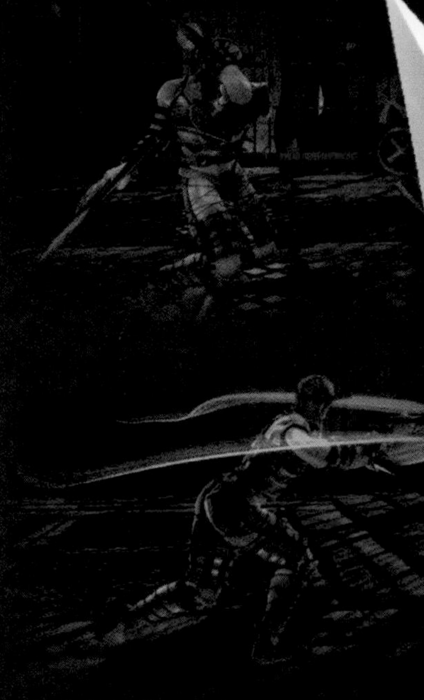

Bio

Age:	50
Birthplace:	Palermo, Kingdom of Naples
Height:	6'0"
Weight:	185 lbs.
Birth Date:	August 25
Blood Type:	A
Weapon:	Katar (Jamadhar) x 2
Weapon Name:	Manas & Ayus
Discipline:	Self-Taught
Family:	Parents: Deceased Four brothers: Killed through warfare Master: Vercci (long deceased)

Manas and Ayus

Voldo's master was a man named Vercci, who traveled the world seeking Soul Edge. On his journeys to the Orient he acquired many strange weapons that became part of his vast treasure hoard.

Manas and Ayus are a pair of Jamadhar, given to Voldo so that he could guard his master's treasure. Over the long years of his vigil, many were the pitiful thieves whose blood was let by their blades. Soul Edge came to use Voldo's fierce loyalty to control him, and now Manas and Ayus are wielded in the cause of evil.

Self-Taught

During his long, lonely vigil protecting his master's treasures in the Money Pit, Voldo's body and soul slowly adapted to the lightless environment of the vault. His eyes lost their sight, but instead he developed the ability to detect enemies in the blackness. His powers of conscious reasoning faded and he came to be guided by pure instinct.

He eventually forgot that he was a man, and his movements have become alien and inhuman. Inexperienced fighters become so confused they do not even realize they are being attacked, and veteran warriors find that their battle experience is for naught in the face of this bizarre opponent.

Signature Techniques

Name	Command	Attack Level	Damage	Notes
Blind Crescent ~Face Away	⇨ⒷⒷ	High, Mid	15, 20	1st attack stuns on counter-hit. Leaves Voldo facing away from enemy.
Hell Claw ~Face Away	⇦ⒷⒶ	Mid, High	25, 10	Leaves Voldo facing away from enemy
Demon Elbow	➔ or ➘ or ➚Ⓑ	Mid	20	Stuns on counter-hit. Input command as fast as possible for Just Frame version (stuns on hit). Input ➔🅑 for additional attack if Elbow hits fallen enemy.
Faceless Wheel ~Down	Backturned ⇩Ⓑ🅚	Low, Mid	20, 40	2nd attack guard Breaks. Leaves Voldo lying on the ground.
Blind Assault	Backturned ➔ or ➘ or ➚Ⓚ	Mid	30	
Single Flap ~Mantis Crawl	⬅🅚	High	26	Stuns on hit. Shifts to Mantis Crawl.
Mantis Crawl	Backturned ⇩Ⓑ+Ⓚ	Mid	20	Shifts to Mantis Crawl
Fool Ritual	Mantis Crawl Ⓑ+Ⓚ	Mid	15	

Horizontal Attacks

Name	Command	Attack Level	Damage	Notes
Scissor Claw	ⒶⒶ	High, High	10, 10	
Grave Digger	ⒶⒷⒷⒷ	Low, Low, Low	5, 5, 5	
Silent Embrace	⇨Ⓐ	High	20	
Scorpion Claw	⇘Ⓐ	Mid	18	Causes recoverable stun on counter-hit
Silent Toe Cleaver	⇩Ⓐ	Sp.Low	10	
Evil Bow	⇗Ⓐ	Low	34	
Jolly Ripper ~Face Away	⇦Ⓐ	High	20	Leaves Voldo facing away from enemy
Shadow Toe Cleaver	While Crouching Ⓐ	Sp.Low	10	
Dusky Nipper	While Rising Ⓐ	High	18	Stuns on counter-hit
Frolicking Brain Shear	Jumping Ⓐ	High	18 or 22 or 26	Damage varies depending on direction jumped in
Blind Scissors	Backturned ⒶⒶ	High, High	10, 10	
Faceless Macabre ~Face Opponent	Backturned ⇨ⒶⒷⒷ	High, Mid, Mid, Mid, Mid	10, 12, 5, 5, 20	Final attack stuns on hit. Leaves Voldo facing enemy.
Lunatic Doll	Backturned ⇘Ⓐ	Mid	10	Causes recoverable stun on counter-hit
Reverse Evil Bow	Backturned ⇩Ⓐ	Sp.Low	10	
Blind Leg Cutter	Backturned ⇗Ⓐ	Low	30	
Scarecrow ~Face Opponent	Backturned ⇦Ⓐ	High	14	Leaves Voldo facing enemy
Blind Leg Cutter	Backturned While Crouching Ⓐ	Sp.Low	10	
Blind Double Claw	Backturned While Rising Ⓐ	Mid	24	

Vertical Attacks

Name	Command	Attack Level	Damage	Notes
Madness Shredder	ⒷⒷ	Mid, Mid	12, 16	
Blind Crescent ~Face Away	⇨ⒷⒷ	High, Mid	15, 20	1st attack stuns on counter-hit. Leaves Voldo facing away from enemy.
Guillotine Scissors	⇘ⒷⒷ	Mid, Mid	24, 36	
Fencer Mantis	⇩Ⓑ	Mid	16	
Asylum Step	⇗Ⓑ	Mid	20	
Asylum Step (Attack Throw)	Against Downed Foe ⇗🅑	Throw	14	Shifts to attack throw on hit against fallen enemy
Hell Claw ~Face Away	⇦ⒷⒶ	Mid, High	25, 10	Leaves Voldo facing away from enemy
Fencer Mantis	While Crouching Ⓑ	Mid	16	
Rat Drill ~Face Away	While Crouching ⇘Ⓑ	Mid	28	Leaves Voldo facing away from enemy
Bad Luck	While Rising Ⓑ	Mid	20	
Bad Luck ~Mantis Crawl	While Rising 🅑	Mid	20	Shifts to Mantis Crawl>
Frolicking Port de Bras	Jumping Ⓑ	Mid	20 or 24 or 28	Damage varies depending on direction jumped in
Lunatic Strike	Backturned ⒷⒷ	Mid, Mid	12, 16	
Blind Pending Thrust	Backturned ⇨Ⓑ	Mid	20	
Blind Pending Thrust ~Mantis Crawl	Backturned ⇨🅑	Mid	20	Shifts to Mantis Crawl>
Back Pendulum	Backturned ⇘Ⓑ	Mid	30	
Faceless Flap ~Down	Backturned ⇩ⒷⓀ	Low, Mid	20, 30	Leaves Voldo lying on the ground
Faceless Wheel ~Down	Backturned ⇩Ⓑ🅚	Low, Mid	20, 40	2nd attack Guard Breaks. Leaves Voldo lying on the ground.
Asylum Step ~Face Opponent	Backturned ⇗Ⓑ	Mid	20	Leaves Voldo facing enemy
Hell Scarecrow Spin ~Face Opponent	Backturned ⇦ⒷⒶⒶ	Mid, High, Mid	20, 10, 20	Leaves Voldo facing enemy
Rat Bounce	Backturned While Crouching Ⓑ	Mid	15	
Blind Toss	Backturned While Rising Ⓑ	Mid	28	Stuns on hit

Kick Attacks

Name	Command	Attack Level	Damage	Notes
Mute High Kick	Ⓚ	High	14	
Jolly Jumping Kick	⇨Ⓚ	High	20	
Mute Mid Kick	↘Ⓚ	Mid	14	
Rat Kick	⇩Ⓚ	Low	12	
Scorpion Tail	↗Ⓚ	Mid	20	
Scorpion Tail ~Face Away	↗🅚	Mid	18	Stuns on hit. Leaves Voldo facing away from enemy.
Silent Stinger	⇦Ⓚ	High	18	Stuns on counter-hit
Silent Stinger ~Death Roll	⇦🅚	High	18	Stuns on counter-hit. Shifts to Superwyrm.
Rat Kick	While Crouching Ⓚ	Low	14	
Lunatic Spin	While Rising Ⓚ	Mid, High	10, 8	
Lunatic Spin ~Face Away	While Rising 🅚	Mid, High	10, 8	Leaves Voldo facing away from enemy
Side Kick ~Down	Jumping Ⓚ	High	18 or 20 or 22	Stuns on hit (except ↙Ⓚ). Damage varies depending on direction jumped in. Leaves Voldo lying on the ground.
Mute Kick	Backturned Ⓚ	High	14	
Spinning High	Backturned ⇨Ⓚ	High	20	
Back Silent Middle	Backturned ↘Ⓚ	Mid	16	
Blind Slide Low	Backturned ⇩Ⓚ	Low	12	
Scorpion Tail	Backturned ↗Ⓚ	Mid	18	Stuns on hit
Mad Slap ~Down	Backturned ⇦ⓀⒶ	Mid, High	20, 30	2nd attack stuns on hit. Leaves Voldo lying on the ground.
Blind Arch	Backturned While Crouching Ⓚ	Low	16	
Blind Drill	Backturned While Rising Ⓚ	High	18	

Simultaneous Press

Name	Command	Attack Level	Damage	Notes
Despair	Ⓐ+Ⓑ	Mid, Mid	10, 10	Stuns on hit
Praying Mantis	⇩Ⓐ+Ⓑ	Mid	30	Stuns on counter-hit
Praying Mantis ~Caliostro Rush	⇩Ⓐ+Ⓑ⇩↘⇨	Mid	30	Stuns on counter-hit
Death Rose	⇦Ⓐ+Ⓑ	Mid, Mid, Mid, Mid	10, 10, 10, 10	
Blind Dive	While Crouching ↘Ⓐ+Ⓑ	High	45	Guard Breaks
Blind Dive (Hold)	While Crouching ↘🅐+🅑	High	70	Unblockable
Guillotine Scissors Alternate	Ⓑ+Ⓚ	Mid	20	
Guillotine Scissors Alternate (Hold)	🅑+🅚	Mid, Mid, Mid	10, 20, 40	
Super Freak	Ⓐ+Ⓚ			Evade properties. Avoids any type of a single attack. May shift into Super Freak Inner, Outer, Retreat, or Lunge.
Super Freak ~Super Freak Lunge	Ⓐ+Ⓚ⇨Ⓐ+Ⓚ			
Super Freak ~Super Freak (Inner or Outer)	Ⓐ+Ⓚ⇩ or ⇧ Ⓐ+Ⓚ			
Super Freak ~Super Freak Retreat	Ⓐ+Ⓚ⇦Ⓐ+Ⓚ			
Super Freak Lunge	⇨Ⓐ+Ⓚ			
Super Freak Lunge ~Mantis Crawl	⇨🅐+🅚			Shifts to Mantis Crawl>
Super Freak (Inner or Outer)	⇩ or ⇧Ⓐ+Ⓚ			
Super Freak (Inner or Outer) ~Mantis Crawl	⇩Ⓐ+Ⓚ⇩			Shifts to Mantis Crawl>
Super Freak (Inner or Outer) ~Mantis Crawl	⇧Ⓐ+Ⓚ⇧			Shifts to Mantis Crawl>
Super Freak Retreat	⇦Ⓐ+Ⓚ			
Super Freak Retreat ~Caliostro Rush	⇦🅐+🅚			Shifts to Caliostro Rush
Rat Bounce	While Crouching Ⓐ+Ⓚ	Sp.Mid	18	
Rat Bounce ~Mantis Crawl	While Crouching 🅐+🅚	Sp.Mid	18	Shifts to Mantis Crawl
Rat Straight ~Face Opponent	Backturned Ⓐ+Ⓑ	High	30	Deflects horizontal and vertical attacks. Leaves Voldo facing enemy.
Freak Roll	Backturned ⇩Ⓐ+Ⓑ	Sp.Mid	23	Stuns on hit
Freak Roll ~Mantis Crawl	Backturned ⇩Ⓐ+ⒷⒼ	Sp.Mid	23	Stuns on hit. Shifts to Mantis Crawl>
Spasm ~Down	Freak Roll ⇩	Low	??	Leaves Voldo lying on ground
Fortune Spasm	Freak Roll During Hit enemy does not Ukemi.	Mid, Mid	17	
Freak Roll ~Down	Fortune Spasm Ⓚ	Low	??	Leaves Voldo lying on the ground
Death Rose ~Face Opponent	Backturned ⇦Ⓐ+Ⓑ	Mid, Mid, Mid, Mid	10, 10, 10, 10	Leaves Voldo facing enemy
Scarecrow ~Face Opponent	Backturned Ⓑ+Ⓚ	Mid	21	Stuns on counter-hit. Leaves Voldo facing enemy.
Taunt	Ⓚ+Ⓖ			

Voldo

8-Way Run

Name	Command	Attack Level	Damage	Notes
Frenzy Dive ~Down	→ or ↘ or ↗Ⓐ	High	26	Leaves Voldo lying on the ground
Frenzy Dive ~Death Roll	→ or ↘ or ↗🅐	High	26	Shifts to Superwyrm
Blind Blade	↓ or ↑Ⓐ	Mid	30	
Elegant Claw	← or ↙ or ↖Ⓐ	High	28	Stuns on hit
Demon Elbow	→ or ↘ or ↗Ⓑ	Mid	20	Stuns on counter-hit. Input command as fast as possible for Just Frame version (stuns on hit). Input → 🅑 for additional attack if Elbow hits fallen enemy.
Katar Gore ~Face Away	↓ or ↑Ⓑ	Mid	34	Stuns on hit. Leaves Voldo facing away from enemy.
Rat Cheeze	↙ or ↖ⒷⒷⒷ	Low, Low, Low	10, 10, 10	
Rat Cheeze Kick ~Down	↙ or ↖ⒷⒷⒷⓀ	Low, Low, Low, High	10, 10, 10, 20	Final attack stuns on hit. Leaves Voldo lying on the ground.
Katar Splitter	←Ⓑ	Mid	20	
Katar Splitter ~Mantis Crawl	←🅑	Mid, Mid	20	Shifts to Mantis Crawl>
Blind Drop ~Face Away	→ or ↘ or ↗Ⓚ	High, Mid	34	Stuns on hit. Leaves Voldo facing away from enemy.
Demon Tail	↓ or ↑Ⓚ	High	36	
Mute Low Kick	↙ or ↖Ⓚ	Low	16	
Single Flap ~Down	←Ⓚ	High	26	Stuns on hit. Leaves Voldo lying on the ground.
Single Flap ~Mantis Crawl	←🅚	High	26	Stuns on it. Shifts to Mantis Crawl>
Gate Opener	→Ⓐ+Ⓑ	Mid, Mid	20, 20	
Gate Prier	→Ⓐ+ⒷⓀ	Mid, High	20, 20	
Mystery Dance	↓ or ↑Ⓐ+Ⓑ			
Web Weaver	←Ⓐ+Ⓚ	High	78	Unblockable
Sliding	While Running Ⓚ	Low	26	
Madness Spin	Backturned → or ↘ or ↗Ⓐ	Mid, Mid	36	
Blind Winder	Backturned ↓ or ↑Ⓐ	Mid	28	Stuns on counter-hit
Lunatic Wheel	Backturned ← or ↙ or ↖Ⓐ	High	21	Stuns on hit
Blind Arch	Backturned →Ⓑ	Mid	24	Stuns on counter-hit
Jolly Slasher	Backturned ↘ or ↗ⒷⒷ	Mid, Mid	16, 18	2nd attack stuns on hit
Red Stitch ~Face Opponent	Backturned ↓ or ↑Ⓑ	Mid	30	Leaves Voldo facing enemy
Blind Pillory Break	Backturned ← or ↙ or ↖Ⓑ	Mid	20	
Blind Pillory Break ~Mantis Crawl	Backturned ← or ↙ or ↖🅑	Mid	20	Shifts to Mantis Crawl>
Blind Assault	Backturned → or ↘ or ↗Ⓚ	Mid	30	
Wyrm Breakdance ~Face Opponent	Backturned ↓ or ↑ⓀⓀ	Low, High	20, 22	1st attack stuns on hit. Leaves Voldo facing enemy.
Wyrm Breakdance ~Mantis Crawl	Backturned ↓ or ↑Ⓚ 🅚	Low, High	20, 22	Shifts to Mantis Crawl>
Blind Heel Kick	Backturned ↙ or ↖Ⓚ	Low	16	
Blind Drop Kick ~Down	Backturned ←Ⓚ		30	Leaves Voldo lying on the ground
Blind Back Strike ~Down	Backturned ←ⓀⒷ+Ⓚ	Low, Mid, Mid, Mid	30, 10, 10, 10	Leaves Voldo lying on the ground

Throws

Name	Command	Attack Level	Damage	Notes
Spinning Umbrella	Ⓐ+Ⓖ	Throw	45	Input Ⓐ to escape
Catacomb Throw	Ⓑ+Ⓖ	Throw	50	Input Ⓑ to escape
Fool's Inquest	Left Side Throw	Throw	50	Same button as throw (Ⓐ or Ⓑ) to escape
Bush Whacker	Right Side Throw	Throw	55	Same button as throw (Ⓐ or Ⓑ) to escape
Sadistic Cross	Back Throw	Throw	60	Same button as throw (Ⓐ or Ⓑ) to escape
Blind Ownership	Backturned Ⓐ+Ⓖ or Ⓑ+Ⓖ	Throw	65	Same button as throw (Ⓐ or Ⓑ) to escape
Jack in the Cage	Backturned ⇨⇨Ⓐ+Ⓖ	Throw	55	Input Ⓐ to escape

Mantis Crawl

Name	Command	Attack Level	Damage	Notes
Mantis Crawl	⇩Ⓑ+Ⓚ	Mid	20	
Mantis Crawl	Backturned ⇩Ⓑ+Ⓚ	Mid	20	
Twisted Salute	Mantis Crawl Ⓐ	Mid, Mid	20 or 30	Deals 20 damage backturned, deals 30 damage and stuns when facing forward
Asylum Breakout	Mantis Crawl Ⓑ	Mid, Low	36	
Blind Drop	Mantis Crawl Ⓚ	Mid	20	
Freak Roll	Mantis Crawl Ⓐ+Ⓑ	Sp.Mid	10	
Freak Roll ~Mantis Crawl	Mantis Crawl Ⓐ+ⒷⒼ	Sp.Mid	10	Shifts to Mantis Crawl>
Spasm ~Down	Freak Roll ⇩	Low	??	Leaves Voldo lying on the ground
Fortune Spasm	Freak Roll During Hit Enemy does not Ukemi	Mid, Mid	10, 17	
Fool Ritual	Mantis Crawl Ⓑ+Ⓚ	Mid	15	Evades horizontal attacks
Fool Ritual (Hold)	Mantis Crawl 🅑+🅚	Mid	30	Evades horizontal attacks
Fanatic Fool	Mantis Crawl Ⓐ+Ⓚ	Mid	20 or 25	20 damage backturned, 25 facing enemy. Stuns on hit.
Mantis Fire Dance	Mantis Crawl ⇨⇨	Low	20	
Death Roll	Mantis Crawl ⇩ or ⇧			Evades vertical attacks

Caliostro Rush

Name	Command	Attack Level	Damage	Notes
Caliostro Rush	⇩⬂⇨			Evades high attacks
Katar Slap	Caliostro Rush ⒶⒶ	High, Mid	15, 21	2nd attack stuns on hit
Snake Eater	Caliostro Rush Ⓑ	Low	25	
Lunatic Flip	Caliostro Rush Ⓚ	Mid	24	Leaves Voldo lying on ground
Blind Dive	Caliostro Rush Ⓐ+Ⓑ	High	45	Guard Breaks
Blind Dive (Hold)	Caliostro Rush 🅐+🅑	High	70	Unblockable
Tomb Implant ~Mantis Crawl	Caliostro Rush Ⓑ+Ⓚ	Mid		Shifts to Mantis Crawl>
Caliostro Rush ~Face Away	Caliostro Rush			Leaves Voldo facing away from enemy
Life Sucker	Caliostro Rush Ⓐ+Ⓖ	Throw	50	Input Ⓐ to escape throw
Centipede Nightmare ~Mantis Crawl	Caliostro Rush Ⓑ+Ⓖ	Throw	50	Input Ⓑ to escape throw. Shifts to Mantis Crawl

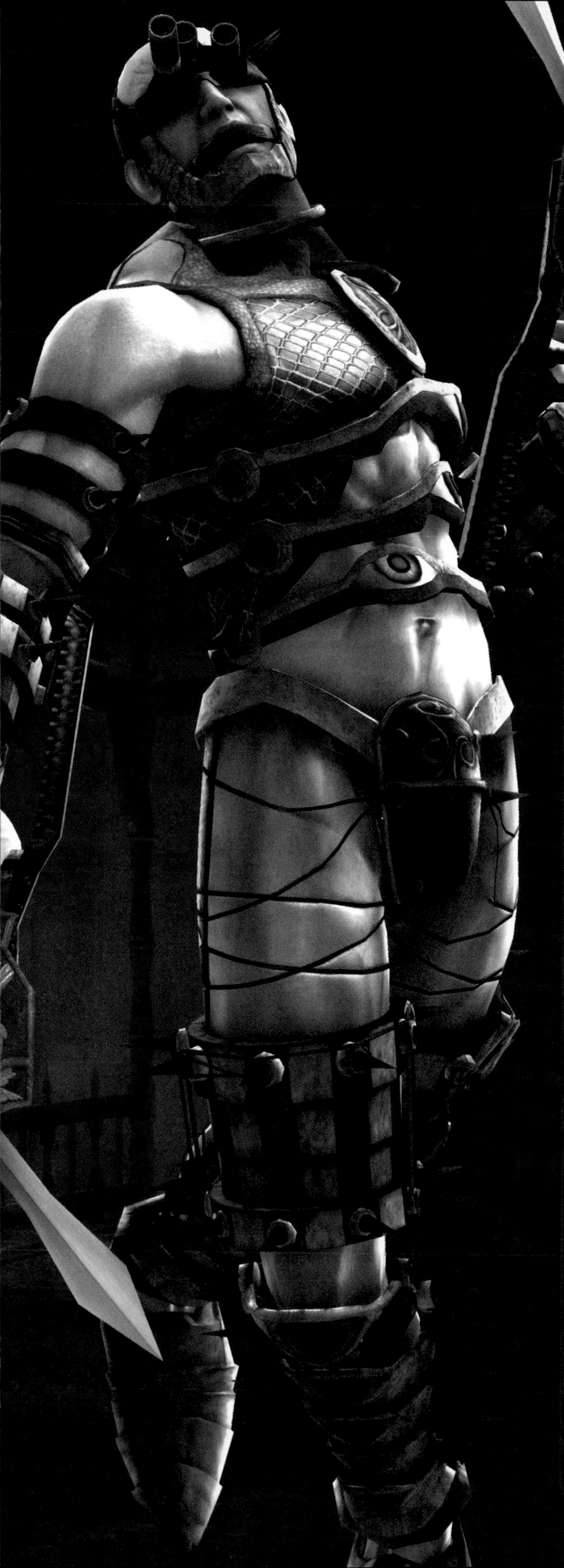

Blind Caliostro Rush

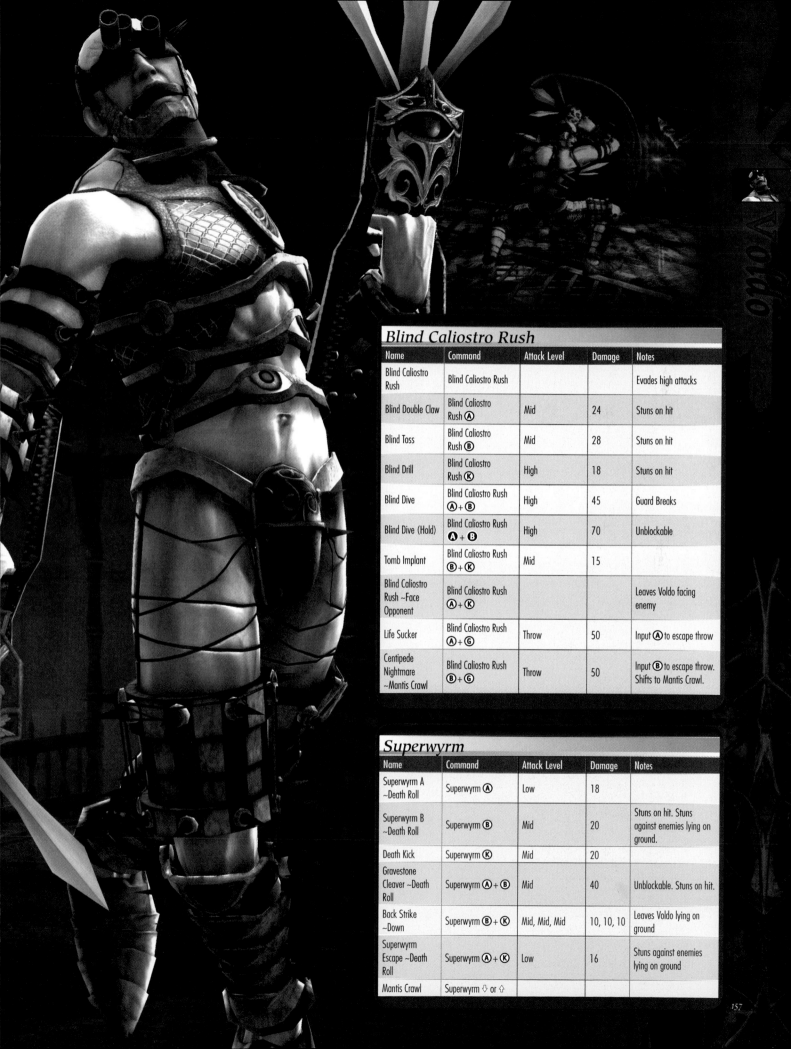

Name	Command	Attack Level	Damage	Notes
Blind Caliostro Rush	Blind Caliostro Rush			Evades high attacks
Blind Double Claw	Blind Caliostro Rush Ⓐ	Mid	24	Stuns on hit
Blind Toss	Blind Caliostro Rush Ⓑ	Mid	28	Stuns on hit
Blind Drill	Blind Caliostro Rush Ⓚ	High	18	Stuns on hit
Blind Dive	Blind Caliostro Rush Ⓐ+Ⓑ	High	45	Guard Breaks
Blind Dive (Hold)	Blind Caliostro Rush 🅐+🅑	High	70	Unblockable
Tomb Implant	Blind Caliostro Rush Ⓑ+Ⓚ	Mid	15	
Blind Caliostro Rush ~Face Opponent	Blind Caliostro Rush Ⓐ+Ⓚ			Leaves Voldo facing enemy
Life Sucker	Blind Caliostro Rush Ⓐ+Ⓖ	Throw	50	Input Ⓐ to escape throw
Centipede Nightmare ~Mantis Crawl	Blind Caliostro Rush Ⓑ+Ⓖ	Throw	50	Input Ⓑ to escape throw. Shifts to Mantis Crawl.

Superwyrm

Name	Command	Attack Level	Damage	Notes
Superwyrm A ~Death Roll	Superwyrm Ⓐ	Low	18	
Superwyrm B ~Death Roll	Superwyrm Ⓑ	Mid	20	Stuns on hit. Stuns against enemies lying on ground.
Death Kick	Superwyrm Ⓚ	Mid	20	
Gravestone Cleaver ~Death Roll	Superwyrm Ⓐ+Ⓑ	Mid	40	Unblockable. Stuns on hit.
Back Strike ~Down	Superwyrm Ⓑ+Ⓚ	Mid, Mid, Mid	10, 10, 10	Leaves Voldo lying on ground
Superwyrm Escape ~Death Roll	Superwyrm Ⓐ+Ⓚ	Low	16	Stuns against enemies lying on ground
Mantis Crawl	Superwyrm ⇩ or ⇧			

Combos

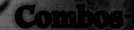

⇨⇨Ⓑ (Just), ⇨⇨Ⓑ (Just), ⇨⇨Ⓑ (Just)	4 hits, 59 Damage, first hit cannot be a counter-hit
Counter-hit While Rising Ⓐ, ⇨ⒷⒷ	3 hits, 50 Damage
Counter-hit ⇩Ⓐ + Ⓑ ⇩⇘⇨, Ⓑ + Ⓚ, Ⓑ	3 hits, 65 Damage
Back-turned ⇩⇘⇨Ⓐ, ⇘Ⓑ, Ⓐ + Ⓑ	3 hits, 73 Damage
Back-turned ⇩⇘⇨Ⓐ, ⇩⇘⇨Ⓑ, ⇙Ⓚ, ⇙Ⓑ	4 hits, 73 Damage
Back-turned ⇦⇦Ⓐ, ⇩⇘⇨Ⓐ, ⇩⇘⇨Ⓑ, ⇙Ⓚ, ⇙Ⓑ	5 hits, 82 Damage
Counter-hit back-turned Ⓑ + Ⓚ, Ⓐ + Ⓑ, ⇨⇨Ⓑ, ⇨⇨Ⓑ (Just), ⇙Ⓑ	6 hits, 64 Damage
During Mantis Crawl Ⓐ, ⇙Ⓑ	2 hits, 40 Damage
During Mantis Crawl Ⓑ + Ⓚ, Ⓑ + Ⓚ	2 hits, 46 Damage
Counter-hit ⇨⇨Ⓐ, Ⓑ, Ⓑ + Ⓚ	5 hits, 56 Damage
Counter-hit ⇦⇦Ⓑ, ⇨⇨	3 hits, 54 Damage
During Superwyrm Ⓐ + Ⓑ, Ⓑ, Ⓑ	3 hits, 64 Damage

Close Range

The bizarre Voldo can fight and defend normally from a back-turned state. This is referred to as his "Blind Stance," which features most of his strongest close-range attacks. Your objective is to pressure your enemy with Voldo's back-turned offense to ultimately land his Blind Winder (Bland Stance~Caliostro Rush Ⓐ), which leads to heavy damage. Start an attack with his Blind Crescent (→ⒷⒷ), Hell Claw (←ⒷⒶ), or Jolly Ripper (←Ⓐ), all of which leave him in a back-turned state. When any of these strings hit, stage a follow-up attack that consists of a throw, ↙Ⓐ, ⒶⒶ, or ↓↘→Ⓐ. Use ⒶⒶ to counter sidesteps, while ↓↘→Ⓐ should be used to hit crouch attempts; if it hits, perform the combo ↓↘→Ⓑ, ↙Ⓚ, ↙Ⓑ. When your opening attacks are blocked, use Voldo's back-turned attacks to stage a counteroffensive. If your enemy attacks out of block-stun with ↓Ⓐ, input Ⓑ+Ⓚ (Scarecrow) to jump over and counter-hit it. Follow up with Ⓐ+Ⓑ, →→Ⓑ, →→Ⓑ(Just), ↙Ⓑ. Use ↓↘→Ⓐ+Ⓖ or Ⓑ+Ⓖ if your enemy knows Ⓑ+Ⓚ is coming. If your opponent goes for ⒶⒶ, input ↓↘→Ⓑ to duck under the attack and punish it with back-turned ↓↘→Ⓑ, ↙Ⓚ, ↙Ⓑ. Deter attempts to sidestep either of the preceding options with a back-turned ⒶⒶ. Keep in mind that any of the aforementioned combos that end with Asylum Step (↙Ⓑ) leaves Voldo directly next to his enemy with an advantage, so stage a follow-up attack when you recover.

Mid Range

Your goal is to establish close range via a knockdown or movement. The means to accomplish this is based on your stance. When you face forward, lure out and punish your foe's missed attacks with the Demon Elbow (→→Ⓑ, Just Frame). It's one of the best whiff punishers available for any character, thanks to its speed and damage output. If it hits, link into a second →→Ⓑ(Just), then hit your fallen enemy with ↙Ⓑ to move into close range. Keep your enemy from sidestepping this move, and others, by using Blind Blade (⇩or ⇧Ⓐ) or Dusky Nipper (While Rising Ⓐ). While Rising Ⓐ is difficult to use while you're moving around, but it leads to far more damage on counter-hit (While Rising Ⓐ, →ⒷⒷ). Use these attacks to scare your enemy into a defensive mode, and then dash into close range.

When you're back-turned, use ← (or ↙ or ↖) Ⓐ to punish missed high moves and to catch enemy sidesteps. If it hits, take advantage of the stun and combo ↓↘→Ⓐ, ↓↘→Ⓑ, ↙Ⓚ, ↙Ⓑ. Though it's powerful, this attack is extremely vulnerable when ducked under, so it's best to use ⇩(or ⇧)Ⓐ only to dissuade sidesteps.

Long Range

As with mid range, your goal is to establish close range. Outside of the Evil Bow (↙Ⓐ), Voldo has very few standard attacks that work from this distance. Instead, rely on his Caliostro Rush (↓↘→) to move in and attack, as it ducks under high attacks. Use its Katar Slap (during Caliostro Rush ⒶⒶ) to stop your enemy from sidestepping around the stance's other options. When enemies are less willing to counter your movements, go for the movement's low Ⓑ option or the mid-hitting Ⓑ+Ⓚ. Also try using the Caliostro's Blind Dive (Ⓐ+Ⓑ) when your enemy is standing; it Guard Breaks your foe and leaves you at an advantage when blocked.

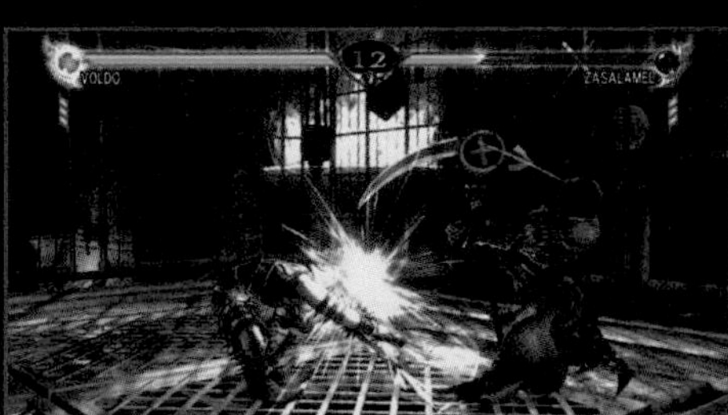

Special Tactics

Okizeme: Anti-Wakeup

The flexible middle attack ↓Ⓐ+Ⓑ↓↘→ shifts directly into Voldo's Caliostro Rush (↓↘→), enabling him to approach his enemy quickly behind an advantage when it is blocked. You can verify whether it hits and choose actions based on the outcome. If it strikes on a normal hit, follow up with the Caliostro Rush's Ⓑ option for a 2 hit combo. If ↓Ⓐ+Ⓑ↓↘→ connects on a counter-hit, perform Ⓑ+Ⓚ, then Ⓑ. When your enemy guards the attack, come out of the Caliostro Rush with its low Ⓑ attack, or its mid-hitting Ⓚ or Ⓑ+Ⓚ attacks. The Ⓑ option is extremely unsafe when blocked, so use it less than the others. The Ⓑ+Ⓚ option launches the enemy and shifts into the Mantis Crawl stance, enabling you to juggle your foe with the Asylum Breakout (during Mantis Crawl Ⓑ). Use the Caliostro's ⒶⒶ string if your enemy tries to sidestep the preceding options. When your enemy is afraid of your mid attacks, go for the Ⓐ+Ⓑ Unblockable attack, which is difficult to counter because of your blocked advantage. Release it early for the Guard Break version to counter your foe's early attempts to attack the charge. To stage a basic two-way guessing game on wakeup, use ↓Ⓐ+Ⓑ↓↘→ combined with ↙Ⓐ, which is a low slash with a similar-looking startup.

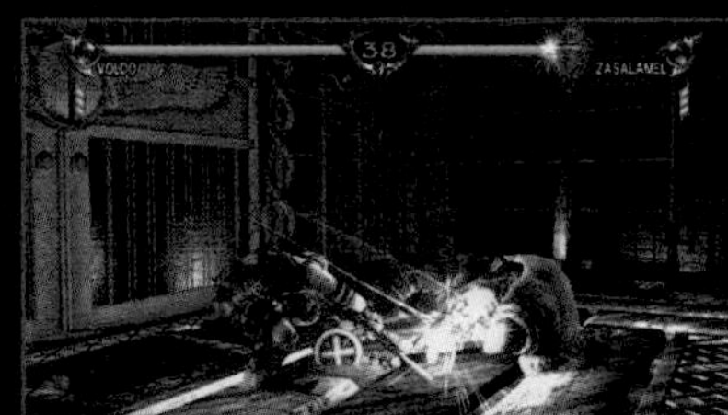

Mantis Crawl

Inputting ↓Ⓑ+Ⓚ manually enters the Mantis Crawl stance, a special fighting style so low to the ground that it avoids high attacks. Though it's difficult to use, this stance has a few applications for countering attacks at close range. For example, as we previously mentioned, ↓Ⓐ+Ⓑ is a very effective mid attack that shifts into the Caliostro Rush. Inputting Ⓑ+Ⓚ during the Caliostro Rush initiates the Tomb Implant, a drop kick that shifts into the Mantis Crawl. This kick launches the enemy into the air when it hits, enabling you to follow up with the Snake Eater (Ⓑ). When blocked, take defensive measures and use the Fool's Ritual (during Mantis Crawl Ⓑ+Ⓚ) to duck under and counter both high and crouching horizontals. To counter verticals used against you, input ↓ or ↑ to sidestep them, then attack with Ⓑ to punish their recovery.

Chai Xianghua

Chai Xianghua

What would life be if we had no courage to attempt anything?
Vincent Willem van Gogh (1853 - 1890)

Bio

Age:	20
Birthplace:	Peking, Ming Empire
Height:	5'0"
Weight:	101 lbs.
Birth Date:	April 2
Blood Type:	B
Weapon:	Chinese Sword
Weapon Name:	No name
Discipline:	Sword style passed down from her mother
Family:	Mother: Deceased Father: Deceased, according to her mother

The training Xianghua had undergone in her homeland had given her the strength to conquer her own emotional frailty. Convinced she would be ready the next time she faced the cursed sword, she hurried west along the Silk Road.

Xianghua's travels took her to a fighting arena in central Asia, where a familiar (and much-missed) face was waiting. She had known all along that if she searched for Soul Edge, she was bound to find him along the way. The arena drew strong fighters from all over, and with them, information. The two of them had been thinking the same. Still, she had never imagined she would find Kilik so soon. As she buried her face against his chest, the tears running down her cheeks spoke more eloquently of her feelings than any words could.

Happily reunited, the two continued west, until they learned that the last of their erstwhile trio, the Okinawan pirate Maxi, was in India. Excited, Xianghua and Kilik changed their course and headed south. But, although they found their old friend just as they had hoped, he would not join them. Xianghua could not take her eyes off Maxi as he walked away; it was as if a permanent shadow had fallen between them, silencing all their pleas for him to stay.

They left India with dampened spirits and eventually reached Europe, where they began the march toward their sinister destination. They had taken this route before, but this time there was one less pair of legs. Xianghua did her best to stay cheerful and keep her worries at bay. Kilik, however, must have had something on his mind, for he often fell silent.

"Kilik?" she called. No response. Xianghua called his name again. This time her sharper tone startled him, and he whirled around. He must have more on his mind than I imagined, she thought, he ought to at least confide in me. "Well, just as long as you're on your toes when it counts," she sulked. Then smiled, "For my sake."

He's concerned about Maxi, too, Xianghua thought. She turned her gaze westward. She and Kilik had not given up on Maxi after he had left, but a search yielded few clues to his whereabouts. They did, however, hear that a man fitting his description had headed toward Ostrheinsburg. Was Maxi looking for Soul Edge in order to seek revenge? If so, she would do everything in her power to stop him. Using that cursed sword to avenge the fallen would bring her friend no salvation.

Xianghua thought back to when the three of them had plunged into the chaotic war between the spirit sword and cursed sword. Thanks to Maxi's cheerful disposition, there had been no shortage of laughs. The young Xianghua and Kilik had found a strong older brother in Maxi. How many times had he gotten them through the worst? But that was a long time ago, and it looked as though Maxi had veered from the path they followed. Nothing stays the same forever.

That went for the two of them as well. Xianghua turned to glance at Kilik beside her. She had no idea how he felt about her, but her heart was quite clear on the matter. But as long as so much remained to be done, she could never say the words. It was like a solemn, unspoken agreement between them.

Another painful truth plagued Xianghua: her unexpected parting with the spirit sword. She may not have known the extent of the blade's power, but it was her late mother's sword—the only remembrance she'd had—and losing it had felt like being cut off from her mother forever. Xianghua could not forget the way the sword fit in her hand so comfortably. That was why she had worked so hard to hone her fighting skills: to feel close to her mother and teacher again.

That's not the only reason, though, she admitted. Deep down the same conviction—no, a deeper conviction—drove Xianghua, and even now she had her goal firmly in sight. Stop Soul Edge. The blade was gathering power, and over the past several years it had left countless victims in its bloody wake. It was only a matter of time before it would prey on the entire world. Last time they faced it, Xianghua and Kilik had lacked the power to destroy the weapon outright. That bitterness still lingered; their failure was to blame for every life the cursed sword had taken since.

(I will cut my own path to destiny. This time, we will eliminate Soul Edge once and for all!)

And so, having turned remorse into resolve, Xianghua pressed on with her head held high and confidence in her step. And when she saw the meteor shower shooting west across the sky one night, she knew the final battle was at hand.

No Name

Xianghua met an aging Master Swordsman (for that was the only name he gave) in her homeland after returning from her battle with Soul Edge, and he entrusted her with this nameless sword. Kilik would have recognized the old man as Edge Master, his teacher, a man who had perfected every discipline.

The blade Edge Master forged for Xianghua suits and serves her just as well as the one she lost during her great battle: the Krita-Yuga, one of the Three Treasures of Ling-Sheng Su Temple and also the spirit sword Soul Calibur in disguise.

Sword Art Inherited from Her Mother

Although Xianghua did not know it, her mother, who was born from the lineage of General Ming, had studied the sword-arts at Ling-Sheng Su Temple. After leaving the temple and returning to the Ming family, her mother gave birth to her (Xianghua). Perhaps because of some difficult part of her training years, Xianghua's mother would not speak of it when she was growing up. No one knew what secret lay in the mother's heart. However, before she left this world, she passed on her sword to her daughter along with some short words.

"Cut open your own path through this ever-changing future."

She took those words of love along with her, and the sword she received was actually the Krita-Yuga. Xianghua knew nothing about the fate of this sword and continued to think of it only as a memento from her mother. As a sword to "cut open her future."

Command List

Signature Techniques

Name	Command	Attack Level	Damage	Notes
Angry Shui Shian	⬂ⒶⓀ	Low, High	18, 20	
Shan Kick	⇦Ⓚ	High	18	
Striking Lian Hua	→Ⓐ	High	30	
Vengeful Lian Hua	←Ⓑ	Mid	38	Stuns on counter-hit
Beautiful Rhythm ~Silent Xia Sheng	Ⓐ🅐	High, High	10, 10	Shifts to Silent Xia Sheng
Twin Rhythm ~Silent Xia Sheng	⬃🅑	Mid	15	Shifts to Silent Xia Sheng
Waterfall	Silent Xia Sheng Ⓑ	Mid	40	Stuns on hit
Rising Cloud	Silent Xia Sheng Ⓚ	Mid	18	
Twisting Lotus Flow	⇩⬃⇦Ⓑ+Ⓖ ⇦⬃⇩Ⓑ	Throw	60	Input Ⓑ to escape

Horizontal Attacks

Name	Command	Attack Level	Damage	Notes
Beautiful Rhythm	ⒶⒶⒷ	High, High, Mid	10, 10, 14	
Beautiful Rhythm ~Laughing Bea Her Hua	ⒶⒶⒷ⇦	High, High, Mid	10, 10, 14	Shifts to Laughing Bea Her Hua
Beautiful Rhythm ~Silent Xia Sheng	Ⓐ🅐	High, High	10, 10	Shifts to Silent Xia Sheng
Lian Hua Twist Left	ⒶⒷ	Mid	18	Stuns on hit
Feng Yun Feint	ⒶⓀⒷ	Mid, Mid, Low	16, 15, 28	2nd attack stuns on counter-hit
Double Feng Yun	ⒶⓀⓀ	Mid, Mid, Mid	16, 15, 28	2nd attack stuns on counter-hit
Feng Yun Feint ~Silent Xia Sheng	Ⓐ🅚	Mid, Mid	16, 15	2nd attack stuns on counter-hit. Shifts to Silent Xia Sheng.
Cross Lian Hua	⇨Ⓐ	High	14	
Angry Shui Shian	⬂ⒶⓀ	Low, High	18, 20	
Rhythm Halt	⇩Ⓐ	Sp.Low	10	
Chai Hua	⬃Ⓐ	Low	18	
Storming Lian Hua	⇦Ⓐ	Mid	20	
Chai Hua Slice	While Crouching Ⓐ	Sp.Low	10	
Muu Jiann Rhythm	While Rising ⒶⒶ	Mid, Mid	16, 20	
Muu Jiann Rhythm ~Silent Xia Sheng	While Rising 🅐	Mid	16	Shifts to Silent Xia Sheng
Sparrow Spin Blade	Jumping Ⓐ	High	22 or 26 or 28	Damage varies depending on direction jumped in
Spinning Jiann Slice	Backturned Ⓐ	High	12	
Spinning Rhythm Halt	While Crouching Backturned Ⓐ	Low	12	

Vertical Attacks

Name	Command	Attack Level	Damage	Notes
Elegant Rhythm	ⒷⒷ	Mid, Mid	12, 14	
Crescent Flow	ⒷⓀ	Mid, Mid	14, 10	
Advancing Rhythm	⇨ⒷⒶ	High, Mid	15, 20	
Pointing Thrust	⇨ⒷⒷ	High, Low	15, 15	
Advancing Rhythm ~Silent Xia Sheng	⇨🅑	High	15	Shifts to Silent Xia Sheng
Feint Wheel Kick	⇨ⒷⓀ	Low, Mid	16, 16	
Feint Wheel Kick ~Sidestep	⇨ⒷⓀ⇧ or ⇩	Low	16	Shifts into sidestep
Lian Hua Upper	⬂Ⓑ	Mid	20	Launches on hit
Rhythm Break	⇩Ⓑ	Mid	14	
Twin Rhythm	⬃ⒷⒷ	Mid, Mid	15, 18	Second attack causes recoverable stun
Twin Rhythm ~Silent Xia Sheng	⬃🅑	Mid	15	Shifts into Silent Xia Sheng
Tzao Lan Hua	⇦ⒷⒷ	Mid, Mid, Mid	16, 14, 20	Final attack stuns on counter-hit
Tzao Lan Hua Feint	⇦Ⓑ⇨Ⓑ	Mid, Mid, High	16, 14, 30	Final attack stuns on hit
Playful Slice	⇧ or ⇩ Ⓑ	Mid	20	
Rhythm Break	While Crouching Ⓑ	Mid	14	
Mei Guei Hua	While Crouching ⬂Ⓑ	Mid	25	
Mei Guei Hue Feint	While Crouching ⬂ⒷⒷ	Low	28	Stuns on hit
Mei Guei Hue Feint ~Silent Xia Sheng	While Crouching ⬂Ⓑ🅑			Shifts into Silent Xia Sheng
Fluttering Lan Se Ren	While Rising Ⓑ	Mid	20	Stuns on hit. Deflects horizontal attacks.
Sparrow Flutter Blade	Jumping Ⓑ	Mid	24 or 28 or 32	Damage varies depending on direction jumped in
Spinning Hua Bann	Backturned Ⓑ	Mid	14	
Spinning Rhythm Break	While Crouching Backturned Ⓑ	Mid	16	

Kick Attacks

Name	Command	Attack Level	Damage	Notes
Yuen Kick	Ⓚ	High	12	
Heh Kick	⇨Ⓚ	High	24	
Chicken Kick	⬂Ⓚ	Mid	14	
Woan Shyong Nibble	⇩Ⓚ	Low	12	
Circle Breaker	⬃Ⓚ	Low	20	
Circle Breaker Feint Divide	⬃ⓀⒶⒶⒷ	Mid, Mid, Mid, Low	22, 15, 18, 28	3rd attack stuns on counter-hit. Input ⬃ⓀⒶ🅐 to shift to Silent Xia Sheng.
Circle Breaker Feint Double Feng Yun	⬃ⓀⒶⒶⓀ	Mid, Mid, Mid, Mid	22, 15, 18, 25	3rd attack stuns on counter-hit. Input ⬃ⓀⒶ🅐 to shift to Silent Xia Sheng.
Shan Kick	⇦Ⓚ	High	18	
Woan Shyong Nibble	While Crouching Ⓚ	Low	12	
Rising Shui Shian	While Rising Ⓚ	Mid	24	
Tiao Wu Kick	Jumping Ⓚ	Mid, Mid	10, 14	
Spinning Yuen Kick	Backturned Ⓚ	Mid	14	
Spinning Woan Shyong Nibble	While Crouching Backturned Ⓚ	Low	12	

Simultaneous Press

Name	Command	Attack Level	Damage	Notes
Muu Jiann	Ⓐ+Ⓑ	Mid, Mid	15, 22	
Muu Jiann ~Silent Xia Sheng	🅐+🅑	Mid	15	Shifts to Silent Xia Sheng
Twin Mei Hua	⇨Ⓐ+Ⓑ	Mid, Mid	18, 22	2nd attack stuns on hit, launches on counter-hit
Yann Divide	⇩Ⓐ+Ⓑ	Low	24	
Yann Divide (Cancel)	⇩Ⓐ+ⒷⒼ			
Reverse Shui Shian	⬃Ⓐ+Ⓑ	Mid	18	Evades high attacks. Stuns on counter-hit.
Reverse Shui Shian ~Down	⬃🅐+🅑			Leaves Xianghua lying in the ground
Muu Jiann Retreat	⇦Ⓐ+Ⓑ	Mid, Mid	20, 30	Deflects high attacks
Muu Jiann Retreat ~Silent Xia Sheng	⇦🅐+🅑	Mid	20	Shifts to Silent Xia Sheng
Shiang Gyh Kwei Feint	While Crouching Ⓐ+Ⓑ	Low	28	
Shiang Gyh Kwei Feint ~Silent Xia Sheng	While Crouching 🅐+🅑			Shifts to Silent Xia Sheng
Mei Hua Divide	While Rising Ⓐ+ⒷⒷ	Low, High, High	10, 10, 30	Final attack stuns on hit
Mei Hua Carve	While Rising Ⓐ+Ⓑ⇩Ⓑ	Low, High, Low	10, 10. 20	
Mei Hua Divide ~Silent Xia Sheng	While Rising 🅐+🅑	Low, High	10, 10	Shifts to Silent Xia Sheng
Guei	When lying facedown Ⓐ+Ⓑ	Low	5	
Guei	When lying face up Ⓐ+Ⓑ	Low	5	
Wild Spin	Ⓑ+Ⓚ	Low	16	Stuns on counter-hit
Muu Jiann Advance	⇨Ⓑ+Ⓚ	Mid, Mid	16, 20	
Muu Jiann Advance ~Silent Xia Sheng	⇨🅑+🅚	Mid	16	Shifts to Silent Xia Sheng
Lower Great Wall	⬂Ⓑ+Ⓚ	Mid	35	
Quake Step	⇩Ⓑ+Ⓚ	Mid(Low)	30(0)	Hits normally and Guard Breaks at close range. From a distance, causes ground burst with large hit radius. Stuns on contact, but inflicts no damage.
Quake Step ~Silent Xia Sheng	⇩🅑+🅚			Shifts into Silent Xia Sheng
Hwu Dye	⬃Ⓑ+Ⓚ	Mid	22	
Muu Ling	⇦Ⓑ+Ⓚ	Mid	60	Unblockable. Input Ⓖ to cancel.
Reverse Chicken Kick	Backturned Ⓑ+Ⓚ	Mid	20	Causes recoverable stun on hit
Circle Breaker	Backturned ⇩Ⓑ+Ⓚ	Low	20	
Hou Lee	Ⓐ+Ⓚ			Evades high attacks
Hou Lee ~Silent Xia Sheng	🅐+🅚			Evades high attacks, shifts into Silent Xia Sheng
Lower Great Wall Punishment	Ⓐ+ⓀⒷ+Ⓚ	Mid	40	
Lower Great Wall	Ⓐ+Ⓚ🅑🅚	Mid	50	Guard Breaks
Lian Hua Kicks	⇩Ⓐ+ⓀⓀ	Low, Mid, Mid	20, 15, 15	
Lian Hua Sweeps	⇩Ⓐ+Ⓚ⇩Ⓚ	Low, Low	20, 24	
Sweet Harmony	⇦Ⓐ+ⓀⒶ	Mid, High	20, 28	Deflects high horizontal attacks
Lian Hua Sweeps ~Silent Xia Sheng	⇦🅐+🅚	Mid	20	Shifts into Silent Xia Sheng
Taunt	Ⓚ+Ⓖ			

8-Way Run

Name	Command	Attack Level	Damage	Notes
Striking Lian Hua	→Ⓐ	High	30	
Li	↘ or ↗Ⓐ	Mid	18	Causes recoverable stun on counter-hit
Spinning Lian Hua	↓ or ↑Ⓐ	Mid, Mid	14, 18	
Ing Hua	↙ or ↖Ⓐ	High	30	
Lan Hua	←ⒶⒶ	Mid, High	20, 24	1st attack stuns on counter-hit
Lan Hua Slice ~Silent Xia Sheng	←🅐	Mid	20	
Playful Rhythm	→ⒷⒷ	Mid, Mid	18, 24	2nd attack stuns on hit
Playful Rhythm ~Laughing Bea Her Hua	→Ⓑ⇦	Mid	18	Shifts to Laughing Bea Her Hua
Playful Rhythm ~Laughing Bea Her Hua	→ⒷⒷ⇦	Mid, Mid	18, 24	Laughing Bea Her Hua
Playful Rhythm ~Silent Xia Sheng	→🅑	Mid	18	Shifts to Silent Xia Sheng
San Jaan	↘ or ↗Ⓑ	Mid, Mid, Mid	15, 12, 18	2nd attack stuns
San Jaan ~Silent Xia Sheng	↘ or ↗🅑	Mid	15	Shifts to Silent Xia Sheng
Lian Hua Cannon	↓ or ↑Ⓑ	Mid	24	
Shan Ji Illusion	↙ or ↖ⒷⒶ	Mid, Mid	24, 30	Deflects high horizontals
Shan Ji Illusion ~Silent Xia Sheng	↙ or ↖🅑	Mid	24	Shifts to Silent Xia Sheng
Shan Ji	↙ or ↖Ⓑ⇩Ⓐ	Mid, Low	24, 20	
Vengeful Lian Hua	←Ⓑ	Mid	38	
Vengeful Lian Hua ~Laughing Bea Her Hua	←Ⓑ⇦	Mid	38	Deflects high horizontals
Woan Shyong Swing	→Ⓚ	Mid	18	
~Bea Her Hua	↘ or ↗ⓀⒶ Ⓑ+Ⓚ	Mid, High	15, 18	Final action deflects horizontal attacks
Mei Hua Kick	↓ or ↑Ⓚ	Mid	24	
Horizon Kick	↙ or ↖Ⓚ	Low	14	
Advancing Tiger Thrust	←ⓀⒷ	Mid, Mid	16, 26	1st attack causes recoverable stun. 2nd attack stuns on hit.
Advancing Tiger Thrust ~Silent Xia Sheng	←🅚	Mid	16	1st attack causes recoverable stun
Great Wall	→ or ↘ or ↗ Ⓐ+Ⓑ	High	32	
Ma Chiueh	↓ or ↙ or ← or ↖ or ↑Ⓐ+Ⓑ	High	30	Stuns on counter-hit
Hou Lee Hua	→ or ↘ or ↗ Ⓑ+Ⓚ	Mid	25 or 35 or 45	Inflicts additional damage the closer it hits
Bea Her Hua	↓ or ↑Ⓑ+Ⓚ			Deflects horizontal attacks
Retreating Bea Her Hua	←Ⓑ+Ⓚ			Deflects vertical attacks
Wei Guang Blade	→ or ↘ or ↗ Ⓐ+Ⓚ	Mid	28	
Di Hui Slash	↙ or ↖Ⓐ+Ⓚ	Low	22	
Sliding	While Running Ⓚ	Low	26	

Throws

Name	Command	Attack Level	Damage	Notes
Yuen Chuei Shaur	Ⓐ+Ⓖ	Throw	55	Input Ⓐ to escape
Long Ling Sheang	Ⓑ+Ⓖ	Throw	55	Input Ⓑ to escape
Tien E Sheang	Left Side Throw	Throw	65	Same button as throw (Ⓐ or Ⓑ) to escape
Yng Dyi Yann	Right Side Throw	Throw	55	Same button as throw (Ⓐ or Ⓑ) to escape
Yuh Luen Shaur	Back Throw	Throw	65	Same button as throw (Ⓐ or Ⓑ) to escape
Shui Long Sheang	Against Crouching Foe ⇩Ⓐ+Ⓖ	Throw	30	
Lo Tsai Shaur ~Reverse Chicken Kick	Against Crouching Foe ⇩Ⓑ+ⒼⒷ+Ⓚ	Throw	10, 22	2nd attack stuns. Input Ⓑ to escape throw.
Twisting Lotus Flow	⇩⬃⇦Ⓑ+Ⓖ ⇦⬃⇩Ⓑ	Throw	20, 40	Input Ⓑ to escape throw

Silent Xia Sheng

Name	Command	Attack Level	Damage	Notes
Silent Xia Sheng	Ⓐ+Ⓚ			Evades high attacks
Splitting Mist	Silent Xia Sheng Ⓐ	High	20	Stuns every 5th time this attack is used
Waterfall	Silent Xia Sheng Ⓑ	Mid	40	Gains Guard Break properties every 5th use. Leaves Xianghua in crouching state.
Rising Cloud	Silent Xia Sheng Ⓚ	Mid	18	Stuns every 5th time this attack is used
Feng Xia Taunt (Earth)	Silent Xia Sheng (Earth) Ⓚ+Ⓖ	High	0	Upgrades Silent Xia Sheng stance to "Heaven" status
Feng Xia Taunt (Heaven)	Silent Xia Sheng (Heaven) Ⓚ+Ⓖ	High	0	Deflects high horizontals. Upgrades Silent Xia Sheng stance to "Blue" status.
Feng Xia Taunt (Blue)	Silent Xia Sheng (Blue) Ⓚ+Ⓖ	Mid	0	Adds one additional Silent Xia Sheng "Blue" stance power up behind current (enables you to use 2 powered up stance attacks in a row).
Raging Wind	Silent Xia Sheng (Heaven) Ⓐ+Ⓖ or Ⓑ+Ⓖ	Throw	40	Same button as throw (Ⓐ or Ⓑ) to escape

Combos

Counter-hit ⬂Ⓑ, ⇨⇨Ⓑ + Ⓚ
2 hits, 52 Damage

⇩ or ⇧ (Neutral) Ⓑ, ⇨⇨Ⓑ + Ⓚ
2 hits, 57 Damage, perform second attack late for full damage

Counter-hit ⬀Ⓐ + Ⓑ, ⬂Ⓑ, ⬂⬂ⓀⒶ
4 hits, 57 Damage

Counter-hit, Ⓑ + Ⓚ, ⒷⓀ
3 hits, 35 Damage

ⒶⒷ, ⒷⓀ
3 hits, 34 Damage

Counter-hit ⬂⬂Ⓐ, Ⓐ + Ⓑ, ⇨⇨Ⓑ + Ⓚ
3 hits, 63 Damage, first stun is escapable

⇦Ⓚ, ⬂Ⓑ
2 hits, 32 Damage

While Rising Ⓑ, ⒷⓀ
3 hits, 38 Damage

During Silent Xia Sheng Ⓐ (spinning state), ⒶⒶ
3 hits, 40 Damage

During Silent Xia Sheng Ⓐ (stun), ⬂Ⓑ, ⇨⇨Ⓑ + Ⓚ
3 hits, 64 Damage

Opponent must be crouching ⇩Ⓑ + ⒼⒷ + Ⓚ (Just), ⇩⇩Ⓑ, ⬂⬂ⓀⒶ
5 hits, 74 Damage Damage

⇦Ⓑ + Ⓚ, ⒷⓀ
3 hits, 78 Damage

Close Range

Xianghua's strongest position is mid range, which enables her to safely fight and inflict heavy damage with little risk of retaliation. She has very few fast mid attacks that lead to heavy damage, and her stance-oriented strings aren't very effective for scoring counter-hits, making her less potent at closer distances. What she does have, however, is just enough reason to occasionally establish this position: her Lo Tsai Shaur (⇩Ⓑ+Ⓖ) crouch throw. This grab, which works only against crouching characters, leads to the giant combo ⇩Ⓑ+ⒼⒷ+Ⓚ (Just), ⇩⇩Ⓑ, ⇨⇨Ⓑ+Ⓚ. To land this throw, it's imperative that you condition your enemy to block low. Careful use of low attacks and standing throws helps to accomplish this, as your enemy's counter to both options is to crouch. Using fast, high strings, which are difficult to deal with without crouching under them, is another means to bait this response. For example, attack with ⒶⒶ to start an offense. Condition your foe with its ⒶⒶⒷ extension, which fully combos if it counter-hits. When the enemy is afraid to attack, perform ⒶⒶ, which shifts into Xiangua's special Silent Xia Sheng stance. Go for a throw afterward, or perform the Rising Cloud (Ⓚ) option to hit your enemy if he's looking for the throw attempt. If you think your adversary will sidestep either of these options, perform the stance's Splitting Mist (Ⓐ) to hit him. If it connects, link ⒶⒶ afterward for a 3-hit combo. As we mentioned, every attack used in this strategy is vulnerable to crouching, except the final hit of the ⒶⒶⒷ string and the Silent Xia Sheng's Ⓚ option. Mix in the low-hitting Angry Shui Shian (⇦ⒶⓀ) and Pointing Thrust (⇨ⒷⒷ) to further toy with your enemy's guard. When you anticipate a crouch, grab your foe with ⇩Ⓑ+Ⓖ to lay down the hurt.

Mid Range

Surprisingly simplistic, yet overwhelmingly effective, Xianghua's mid-range options revolve around the Lian Hua Cannon (⇩ or ⇧(neutral)Ⓑ), her strongest mid-range attack. This unique mid slash dodges vertical attacks, counters sidesteps, launches on normal hit, has a massive area of affect, and is completely safe to punishment when guarded. Use it to stop anticipated movement and vertical slashes. Its only weakness is against fast horizontals, which counter it cleanly. To compensate, use ⇦ⒶⓀ, which ducks under high attacks, hits low, and fully combos if it counter-hits. It also happens to hit sidesteps.

Knowing this, your plan is to rapidly move in and out of your enemy's attack range to lure him or her into going for aggressive actions. If your challenger whiffs any attacks, punish him or her with ⬇ or ⬆Ⓑ—juggle with ⇨⇨Ⓑ+Ⓚ after the hit. If your enemy tries to stop your backward movement with long-range attacks, or if he or she is reliant on 8-Way Run to approach you, use ⇩(neutral)Ⓑ to launch your enemy. Follow up with a ⇨⇨Ⓑ+Ⓚ to perform a 2-hit combo.

Long Range

Xianghua has very few effective options at this distance, making your priority to move into mid range. The safest way to tackle this problem is to slowly work your way in via movement. It's possible to use risky movement types, like Hou Lee (Ⓐ+Ⓚ), to help you with this process. Most opposing characters use horizontals with a lot of range from this distance. Though it's risky, Hou Lee moves Xianghua forward while slipping under these attacks, which you can punish with the movement's Ⓑ+Ⓚ attack. When your opponent is afraid of the attack, roll toward him or her and throw when you recover.

Special Tactics

Okizeme: Anti-Wakeup

A flexible method to attack fallen enemies is with the ⇗ⓀⒶⒶ string. This mid attack is a 3-hit combo with three extensions: the low Circle Breaker Feint Divide (⇗ⓀⒶⒶⒷ); the mid-hitting Circle Breaker Feint Double Feng Yun (⇗ⓀⒶⒶⓀ); or simply shift into the Silent Xia Sheng stance (⇗ⓀⒶⒶ). Attack with the first three hits of the string, then vary between the three extensions based on your enemy's guarding habits.

When you attack low, use the Lian Hua Sweeps (⇩Ⓐ+Ⓚ⇩Ⓚ) or Lian Hua Kicks (⇩Ⓐ+ⓀⓀ), a low kick with both mid and low ending attacks. Both variations of the string combo on a normal hit, so vary between them to throw off your enemy's guarding habits.

A second useful low attack is Yann Divide (⇩Ⓐ+Ⓑ). You can fake this slash by inputting ⇙Ⓐ+ⒷⒼ, leaving Xianghua in a back-turned state. From there, mix up your actions between her ⇩Ⓑ+Ⓖ throw or her Reverse Chicken Kick (back-turned Ⓑ+Ⓚ). The Reverse Chicken Kick stuns on contact, enabling you to link ⒷⒷ afterward.

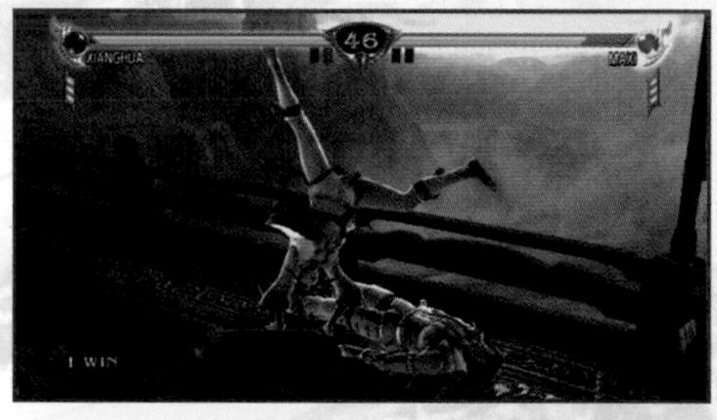

Silent Xia Sheng Stance

Several of Xianghua's strings shift into the Silent Xia Sheng stance. This allows her to launch a varied offense after a variety of attacks. The basis of the stance is stopping enemy counter options and then using the stance's Raging Wind throw (during Silent Xia Cheng "Heaven" Ⓐ+Ⓖ or Ⓑ+Ⓖ) when the opponent is afraid to act. However, its throw options are available only during the "Heaven" variation of the stance, which Xianghua enters every third time the stance is used. In addition to this, Xianghua flashes blue every fifth time she enters the stance, bestowing its three attacks with a special hit state: the Ⓐ and Ⓚ options stun on hit, the Ⓑ option gains Guard Break properties. After entering the special state once, and then using one of its attacks, you need to enter the stance only three times to gain the upgrade again. As a rule of thumb, once you've entered the blue flash state, you continue to enter that state until you use a Silent Xia Sheng attack that takes advantage of its bonuses. The same goes for the "Heaven" version of the stance—once you've used the stance three times, the Raging Wind throw will always be available until you finally use it, in which case you must use the stance three times before it becomes available again.

The Feng Xia Taunt (during Silent Xia Sheng Ⓚ+Ⓖ) is a second method of upgrading the stance. Inputting the command during the stance's "Earth" stage (the first or second time the stance is used) upgrades the stance to its "Heaven" status, allowing you to use the Raging Wind throw. Performing the command while in "Heaven" upgrades the stance to its blue flashing state. You can also use the taunt when the stance is at its strongest, stacking a second blue state directly behind the one already obtained. This allows you to use two upgraded Silent Xia Sheng attacks in a row. Unfortunately, all versions of the Feng Xia Taunt deal no damage on hit, making them extremely risky maneuvers to ever commit to.

Though the stance's erratic nature makes attacking effectively with it difficult, it's quite powerful in its "Blue Flash" stage, which allows both the Raging Wind throw and the upgraded Silent Xia Sheng attacks. For example, its Rising Cloud (Ⓚ) is a mid attack useful for stopping your enemy's immediate attacks. It's linear, so if your enemy tries to sidestep it, use the Splitting Mist (Ⓐ) option to strike your foe's movement. If it hits, link into ⒶⒶ afterward for a 3-hit combo. If its special stun properties occur, link into ⇦Ⓑ, then ⇨⇨Ⓑ+Ⓚ. Start using the Ⓐ+Ⓖ or Ⓑ+Ⓖ throw options when your enemy is afraid of everything else.

Yoshimitsu

To obey the will of Heaven is to accept righteousness as the standard.
"Mozi"

Bio

Age:	Unknown
Birthplace:	He does not speak of it (Base of Mt. Fuji, Japan)
Height:	Unknown
Weight:	Unknown
Birth Date:	Unknown
Blood Type:	Unknown
Weapon:	Katana x 2
Weapon Name:	Yoshimitsu
Discipline:	Manji Ninjitsu
Family:	Entire clan: Massacred by a man of influence Now belongs to a clan of chivalrous thieves called the Manjitou.

Yoshimitsu

Whenever the world falls into chaos, none suffer more than the poor. Thus it was that a band of chivalrous thieves known as the Manjitou traveled the world, relieving the wealthy of the riches they hoarded and raiding their treasure-laden tombs on behalf of the less fortunate.

At the moment, Yoshimitsu, their leader, tarried in a valley enclosed by tall mountains overlooking Europe, waiting for his men to assemble. Yoshimitsu had lost several good companions in their last attempt to collect a piece of Soul Edge, and all for naught; the shard itself had vanished, dashing any hopes of success. At the same time, one of his officers—a man Yoshimitsu trusted greatly—had gone missing as well. The subsequent search had led Yoshimitsu west across the continent, to this valley.

Yoshimitsu let his thoughts lead him back to when he had first set foot in these lands and saw the girl dancing in the moonlight. She had radiated evil from the giant, blood-soaked ring blade she carried to her flock of black-winged servants, who had seemed to melt into the dark of night. And then, during the brief moment a passing cloud had hung over the moon, she had vanished. Yoshimitsu had spotted his officer and ran to his side.

"Chief, forgive me... I failed you." Every breath came as a gasp.

"No," replied Yoshimitsu. "I caught a glimpse of her. There was nothing human about that one. You've done me proud just by staying alive." The girl's eyes had sickened Yoshimitsu the most, the way they'd glistened with evil. He had not dared peer through those windows to see what black heart possessed that mad mistress of ravens. Now, if a monster like her had stolen the shard, where would she head next? Soul Edge crept back into Yoshimitsu's thoughts.

He spent the next several days rescuing his officer from the brink of death. Meanwhile, the man's reports confirmed Yoshimitsu's fears. The girl had treated her pursuer with scorn; rather than attempting to shake him off, she had tried to provoke him on more than one occasion. Then, during one of these exchanges, the officer had heard Soul Edge's name escape her lips. He had continued to chase her to this valley, but despite being one of Manjitou's most able warriors, he had not been prepared when the girl suddenly decided to whirl about and take the offensive.

Soul Edge, the cursed sword. Those words held such an ominous ring. Yoshimitsu recalled his last search for the blade, how it had been paved with rage and terror and despair. He had formed the Manjitou to break Soul Edge's cycle of negative power and protect people from the ravages of war. He had done his best, but now it seemed he would have to destroy this menace at its source.

Tending his officer's injuries had cost Yoshimitsu much time, but he used the delay to summon the rest of the Manjitou to continue reconnaissance. Where was the cursed sword? What were the grotesque monsters under its control doing now? As information flowed in from across the land, Yoshimitsu analyzed it and began to form a bold and elaborate plan.

And now, his men were beginning to gather.

Yoshimitsu issued orders to each of them in turn. First they would strike the evil forces in Ostrheinsburg who wished malice on mankind. Then they would go after Soul Edge. The Manjitou's greatest campaign ever was about to commence.

Yoshimitsu

A special katana forged by secret means handed down through the Manji clan. It became the last of its kind with the demise of the clan.

Soul Edge's malice filled the blade and turned it demonic, but Yoshimitsu was able to keep the evil in check by giving the sword his own name.

Manji Ninjutsu

Member of the secretive Manji clan from the base of Mt. Fuji. One legend says that they guarded "something dangerous" that they prevented from reaching the outside world. But the clan fell into a trap and were all destroyed. Only one survived.

The final inheritor of Manji Ninjjtsu, Yoshimitsu roamed the world, a prisoner of thoughts of revenge, but he finally realized that his ambition would only lead to further revenge.

He formed a group of friendly thieves called the "Manjitou" and used his ninjutsu skill to help the weak.

His movement is the extremely mysterious, phantasmagoric fencing skill.

Command List

Signature Techniques

Name	Command	Attack Level	Damage	Notes
Golden Shrine	↘ⒶⒷ	Mid, Mid	16, 24	Combos on counter-hit, 1st hit crumples on counter-hit, 2nd hit launches
Door Knocker	→Ⓐ+ⒷⒷⒷⒷ	Mid, High, High, Mid	16, 8, 8, 20	Combos on counter-hit, causes back slide
Double Blade	↘Ⓑ+ⓀⒷ (Just)	Mid, Mid	20, 20 (30)	Combos on counter-hit, 2nd hit bounces on counter-hit and does extra damage if input as a Just Frame
Lunging Sweep	While Crouching ↘Ⓚ	Low	20	Knocks down
Passing Light ~Intimidation	➡Ⓑ	Mid	28	Launches, shifts to Intimidation
Intimidation	→Ⓑ+Ⓚ			Shifts to Intimidation
Dark Cross	Intimidation Ⓐ	Mid	30	Causes backflop
Ashura Blade	Intimidation Ⓑ	Mid, Mid, Mid	10, 20, 30	Combos naturally, 3rd hit knocks down, leaves Yoshimitsu backturned

Horizontal Attacks

Name	Command	Attack Level	Damage	Notes
Rapid Gale	ⒶⒶ	High, High	12, 10	Combos naturally
Ear Slicer	ⒶⒷ+Ⓚ	High	30	Crumples on counter-hit
Gale	→Ⓐ	High	14	
Golden Shrine	↘ⒶⒷ	Mid, Mid	16, 24	Combos on counter-hit, 1st hit crumples on counter-hit, 2nd hit launches
Parting Grass	↓Ⓐ	Sp.Low	10	
Manji Carve Fist	↓ⒶⒷ	Sp.Low	8	Causes recoverable stun on counter-hit
Stone Fist ~Down	↙ⒶⒶⒶⒶⒶ	Mid, Mid, Mid, Mid, Mid	10, 6, 8, 6, 10 (20)	First 3 hits combo naturally, Just Frame inputs increase final hit damage, make it into Guard Break, performing final hit leaves Yoshimitsu dizzy
Stone Backhands ~Down	←ⒶⒶⒶⒶⒶ	High, High, High, High, High	12, 8, 10, 8, 10 (20)	First 3 hits combo naturally, Just Frame inputs increase final hit damage, make it into Guard Break, performing final hit leaves Yoshimitsu dizzy
Sword Sweep	↓↙←Ⓐ	Low	30	Causes backflop
Parting Grass	While Crouching Ⓐ	Sp.Low	10	
Manji Carve Fist	While Crouching ⒶⒷ	Sp.Low	8	Causes recoverable stun on counter-hit
Exorcism Fist	While Rising Ⓐ	Mid	16	Backturns Yoshimitsu and foe
Spiral Blade	Jumping Ⓐ	Low	30	
Reverse Splinter Gale	Backturned Ⓐ	High	12	
Reverse Grass Part	While Crouching Backturned Ⓐ	Low	12	Leaves Yoshimitsu in crouching state

Vertical Attacks

Name	Command	Attack Level	Damage	Notes
Rapid Grace	ⒷⒷ	Mid, Mid	14, 16	Combos naturally
Ninja Blade Rush	ⒷⒶ	Mid	14	Extra damage and knockdown on counter-hit
Ninja Blade Rush (Counter)	Counter-hit ⒷⒶ	Mid	66	
Ominous Twilight	→Ⓑ	Mid	16	Causes recoverable stun on counter-hit
Clansmen	↘Ⓑ	Mid	26	Launches
Autumn Drizzle	↓Ⓑ	Mid	16	
Death Slash	↙Ⓑ	Mid	20	
Death Slash (Hold)	↙🅑	Mid	40~80	Unblockable, damage increases the longer input is held
Spine Divide	←Ⓑ	Mid	30	Causes backward crumple
Moon Sault Slayer	↓↘→Ⓑ	Mid	60	Unblockable, knocks down
Snowflake	While Crouching Ⓑ	Mid	16	
Heretic Sword	While Rising Ⓑ	High	28	Causes backward crumple
Quarter Moon	Jumping Ⓑ	Mid	26	
Reverse Drizzle	Backturned Ⓑ	Mid	16	
Reverse Snowflake	While Crouching Backturned Ⓑ	Mid	18	Leaves Yoshimitsu in crouching state

Kick Attacks

Name	Command	Attack Level	Damage	Notes
Side Kick	Ⓚ	High	12	
Zig-Zag	→ⓀⓀ	High, Mid	35, 35	Both hits knock down
Double Zig	→Ⓚ↓Ⓚ	High, Low	35, 20	Combos naturally, knocks down
Mid Kick	↘Ⓚ	Mid	14	
Sweep Kick	↓Ⓚ	Low	12	
Kangaroo Kick	↙Ⓚ	Mid	30	Launches
Bullet Cutter	←ⓀⒷ	Mid, Mid	24, 22	Combos naturally, 1st hit knocks down
Bullet Cutter (Hold)	←Ⓚ🅑	Mid, Mid	24, 40~80	1st hit knocks down, 2nd hit is Unblockable, damages increases the longer input is held
Lunging Sweep	While Crouching ↘Ⓚ	Low	20	Knocks down
Sweep Kick	While Crouching Ⓚ	Low	12	
Spinning Low Kick ~Down	While Crouching ↙ⓀⓀⓀⓀⓀ	Low, Low, Low, Low, Low	20, 4, 6, 4, 10 (20)	First 3 hits combo naturally, Just Frame inputs increase final hit damage, make it into Guard Break, performing final hit leaves Yoshimitsu dizzy
Twirling Wind	While Rising Ⓚ	High	20	Causes backflop on counter-hit
Manji Jump Kick	Jumping Ⓚ	Mid	22	Knocks down
Reverse Koragashi	Backturned Ⓚ	High	14	
Reverse Dust Banishment	While Crouching Backturned Ⓚ	Low	12	Knocks down

Yoshimitsu

Simultaneous Press

Name	Command	Attack Level	Damage	Notes
Poison Breath	Ⓐ+Ⓑ	High	30	Causes crumple
Bad Stomach	Ⓐ+Ⓑ	High	30	Delays release of noxious fumes
Backflip Kick	Ⓐ+ⒷⓀ	Mid	20	Knocks down
Door Knocker	→Ⓐ+ⒷⒷⒷⒷ	Mid, High, High, Mid	16, 8, 8, 20	Combos on counter-hit, causes back slide
Kamikaze	↘Ⓐ+Ⓑ	Mid	20	Knocks down
Kamikaze ~Flea Walk ~Flea	↘Ⓐ+Ⓑ	Mid, Low, Low, Low, Low	20, 1x4	Combos naturally, shifts to Flea
Kamikaze Feint ~Preparation	↘Ⓐ+ⒷⒼⒼ			Trick movement, shifts to Preparation
Digging Cyclone	↓Ⓐ+ⒷⒷ	Mid, Mid	18, 12	Combos on counter-hit
Digging Cyclone ~Flea	↓Ⓐ+Ⓑ	Mid	18	Shifts to Flea
Spinning Evade ~Down	←Ⓐ+ⒷⒷⒷⒷⒷⒷⒷ			Spin counter-clockwise around foe, performing final hit leaves Yoshimitsu dizzy
Deathcopter	↑Ⓐ+Ⓑ	Mid	80	Unblockable, knocks down
Deathcopter Attack	Deathcopter ↓ or Ⓖ	Mid	40~80	Causes Deathcopter to fall prematurely, deals more damage the longer you wait
Deathcopter Trick	Deathcopter ←	Mid	40	Unblockable, knocks down, strikes behind foe
Deathcopter Trick ~Dragonfly	Deathcopter Ⓑ+Ⓚ			Shifts to Dragonfly
Poison Breath	Backturned Ⓐ+Ⓑ	High	30	Causes crumple
Bad Stomach	Backturned Ⓐ+Ⓑ	High	30	Causes crumple
Backflip Kick	Backturned Ⓐ+ⒷⓀ	Mid	20	Knocks down
Flea	Ⓑ+Ⓚ			Shifts to Flea
Intimidation	→Ⓑ+Ⓚ			Shifts to Intimidation
Double Blade	↘Ⓑ+ⓀⒷ (Just)	Mid, Mid	20, 20 (30)	Combos on counter-hit, 2nd hit bounces on counter-hit and does extra damage if input as a Just Frame
Meditation	↓Ⓑ+Ⓚ			Shifts to Meditation
Cyclone Lift	↗Ⓑ+Ⓚ	Mid	14	Crumples on counter-hit
Preparation	←Ⓑ+Ⓚ			Shifts to Preparation
Steel Wind	↗Ⓑ+ⓀⓀ	Mid, Mid	22, 22	Combos naturally, both hits knock down
Steel Wind (Delay)	↗Ⓑ+ⓀⓀ	Mid, Mid	22, 22	Combos naturally, both hits knock down
Steel Wind	↗Ⓑ+Ⓚ← (During Hit)	Mid	22	Knocks down, hops backward
Somersault ~Dragonfly	↗Ⓑ+ⓀⓀⒼ	Mid	22	Knocks down, shifts to Dragonfly
Manji Dragonfly	↑Ⓑ+Ⓚ			Shift to Dragonfly
Meditation	While Crouching Ⓑ+Ⓚ			Shift to Meditation
Flea	Backturned Ⓑ+Ⓚ			Shifts to backturned Flea
Meditation	Backturned ↓Ⓑ+Ⓚ			Shifts to backturned Meditation
Manji Dragonfly	Backturned ↑Ⓑ+Ⓚ			Shifts to backturned Dragonfly
Healing ~Meditation	(While down, facing up) Ⓑ+Ⓚ			Wakes up, shifts to Meditation
Yoshimitsu Flash	Ⓐ+Ⓚ			Guard Impact
Back Hand	→Ⓐ+Ⓚ	High	18	
Soul Siphon	→Ⓐ+Ⓚ←	High	18, 29	Combos on counter-hit, drains foe's life and gives it to Yoshimitsu
Soul Harvest	→Ⓐ+Ⓚ	High	18, -29	Combos on counter-hit, drain's Yoshimitsu's life and gives it to foe
Standing Suicide	↓Ⓐ+Ⓚ	Mid	90	Unblockable, knocks down, deals damage to both characters
Manji Blood Petals	↓Ⓐ+ⓀⒶⒶⒶⒶⒶ	Mid x6	90, 20, 15, 10, 5, 30	Unblockable, every hit knocks down, mash Ⓐ repeatedly to repeat last hit
Iron-Fist Possession	←Ⓐ+Ⓚ			
Rising Kite ~Super Dragonfly	↑Ⓐ+Ⓚ	Mid, Mid, Mid	20	Causes crumple, shifts to Super Dragonfly
Standing Suicide	Backturned ↓Ⓐ+Ⓚ	Mid	90	Unblockable, knocks down, deals damage to both characters
Manji Blood Petals	Backturned ↓Ⓐ+Ⓚ ⒶⒶⒶⒶⒶ	Mid x6	90, 20, 15, 10, 5, 30	Unblockable, every hit knocks down, mash Ⓐ repeatedly to repeat last hit
Rising Kite ~Super Dragonfly	Backturned ↑Ⓐ+Ⓚ	Mid, Mid, Mid	20	Knocks down, shifts to Super Dragonfly
Greetings	Ⓚ+Ⓖ			

8-Way Run

Name	Command	Attack Level	Damage	Notes
Kabuki	→ or ↘ or ↗Ⓐ	Mid	24	Crumples on counter-hit
Flagstaff	↓ or ↑Ⓐ	Mid	32	Sideturns on normal hit, knocks down on counter-hit
Asura Sweeper	↙ or ↖Ⓐ	Low	26	Causes backflop on counter-hit
Lightning Blade	←Ⓐ	Mid	22	Spins foe
Passing Light	→Ⓑ	Mid	28	Launches
Passing Light ~Intimidation	→🅑	Mid	28	Launches, shifts to Intimidation
Firmiana Shark Attack Combo	↘ or ↗ⒷⒷ+ⓀⒶ+ⒷⓀ	Mid, Mid, High, Mid	26, 30, 10, 18	First hit launches on counter-hit, 4th hit launches
Deathcopter	↘ or ↗ⒷⒷ+Ⓚ🅐+🅑	Mid, Mid, High, Mid	26, 30, 10, 80	First hit launches on counter-hit, shifts to Deathcopter
Firmiana Shark Attack Combo	↘ or ↗Ⓑ🅑+🅚Ⓐ+ⒷⓀ	Mid, Mid, High, Mid	26, 30, 10, 18	First hit launches on counter-hit, 2nd hit turns Yoshimitsu, 4th hit launches
Deathcopter	↘ or ↗Ⓑ🅑+🅚🅐+🅑	Mid, Mid, High, Mid	26, 30, 10, 80	First hit launches on counter-hit, 2nd hit turns Yoshimitsu, shifts to Deathcopter
Side Blow	↓ or ↑Ⓑ	Sp.Low	20	Crumples on counter-hit
Side Blow ~Intimidation	↓ or ↑ⒷⒼ			Shifts to Intimidation
Hell Gate	↙ or ↖Ⓑ	Mid	24	Knocks down on counter-hit
Sword Impale	←Ⓑ	Mid	130	Unblockable, knocks down
Spinning Sword	←ⒷⒶ	Mid x6	25x6	Knocks down
Spinning Sword (Cancel)	←ⒷⒶⒼ	Mid	25, 25	Knocks down
Helm Splitter	←ⒷⒷ	High	20	Crumples on counter-hit
Knee Bash	→Ⓚ	Mid	24	Knocks down
Hayabusa	↘ or ↗Ⓚ	Mid	18	Launches
Slingshot	↓ or ↑Ⓚ	Mid	30	Knocks down
Bullet Cutter	← or ↙ or ↖ⓀⒷ	Mid, Mid	24, 22	Combos naturally, 1st hit knocks down
Bullet Cutter (Hold)	← or ↙ or ↖Ⓚ🅑	Mid, Mid	24, 40~80	1st hit knocks down, 2nd hit is Unblockable
Crying Spirit Sword	8-Way Run Any Direction Ⓐ+Ⓑ	Mid	34	Causes crumple
Crying Spirit Sword (Cancel)	8-Way Run Any Direction Ⓐ+ⒷⒼ			Cancels attack
Crying Spirit Sword ~Flea	8-Way Run Any Direction Ⓐ+ⒷⒷ+Ⓚ			Shifts to Flea
Crying Spirit Sword ~Meditation	8-Way Run Any Direction Ⓐ+Ⓑ⇩Ⓑ+Ⓚ			Shifts to Meditation
Crying Spirit Sword to Death	8-Way Run Any Direction Ⓐ+Ⓑ⇩Ⓑ	Low	20	
Firmiana Shark Attack Combo	→ or ↘ or ↗Ⓑ+ⓀⒶ+ⒷⓀ	Mid, High, Mid	30, 10, 18	3rd hit launches
Deathcopter	→ or ↘ or ↗Ⓑ+Ⓚ🅐+🅑	Mid, High, Mid	30, 10, 80	Shifts to Deathcopter
Firmiana Shark Attack Combo	→ or ↘ or ↗🅑+🅚Ⓐ+ⒷⓀ	Mid, High, Mid	30, 10, 18	1st hit turns Yoshimitsu, 3rd hit launches
Deathcopter	→ or ↘ or ↗🅑+🅚🅐+🅑	Mid, High, Mid	30, 10, 80	1st hit turns Yoshimitsu, shifts to Deathcopter
Cyclone Lift	↙ or ↖Ⓑ+Ⓚ	Mid	14	Crumples on counter-hit
Ninja Sun Flare	← or ↓ or ↑Ⓑ+Ⓚ	Mid	40	Knocks down
Ninja Sun Flare (Cancel)	← or ↓ or ↑Ⓑ+ⓀⒼ			Cancel attack
Ninja Sun Flare ~Flea	← or ↓ or ↑Ⓑ+ⓀⒷ+Ⓚ			Shift to Flea
Ninja Sun Flare ~Meditation	← or ↓ or ↑Ⓑ+Ⓚ⇩Ⓑ+Ⓚ			Shift to Meditation
Fake Turning Suicide	→Ⓐ+Ⓚ			Leaves Yoshimitsu backturned
Turning Suicide	→🅐+🅚	Mid	110	Unblockable, deals damage to both characters
Manji Blood Petals	→🅐+🅚ⒶⒶⒶⒶⒶ	Mid x6	110, 20, 15, 10, 5, 30	Unblockable, every hit knocks down, deals damage to both characters
Double Suicide	→🅐+🅚Ⓐ+Ⓚ	Mid, Mid	110, 140	Unblockable, deals damage to both characters
Sliding	While Running Ⓚ	Low	26	Knocks down

Throws

Name	Command	Attack Level	Damag	otes
Jaw Smash	Ⓐ+Ⓖ	Throw	55	Ⓐ to break throw
Jumping Body Slam	Ⓑ+Ⓖ	Throw	55	Ⓑ to break throw
Wheels of Hell	Left Side Throw	Throw	60	Ⓐ or Ⓑ to break throw
Puppet Dance	Right Side Throw	Throw	63	Ⓐ or Ⓑ to break throw
Tornado Drop	Back Throw	Throw	68	
Rainbow Drop	⇩⇙⇦Ⓐ+Ⓖ	Throw	68	Ⓐ to break throw
Soul Siphon	Ⓑ+Ⓖ⇨	Throw	-29	Gives foe Yoshimitsu's health
Soul Harvest	Ⓑ+Ⓖ⇦	Throw	29	Drains health from foe

Flea

Name	Command	Attack Level	Damage	Notes
Flea	Ⓑ+Ⓚ			Shifts to Flea
Rolling Spark	Flea Ⓐ	Low	28	Returns to normal stance
Skull Splitter	Flea Ⓑ	Mid	20	Launches on counter-hit
Skull Splitter (Hold)	Flea Ⓑ	Mid	30	Launches
Rising Flea ~Dragonfly	Flea Ⓚ	Mid	30	Launches, shifts to Dragonfly
Dead Flea	Flea Ⓚ	Low	20	Lies down
Mine Spark	Flea Ⓐ+Ⓑ	Sp.Low	10	
Flea Roll	Flea Ⓑ+Ⓚ			Rolls forward, returns to normal stance
Meditation	Flea ⇩Ⓑ+Ⓚ			Shifts to Meditation
Manji Dragonfly	Flea ⇧Ⓑ+Ⓚ			Shifts to Dragonfly
Flea Digger	Flea ⇩Ⓐ+Ⓚ			Avoids high attacks and throws
Flea Hop (High)	Flea ⇖ or ⇧ or ⇗ Ⓐ+Ⓚ	Mid	40	Knocks down
Flea Hop (Low)	Flea (⇦ or ⇨) Ⓐ+Ⓚ	Mid	20	Knocks down
Flea Rush	Flea ⇨⇨ or ⇨➡	Low, Low, Low	10, 10, 10	Combos naturally
Oni Killer	Flea ⒼⒶ+Ⓖ	Throw	65	Ⓐ to break throw
Nimbus	Flea ⒼⒷ+Ⓖ	Throw	65	Ⓑ to break throw

Intimidation

Name	Command	Attack Level	Damage	Notes
Intimidation	⇨Ⓑ+Ⓚ			Shifts to Intimidation
Dark Cross	Intimidation Ⓐ	Mid	30	Causes backflop
Ashura Blade	Intimidation Ⓑ	Mid, Mid, Mid	10, 20, 30	Combos naturally, 3rd hit knocks down, leaves Yoshimitsu backturned
Whirlwind	Intimidation Ⓚ	High	14	
Whirlwind ~Preparation	Intimidation Ⓚ	High	14	Shifts to Preparation
Flea	Intimidation Ⓑ+Ⓚ			Shifts to Flea
Manji Dragonfly	Intimidation ⇧Ⓑ+Ⓚ			Shifts to Dragonfly

Preparation

Name	Command	Attack Leve	amage	Notes
Preparation	⇦Ⓑ+Ⓚ			Backturns and shifts to Prepartion
Broken Promise	Preparation Ⓐ	Low	16	Knocks down
Perilous Spirit	Preparation ⒷⓀ	Mid, Mid	10, 10, 10	Combos naturally, launches
Back Handspring	Preparation Ⓚ	Mid	20	Knocks down, leaves Yoshimitsu backturned
Divine Truth	Preparation Ⓐ+Ⓑ Ⓐ or Ⓑ			Leaves Yoshimitsu backturned
Flea	Preparation Ⓑ+Ⓚ			Shifts to backturned Flea
Healing	Preparation ⇨Ⓑ+Ⓚ			
Meditation	Preparation ⇩Ⓑ+Ⓚ			Shifts to backturned Meditation
Intimidation	Preparation ⇦Ⓑ+Ⓚ			Shifts to backturned Intimidation
Manji Dragonfly	Preparation ⇧Ⓑ+Ⓚ			Shifts to backturned Dragonfly
Suicide Preparation	Preparation Ⓐ+Ⓚ	Mid	90	Unblockable, knocks down, damages both characters
Manji Blood Petals	Preparation Ⓐ+Ⓚ ⒶⒶⒶⒶⒶ	Mid x6	90, 20, 15, 10, 5, 30	Unblockable, every hit knocks down, mash Ⓐ repeatedly to repeat last hit
Oni Killer	Preparation ⒼⒶ+Ⓖ	Throw	65	Ⓐ to break throw
Nimbus	Preparation ⒼⒷ+Ⓖ	Throw	65	Ⓑ to break throw

Meditation

Name	Command	Attack Level	Damage	Notes
Meditation	⇩Ⓑ+Ⓚ			Shifts to Meditation
Warp Rolling Shark	Meditation Ⓐ	Low	28	Teleports behind foe if close, leaves Yoshimitsu in crouching state
Warp Moon Slayer	Meditation Ⓑ	Mid	35	Unblockable, knocks down, teleports behind foe if close
Warp Kangaroo Kick	Meditation Ⓚ	Mid	30	Launches, teleports behind foe if close
Extermination	Meditation Ⓐ+Ⓑ		10	Counters mid vertical slashes with an Unblockable tackle
Raging Kneel Head	Meditation ⇨Ⓐ+Ⓑ or ⇦Ⓐ+ⒷⒶ+Ⓑ	Low	24	Leaves Yoshimitsu floored
Warp	Meditation ⇩Ⓐ+Ⓑ			Warps behind foe
Flea	Meditation Ⓑ+Ⓚ			Shifts to Flea
Healing	Meditation ⬇Ⓑ+Ⓚ			Replenishes life
Manji Dragonfly	Meditation ⇧Ⓑ+Ⓚ			Shifts to Dragonfly
No Fear	Meditation Ⓐ+Ⓚ	Mid	90	Unblockable, knocks down, damages both characters
No Fear(Hold)	Meditation Ⓐ+Ⓚ	Mid, Mid	90	Unblockable, knocks down, damages both characters
Manji Blood Star	Meditation Ⓐ+ⓀⒶ	Mid, Mid	90, 50	Unblockable, every hit knocks down, mash Ⓐ to continue repeating follow-up
Oni Killer	Meditation ⒼⒶ+Ⓖ	Throw	65	Ⓐ to break throw
Nimbus	Meditation ⒼⒷ+Ⓖ	Throw	65	Ⓑ to break throw

Manji Dragonfly

Name	Command	Attack Level	Damage	Notes
Manji Dragonfly	⇧Ⓑ+Ⓚ			Shifts to Dragonfly
Flag Slap ~Dragonfly	Manji Dragonfly Ⓐ	Mid	26	Guard Break, spins foe on normal hit, crumples on counter-hit
Mt. Oni	Manji Dragonfly Ⓑ	Mid	24	Causes crumple
Autumn Sweeper	Manji Dragonfly Ⓚ	Low	26	Causes backflop, leaves Yoshimitsu in crouching state
Spirit Away	Manji Dragonfly Against Airborne Foe Ⓐ+Ⓑ	Throw	45	
Flea	Manji Dragonfly Ⓑ+Ⓚ			Shifts to Flea
Meditation	Manji Dragonfly ⇩Ⓑ+Ⓚ			Shifts to Meditation
Manji Dragonfly (Quick Move)	Manji Dragonfly ⇨ or ⇦ or ⇩ or ⇧ Ⓐ+Ⓑ			Moves more quickly but expends HP
Oni Killer	Manji Dragonfly ⒼⒶ+Ⓖ	Throw	65	Ⓐ to break throw
Nimbus	Manji Dragonfly ⒼⒷ+Ⓖ	Throw	65	Ⓑ to break throw

Super Manji Dragonfly

Name	Command	Attack Level	Damage	Notes
Super Dragonfly	Manji Dragonfly ⇧Ⓑ+Ⓚ			Shifts to Super Dragonfly, expends HP
Parachute Spinner	Super Manji Dragonfly Ⓐ	Mid, Mid	30, 30	Knocks down
Mt. Devil Divider	Super Manji Dragonfly Ⓑ	Mid	41	Unblockable, causes forward crumple
Acrobatic Bliss	Super Manji Dragonfly ⓀⓀ	Low	26	Causes foe to stagger
Spinning Fall ~Flea	Super Manji Dragonfly Ⓑ+Ⓚ	Mid	60	Unblockable, knocks down, shifts to Flea
Daruma Drop ~Meditation	Super Manji Dragonfly ⇩Ⓑ+Ⓚ	Mid	40, 30	Guard Break, knocks down, shifts to Meditation
Manji Dragonfly	Super Manji Dragonfly ⇧Ⓑ+Ⓚ			Shifts to Dragonfly
Paradise Death	Super Manji Dragonfly Ⓐ+Ⓚ	Mid	140	Unblockable, knocks down, deals damage to both characters
Super Manji Dragonfly (Quick Move)	Super Manji Dragonfly ⇨ or ⇦ or ⇩ or ⇧Ⓐ+Ⓑ			Move more quickly at the cost of HP
Oni Killer	Super Manji Dragonfly ⒼⒶ+Ⓖ	Throw	65	Ⓐ to break throw
Nimbus	Super Manji Dragonfly ⒼⒷ+Ⓖ	Throw	65	Ⓑ to break throw

Combos

While Crouching ⬂Ⓚ, While Crouching Ⓑ
2 hits, 32 damage
⇩⬃⇦Ⓐ, ⇨⇨Ⓑ
2 hits, 51 damage
8 Way Run Ⓐ + Ⓑ, ⬂Ⓑ
2 hits, 56 damage
⬊ or ⬈Ⓚ, ⒶⒷ + Ⓚ
2 hits, 43 damage
⇦Ⓑ, ⬂Ⓑ
2 hits, 48 damage
➡Ⓑ, Ⓑ
4 hits, 67 damage
⬃Ⓚ (or Meditation Ⓚ), ⇧Ⓐ + Ⓚ
4 hits, 78 damage, shifts to Super Dragonfly, pause briefly and hit Ⓐ to potentially add another hit even if the foe air recovers
Counter-hit ⬂ⒶⒷ, ⬂⬂ⒷⒷ + Ⓚ
4 hits, 67 damage
Counter-hit Ⓐ + Ⓑ, ⒷⒶ
2 hits, 85 damage
Counter-hit Ⓐ + Ⓑ, ⬂Ⓑ + ⓀⒷ (Just), ⇨Ⓚ
4 hits, 88 damage
Counter-hit ⒶⒷ + Ⓚ, ⬂ⒶⒷ, ⇨Ⓚ
4 hits, 83 damage
Counter-hit ⇨Ⓐ + ⒷⒷⒷⒷ, ⬂Ⓑ
5 hits, 73 damage
Counter-hit ⬇ or ⬆Ⓑ, ⬂Ⓑ, ⇨Ⓚ
3 hits, 70 damage
Counter-hit ⬈ or ➡ or ⬊Ⓐ, ⇨Ⓐ + ⒷⒷⒷⒷ
5 hits, 47 damage
Flea Ⓚ, Dragonfly Ⓐ + Ⓑ
2 hits, 66 damage
Counter-hit While Rising Ⓚ, ⬂Ⓑ, ⇨Ⓚ
3 hits, 70 damage
Flea ⇦ or ⬁ or ⇧ or ⬀ or ⇨Ⓐ + Ⓚ, Ⓐ + Ⓑ
2 hits, 33~50 damage
Dragonfly Ⓚ, ⬃ⓀⓀⓀⓀ
5 hits, 51 damage
Dragonfly Ⓐ, Ⓚ
2 hits, 46 damage
Dragonfly Ⓑ, ⬂Ⓑ, ⇨Ⓚ
3 hits, 70 damage
Counter-hit Dragonfly Ⓐ, Ⓑ, ⬂Ⓑ, ⒶⒷ + Ⓚ (wall hit), ⬂ⒶⒷ (wall hit), ⬂Ⓑ
9 hits, 106 damage

Close Range

Yoshimitsu comes equipped with tons of great close-range attacks, many of which are mid and circular. This allows him to simultaneously deter sidesteps and crouching, which also opens the door for his powerful Rainbow Drop throw (⇩⇙⇦Ⓐ+Ⓖ), as well as his devious stance tricks and Unblockables. His attacks are much more limited from far away, so get into phone booth range and then make the most of your time there. Like most characters, Yoshimitsu's Rapid Gale (ⒶⒶ) is a basic string that hits high for a 2-hit combo, and it catches side movement. Double Zig (⇨Ⓚ⇩Ⓚ) is also effective for stopping 8-Way Run and sidestep attempts. The first hit is high and knocks down, while the second is low and will juggle if the first kick hits. If foes either block correctly or crouch under the first hit altogether, use ⇨ⓀⓀ instead. It follows the high kick with a mid kick that knocks down as well, and it punishes crouching opponents. Enemies may grow savvy to ⒶⒶ and ⇨Ⓚ, so use Sword Sweep (⇩⇙⇦Ⓐ) as another option for killing sidesteps. This attack crouches under high attacks and hits low, scoring a knockdown. From here, you can score an extra guaranteed hit with Passing Light~Intimidation (⇨⇨Ⓑ). As another close-range option, keep in mind Soul Siphon (⇨Ⓐ+Ⓚ⇦), a high-hitting spin punch that transitions naturally into an interesting life-draining throw. If the spinning punch lands as a counter-hit, the throw will combo and leave your foe backturned.

Yoshimitsu has a few unique moves, which are a huge part of his close-range offense. Stone Fist (⇙Ⓐx1~5), Stone Backhands (⇦Ⓐx1~5), and Spinning Low Kick (While Crouching ⇙Ⓚx1~5) are moves that spin Yoshimitsu rapidly, striking either high, mid, or low over and over. Each of these moves combos up to three hits on normal hit, or up to five hits on counter-hit. Plus, every input after the first one can register as a Just Frame, flashing Yoshimitsu white. If the final hit of each sequence is a Just Frame, it also registers as a Guard Break. All of them snuff side movement, and each can be stopped at any time. If you perform all five swings with any of these attacks, Yoshimitsu will be too dizzy to go on and will collapse to the ground, leaving him briefly vulnerable. So, avoid actually finishing these strings; ⇦Ⓐ+ⒷⒷⒷⒷⒷⒷⒷ Spinning Evade works much the same way, although it is not an attack. Instead, use them frequently to pressure the opponent, and stop at random times to go for mix-ups. Both ⇙Ⓐx1~4 and While Crouching ⇙Ⓚx1~4 leave Yoshimitsu briefly in a crouching state, allowing you to easily perform While Crouching or While Rising moves. While Crouching ⇘Ⓚ floors enemies if they don't guard low. Exorcism Fist (While Rising Ⓐ) nails crouching or sidestepping enemies and back-turns them, granting you a big advantage. Alternatively, you can perform a throw. Exorcism Fist leaves Yoshimitsu in a back-turned state, so if opponents guard it, use back-turned ⇩Ⓚ to sweep them even on normal hit, or simply block—Yoshimitsu is safe from guaranteed retaliation.

When your opponent isn't sure whether to guard high, low, or watch out for throws, the door is open for launch attempts. Golden Shrine (⇘ⒶⒷ) is an excellent option. While this double-mid string doesn't combo on normal hit, it can be delayed and verified on counter-hit or against crouching characters. Train yourself to eyeball whether ⇘Ⓐ counters or strikes a crouching opponent before you perform the Ⓑ follow-up and then juggle. Likewise, delaying the Ⓑ strike as long as possible may bait a character that either blocked or simply got hit normally into attacking during the gap, thus scoring a counter-hit. As another counter-hit tool, keep in mind Ninja Blade Rush (ⒷⒶ), a mid-striking shoulder that naturally becomes a special samurai slice only on counter-hit.

Mid Range

Many of Yoshimitsu's attacks have limited range, making him somewhat less effective the further he gets from his opposition. He must focus on a few choice attacks and his deceptive stance options as he tries to get in close. Stand on the edge of your foe's range and wait for him to grow anxious and whiff an attack. Then knock your opponent to the ground with Bullet Cutter (⇦ⓀⒷ). This mid-hitting string combos even on normal hit. You can charge the Ⓑ press, turning the follow-up string into an Unblockable that grows stronger the longer you hold it. This can be useful if ⇦Ⓚ is blocked and your foes hesitate, or if ⇦Ⓚ knocks them down and they fail to roll to the side on wakeup. If you wish, you can access this same Unblockable by itself with ⇙Ⓑ. As another mid-striking poke option from mid range, use Sword Impale (←Ⓑ). This command starts a linear, *extremely* damaging Unblockable, but the enemy has ample opportunity to simply poke you or sidestep. That's part of the trick, though. Input ←ⒷⒷ for a high-striking sword slash with great range that staggers on counter-hit. Alternatively, ←Ⓐ is a helicopter blade spin that can nail foes if they sidestep or rush in; press Ⓖ to cancel this helicopter spin. You can also input ←ⒷⒼ to simply fake the Unblockable, keeping enemies on their toes. Speaking of Unblockables, at mid range Yoshimitsu has an effective tool, provided he has at least half his life to burn. Turning Suicide (→Ⓐ+Ⓚ) causes him to rush forward, turn his back to the enemy, and then run *himself* through, stabbing the enemy in the process! This Unblockable is lightning fast, but the speed comes at a high price. Yoshimitsu damages himself just as heavily as the enemy! This can be a fantastic tool to quickly end matches if you have more than half of your life and your opponent does not. But beware, as Yoshimitsu can easily shoot himself in the proverbial foot by missing with this risky attack. With all these linear options, Yoshimitsu needs some circular moves to keep the enemy from simply sidestepping. Asura Sweeper (↙ or ↖Ⓐ) is a good circular low that knocks down on counter-hit. Dark Cross (⇨Ⓑ+ⓀⒶ) is a mid with sneaky range and evasive properties—Yoshimitsu backsteps during its execution and ducks under high attacks on the way in. This attack crumples on counter-hit, leading to a combo.

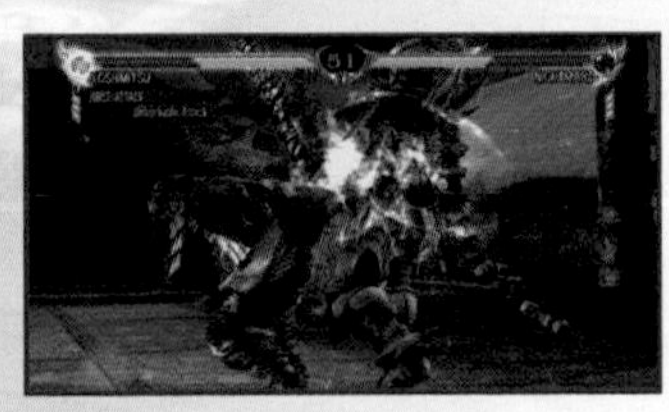

Long Range

From a distance, Yoshimitsu must be patient and rely on ⇦Ⓚ and his special stances to get in close. Use Ninja Sun Flare (← or ↓ or ↑Ⓑ+Ⓚ) to roll in from afar, and slash with a mid that knocks down. Press Ⓖ to cancel this attack prematurely and go for a throw or a While Rising attack from the roll. You can also shift from the roll directly to Flea or Meditation. Crying Spirit Sword is a similar attack. It also strikes mid, causing a crumple that leads to a combo. But you can also press Ⓖ to cancel this move, or interrupt it with Flea or Meditation stance. Deathcopter (⇧Ⓐ+Ⓑ) also allows for variation moving in and attacking from a distance. On its own, it's an Unblockable. By pressing Ⓑ+Ⓚ, the Unblockable is faked and Yoshimitsu enters Manji Dragonfly. Tap ⇩ to drop and strike with the Unblockable early, or ⇦ to fly over the foe and fall from the other side. Alternatively, fly in with his Super Manji Dragonfly stance (⇧Ⓑ+Ⓚx2, or ⇧Ⓐ+Ⓚ, then Ⓐ+Ⓑ to fly faster in midair) before you drop on your enemy with Ⓐ for a circular attack, Ⓑ for a linear Unblockable, ⇩Ⓑ+Ⓚ for a Guard Break that leads to Meditation stance, or ⒼⒶ or Ⓑ+Ⓖ for a special Dragonfly throw. Beware that using Super Manji Dragonfly drains HP, however.

Yoshimitsu

Special Tactics

Okizeme: Anti-Wakeup

Against waking enemies, ⇨Ⓑ+ⓀⒶ and ⇘ⒶⒷ are excellent options. Both lead to combos on counter-hit, and they have evasive properties or can be verified. Mixing up between these and While Crouching ⇘Ⓚ or ⇙Ⓚx1~4 keeps Yoshimitsu in control against foes trying to rise from knockdowns. From a few steps away with a big life lead, go for →Ⓐ+Ⓚ to end a round quickly if you're gutsy. Or start up Yoshimitsu's ←Ⓑ Unblockable and either let it go or interrupt with Ⓐ to start the wide-hitting Spinning Sword.

Stance and Deliver

Yoshimitsu can enter many special stances at almost any time. He can also transition between them at will. Flea (Ⓑ+Ⓚ) features Yoshimitsu balancing and walking on his swords. He can hop around and perform a few exclusive moves. Intimidation (⇨Ⓑ+Ⓚ) stance has him lower his shoulder and glare at his foe, ready to perform quick strikes, like Dark Cross (Ⓐ). In Preparation (⇦Ⓑ+Ⓚ), he turns his back to the enemy and can perform a few unique moves, like Perilous Spirit (ⒷⓀ) or his Suicide Preparation Unblockable (Ⓐ+Ⓚ). He can also enter any other stance from a back-turn. In Meditation (⇩Ⓑ+Ⓚ), Yoshimitsu squats on the ground. Here, he has many moves that teleport around his foe. He can also heal (↓Ⓑ+Ⓚ). Finally, the Manji Dragonfly (⇧Ⓑ+Ⓚ) and Super Manji Dragonfly (⇧Ⓑ+Ⓚx2 or ⇧Ⓐ+Ⓚ) allow Yoshimitsu to take to the skies, hovering above his foes before dropping on them. He can fly quickly in the air by holding Ⓐ+Ⓑ, but beware; not only is it easy to accidentally fly off the stage's edge, but Yoshimitsu also loses life gradually while he's in his Dragonfly flight!

Hong Yun-seong

Hong Yun-seong

The greatest pleasure in life is doing what people say you cannot do.

Walter Bagehot (1826–1877)

Hong Yun-seong

Bio	
Age:	18
Birthplace:	Jirisan, Korea
Height:	5'9"
Weight:	159 lbs.
Birth Date:	April 16
Blood Type:	O
Weapon:	Chinese sword
Weapon Name:	White Storm
Discipline:	Seong Style Long Sword (with some personal style mixed in)
Family:	Father: Died from illness Mother: Whereabouts unknown Master: Seong Han Myong

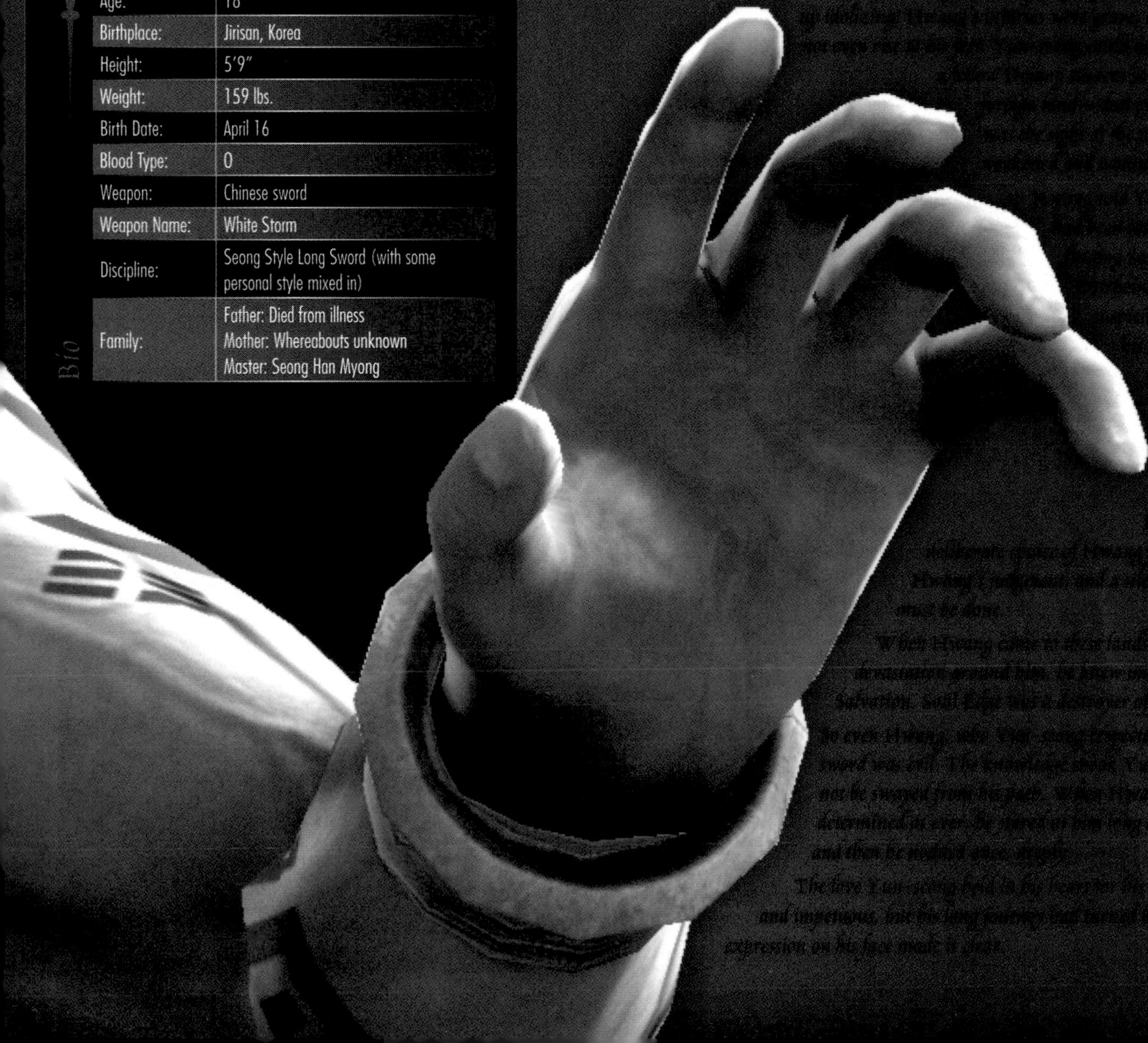

Hwang made a decision. He would place his trust in this younger disciple. He knew that sometimes, [illegible] potential of its youth.

Hwang told Yun-seong everything he knew about Soul Edge, and then gave him a grave warning: [illegible] reckoning. He then told the young man the single fact that Yun-seong had been unable to fathom: [illegible] was a single swordswoman. And though she had defeated him in battle, she spared his life and let him go free.

"She, too, was fighting to protect the weak. I could see it in her eyes."

Once he had finished his tale, Hwang smiled at Yun-seong encouragingly.

"Go, and find your own answer."

With courage and conviction he had never before known, Yun-seong turned toward Ostrheinsburg. He would [illegible]

White Storm

A single Chinese sword passed down through the house of Seong, said to reflect its wielder's innermost heart in its blade.

Yun-seong received the sword from Mi-na, the Seong family's only daughter. He used the reflection of himself in its blade to determine his next course of action, which was to set out in search of Soul Edge. Rather than compare himself to others, he would do what he alone could. White Storm became his compass; many times afterward he would look into its blade for guidance at the crossroads of his life.

Incidentally, he does not realize he walked off with White Storm without permission; he believes Mi-na entrusted him with the weapon, and has never given it another thought.

Seong-Style Longsword Technique (Probably Also Own Style)

Seong is a swordsman of good, honorable lineage. However, his kicking techniques defy categorization. In the dojang he was told that he still had work to do, but as he gained actual fighting experience, his natural rhythm and tendencies began to come to the surface. Nothing can be protected by ceremony alone. Unless it is accompanied by power, faith is nothing more than talk. On his journey seeking Soul Edge, this was the lesson Yun-seong learned. No enemy that faced him and his blade would convince him otherwise.

His distinctive sword style is both sure and also adaptive to the situation at hand. When he finally achieves his goal, he can only then look back and feel worthy of his name.

Command List

Signature Techniques

Name	Command	Attack Level	Damage	Notes
Avenging Claws	⇨ⒷⒷ	Mid, Mid	26, 35	2nd attack Guard Breaks, stuns on hit
Steel Tiger Kick	⇦ⒷⓀ	Mid, Mid, High	16, 15, 18	2nd input can be delayed (additional damage). Final attack shifts into Crane's Rising Kick on counter-hit.
Ragged Fangs	ⓀⓀⒷ	High, High, Mid	8, 10, 16	
Rising Claws	⇩⇘⇨ⓀⓀ	Mid, High	13, 13	
Tempest Kick	➘ or ➚ⒶⓀ	High, Mid	18, 20	1st attack stuns on hit
Dancing Dragon ~Crane	⇩ⒷⓀ	Mid, High	14, 28	Shifts to Crane
Fluttering Crane Kick ~Crane	⇘🅚	Mid	22	Shifts to Crane
Magnificent Heavens ~Crane	➘ or ➚🅑	Mid	30	Shifts to Crane
Rising Blade Kick	Crane ⇧Ⓚ	Mid	20(35)	Shifts into additional attack against aerial enemies
Stone Cleaver	Crane Ⓐ+Ⓑ	Mid	28	Stuns on hit

Horizontal Attacks

Name	Command	Attack Level	Damage	Notes
Branding Blade	ⒶⒶ	High, High	10, 10	
Blazing Blade	⇨Ⓐ	High	22	Causes recoverable stun on hit
Blazing Blade ~Crane	⇨🅐	High	22	Causes recoverable stun on hit, shifts to Crane
Leg Cutter	⇘Ⓐ	Mid	20	Causes stun on counter-hit
Twisting Coils	⇩Ⓐ	Sp.Low	10	
Torso Cutter	⇗Ⓐ	Mid	17	Stuns on counter-hit. Evades high attacks.
Illusion Blade	⇦Ⓐ	High	16	Evades high attacks
Parting Blade	While Crouching Ⓐ	Sp.Low	10	
Dual Rage Kick	While Rising ⒶⓀⓀ	High, High Mid	18, 16, 24	1st attacks stuns on counter-hit. Final attack stuns on hit.
Dual Rage Kick ~Crane	While Rising 🅐	High	18	Stuns on counter-hit. Shifts to Crane.
Upper Bite	Jumping Ⓐ	High	20 or 24 or 28	Damage varies depending on direction jumped in
Reverse Backhand Blade	Backturned Ⓐ	Low	12	
Reverse Blade	While Crouching Backturned Ⓐ	Low	12	

Vertical Attacks

Name	Command	Attack Level	Damage	Notes
Burning Sky	ⒷⒷ	Mid, Mid	14, 16	
Avenging Claws	⇨ⒷⒷ	Mid, Mid	26, 35	2nd attack Guard Breaks, stuns on hit
Avenging Claws ~Crane	⇨🅑	Mid	26	Shifts to Crane
Crashing Blade	⇘Ⓑ	Mid	24	
Dancing Dragon ~Crane	⇩ⒷⓀ	Mid, High	14, 28	Shifts to Crane
Piercing Thrust	⇗Ⓑ	Low	20	
Steel Tiger Kick	⇦ⒷⓀ	Mid, Mid, High	16, 15, 18	Final attack shifts into Crane's Rising Kick on counter-hit
Steel Tiger Kick (Delay)	⇦ⒷⓀ (Delay)	Mid, Mid, High	16, 15, 18	Final attack shifts into Crane's Rising Kick on counter-hit
Wolverine Blade	While Crouching Ⓑ	Mid	16	
Viper Lunge	While Rising Ⓑ	High	22	
Swatting Claw	Jumping Ⓑ	Mid	22 or 26 or 30	Damage varies depending on direction jumped in
Reverse Upper Blade	Backturned Ⓑ	Mid	16	
Reverse Cleaver	While Crouching Backturned Ⓑ	Mid	18	

Kick Attacks

Name	Command	Attack Level	Damage	Notes
Ragged Fangs	ⓀⓀⒷ	High, High, Mid	8, 10, 16	
Dual Cry Kick	⇨ⓀⓀ	High, Mid	16, 24	2nd attack stuns on hit
Dual Cry Kick (Delay)	⇨ⓀⓀ (Delay)	High, Mid	16, 24	2nd attack stuns on hit
Dual Cry Kick (Cancel)	⇨ⓀⒼ			
Dual Cry Kick ~Crane	⇨Ⓚ🅖			Shifts to Crane
Lone Bell	⇨ⓀⒼⓀ	Mid	24	Stuns on hit
Fluttering Crane Kick	⇘Ⓚ	Mid	22	
Fluttering Crane Kick ~Crane	⇘🅚	Mid	22	Shifts to Crane
Viper Sweep	⇩Ⓚ	Low	12	
Echo Kick	⇙ⓀⓀ	Low, High	15, 22	
Echo Kick ~Crane	⇙ⓀⓀⒼ	Low	15	
Whispering Kick	⇙Ⓚ⇩Ⓚ	Low, Low	15, 24	
Ripping Fang	⇦Ⓚ	Mid	18	
Rising Claws	⇩⇘⇨ⓀⓀ	Mid, High	13, 13	
Viper Sweep	While Crouching Ⓚ	Low	12	
Rising Hook Heel	While Rising Ⓚ	Mid	20	Stuns on hit
Phoenix Ascension	Jumping ⓀⓀⓀ	High, High, Mid	20, 15(25), 30(40)	Input with Just Frame timing for additional damage. Causes final hit to ground stun enemy.
Reverse Fang	Backturned Ⓚ	High	10	
Reverse Viper Sweep	While Crouching Backturned Ⓚ	Low	12	

Simultaneous Press

Name	Command	Attack Level	Damage	Notes
Heaven's Path	Ⓐ+Ⓑ	Mid, Mid	15, 25	
Heaven's Path (Additional Attack)	Ⓐ+Ⓑ, Ⓑ (Press Repeatedly)	Mid, Mid, High	15, 25, 30	Final attack Guard Breaks
Waving Flame	⇨Ⓐ+Ⓑ	Mid, Mid	15, 14	Deflects mid horizontals. 2nd attack stuns on counter-hit.
Crane	Ⓑ+Ⓚ			Evades vertical attacks. Initiates attack after dodge. Input Ⓚ during attack for special attack.
Falling Peak	⇩Ⓑ+Ⓚ	Mid	26	Stuns on hit
Wagging Tail	⇦Ⓑ+Ⓚ	Mid	25	Causes recoverable stun on hit
Pouncing Claws	⇗Ⓑ+Ⓚ	Mid	28	
Wagging Tail	Backturned Ⓑ+Ⓚ	Mid	20	Guard Breaks. Causes recoverable stun on hit.
Sweeping Wave	Ⓐ+Ⓚ	Mid, Low	15, 18	Leaves Yun-Seong in crouching state
Taunt	Ⓚ+Ⓖ			

8-Way Run

Name	Command	Attack Level	Damage	Notes
Diving Viper	→Ⓐ	High	30	
Tempest Kick	↘ or ↗ⒶⓀ	High, Mid	18, 20	1st attack stuns on hit
Willow Dance	↓ or ↑ⒶⒷ	High, High, Mid	10, 10, 20	
Willow Dance (Cancel)	↓ or ↑ⒶⒷⒼ	High, High	10, 10	
Submerged Blade	↙ or ↖Ⓐ	Low	24	
Burning Ember	←Ⓐ	Mid	26	Causes recoverable stun on counter-hit
Tempest Blade	→Ⓑ	Mid	34	Stuns on hit
Magnificent Heavens	↘ or ↗Ⓑ	Mid	30	
Magnificent Heavens ~Crane	↘ or ↗🅑	Mid	30	Shifts to Crane
Eclipse Blade	↓ or ↑Ⓑ	Mid	25	
Opening Void Thrust	↙ or ↖Ⓑ	Low	28	
Vengeful Thrust	←Ⓑ	Mid	30	Causes recoverable stun on hit
Crushing Heel	→Ⓚ	Mid	24	Stuns on hit
Crane Kick	↘ or ↗Ⓚ	Mid	14	Stuns on counter-hit
Crane Kick ~Crane	↘ or ↗🅚	Mid	14	Stuns on counter-hit. Shifts to Crane.
Roundhouse Kick	↓ or ↑Ⓚ	High	35	
Raging Talons	↙ or ↖Ⓚ	Mid, Mid	13, 17	Both attacks stun on hit
Tiger Cannon Kick	←Ⓚ	High	34	
Roaring Flame	→Ⓐ+Ⓑ	Mid	40	Stuns on hit
Cresting Wave	→Ⓑ+Ⓚ	Mid	20	
Fire Storm	←Ⓑ+Ⓚ	Mid	85	Unblockable. Input Ⓖ to cancel.
Blazing Tempest	←🅑+🅚	Mid	30	Guard Breaks. Causes recoverable stun on hit.
Sliding	While Running Ⓚ		26	

Throws

Name	Command	Attack Level	Damage	Notes
Death Dance	Ⓐ+Ⓖ	Throw	50	Input Ⓐ to escape
Death Blade	Ⓑ+Ⓖ	Throw	50	Input Ⓑ to escape
Burning Cradle	Left Side Throw	Throw	55	Same button as throw (Ⓐ or Ⓑ) to escape
Drac Slayer	Right Side Throw	Throw	68	Same button as throw (Ⓐ or Ⓑ) to escape
Spine Destroyer	Back Throw	Throw	60	Same button as throw (Ⓐ or Ⓑ) to escape

Crane

Name	Command	Attack Level	Damage	Notes
Crane	Ⓑ+Ⓚ			Evades vertical attacks. Initiates attack after dodge. Input Ⓚ during attack for special attack.
Circling Wing	Crane Ⓐ	High	24	Stuns on hit. Shifts to Crane.
Crown Strike	Crane Ⓑ	High	10	
Rising Kick	Crane Ⓚ	Mid	25	Shifts to Crane. Launches on counter-hit.
Rising Kick (Cancel)	Crane ⓀⒼ			Shifts to Crane
Crane Shredder	Crane ⇩ⓀⓀ	Low, High	12, 24	
Rising Blade Kick	Crane ⇧Ⓚ	Mid	20(36)	Shifts into additional attack against aerial enemies
Stone Cleaver	Crane Ⓐ+Ⓑ	Mid	28	Stuns on hit
Stone Cleaver (Hold)	Crane 🅐+🅑	Mid	38	
Coiling Viper Thrust	Crane Ⓑ+Ⓚ	Mid	45	Guard Breaks
Coiling Viper Thrust (Cancel)	Crane Ⓑ+ⓀⒼ			Leaves Yun-Seong in crouching state
Crane Flip ~Crane	Crane 🅑+🅚			Shifts to Crane
Leg Sweep	Crane Ⓐ+Ⓚ	Low	24	
Crane Flip	Backturned Crane Ⓑ+Ⓚ			
Crane Flip ~Crane	Backturned Crane 🅑+🅚			

Combos

Counter-hit ⬂🅚, Ⓑ
2 hits, 36 Damage
➘ (or ➚) 🅑, ⇧Ⓚ
3 hits, 68 Damage
Counter-hit ⬃Ⓐ, While Rising Ⓚ, ⇨⇨Ⓚ
3 hits, 55 Damage
During Crane Ⓐ, Ⓑ, ⇦ⒷⓀ (delayed)
6 hits, 64 Damage
During Crane Ⓐ, Ⓚ, ⇧Ⓚ
3 hits, 70 Damage
During Crane Counter-hit ⇩ⓀⓀ, Ⓐ + Ⓑ
3 hits, 58 Damage
Ⓐ + Ⓚ, ⇨⇨Ⓚ
3 hits, 47 Damage
⇨⇨Ⓑ + Ⓚ, ⇧ⓀⓀⓀ (Just)
4 hits, 68 Damage
⇩⬂⇨ⓀⓀ, ⇧ⓀⓀⓀ (Just)
5 hits, 64 Damage
Counter-hit ⇦⇦Ⓐ, ⇨Ⓐ + Ⓑ, ⬂🅚, Ⓑ, ⇦ⒷⓀ (Delay)
9 hits, 89 Damage, first stun is escapable

Close Range

Counter your enemies' sidestep attempts or scare them into crouching, Yun-Seong's only means of dealing heavy damage. Pressure your foe with Yun-Seong's horizontal ⒶⒶ string, closely watching whether the attack hits. If it connects, attack with Ragged Fangs (ⓀⓀⒷ) to stop immediate standing attacks. Use Torso Cutter (↙Ⓐ) to counter standing attacks and sidesteps. Or use a throw or Yun-Seong's Echo Kick (↙ⓀⓀ) string. If ↙Ⓐ connects as a counter-hit, perform While Rising Ⓚ then →→Ⓚ for a 3-hit combo. If your enemy blocks your string, use the Vengeful Thrust (←←Ⓑ) to dodge and counter most low and high attacks. When you anticipate a sidestep or a vertical attack, strike with the Willow Dance (⇩or⇧Ⓐ). Successfully hitting a sidestep causes a counter-hit, enabling you to verify the hit and chain into its Ⓑ extension (⇗ⒶⒷ) for a 3-hit combo. If the first two hits are blocked, you have several options: recover and take a defensive stance, input ⇗ⒶⒷⒼ to fake the third hit and go for a throw, or simply perform the entire string if your enemy is expecting the fake.

When you believe your enemy wants to duck under your high strings, nail the foe with the combo Steel Tiger Kick (←ⒷⓀ). Though it's risky because of its vulnerability when guarded, it may be worth taking a chance to go for Yun-Seong's Rising Claws (↓↘→]ⓀⓀ), a 2-hit launcher that allows for juggle combos. Pursue your enemy with ↑ⓀⓀⓀ(Just) to perform a 5-hit combo.

Mid Range

Lure your enemy into using 8-Way Run or a sidestep. Yun-Seong's most damaging combos start off of attacks that stop these maneuvers. Pressure your enemy with Yun-Seong's Opening Void Thrust (⇗ (or ⇘)Ⓑ) low attack, or his mid Avenging Claws (→ⒷⒷ). The second hit of →ⒷⒷ is a Guard Break, so if your enemy blocks it, stage a secondary attack with the same moves. When you anticipate that your foe will sidestep any of these strikes, perform the Burning Ember (⇦Ⓐ) to counter-hit, causing a recoverable stun that leads to a possible combo; follow-up with →Ⓐ + Ⓑ, ↘Ⓚ, Ⓑ, ←ⒷⓀ(Delay). Your enemy can sidestep the second hit of →ⒷⒷ after blocking the first. If you anticipate this action, input →Ⓑto shift to his Crane stance, then perform its Circling Wing (Ⓐ) to stun the opponent. This leads to the combo: during Crane Ⓐ, Ⓑ, ←ⒷⓀ (delayed). It deals massive damage and leaves you in the Crane stance at an advantage, so stage a second attack with its Leg Sweep (Ⓐ + Ⓚ) or Rising Kick (Ⓚ) options.

Long Range

This is Yun-Seong's worst position. His options at this distance are limited to his ⇗(or ⇘)Ⓑ low slash, or his ←←Ⓐ. As we mentioned, ←←Ⓐ is used to counter sidesteps, which leads to a recoverable stun on counter-hit. Use this to discourage 8-Way Run and to train your enemy into blocking high, which then enables you to use ⇗Ⓑ to attack. Use the fear of either attack to move into mid range.

Special Tactics

Okizeme: Anti-Wakeup

The Steel Tiger Kick (←ⒷⓀ) is Yun-Seong's most important mid attack. The entire string combos even when the Ⓚ segment is input very late, enabling you to verify that ←Ⓑ hits before you do the extension. Though it's unsafe, delaying the string's input also makes it difficult for the enemy to know whether you'll do the kick extension. As an interesting extra, if the final hit happens to strike as a counter-hit, Yun-Seong shifts directly into the Crane Stance's Rising Kick. This is specifically useful for stun-based combos using the delayed version of kick, which doesn't knock the enemy into the air and allows for the Rising Kick to combo. When your foe is wary of ←ⒷⓀ, strike with the low ⇗(or ⇘)Ⓑ to catch him or her standing.

Crane Stance

Yun-Seong's evasive Crane stance (Ⓑ + Ⓚ), which dodges vertical attacks, also enables him to stage a varied offense from a myriad of techniques. The strongest of his opening attacks are his Avenging Claws (→Ⓑ) and the Fluttering Crane Kick (↘Ⓚ). The Crane options to use greatly depend on the distance from which you're fighting. The long-distance slash →Ⓑ is good for luring your enemy into sidestepping. After it's blocked, shift into the Crane's Crown Strike (Ⓑ) to stop your foe's immediate attempts to retaliate. If you anticipate that your opponent will try to crouch under the Ⓑ attack, use the mid-hitting Rising Kick (Ⓚ) or Stone Cleaver (Ⓐ + Ⓑ). Use the low Ⓐ + Ⓚ to sweep adversaries looking for mid attacks. When you finally anticipate that your enemy will sidestep to escape the preceding options, shift into the Ⓐ option to stun him or her for a combo. Against defensive players cautious of your Ⓐ option, you can use the Crane's leaping Coiling Viper Thrust (Ⓑ + Ⓚ) Guard Break. If your enemy blocks it, immediately attack with ⒷⒷ to score an unavoidable combo. You can fake Ⓑ + Ⓚ by pressing the Ⓖ button while Yun-Seong is jumping, a tricky option for landing throws when your opponent is afraid of the attack.

The ↘Ⓚuses fewer of the stance's attacks. If it connects on a counter-hit, attack with the Crane's Ⓑ attack to score a 2-hit combo. When guarded, attack with Ⓐ+Ⓚ to duck under and sweep standing horizontal attacks, or simply stand idle to dodge vertical counterattacks. If you successfully dodge a slash, input ⓀⓀ to perform a special hit-throw combo. Attack with the low ↓ⓀⓀ or the mid Ⓚ attack when your enemy is afraid of your defensive options.

Unfortunately, the Crane stance has one crippling flaw: it has absolutely no means to counter crouching Ⓐ attacks when it's used at close distances. In other words, a blocked ↘Ⓚmeans your enemy can always perform crouching Ⓐ to stop any of your Crane stance options. To compensate, use the command ↘Ⓚ to perform the attack without switching to the Crane stance, and then use Guard Impacts to counter your foe's attack. When the enemy isn't willing to attack anymore, go back to shifting into the Crane stance.

Zasalamel

That you cannot end, that makes you great...

"West-östlicher Diwan," Johann Wolfgang von Goethe (1749 – 1832)

Bio

Age:	Unknown, for he has lived many lives
Birthplace:	More than one, for he has lived many lives
Height:	5'11" (in this life)
Weight:	170 lbs. (in this life)
Birth Date:	May 5 (in this life)
Blood Type:	B (in this life)
Weapon:	Death Scythe
Weapon Name:	Kafziel
Discipline:	Self-Taught
Family:	Long since deceased

Zasalamel

This is it, he thought, this power will put an end to my cursed life once and for all!

Zasalamel felt certain of it as he stood before the opposing swords' rush of power. At last he would be able to escape the [illegible] that forced him to endlessly repeat life and death. The torrential forces produced by the spirit sword and the cursed sword [illegible] cathedral to its ruin; in the aftermath all would be devoured—the transmigrator, Zasalamel, included.

The swords had memories. Soul Edge's were ancient and bloody, marked by the screams of countless souls. Soul Calibur's [illegible] defended it, and its countless heroic wielders throughout history. As his mind melted into the [illegible] of power, [illegible] he learned the truth. He saw why the spirit sword had been created. He saw what it really was. And he witnessed the [illegible]

It was too late for any of that to matter.

But then, just as he was about to let go of life and pass into nothingness, a wondrous vision appeared before him like [illegible] at the unknown vista: towering structures that seemed to reach as high as heaven itself, steel boats that flew freely through [illegible] striking out moonward, then the achievement of that goal. And the creation of new life, the province of the gods themselves.

He was witnessing the future, the sum of all human potential.

With the very last fragment of his being, Zasalamel clung to the new desires awakening within him. For so long he had been [illegible] nothing more to learn; resignation had robbed him of all feeling. Never in his wildest dreams had he expected to encounter anything [illegible] shake him out of that apathy. But neither had he expected the future to hold such wonders, to shine so brightly! It was a [illegible] time in countless ages, the will to live swelled within him. Zasalamel had to be there when that vision became a reality! He had [illegible] And more than anything else, he wanted to be the shepherd that led mankind to those greater heights.

Zasalamel gathered up the broken pieces of his mind, and within the torrential forces he focused on rebuilding his self. [illegible] around him, tossing him about. With the power of Soul Calibur and Soul Edge, he thought, I can guide history in any direction [illegible] same power he had dreamed would bring him to death now brought him new hope. He tried to draw the opposing swords' [illegible] consciousness, but then he saw a dark, gaping chasm before him. Within a moment's passing, the abyss opened wider and [illegible] swallow Zasalamel whole.

The next moment, instinct took over and he released the swords' power. Eerie howls rose from the mass as it receded back [illegible] Zasalamel turned his thoughts back to rebuilding himself. It pained him that he was missing this chance to claim the two swords' [illegible] would serve him little if he could not escape back into the living world; living came first. The torrents subsided, and [illegible] moment, Zasalamel turned toward it, and with admiration—his first emotion in countless years—he [illegible]

His feet touched the ground. Zasalamel glanced around and took in the wasteland surrounding him. [illegible] Not a trace of it remained, nor of the swords. Where had they gone? Where had Nightmare and Siegfried gone [illegible]

Perhaps it would be in my best interest to find out, he mused.

Zasalamel felt so untroubled. As he gazed across the barren land, he took a deep breath. This was a new beginning. [illegible] He shut his eyes and the vista appeared before him. The future felt so definite, so real. He paused to relish [illegible] remained of the man who had so longed for death.

He had temporarily lost track of the passage of time, but after rejoining the flow of [illegible] only a few days had passed. Once he had calmed his emotions, he began to pick up on [illegible] sword. Both were exceedingly agitated; another clash was not far off.

Zasalamel remembered the abyss that had opened before him. [illegible] become. Half himself, half something not himself, he supposed. Though he had [illegible] experience. And yet, being able to observe the nature of the swords up close [illegible] that knowledge, surely next time, he would be able to bend Soul Calibur and Soul Edge to his will.

Yet someone stood between him and that goal, the man Zasalamel [illegible] from his sleep deep within the spirit sword with strength [illegible] of the spirit sword, Zasalamel knew who the man was [illegible] Zasalamel also came to a realization. He had been [illegible] "We who know of the sword's power must never wield it" [illegible] merely been worried their weapon would be used for evil [illegible] the Hero King, may be able to summon forth the [illegible]

Fascinating, Zasalamel thought.

Such a mighty being was a worthy foe to stand between [illegible] stretched to the ends of eternity, he would [illegible] Then, he would chase history from the [illegible] to the world, and lead humanity [illegible] What he did, he did for the sake of [illegible] future, his destined world.

Kafziel

This great scythe bears the name of an ancient Angel of Death, and Zasalamel never parts with it. After every reincarnation, he takes Kafziel in hand to serve his purpose. The beginnings of this icon of Death are unclear; all we can know for sure is that like its master, it has returned to life countless times. In the vast annals of history left to us, we find here and there figures who are almost certainly Zasalamel, always wielding the telltale scythe.

Master and blade, both witnesses to an eternity of happenings on earth. Considering the many people who have fallen victim to the weapon, its name seems quite appropriate.

Own Style

The skill with which Zasalamel swings his great scythe was refined over his many lives, but was originally passed down from his tribe.

His tribe can trace their history to the birth of the Spirit sword. He hails from an ancient tribe that was tasked with the protection of Soul Calibur. But the tribe had a law that stated that "any man who was to touch the sword will never be allowed to touch it again."

This giant knight who had left so many legends behind him also had many dramatic endings to his life as well... Could he not sense the secret maneuvers that happened in the shadows? The tribe which guards the Spirit Sword will continue forever. However, that cold blade may still live inside the banished one, Zasalamel alone.

Command List

Signature Techniques

Name	Command	Attack Level	Damage	Notes
Damnation of Ereshkigal	⇨ⒶⒷ	High, High	14, 10	Combos on counter-hit, leaves Zasalamel back-to-back
Judgement of Nergal	⇦Ⓐ During Counter-Hit Ⓑ (Just) ⇩ or ⇧Ⓐ	High, Sp.Mid, Throw	16, 5, 10	Requires Just Frame input just after 2nd hit of first attack
Marduk's Scythe of Conviction	⬃ⒷⒷⒶ	Mid, Mid, High, Sp.Mid	13, 16, 20	Combos on counter-hit
Enkidu's Bravery	⇨ⓀⒷ	High, Mid	15, 20	Combos naturally
Shamhat's Allure	While Crouching Ⓚ	Low	10	Leaves Zasalamel in crouching state
Nergal's Talon	→ⒷⒷ	Mid, Low	16, 17	Combos naturally
Prayer to Belit-ili (Draw)	← or ↙ or ↖Ⓑ⇦	Mid	30	Launches
Wrath of Tiamat	→Ⓐ+Ⓑ	Mid	42	Knocks down

Horizontal Attacks

Name	Command	Attack Level	Damage	Notes
Chained Sickle of Shamash	ⒶⒶ	High	10, 12	Combos naturally
Damnation of Ereshkigal	⇨ⒶⒷ	High, High	14, 10	Combos on counter-hit, leaves Zasalamel back-to-back
Hook of Namtar	⬂ⒶⒷ	Mid, Mid	14, 18	Combos naturally, knocks down on counter-hit
Mutter of Bashm	⇩Ⓐ	Sp.Low	10	
Talon of Zu	⬃ⒶⒷ	Low, Low	18, 18	Combos naturally, knocks down
Ilabrat's Sapara	⇦Ⓐ	High, Sp.Mid	16, 5	Combos naturally
Judgement of Nergal	⇦Ⓐ During Counter-Hit Ⓑ (Just) ⇩ or ⇧Ⓐ	High, Sp.Mid, Throw	16, 5, 10	Requires Just Frame input just after 2nd hit of first attack
Roar of Nergal	⇦Ⓐ During Counter-Hit Ⓑ (Just) Ⓑ	High, Sp.Mid, Throw	16, 5, 10	Requires Just Frame input just after 2nd hit of first attack
Mutter of Bashm	While Crouching Ⓐ	Sp.Low	10	
Great Scythe of Shamash	While Rising Ⓐ	High	18	Spins foe
Great Scythe of Shamash (Draw)	While Rising Ⓐ⇦	High	18	Spins foe, pulls them close
Shamash the Just	Jumping Ⓐ	Low	20	Leaves Zasalamel in crouching state
Shamash's Glance	Backturned Ⓐ	High	12	
Sin's Glare	While Crouching Backturned Ⓐ	Low	14	Leaves Zasalamel in crouching state

Vertical Attacks

Name	Command	Attack Level	Damage	Notes
Ea's Twin Hammers	ⒷⒷ	Mid, Mid	10, 10	Combos naturally
Ea's Twin Hammers (Draw)	ⒷⒷ⇦	Mid, Mid	10, 20	Combos naturally, pulls foe close
Adoration of Gilgamesh	ⒷⓀ	Mid, Mid	12, 16 (18)	Combos naturally, does extra damage with Just Frame input
Curse of Nergal	⇨ⒷⒶ	Mid, High	20, 20	Combos naturally, backturns foe
Paean to Ishtar	⬂Ⓑ	Mid	20	Launches, input ⇦ immediately to draw them closer
Ea the Grand Ruler	⇩Ⓑ	Mid	14	Leaves Zasalamel in crouching state
Ea the Grand Ruler (Draw)	⇩Ⓑ⇦	Mid	20	Pulls foe close, leaves Zasalamel in crouching state
Marduk's Scythe of Conviction	⬃ⒷⒷⒶ	Mid, Mid, High, Sp.Mid	13, 16, 20	Combos on counter-hit
Sacred Rite of Ishtar	⇦Ⓑ	Mid	10	
Sacred Rite of Ishtar (Additional attack)	⇦Ⓑ During Counter-Hit Ⓑ (Just)	Mid, Mid, High	12, 10, 6	Combos naturally, launches
Ea the Grand Ruler	While Crouching Ⓑ	Mid	14	
Grand Air (Draw)	While Crouching Ⓑ⇦	Mid	20	Pulls foe close
Prayer to Ishtar	While Crouching ⬂Ⓑ	Mid	26	Launches
Belit-Sheri's Spear	While Rising Ⓑ	Mid	15, 30	Combos naturally, knocks down
Belit-Sheri's Condemnation	While Rising Ⓑ⇨	Mid	15, 8	Combos naturally, knocks foe away
Anu the Radiant	Jumping Ⓑ	Mid	24	
Ea's Glance	Backturned Ⓑ	Mid	14	
Ea's Glare	While Crouching Backturned Ⓑ	Mid	14	Leaves Zasalamel in crouching state

Kick Attacks

Name	Command	Attack Level	Damage	Notes
Will of Gilgamesh	ⓀⓀ	High, Low	10, 10	Combos naturally
Enkidu's Bravery	⇨ⓀⒷ	High, Mid	15, 20	Combos naturally
Lugalbanda's Protection	⬂Ⓚ	Mid	15	
Shamhat's Allure	⇩Ⓚ	Low	10	Leaves Zasalamel in crouching state
Wisdom of Utnapishtim	⬃Ⓚ	Low	14	
Siduri's Warning	⇦Ⓚ	Mid	20	
Shamhat's Allure	While Crouching Ⓚ	Low	10	Leaves Zasalamel in crouching state
Devotion to Ninsun	While Rising Ⓚ	High	16	Sideturns foe
Enkidu the Valiant	Jumping Ⓚ	High	20	Knocks down
Gilgamesh's Glance	Backturned Ⓚ	High	16	
Shamhat's Glare	While Crouching Backturned Ⓚ	Low	12	Knocks down, leaves Zasalamel in crouching state

Simultaneous Press

Name	Command	Attack Level	Damage	Notes
Tiamat's Frenzy	Ⓐ+Ⓑ	Mid, Mid, Mid	14, 16, 20	Last 2 hits combo naturally, all hits combo on counter-hit
Marduk's Thunder	⇨Ⓐ+ⒷⒷ	Mid, Mid, Mid	10, 10, 25	First 2 hits combo naturally, all hits combo on counter-hit
Marduk's Thunder (Hold)	⇨Ⓐ+ⒷⒷ	Mid, Mid, Mid	10, 10, 35	First 2 hits combo naturally, 3rd hit is Guard Break
Offering to Kishar	⇦Ⓐ+Ⓑ	High	36	Hit throw against airborne foes
Command of Tiamat	Ⓑ+Ⓚ	Mid	12	Crumples and taunts on counter-hit
Breath of Mushussu	⇨Ⓑ+Ⓚ	High, Sp.Mid	15, 5	Combos naturally, 2nd hit is Guard Break
Judgement of Nergal	⇨Ⓑ+Ⓚ During Counter-Hit Ⓑ ⇩ or ⇧Ⓐ	High, Sp.Mid, Throw	18, 5, 3, 2, 2, 14	Requires Just Frame Ⓑ input during 2nd hit
Roar of Nergal	⇨Ⓑ+Ⓚ During Counter-Hit ⒷⒷ	High, Sp.Mid, Throw	18, 5, 3, 2, 2, 11	Requires Just Frame Ⓑ input during 2nd hit
Asushunamir's Spear	⇩Ⓑ+Ⓚ	Low	28	
Asushunamir's Spear (Hold)	⇩Ⓑ+Ⓚ	Low	28	Causes crumple
Confession to Lahamu	⇦Ⓑ+Ⓚ	Mid, Mid	20, 20	Launches, combos on counter-hit
Adad's Great Shears	Backturned Ⓑ+Ⓚ	Mid, Mid	16, 20	Combos on counter-hit, 2nd hit is Guard Break
Adad's Great Shears (Hold)	Backturned Ⓑ+Ⓚ	Mid, Mid	18, 35	Combos on counter-hit, 2nd hit is Guard Break
Anshar's Halberd	Ⓐ+Ⓚ	High	35	Guard Break, spins foe
Taunt	Ⓚ+Ⓖ			

8-Way Run

Name	Command	Attack Level	Damage	Notes
Sin's Execution Scythe	➡ or ⬊ or ⬈Ⓐ	Mid	28 (26)	
Nergal's Anguish	⬇ or ⬆Ⓐ	High	24	Sidesteps and sideturns foe
Adad's Sickle Sword	⬅ or ⬋ or ⬉Ⓐ	High, Sp.Mid	16, 5	Combos naturally
Judgement of Nergal	⬅ or ⬋ or ⬉Ⓐ During Counter-Hit Ⓑ ⇩ or ⇧Ⓐ	High, Sp.Mid, Throw	18, 5, 6, 2, 2, 21	Requires Just Frame Ⓑ input during 2nd hit
Roar of Nergal	⬅ or ⬋ or ⬉Ⓐ During Counter-Hit ⒷⒷ	High, Sp.Mid, Throw	18, 5, 6, 2, 2, 15	Requires Just Frame Ⓑ input during 2nd hit
Nergal's Talon	➡ⒷⒷ	Mid, Low	16, 17	Combos naturally
Ea's Judgment	⬊ or ⬈Ⓑ	Mid	28	Knocks down
Ea's Judgment (Draw)	⬊ or ⬈Ⓑ⇦	Mid	26	Knocks down and pulls foe close
Lilitu's Needle	⬇ or ⬆Ⓑ	Low	16	
Prayer to Belit-ili	⬅ or ⬋ or ⬉Ⓑ	Mid	26	Knocks down
Prayer to Belit-ili (Draw)	⬅ or ⬋ or ⬉Ⓑ⇦	Mid	30	Launches
Triumph of Gilgamesh	➡ or ⬊ or ⬈Ⓚ	High	21	Knocks down
The Ark of Utnapishtim	⬇ or ⬆ⓀⓀ	High, High	10, 10	Combos naturally, knocks down
Enkidu's Frenzy	⬋ or ⬉Ⓚ	Low	14	Leaves Zasalamel in crouching state
Enkidu's Karma	⬅Ⓚ	High	28	Knocks down
Wrath of Tiamat	➡Ⓐ+Ⓑ	Mid	42	Knocks down
Blessing for Lahamu	➡Ⓑ+Ⓚ	Mid	26	Launches
Tiamat's Rampage	⬅Ⓑ+Ⓚ	Mid	16, 16, 30	Unblockable, combos naturally, knocks down
Urshanabi's Crossing	While Running Ⓚ	Low	26	Knocks down

Throws

Name	Command	Attack Level	Damage	Notes
Ereshkigal the Ruthless	Ⓐ+Ⓖ	Throw	48	Ⓐ to break throw
Kingu the Sly Lord	Ⓑ+Ⓖ	Throw	45	Ⓑ to break throw
Ea of the Abyss	Left Side Throw	Throw	52	Ⓐ or Ⓑ to break throw
Apsu the Origin	Right Side Throw	Throw	60	Ⓐ or Ⓑ to break throw
Marduk the Tempest	Back Throw	Throw	57	

Combos

⇙Ⓑ⇦, ⇦Ⓐ + Ⓑ	
4 hits, 52 damage	
Ⓐ + Ⓚ, ⇨Ⓐ + ⒷⒷ	
4 hits, 64 damage	
While crouching ⇙Ⓑ, ⇨⇨Ⓐ + Ⓑ	
2 hits, 61 damage	
➡Ⓑ + Ⓚ, ⇦Ⓐ + Ⓑ	
4 hits, 58 damage	
Ⓐ + Ⓚ, ⇨Ⓐ + Ⓑ (recoverable stun), ⇙Ⓑ (wall hit), ⇨ⒷⒶ	
7 hits, 74 damage, ends with enemy back-turned in corner	
Counter-hit ⇦Ⓑ + Ⓚ, back-turned Ⓑ + Ⓚ	
4 hits, 62 damage	
Counter-hit ⇦ⒷⒷ (Just), back-turned Ⓑ + Ⓚ	
5 hits, 58 damage	

Close Range

Zasalamel fights quite unlike any other combatant. He comes equipped with a vast suite of multi-hit attacks that snag enemies and drag them close on contact. Many of his attacks are unsafe from retaliation if guarded. However, the unusual, staggered nature of many of his strikes means that he's often guarded incorrectly, and he scores counter-hits during built-in gaps in his sequences. Nevertheless, simply because the enemy might guard correctly and retaliate with quick strikes, close range is not Zasalamel's forte. Like most characters, he has Ⓐ and Ⓑ strings to stop sidestepping and crouching opponents: the Twin Blades of Shamash (ⒶⒶ) and Ea's Twin Hammers (ⒷⒷ←). But neither is safe if blocked. In close range, you can use the Adoration of Gilgamesh (ⒷⓀ) as a slightly safer, slightly higher-damage replacement for Ea's Twin Hammers. And there's even a Just Frame version for extra damage—hit Ⓚ with perfect timing. But this move isn't completely safe if guarded. You can use the Hook of Namtar (↘ⒶⒷ) to stop side movement in close, and its awkward motion might even bait sidesteps or score counter-hits between the first and second attacks. Marduk's Thunder (→Ⓐ + ⒷⒷ or Ⓑ) is a powerful attack. This three-stage linear sequence combos on counter-hit and is actually safe from counterattack if guarded, a rare trait for Zasalamel's close-range options. If you wish, you can delay the third hit into a Guard Break to make sure your foe is paying attention. Keep Paean to Ishtar (↘Ⓑ←) in mind to snag crouching foes. This launcher pops the opponent up into the air, where you can juggle quickly with either ←Ⓐ + Ⓑ or →→Ⓐ + Ⓑ. The second choice sends Zasalamel flying over your foe's head and leaves him in a back-turned state, where he can access his Spark of Marduk (Ⓑ + Ⓚ or Ⓑ+Ⓚ). This is a two-part mid attack, the second hit of which is a Guard Break that can be charged! After juggling with →→Ⓐ + Ⓑ, Zasalamel is in position to use this attack. Finally, note ⓀⒼ up close. Basic attacks can often be canceled by pressing Ⓖ quickly. Zasalamel's guard-canceled Ⓚ is one of the most exaggerated-looking guard cancels in the game. If your opponent knows that most of Zasalamel's attacks can simply be blocked and punished, he or she may play more passively. Use ⓀⒼ to get your foe to clam up, and then throw him.

Mid Range

Zasalamel is safer from mid range. Even if his attacks are technically unsafe when guarded, he's likely be too far away for the enemy to take advantage. The Blessing for Lahamu (⇨Ⓑ+Ⓚ) is a leaping launcher useful from mid range for the same reason as ↘Ⓑ: to nail careless or crouching foes before juggling them. Surprisingly, it's not as vulnerable to counterattack as even some of Zasalamel's basic standing strings. Besides launching moves, →ⒷⒶ is a useful poke string from mid range against crouching foes. It hits mid-to-high and back-turns the enemy on hit, granting Zasalamel huge advantage to go for a back throw or launcher. To deter circular movement, use Anshar's Halberd (Ⓐ+Ⓚ), a high-striking, surprisingly fast circular Guard Break. If it hits, you can link Marduk's Thunder for a 4-hit combo. The mid-hitting Great Scythe of Shamash (⇨Ⓐ) is also good for stopping sidesteps without giving the enemy a way out through crouching. It's vulnerable to attack if guarded, so be sure to use it from the edge of its range. For a low option, try Nergal's Talon (⇨ⒷⒷ), a mid-to-low hitting scythe drag that's difficult to block, and it's safe if guarded.

Long Range

Zasalamel has a sweet spot in mid range where all of his attacks are useful and are less vulnerable than at close range. At long range, many of these moves no longer reach. But he still has a few tools. Tiamat's Rage (⇨Ⓐ+Ⓑ) is a forward-flipping scythe spin that floors the enemy with a mid strike. While it's usually useful in juggles or against waking opponents, it can also serve as a long-distance poke if the enemy is careless at whiffing attacks. Zasalamel has a great long-distance sweeping sequence in ↙ⒶⒷ. Both hits are low, the opponent is dragged closer on a successful hit, and the sequence is safe to counterattack if blocked. Also, if the enemy blocks the first hit and then tries to retaliate, the second hit launches him into the air in prime position for a juggle. Keep in mind Zasalamel's Unblockable Tiamat's Rampage (⇦Ⓑ+Ⓚ). While it's unusually telegraphed, you can easily cancel it by tapping Ⓖ. Simply starting this attack and then canceling it from long range forces your enemy to take some sort of evasive action, preventing the foe from doing whatever else he had in mind. Canceling it frequently can also bait your opponent, possibly increasing the chance of a successful hit when you don't cancel it!

Special Tactics

Okizeme: Anti-Wakeup

Zasalamel has great options against a floored opponent. Mix up your foe as he or she rises with either the Ⓐ+Ⓚ Guard Break, the ↙ⒶⒷ sweep, or the ⇨Ⓑ+Ⓚ launcher. The first two punish opponents who try to rise and guard high, while the launcher punishes those who rise and guard low. Also, ⇨Ⓐ+Ⓑ is good against floored foes. It strikes your opponent's body on the ground if he or she doesn't get up quickly. It also floors your foe again if he or she rises and does anything other than guard high. If your enemy is wary of these options, Zasalamel can simply guard cancel Ⓚ, then throw.

Stab Happy

Zasalamel's attacks can best be described as unconventional. His many scythe strikes frequently hit as they retract, dragging foes along the blade for two or three hits. Great examples include ←Ⓐ, ↘ⒶⒷ, ↙ⒶⒷ, →Ⓑ+Ⓚ, and ←Ⓑ+Ⓚ. When these moves are successful, Zasalamel is usually close to his foe and sitting on a significant advantage, so use the opportunity to stage a follow-up attack, such as going for a launcher or a throw.

Algol

Our birth is but a sleep and a forgetting:
The soul that rises with us, our life's star,
Hath had elsewhere its setting,
And cometh from afar...

"Intimations of Immortality," William Wordsworth (1770 - 1850)

Bio

Age:	Frozen in time
Birthplace:	An ancient dynasty whose name has been lost to history
Height:	Whatever he wills it to be
Weight:	Whatever he wills it to be
Birth Date:	Meaningless now
Blood Type:	Only pure power courses through him
Weapon:	Assimilated Soul Calibur & Soul Edge
Weapon Name:	Soul Calibur & Soul Edge
Discipline:	Command of the Flow of Power
Family:	All in the past

Algol

Clean. [illegible]

The Hero King was a great man, but he was [illegible]

period, the evil sword had reduced the [illegible]

But alas, with [illegible]

As for Soul Edge, by the time the [illegible]

return to the world someday [illegible]

own sins, he wished [illegible] to create a "spirit sword." [illegible]

purifying the shards of Soul Edge that remained, the King [illegible]

At least, that is how the legend goes.

But is it what really happened? The elaborate carvings [illegible] gifted historians can stare at a statue's front [illegible] from every angle, and still [illegible] and ultimately survive the rigors of history.

Rest assured, though, herein lies the legend's truth.

The Hero King chose for the ritual to take place in the Tower of Glory, [illegible] earlier. Using every last ounce of his life and strength, the king [illegible] ritual. And at its base, in the carnage, the king's subjects found [illegible] had ended in failure.

However, at least one man had seen that this would happen, a sage who had [illegible] ambition. He wanted to be the strongest, he wanted to be [illegible] that, if it brought peace to the world. But just because those [illegible] sword found at the base of the tower actually contained the soul of the king himself. [illegible] and thirst for power had come to rest within the blade. If someone weak in spirit were to try to wield that weapon...

"This sword is even more dangerous than the last," thought the sage.

Though the newborn blade's limitless power had not yet been [illegible] stop Soul Edge should it return. After much consideration, in the end the sage decided to carry on as the Hero King [illegible]

The sage and the king's few closest advisors sealed the king's soul securely inside the blade and attempted to [illegible] of two treasures to accomplish this: a "rod that absorbs all power," to strengthen the sword, and a [illegible]

As the sage and the royal advisors toiled in the Tower of Glory, the sword gradually took on the [illegible] could be called a spirit sword, they decided to take the fledgling blade out of the tower. Its spirit power [illegible] nurtured for many long years. And above all else, Algol's soul must be kept contained. [illegible] disappeared into the shadows of history, leaving the people with these final words: "The Hero King has [illegible] To keep it from falling into the wrong hands and prepare it for the coming of Soul Edge. [illegible]"

And so the Hero King, Algol, slept for many years. None disturbed him. It was as if he slumbered [illegible] death-like state, with naught but the endless universe of his consciousness surrounding him. The spirit [illegible] history, and while there may have been times the clamor brought Algol drifting up out of the abyss of sleep [illegible] Not even once.

Then, almost an eternity later, came the sixteenth century.

When the two swords first came into mystical contact with each other in the Embrace of Souls, the Hero King [illegible] the guardians of the spirit sword had fashioned for him. As Algol slept, Soul Edge's [illegible] turbulent world, the clang of weapons, blood raining down. The endless cycle of war and strife [illegible] until at long last, he woke.

But immediately after that, the two swords crashed together one last time in a violent [illegible] resting place. Half-soul, half-mind (and only half-awake), Algol nonetheless craved [illegible] sword, he began to look for a way to manifest himself in the tangible world. After [illegible] to do it.

Without warning, an enormous tower appeared in Ostrheinsburg. The Tower of Glory [illegible] tremendous power, it had been reconstructed as a Tower of Remembrance. [illegible] physical form. But his return was not perfect; his new body was made of [illegible] Retaining this form consumed much of the power he had stolen, and if it ran out, the tower and the Hero King [illegible] like a mirage.

Algol needed more power. Very soon, the spirit sword and the cursed sword would [illegible] his own. He knew his overwhelming desire would resonate fiercely with the two blades and [illegible]

"Come to me! Show me your power!"

The desire for battle filled Algol's heart. He had absolute confidence in his [illegible] His feelings were the same as they had been during the days when he had ruled the land.

How much had thousands of years of oblivion changed the heart of Algol, the Hero King [illegible] who had challenged Soul Edge and sought a more righteous weapon. This new Algol [illegible] And if he managed to claim either, there was no question he would become the greatest [illegible] would conquer the world.

Atop the Tower of Remembrance, Algol waited to see who would come. Not that it mattered, [illegible] would be powerful. And once they had revealed that power, they would [illegible]

Soul Calibur and Soul Edge

The pure power of Soul Calibur and Soul Edge gives the resurrected Algol physical form in this world. Despite being under his command, their essential nature remains unchanged. Thus, Algol is able to devour souls and take their power.

The Hero King longs for the days when the fight was everything and each day was spent proving his might. Battle has quite literally become his daily nourishment, and each victory only makes him tougher.

Flow of Power Method

Although he was resurrected, Algol is still no human. It is made up of the malice that Soul Edge has accumulated over thousands of years. Although Soul Calibur is charged with the mission of correcting the imbalance, it is still just a part of Soul Edge.

Power courses in a torrent through his body. Algol uses his tenacious spiritual power to hold back the enormous power that would destroy all. By controlling all of this power, he is not held back by any normal boundaries and can use any fighting technique he can imagine. Equipped with a battle sense that can only be likened to great kings of ancient times, he can turn any part of his body into a blade and can attack the enemy's very soul.

It would be no exaggeration to say that Algol exists simply to maintain his high and unassailable position.

Command List

Signature Techniques

Name	Command	Attack Level	Damage	Notes
Alnilam Wezen	⇨ⒶⒶⒷ	High, High, Mid	10, 8, 18	Combos naturally, launches
Suhail Sheratan	⇨⇩⇘ⒶⒷⓀ	High, Mid, Mid	16, 20, 20	Combos naturally, knocks down
Thalthah Qarn	⇨ⒷⒷⒷ	High, Mid, Mid	14, 10, 20	First 2 hits combo naturally, all hits combo on counter-hit, 3rd hit crumples
Alshain Najm	⇨⇩⇘Ⓑ	Mid	30	Launches
Eltanin Nath (Menancing Eye) (Hold)	⇨🅐+🅑	Sp.Mid	15	Fires slow linear orb
Marfic Eltanin Nath (Hold)	⇩Ⓐ+Ⓚ During Hit 🅐+🅑	Low Sp.Mid	20, 10	1st hit knocks down
Metallah Mufrid	➡ⒷⒶ	Mid, Mid	12, 15	Combos naturally, causes spinning knockdown
Nath Tawr	↘ or ↗Ⓑ	Mid	26	Launches
Sham Gienah	➡Ⓐ+Ⓑ	Mid, Mid, Mid, Mid	4x10	Combos naturally, knocks down
Albali Alkes	⇨⇨Ⓐ+Ⓖ	Throw	65	Ⓐ to break throw, leaves Algol backturned

Horizontal Attacks

Name	Command	Attack Level	Damage	Notes
Chertan Aladfar	ⒶⒶ	High, High	10, 12	Combos naturally
Qadim Thuban	ⒶⒷ	Mid	30	Causes back slide
Alnilam Wezen	⇨ⒶⒶⒷ	High, High, Mid	10, 8, 18	Combos naturally, launches
Theemin Lesuth	⇘ⒶⒶ	Mid, Mid	18, 22	Combos naturally, both hits cause crumple
Hadar Saiph	⇩Ⓐ	Sp.Low	10	Leaves Algol in crouching state
Saiph Caph	⇙Ⓐ	Low	18	
Mirfak Aladfar	⇦ⒶⒶ	High, High	16, 20	Combos naturally, 2nd hit is Guard Break, leaves Algol backturned
Alshain Nizk	⇨⇩⇘ⒶⒷ	High, Mid	16, 20	Combos naturally, knocks down
Suhail Sheratan	⇨⇩⇘ⒶⒷⓀ	High, Mid, Mid	16, 20, 20	Combos naturally, knocks down
Hadar Saiph	While Crouching Ⓐ	Sp.Low	10	Leaves Algol in crouching state
A rab Saiph	While Rising Ⓐ	High	20	Sideturns foe
Alrakis Saiph	Jumping Ⓐ	High	24	
Adhil Caph	Backturned Ⓐ	High	12	
Alioth Saiph	While Crouching Backturned Ⓐ	Sp.Low	12	Leaves Algol in crouching state

Vertical Attacks

Name	Command	Attack Level	Damage	Notes
Beemin Acubens	ⒷⒷ	Mid, Mid	14, 16,	Combos naturally
Thalthah Qarn	⇨ⒷⒷⒷ	High, Mid, Mid	14, 10, 20	First 2 hits combo naturally, all hits combo on counter-hit, 3rd hit crumples
Ras Algethi	⇘ⒷⒷ	Mid, Mid	26, 30	Combos naturally, 1st hit launches, 2nd hit knocks down
Ras Algethi ~Qamar I'klil	⇘Ⓑ⇦⇙⇩⇘⇨	Mid	26	Launches, flips forward
Matar Acubens	⇩Ⓑ	Mid	16	Leaves Algol in crouching state
Awwal Qarn	⇙Ⓑ	Mid	20	Causes crumple
Qarn Eltanin Nath	⇦Ⓑ During Hit Ⓐ+Ⓑ	High Sp.Mid	12, 10	Combos naturally
Qarn Eltanin Nath (Hold)	⇦Ⓑ During Hit 🅐+🅑	High Sp.Mid	12, 10	
Alshain Najm	⇨⇩⇘Ⓑ	Mid	30	Launches
Hadar Acubens	While Crouching Ⓑ	Mid	16	Leaves Algol in crouching state
Qadim Sulafat	While Crouching ⇘Ⓑ	Mid	18	Leaves Algol in crouching state
Alruccaba Vega	While Crouching ⇧Ⓑ	Mid	20	Knocks down
Alruccaba Vega (Hold)	While Crouching ⇧🅑	Mid	30	Guard Break, causes back flop
Haris Shaula	While Rising Ⓑ	Mid	22	Launches
Alrakis Vega	Jumping Ⓑ	Mid	22	
Adhil Acubens	Backturned Ⓑ	Mid	16	
Alioth Acubens	While Crouching Backturned Ⓑ	Mid	18	Leaves Algol in crouching state

Throws

Name	Command	Attack Level	Damage	Notes
Alphard Maliki	Ⓐ+Ⓖ	Throw	55	Ⓐ to break throw
Mirzam Kochab	Ⓑ+Ⓖ	Throw	55	Ⓑ to break throw
Mufrid I'klil	Left Side Throw	Throw	65	Ⓐ or Ⓑ to break throw
Gienah Meissa	Right Side Throw	Throw	60	Ⓐ or Ⓑ to break throw
Sadalmelek Alchiba	Back Throw	Throw	68	
Albali Alkes	⇨⇨Ⓐ+Ⓖ	Throw	65	Ⓐ to break throw, leaves Algol backturned

Simultaneous Press

Name	Command	Attack Level	Damage	Notes
Alaraph Achernar	Ⓐ+Ⓑ	Mid	30	Crumples
Eltanin Nath (Menancing Eye)	⇨Ⓐ+Ⓑ	Sp.Mid	15	Fires linear orb
Eltanin Nath (Menancing Eye) (Hold)	⇨🅐+🅑	Sp.Mid	15	Fires slow linear orb
Eltanin Nath (Heavenly Gaze)	⇩Ⓐ+Ⓑ	Sp.Mid	10	Fires downward orb
Eltanin Nath (Fearless Reflection) (Hold)	⇩🅐+🅑	Sp.Mid	10	Fires slow downward orb
Eltanin Nath (Fearless Reflection)	⇧Ⓐ+Ⓑ	Sp.Mid	20	Fires upward orb
Eltanin Nath (Water Mirror) (Hold)	⇧🅐+🅑	Sp.Mid	20	Fires slow upward orb
Rastaban Nath (Dual Wings)	⇦Ⓐ+Ⓑ	Sp.Mid	10	Fires orbs laterally
Rastaban Nath (Dual Wings) (Hold)	⇦🅐+🅑	Sp.Mid	10	Fires slow orbs laterally
Alphecca I'klil Nath	⇩⇙⇦Ⓐ+Ⓑ	Mid	60	Unblockable, huge orb
Eltanin Nath (Call of Earth)	While Crouching Ⓐ+Ⓑ	Sp.Mid	15	Fires low orb
Eltanin Nath (Call of Earth) (Hold)	While Crouching 🅐+🅑	Sp.Mid	15	Fires slow low orb
Alaraph Achernar	Backturned Ⓐ+Ⓑ	Mid	30	Knocks down, leaves Algol backturned
Alnair Alterf	Ⓑ+Ⓚ	Mid, Mid, Mid, Mid, Mid	10x5	Combos naturally, knocks down, strikes behind Algol
Shams Asad	⇨Ⓑ+Ⓚ	Mid	20	Fires large stationary orb
Alaraph Anchentenar	⇩Ⓑ+Ⓚ	Mid, Mid	20, 30	Combos naturally, knocks down
Almach Najm	⇧Ⓑ+Ⓚ	Mid	20	Knocks down, hit throw against airborne foes
Almach Najm (Attack Throw)	Against Airborne Foe ⇧Ⓑ+Ⓚ		50	
Sadalsuud Markab	⇦Ⓑ+Ⓚ	Mid		
Alnair Alterf	Backturned Ⓑ+Ⓚ	Mid, Mid, Mid, Mid, Mid	5x10	Combos naturally, knocks down, strikes behind Algol
Sabik Sheratan	Ⓐ+Ⓚ			Teleports behind foe
Thuban Duhr	⇖ or ⇧ or ⇗Ⓐ+Ⓚ	Mid	30	Leaps upward
Thuban Kalb Nath	⇖ or ⇧ or ⇗Ⓐ+Ⓚ ⒷⒷⒷⒷ	Sp.Mid, Sp.Mid, Sp.Mid, Sp.Mid	10x4	Leaps upward, fires 4 orbs
Shams Qadam	⇖ or ⇧ or ⇗ Ⓐ+ⓀⓀ	Mid	20	Knocks down
Marfic Eltanin Nath	⇩Ⓐ+Ⓚ During Hit Ⓐ+Ⓑ	Low, Sp.Mid	20, 10	1st hit knocks down
Marfic Eltanin Nath (Hold)	⇩Ⓐ+Ⓚ During Hit 🅐+🅑	Low, Sp.Mid	20, 10	1st hit knocks down
Sabik Sheratan	Backturned Ⓐ+Ⓚ			Teleports behind foe, remains backturned
Taunt	Ⓚ+Ⓖ			

8-Way Run

Name	Command	Attack Level	Damage	Notes
Alderamin Lesuth	→ or ↘ or ↗Ⓐ	High	30	
Adib Saiph	↓ or ↑Ⓐ	Mid	26	Knocks down on normal hit, causes crumple on counter-hit
Qamar Aladfar	↙ or ↖Ⓐ	Low	22	Causes spinning fall
Alya Said	←Ⓐ	High	28	Backturns foe
Metallah Mufrid	→ⒷⒶ	Mid, Mid	12, 15	Combos naturally, causes spinning knockdown
Nath Tawr	↘ or ↗Ⓑ	Mid	26	Launches
Murzim Sinn	↓ or ↑Ⓑ	Mid	34	Guard Break, causes low crumple
Thaniah Qarn	↙ or ↖Ⓑ	Low	20	
Khawwar Sinn	←Ⓑ	Mid	24	Knocks down on counter-hit
Kaffaljidhma Ruchbah	→ or ↘ or ↗Ⓚ	Mid	18	
Dubhe Rukbat	↓ or ↑Ⓚ	High	22	Spins foe
Wezen Rigil	↙ or ↖Ⓚ	Low	16	
Hamal Marfic	←Ⓚ	Mid	18	
Sham Gienah	→Ⓐ+Ⓑ	Mid, Mid, Mid, Mid	4x10	Combos naturally, knocks down
Rastaban Nath (Double Threat)	↓ or ↑Ⓐ+Ⓑ	Sp.Mid, Sp.Mid	10, 10	Fires two orbs while strafing
Almach Waraqa	→Ⓑ+Ⓚ	Mid, Mid	20, 20	Combos naturally, knocks down
Sham Scheat	While Running Ⓚ	Low	26	Knocks down

Kick Attacks

Name	Command	Attack Level	Damage	Notes
Menkar Pherkad	Ⓚ	High	14	
Menkar Scheat	Ⓚ⇨	Mid	10	
Dhih Tarf	⇨ⓀⓀ	High, Mid	12, 16	Combos naturally
Dhih Tarf (Hold)	⇨Ⓚ🅚	High, Mid	12, 26	Combos on counter-hit, 2nd hit is Guard Break that causes crumple
Pherkad Rigil	⇘Ⓚ	Mid	16	
Fil Qadam	⇩Ⓚ	Low	14	Leaves Algol in crouching state
Tawr Rigil	⇙Ⓚ	Low	16	
Nimr Marfic	⇦Ⓚ	High	18	Spins foe
Nimr Marfic (Hold)	⇦🅚	High	22	Spins foe
Cursa Scheat	While Crouching Ⓚ	Low	14	
Theemin Menkar	While Rising Ⓚ	Mid	16	
Theemin Menkar (Hold)	While Rising 🅚	Mid, High	12, 18	Combos naturally, knocks down
Algorab Skat	Jumping Ⓚ	Mid	20	Knocks down
Adhil Menkar	Backturned Ⓚ	High	16	
Alioth Cursa	While Crouching Backturned Ⓚ	Low	16	Knocks down

Qamar I'klil

Name	Command	Attack Level	Damage	Notes
Qamar I'klil	⇦⇙⇩⇘⇨			Flips forward
I'klil Akrab	Qamar I'klil Ⓐ	High	30	Causes backward crumple
I'klil Uf"uwan	Qamar I'klil Ⓑ	Mid	22	Knocks down
I'klil Shams	Qamar I'klil Ⓚ	Low	18	Knocks down
Thuban Algieba Nath	Qamar I'klil Ⓐ+Ⓑ	Sp.Mid	15	Fires downward orb
Thuban Algieba Nath (Hold)	Qamar I'klil 🅐+🅑	Sp.Mid	15	Fires slow downward orb
Alnair Zubra	Qamar I'klil Ⓑ+Ⓚ	Mid	30	Knocks down, leaves Algol backturned

Combos

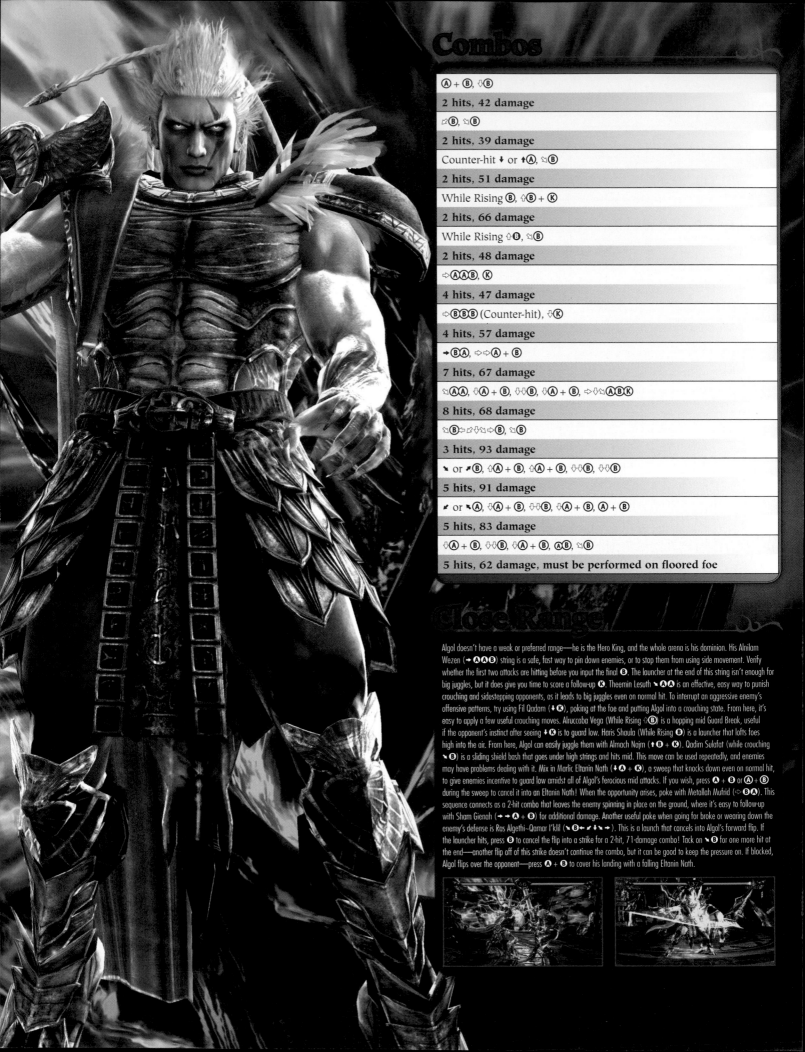

Ⓐ + Ⓑ, ⇩Ⓑ	2 hits, 42 damage
⬃Ⓑ, ⬂Ⓑ	2 hits, 39 damage
Counter-hit ↓ or ↑Ⓐ, ⬂Ⓑ	2 hits, 51 damage
While Rising Ⓑ, ⇧Ⓑ + Ⓚ	2 hits, 66 damage
While Rising ⇧Ⓑ, ⬂Ⓑ	2 hits, 48 damage
⇨ⒶⒶⒷ, Ⓚ	4 hits, 47 damage
⇨ⒷⒷⒷ (Counter-hit), ⇩Ⓚ	4 hits, 57 damage
→ⒷⒶ, ⇨⇨Ⓐ + Ⓑ	7 hits, 67 damage
⬂ⒶⒶ, ⇩Ⓐ + Ⓑ, ⇩⇩Ⓑ, ⇩Ⓐ + Ⓑ, ⇨⇩⬂ⒶⒷⓀ	8 hits, 68 damage
⬂Ⓑ⇦⬃⇩⬂⇨Ⓑ, ⬂Ⓑ	3 hits, 93 damage
↘ or ↗Ⓑ, ⇧Ⓐ + Ⓑ, ⇧Ⓐ + Ⓑ, ⇩⇩Ⓑ, ⇩⇩Ⓑ	5 hits, 91 damage
↙ or ↖Ⓐ, ⇩Ⓐ + Ⓑ, ⇩⇩Ⓑ, ⇩Ⓐ + Ⓑ, Ⓐ + Ⓑ	5 hits, 83 damage
⇩Ⓐ + Ⓑ, ⇩⇩Ⓑ, ⇩Ⓐ + Ⓑ, ⒶⒷ, ⬂Ⓑ	5 hits, 62 damage, must be performed on floored foe

Close Range

Algol doesn't have a weak or preferred range—he is the Hero King, and the whole arena is his dominion. His Alnilam Wezen (→ ⒶⒶⒷ) string is a safe, fast way to pin down enemies, or to stop them from using side movement. Verify whether the first two attacks are hitting before you input the final Ⓑ. The launcher at the end of this string isn't enough for big juggles, but it does give you time to score a follow-up Ⓚ. Theemin Lesuth ↘ⒶⒶ is an effective, easy way to punish crouching and sidestepping opponents, as it leads to big juggles even on normal hit. To interrupt an aggressive enemy's offensive patterns, try using Fil Qadam (↓Ⓚ), poking at the foe and putting Algol into a crouching state. From here, it's easy to apply a few useful crouching moves. Alruccaba Vega (While Rising ⇧Ⓑ) is a hopping mid Guard Break, useful if the opponent's instinct after seeing ↓Ⓚ is to guard low. Haris Shaula (While Rising Ⓑ) is a launcher that lofts foes high into the air. From here, Algol can easily juggle them with Almach Najm (↑Ⓑ + Ⓚ). Qadim Sulafat (while crouching ↘Ⓑ) is a sliding shield bash that goes under high strings and hits mid. This move can be used repeatedly, and enemies may have problems dealing with it. Mix in Marlic Eltanin Nath (↓Ⓐ + Ⓚ), a sweep that knocks down even on normal hit, to give enemies incentive to guard low amidst all of Algol's ferocious mid attacks. If you wish, press Ⓐ + Ⓑ or Ⓐ+Ⓑ during the sweep to cancel it into an Eltanin Nath! When the opportunity arises, poke with Metallah Mufrid (⇨ⒷⒶ). This sequence connects as a 2-hit combo that leaves the enemy spinning in place on the ground, where it's easy to follow-up with Sham Gienah (→→Ⓐ + Ⓑ) for additional damage. Another useful poke when going for broke or wearing down the enemy's defense is Ras Algethi~Qamar I'klil (↘Ⓑ←↙↓↘→). This is a launch that cancels into Algol's forward flip. If the launcher hits, press Ⓑ to cancel the flip into a strike for a 2-hit, 71-damage combo! Tack on ↘Ⓑ for one more hit at the end—another flip off of this strike doesn't continue the combo, but it can be good to keep the pressure on. If blocked, Algol flips over the opponent—press Ⓐ + Ⓑ to cover his landing with a falling Eltanin Nath.

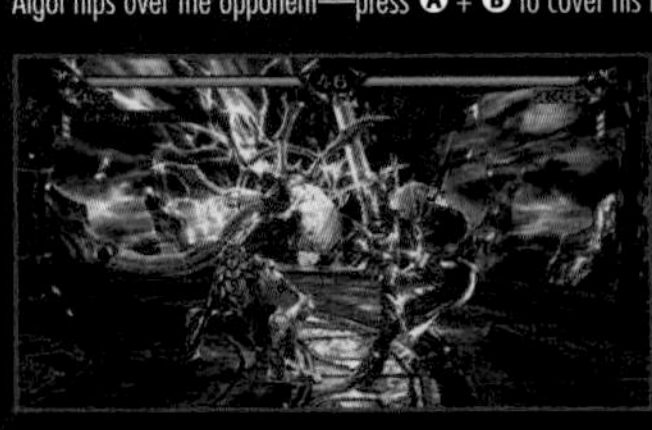

Mid Range

Algol remains powerful at mid range. His ↓🅐 + 🅚 Marlic sweep has enough reach to remain useful from several steps away, serving as a low-hitting knockdown tool. Qamar Aladfar (⬃ or ⬂🅐) is another low option that leads to devastating juggles (consult the Combo section). Nath Tawr (⬂ or ⬀🅑) is Algol's best launcher, lofting foes higher than While Rising 🅑 while working from further away. Mirfak Aladfar (← 🅐🅐) is a high, two-part backspin slash that snags enemies from a dramatic range; if guarded, the second hit is actually a Guard Break! This sequence can be crouched or avoided through side movement, but its erratic motion sometimes catches foes even when they dodge with sidesteps. From a few steps away, Algol can also employ his Eltanin Nath both as a linear attack and to deter side movement. Firing two lateral Eltanin Nath with ← 🅐 + 🅑 and then performing a mid linear attack, like Alaraph Achernar (🅐 + 🅑, calling forth facsimiles of both Soul Edge and Soul Calibur), insures that the enemy briefly has no attack angle to get at Algol.

Long Range

At long range, Algol reigns supreme. Eltanin Nath give him ranged options that no character can completely manage. Algol can simply play keep away with these projectiles if he chooses, making the battle extremely difficult for the other party. Eltanin Nath can be guarded, but they cannot be Repelled or Parried, forcing the enemy to dodge them or deal with them defensively. His upward jump (↑🅐 + 🅚) can lead to either a barrage of four Eltanin Nath directed downward (press 🅑 repeatedly) or a quick dive kick that knocks down (🅚). Algol also has options to get in close quickly whenever he feels the need. Sabik Sheratan (🅐 + 🅚) causes Algol to teleport quickly to the other side of the foe, while ← ↙ ↓ ↘ → executes the Qamar I'klil leap, carrying him a tremendous distance. By inputting commands just after he leaves the ground, he can use the jump aggressively and as a means of transportation. Use 🅑 to make him land with I'klil Ul'uwan, a mid that knocks down the enemy. Choosing 🅚 makes him land and transition into I'klil Shams, a low-hitting slide kick. Using 🅐 + 🅑 after jumping causes Algol to perform Thuban Algieba Nath (a downward Eltanin Nath) just before landing, in the direction from which he just leapt. This is useful if you actually jump over the enemy. Finally, 🅑 + 🅚 makes Algol land with his Alnair Zubra attack, a fierce attack directed behind Algol. All of Algol's leaping attacks are also useful up close, as you can cancel his ↘🅑 Ras Algethi into the leap. If the enemy is launched, press 🅑! If blocked, use the 🅐 + 🅑 or 🅑 + 🅚 options.

You can make both the forward jump and the teleport safer by firing slow Eltanin Nath beforehand, forcing the enemy to think twice before attacking Algol. Eltanin Nath can actually enhance Algol's attacks, too. His forward-leaping attacks usually just floor the enemy on contact. However, if they strike just as an Eltanin Nath does, you can score combos that are not possible otherwise. For example, toss a slow Eltanin Nath and then time ← ↙ ↓ ↘ → 🅚 to strike just before the orb. If you execute this correctly, the enemy is bounced into prime juggle position directly above Algol.

Special Tactics

Okizeme: Anti-Wakeup

Algol is in a very comfortable position against a grounded opponent. His ↓🅐 + 🅚 Marlic sweep lets him strike low, either kicking opponents while they're down or sending them back into the dirt if they rise and guard high in fear of mids. Similarly, ↓🅚 strikes downed opponents. Though the damage is poor, Algol is placed in a crouching state from which he can easily go for While Rising 🅑 to launch or While Rising ⇧Ⓑ to Guard Break just as foes rise in front of him. Murzim Sinn (⇩ or ⇧🅑) is a mid-hitting Guard Break that serves as a triple option. It strikes downed enemies, nails opponents who rise and guard low (perhaps in fear of ↓🅐 + 🅚), and Guard Breaks those who rise and block high. If it hits, the foe will crumple—bounce him or her into the air with ↓🅐 + 🅑 and juggle from there. It's also vital to many juggle combos because of the special floored stun it causes against airborne foes.

You can also use Eltanin Nath against floored foes. Simply place Eltanin Nath above and around them while they rise, forcing them to guard. Eltanin Nath can also lead to big-damage juggles against grounded foes. For this reason, it's smart to use slow, downward-aimed ↓Ⓐ + Ⓑ Eltanin Nath on occasion. If these lazy projectiles strike a floored character, he or she gets bounced up in the air, ready to be juggled!

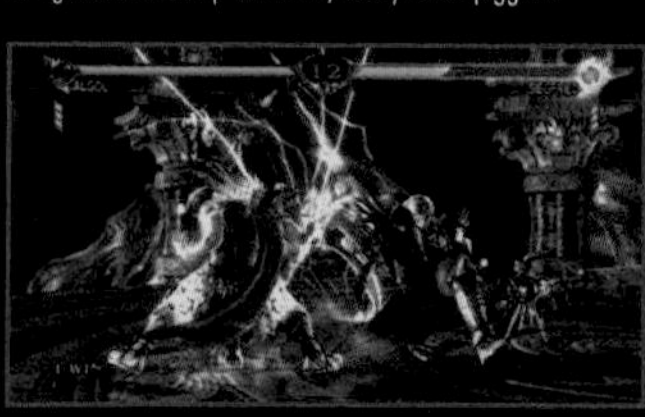

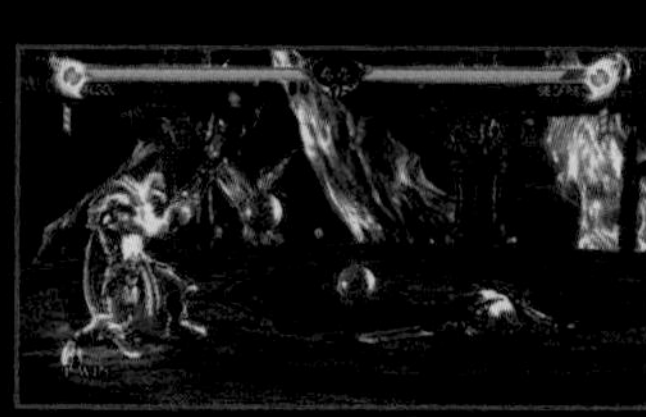

Special Tactics (cont.)

Eltanin Nath

While characters like Ivy and Astaroth have long reach, and others like Cervantes and The Apprentice even have arena-length projectiles, no one commands long distance quite like Algol. He can summon up to four Eltanin Nath at a time—if more are summoned, the first one fired simply disappears. These orb-like projectiles continue until they hit a wall and then proceed to bounce around the stage. They dissipate eventually but, until they do, they represent a threat to the opponent and a boon for Algol. Eltanin Nath control space, act as shields against attacking Algol from certain angles, and can extend or create combos. Most variations can be fired quickly or slowly. Unless you're firing a quick Eltanin Nath for a reason, slow versions tend to be more effective, as they present a longer-lasting impediment to the enemy. Algol can fire a few slow, linear ones and simply travel behind them, getting in for free. He can fire pairs laterally, covering his flanks and giving enemies something to think about before they try sidestepping or using 8-Way Run. He can fire then teleport behind the enemy (🅐 + 🅚), or use his Qamar I'klil leap (← ↙ ↓ ↘ →). Essentially, Eltanin Nath make everything Algol does safer, and you should keep them onscreen as much as possible. Downward Eltanin Nath that strike fallen foes even bounce them up into the air, in position to get juggled! Finally, it's possible to juggle enemies with numerous Eltanin Nath in certain areas. If you launch the enemy with ⬂ or ⬀🅑 near a wall, at a sharp angle to it rather than facing it, juggle repeatedly with ↑🅐 + 🅑 Eltanin Nath. Depending on the positions of Algol and the enemy relative the wall, it's possible to score ten or more consecutive hits with vertical orbs! You should be close to a wall, but not so close that ⬂ or ⬀🅑 scores a wall hit. Also, do not face the wall straight on, or the upward orbs simply the end juggle by scoring a wall hit. Eltanin Nath place the enemy into a juggle state that prevents Aerial Control, and the wall keeps the foe from drifting away too quickly, as they would if you attempted this in the middle of the arena. If your friends cry foul, remind them that they can always pick Algol as well—then be sure to hide any nearby blunt objects!

Eltanin Nath Type	Eltanin Nath Command	Notes
Menacing Eyes	⇨(Ⓐ+Ⓑ or 🅐 + 🅑)	Algol fires a fast or slow linear Eltanin Nath
Heavenly Gaze	⇩Ⓐ+Ⓑ	Algol fires an Eltanin Nath downward
Fearless Reflection	⇩🅐 + 🅑	Algol fires a slow Eltanin Nath downward
Fearless Reflection	⇧Ⓐ+Ⓑ	Algol fires an Eltanin Nath upward
Water Mirror	⇧🅐 + 🅑	Algol fires a slow Eltanin Nath upward
Call of Earth	While crouching (Ⓐ+Ⓑ or 🅐 + 🅑)	Algol crouches and fires a fast or slow Eltanin Nath
Dual Wings	⇦(Ⓐ+Ⓑ or 🅐 + 🅑)	Algol fires two fast or slow Eltanin Nath outward
Rastaban Nath (Double Threat)	↓ or ↑Ⓐ+Ⓑ	Algol strafes and fires 2 Eltanin Nath
Marlic Eltanin Nath	⇩Ⓐ+Ⓚ(Ⓐ+Ⓑ or 🅐 + 🅑)	Algol sweeps and fires a fast or slow Eltanin Nath
Qarn Eltanin Nath	⇦Ⓑ(Ⓐ+Ⓑ or 🅐 + 🅑)	Algol strikes high then fires a fast or slow Eltanin Nath
Thuban Kalb Nath	⬁ or ⇧ or ⬀Ⓐ+Ⓚ, ⒷⒷⒷⒷ	Algol leaps and fires up to 4 Eltanin Nath
Thuban Algieba Nath	⇦⬃⇩⬂⇨(Ⓐ+Ⓑ or 🅐 + 🅑)	Algol leaps forward and fires an Eltanin Nath in the opposite direction
Alphecca I'klil Nath	⇩⬃⇦Ⓐ+Ⓑ	Algol leaps and fires one huge Unblockable Eltanin Nath

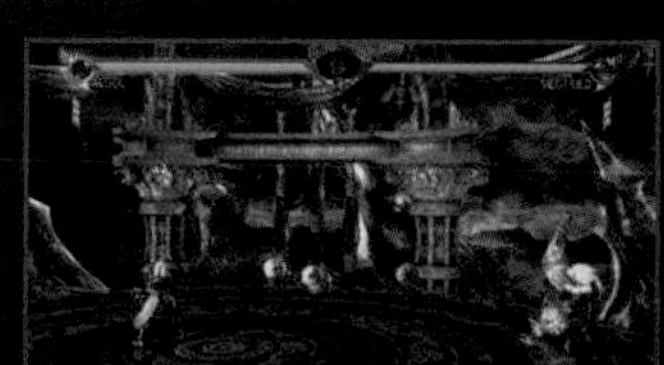

Angol Fear

Once, there was a man who, despondent over life and the world, entreated the distant heavens to curse all existence at the moment of his death.

While alive, the man had distinguished himself as a prophet. By achieving a momentary connection to the vast annals of history that slept in the abyss of the cosmos, he was able to learn about events from the past and future in great detail. But, mantled as he was in deep despair and resentment, the man used his supernatural link in an attempt to send his regrets into the core of the universe. Until, at last, he made a pact with the Will of the Cosmos: destroy the degenerate planet Earth.

Without giving the matter any further thought, the Will of the Cosmos made its decision. The world would be destroyed, after a five-hundred-year grace period. During that time the Earth's doomed inhabitants might try to change their wicked ways.

However, no sooner had the man died, than Earth received a visitor. And while she was a marshal in direct service to the Will of the Cosmos—invested with the power to punish on Its behalf—she had not, strictly speaking, been tasked with the Earth's destruction. Instead, she descended upon Earth to investigate. Five hundred years from now, when the one tasked to destroy the planet arrived, would he or she find Earth—this land where swords spirit and cursed waged endless battle—worthy?

And depending on what she found there might be no need to wait for the appointed executioner to arrive. The day she judged Earth unworthy, why, that would be the day of judgment.

Bio

Age:	About 14,800
Birthplace:	Core of the Macrocosm
Height:	5'10" (variable)
Weight:	1.44 tons (variable) *Adaptation to Earth incomplete
Birth Date:	Beyond reckoning on the Earth's calendar
Blood Type:	None
Weapon:	Planet
Weapon Name:	Lucifer's Spear Black
Family:	Psycho-familial unit (Her kind is not communal by nature.)

Command List

Signature Techniques

Name	Command	Attack Level	Damage	Notes
Whirling Fangs	ⒶⒶⒷ	High, High, Mid	12,10,20	Fully combos on counter-hit
Strangling Slash	⬂Ⓐ	Mid	20(22)	Causes stun on counter-hit from max range
Thrusting Fang	⇨ⒷⒷ	Mid, Mid	15(20),30	1st attack causes recoverable stun on normal hit from max range, 2nd hit always stuns.
Check Mate	⇦ⓀⒷ	Mid, Mid	14,16	2nd attack stuns on hit. Deflects high attacks.
Double Hilt	⇨Ⓑ+Ⓚ	High, High	10,16	Stuns on counter-hit
Lightning Fang	While Crouching ⬃Ⓑ	Low	15	
Liquid Rising	While Crouching ⬃ⓀⓀ	Low, Mid	14,18	2nd attack stuns on hit
Lightning Thrust	➡Ⓑ	High	15(25)	Stuns and inflicts additional damage from max range

Vertical Attacks

Name	Command	Attack Level	Damage	Notes
Meteor Shower	ⒷⒷⒷ	Mid, Mid, Mid	15, 15(18), 28	2nd attack causes recoverable stun at max range. 3rd attack stuns on hit.
Retreating Divide	Ⓑ⇦Ⓑ	Mid, High	15, 14	Shifts into back jump on hit
Hidden Fang	⇨ⒷⒶ	Mid, Low	15(20), 20	1at attack causes recoverable stun at max range
Thrusting Fang	⇨ⒷⒷ	Mid, Mid	15(20), 30	1st attack stuns at max range. 2nd attack stuns on hit.
Lifting Heavens	⬂Ⓑ	Mid	19	Launches at max range
Thrust Kick	⬂ⒷⓀ	Mid	20	
Air Parting	⇩Ⓑ	Mid	16	
Dancing Fang Sweep	⬃ⒷⒶ	Mid, Low	14, 24	
Back Step Fang	⬃ⒷⒷ	Mid, High	14, 10	
Dancing Blade Kick	⬃ⒷⓀ	Mid, Mid	14, 30	
Retreating Fang	⇦Ⓑ	High	13	Shifts into back dash on counter-hit
Air Parting	While Crouching Ⓑ	Mid	16	
Lightning Fang	While Crouching ⬃Ⓑ	Low	15	
Lifting Wing	While Rising Ⓑ	Mid	20(25)	Launches at max range
Giant Air Parting	Jumping Ⓑ	Mid	28 or 32 or 36	Damage varies depending on direction jumped in
Reverse Air Parting	Backturned Ⓑ	Mid	17	
Reverse Air Parting	While Crouching Backturned Ⓑ	Mid	16	

Horizontal Attacks

Name	Command	Attack Level	Damage	Notes
Whirling Fangs	ⒶⒶⒷ	High, High, Mid	12,10,20	Fully combos on counter-hit
Hilt Kick	⇨ⒶⓀ	Mid, High	10, 18	2nd attack stuns on counter-hit
Strangling Slash	⬂Ⓐ	Mid	20(22)	Stuns on counter-hit from max range
Root Fang	⇩Ⓐ	Low	10(20)	Deals additional damage from max range
Fang Sweep	⬃Ⓐ	Low	18(26)	
Shadow Step Slice	⇦Ⓐ	Low	14	
Knee Slicer	While Crouching Ⓐ	Sp.Low	12	
Twin Fang Strike	While Rising ⒶⒶ	Mid Mid	14, 16	
Giant Fang	Jumping Ⓐ	Mid	24 or 26 or 28	Damage varies depending on direction jumped in
Reverse Dance Blade	Backturned Ⓐ	High	14	
Reverse Biting Strike	While Crouching Backturned Ⓐ	Low	22	

Kick Attacks

Name	Command	Attack Level	Damage	Notes
Snap Kick	Ⓚ	High	12	
Celestial Kick	⇨Ⓚ	Mid, High	10, 20	Deflects mid attacks
Belly Crush Spin Kick	⬂ⓀⓀ	Mid, High	12, 15	2nd hit stuns on counter hit
Earth Kick	⇩Ⓚ	Low	12	
Rock Breaker	⬃Ⓚ	Low	16	
Check Mate	⇦ⓀⒷ	Mid, Mid	14, 16	2nd attack stuns on hit, deflects high attacks
Check Mate (Delay)	⇦ⓀⒷ	Mid, Mid	14, 16	2nd attack stuns on hit, deflects high attacks
Earth Kick	While Crouching Ⓚ	Low	12	
Liquid Rising	While Crouching ⬃ⓀⓀ	Low, Mid	14, 18	2nd attack stuns on hit. 1st attack doesn't knockdown from max range.
Shattering Kick	While Rising Ⓚ	Mid	24	
Giant Rising Kick	Jumping Ⓚ	Mid	12 or 14 or 16	Damage varies depending on direction jumped in
Reverse Snap Kick	Backturned Ⓚ	High	14	
Reverse Earth Kick	While Crouching Backturned Ⓚ	Low	12	

Simultaneous Press

Name	Command	Attack Level	Damage	Notes
Double Fang	Ⓐ+Ⓑ	High, High	10, 30	
Fang Barrage	⇨Ⓐ+Ⓑ	Mid, Mid, Mid	10, 10, 30	
Opening Treasure	⇘Ⓐ+Ⓑ	Low	10, 5, 12	Shifts into hit throw at close distances. Input Ⓐ to escape second attack.
Sweeping Blade	⇩Ⓐ+Ⓑ	Low	30(36)	
Sweeping Blade (Cancel)	⇩Ⓐ+ⒷⒼ			
Holding Treasure	⇙Ⓐ+Ⓑ	Low	10, 7, 7, 21	Shifts into hit throw at close distances. Input Ⓑ to escape final attack.
Dancing Crane	⇦Ⓐ+ⒷⒶⒷ	Mid, Mid, Mid, Mid, High, Mid	10, 10, 15, 25	Final hit Guard Breaks
Dancing Crane (Cancel)	⇦Ⓐ+ⒷⒶⒷⒼ	Mid, Mid, Mid, Mid, Mid	10, 10, 15	
Heavy Crane	⇦Ⓐ+Ⓑ ⇦Ⓐ+Ⓑ	Mid x8	10, 10, 11, 14, 14, 14	
Seong's Crushing Long Blade	⇗Ⓐ+Ⓑ	Mid	140	Unblockable
Seong's Quick Long Blade(Cancel)	⇗Ⓐ+ⒷⒼ			
Seong's Quick Long Blade	⇗Ⓐ+ⒷⒷ	Mid	50	Guard Break
Radiant Wing	⇧Ⓐ+Ⓑ	Mid	25	
Heaven's Wheel	Ⓑ+Ⓚ	Mid, Mid	19, 28	1st attack stuns on hit
Double Hilt	⇨Ⓑ+Ⓚ	High, High	10, 16	2nd attack stuns on counter hit
Glory Fan	⇩Ⓑ+Ⓚ	Mid, Mid, Mid	15, 26	1at attack stuns on hit
Glory Fan (Cancel)	⇩Ⓑ+ⓀⒼ	Mid	15	Stuns on hit
Retreating Sands	⇦Ⓑ+Ⓚ	Mid, Mid, Mid	10, 10, 10	Final hit stuns. Deflects mid vertical attacks
Leaping Horse Vault	⇖ or ⇧ or ⇗ Ⓑ+Ⓚ⇦ or ⇨ Ⓑ ⇦ or ⇨ Ⓑ	Mid, Mid, Mid	18, 16, 23	
Leaping Horse Vault	Backturned Ⓑ+Ⓚ	Mid	20	Stuns on hit
Circular Blade Kick	Ⓐ+Ⓚ	Mid	30	
Dark Curtain	⇩Ⓐ+Ⓚ	Low, High	16, 25	
Power Fang Sweep	⇦Ⓐ+Ⓚ	Low, Low	10, 20	
Taunt	Ⓚ+Ⓖ			

8-Way Run

Name	Command	Attack Level	Damage	Notes
Circular Heaven Slash	→Ⓐ	Mid	18(28)	Inflicts additional damage from max range
Heavy Willow Divide	↘ or ↗ⒶⒶ	Mid, Mid	15, 26	
Strangling Flower	↓ or ↑Ⓐ	High, High	10, 12	
Sparrow Sweep	↙ or ↖Ⓐ	Low	14	
Wing Cross	←ⒶⒶ	Mid, Low	14, 16	
Wing Cross (Delay)	←ⒶⒶ	Mid, Low	14, 16	
Lightning Thrust	→Ⓑ	High	15(25)	Inflicts additional damage and stuns on hit from max range
Lifting Heavens	↘ or ↗Ⓑ	Mid	19	Launches on hit from max range
Shadow Fang	↓ or ↑Ⓑ	Low	10(18)	
Top Hammer Fang	↙ or ↖Ⓑ	Mid	15(25)	Stuns on hit. Deals additional damage and longer stun from max range.
Roaring Heaven	←Ⓑ	Mid	20(36)	Guard Break
Circular Heaven Spin Kick	→ⓀⓀⓀ	Mid, Mid, High	14, 12, 20	1st hit causes recoverable stun on counter hit, 3rd hit causes stun on counter hit
Circular Heaven Spin Kick (Delay)	→ⓀⓀⓀ	Mid, Mid, High	14, 12, 20	1st hit causes recoverable stun on counter hit, 3rd hit causes stun on counter hit
Spring Splash Esoterica	↘ or ↗ⓀⒷ	Mid, Mid	12, 20	
Dark Sweep	↓ or ↑Ⓚ	Low	18	
Thunder Kick	← or ↙ or ↖Ⓚ	Mid	26	Stuns on hit
Spinning Divide	→Ⓐ+Ⓑ	Mid	34	
Power Spinning Divide	←Ⓐ+Ⓑ	Mid	44	
Sliding	While Running Ⓚ	Low	26	

Throws

Name	Command	Attack Level	Damage	Notes
Dropping Embrace	Ⓐ+Ⓖ	Throw	55	Input Ⓐ to escape
Crushing Soul	Ⓑ+Ⓖ	Throw	50	Input Ⓑ to escape
Riding Mustang	Left Side Throw	Throw	65	Same button as throw (Ⓐ or Ⓑ) to escape
Mi-na Frankensteiner	Right Side Throw	Throw	60	Same button as throw (Ⓐ or Ⓑ) to escape
Stalk Cutter	Back Throw	Throw	68	Same button as throw (Ⓐ or Ⓑ) to escape

Combos

⇘Ⓑ, ⇧Ⓐ + Ⓑ
2 hits, 51 damage, ↘Ⓑ must hit from max distance
⇘Ⓑ, ⇨⇨Ⓑ, While Crouching ⇗Ⓑ
3 hits, 63 Damage, →→Ⓑ must hit from max range
Counter-hit ⇦ⓀⒷ, ⇘ⓀⓀ, ⇘⇘ⓀⒷ
6 hits, 66 Damage
⇨Ⓚ, ⇨ⒶⓀ
4 hits, 49 Damage
⇦Ⓑ + Ⓚ, ⇘Ⓑ
4 hits, 43 Damage
⇦Ⓐ + Ⓚ, ⇘Ⓑ
3 hits, 44 Damage
Counter-hit ⇨Ⓚ, ⇧Ⓐ + Ⓑ
3 hits, 46 Damage
Counter-hit ⇨⇨ⓀⓀⓀ, ⇨Ⓑ + Ⓚ, ⇘⇘ⓀⒷ
7 hits, 65 Damage
↙ or ↖Ⓑ, ⇨⇨ⓀⓀⓀ, ⇨Ⓑ + Ⓚ, ⇘⇘ⓀⒷ
8 hits, 71 Damage, replace ↘↘ⓀⒷ with ↘Ⓑ against small characters

Close Range

Angol Fear shares the same move set as Seong Mi-na. The only difference is that her active attack range is slightly shorter, making her far less effective from further away. This leaves Angol Fear at a disadvantage, because Seong's move set revolves around keeping her foe at a distance. Because of this, your active fighting range is slightly closer than Seong's. This doesn't change the move set's biggest weakness though, which is close-range fighting. Your goal is to keep your attacks short and to look for a moment to move out to mid or long range. Use abilities like the high-deflecting Checkmate (⇦ⓀⒷ) to counter your enemy's speedy horizontal attacks. If you block one of your opponent's moves, use a back step or Back Step Fang (⇙ⒷⒷ) to escape to your ideal fighting distance (long or middle range).

Mid Range

Use Angol Fear's ⒶⒶ string to deter sidesteps and to stop mid attacks preemptively. Chain into its Ⓑ extension (ⒶⒶⒷ) if it connects on a counter-hit. If ⒶⒶ is blocked, use ⇦ⓀⒷ as a defensive measure to stop high attacks, or chain into the ⒶⒶⒷ extension if your opponent isn't looking for the third hit. When your enemy is looking to crouch under this string, attack with Lifting Heavens (⇘Ⓑ) to launch crouching characters for a combo—juggle your enemy with ⇧Ⓐ+Ⓑ. Another way to deter crouching is to use Thrusting Fang (⇨ⒷⒷ) or Hidden Fang (⇨ⒷⒶ). Both strings start with the same mid attack and end with either a mid or low strike. Mix between both attack types to keep your enemy's guard soft.

Long Range

Smart opponents will circle around your linear attacks, which are your most damaging options. Dissuade their side movements with the Sparrow Sweep (↙ or ↖Ⓐ) or Circular Heaven Slash (→Ⓐ). Replace these attacks with the damage-heavy Heavy Willow Divide (↘ or ↗ⒶⒶ) string when you're certain of a sidestep, though this option is vulnerable when blocked. When your enemy is wary of circular attacks, look for him or her to back away from your striking range. Use Lightning Thrust (→Ⓑ) to counter this reaction, which knocks down on counter-hit and allows for an unavoidable crouching ⇙Ⓑ follow-up.

Special Tactics

Okizeme: Anti-Wakeup

Your most used anti-wakeup mid attack is Wing Cross (←ⒶⒶ). Its mid-to-low hit progression is also difficult to defend against. It leaves Angol Fear in a crouching state, enabling you to follow up with While Rising Ⓚ, a throw, or Liquid Rising (While Crouching ⇙ⓀⓀ). These options are reliable only if the opening string hits, otherwise you're at too great of a disadvantage to safely attack.

Your low attacks of choice are Power Fang Sweep (⇦Ⓐ+Ⓚ) and Dark Curtain (⇩Ⓐ+Ⓚ). The ⇦Ⓐ+Ⓚ attack is safe to retaliation when blocked, but its overall starting period is much longer. It also leads to a short combo consisting of ⇩Ⓐ+Ⓚ, then ⇘Ⓑ. The ⇩Ⓐ+Ⓚ attack inflicts more damage and comes out faster, but the second hit whiffs against crouching opponents, leaving it vulnerable when blocked. Both options are easy to read, in which case use Opening Treasure (⇘Ⓐ+Ⓑ) or Holding Treasure (⇙Ⓐ+Ⓑ). Both of these are special low hits with throw extensions. It's possible for the enemy to escape the throw segments, so vary between both options to keep this from happening.

Varied Range Property

Like Seong Mi-na, many of Angol Fear's moves have stronger properties when performed from maximum range. For example, her ⇘Ⓑ doesn't knock down the enemy if performed at point-blank range. However, it launches the enemy into the air and inflicts more damage if only the very tip of her weapon hits. This makes Angol Fear weaker at close distances. Keep away from your enemy to fight on your best terms.

Ashlotte

Ashlotte Maedel

Maedel

The heathens had been pushed by Astaroth to the brink of annihilation, and the cult's survivors did their best amidst the confusion to preserve their lives. Thus it was that two priests who outlived the struggle came up with this plan: Astaroth, who had brought this great misfortune, must be put down. Since attempts to control the golem—created based on a human being—had ended in failure, then what they needed was a soldier devoid of a soul.

After many months, she (or technically, "it," since the creation was not strictly alive) was complete. An artistic mass of gears and shafts locked together in an intricate and arcane configuration—what the world to come might call a "machine"—made this executioner doll tick, while features of unparalleled grace masked the inorganic stuffing within. However, though she appeared to talk and act just like a real human, they had stripped her of the needless murmurs of emotion, and adapted her to the sole purpose of eradicating the traitor. The heathens had put their all into this "Iron Maiden," pushing their technology to the limit to create a true masterpiece.

Ashlotte emerged beneath the light of the sun and sent tremors through the half-collapsed underground shrine with every movement. At last, unable to bear its own weight, the shrine crumbled into ruin. But not even the resulting roar fazed her. She simply set off across the desert to complete her appointed task, disappearing, at last, into the horizon.

Ashlotte Maedel

Bio

Age:	Recently born
[redacted]	Unknown (Ruins of a nameless, hidden shrine of the Heretical Order Fygul Cestemus)
Height:	4'9"
[redacted]	439 lbs.
Birth Date:	March 9
[redacted]	Sacred oil blessed by incantation
Weapon:	Ax
[redacted]	Krnielk
Family:	The two priests of the heathen cult are her creators.

Command List

Signature Techniques

Name	Command	Attack Level	Damage	Notes
Hades Control	←Ⓐ	High	24	Floors on counter-hit
Poseidon Tide Rush (Attack Throw)	↓↙←Ⓐ	Mid	80	Hit Throw
Hades Ax	ⒷⒷ	Mid, Mid	20, 30	Combos on counter-hit
Bear Fang	←Ⓑ	Mid	20	Knocks down on counter-hit
Dark Tamer	↘ⓀⒶ	Mid, High	18, 36	Combos on counter-hit, 2nd hit knocks down
Titan Ax	Ⓐ+Ⓑ	Mid	25 (48)	Knocks down from long range
Hades Cannon	↓ or ↑Ⓑ	Mid	55 (20)	Launches, does less damage but launches overhead by inputting ↓ or ↑Ⓑ←
Bull Rush	→Ⓚ	Mid	26~48	Knocks down
Wicked Judgement	→↘↓↙←Ⓐ+Ⓖ	Throw	63	Ⓐ breaks throw

Horizontal Attacks

Name	Command	Attack Level	Damage	Notes
Annihilation (Hold)	Ⓐ	High	16	Leaves foe backturned
Annihilation	ⒶⒶ	High, High	16, 24	
Annihilation (Delay)	ⒶⒶ	High, High	16, 24	
Annihilation (Hold)	ⒶⒶ	High, High	16, 24	Leaves foe backturned
Destruction	ⒶⒷ	High, Mid	16, 20	Combos naturally
Destruction (Delay)	ⒶⒷ	High, Mid	16, 20	2nd hit crumples on counter-hit
Grip Shot to Ax Volcano	→ⒶⒷ	High, Mid	10, 20	Combos on counter-hit, 2nd hit launches
Grip Shot to Ax Volcano (Delay)	→ⒶⒷ	High, Mid	10, 20	2nd hit launches
Minotaur Crush	↘Ⓐ	Mid	18	Causes recoverable stun on counter-hit
Hades Break	↓Ⓐ	Low	14	
Discus	↙Ⓐ	Low	25	Knocks down, leaves Ashlotte in crouching state
Double Discus	↙ⒶⒶ	Low, Low	35, 35	Both hits knock down, leaves Ashlotte in crouching state
Discus Breaker	↙ⒶⒷ	Low, Mid	35, 70	1st hit knocks down, 2nd hit is a Guard Break that launches
Hades Control	←Ⓐ	High	24	Floors on counter-hit
Hades Control (Hold)	←Ⓐ	High	24	Leaves foe backturned
Poseidon Tide Rush (Attack Throw)	↓↙←Ⓐ	Mid	80	Hit Throw
Poseidon Tide Rush	↓↙←ⒶⒶⒶⒶⒶⒶ	Mid, Mid, Mid, Mid, Mid Mid	30, 8, 8, 8, 8, 8	Combos naturally
Hades Break	While Crouching Ⓐ	Low	14	Leaves Ashlotte in crouching state
Reverse Spiral Ax	While Rising Ⓐ	High	30	Knocks down
Great Annihilation	Jumping Ⓐ	High	30	Knocks down
Reverse Ax Split	Backturned Ⓐ	Low	18	
Lower Hades Split	While Crouching Backturned Ⓐ	Low	22	Leaves Ashlotte in crouching state

Vertical Attacks

Name	Command	Attack Level	Damage	Notes
Hades Ax	ⒷⒷ	Mid, Mid	20, 30	Combos on counter-hit
Hades Ax (Hold)	ⒷⒷ	Mid, Mid	20, 40	Guard Break, 2nd hit launches
Ax Side Cannon	→Ⓑ	Mid	20	Crumples on counter-hit
Ax Volcano	↘Ⓑ	Mid	32	Launches
Ax Volcano (Hold)	↘Ⓑ	Mid	44	Unblockable, launches
Hades	↓Ⓑ	Mid	20	Leaves Ashlotte in crouching state
Hades (Hold)	↓Ⓑ	Mid	35	Guard Break, leaves Ashlotte in crouching state
Ax Grave	↙Ⓑ	Low	24	Knocks down, leaves Ashlotte in crouching state
Bear Fang	←Ⓑ	Mid	20	Knocks down on counter-hit
Bear Fang (Hold)	←Ⓑ	Mid	45	Knocks down
Dark Split	While Crouching Ⓑ	Mid	22	Leaves Ashlotte in crouching state
Hades Rising	While Rising Ⓑ	Mid	30	
Greater Divide	Jumping Ⓑ	Mid	28	Knocks down
Reverse Dark Split	Backturned Ⓑ	Mid	22	
Lower Dark Split	While Crouching Backturned Ⓑ	Mid	24	Leaves Ashlotte in crouching state

Kick Attacks

Name	Command	Attack Level	Damage	Notes
Moloch's Vise	Ⓚ	High	14	
Valorion	Ⓚ	High	34	Hit Throw
Hades Knee	→Ⓚ	Mid	18	Knocks down on counter-hit
Dark Tamer	↘ⓀⒶ	Mid, High	18, 36	Combos on counter-hit, 2nd hit knocks down
Dark Tamer (Delay)	↘ⓀⒶ	Mid, High	18, 36	Combos on counter-hit, 2nd hit knocks down
Dark Tamer (Hold)	↘ⓀⒶ	Mid, High	38, 36	Combos on counter-hit, 2nd hit knocks down
Dark Tamer (Hold)	↘ⓀⒶ	Mid, Mid	18, 26	
Dark Tamer (Hold)	↘ⓀⒶ	Mid, Mid	38, 26	
Bull Low Kick	↓Ⓚ	Low	10	
Reverse Tamer	↙ⓀⒶ	Low, High	26, 30	Combos on counter-hit, 2nd hit knocks down
Command Kicks	←ⓀⓀ	Mid, Mid, Mid, Mid	15, 15, 15, 15	
Bull Kick	While Crouching Ⓚ	Low	10	Leaves Ashlotte in crouching state
Bull Rush	While Crouching ↘Ⓚ	Mid	28	Knocks down
Bull Rush (Hold)	While Crouching ↘Ⓚ	Mid	31	Launches
Rising Cyclone	While Rising ⓀⒶ	Mid, Low	18, 30	Combos on counter-hit, 1st hit crumpes on counter-hit, 2nd hit knocks down
Great Kick	Jumping Ⓚ	Mid	16	
Reverse Bull Kick	Backturned Ⓚ	High	16	
Lower Sweep	While Crouching Backturned Ⓚ	Low	16	Knocks down, leaves Ashlotte in crouching state

Simultaneous Press

Name	Command	Attack Level	Damage	Notes
Titan Ax	Ⓐ+Ⓑ	Mid	25 (48)	Knocks down from long range
Offering	⇘Ⓐ+Ⓑ	Mid	35	Hit Throw on counter-hit
Offering (Hold)	⇘🅐+🅑	Mid	35	Hit Throw
Breath of Hades	⇦Ⓐ+Ⓑ	Mid	20	Knocks down
Breath of Hades (Hold)	⇦🅐+🅑	Mid	50	Unblockable
Guard Crusher	Ⓑ+Ⓚ	High	20	Leaves foe backturned
Body Splash	⇨Ⓑ+Ⓚ	High	28	Deflects vs. high & mid slashes
Body Splash (Hold)	⇨🅑+🅚	High	38	Deflects vs. high & mid slashes
Hades Crush	⇩Ⓑ+Ⓚ	Mid	15	
Hades Crush ~Maelstrom Divide	↓Ⓑ+ⓀⒶ+Ⓖ	Mid, Throw	15, 30	
Hades Crush ~Hades Destroyer	⇩Ⓑ+ⓀⒷ+Ⓖ	Mid, Throw	15, 25	
Hades Crush ~Bludgeoning Crush	↓Ⓑ+Ⓚ↓Ⓐ+Ⓖ	Mid, Throw	20, 35	
Hades Crush ~Drop of Lava	⇩Ⓑ+Ⓚ⇩Ⓑ+Ⓖ	Mid, Throw	20, 45	
Ax Lower Cannon	⇦Ⓑ+Ⓚ	Low, Low, Low	8, 8, 22	Knocks down, leaves Ashlotte in crouching state
Ax Lower Cannon (Additional attack)	⇦Ⓑ+ⓀⒷ	Low, Low, Low	8, 8, 22, 39	Hit Throw
Flying Divide	⇗Ⓑ+Ⓚ	Mid	45	Knocks down
Flying Divide (Hold)	⇗🅑+🅚	Mid	55	Guard Break
Demented Moon	⇩⇘⇨Ⓑ+Ⓚ	Mid	110	Unblockable, launches
Side Divide	Backturned Ⓑ+Ⓚ	Mid	27	Leaves Ashlotte backturned, crumples on counter-hit
Taunt	Ⓚ+Ⓖ			

8-Way Run

Name	Command	Attack Level	Damage	Notes
Ares Spiral Rage	→ⒶⒷ	Mid, Mid	18, 26	Combos on counter-hit, 2nd hit launches
Ax Blow	↘ or ↗Ⓐ	Mid	26	Causes recoverable stun
Poseidon Crest	↓ or ↑ⒶⒶ	Mid, Mid	16, 16	Combos naturally
Discus	↙ or ↖Ⓐ	Low	25	Knocks down, leaves Ashlotte in crouching state
Hades Divide	←Ⓐ	Mid	20	Leaves foe backturned on normal hit, floors on counter-hit
Hades Divide (Hold)	←🅐	Mid	20	Spins foe
Ax Crash	→Ⓑ	High	35 (45)	Knocks down on counter-hit from long range
Ax Volcano	↘ or ↗Ⓑ	Mid	34	Launches
Ax Volcano (Hold)	↘ or ↗🅑	Mid	44	Unblockable, launches
Hades Cannon	↓ or ↑Ⓑ	Mid	55 (20)	Launches, does less damage but launches overhead by inputting ↓ or ↑🅑⇦
Azazel Tackle	↙ or ↖ⒷⓀ	Mid, Mid	36, 30	1st hit aims off-axis
Canyon Creation	←Ⓑ	Mid	40	Knocks down, leaves Astaroth in crouching state
Canyon Creation (Hold)	←🅑	Mid	70	Unblockable, leaves Astaroth in crouching state
Bull Rush	→Ⓚ	Mid	28	Knocks down
Bull Rush (Hold)	→🅚	Mid	50	Launches
Hades Rush	↘ or ↗Ⓚ	Mid	26	Aims off-axis
Hades Rush (Hold)	↘ or ↗🅚	Mid	19	Aims off-axis, launches
Stamp of Hades	↓ or ↑Ⓚ	Mid	30	
Stamp of Hades (Hold)	↓ or ↑🅚	Mid	28	Launches, causes tremor that staggers nearby foes
Lower Command Kick	← or ↙ or ↖Ⓚ	Mid	30	Crumples on counter-hit, leaves Ashlotte in crouching state
Titan Swing	↓ or ↑Ⓐ+Ⓑ	High	40 (50)	Knocks down, does extra damage from max range
Titan Swing (Hold)	↓ or ↑🅐+🅑	High	60	Unblockable
Sliding	While Running Ⓚ	Low	22	Knocks down

Throws

Name	Command	Attack Level	Damage	Notes
Maelstrom Divide	Ⓐ+Ⓖ	Throw	55	Ⓐ to break throw
Hades Destroyer	Ⓑ+Ⓖ	Throw	50	Ⓑ to break throw
Beat Down	Left Side Throw	Throw	78	Ⓐ or Ⓑ to break throw
On Silent Wings	Right Side Throw	Throw	62	Ⓐ or Ⓑ to break throw
Death Crush	Back Throw	Throw	70	
Plunging Crush	Against Crouching Foe ↘Ⓐ+Ⓖ	Throw	50	Ⓐ to break throw
Flood of Lava	Against Crouching Foe ⇘Ⓑ+Ⓖ	Throw	60	Ⓑ to break throw
Bludgeoning Crush	Against Crouching Foe ↓Ⓐ+Ⓖ	Throw	50	Ⓐ to break throw
Drop of Lava	Against Crouching Foe ⇩Ⓑ+Ⓖ	Throw	60	Ⓑ to break throw
Wicked Judgement	→↘↓↙←Ⓐ+Ⓖ	Throw	63	Ⓐ to break throw
Flight of the Wicked	⇨⇘⇩⇙⇦Ⓑ+Ⓖ	Throw	33	Ⓑ to break throw
Wrath of the Damned	Against Airborne Foe Ⓐ+Ⓖ	Throw	30	
Titan Bomb	Against Airborne Foe ⇩⇧Ⓑ+Ⓖ	Throw	88 (94)	Does more damage with perfect input
Brutal Grasp	Against Downed Foe's Head ⇙Ⓐ+Ⓖ or ⇙Ⓑ+Ⓖ	Throw	30	Leaves foe standing, Ⓐ or Ⓑ to break throw
Wrath of the Damned	Against Downed Foe ⇩Ⓑ+ⓀⒶ+Ⓖ	Mid, Throw	14, 30	
Burial	Against Downed Foe ↓Ⓐ+Ⓚ	Throw	35	

Combos

ⒶⒷ (delay, Counter-hit), ⇩Ⓑ + Ⓖ
2 hits, 84 damage
⇩⇩Ⓑ⇦, ⇩⇧Ⓑ + Ⓖ
2 hits, 90 damage
⇨⇘⇩⇙⇦Ⓑ + Ⓖ, ⇩⇧Ⓑ + Ⓖ
1 hit, 70 damage
⇨⇘⇩⇙⇦Ⓑ + Ⓖ, Ⓐ + Ⓖ (Wall Hit), ⇩Ⓐ + Ⓖ (Wall Hit), ⇙Ⓐ (or Ⓑ) + Ⓖ
5 hits, 88 damage, start with foe's back near wall, leaves foe standing
Counter-hit ⇨Ⓚ, ⇩Ⓐ + Ⓚ
2 hits, 56 damage
←Ⓐ, ⒶⒷ, (pause) ⇙Ⓐ (orⒷ) + Ⓖ
4 hits, 59 damage, leaves foe standing at close range
⇘Ⓑ, ⇩⇧Ⓑ + Ⓖ
2 hits, 112 damage, Unblockable
Ⓑ + Ⓖ (Wall Hit), ⇙Ⓐ (orⒷ) + Ⓖ
3 hits, 80 damage, begin with foe's back near wall, leaves foe standing
⇦⇦Ⓐ, ⇨⇨ⒶⒷ, ⇩⇧Ⓑ + Ⓖ
4 hits, 82 damage
ⒷⒷ, ⇩⇧Ⓑ + Ⓖ
2 hits, 110 damage, delayed Ⓑ must hit
⇙ⒶⒷ, Ⓐ + Ⓖ (Wall Hit), ⇩Ⓐ + Ⓖ (Wall Hit), ⇙Ⓐ (or Ⓑ) + Ⓖ
6 hits, 158 damage, start with Ashlotte's back to wall, delayed Ⓑ must hit
⇩⇘⇨Ⓑ + Ⓚ, ⇩⇧Ⓑ + Ⓖ
2 hits, 180 damage, Unblockable

Close Range

Astaroth's would-be assassin was fashioned from the same cloth—Ashlotte shares her quarry's moves. However, her smaller frame changes her gameplay somewhat; a smaller character means a reduced throw reach and shorter range on attacks. Nevertheless, the same general strategy Astaroth uses can still be applied to Ashlotte with some modifications. As with Astaroth, Ashlotte is lacking at close range, thanks to slow wind-up on most of her significant attacks. If enemies try to overwhelm you in close, use the Hades Knee (⇨Ⓚ) during openings to knock them back, or the Minotaur Crush (⇘Ⓐ) to potentially stun them. If the enemy is aggressive with high attacks, trying to pin Ashlotte down, use the Reverse Tamer (⇙ⓀⒶ) to counter-hit and send your foe flying away. But apply it sparingly; its startup doesn't actually avoid high attacks and it combos only on counter-hit. If the second hit whiffs over a crouching opponent, Ashlotte could be in trouble. An alternative to stop high strings is to use the Rising Cyclone (While Rising ⓀⒶ), a mid-to-low string that combos on counter-hit, doesn't leave Ashlotte vulnerable, and may sweep opponents even if they guard the first hit correctly.

When mounting your offense at close range, use the Grip Shot to Ax Volcano (⇨ⒶⒷ) to stage a mix-up between a throw or a launch attempt. Perform ⇨Ⓐ on its own, then throw against guarding foes. Eventually, they'll try hitting you back after blocking ⇨Ⓐ, allowing you to input ⇨ⒶⒷ to counter-hit them. Hades Ax (ⒷⒷ) is also powerful at close range. Perform it normally several times to condition the opponent. Then perform ⒷⒷ to change the second attack into a Guard Break that bounces your foe into the air if it actually connects. Both Ⓐ+Ⓖ and ⇩⇧Ⓑ+Ⓖ can connect as air throws from this bounce, causing huge damage.

Mid Range

At mid range, quick attacks are less likely to pin Ashlotte. Her Ax Crash (➔Ⓑ) and Ax Grave (⇙Ⓑ) are great pokes from here. Opponents may eat Ax Grave frequently if they're worried about Ashlotte's damaging moves that they must guard or repel while standing. To stop side movement, use ⒶⒶ or Destruction (ⒶⒷ), a high-to-mid 2-hit combo even on normal hit. You can delay the second hit ever so slightly, perhaps baiting a counterattack that you can then counter-hit, leading to a useful stagger. You have several options if you anticipate the foe crouching under the Ax Crash or the first hit of Destruction. You can use one of Ashlotte's leaping anti-crouch throws (⇘Ⓐ or Ⓑ+Ⓖ). Another option is Poseidon Tide Rush, a mid-striking hit throw with a bit of wind-up performed with ⇩⇙⇦Ⓐ. Finally, you can use Ax Volcano (⇘Ⓑ) or Hades Divide (⬅Ⓐ). In particular, the Hades Divide is very important—it snuffs side movement, nails crouching opponents, and you can charge it by holding Ⓐ. If the fully-charged version strikes the enemy, it sends them into a spinning stagger, letting you follow with ⇨⇨ⒶⒷ, ⇩⇧Ⓑ+Ⓖ!

Long Range

Ashlotte shines from long range, where she has an extremely solid mix-up game between circular attacks that always cause knockdowns and are not consistently avoidable via side movement. The Titan Ax (Ⓐ+Ⓑ) is her baseline poke from a distance. It inflicts significant Soul Gauge damage if guarded, and it nails crouching foes or those using 8-Way Run. Opponents worried about the Titan Ax are open to Discus (⇙Ⓐ), an axe sweep that knocks down and can be charged to execute built-in follow-ups. Foes must guard low twice against the double sweep ⇙ⒶⒶ, while ⇙ⒶⒷ is a low-to-mid Guard Break that bounces the enemy if it actually hits, giving you a chance to air throw! Both follow-ups are very fast and hard for opponents to manage if you mix them up well, frequently sprinkling in Titan Ax to remind opponents that it's there. Keep Bull Rush (⇨⇨Ⓚ) in mind as well. The beginning of this mid-hitting shoulder rush, which you can charge for more damage, is easy to confuse with the beginning animation of ⇙Ⓐ or Ⓐ. If the opponent guards low, thinking the Discus sweep is coming, the Bull Rush will bowl them over. With the opponent worried about the combination of Titan Ax, Discus, and Bull Rush, keep Hades Cannon (⬇ or ⬆Ⓑ) ready as well. Like many of Ashlotte's moves, this attack inflicts tons of Soul Gauge damage if blocked, causing enough blockstun to leave Ashlotte totally safe. If it actually hits, this move sends the enemy flying, putting Ashlotte back into her favorite position (far away) and possibly causing a Ring Out.

Special Tactics

Okizeme: Anti-Wakeup

Ashlotte has tools to terrorize rising opponents even from a distance. Titan Ax and Discus both have enough range to put enemies right back on the floor if they guard incorrectly as they rise from a distance. Up close, Ashlotte can use her ground hit throw (⇩Ⓐ+Ⓚ) to haul up foes before smacking them back down. If an opponent is floored with his head near Ashlotte, use ⇙Ⓐ or Ⓑ+Ⓖ to pull him to his feet after you smack him up a bit. This ground throw gives Ashlotte huge advantage but, because she's smaller than Astaroth, a throw attempt after this ground throw will whiff. Instead, make enemies guess between the Hades Knee, Ax Grave, or Discus. The Hades Knee (⇨Ⓚ) will counter-hit anything they try. If you feel a foe will just guard standing, mix in Ax Grave (⇙Ⓑ) to knock him down again, or Discus (⇙Ⓐ) if you feel he'll try to sidestep Ax Grave.

Landing Throws

Throws most often land against opponents that are passive or at a disadvantage. This usually happens after you've conditioned them to guard in certain situations, or after you've blocked their attacks up close. Throws are also useful to snag characters using 8-Way Run, or to catch opponents after they've sidestepped up close. Condition grounded opponents to wake up guarding, afraid of mix-ups between mid and low attacks. Then simply throw them as they rise. Successfully mixing throws into your game also benefits your attacks, as the opponent has one more threat to worry about. Against advanced players who attempt to break throws, mix between grapples that use either Ⓐ or Ⓑ in their commands, adding another layer to the guessing game. Ashlotte (along with Astaroth, her template and prey) has many throws that can lead from one to another, especially near a wall. Her Ⓐ+Ⓖ and ⇩⇧Ⓑ+Ⓖ air throws can create Wall Hits (Ⓐ+Ⓖ is virtually guaranteed if Ashlotte's back is near a wall, while ⇩⇧Ⓑ+Ⓖ must smack the foe into the ground at a slight angle). ⇨Ⓚ, ⇨⇨Ⓚ, ⇘Ⓑ, and counter-hit ⇦⇦Ⓐ are useful attacks that cause Wall Hits, too. And while foes crumple from most Wall Hits, Ashlotte can freely tack on her ⇩ and ⇘Ⓐ+Ⓖ crouch throws. Then, if the foe slumps off the wall with his or her face toward Ashlotte, she can finish with a guaranteed ⇙Ⓐ(or Ⓑ)+Ⓖ ground throw, pulling the foe right back to where they started—between Ashlotte and a wall!

Hades Crush: ⇩Ⓑ + Ⓚ

The mid-hitting stomp ⇩Ⓑ+Ⓚ staggers the enemy if it lands as a counter-hit. It's also one of the only attacks in the game that leads directly into many different throw options. Input Ⓐ+Ⓖ, Ⓑ+Ⓖ, ⇩Ⓐ+Ⓖ, or ⇩Ⓑ+Ⓖ immediately after ⇩Ⓑ+Ⓚ to chain into the desired throw. This move acts as a built-in tick into throw for Ashlotte at close range, and even *guarantees* a follow-up standing throw if the stomp counter-hits, causing big damage. Against floored opponents, ⇩Ⓑ+Ⓚ, Ⓐ+Ⓖ bounces the opponent up off the ground into an air throw!

Kamikirimu
Kamikirimusi

si

Once, during the Heian Period, there was an oni girl whose reckless destruction of the capital caused her and her [illegible] be magically restrained by an onmyodo practitioner. The way she saw it, they were simply following the [illegible] born with. Why did humans have to be so terribly narrow-minded? Still, having been given a thorough [illegible] Kamikirimusi decided to be good and submit to her restraints.

One day, she realized she had control of her body again. The restraints were gone. Merrily, her friends [illegible] had been their place of confinement. But wait, she thought, our captor told us we must stay longer! [illegible] honest by nature as she was, she decided to keep her promise and wait quietly in the pit for the appointed time to come.

Six hundred years passed in this way. Japan had now entered a period of civil war, and nearly all the supernatural [illegible] capital was gone. Kamikirimusi's friends were nowhere in sight; they had either been vanquished, or faded away [illegible] way she was finally free. As she took her first steps, something reached her ears: some power beyond that of [illegible] magical; closer in nature to one of her kind; a great power that could set the world trembling.

Drawn to it, she took another step, then another. New friends were waiting, she could feel it.

Bio

Age:	Over 600
Birthplace:	Kyoto, Japan
Height:	5'0"
Weight:	Unknown
Birth Date:	Unknown
Blood Type:	Unknown
Weapon:	Kanabo
Weapon Name:	Denryu Bakuha
Family:	The spirits she once ran wild with have already been purified. Now she is all alone.

Kamikirimusi

Command List

Horizontal Attacks

Name	Command	Attack Level	Damage	Notes
Slash Cross	ⒶⒶⒷ	High, High, Mid	14, 16, 30	3rd hit stuns
Slash Cross (Delay)	ⒶⒶⒷ	High, High, Mid	14, 16, 30	3rd hit stuns
Slash Cross ~Night Side Stance	🅐	High	14	Shifts to Night Side Stance
Triple Grounder	Ⓐ⇩ⒶⒶ	High, Low, Low	14, 18, 28	
Bloody Hilt	ⒶⒷ	High	22	
Bloody Hilt ~Night Side Stance	Ⓐ🅑	High	22	Shifts to Night Side Stance
Quick Neck Buster	ⒶⒼⒶ	High	30(35)	Guard Breaks. Perform input as fast as possible for additional damage.
Quick Temple Buster	⇨Ⓐ	High	28	
Mail Crusher	⇘ⒶⒶ	Mid, Mid	20, 280	1st attack stuns on counter-hit
Death Grounder	⇘Ⓐ⇩Ⓐ	Mid, Low	20, 26	1st attack stuns on counter-hit
Death Grounder ~Grim Stride	⇘Ⓐ⇩Ⓐ⇨	Mid, Low	20, 26	1st attack stuns on counter-hit. Shifts into Grim Stride.
Jade Slicer	⇩Ⓐ	Low	18	
Shadow Slicer	⇙Ⓐ	Low	32	
Shadow Slicer (Hold)	⇙🅐	Low	52	Guard Breaks
Jade Crusher	⇙ⒶⓀ	High	60	
Shadow Slicer ~Grim Stride	⇙Ⓐ⇨	Low	32	Shifts into Grim Stride
Back Blade	⇦Ⓐ	High	36	Guard Breaks, stuns on hit
Leg Slash	While Crouching Ⓐ	Low	12	
Death Rage	While Rising ⒶⒶ	Mid, Mid	20, 35	
Death Rage ~Grim Stride	While Rising ⒶⒶ→	Mid	20	Shifts to Grim Stride
Fatal Spin Slash	Jumping Ⓐ	High	28 or 30 or 32	Damage varies depending on direction jumped in
Turning Head Slash	Backturned Ⓐ	High	18	
Turning Leg Slash	While Crouching Backturned Ⓐ	Low	14	

Signature Techniques

Name	Command	Attack Level	Damage	Notes
Right Slasher	→ or ↘ or ↗Ⓐ	High	34	
Rook Splitter	↓ or ↑Ⓑ	Mid	40	
Shadow Slicer ~Grim Stride	⇙Ⓐ⇨	Low	32	Shifts to Grim Stride
Ether Splitter ~Grim Stride	↘ or ↗Ⓑ⇨	Mid	21	Shifts to Grim Stride
Grim Launcher ~Night Side Stance	Grim Stride 🅑	Mid	32	Launches on counter-hit
Soul Wave	Grim Stride Ⓐ+Ⓑ	Mid	30	Leaves Kamikirimusi in powered up state
Death Smash ~Night Side Stance	⇘🅑	Mid	18(28)	Shifts to Night Side Stance. Guard Breaks when powered up. Launches and deals additional damage at close distances.
Night Side Stance	While Standing or While Crouching Ⓑ+Ⓚ			
Cannonball Feint ~Night Side Stance	Night Side Stance 🅐	Mid	20	Shifts to Night Side Stance
Skull Chopper	Night Side Stance ⒷⒶ	High	32(42)	Input as fast as possible for additional damage

Vertical Attacks

Name	Command	Attack Level	Damage	Notes
Knight Breaker	ⒷⒷⒷ	Mid, Mid, Mid	15, 12, 27	3rd attack stuns on hit. String fully combos on counter-hit.
Backspin Temple Buster	ⒷⒶ	High	28	Stuns on hit
Backspin Temple Buster ~Grim Stride	ⒷⒶ⇨	High	28	Stuns on hit. Shifts to Grim Stride.
Quick Revenge	⇨Ⓑ	Mid	20	
Quick Revenge (Additional attack)	⇨Ⓑ During Hit Ⓑ (Just)	Mid, Mid	20, 23	Guard Breaks when Kamikirimusi is powered up
Death Smash	⇘Ⓑ	Mid	18(28)	Launches and deals additional damage at close distances. Guard Breaks when Kamikirimusi is powered up.
Death Smash ~Night Side Stance	⇘Ⓑ	Mid	18(28)	Shifts to Night Side Stance. Launches and deals additional damage at close distances. Guard Breaks when Kamikirimusi is powered up.
Shadow Buster	⇩Ⓑ	Mid	20	
Reaver	⇗Ⓑ	Mid	24	Stuns on counter-hit
Reaver ~Night Side Stance	⇗Ⓑ	Mid	24	Stuns on counter-hit. Shifts to Night Side Stance.
Midnight Launcher	⇦Ⓑ	Mid	38	Guard Breaks
Split Buster	While Crouching Ⓑ	Mid	23	
Death Horn Charge	While Crouching ⇘Ⓑ	Mid	55	
Upper Claw	While Rising Ⓑ	Mid	18	Stuns on counter-hit. Always stuns when Kamikirimusi is powered up.
Upper Claw ~Night Side Stance	While Rising Ⓑ	Mid	18	Stuns on counter-hit. Shifts into Night Side Stance.
Fatal Buster	Jumping Ⓑ	Mid	26 or 28 or 30	Damage varies depending on direction jumped in
Turning Sword Buster	Backturned Ⓑ	Mid	20	
Turning Shadow Buster	While Crouching Backturned Ⓑ	Mid	22	

Throws

Name	Command	Attack Level	Damage	Notes
Shoulder Claw Throw	Ⓐ+Ⓖ	Throw	55	Input Ⓐ to escape
Soul Devour	Ⓑ+Ⓖ	Throw	50	Input Ⓑ to escape
Doom's Invitation	Left Side Throw	Throw	55	Same button as throw (Ⓐ or Ⓑ) to escape
Unholy Terror	Right Side Throw	Throw	65	Same button as throw (Ⓐ or Ⓑ) to escape
Witch Hunt	Back Throw	Throw	65	Same button as throw (Ⓐ or Ⓑ) to escape
Flap Jack	While Crouching Ⓐ+Ⓖ	Low	30	Input Ⓐ to escape
Over Toss	While Crouching Ⓑ+Ⓖ	Low	20	Input Ⓑ to escape
Soul Smasher	Against Downed Foe ⇩Ⓐ+Ⓑ	Throw	32	Leaves Kamikirimusi in powered up state

Simultaneous Press

Name	Command	Attack Level	Damage	Notes
Soul Wave	Ⓐ+Ⓑ	Mid	30	Nullifies 1 hit (Kamikirimusi still receives damage, but continues attack), deflects all following attacks after first nullification. Leaves Kamikirimusi in powered up state.
Dark Soul Impact	⇘Ⓐ+Ⓑ	Low	34	
Soul Smasher	⇩Ⓐ+Ⓑ	Mid	10(32)	Performs special hit throw against fallen enemies (leaves Kamikirimusi powered up after it hits)
Soul Blaze	⇦Ⓐ+Ⓑ	Mid	48	Unblockable. Input Ⓖ to cancel.
Soul Wave	Backturned Ⓐ+Ⓑ	Mid	30	Leaves Kamikirimusi in powered up state
Night Side Stance	While Standing or While Crouching Ⓑ+Ⓚ			
Bloody Jade Impact	⇩Ⓑ+Ⓚ	Mid	30	Guard Breaks
Dark Bite	Backturned Ⓑ+Ⓚ	High	43	Special hit throw. Can grab airborne enemies.
Dark Bite	Ⓐ+Ⓚ	High	40	
Taunt	Ⓚ+Ⓖ			

8-Way Run

Name	Command	Attack Level	Damage	Notes
Right Slasher	→ or ↘ or ↗Ⓐ	High	34	
Shadow Cross Divide	↓ or ↑ⒶⒷ	High, Mid	18, 28	2nd attack stuns on hit
Alternate Cross	← or ↙ or ↖Ⓐ	High	36	
Hell Slayer	→Ⓑ	Mid	36	Guard Breaks when Kamikirimusi is powered up
Ether Splitter	↘ or ↗Ⓑ	Mid	21	
Ether Splitter ~Grim Stride	↘ or ↗Ⓑ⇨	Mid	21	Shifts to Grim Stride
Rook Splitter	↓ or ↑Ⓑ	Mid	40	
Darkness Impact	↙ or ↖Ⓑ	Low	26	
Shadow Breaker	←ⒷⒷ	Mid, Mid	30, 33	2nd attack stuns on ground hit
Shadow Breaker ~Night Side Stance	←ⒷⒷ	Mid, Mid	30, 33	2nd attack stuns on ground hit. Shifts to Night Side Stance.
Shoulder Rush	→ or ↘ or ↗Ⓚ	Mid	20	
Shoulder Rush ~Grim Stride	→ or ↘ or ↗Ⓚ⇨	Mid	20	Shifts into Grim Stride
Jade Smasher	↓ or ↑Ⓚ	Mid	28	
Jade Smasher ~Grim Stride	↓ or ↑Ⓚ⇨	Mid	28	Shifts into Grim Stride
Darkside Kick	↙ or ↖Ⓚ	Mid	24	
Drop Kick	←Ⓚ	High	46	Guard Breaks
Flying Edge	→Ⓐ+Ⓑ	Mid	48	
Cannonball Splitter	→Ⓑ+Ⓚ	Mid, Mid, Mid	10, 10, 25	Leaves Kamikirimusi in crouching state
Sliding	While Running Ⓚ	Low	26	

Kick Attacks

Name	Command	Attack Level	Damage	Notes
Dark High Kick	Ⓚ	High	14	
Jade Strike	⇨Ⓚ	High	21	
Dark Middle Kick	↘Ⓚ	Mid	16	
Dark Middle Kick (Hold)	↘🅚	Mid	30	
Stomping	⇩Ⓚ	Low	14	
Stomping (Hold)	⇩🅚	Low	22	Unblockable
Grind Low Kick	↙Ⓚ	Low	12	
Double Death Claw	⇦ⓀⓀ	Mid, High	16, 25	Second attack may be delayed, fully combos on counter-hit
Double Death Thrust	⇦🅚Ⓑ	Mid, Mid	18, 21	
Double Death Thrust (Additional attack)	⇦🅚Ⓑ During Hit Ⓑ (Just)	Mid, Mid, Mid	20, 21, 23	
Grind Low Kick	While Crouching Ⓚ	Low	12	
Phantom Knee	While Rising Ⓚ	Mid	22	
Fatal Brave Kick	Jumping Ⓚ	Mid	14 or 18 or 20	Damage varies depending on direction jumped in
Turning Dark High Kick	Backturned Ⓚ	High	18	
Turning Dark Low Kick	While Crouching Backturned Ⓚ	Low	12	

Grim Stride

Name	Command	Attack Level	Damage	Notes
Grim Stride	⇩↘⇨			
Grim Fang	Grim Stride Ⓐ	High	18	Stuns on counter-hit. Deflects mid attacks.
Grim Launcher	Grim Stride Ⓑ	Mid	32	Launches on counter-hit
Grim Launcher ~Night Side Stance	Grim Stride 🅑	Mid	32	Launches on counter-hit. Shifts to Night Side Stance.
Grim Launcher ~Grim Stride	Grim Stride Ⓑ⇨	Mid	32	Shifts to Grim Stride
Grim Roundhouse	Grim Stride ⓀⓀ	Mid, High	10, 13	
Soul Wave	Grim Stride Ⓐ+Ⓑ	Mid	30	Leaves Kamikirimusi in powered up state

Night Side Stance

Name	Command	Attack Level	Damage	Notes
Night Side Stance	While Standing or While Crouching Ⓑ+Ⓚ			
Cannonball Feint	Night Side Stance Ⓐ	Mid	20	
Cannonball Feint ~Night Side Stance	Night Side Stance 🅐	Mid	20	Shifts into Night Side Stance
Phantom Impact	Night Side Stance Ⓑ	Low	28	
Skull Chopper	Night Side Stance ⓑⒶ	High	32(42)	Perform input as fast as possible for additional damage (Just)
Night Front Kick	Night Side Stance Ⓚ	High	16	Stuns on counter-hit
Phantom Splitter	Night Side Stance Ⓐ+Ⓑ	Mid	26	Guard Breaks when Kamikirimusi is powered up
Grim Stride	Night Side Stance ⇩↘⇨			

Combos

↙🅑, Ⓚ
2 hits, 40 Damage
Counter-hit ↙🅑, Ⓐ + Ⓑ, ⇩Ⓐ + Ⓑ
3 hits, 68 Damage
While Rising 🅑, ⓑⒶ (Just)
2 hits, 51 Damage
Counter-hit While Rising 🅑, Ⓐ + Ⓑ, ⇩Ⓐ + Ⓑ
3 hits, 61 Damage
↘🅑, ⓑⒶ
2 hits, 61 Damage
⇨⇨Ⓐ, ⇩↘⇨ⓀⓀ
3 hits, 54 Damage
↙Ⓐ➡, ⓀⓀ
3 hits, 53 Damage
⇨⇨Ⓑ, Ⓐ + Ⓚ
2 hits, 68 Damage
⇨⇨Ⓑ, While Rising 🅑, ⓑⒶ (Just)
3 hits, 79 Damage, input ⇩🅖🅑 to quickly perform While Rising attack
↘ or ↗Ⓑ ➡, Ⓑ + Ⓚ
3 hits, 56 Damage
⇩↘⇨, Ⓑ ➡, ⓀⓀ
3 hits, 51 Damage
Counter-hit ⇩↘⇨, Ⓐ, ⇦ⓀⓀ
3 hits, 49 Damage
ⓑⒶ ➡, Ⓐ, ⓐ🅑, Ⓚ, ⇩Ⓐ + Ⓑ
5 hits, 77 Damage, must be performed against wall

Close Range

Kamikirimusi shares the same move set as the ever-vivid Nightmare. Unfortunately, her short limbs give her less range than her counterpart. This makes her less effective than Nightmare, whose main focus is ranged attacks. Kamikirimusi's close range options are potent, but their slow speed makes it difficult to use them when she isn't sitting on a heavy advantage. To compensate, rely on scoring knockdowns, making the most out of her anti-wakeup attacks, and moving out to mid range when possible. Careful use of her defensive options is your main means to achieve this. For example, Upper Claw (While Rising Ⓑ) is one of the best ways to stop high attacks. If it strikes as a counter-hit, launch your enemy with Ⓐ + Ⓑ, then juggle with ↓Ⓐ + Ⓑ. This combo knocks your enemy down next to you, the perfect position for staging an anti-wakeup attack. Her Soul Wave (Ⓐ + Ⓑ) explosion, which deflects high strikes while blasting your foe away from you, also stops high attacks. Use the breathing room to establish mid range.

If the above options aren't reliable, fall back on Guard Impacts and sidesteps to avoid incoming attacks. Back-step out of attack range or use ⇨Ⓚ⇨ to shift into an aggressive posture when you see a gap in your foe's offense. Her ⒶⒷ is also useful for switching into an aggressive stance. If it hits your enemy, link into the Night Side Stance's Night Front Kick (Ⓚ) attack to knock him or her down. When blocked, take advantage of the stance's Phantom Impact (Ⓑ) and Cannonball Feint Ⓐ options to stage a basic 2-way guessing game.

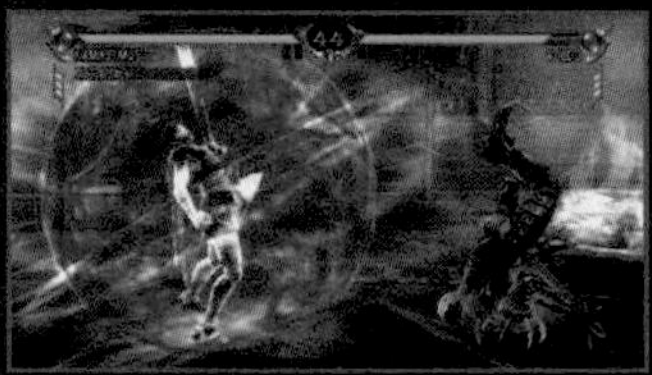

Mid Range

Stop your enemy from relying on 8-Way Run and sidesteps. Doing so enables you to use Kamikirimusi's powerful linear attacks. Use Shadow Cross Divide (⇩ or ↑ⒶⒷ) or Ⓐ to deter side movement. The first option inflicts more damage than the second, but it leaves you vulnerable when it's blocked. Rely more on the safe Ⓐ slash, a horizontal attack that shifts into her Night Side Stance. Its purpose is to both deter sidesteps and start a varied offense. Attack with Ⓐ, then use the Night Side Stance's mid-hitting Ⓐ or low-hitting Ⓑ to stage a basic 2-way guessing game. The Ⓐ option counters sidesteps and shifts back into the Night Side Stance. If the slash hits your enemy, link into the Night Front Kick (during Night Side Stance Ⓚ) to score a 2-hit combo. The Ⓚ follow-up also stops your foe's attempts to attack your recovery if Ⓐ is guarded. Note that the Night Side Stance can also shift into the Grim Stride. Use it to quickly approach and surprise your enemy with its many options.

Because the aforementioned circular attacks hit high, your opponent can counter both options by crouching. Use this to your advantage and attack with the mid strings ↘ⒶⒶ and ↘Ⓐ↓Ⓐ. The ↘Ⓐ↓Ⓐ string shifts into the Grim Stride, enabling you to combo ⓀⓀ on a successful hit. If your enemy is near a wall, go for the Quick Revenge (→Ⓑ during hit Ⓑ mid attack, which inflicts massive damage while also setting up a wall stun. Vary between these actions and Kamikirimusi's potent low attacks, like Darkness Impact (⇙ or ⇘Ⓑ) or Shadow Slicer (↙Ⓐ).

Long Range

Kamikirimusi's range game suffers in contrast to Nightmare's due to her shorter reach. Focus on careful footwork and passive play in order to move into mid range. Dance in and out of your enemy's maximum range to coerce whiffed attacks. When opponents miss with an attack, punish them with ⇘ (or ⇙) Ⓑ⇨, Ⓑ + Ⓚ. If you time ⇘Ⓑ⇨ poorly and your enemy guards it, use the Grim Slide to move into close range. Come out of the movement with its Ⓐ option (deflecting high and mid attacks), the mid-hitting Ⓑ option, or let the slide recover and perform the Flap Jack (↓Ⓐ + Ⓖ).

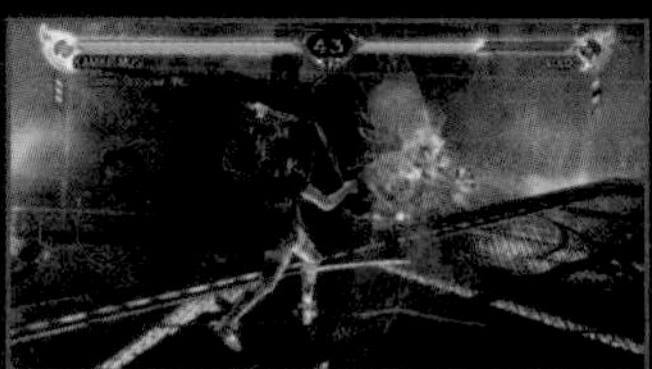

Special Tactics

Okizeme: Anti-Wakeup

Like Nightmare, Kamikirimusi's anti-wakeup game revolves around her Shadow Slicer (↙Ⓐ) and Midnight Launcher (←Ⓑ). The damaging low attack ↙Ⓐ shifts into the Grim Stride (↙Ⓐ⇨), while ←Ⓑ is a mid Guard Break attack that launches your foe into the air. Both moves have a blue lightning effect during their wind-up period, making it difficult to distinguish between both attack types. If ↙Ⓐ hits, shift into the Grim Slide and link ⓀⓀ for a damaging combo.

The mid-hitting Reaver ↙Ⓑ is also a worthy option. It shifts directly into Night Side Stance, allowing you to link a Night Front Kick (during Night Side Stance Ⓚ) if ↙Ⓑ successfully hits. If ↙Ⓑ is blocked, mix-up between the Night Side Stance's low (Ⓑ) and mid (Ⓐ) options. The Ⓐ option shifts back into the Night Side Stance, enabling you to combo its Ⓚ attack if Ⓐ hits. Furthermore, if ⒶⒷ manages to connect as a counter-hit, link directly into the Night Side Stance's Ⓐ + Ⓑ launcher. Then stab your falling foe with ↓Ⓐ + Ⓑ for a 3-hit combo. This leaves your enemy directly next to you, enabling you to go for ↙Ⓑ again or a low attack.

Use the Flap Jack (↓Ⓐ + Ⓖ or ↓Ⓑ + Ⓖ) as your main low attack. Both versions of the throw have different properties. The ↓Ⓐ + Ⓖ version is useful for scoring a Ring Out near an arena's edge.

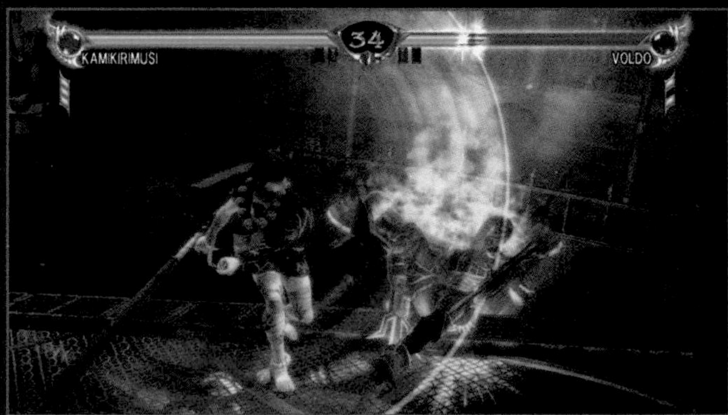

Grim Stride Options

The command ↓↘→ performs the Grim Stride, a speedy forward movement designed to move Kamikirimusi quickly into close range. Three attacks are available within this movement: the high Grim Fang (Ⓐ), the Grim Launcher (Ⓑ), and the combo-oriented Grim Roundhouse (ⓀⓀ). The Grim Fang is the most important of these options, as it nails sidesteps, stuns on counter-hit, and deflects mid and high attacks. Use it to counter your enemy's attempts to stop the Grim Stride. On a successful counter-hit, link into ← ⓀⓀ for a 3-hit combo. The Grim Fang is a high hit, so your foe may counter by crouching or guarding. If you expect an opponent to crouch, use the Grim Launcher mid attack. Hold ⇨ if it hits and perform the Grim Roundhouse to combo your fallen enemy.

The Grim Stride leaves Kamikirimusi in a crouching state near the end of its recovery. This is particularly useful for initiating the low Flap Jack throw (↓Ⓐ + Ⓖ or ↓Ⓑ + Ⓖ). Use this technique when your adversary is wary of the mid-hitting Grim Launcher.

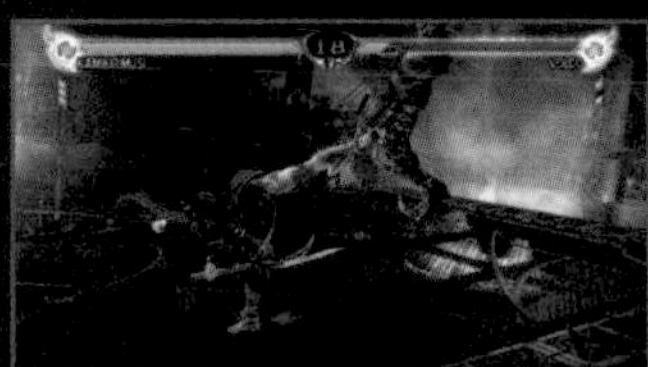

Scheherazade

Bio

Age:	She does not keep count, but young among her people
Birthplace:	Reclusive village
Height:	5'2"
Weight:	93 lbs.
Birth Date:	12th day under the Chanting Moon
Blood Type:	Unknown
Weapon:	Rapier
Weapon Name:	Alf Layla Wa Layla
Family:	The stubborn elders in the woods

zade

Once there was a war between two swords that shook the world. To Scheherazade, storyteller of her people, this tale held great interest. And so she slipped past the watchful eyes of the elders who had concealed themselves in the woods' deepest depths so long ago, and went off into the outside world. And though she found herself tangled up in countless troubles, she still managed to sate her vast curiosity, only to be taken back to the woods again in the end.

Had curiosity been her only crime, her transgression might have been overlooked. However, she had gone too far: forbidden love! Normally the price would have been death, but Scheherazade was instead locked away in an arboreal prison. There she spent an eternity thinking of the man she loved—a young warrior who would become the founding father of Wolfkrone. Eventually, her time was served, and the elders opened her prison door. But Scheherazade showed no signs of remorse. Instead she ran yet again from the confines of the woods, leaving the elders crying woefully in her wake.

Her people lived much, much longer lives than humans. The vicissitudes of the outside world were swift as a shallow brook. Surely her beloved had departed this life long ago, but he must have left some legacy, and she was determined to find out what it was for herself. After all, what storyteller fails to see her own tale through to the end?

Scheherazade

Command List

Signature Techniques

Name	Command	Attack Level	Damage	Notes
Graceful Cutter	⬃Ⓐ	Low	18	
Triple Botta in Tempo	⇨ⒷⒷⒷ	High, High, Mid	10, 5, 15	Fully combos on counter-hit
Decussate Strike	⬂ⒷⒶ	Mid, Low	20, 26	1st attack stuns on hit
Helm Splitter	⇦ⒷⒷ	High, Mid	14, 16	1st attack stuns on counter-hit, 2nd attack may be delayed
Bella Donna	⬃ⓀⒶ	High, High	12, 12	2nd attack causes recoverable stun on hit, stuns on counter-hit
Advance Splitter Crescendo	➡ⒷⒶ	Mid, High	20, 30	2nd attack Guard Breaks and stuns on hit
Soaring Flutter	➘ or ➚Ⓑ	Mid	22	
High Arc	8-Way Run Any Direction Ⓐ+Ⓑ	Mid	26	
Amaryllis Spiral	Amaryllis Spin ⓀⒶ (Just)	Mid, High	10, 9	
Night Toe Kick	Lilith ParryⓀ	Mid	20	

Horizontal Attacks

Name	Command	Attack Level	Damage	Notes
Attack au Fer	ⒶⒶ	High, High	8, 10	
Flash Needle	ⒶⒷ	High, Low	8, 10	
Hilt Strike	⇨Ⓐ	High	12	
Air Blade	⬂Ⓐ	Mid	14	
Twirling Talon	⇩Ⓐ	Sp.Low	8	Leaves Scheherazade in crouching state
Graceful Cutter	⬃Ⓐ	Low	18	
Heavy Mandritti	⇦Ⓐ	High	18	Evades vertical attacks
Twirling Talon	While Crouching Ⓐ	Sp.Low	8	
Merciless Stramazone	While Rising Ⓐ	High	20	
Sky Botte	Jumping Ⓐ	High	16 or 18 or 20	Damage varies depending on direction jumped in
Turning Attack au Fer	Backturned Ⓐ	High	10	
Low Turn Attack au Fer	While Crouching Backturned Ⓐ	Sp.Low	12	Leaves Scheherazade in crouching state

Vertical Attacks

Name	Command	Attack Level	Damage	Notes
Dui Montante	ⒷⒷ	Mid, Mid	10, 12	
Triple Botta in Tempo	⇨ⒷⒷⒷ	High, High, Mid	10, 5, 15	Fully combos on counter-hit
Double Botta in Tempo ~Amaryllis Spin	⇨ⒷⒷ⇩⬂⇨	High, High	10, 5	Shifts into Amaryllia
Decussate Strike	⬂ⒷⒶ	Mid, Low	20, 26	
Fendante	⇩Ⓑ	Mid	14	Leaves Scheherazade in crouching state
Grave Needle	⬃Ⓑ	Low	16	
Helm Splitter	⇦ⒷⒷ	High, Mid	14, 16	1st attack stuns on counter-hit, 2nd attack may be delayed
Crouching Montante	While Crouching Ⓑ	Mid	12	
Advance Slicer	While Crouching ⬂Ⓑ	Mid	24	Stuns on hit
Shadow Stinger	While Crouching ⬃Ⓑ	Low	24	
Frigid Tap	While Rising Ⓑ	High	16	Causes recoverable stun on hit
Sky Agente	Jumping Ⓑ	Mid	14 or 16 or 18	Damage varies depending on direction jumped in. Stuns on hit (except for ⬂Ⓑ).
Turning Montante	Backturned Ⓑ	Mid	12	
Low Turn Montante	While Crouching Backturned Ⓑ	Mid	16	Leaves Scheherazade in crouching state

Kick Attacks

Name	Command	Attack Level	Damage	Notes
Venom High Kick	Ⓚ	High	8	
Venom Swing Kick	⇨Ⓚ	High	14	Causes recoverable stun on hit
Venom Swing Kick ~Amaryllis Spin	⇨Ⓚ⇩⬂⇨	High	14	Causes recoverable stun on hit, shifts into Amaryllis
Venom Side Kick	⬂Ⓚ	Mid	14	
Sweep Kick	⇩Ⓚ	Low	10	Leaves Scheherazade in crouching state
Bella Donna	⬃ⓀⒶ	High, High	12, 12	2nd attack causes recoverable stun
Dual Stinger Kick	⇦ⓀⓀ	High, Mid	12, 14	
Sweep Kick	While Crouching Ⓚ	Low	10	
High Back Kick	While Rising Ⓚ	Mid	18	
Dark Moon	Jumping Ⓚ	Mid	12 or 14 or 16	Damage varies depending on direction jumped in
Turning Venom High Kick	Backturned Ⓚ	High	10	
Turning Sweep Kick	While Crouching Backturned Ⓚ	Low	14	

Simultaneous Press

Name	Command	Attack Level	Damage	Notes
Biondetta Parry	Ⓐ+Ⓑ			Deflects high attacks
Assalto Montante Crescendo	⇨Ⓐ+ⒷⒶ	Mid, Mid, Low	10, 14, 16	2nd attack stuns on counter-hit
Assalto Montante ~Amaryllis Spin	⇨Ⓐ+Ⓑ⇩⬂⇨	Mid, Mid	10, 14	2nd attack stuns on counter-hit, shifts into Amaryllis
Silent Curtsey	⇩Ⓐ+Ⓑ	Low	20	
Bloody Funeral	⇦Ⓐ+Ⓑ	Mid	45	Unblockable
Bloody Funeral ~Amaryllis Spin	⇦Ⓐ+ⒷⒼ			Unblockable. Shifts into Amaryllis
Dark Abyss	⇧Ⓐ+Ⓑ	Mid	28	Stuns on hit
Frigid Stramazone	While Crouching Ⓐ+ⒷⒶ	Mid, Mid	12, 12	2nd attack may be delayed. Both attacks stun on counter-hit.
Lilith Parry	Ⓑ+Ⓚ			Deflects mid attacks
Falling Prayer	⇨Ⓑ+Ⓚ	Mid	30	Causes recoverable stun on hit
Silent Impale	⇩Ⓑ+Ⓚ	Low	20	Stuns on hit
Stocatta Rampage Crescendo	⇦Ⓑ+ⓀⒷ	Mid x9	5 (first 8 hits), 20	Stuns on hit (8th and 9th attack)
Circular Blitz	Backturned Ⓑ+Ⓚ	Mid	20	Stuns on hit
Circular Blitz ~Amaryllis Spin	Backturned Ⓑ+Ⓚ⇩⬂⇨	Mid	20	Shifts into Amaryllis
Crest Form	Ⓐ+Ⓚ			Evades low attacks
Taunt	Ⓚ+Ⓖ			

8-Way Run

Name	Command	Attack Level	Damage	Notes
Descending Talon	→ or ↘ or ↗Ⓐ	Mid	30	Stuns on hit
Silent Saber	↓ or ↑Ⓐ	High	26	
Heartless Needle	↙ or ↖Ⓐ	Mid	22	
Squalambrato Concierto Crescendo	←ⒶⒷⒶ	Mid, Mid, High	18, 11, 30	3rd attack stuns on hit. 1st attack stuns on counter-hit.
Advance Splitter Crescendo	→ⒷⒶ	Mid, High	20, 30	3rd attack stuns on hit
Advance Splitter ~Step	→Ⓑ⇩ or ⇧	Mid	20	Shifts into sidestep
Soaring Flutter	↘ or ↗Ⓑ	Mid	22	
Broken Thrust	↓ or ↑Ⓑ	Mid	24	
Broken Thrust ~Broken Thrust	↓ or ↑Ⓑ⇩ or ⇧Ⓑ	Mid, Mid	24	Shifts into additional Broken Thrust
Broken Thrust ~Amaryllis Spin	↓ or ↑Ⓑ⇩⬂⇨	Mid	24	Shifts into Amaryllis
Shadow Evade	↓ or ↑ⒷⒼ			
Crimson Slicer	↓ or ↑ⒷⒼⒶ	High	18	
Assault Blade	↓ or ↑ⒷⒼⒷ	Mid	28	Causes recoverable stun
Dread Coffin	← or ↙ or ↖Ⓑ	Mid	25	Stuns on hit
Dread Coffin ~Stocatta Rampage Crescendo	← or ↙ or ↖ Ⓑ Counter-hit During Hit Ⓑ	Mid x10	25, 5 (first 8 hits), 20	Stuns on hit (1st, 8th and 9th)
Night Round Kick	→ or ↘ or ↗Ⓚ	High	22	
Venom Swing Kick	↓ or ↑Ⓚ	Mid	18	
Venom Swing Kick ~Amaryllis Spin	↓ or ↑Ⓚ⇩⬂⇨	Mid	18	Shifts into Amaryllis
Unholy Kick	← or ↙ or ↖Ⓚ	High	30	Leaves Scheherazade facing backwards
High Arc	8-Way Run Any Direction Ⓐ+Ⓑ	Mid	26	
Bleak Touch	→Ⓑ+Ⓚ	Mid	18	Causes recoverable stun on hit
Bleak Touch ~Amaryllis Spin	→Ⓑ+Ⓚ During Hit ⇩⬂⇨	Mid	18	Causes recoverable stun on hit, shifts into Amaryllis
Sliding	While Running Ⓚ	Low	26	

Throws

Name	Command	Attack Level	Damage	Notes
Forget Me Not	Ⓐ+Ⓖ	Throw	48	Input Ⓐ to escape
Ephemeral Wing	Ⓑ+Ⓖ	Throw	45	Input Ⓑ to escape
A Lesson in Massacre	Left Side Throw	Throw	52	Same button as throw (Ⓐ or Ⓑ) to escape
Undertaker	Right Side Throw	Throw	50	Same button as throw (Ⓐ or Ⓑ) to escape
Pure Sacrifice	Back Throw	Throw	58	Same button as throw (Ⓐ or Ⓑ) to escape

Amaryllis

Name	Command	Attack Level	Damage	Notes
Amaryllis Spin	⇩⇘⇨			
Scarlet Night	Amaryllis Spin Ⓐ	Mid, High	15, 20	
Stocatta Slicer	Amaryllis Spin Ⓑ Rapidly	Mid, Mid, Mid, Mid, Mid	5 (first 5 hits), 20	Stuns on final hit
Amaryllis Spiral	Amaryllis Spin ⓀⒶ (Just)	Mid, High	10, 12	
Frigid Moon	Amaryllis Spin ⓀⓀ	Mid, Mid	10, 12	

Biondetta Parry

Name	Command	Attack Level	Damage	Notes
Biondetta Parry	Ⓐ+Ⓑ			Deflects high attacks
Aurora Talon	Biondetta Parry Ⓐ	Mid	30	Stuns on hit
Hidden Thorn	Biondetta Parry Ⓑ	Mid	20	Stuns on hit
Silent Sweep	Biondetta Parry Ⓚ	Low	24	
Lilith Parry	Biondetta Parry Ⓑ+Ⓚ			
Crest Form	Biondetta Parry Ⓐ+Ⓚ			
Amaryllis Spin	Biondetta Parry ⇩⇘⇨			

Lilith Parry

Name	Command	Attack Level	Damage	Notes
Lilith Parry	Ⓑ+Ⓚ			Deflects mid attacks
Arctic Night	Lilith Parry Ⓐ	Mid	16	
Frost Blade	Lilith Parry Ⓑ	High	10	Causes recoverable stun on counter-hit
Night Toe Kick	Lilith Parry Ⓚ	Mid	20	
Biondetta Parry	Lilith Parry Ⓐ+Ⓑ			
Crest Form	Lilith Parry Ⓐ+Ⓚ			
Amaryllis Spin	Lilith Parry ⇩⇘⇨			

Crest Form

Name	Command	Attack Level	Damage	Notes
Crest Form	Ⓐ+Ⓚ			Evades low attacks
Heel Cutter	Crest Form Ⓐ	Low	12	
Vermillion Fang	Crest Form Ⓑ	Mid, Mid	40	Unblockable
Soaring Dance	Crest Form Ⓚ	Mid, Mid	18, 24	Stuns on hit
Biondetta Parry	Crest Form Ⓐ+Ⓑ			
Lilith Parry	Crest Form Ⓑ+Ⓚ			
Amaryllis Spin	Crest Form ⇩⇘⇨			

Combos

⇘ⒷⒶ, ⇘⇘Ⓑ

3 hits, 59 Damage

Counter-hit ⇦Ⓐ, ⇨⇨Ⓐ + Ⓑ

2 hits, 39 Damage

⇨⇨Ⓐ, ⇘ⒷⒶ, ⇘⇘Ⓑ

4 hits, 78 Damage

⇨⇨Ⓐ + Ⓑ, Ⓑ + Ⓚ, ⇘↘Ⓑ

3 hits, 62 Damage

Ⓐ + ⒷⓀ, ⇨ⒷⒷ

3 hits, 35 Damage

Ⓐ + ⒷⒷ, ⇘ⒷⒶ, ⇘⇘Ⓑ

4 hits, 68 Damage

↑ or ↓ⒷⒼ, Ⓑ, ⇨⇨ⒷⒶ

3 hits, 60 Damage, first stun is escapable

↘Ⓑ, ⇨⇨Ⓑ + Ⓚ, ⇩⇘⇨ⓀⓀ

4 hits, 52 Damage

⇦Ⓐ + Ⓑ, ⇨⇨Ⓐ + Ⓑ

2 hits, 63 Damage

⇦⇦Ⓚ, ⇧Ⓐ + Ⓑ

2 hits, 55 Damage

Backturned Ⓑ + Ⓚ, ⇩Ⓚ

2 hits, 30 Damage, Ⓑ + Ⓚ must hit enemy's front side

Backturned Ⓑ + Ⓚ, ⇙ⓀⒶ, ⇩Ⓑ

4 hits, 47 Damage, Ⓑ + Ⓚ must hit enemy's back

⇦Ⓐ + Ⓑ (wall hit), ⇘↘Ⓑ, ⇨⇨Ⓐ + Ⓑ, Ⓑ + Ⓚ, ⇘↘Ⓑ

7 hits, 85 Damage, must be done near wall

Close Range

Scheherazade shares the same move list as Amy, but with a slight range increase thanks to her body and sword size. This makes Scheherazade a slightly more effective character than Amy.

Start your attacks with ⇨ⒷⒷ. Chain into its Ⓑ follow-up if it connects on a counter-hit. If ⇨ⒷⒷ is guarded, shift into the Amaryllis movement (⇨ⒷⒷ⇩⇘⇨) and go for either Its Stocatta Slicer (ⒷⒷ) option, or throw as the movement recovers. Note that ⇨ⒷⒷ is vulnerable to sidesteps and whiffs against crouching opponents, so take measures to counter both options. Use Decussate Strike (⇘ⒷⒶ) to hit crouching foes and ⒶⒶ to stop sidesteps. When the enemy begins to stand again, mix in throws and Silent Impale (⇩Ⓑ+Ⓚ) to keep your offense varied.

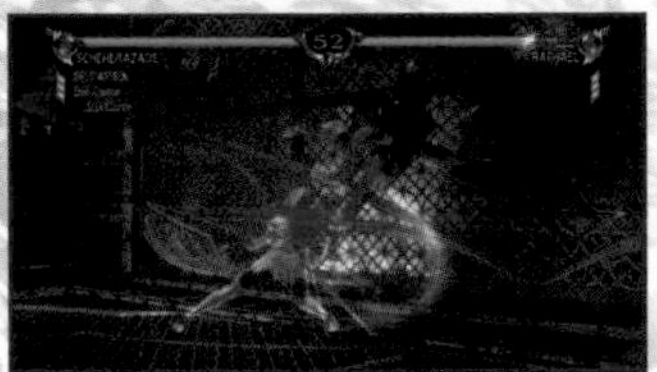
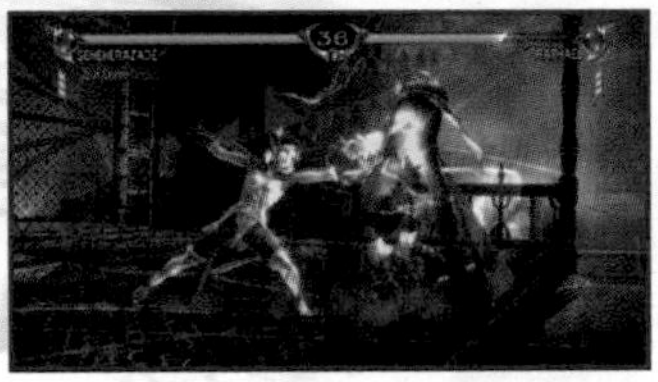

Mid Range

Like Amy, Scheherazade's stronger attacks are linear, so take measures to keep your foe from sidestepping. Use the Heavy Mandritti (⇦Ⓐ) or Silent Saber (↓or↑Ⓐ) to counter-hit sidesteps. The slowest of these options is ⇦Ⓐ, but it leads to bigger damage as a counter-hit. Attack your stunned enemy with High Arc (8-Way Run any direction Ⓐ+Ⓑ) afterward. Your enemy's counter to both of these tactics is to crouch. Use this opportunity to strike with mid attacks, such as the Advance Splitter Crescendo (→Ⓑ) or Soaring Flutter (↘Ⓑ). The mid attack Falling Prayer (⇨Ⓑ+Ⓚ) is also worthwhile, as it ducks under high attacks, catches backward movement, and causes a recoverable stun.

Long Range

Scheherazade lacks the attacks necessary to compete at this distance, so your objective is to move into mid or close range. The safest way to accomplish this is to wait for enemies to make a mistake, enabling you to knock them down. Use Scheherazade's fast walking speed to move rapidly in and out of your adversary's attack range. If the foe mistakenly attacks, punish the missed move with ↘Ⓑ or →Ⓐ+Ⓑ to score a combo and a knockdown. If your enemy is afraid to stick out attacks, use ⇩⇘⇨ to quickly approach him or her. Go for the Ⓑ option or a throw when you recover. Use ⇩⇘⇨Ⓐ to catch your foe's attempts to sidestep around this maneuver.

Special Tactics

Okizeme: Anti-Wakeup

Normally, the first hit of Assalto Montante Crescendo (⇨Ⓐ+Ⓑ) misses when Amy uses it, lowering its overall worth. However, Scheherazade's improved range allows all three hits to combo together on a normal hit. When combined with its ability to shift into the Amaryllis on the second hit, this attack combo becomes quite useful against downed enemies. Verify when it's blocked and shift into the Amaryllis' mid-hitting ⒷⒷ string to trick enemies looking for the final low hit.

As an alternate attack method, use the ⇘ⒷⒶ combo against downed enemies. When your enemy is wary of this move, attack with the low attacks Silent Impale (⇩Ⓑ+Ⓚ) or Silent Curtsey (⇩Ⓐ+Ⓑ). The first option leads to a small combo consisting of ⇩Ⓑ+Ⓚ, then While Crouching ⇗Ⓑ, so use it often.

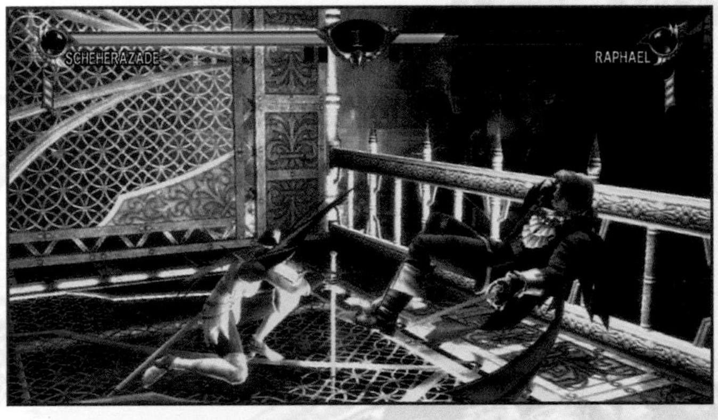

Amaryllis

Like Amy, Scheherazade's Amaryllis (⇩⇘⇨) causes her to slide forward at a high speed. This movement ducks under high attacks and grants access to three unique attacks. Its Stocatta Slicer (ⒷⒷ) attack is the fastest option out of the Amaryllis; use it to stop your enemy's early attempts to attack. When your enemy is nervous to act, use the Amaryllis to slip into range for a throw. In cases where enemies use sidesteps to avoid both the attack and the throw, use the circular Scarlet Night (Ⓐ) option to hit them. Finally, use the Frigid Moon (ⓀⓀ) attack mainly for combos, like ↘Ⓑ, ⇨⇨Ⓑ+Ⓚ⇩⇘⇨ⓀⓀ. Its special Just Frame variation, ⇩⇘⇨ⓀⒶ, ends with a safe high attack capable of hitting enemies into walls. Use it when you have your enemy cornered.

Scheherazade

The vengeful spirit whispered into the woman's [illegible]

The woman was a mere killer, one who had never truly [illegible] challenging, after all. So the [illegible] saying went [illegible] one must reap what one has sown. [illegible] the woman would [illegible] name, none can say—the world was calling her "Shura" [illegible].

The spirit was in search of a powerful body so that it might [illegible] from the [illegible] they wandered from one strong warrior to the next, each stronger [illegible].

"Heh heh, the day I find the perfect body is the day I tear you to pieces, woman."

"Oh, so you say. But I'm beginning to wonder if anyone out there is strong enough [illegible]

Bio

Age:	She has forgotten
Birthplace:	Suwa, Japan
Height:	She has never measured herself
Weight:	Or weighed herself
Birth Date:	She can't remember
Blood Type:	AB
Weapon:	Samurai Sword x 2
Weapon Name:	Raijin-Maru, Fujin-Maru
Family:	She is possessed by the vengeful spirit of a demon she once slew. Any other family, she has forgotten.

Shura

Signature Techniques

Name	Command	Attack Level	Damage	Notes
Wave Break	⇗Ⓐ	Low	26	Knocks down, leaves Shura in crouching state
Cannonball Lifter	⇘Ⓑ	Mid	18 (24)	Launches and does extra damage at close range
Bloody Hilt Kick	⇦ⒷⓀ	Mid, High	16, 22	Combos on counter-hit, 2nd hit leaves both characters backturned
Scissor Wave	⇘Ⓐ+Ⓑ	Mid, Mid	15, 12	
Flying Dutchman	While Crouching Ⓐ+ⒷⒷ (Mash)	Mid, Mid, Mid, Mid, Mid, Mid, Mid	6, 6, 6, 6, 6, 6, 20	Guard Break
Law of Pirates	While Rising ⒷⒷ	Mid, Mid	15, 35	1st hit launches, 2nd hit launches on counter-hit, leaves Shura in crouching state
Lagging Wave	➡Ⓐ	High	30	Knocks down
Bile Lunges	➡Ⓑ	Mid	25, (48)	Hit throw if close
Geo Da Ray	Dread Charge Ⓑ	Mid	30	Launches, hold Ⓑ to redirect off walls

Kick Attacks

Name	Command	Attack Level	Damage	Notes
Anchor Kick	Ⓚ	High	14	
Anchor Knee Kick	⇨Ⓚ	Mid	16	
Anchor Middle Kick	⇘Ⓚ	Mid	15	
Anchor Bow Kick	⇩Ⓚ	Low	11	Leaves Shura in a crouching state
Anchor Marooned Kick	⇗Ⓚ	Low	18	Leaves Shura in a crouching state
Anchor Steep Kick	⇦ⓀⓀ	High, Mid	16, 16	Combos on counter-hit
Vile Slide	⇦⇩⇙Ⓚ	Low	25	Crumples on counter-hit
Vile Tornado	⇦⇩⇙ⓀⒷⒷ	Low, High, High	10, 20, 20	First 2 hits combo, 3rd hit is Unblockable
Anchor Bow Kick	While Crouching Ⓚ	Low	11	Leaves Shura in a crouching state
Anchor Revive Kick	While Rising Ⓚ	Mid	21	
Cannon Launch Kick	Jumping Ⓚ	Mid	18	
Aft Anchor Kick	Backturned Ⓚ	High	16	
Sub Anchor Bow Kick	While Crouching Backturned Ⓚ	Low	12	Knocks down, leaves Shura in crouching state

Horizontal Attacks

Name	Command	Attack Level	Damage	Notes
Soul Swing	ⒶⒶ	High, High	10, 11	Combos naturally
Pirate's Cross	ⒶⒷ	High, Mid	10, 25	
Anchor Gusty Kick	ⒶⓀ	High	28	
Gentle Wave	⇨Ⓐ	High	14	Leaves foe sideturned
Scissor Lifter	⇘ⒶⒷ	Low, Mid	14, 16	Just Frame Ⓑ for extra damage and launch
Laser Wave	⇩Ⓐ	Sp.Low	10	
Wave Break	⇗Ⓐ	Low	26	Knocks down
Crush Keel	⇦Ⓐ	High	17	Backturns foe on normal hit, crumples foe on counter-hit
Crush Keel (Hold)	⇦🅐	High	17	Crumples foe
Laser Wave	While Crouching Ⓐ	Sp.Low	10	
Cursed Blow	While Rising Ⓐ	Mid	18	Spins foe
Soul Wipe Riptide	Jumping Ⓐ	High	24	
Aft Soul Wipe	Backturned Ⓐ	High	12	
Sub Laser Wave	While Crouching Backturned Ⓐ	Low	14	

Vertical Attacks

Name	Command	Attack Level	Damage	Notes
Wild Storm	ⒷⒷⒷ	Mid, Mid, Mid	13, 13, 24	Combos on counter-hit, knocks down
Storm Flare	ⒷⒷ⇦Ⓑ+Ⓚ	Mid, Mid, Mid	13, 13, 45	First 2 hits combo naturally, 3rd hit is a Guard Break
Surprise Wave	ⒷⒶ	High	16	Causes foe to spin and crumple on counter-hit, teleports Shura if struck during retraction by high slashes
Head Snap Kick	ⒷⓀ	Mid	28	Knocks down
Storm Generate	Ⓑ⇩	Sp.Mid	5	Hit throw against airborne foes
Storm Generate (Attack Throw)	Against Airborne Foe Ⓑ⇩		20	Hit Throw against airborne foes
Sail Nautilus (Hold)	⇨🅑	Mid	25	Crumples foe
Sail Nautilus	⇨ⒷⒷ	Mid, Mid	20. 25	Combos on counter-hit
Sail Nautilus (Hold)	⇨Ⓑ🅑	Mid, Mid	20, 15, 15, 20	Last 3 hits combo naturally
Cannonball Lifter	⇘Ⓑ	Mid	18 (24)	Launches and does extra damage at close range, press Ⓑ for follow-up attack during counter-hit
Cannonball Lifter (Follow-up Attack 1)	Counter-hit ⇘ⒷⒷ (Just)	Mid, Mid	28, 35	
Cannonball Lifter (Follow-up Attack 2)	Counter-hit ⇘Ⓑ ⇦Ⓑ (Just)	Mid, Mid	28, 20	
Spike Anchor	⇩Ⓑ	Mid	20	Leaves Shura in crouching state
Bloody Hoist	⇗Ⓑ	Mid	24	Knocks down, leaves Shura in crouching state
Bloody Hilt Kick	⇦ⒷⓀ	Mid, High	16, 22	Combos on counter-hit, 2nd hit leaves both characters backturned
Slay Storm	While Crouching Ⓑ	Mid	16	Leaves Shura in crouching state
Law of Pirates	While Rising ⒷⒷ	Mid, Mid	15, 35	1st hit launches, 2nd hit launches on counter-hit, leaves Shura in crouching state
Deck Lifter	Jumping Ⓑ	Mid	20	Launches
Aft Blade Storm	Backturned Ⓑ	Mid	15	
Sub Slay Storm	While Crouching Backturned Ⓑ	Mid	18	Leaves Shura in crouching state

Simultaneous Press

Name	Command	Attack Level	Damage	Notes
Full Sail Hoist	Ⓐ+Ⓑ	Mid	18	Causes recoverable stun
Gale Slash	⇨Ⓐ+ⒷⒷ	Mid, Mid	14, 20 (30)	Extra hit and damage with Just Frame input on 2nd hit
Scissor Wave	⬂Ⓐ+Ⓑ	Mid, Mid	12, 15	
Fregata Slicer	⇩Ⓐ+Ⓑ	Mid	20	Crumples foe on counter-hit, leaves Shura in a crouching state
Eternal Curse	⬀Ⓐ+Ⓑ	Mid	30	Unblockable, launches
Dark Geo Da Ray	⇦Ⓐ+Ⓑ	Mid, Mid, Mid	10, 20, 22	Guard Break, launches
Iceberg Circular	⇧Ⓐ+Ⓑ	Mid	28	Launches
Flying Dutchman	While Crouching Ⓐ+Ⓑ	Mid, Mid, Mid, Mid, Mid, Mid, Mid	6, 6, 6, 6, 6, 6, 20	
Flying Dutchman	While Crouching Ⓐ+ⒷⒷ (Mash)	Mid, Mid, Mid, Mid, Mid, Mid, Mid	6, 6, 6, 6, 6, 6, 20	Guard Break
Pirate's Tactics	Ⓑ+Ⓚ			Deflects vertical slashes and teleports Shura behind foe
High Tide Anchoring	⇩Ⓑ+Ⓚ	Mid	33	
High Tide Anchoring (Hold)	⇩🅑+🅚	Sp.Mid	38	Knocks down
Shadow Flare	⇦Ⓑ+Ⓚ	Mid	45	Guard Break
Shadow Flare (Hold)	⇦🅑+🅚	Mid	45	Guard Break, falls behind foe
Killer X Crawler	⇧Ⓑ+Ⓚ	Mid	36	Knocks down
Pressure Astern	⇧🅑+🅚	Mid	28	Knocks down
Aft Dread Pressure	Backturned Ⓑ+Ⓚ	Mid	20	
Pirate's Scheme	Ⓐ+Ⓚ			Deflects horizontal high and mid slashes and teleports Shura behind foe
Genocidal Culverin	⇨Ⓐ+Ⓚ	High	60	Unblockable
Anchor Bow Heel	⇦Ⓐ+Ⓚ	Mid	25	Launches on counter-hit, deflects vs. horizontal high and mid slashes
Bloody Culverin	⇧Ⓐ+Ⓚ	High	15	Unblockable
Dark Flame	Backturned Ⓐ+Ⓚ			Teleports behind foe, facing them
Dark Flame (Hold)	Backturned 🅐+🅚			Teleports behind foe, backturned
Taunt	Ⓚ+Ⓖ			

8-Way Run

Name	Command	Attack Level	Damage	Notes
Lagging Wave	→Ⓐ	High	30	Knocks down
Dishonest Wave	↘ or ↗Ⓐ	High	35	Knocks down, deflect vs. horizontal high slashes
Bridgette Slice	↓Ⓐ	Mid, High	15, 20	Knocks down
Tornado Slice	↑Ⓐ	High, Mid	15, 20	Knocks down
Gibbering Torpedo	↙ or ↖ⒶⒶ	Low, Low	15, 27	Combos on counter-hit, 2nd hit launches
Gibbering Pressure	↙ or ↖ⒶⒷ	Low, Mid	15, 25	
Merciless Wave	←Ⓐ	High	38	Knocks down
Cannonball Split	←ⒶⒷ	Mid	43	Hit throw
Merciless Needle	←ⒶⒷⒷ	Mid, Mid	X, 16	Follow-up if hit throw is blocked
Bile Lunges	→Ⓑ	Mid	25, (48)	Becomes hit throw if close enough
Cannonball Lifter	↘ or ↗Ⓑ	Mid	18 (24)	Launches and does extra damage from close range
Storm Nest	↓ or ↑Ⓑ	Low	15	Crumples on counter-hit
Storm Nest (Attack Throw)	Against Downed Foe ↓ or ↑Ⓑ		25	Hit throw against downed foes, launches
Riot Storm	↙ or ↖Ⓑ	Mid	34	Launches on counter-hit
Bow Breaker	←Ⓑ	Mid	35	
Head Scratch Kick	→ or ↘ or ↗Ⓚ	Mid	16	Crumples on counter-hit
Anchor Side Kick	↓ or ↑Ⓚ	Mid	22	Deflects vs. horizontal highs and mids
Anchor Swirl Kick	↙ or ↖Ⓚ	Low	22	
Galleon Sinker	←Ⓚ	Mid	28	Causes back slide on counter-hit
Windmill	→Ⓐ+Ⓑ	Mid, High	15, 15	Launches
Cross Bone Divider	←Ⓐ+Ⓑ	Mid	35	Launches
Cross Bone Divider (Hold)	←🅐+🅑	Mid	50	Unblockable, launches
Sliding	While Running Ⓚ	Low	26	Knocks down

Throws

Name	Command	Attack Level	Damage	Notes
Sadistic Cross	Ⓐ+Ⓖ	Throw	50	Ⓐ to break throw
Turbulence Lift	Ⓑ+Ⓖ	Throw	10	Launches
Figurehead Break	Left Side Throw	Throw	55	Ⓐ to break throw
Jolly Roger Hoist	Right Side Throw	Throw	58	Ⓑ to break throw
Flush Flood	Back Throw	Throw	60	
Curse of the Ancient Mariner	While Crouching ⬂⇩⬃Ⓑ+Ⓖ	Throw	69	Ⓑ to break throw

Dread Charge

Name	Command	Attack Level	Damage	Notes
Dread Charge	⇩⇙⇦			Initiates Dread Charge
Dread Slash	Dread Charge Ⓐ	High	55	Unblockable
Geo Da Ray	Dread Charge Ⓑ	Mid	30	Launches, hold Ⓑ to redirect off walls
Geo Da Ray	Dread Charge Ⓑ (Perfect ⇩⇙⇦ Ⓑ input)	Mid	17, 10, 6	Launches
Geo Da Ray	Dread Charge Ⓑ (Perfect ⇩⇙⇦Ⓑ input)⇩⇧Ⓑ	Mid, Mid	17, 10, 6, 18	
Geo Da Ray	Dread Charge ⇩ or ⇧Ⓑ		30	Aims off-axis
Rolling Slapper	Dread Charge Ⓚ	Mid	20, 20	
Tornado Swell	Dread Charge Ⓑ+Ⓚ		22, 22, 22	
Anchor Whirlpool	Dread Charge Ⓐ+Ⓚ	Low	20	Knocks down
Dark Flame	Dread Charge ⇨			Teleports forward

Combos

⇘Ⓑ, ⇧Ⓐ + Ⓚ, Ⓑ⇩
3 hits, 52 damage
Counter-hit ⇘Ⓑ, ⇩⇙⇦, Ⓑ + Ⓚ
4 hits, 79 damage
Ⓑ + Ⓖ, Ⓑ + Ⓚ (late)
4 hits, 55 damage
While Rising Ⓐ, ⇦ⓀⓀ
3 hits, 45 damage
⇘ⒶⒷ (Just), ⇧Ⓐ + Ⓚ, ⒶⒶ
6 hits, 51 damage
⇨⇨Ⓑ (Wall Hit), ⒷⒷⒷ (Wall Hit), ⇩Ⓑ + Ⓚ
8 hits, 96 damage
⇦⇦Ⓐ + Ⓑ, ⇩⇙⇦, Ⓑ + Ⓚ
4 hits, 86 damage
Counter-hit ⒷⒶ, ⇩Ⓐ + Ⓑ, While Rising Ⓐ, ⇦ⓀⓀ (Wall hit), ⇘Ⓑ, ⇩⇙⇦, Ⓑ + Ⓚ
10 hits, 90 damage

Close Range

Shura is a handful up close. Between Soul Swing (ⒶⒶ) and Wild Storm (ⒷⒷⒷ), she can stop enemies from using side movement or crouching. The Wild Storm is a strong 3-hit combo if it strikes as a counter-hit or against a crouching foe. Learn to confirm whether the enemy is guarding ⒷⒷ before the third Ⓑ press, as Shura is vulnerable if the full string is guarded. The Cannonball Lifter (↘Ⓑ) is also useful for punishing crouching enemies. At close range, it launches on normal or counter-hit. As with the Wild Storm, it's useful to train yourself to eyeball the outcome. If ↘Ⓑ lands as a normal hit, juggle with ↑Ⓐ + Ⓚ, ↘Ⓐ + Ⓑ. However, if it strikes as a counter-hit, the enemy will be launched much higher, allowing you to juggle with ↓↙←, Ⓑ + Ⓚ for Shura's Dread Charge Tornado Swell. Verifying whether the Cannonball Lifter lands as a counter-hit, and then actually performing the Tornado Swell quickly enough to juggle, takes practice. This juggle inflicts far more damage though, making it worth your while.

Apart from these attacks, use Scissor Wave (↘Ⓐ + Ⓑ) and Fregata Slicer (↓Ⓐ + Ⓑ) as your main pokes up close. Both are mid-striking slashes. Scissor Wave simply serves as a great interruption move, hitting twice without leaving Shura vulnerable if guarded. Fregata Slicer is slightly slower, but also safe if blocked, and it leads to enormous combos on counter-hit. Shura is left in a crouching animation after Fregata Slicer, making While Rising attacks easy to perform by simply pressing a button. Fregata Slicer as a counter-hit causes the enemy to stagger, letting you combo with While Rising Ⓐ, ←ⓀⓀ. If the enemy is knocked into the wall by ←ⓀⓀ, it's party time. Tack on ⒷⒷⒷ for easy, heavy extra damage before going for ground hits, or try ↘Ⓑ to launch your foe into Tornado Swell or Bloody Culverin (↑Ⓐ + Ⓚ) to Storm Generate (Ⓑ↓). Finally, while it's not as great a poke as Fregata Slicer, note that the high-hitting Surprise Wave (ⓞⒶ) spins the enemy on counter-hit, from which you can land Fregata Slicer into this same sequence.

Mid Range

Shura standing a couple steps away from her foe isn't any less threatening. Wild Storm can still hit from a surprising range, and while the Cannonball Lifter isn't as effective from a distance, she has a few other tools that easily lead to juggles from mid range. Scissor Lifter (↘ⒶⒷ) is a low-to-mid linear string that can be difficult to guard properly, and it combos even on normal hit, flipping foes over Shura's head. Input Ⓑ with perfect timing—just as ↘Ⓐ contacts the enemy—and Shura adds an extra canned hit before leaving opponents floating at a perfect juggle height. Combo them with ↑Ⓐ + Ⓚ, ⒶⒶ. Enemies can avoid Scissor Lifter with sidesteps or 8-Way Run, so mix in Gibbering Torpedo (⇗ or ⇘ⒶⒶ) and Gibbering Pressure (⇗ or ⇘ⒶⒷ) to discourage side movement. Gibbering Torpedo hits low twice and launches even on normal hit, letting you juggle with ↘Ⓐ + Ⓑ. It's unsafe if guarded, but that's what Gibbering Pressure is for. The first hit is the same, but the second hit is a mid that strikes foes if they expected to guard all of Gibbering Torpedo.

Merciless Wave (←←Ⓐ) and Merciless Needle (←← ⒶⒷⒷ) are also excellent from mid range. Merciless Wave is a sweeping high slash that floors foes using side movement. Merciless Needle actually fakes a Merciless Wave before going for a hit throw that nails crouching enemies. If Merciless Needle is guarded, Shura just forces the opponent to block two mids that don't leave her vulnerable.

Long Range

Shura remains versatile from afar, though her versatility at great distances mostly involves getting close easily. Her Genocidal Culverin (→Ⓐ+Ⓚ) is a relatively fast full-screen Unblockable useful to catch foes napping. It also counter-hits uselessly whiffed pokes from great range. If the enemy gets too close to a ring edge and you're far enough away to try Genocidal Culverin without getting horribly punished for missing, go for it—the move easily causes a Ring Out if it hits. Shadow Flare (←Ⓑ+Ⓚ) allows Shura to instantly teleport above the enemy's head from any range before falling onto him or her with a Guard Break. It's easily sidestepped, but it can still be useful against foes not expecting it or those who are a little careless with attacks at range. If you'd like to essentially fake the Shadow Flare and simply stay where you are, perform ←Ⓑ+Ⓚ. Shura will simply Shadow Flare in place, but this might be just enough to make enemies nervous, allowing subsequent attacks to hit. Shura's Geo Da Ray (↓↙← to initiate Dread Charge then Ⓑ, or ←Ⓐ+Ⓑ) can also cross an entire arena in an instant, sending the enemy flying into a position to be juggled (Ⓖ briefly to face the launched body, then Ⓑ↓) if they don't guard standing or sidestep. Be careful using this move on stages without walls, as Shura will fly off a stage without hesitation if you tell her to!

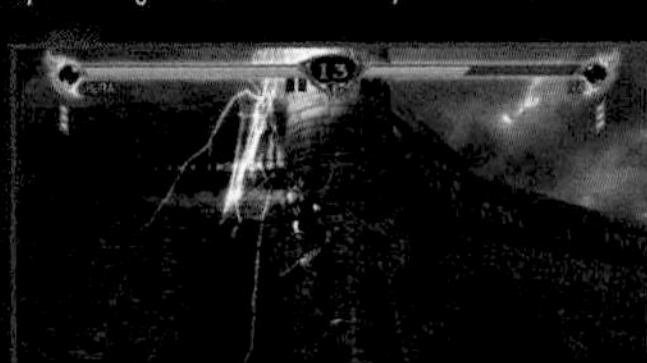
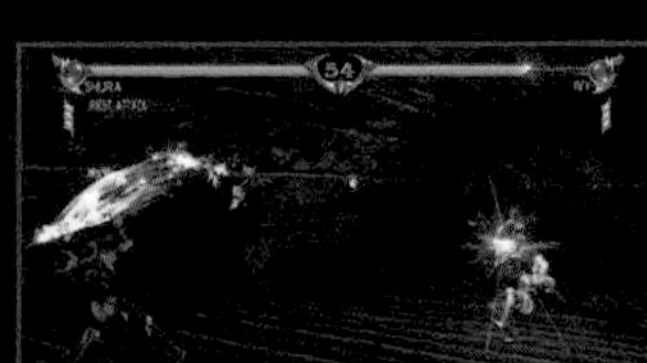

Special Tactics

Okizeme: Anti-Wakeup

Shura's numerous middles and lows that lead directly to staggers or launches are as useful on waking enemies as they are against standing ones. Besides mixing them up with Gibbering Torpedo versus Cannonball Lifter as they rise, Shura can also use her Dread Charge (↓↙←) to pressure floored opponents. If you sense they'll Ukemi, try using a Geo Da Ray to nail them quickly. Pressure Astern (↗Ⓑ+Ⓚ), a leaping slash with great range, also works well for this purpose. If you think the opponent will wait and rise slowly, initiate a Dread Charge and then make him guess between dealing with Shura's Anchor Whirlpool Ⓐ+Ⓚ sweep or her Dread Slash (Ⓐ) Unblockable. If your foe is *really* taking his time, pick him up off the ground into a juggle combo with Storm Nest (⇩or⇧Ⓑ).

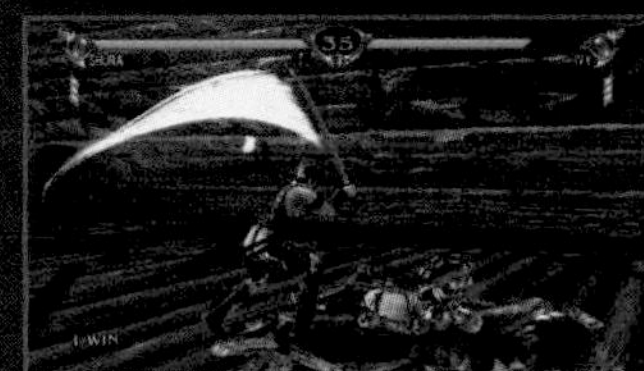

Dread Charge

Initiate the Dread Charge with ↓↙←. Shura briefly shifts her stance, opening up a few unique offensive options. The low-hitting sweep Ⓐ+Ⓚ floors the foe, while Ⓐ is a high Unblockable. Using Ⓑ initiates the torpedo-like Geo Da Ray, which you can also direct into the fore- or background by holding ↓ or ↑. This can be useful as a fake or to obtain better arena position. Hold → to teleport from a Dread Charge closer to the opponent. Finally, Ⓑ+Ⓚ from a Dread Charge initiates the Tornado Swell, a high-flying blade spin that is excellent in juggles, provided the enemy is lofted high enough to allow Tornado Swell to connect. Counter-hit ↘Ⓑ or ←←Ⓐ+Ⓑ are examples of launchers that Tornado Swell can follow. Input ↓↙←, Ⓑ+Ⓚ as quickly as possible in order to execute the attack fast enough to juggle. Finally, while it's difficult, a perfect ↓↙←Ⓑ input produces an instant Just Frame Geo Da Ray. If this hits, input ↓↑Ⓑ for a high-flying follow-up slash!

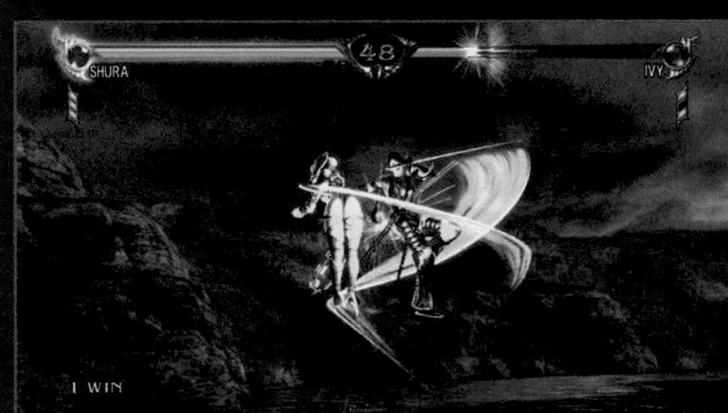

Darth Vader

Bio

Age:	Unknown
Birthplace:	Planet Tatooine
Height:	6'8"
Weight:	300 lbs.
Birth Date:	Unknown
Blood Type:	Unknown (Midi-chlorian Count: 20,000+)
Weapon:	Lightsaber
Weapon Name:	Unknown
Discipline:	Djem So
Family:	Emperor Palpatine (Master)

A long time ago in a galaxy far, far away....

During a battle between the Galactic Empire and the Rebel Alliance, [illegible] Emperor Palpatine sensed a faint ripple of power. [illegible] investigation in secret.

The ripple came from somewhere [illegible] something strange [illegible] in the universe as well.

[illegible] Darth Vader had been searching [illegible] from a different dimension [illegible] the disturbance. Could this unknown power be utilized?

With that possibility in mind, Darth Vader arranged for the readying of [illegible] a dimensional portal had opened. After waiting for conditions to stabilize, Darth Vader [illegible] galaxy.

He searched for the origins of the wave of power and arrived at a planet. The planet was in [illegible] two forces with opposite natures. The conflicting nature of the dissonant forces [illegible] swords were not their true form—they were beings that [illegible].

Darth Vader had not a doubt in his mind. He would be able to wield these forces—Soul Calibur and Soul Edge—[illegible] were in his hands, these two contrasting swords would enable him to rule the galaxy.

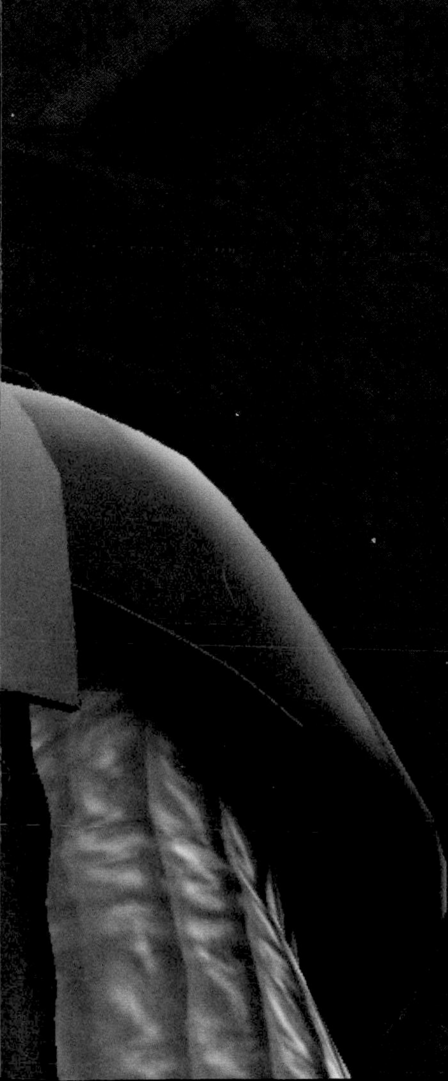

Darth Vader

Command List

Signature Techniques

Name	Command	Attack Level	Damage	Notes
Mustafar Tide	⇦ⒶⒶ	Low, High	16, 23	
Imperial Buster	⇨ⒷⒷ	Mid, Mid	11, 18	
Hilt Strike	⇙ⒷⒶ	Mid, High	18. 22	
Imperial Rise	➡Ⓑ	Mid	28	Launches on hit
Dark Splitter	⬇ or ⬆Ⓑ	Mid	31	Stuns on hit
Force Impact	Ⓐ+Ⓑ	High	50	Unblockable. Depletes Force.
Sith Impale	⇘Ⓑ+Ⓚ	Mid	20	Stuns on hit. Depletes Force.
Force Hang ~Saber Strike	Against Downed Foe ⇦Ⓐ+Ⓑ ⇨Ⓐ+Ⓑ	Throw, Mid	15, 20	Depletes Force
Force Grip	Ⓑ+ⒼⒶ+Ⓑ	Throw	15, 40	Depletes Force

Horizontal Attacks

Name	Command	Attack Level	Damage	Notes
Sith Strike	ⒶⒶ	Low, High	14, 16	
Deadly Strike	⇨Ⓐ	High	14	
Dark Strike	⇘Ⓐ	Mid	18	
Low Strike	⇩Ⓐ	Low	21	
Sinking Strike	⇙Ⓐ	Low	27	
Mustafar Tide	⇦ⒶⒶ	Low, High	16, 23	
Low Strike	While Crouching Ⓐ	Sp.Low	12	
Break Slash	While Rising Ⓐ	High	27	
Annihilation "Force Impact"	While Rising ⒶⒼ Ⓐ+Ⓑ	Low, High	14, 50	2nd attack is unblockable. Depletes Force.
Annihilation "Force Cannon"	While Rising ⒶⒼ ⇙Ⓐ+Ⓑ	Low, Mid	14, 70	2nd attack is unblockable, stuns on hit. Depletes Force.
Jumping Slash	Jumping Ⓐ	High	22 or 24 or 26	Damage varies depending on direction jumped in
Back Strike	Backturned Ⓐ	High	16	
Back Low Strike	While Crouching Backturned Ⓐ	Low	14	

Throws

Name	Command	Attack Level	Damage	Notes
Dark Glory	Ⓐ+Ⓖ	Throw	50	Input Ⓐ to escape
Force Grip	Ⓑ+ⒼⒶ+Ⓑ	Throw	15, 40	Input Ⓑ to escape. Depletes Force.
Law of the Empire	Left Side Throw	Throw	55	Same button as throw (Ⓐ or Ⓑ) to escape
Crimson Slayer	Right Side Throw	Throw	60	Same button as throw (Ⓐ or Ⓑ) to escape
Honor of Sith	Back Throw, Ⓐ+Ⓑ	Throw	30, 30	Same button as throw (Ⓐ or Ⓑ) to escape. Depletes Force.
Force Hang ~Saber Strike	Against Downed Foe ⇦Ⓐ+Ⓑ ⇨Ⓐ+Ⓑ	Throw, Mid	15, 20	
Force Hang ~Draw	Against Downed Foe ⇦Ⓐ+Ⓑ ⇦Ⓐ+Ⓑ	Throw		
Force Hang ~Force Impact	Against Downed Foe ⇦Ⓐ+ⒷⒶ+Ⓑ ⇨Ⓐ+Ⓑ	Throw, High	50	2nd attack is unblockable. Depletes Force.
Force Hang ~Force Cannon	Against Downed Foe ⇦Ⓐ+ⒷⒶ+Ⓑ ⇙Ⓐ+Ⓑ	Throw, Mid	70	2nd attack is unblockable, stuns on hit. Depletes Force.

Vertical Attacks

Name	Command	Attack Level	Damage	Notes
Tempest Breaker	ⒷⒷ	Mid, Mid	16, 24	Fully combos on counter-hit. 2nd attack causes recoverable stun on hit.
Imperial Buster	⇨ⒷⒷ	Mid, Mid	11, 18	
Imperial Storm "Force Impact"	⇨Ⓑ ⒷⒼⒶ+Ⓑ	Mid, Low, High	11, 18, 50	2nd attack causes recoverable stun on hit. 3rd attack is unblockable. Depletes Force.
Imperial Storm "Force Cannon"	⇨Ⓑ ⒷⒼ⇙ Ⓐ+Ⓑ	Mid, Low, Mid	11, 18, 70	2nd attack causes recoverable stun on hit. 3rd attack is unblockable, causes stun. Depletes Force.
Charging Thrust	⇘Ⓑ	Mid	20	
Sith Rampage	⇩Ⓑ	Mid	18	
Hilt Strike	⇙ⒷⒶ	Mid, High	12. 22	
Dark Side Blow	⇦Ⓑ	Mid	24	
Star Splitter	While Crouching Ⓑ	Mid	16	
Droid Breaker	While Rising Ⓑ	Mid	23	
Jumping Splitter	Jumping Ⓑ	Mid	22 or 25 or 28	Damage varies depending on direction jumped in
Back Cutter	Backturned Ⓑ	Mid	18	
Back Splitter	While Crouching Backturned Ⓑ	Mid	19	

Kick Attacks

Name	Command	Attack Level	Damage	Notes
Cyborg Kick	Ⓚ	High	14	
Neck Crush	⇨Ⓚ	Mid	16	
Sith Crusher	⇘ⓀⒷ	Mid, Mid	12, 16	1st attack stuns against fallen enemies (⇘Ⓚ cannot be performed by itself for this to work)
Leg Sweep	⇩Ⓚ	Low	15	
Knee Breaker	⇗Ⓚ	Low	14	
Dark Side Smash	⇦Ⓚ	Mid	18	Causes recoverable stun on hit
Leg Sweep	While Crouching Ⓚ	Low	15	
Knee Blast	While Rising Ⓚ	Mid	19	
Jumping Toe Kick	Jumping Ⓚ	Mid	21	
Back Kick	Backturned Ⓚ	High	16	
Back Sweep	While Crouching Backturned Ⓚ	Low	12	

Simultaneous Press

Name	Command	Attack Level	Damage	Notes
Force Impact	Ⓐ+Ⓑ	High	50	Unblockable. Depletes Force.
Force Parry	⇨Ⓐ+Ⓑ (During Impact; Ⓐ or Ⓑ For Additional Attack)	High or Mid	20 or 36	Ⓐ attack Guard Breaks and stuns on hit. Ⓑ attack is an unblockable. Depletes Force.
Force Parry	⇘Ⓐ+Ⓑ (During Impact; Ⓐ or Ⓑ For Additional Attack)	High or Mid	20 or 36	Ⓐ attack Guard Breaks and stuns on hit. Ⓑ attack is an unblockable. Depletes Force.
Force Crush	⇩Ⓐ+Ⓑ	S.Mid		Causes ground stun on aerial hit. Depletes Force.
Force Crush	⇩Ⓐ+Ⓑ	Mid	18	Depletes Force
Force Cannon	⇗Ⓐ+Ⓑ	Mid	70	Unblockable, stuns on hit. Depletes Force.
Force Hang	⇦Ⓐ+Ⓑ	Sp.Mid		Depletes Force.
Dark Vortex	⇩⇘⇨Ⓐ+Ⓑ	Mid, Mid, Mid, Mid	10, 25	Final attack Guard Breaks. Depletes Force.
Dark Vortex (Hold)	⇩⇘⇨Ⓐ+Ⓑ	Mid x7	10, 7, 5, 5, 5...8, 25	Final attack Guard Breaks. Continues attack and depletes Force for as long as command is held.
Rising Strike	While Crouching Ⓐ+Ⓑ	Mid	33	Guard Breaks
Reign of Terror	Ⓑ+ⓀⒷⒷ	Mid, Mid, Mid	16, 14, 24	Depletes Force
Sith Impale	⇘Ⓑ+Ⓚ	Mid	20	Stuns on hit, depletes Force
Star Breaker	⇩Ⓑ+Ⓚ	Mid	22	Stuns on hit, ground hit and aerial hit. Depletes Force.
Ground Scrape	⇦Ⓑ+Ⓚ	Low	24	Depletes Force
Rising Slash	While Rising Ⓑ+Ⓚ	Mid	28	Stuns on hit, depletes Force
Sudden Thrust	Backturned Ⓑ+Ⓚ	Mid	16	Stuns on hit
Horizontal Slice	Ⓐ+ⓀⒶ	Low, High	16, 18	Depletes Force
Taunt	Ⓚ+Ⓖ			

8-Way Run

Name	Command	Attack Level	Damage	Notes
Jedi Killer	→Ⓐ	High	26	
Jedi Killer	↘Ⓐ	High	26	
Jedi Killer	↗Ⓐ	High	26	
Hilt Thrust	↓ or ↑Ⓐ	High	15	
Buster Combo	↙ or ↖ⒶⒷ	Low, Mid	13, 32	
Vader Slash	←Ⓐ	High	19	
Imperial Rise	→Ⓑ	Mid	28	Launches on hit
Imperial Assault "Force Impact"	→ⒷⒼⒶ+Ⓑ	Mid, High	16, 50	2nd attack is unblockable, stuns on hit. Depletes Force.
Imperial Assault "Force Cannon"	→ⒷⒼ⇗Ⓐ+Ⓑ	Mid, Mid	16, 70	2nd attack is unblockable, stuns on hit. Depletes Force.
Dark Rise	↘ or ↗Ⓑ	Mid	26	
Dark Splitter	↓ or ↑Ⓑ	Mid	31	Stuns on hit
Imperial Strike "Force Impact"	↓ or ↑ⒷⒼ Ⓐ+Ⓑ	Mid, High	16, 50	2nd attack is unblockable. Depletes Force.
Imperial Strike "Force Cannon"	↓ or ↑ⒷⒼ⇗ Ⓐ+Ⓑ	Mid, Mid	16, 70	2nd attack is unblockable, stuns on hit. Depletes Force.
Tornado Splitter	↙ or ↖Ⓑ	Mid	35	Launches on hit
Dark Lord "Force Impact"	←ⒷⒶ+Ⓑ	Mid, High	22, 50	2nd attack is unblockable. Depletes Force.
Dark Lord "Force Cannon"	←Ⓑ⇗Ⓐ+Ⓑ	Mid, Mid	22, 70	2nd attack is unblockable, stuns on hit. Depletes Force.
Face Buster	→ or ↘ or ↗Ⓚ	Mid	22	
Skull Buster	↓ or ↑Ⓚ	Mid	25	
Body Breaker	↙ or ↖Ⓚ	Low	20	
Flip Kick	←Ⓚ	Mid	21	
Life Shaker	8-Way Run Any Direction Ⓐ+Ⓑ	Mid	13	Guard Breaks, stuns on hit. Depletes Force.
Rising Break	↘ or ↗Ⓑ+Ⓚ	Mid	28	Depletes Force
Dark Launcher "Force Impact"	←Ⓑ+ⓀⒶ+Ⓑ	Mid, High	22, 50	Launches on hit. 2nd attack is unblockable. Depletes Force.
Dark Launcher "Force Cannon"	←Ⓑ+Ⓚ⇗ Ⓐ+Ⓑ	Mid, Mid	22, 70	Launches on hit. 2nd attack is unblockable, stuns on hit. Depletes Force.
Jedi Slaughter	→Ⓐ+Ⓚ	High	30	Depletes Force
Jedi Slaughter	↘Ⓐ+Ⓚ	High	30	Depletes Force
Jedi Slaughter	↗Ⓐ+Ⓚ	High	30	Depletes Force
Fear Strike	↓ or ↑Ⓐ+Ⓚ	Mid	35	Depletes Force
Jedi Execution	←Ⓐ+Ⓚ	High	30	Depletes Force
Sliding Kick	While Running Ⓚ	Low	26	

Close Range

Darth Vader is an offensive powerhouse, best from mid range, but he has tools to work with up close and from a distance as well. A quick and safe way to start your offense is with Darth Vader's ⒶⒶ string. Use it to preemptively stop your opponent's sidesteps or attacks. If it hits your enemy, use the advantage to stage a second attack consisting of a throw, ⒷⒷ, or ←Ⓑ + Ⓚ. If ⒷⒷ connects as a counter-hit, use the recoverable stun it causes to go for the Sith Impale (↘Ⓑ + Ⓚ), Ground Scrape, or simply dash forward and throw your enemy. If the Sith Impale hits, immediately input ←←Ⓑ to score a 2-hit combo. Take a defensive stance when ⒶⒶ is blocked, either by guarding or using Vader's →Ⓐ + ⒷⒷ and ↘Ⓐ + ⒷⒷ deflect moves to stop incoming offense. Your opponent may try to crouch under ⒶⒶ to score a counterattack. Anticipate these attempts and counter them with a powerful mid attack, like the Dark Lord (←←Ⓑ).

When attacking with ←←Ⓑ, use the command ←←ⒷⒶ + ⒷⒼ. For the cost of a little Force, this command strings the Dark Lord into its Force Eruption extension, and then immediately cancels it. This not only makes the attack safe to punishment when blocked, but also makes it easier to juggle your enemy when it successfully hits. When it connects, go for this combo: ←←ⒷⒶ + Ⓑ, Ⓖ, ↓Ⓑ + Ⓚ, then →→Ⓑ.

You can also use the same cancellation method to greatly enhance other attacks. For example, the Imperial Storm "Force Eruption" (→ⒷⓑⒼⒶ + Ⓑ) string's final attack can also be cancelled in the same manner (→ⒷⓑⒼⒶ + Ⓑ, then Ⓖ). Using this command leaves you with a slight advantage when the string is blocked, allowing you to stage a secondary attack afterward; go for →ⒷⓑⒼ again, ⒶⒶ, or a throw. This string also causes a recoverable stun on a successful hit, opening the window for massive follow-up combinations, like →ⒷⓑⒼⒶ + ⒷⒼ, ←←ⒷⒶ + ⒷⒼ, ↓Ⓑ + Ⓚ, →→Ⓑ. Its only weakness is its second high hit, so condition your enemy into standing with the Imperial Buster (→ⒷⒷ) to deter crouching.

Combos

⇦⇦Ⓑ, ⇦⇦Ⓑ
2 hits, 37 Damage
⇨⇨Ⓐ + Ⓚ, ⇨⇨Ⓑ
2 hits, 49 Damage
⇦⇦ⒷⒶ + Ⓑ, Ⓖ, ⇩Ⓑ + Ⓚ, ⇨⇨Ⓑ
4 hits, 62 Damage, Ⓖ input cancels Unblockable
⬂Ⓑ, ⇦Ⓐ + Ⓑ⇦Ⓐ + Ⓑ, Ⓑ + Ⓚ, ⬂ⓀⒷ
4 hits, 57 Damage
⇨⇨Ⓐ + Ⓑ, ⬂ⓀⒷ
3 hits, 30 Damage
While Rising Ⓑ + Ⓚ, ⬂ⓀⒷ
3 hits, 45 Damage
⬂Ⓑ + Ⓚ, ⇦⇦ⒷⒶ + Ⓑ, Ⓖ, ⇩Ⓑ + Ⓚ, ⇨⇨Ⓑ
4 hits, 63 Damage, Ⓖ input cancels Unblockable
⇦⇦Ⓑ + Ⓚ, ⇩Ⓑ + Ⓚ, ⇨⇨Ⓑ
4 hits, 74 Damage
⇨⇨ⓑⒼⒶ + Ⓑ, Ⓖ, Ⓚ
2 hits, 30 Damage
Guard Impact attack with ⇨Ⓐ + ⒷⒶ, then link ⬃ⒷⒶ
3 hits, 47 Damage

Mid Range

Your strategy is to look for opportunities to land the Sith Impale (↘Ⓑ + Ⓚ), Charging Thrust (↘Ⓑ), or to force enemies to guard the Imperial Strike (⇩ or ⇧ⓑⒼ). To do this, dissuade them from using circular movement with Vader's Buster Combo (⇗ or ⇖ⒶⒷ). Both strikes link together on counter-hit, knocking down the opponent for heavy damage. Furthermore, the second slash is a mid attack, which counters attempts to crouch under the first high slash. Use this technique to scare your enemy into fighting on a linear path, which makes it easier not only to attack with vertical slashes, but also to dodge enemy attack.

If you believe your enemy wants to make an aggressive movement, attack with ↘Ⓑ to stop it. On a successful hit, immediately input ←Ⓐ + Ⓑ←Ⓐ + Ⓑ, back-turned Ⓑ + Ⓚ, then ↘ⓀⒷ to blast your foe with a 4-hit combo. If your opponents are luring out ↘Ⓑ and countering it preemptively, move into attack range to bait their attack, then back-dash out of its range. Punish their whiffed attack with ↘Ⓑ + Ⓚ, which leads to the combo ↘Ⓑ + Ⓚ, ←←ⒷⒶ + Ⓑ, Ⓖ, ↓Ⓑ + Ⓚ[redacted]Ⓑ.

When you[redacted]ry is afraid to mount an offense, attack with the Imperial Strike. Inputting the command ⇩ⓑⒼⒶ + ⒷⒼ performs the Force Eruption variation of the technique and then immediately cancels it into a forward dash. Because the initial attack causes an absolutely massive stun on hit or guard, the dash cancellation allows you to stage an airtight follow-up attack that is almost completely inescapable via sidesteps or attacks—although enemies can still use Guard Impacts. Attack with the mid ↘Ⓑ + Ⓚ, low ←Ⓑ + Ⓚ, or simply throw when you recover. Also try attacking with the flexible →ⒷⓑⒼ afterward, which leads to additional high-pressure cancellation antics.

Long Range

Your game plan is to land either Vader's ←←Ⓑ or ⇗Ⓐ. An effective way to do this is to use the Force to scare your enemy into vulnerable positions. For instance, ←Ⓐ + Ⓑ pulls the enemy toward you on a hit, leaving you with a small advantage to exploit. It's fast, it boasts a long attack range, and it costs very little of your Force gauge to use. Initiate it to drag opp[redacted] you whenever they aren't using side movement. If it hits, use the advantage to stage an attack. At max d[redacted]Ⓑ + Ⓚ to stop their attempts to regain ground after the attack. If your enemy likes to sidestep the ↘Ⓑ [redacted] option, use ↙Ⓐ after pulling him or her in to counter it. When your foe is afraid of both attack types, run in and go for a throw attempt.

Vader's Ⓐ + Ⓑ blast is also useful for the same reason. This Unblockable has extremely fast startup and massive attack range, but it misses against side movement and crouching. To compensate for this, initiate the blast and cancel it before it fires by inputting Ⓐ + ⒷⒼ. This scares the opponent into taking a defensive measure, which you can then counter after Vader recovers from the cancellation's forward dash. Punish sidestep attempts with ⇗Ⓐ, or knock crouching enemies into the air with ←←Ⓑ.

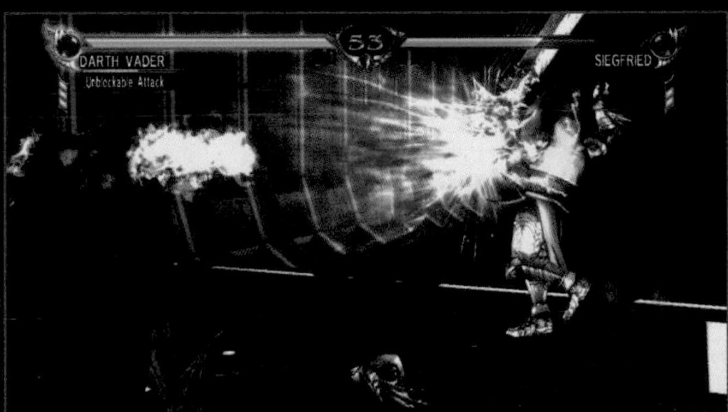

Special Tactics

Okizeme: Anti-Wakeup

Vader's low attacks are lackluster at best, so instead mix between throws and his many powerful mid attacks. The Imperial Strike and Dark Lord are the most effective of these attacks, leading to either big damage or flexible follow-up options. Another option is the Life Shaker (During 8-Way Run Ⓐ + Ⓑ), a mid attack that Guard Breaks. If it hits, perform a 3-hit combo by linking after the stun with ↘ⓀⒷ. If your enemy guards, stage a secondary attack consisting of Ⓐ + ⓀⒶ, ←Ⓑ + Ⓚ, ↘Ⓑ + Ⓚ, or run up and throw your opponent. Use the Ⓐ + ⓀⒶ option to counter your enemies' earliest attempts to sidestep after they leave blockstun; this conditions your foe, at which point you can exploit the other options.

"I Find Your Lack of Faith Disturbing..."

The shrouded Darth Vader has a small blue bar called the Force Gauge under his health meter. This meter depletes when you perform his special Force attacks. If you use Force techniques when the Force Gauge is empty, Vader enters a heavy recovery period that leaves him open to attack. Avoid using his powers whenever the gauge is low. Build meter by playing aggressively, hitting your enemy with attacks or forcing them to guard your moves.

One of Vader's more interesting Force powers is his ←Ⓐ + Ⓑ, which causes a special state when used against an enemy laying on the ground. Inputting different commands during this state causes Vader to manipulate his enemy in three different ways: Ⓐ + Ⓑ lifts enemies into the air and hits them with a Force blast, →Ⓐ + Ⓑ stabs enemies and tosses them aside, and ←Ⓐ + Ⓑ pulls them close, leaving them vulnerable to attack. The most useful of these options is ←Ⓐ + Ⓑ, as it leaves the enemy vulnerable to Vader's back-turned Ⓑ + Ⓚ, thus allowing additional hits afterward. You can use this ability after several attacks to extend your combos dramatically. The easiest opening is to land a counter-hit ⒷⒷ string, then immediately perform ←Ⓐ + Ⓑ to pick up your foe off the ground. You can then perform combos like counter-hit ⒷⒷ, ←Ⓐ + Ⓑ←Ⓐ + Ⓑ, back-turned Ⓑ + Ⓚ, ⒷⒷ, →→Ⓑ. This combo alone inflicts a massive 147 damage!

Yoda

A long time ago in a galaxy far, far away....

Jedi Master Yoda, who was considered by some to be a living legend, remained hidden on the planet Dagobah in order to evade persistent pursuers after the rise of the Empire. For many years, Yoda had lived on that planet of mud and swampland.

One day, he noticed a faint wave of power that shook the very foundations of the universe. He looked up into the sky to try and see what was happening, but had no means of discerning it. The wave of power was weak and quickly became undetectable. Though it had been an unmistakable disturbance, he surmised that it was not a huge problem. The movements of the Galactic Empire were of more concern. The Empire had taken control of the galaxy, and many suffered under its tyranny.

However, as the days passed, the strength of the wave increased. It could now be felt constantly as a distortion in the universe. Soon after, Darth Vader, the Empire's Dark Lord, made his move. Yoda sensed that it was time for him to act as well, for if the Empire was becoming involved, then so must he. Leaving Dagobah meant that his safety would be compromised, but there were no Jedi left with the power to stop Darth Vader.

In the course of his journey, Yoda sensed that Darth Vader had become involved with the disturbance. Vader's motive was now clear. There was something on the other side that created this disturbance, and the Empire was attempting to gain control of that power. If left unchecked, Vader may return to their universe with a huge calamity.

Without hesitation, Yoda made his decision and jumped into the disturbance himself. No matter what may lay waiting for him, he knew he had to stop the Empire's scheme.

Yoda

Bio

Age:	900 years old
Birth Place:	Unknown
Height:	2'2"
Weight:	Unknown
Birth Date:	Unknown
Blood Type:	Unknown (Midi-chlorian Count: approx. 20,000)
Weapon:	Lightsaber
Weapon Name:	Unknown
Discipline:	Ataru
Family:	Unknown

Command List

Signature Techniques

Name	Command	Attack Level	Damage	Notes
Ataru Windmill	↘ⒷⒷ	Mid, Mid	16, 20	1st hit launches
Swing Kick	←Ⓚ	Mid	20	Causes backward crumple
Ataru Combo	Ⓐ+ⒷⒷ	High, Mid	14, 20	
Charge Slash	→Ⓐ+Ⓚ	Low	20	Knocks down
Ataru Combo	→ or ↘ or ↗ⒶⒶ	Mid, Low	18, 16	Knocks down
Whirlwind Strike	↓ or ↑Ⓐ	High	15	Spins foe
Force Cancel ~Ataru Combo	Cancel From Flip or Flipping Attack →Ⓑ+ⓀⒷ	Mid, Mid	14, 20	Knocks down
Force Cancel ~Twirling Divide	Cancel From Flip or Flipping Attack ↓ or ↑Ⓑ+Ⓚ	Mid	20	Launches
Tector Shake	↓↑Ⓑ+Ⓖ	Throw	25	

Horizontal Attacks

Name	Command	Attack Level	Damage	Notes
Double Strike	ⒶⒶ	High, High	8, 8	
Charge Slash	→Ⓐ	Mid	16	
Jedi Slash	↘Ⓐ	Mid	14	Backturns foe
Jedi Slice	↓Ⓐ	Sp.Low	8	
Jedi Strike	↙Ⓐ	Low	14	
Droid Buster	←Ⓐ	High	20	Backturns foe, crumples foe on counter-hit
Aerial Strike	Jumping Ⓐ	High	14	Backturns foe
Back Double Strike	Backturned Ⓐ	High	10	
Back Slice	Backturned ↓Ⓐ	Sp.Low	10	

Vertical Attacks

Name	Command	Attack Level	Damage	Notes
Double Split	ⒷⒷ	Mid, Mid	12, 12	
Charge Strike	→Ⓑ	Mid	24	Guard Break
Ataru Windmill	↘ⒷⒷ	Mid, Mid	16, 20	1st hit launches
Dagobah Strike	↓Ⓑ	Mid	12	
Dagobah Divide	↙Ⓑ	Mid	14	Crumples foe on counter-hit
Piercing Thrust	←Ⓑ	High	18	
Council Judgement	↓↘→ⒷⒷⒷⒷⒷⒷ	Mid, Mid, Mid, Mid, Mid, Mid	16, 8, 8, 9, 6, 10	1st hit launches, input Ⓑ rhythmically for all six hits
Aerial Pierce	Jumping Ⓑ	Mid	16	
Back Double Split	Backturned Ⓑ	Mid	14	
Back Dagobah Divide	Backturned ↓Ⓑ	Mid	14	

Kick Attacks

Name	Command	Attack Level	Damage	Notes
High Kick	Ⓚ	High	10	
Hopping Kick	⇨Ⓚ	High	16	Knocks down
Waist Breaker	⬂Ⓚ	Mid	12	Back slides on counter-hit
Heel Kick	⇩Ⓚ	Low	10	
Flip Kick	⬃Ⓚ	Mid	18	Causes back flop
Swing Kick	⇦Ⓚ	Mid	20	Causes backward crumple
Dagobah Dance	⇩⬂⇨ⓀⓀⒷ	Mid, Mid, Mid	10, 10, 20	Knocks down
Dagobah Dance (Cancel)	⇩⬂⇨ⓀⒼ			Forward roll without attacking
Dagobah Roll	⇩⬂⇨🅚ⓀⒷ	Mid, Mid, Mid	10, 10, 20	Knocks down
Heavy Kick	Jumping Ⓚ	Mid	22	Knocks down
Back High Kick	Backturned Ⓚ	High	12	
Back Heel Kick	Backturned ⇩Ⓚ	Low	12	Knocks down

Simultaneous Press

Name	Command	Attack Level	Damage	Notes
Ataru Combo	Ⓐ+ⒷⒷ	High, Mid	14, 20	
Ataru Strike	⇩Ⓐ+Ⓑ	Mid	50	Unblockable
Force Parry	Ⓑ+Ⓚ (During Impact: Ⓐ+Ⓑ For Additional Attack)		20	
Back Slash	Backturned Ⓑ+Ⓚ	Mid	16	Guard Break, causes crumple
Spiral Attack	Ⓐ+Ⓚ	Mid	14, 14	Knocks down
Charge Slash	⇨Ⓐ+Ⓚ	Low	20	Knocks down
Taunt	Ⓚ+Ⓖ			

8-Way Run

Name	Command	Attack Level	Damage	Notes
Ataru Combo	→ or ↘ or ↗ⒶⒶ	Mid, Low	18, 16	Knocks down
Whirlwind Strike	↓ or ↑Ⓐ	High	15	Spins foe
Jedi Master Combo	← or ↙ or ↖ⒶⒷ	Low, Mid	16, 30	2nd hit is Guard Break that launches
Ataru Combo	→ or ↘ or ↗ⒷⒷ	Mid, Mid	14, 20	Knocks down
Twirling Divide	↓ or ↑Ⓑ	Mid	20	Launches
Aerial Divide	← or ↙ or ↖Ⓑ	Mid	18	
Forward Flip	→Ⓚ			Movement
Horizontal Flip	↓ or ↑Ⓚ			Movement
Back Flip	←Ⓚ			Movement
Sliding Kick	While Running Ⓚ	Low	20	Knocks down

Throws

Name	Command	Attack Level	Damage	Notes
Jedi Wisdom	Ⓐ+Ⓖ	Throw	40	Ⓐ to break throw
Meteor Trample	Ⓑ+Ⓖ	Throw	40	Ⓑ to break throw
Justice Strike	Left Side Throw	Throw	50	Ⓐ or Ⓑ to break throw
Jedi Rush	Right Side Throw	Throw	50	Ⓐ or Ⓑ to break throw
Dagobah Storm	Back Throw	Throw	60	
Tector Shake	⇩⇧Ⓑ+Ⓖ	Throw	25	

Force Cancel

Name	Command	Attack Level	Damage	Notes
Forward Flip	⇨⇨ or →Ⓚ			Movement
Ataru Combo	During Front Flip ⒶⒶ	Mid, Low	18, 16	Knocks down
Ataru Combo	During Front Flip ⒷⒷ	Mid, Mid	14, 20	Knocks down
Aerial Kick	During Front Flip Ⓐ+Ⓑ	Mid	24	
Horizontal Flip	⇩⇩ or ⇧⇧ or ↓Ⓚ or ↑Ⓚ			Movement
Whirlwind Strike	During Side Flip Ⓐ	High	15	Spins foe
Twirling Divide	During Side Flip Ⓑ	Mid	20	Launches
Side Levitation Kick	During Side Flip Ⓐ+Ⓑ	Mid	24	
Back Flip	⇦⇦ or ←Ⓚ			Movement
Jedi Master Combo	During Back Flip ⒶⒷ	Low, Mid	16, 30	2nd hit is Guard Break that launches
Aerial Divide	During Back Flip Ⓑ	Mid	18	
Levitation Kick	During Back Flip Ⓐ+Ⓑ	Mid	20	
Force Cancel ~Forward Flip	Cancel From Flip or Flipping Attack ⇨Ⓚ			Movement
Force Cancel ~Ataru Combo	Cancel From Flip or Flipping Attack ⇨Ⓐ+ⓀⒶ	Mid, Low	18, 16	Knocks down
Force Cancel ~Ataru Combo	Cancel From Flip or Flipping Attack ⇨Ⓑ+ⓀⒷ	Mid, Mid	14, 20	Knocks down
Force Cancel ~Horizontal Flip	Cancel From Flip or Flipping Attack ⇩ or ⇧Ⓚ			Movement
Force Cancel ~Whirlwind Strike	Cancel From Flip or Flipping Attack ⇩ or ⇧Ⓐ+Ⓚ	High	15	Spins foe
Force Cancel ~Twirling Divide	Cancel From Flip or Flipping Attack ⇩ or ⇧Ⓑ+Ⓚ	Mid	20	Launches
Force Cancel ~Back Flip	Cancel From Flip or Flipping Attack ⇦Ⓚ			Movement
Force Cancel ~Jedi Master Combo	Cancel From Flip or Flipping Attack ⇦Ⓐ+ⓀⒷ	Low, Mid	16, 30	2nd hit is Guard Break that launches
Force Cancel ~Aerial Divide	Cancel From Flip or Flipping Attack ⇦Ⓑ+Ⓚ	Mid	18	

Close Range

Yoda's tiny frame in relation to other Soul Calibur combatants belies his true strength. This mercurial Jedi Master is at home up close, using his speed and unconventional attacks to overwhelm the opposition. As Yoda himself says, size matters not. His lack of stature actually rates as an advantage—most high attacks and throws miss Yoda, and characters with strong juggle combos may find that they don't work on this Jedi Master! His individual attacks don't inflict much damage, but his throws are useful and his unique attacks can be difficult for foes to manage. Like Darth Vader and The Apprentice, he has a Force gauge just under his health bar that dictates his use of Force powers. Yoda most frequently needs Force power for his Force Cancel attacks in midair.

Use Jedi Slash (⬂Ⓐ) as a catchall poke from close range. This attack is a quick mid slash that snuffs side movement, while back-turning the enemy even as a normal hit. Use the advantage gained from your foe's back-turned state to press your offense further, making your adversary guess between guarding attacks and breaking throws. Droid Buster (⇦Ⓐ) is also great; this circular slash stops 8-Way Run and sidesteps while back-turning the enemy as a normal hit. If it strikes as a counter-hit, the enemy crumples to the ground, allowing you to land a follow-up hit for free. Droid Buster is high, however, so it can be avoided through crouching.

If you anticipate the enemy crouching, use Ataru Windmill (⬂Ⓑ or ⬂Ⓑ + Ⓚ) to strike and launch him or her. Both attacks are linear mids. The ⬂Ⓑ option allows you to hit Ⓑ again for a second hit, or you can input commands for Yoda's Force Cancel attacks. This is useful to safeguard Yoda if the opponent blocks correctly. The ⬂Ⓑ + Ⓚ alternative automatically enters Yoda's Force Cancel state; if you simply input ⬂Ⓑ + Ⓚ, Yoda strikes upward and launches the enemy, then flips to the side and strikes again, juggling your foe. From here, you can input Force Cancel commands to continue the juggle, even if the enemy tries to Aerial Recover, if you direct Yoda in the same direction they choose!

Once your opponent is worried about these options, not to mention throws, it's time to use Ⓐ + ⒷⒷ. Yoda swirls upward with a high attack that nails side movement, then he performs a linear mid strike that actually flips over your foe's body if you perform it close enough. This is a 2-hit combo even on normal hit, and Yoda can follow the second hit with his Force Cancel options. You have several options if the enemy is guarding: You can land and go for a throw. You can also perform Yoda's extremely fast back-turned Guard Break (Ⓑ + Ⓚ), as Yoda lands on the other side facing away. Or you can use ⇩Ⓚ for a back-turned sweep that knocks down even as a normal hit.

Yoda can use Force Cancel options instead of landing to confuse enemies further. Input Ⓚ (with a direction) immediately after Ⓐ + ⒷⒷ before Yoda hits the ground to Force Cancel in your chosen direction without attacking. From here, immediately press Ⓐ + Ⓑ for the diving Aerial Kick if you flip directly toward your foe. If you flip to the side or backward, this performs the floating Levitation Kick. The Levitation Kick is interesting; it's a mid-striking attack that causes Yoda to bounce off his foe. As he bounces, you can make him fall backward with Ⓑ or Ⓐ (Ⓑ), or input Ⓐ + Ⓑ to send him flying back at your enemy with another kick! Alternatively, after Ⓐ + ⒷⒷ you can use Yoda's many other Force Cancel options to keep the enemy guessing. Use Ⓐ + Ⓚ with or without a direction to fall with a circular mid slash. If you use Ⓐ + Ⓚ to Force Cancel toward your foe with a slash, press Ⓐ to land with a low sweep. If you use Ⓐ + Ⓚ to flip away from the enemy, press Ⓑ to land and immediately spring forward into the Jedi Master Combo, an arcing Guard Break that launches enemies if it connects! Finally, keep Ⓑ + Ⓚ and Ⓐ + Ⓚ in mind as Force Cancel options after Ⓐ + ⒷⒷ and most other attacks where Yoda leaps into the air. You can perform them in any direction. Using Force Cancel, you can land combos like Ⓐ + ⒷⒷ (striking up close and crossing over the opponent's body), ⇨Ⓑ + ⓀⒷ. Watch out for ring edges—getting overly ambitious with Force Cancel can easily lead to inadvertent Ring Out losses!

Combos

⬂Ⓑ, ⇨Ⓑ + ⓀⒷ
3 hits, 43 damage
⬂Ⓑ + Ⓚ (both hits), ⇧Ⓐ + Ⓚ, ⇧Ⓐ + Ⓚ, ⇧Ⓐ + Ⓚ
5 hits, 58 damage, requires full Force. Enemy can Aerial Recover out, but angle of Yoda's attacks makes it difficult
Ⓐ + ⒷⒷ, ⇨Ⓑ + Ⓚ, ⇧Ⓑ + Ⓚ (⇦Ⓑ + Ⓚ when facing left), ⇨Ⓑ + ⓀⒷ
5 hits, 62 damage
⬇ or ⬆Ⓐ, ⇩Ⓐ + Ⓚ, ⇨Ⓐ + ⓀⒶ
4 hits, 50 damage
⬇ or ⬆Ⓐ, ⇩Ⓐ + Ⓚ, ⇨ⓀⒶ + Ⓑ, ⬂Ⓑ
4 hits, 53 damage
⬇ or ⬆Ⓐ, ⇩Ⓐ + Ⓚ, ⇨Ⓑ + Ⓚ, ⇨Ⓑ + Ⓚ, ⇨Ⓑ + ⓀⒷ
5 hits, 56 (62) damage, requires full Force

Mid Range

Yoda's versatility at close range is balanced by fewer options at greater distance. His most useful ranged attacks focus on getting inside quickly. Use ↘ or ↗ⒶⒶ to perform his leaping mid-to-low circular slash attack. Or use →ⒷⒷ to flip forward with a 2-hit linear mid combination. You can initiate Force Cancels immediately after →Ⓑ to transition quickly from mid range into Yoda's manic close-range offense. Charge Strike (⇨Ⓐ) is also useful as a forward-leaping attack that doesn't go quite as high as most of his flipping attacks; it strikes mid. Charge Strike (⇨Ⓑ) is a forward-flopping Guard Break that knocks down if it hits, and it has surprising range. However, be careful with its use, as Yoda is very vulnerable to side movement during this attack, and enemies can crouch under it. Use ⇘Ⓚ for a less risky poke from mid range. This mid-striking kick knocks down the enemy on counter-hit and, unlike the other options listed here, it doesn't require Yoda to commit to aerial or flopping movement.

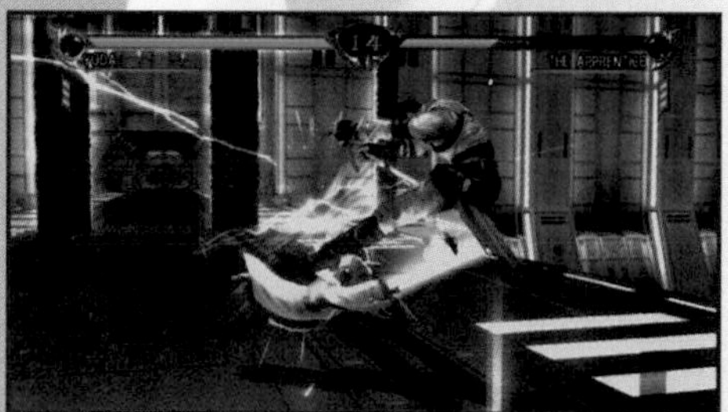

Long Range

As with mid ranges, Yoda's primary objective from afar is to get within range of his throws and Force Cancel attacks. Inputting ↙ or ↖ⒶⒷ performs the Jedi Master Combo, a slow, circular back-flip slash into a forward-leaping Guard Break that strikes mid and launches on a successful hit. This move telegraphs itself to the extreme, but you can use this to your advantage by performing ↙Ⓐ from a distance and *not* doing the Guard Break follow-up, causing your opponent to brace for an attack that you don't actually use. Land a few different threats while your foe is wary of the Guard Break, and then use it when he or she isn't sure what you'll do. Spiral Attack (Ⓐ+Ⓚ) is a spinning, 2-hit mid kick that knocks down even as a normal hit, even from a very long distance. Stage a long-range guessing game between this and Charge Slash (⇨Ⓐ+Ⓚ), a forward-leaping low slash that knocks down even as a normal hit. This is Yoda's best low attack. If the opponent expects one of these options, he'll get floored by the other. Finally, keep the Dagobah Dance sequence (⇩⇘⇨ⓀⓀⒷ) in mind. This command executes a forward roll into a two-part rising kick that ends in a downward slash. The whole sequence creates a 3-hit combo if it strikes the enemy. But your opponent can Aerial Recover away after the kicks, potentially causing the Ⓑ slash to miss. Just use ⇩⇘⇨ⓀⓀ to be safe, tacking on Ⓑ only to protect Yoda on the way down from his kicks if blocked. If you input ⇩⇘⇨Ⓚ, Yoda rolls forward, holding off on his kicks until you release Ⓚ. If you'd rather just stop rolling, press Ⓖ. Use this to stop short and throw occasionally, thus keeping the enemy guessing.

Special Tactics

Okizeme: Anti-Wakeup

The biggest hole in Yoda's offense is that he cannot threaten low very well. This gives his enemy little incentive on wakeup to do anything but use rising attacks or guard high. Abuse ⇨Ⓐ+Ⓚ against rising enemies to remind them that he *can* attack low, scoring knockdowns if they simply choose to guard standing. You can also surprise them occasionally with Yoda's ⇨Ⓑ flopping Guard Break as they get up. Yoda's throws are also very useful, so grab enemies frequently, especially as they rise.

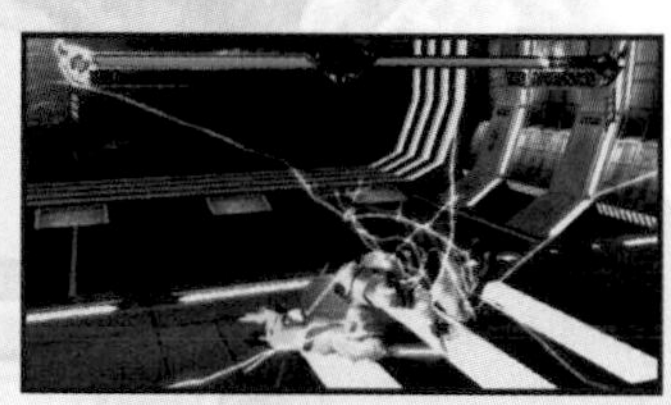

Masterful Movement

Quick movements work differently for this Jedi Master than for other characters. His 8-Way Run is a hobbling step, not useful for repositioning or evading attacks. He also lacks sidesteps and dashes. At 900 years of age, Yoda isn't as sprightly on the ground as most. But the air, where Yoda can perform acrobatic flips using his Force power, is a very different story. There are two ways to initiate Yoda's flips: ⇦⇦, ⇨⇨, ⇩⇩, and ⇧⇧ (double-tap inputs); or ←Ⓚ, →Ⓚ, ↓Ⓚ, and ↑Ⓚ (8-Way Run inputs). Either way, Yoda leaps into the air in the desired direction, changing his position rapidly while avoiding low attacks. Yoda has many options while airborne.

Flip Direction	Attack Command	Notes
⇨	ⒶⒶ	Circular mid-to-low attack
⇨	ⒷⒷ	Two linear mid attacks; can Force Cancel after single Ⓑ
⇨	Ⓐ+Ⓑ	Aerial Kick
⇩, ⇦, or ⇧	Ⓐ+Ⓑ	Levitation Kick (can be repeated)
⇦	Ⓑ	Linear mid slash
⇦	ⒶⒷ	Circular mid slash to forward-leaping mid launcher (Guard Break)
⇩ or ⇧	Ⓐ	Circular high slash; can Force Cancel
⇩ or ⇧	Ⓑ	Linear mid slash that launches; can Force Cancel

The Whirling Dervish

Yoda's Force meter can be used for his Force Parry: Ⓑ+Ⓚ just as an incoming attack hits Yoda, then Ⓐ+Ⓑ. But it's much more useful for powering his aerial offense. By inputting different commands after attacks that leave him airborne, Yoda will flash green and redirect his attack. The commands are any direction and Ⓚ to flip without attacking, or any direction and Ⓐ+Ⓚ or Ⓑ+Ⓚ to flip with either a horizontal or vertical attack. This can be used for combos to confuse the enemy or to continue pressuring them when an initial attack is guarded. Force Cancel Twirling Divide ⇩ or ⇧Ⓑ+Ⓚ, a mid that launches enemies just like ↓ or ↑Ⓑ, is useful for pressure. Likewise, Force Cancel Whirlwind Strike ⇩ or ⇧Ⓐ+Ⓚ, a high that spins the enemy on contact just like ↓ or ↑Ⓐ, is equally handy, and it can be linked into itself! Force Cancel ⇨Ⓐ+ⓀⒶ is great for staging a mid-to-low mix-up. If the opponent begins guarding the low strike, simply use Force Cancel ⇨Ⓐ+Ⓚ on its own, then land and use a mid, such as ⇘ⒷⒷ. Force Cancel ⇨Ⓑ+Ⓚ is great for creating and extending combos, as it combos into itself as long as Yoda has Force to expend. It can be hard getting used to inputting Yoda's commands so quickly, but the effort pays off. Remember: Try not. Do. Or do not. There is no try. Yoda is less combo-oriented than any other character, and instead depends more on a flurry of single strikes and 2-to-3-hit combos stemming from Force Cancel options. Consult the Close Range section for many Force Cancel applications in Yoda's offense.

The Apprentice

The Apprentice

Bio

Age:	Unknown
Birth Place:	Planet Kashyyyk
Height:	6'1"
Weight:	178 lbs.
Birth Date:	Unknown
Blood Type:	Unknown
Weapon:	Lightsaber
Weapon Name:	Unknown
Discipline:	Self-Taught
Family:	Father (deceased), Darth Vader (Master)

A long time ago in a galaxy far, far away...

He was raised in secret as the apprentice of Darth Vader, Dark Lord of the Sith. [illegible] *immeasurable potential. Darth Vader saw his natural aptitude and raised him to* [illegible]

He became the Dark Lord's shadow, performing secret missions at his behest. Upon [illegible] *a new order. A gate to another dimension was about to open in space. He was* [illegible] *was causing the disturbance.*

Upon reaching the area of space in question and confirming the dimensional [illegible] *passageway. The wave of power grew stronger right before his eyes, and the* [illegible] *space. When the dimensional portal opened, The Apprentice entered without* [illegible]

There, in that other galaxy, he encounters two swords that possess opposing powers.

The Apprentice

Command List

Signature Techniques

Name	Command	Attack Level	Damage	Notes
Apprentice Combo	ⒶⒶⒷ	High, High, Mid	10, 8, 16	First 2 hits combo naturally, all 3 hits combo on counter-hit
Storm Breaker	⇨ⒷⒷⓀ	Mid, High, High	11, 12, 22	Combos on counter-hit, knocks down
Triple Kick	⇩ⓀⒷ	Low, Mid	15, 22	Combos on counter-hit, knocks down
Force Blast	⇩Ⓐ+Ⓑ	Sp.Mid	26	Guard Break, launches, uses 50% Force
Force Wave Combo	→ or ↘ or ↗ⒶⒷ	High, Low	16, 28	Combos naturally, shoots Force Wave, expends 40% Force
Force Blast Combo	↘ or ↗ⒷⒷ	Mid, Sp.Mid	18, 18	Combos naturally, 2nd hit is Guard Break, launches, expends 60% Force
Galactic Breaker	→Ⓐ+ⒷⒷ	Mid, Mid	15, 15	Combos naturally, causes crumple, 2nd hit expends 40% Force
Force Lightning	←Ⓐ+Ⓑ	Mid x6	10x6	Unblockable, knocks down, expends 50% Force
Star Raid Lightning	During Force Levitation Ⓑ+Ⓚ	Mid, Mid, Mid, Mid, Mid, Mid	8x6	Knocks down, expends 60% Force

Horizontal Attacks

Name	Command	Attack Level	Damage	Notes
Apprentice Combo	ⒶⒶⒷ	High, High, Mid	10, 8, 16	First 2 hits combo naturally, all 3 hits combo on counter-hit
Dark Side Fang	⇨Ⓐ	High	18	Sideturns foe
Sinking Saber	⇘Ⓐ	High	12	
Piercing Strike	⇩Ⓐ	Sp.Low	10	
Vortex Saber	⇗Ⓐ	High	24	Spins foe
Hilt Blow	⇦Ⓐ	High	16	Causes recoverable stun on normal hit, knocks down on counter-hit
Sinking Strike	While Crouching Ⓐ	Sp.Low	10	
Blinding Saber	While Rising Ⓐ	High	26	Backturns foe
Jumping Saber Slice	Jumping Ⓐ	High	24	
Back Strike	Backturned Ⓐ	High	12	
Back Sinking Saber	While Crouching Backturned Ⓐ	Sp.Low	12	Puts Apprentice in crouching state

Vertical Attacks

Name	Command	Attack Level	Damage	Notes
Mist Splitter	ⒷⒷ	Mid, Mid	14, 14	Combos naturally
Storm Breaker	⇨ⒷⒷⓀ	Mid, High, High	11, 12, 22	Combos on counter-hit, knocks down
Storm Breaker	⇨Ⓑ⇘Ⓑ	Mid, Mid	11, 16	Combos on counter-hit, 2nd hit launches
Storm Breaker ~Force Levitation	⇨Ⓑ⇘Ⓑ⇧	Mid, Mid	11, 16	Combos on counter-hit, 2nd hit launches, leaps upward
Mist Splitter ~Force Grab	⇨ⒷⒶ+Ⓑ	Mid, High	11	Pulls foe close
Star Divide	⇘Ⓑ	Mid	20	Launches
Star Divide ~Force Levitation	⇘Ⓑ⇧	Mid	20	Launches, leaps upward
Mist Slicer	⇩Ⓑ	Mid	14	
Side Saber	⇗Ⓑ	Mid	20	Causes back flop
Piercing Thrust	⇦Ⓑ	Mid	18	
Force Wave	⇩⇘⇨Ⓑ	Low	28	Knocks down, expends 30% Force
Mist Slicer	While Crouching Ⓑ	Mid	14	
Dark Cutter	While Rising Ⓑ	Mid	22	Causes backward crumple
Jumping Saber Strike	Jumping Ⓑ	Mid	26	
Back Slicer	Backturned Ⓑ	Mid	16	
Backside Mist Slicer	While Crouching Backturned Ⓑ	Mid	18	Leaves Apprentice in crouching state

Kick Attacks

Name	Command	Attack Level	Damage	Notes
Face Crush	Ⓚ	High	12	
Throat Crush	⇨Ⓚ	High	16	
Knee Drive	⇘Ⓚ	Mid	10	Crumples on counter-hit
Triple Kick	⇩ⓀⒷ	Low, Mid	15, 22	Combos on counter-hit, knocks down
Triple Kick	⇙ⓀⓀⓀ	High, Mid, High	8, 8, 14	Combos naturally
Neck Breaker	⇦Ⓚ	High	20	Spins foe
Foot Crush	While Crouching Ⓚ	Low	10	
Flipping Saber Throw	While Crouching ⇧ⓀⒶ	Mid, Mid, High, High	10, 10, 20, 20	Combos naturally, knocks down, expends 40% Force
Jaw Crush	While Rising Ⓚ	Mid	16	
Summersault Kick	Jumping Ⓚ	Mid	18	
Back Face Crush	Backturned Ⓚ	High	14	
Back Foot Crush	While Crouching Backturned Ⓚ	Low	14	Knocks down, puts Apprentice in crouching state

Simultaneous Press

Name	Command	Attack Level	Damage	Notes
Force Grab	Ⓐ+Ⓑ	High		Pulls foe close, expends 15% Force
Force Blast	⇩Ⓐ+Ⓑ	Sp.Mid	26	Guard Break, launches, expends 50% Force
Force Blast ~Force Levitation	⇩Ⓐ+Ⓑ⇧	Sp.Mid	26	Guard Break, launches, expends 50% Force, leaps upward
Kashyyyk Raid	Ⓑ+ⓀⒷⒷ ⒷⒷ	High, High, High, High, High	8, 5, 5, 5, 5	Combos naturally, knocks down
Kashyyyk Storm	Ⓑ+ⓀⒷ⇨Ⓑ ⒷⓀ	High, High, Mid, High, High	8, 5, 10, 10, 22	Combos on counter-hit, knocks down
Kashyyyk Storm	Ⓑ+ⓀⒷ⇨Ⓑ ⇘Ⓑ	High, High, Mid, Mid	8, 5, 16, 10	Combos on counter-hit, launches
Kashyyyk Storm ~Force Levitation	Ⓑ+ⓀⒷ⇨Ⓑ ⇖Ⓡ⇧	High, High, Mid, Mid	8, 5, 10, 16	Combos on counter-hit, launches, leaps upward
Kashyyyk Storm ~Force Grab	Ⓑ+ⓀⒷ⇨Ⓑ Ⓐ+Ⓑ	High, High, Mid, High	8, 5, 10	Combos on counter-hit, pulls foe close
Knee Buster	⇩Ⓑ+Ⓚ	Low	10	Just Frame input of Ⓑ on hit produces Kashyyyk Storm
Back Flip Kick	Backturned Ⓑ+Ⓚ	Mid, Mid	10, 10	Guard Break
Force Flip	⇨Ⓐ+Ⓚ			Leaps forward, lands facing same direction
Force Flip	⇩ or ⇧Ⓐ+Ⓚ			Leaps laterally
Force Flip	⇦Ⓐ+Ⓚ			Leaps forward, lands facing opposite direction
Counter Saber Throw	Backturned Ⓐ+Ⓚ Ⓐ+Ⓑ	High, High	10, 10	Leaps backward, knocks down
Taunt	Ⓚ+Ⓖ			

8-Way Run

Name	Command	Attack Level	Damage	Notes
Force Wave Combo	→ or ↘ or ↗ⒶⒷ	High, Low	16, 28	Combos naturally, shoots Force Wave, expends 40% Force
Charging Saber Strike	↓ or ↑Ⓐ	Mid	28	
Saber Smash	← or ↙ or ↖Ⓐ	High	24	Knocks down
Mist Cutter	→Ⓑ	Mid	30	Launches
Force Blast Combo	↘ or ↗ⒷⒷ	Mid, Sp.Mid	18, 18	Combos naturally, 2nd hit is Guard Break, expends 60% Force, launches
Force Blast Combo ~Force Levitation	↘ or ↗ⒷⒷ⇧	Mid, Sp.Mid	18, 18	Combos naturally, 2nd hit is Guard Break, expends 70% Force, launches, leaps upward
Heat Cutter	↓ or ↑Ⓑ	Mid	18	Knocks down, leaves Apprentice in crouching state
Celestial Hammer	← or ↙ or ↖Ⓑ	Mid	24	Knocks down
Body Breaker	→Ⓚ	High	22	Knocks down
Hook Kick	↘ or ↗Ⓚ	Mid	20	Causes crumple
Head Assault	↓ or ↑ⓀⓀ	High, High	14, 18	Combos naturally, knocks down
Spinning Kick	↙ or ↖Ⓚ	High	22	Knocks down
Leg Sweep	←Ⓚ	Low	18	Launches
Galactic Breaker	→Ⓐ+ⒷⒷ	Mid, Mid	15, 15	Combos naturally, causes crumple, expends 30% Force
Force Lightning	←Ⓐ+Ⓑ	Mid x6	10x6	Unblockable, knocks down
Meteor Strike	→Ⓑ+Ⓚ	Mid, Mid	8, 20	Combos naturally, knocks down, expends 50% Force
Sliding Kick	While Running Ⓚ	Low	26	Knocks down

Throws

Name	Command	Attack Level	Damage	Notes
Dark Widow	Ⓐ+Ⓖ	Throw	55	Ⓐ to break throw
Force Impact	Ⓑ+Ⓖ	Throw	55	Ⓑ to break throw
Black Banishment	Left Side Throw	Throw	60	Ⓐ or Ⓑ to break throw
Deadly Expulsion	Right Side Throw	Throw	60	Ⓐ or Ⓑ to break throw
Operation	Back Throw	Throw	65	

Special

Name	Command	Attack Level	Damage	Notes
Force Levitation	Ⓐ+Ⓚ			Leaps upward
Levitation Combo	During Force Levitation ⒶⒶ ⒷⒷ	High, High, Mid, Mid	14, 10, 10, 25	Aerial combo
Aerial Saber Throw	During Force Levitation ⒶⒶ Ⓐ+Ⓑ	High, High, Mid, Mid	10, 10, 16, 24	Aerial combo
Star Raid Lightning	During Force Levitation Ⓑ+Ⓚ	Mid, Mid, Mid, Mid, Mid, Mid	8x6	Knocks down

Close Range

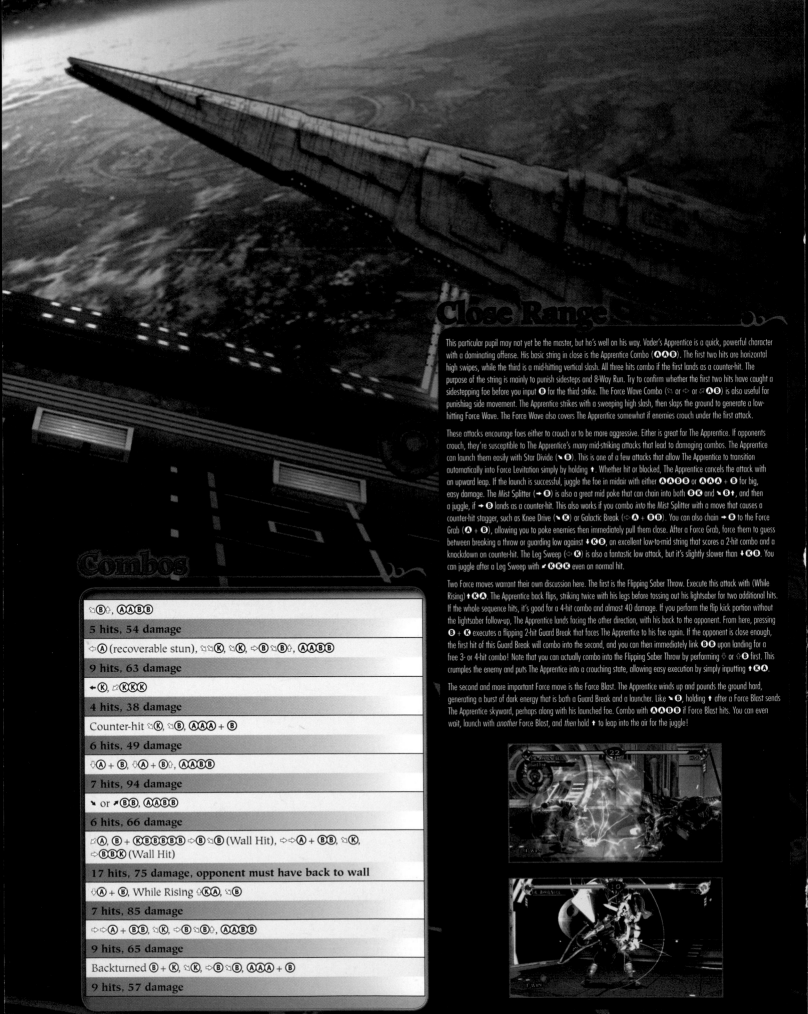

This particular pupil may not yet be the master, but he's well on his way. Vader's Apprentice is a quick, powerful character with a dominating offense. His basic string in close is the Apprentice Combo (ⒶⒶⒷ). The first two hits are horizontal high swipes, while the third is a mid-hitting vertical slash. All three hits combo if the first lands as a counter-hit. The purpose of the string is mainly to punish sidesteps and 8-Way Run. Try to confirm whether the first two hits have caught a sidestepping foe before you input Ⓑ for the third strike. The Force Wave Combo (⇘ or ⇨ or ⇗ⒶⒷ) is also useful for punishing side movement. The Apprentice strikes with a sweeping high slash, then slaps the ground to generate a low-hitting Force Wave. The Force Wave also covers The Apprentice somewhat if enemies crouch under the first attack.

These attacks encourage foes either to crouch or to be more aggressive. Either is great for The Apprentice. If opponents crouch, they're susceptible to The Apprentice's *many* mid-striking attacks that lead to damaging combos. The Apprentice can launch them easily with Star Divide (↘Ⓑ). This is one of a few attacks that allow The Apprentice to transition automatically into Force Levitation simply by holding ↑. Whether hit or blocked, The Apprentice cancels the attack with an upward leap. If the launch is successful, juggle the foe in midair with either ⒶⒶⒷⒷ or ⒶⒶⒶ + Ⓑ for big, easy damage. The Mist Splitter (→Ⓑ) is also a great mid poke that can chain into both ⒷⓀ and ↘Ⓑ↑, and then a juggle, if →Ⓑ lands as a counter-hit. This also works if you combo *into* the Mist Splitter with a move that causes a counter-hit stagger, such as Knee Drive (↘Ⓚ) or Galactic Break (⇨Ⓐ + ⒷⒷ). You can also chain →Ⓑ to the Force Grab (Ⓐ + Ⓑ), allowing you to poke enemies then immediately pull them close. After a Force Grab, force them to guess between breaking a throw or guarding low against ↓ⓀⒷ, an excellent low-to-mid string that scores a 2-hit combo and a knockdown on counter-hit. The Leg Sweep (⇦Ⓚ) is also a fantastic low attack, but it's slightly slower than ↓ⓀⒷ. You can juggle after a Leg Sweep with ↙ⓀⓀⓀ even on normal hit.

Two Force moves warrant their own discussion here. The first is the Flipping Saber Throw. Execute this attack with (While Rising) ↑ⓀⒶ. The Apprentice back flips, striking twice with his legs before tossing out his lightsaber for two additional hits. If the whole sequence hits, it's good for a 4-hit combo and almost 40 damage. If you perform the flip kick portion without the lightsaber follow-up, The Apprentice lands facing the other direction, with his back to the opponent. From here, pressing Ⓑ + Ⓚ executes a flipping 2-hit Guard Break that faces The Apprentice to his foe again. If the opponent is close enough, the first hit of this Guard Break will combo into the second, and you can then immediately link ⒷⒷ upon landing for a free 3- or 4-hit combo! Note that you can actually combo into the Flipping Saber Throw by performing ⇩ or ⇧Ⓑ first. This crumples the enemy and puts The Apprentice into a crouching state, allowing easy execution by simply inputting ↑ⓀⒶ.

The second and more important Force move is the Force Blast. The Apprentice winds up and pounds the ground hard, generating a burst of dark energy that is both a Guard Break and a launcher. Like ↘Ⓑ, holding ↑ after a Force Blast sends The Apprentice skyward, perhaps along with his launched foe. Combo with ⒶⒶⒷⒷ if Force Blast hits. You can even wait, launch with *another* Force Blast, and *then* hold ↑ to leap into the air for the juggle!

Combos

⇘Ⓑ⇧, ⒶⒶⒷⒷ	**5 hits, 54 damage**
⇦Ⓐ (recoverable stun), ⇘⇘Ⓚ, ⇘Ⓚ, ⇨Ⓑ ⇘Ⓑ⇧, ⒶⒶⒷⒷ	**9 hits, 63 damage**
←Ⓚ, ⇗ⓀⓀⓀ	**4 hits, 38 damage**
Counter-hit ⇘Ⓚ, ⇘Ⓑ, ⒶⒶⒶ + Ⓑ	**6 hits, 49 damage**
⇩Ⓐ + Ⓑ, ⇩Ⓐ + Ⓑ⇧, ⒶⒶⒷⒷ	**7 hits, 94 damage**
↘ or ↗ⒷⒷ, ⒶⒶⒷⒷ	**6 hits, 66 damage**
⇗Ⓐ, Ⓑ + ⓀⒷⒷⒷⒷⒷ ⇨Ⓑ ⇘Ⓑ (Wall Hit), ⇨⇨Ⓐ + ⒷⒷ, ⇘Ⓚ, ⇨ⒷⒷⓀ (Wall Hit)	**17 hits, 75 damage, opponent must have back to wall**
⇩Ⓐ + Ⓑ, While Rising ⇧ⓀⒶ, ⇘Ⓑ	**7 hits, 85 damage**
⇨⇨Ⓐ + ⒷⒷ, ⇘Ⓚ, ⇨Ⓑ ⇘Ⓑ⇧, ⒶⒶⒷⒷ	**9 hits, 65 damage**
Backturned Ⓑ + Ⓚ, ⇘Ⓚ, ⇨Ⓑ ⇘Ⓑ, ⒶⒶⒶ + Ⓑ	**9 hits, 57 damage**

Mid Range

The Apprentice prefers to be in the opponent's face, counter-hitting or launching foes into painful juggles or abusing the powers of Force Blast. Unlike most characters, he doesn't have to be concerned with forcing his way inside; he can make his enemy come to him! Use the Force Grab with Ⓐ + Ⓑ to pull standing enemies close, where you can immediately go for a throw, a launch, or a sweep. If you prefer a more proactive offense, use the Galactic Break (⇨Ⓐ + ⒷⒷ), a lunging two-part mid attack that leads directly to big juggles. Link ➔Ⓑ↘Ⓑ↑, ⒶⒶⒷⒷ after Galactic Break. If your foe guards Galactic Break, you're right back where you want to be: in his or her face. Even from a few steps away the Force Blast (↓Ⓐ + Ⓑ) remains effective, as The Apprentice steps forward in his delivery. His Force Wave (↓↘➔Ⓑ) and Star Raid Lightning (Ⓐ + Ⓚ, Ⓑ + Ⓚ) are also effective from a few steps away, at the edge of strike range. Side movement can thwart every move we've discussed here except the Force Blast, so deter this with the Charging Saber Strike (⇩ or ⇧Ⓐ). The Apprentice slides forward with a delayed mid attack that enemies can neither crouch under nor sidestep.

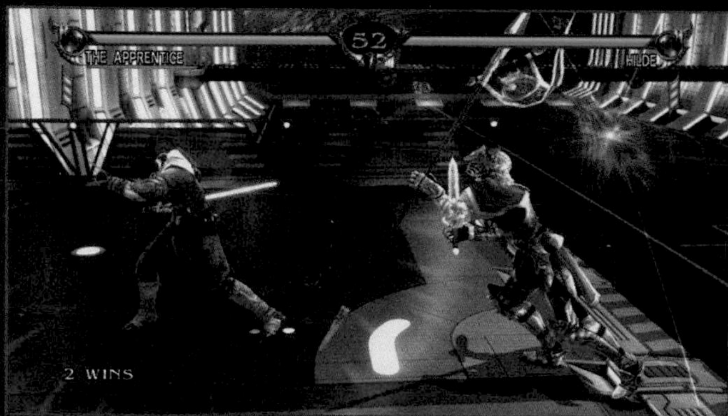

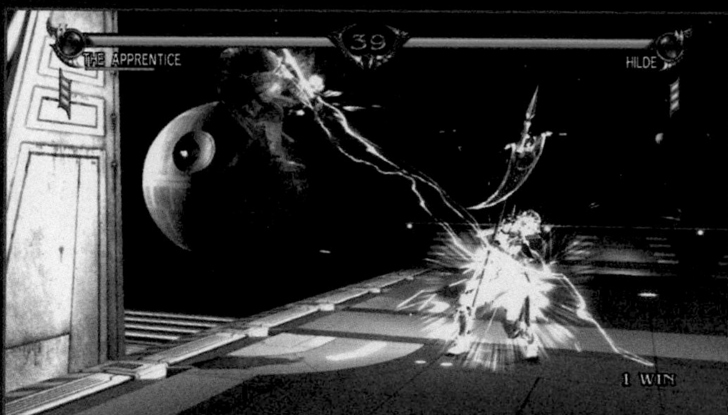

Long Range

From far away, focus on waiting for enemies to give you an opening, then rush into it. Hang back and feed them Force Waves (↓↘➔Ⓑ). Note that this move can cause a Soul Crush even from all the way across the arena. So, if the enemy chooses to guard rather than step around them, more power to you. You may even get a chance to surprise them with a Critical Finish from across an entire stage! You can also produce Force Waves with the Force Wave Combo string (⇘ or ⇨ or ⇗ⒶⒷ). This can work in your favor, as the enemy may see you whiff the first attack in the string and figure it's time to rush forward and punish you. The foe may just run directly into the follow-up Force Wave. Also, remember The Apprentice's ←←Ⓐ + Ⓑ Unblockable. While it has a lengthy start-up and can be sidestepped easily, it's still worth remembering if the opponent plays extreme keep away or lets his attention lapse.

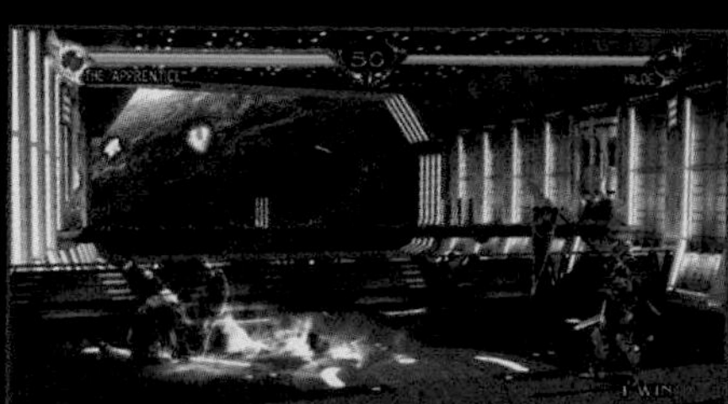

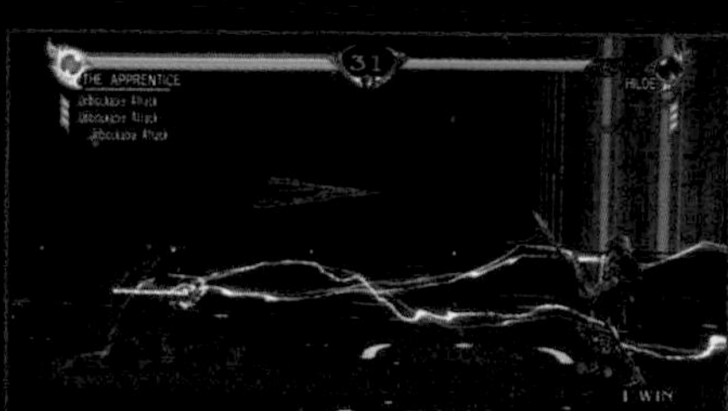

Special Tactics

Okizeme: Anti-Wakeup

Demoralize waking opponents by using the Force Blast as they rise. With proper timing, it blows out any rising attacks they try and Guard Breaks them. Otherwise, mix them up between run-up throws, ↘Ⓑ into a juggle combo, and ←←Ⓚ into ↙ⓀⓀⓀ. The rising adversary must treat all three of these options and the Force Blast differently. Thus, there is no clear solution when rising against The Apprentice. Force Waves also strike grounded enemies and can be useful for scoring follow-up hits after you knock foes away from you.

Force Levitation

The Apprentice can use the dark side of the Force to hurl himself vertically, following his opponent after many launching moves. From here, he can employ the dark side to generate a lightning storm, or combo from an aerial chain into a falling stab or lightsaber toss. From mid and long range, simply using Ⓐ + Ⓚ, then Ⓑ + Ⓚ for Star Raid Lightning can be an effective and threatening poke from above. The other commands are useful for launching foes into damaging combos, or for pressuring them from the ground before feeding them electricity from above. You can also input ↓ or ↑Ⓐ + Ⓚ, making The Apprentice leap laterally into the foreground or background. This can be useful for avoiding attacks at long range or obtaining better ring position, but he lacks the offensive options from these leaps that he has with standard Force Levitation.

Force Levitation Commands
Ⓐ+Ⓚ
⇘Ⓑ⇧
⇩Ⓐ+Ⓑ⇧
⇨Ⓑ⇘Ⓑ⇧
↘ or ↗ⒷⒷ⇧

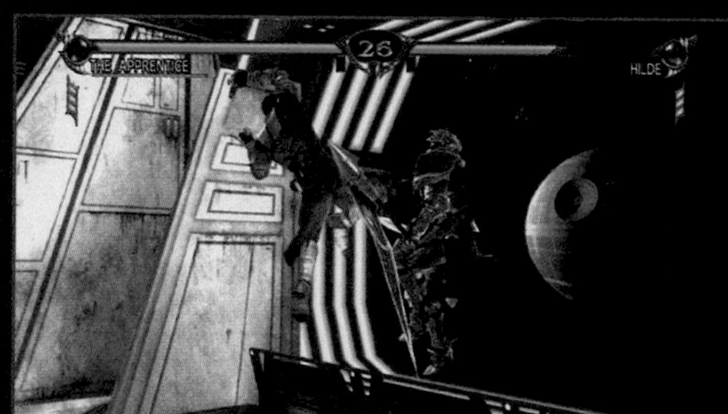

The Apprentice

SOULCALIBUR IV

Official Strategy Guide

Written by Adam Deats and Joe Epstein

DK/BradyGames, a division of Penguin Group (USA) Inc.
800 East 96th Street, 3rd Floor
Indianapolis, IN 46240

ISBN-13: 978-0-7440-1006-0
ISBN-10: 0-7440-1006-3

Printing Code: The rightmost double-digit number is the year of the book's printing; the rightmost single-digit number is the number of the book's printing. For example, 08-1 shows that the first printing of the book occurred in 2008.
11 10 09 08 4 3 2 1

Credits

TITLE MANAGER
Tim Fitzpatrick
SCREENSHOT EDITOR
Michael Owen
BOOK DESIGNER
Brent Gann
COVER AND FOLDOUT DESIGNER
Carol Stamile
PRODUCTION DESIGNERS
Areva
Tracy Wehmeyer

BradyGAMES Staff

PUBLISHER
David Waybright
EDITOR-IN-CHIEF
H. Leigh Davis
LICENSING DIRECTOR
Mike Degler
MARKETING DIRECTOR
Debby Neubauer
INTERNATIONAL TRANSLATIONS
Brian Saliba

Namco Bandai Games America Staff

Ben Rinaldi
Ryota Toyama
Wayne Shiu

SPECIAL THANKS TO NBGA QA:
Jesus Barragan
Damon Bernal
Nikolas Carey
Brian Ellak
Tad Hirabayashi
Kenrick Mah
Mike Peterson
Geoff Tuttle

Acknowledgments

BradyGAMES sincerely thanks everyone at NAMCO BANAI Games for a great addition to the Soulcalibur series, and special thanks to Ben Rinaldi and the entire team for their generous support during this project. Thank you!

Joe Epstein: Big thanks to the entire staff at BradyGAMES, who did their best to make us feel at home while we toiled in the *Soulcalibur IV* mines. In particular, I'd like to thank: Brian Shotton, for the scotch and skillet cookies (in spirit!); Michael Owen, for the batteries, hardware, and pictures; Chris, Sara, and Lars Hausermann, for the hospitality; Brent Gann, for the pretty designs and soft tissues (Brent: I'm sorry I stole your tissues); Tim Fitzpatrick, for putting up with constant revisions with a smile; Mike Degler, for his diligence; Adam Deats, for complaining very little about the month I spent using my detestable Yoda impersonation to lament, "still burns, the soul does," among other things—also, for at one point writing that the player should "use sidesteps to sidestep."; Leigh Davis, for the bakery suggestion, which we took at least 10 times; Stacey Beheler, for the life-saving fan and the snacks; Finally, Tim in the lobby cafe, with the hazelnut coffee.

Adam Deats: I would like to thank the entire BradyGAMES crew for their hospitality during our stay in Indianapolis, the folks at Namco for their /unyielding / support, Joe Epstein for the gift of song, Paradise for cookies, and Jennifer Fleming for her love and phone calls. No thanks goes to Indianapolis weather, hotel TV, bad teeth, and mesenteric lymphadenitis. What a thrill.